Chewing Sand

a process for understanding counter insurgency operations

Dean Nosorog

Editor

McGraw Hill **Custom Publishing**

Boston   Burr Ridge, IL   Dubuque, IA   Madison, WI   New York   San Francisco   St. Louis
Bangkok   Bogotá   Caracas   Lisbon   London   Madrid
Mexico City   Milan   New Delhi   Seoul   Singapore   Sydney   Taipei   Toronto

Chewing Sand
A Process for Understanding Counter Insurgency Operations

McGraw-Hill's Custom Publishing consists of products that are produced from camera-ready copy. Peer review, class testing, and accuracy are primarily the responsibility of the author(s).

1 2 3 4 5 6 7 8 9 0   QSR QSR   0 9 8 7 6 5

ISBN 0-07-353978-3

McGraw-Hill Editor: Ann Jenson
Production Editor: Nina Meyer
Cover Photo by SFODA 534: U.S. forces and indigenous allies captured this enemy soldier along with several thousand others near the city of Qonduz, Afghanistan in November of 2001. Qonduz marked OPERATION ENDURING FREEDOM's turning point in Northern Afghanistan from an insurgent to a counterinsurgent conflict.
Cover Design: Fairfax Hutter
Printer/Binder: Quebecor World

TABLE OF CONTENTS

PREFACE

Chewing Sand is an anthology of readings relevant to the study of counterinsurgency operations. I have combined these various works for students to examine as part of the *Counterinsurgency Operations* course at the United States Military Academy. The course includes only forty lessons, and as a result, I chose readings very carefully in order to empower the students with a comprehensive understanding of the fundamental origins, solutions, and tools available for the military scientist. Since I did not choose the readings for their entertainment value, a few are quite dry, and hence the title, *Chewing Sand*.

These readings fit into specific course and lesson objectives, and some of those are less apparent to the reader than others. Nevertheless, if one approaches each work with the question, "So what does this mean to me in a counterinsurgency war," then one will inevitably find great value just from each author's insights. Thus, I think the value added makes reading these works worth choking down a periodic mouthful of sand. The texts required for this course that are not inside *Chewing Sand* are Che Guevara's *Guerrilla Warfare* and other assorted U.S. Army field manuals.

This forty lesson seminar comprises three sub-courses: *Insurgency*; *Counterinsurgency operations*; and *Case studies*. In the first sub-course, *Insurgency*, this program will work to develop a theoretical, strategic, operational, and tactical understanding of insurgencies. Students will begin by exploring one reading from each of the three basic types of revolutionary theory [see authors Goodwin, McAdam, and Taylor]. Revolutionary theory is the academic study of how and why revolutions—often waged by insurgencies—begin. These readings are dry, but they give us a theoretical understanding of the various origins of the entire conflict that this seminar investigates. Readers will probably note that there are always social, political, or economic beginnings to insurgencies, not military ones. If the counterinsurgent does not address the non-military reasons why insurgents fight, then there will likely be no end to either recruits or other insurgencies that are willing to fight. Therefore, understanding the fundamental origins to revolution is critical to success, and these concepts will echo throughout this course.

Next, students will examine insurgent strategies in three ways. First, they will compare exhaustion strategies that typify insurgent and counterinsurgent success to annihilation strategies that both Clausewitz and U.S. warfighting doctrine emphasize [see Craig]. Insurgencies often appear militarily weaker than their enemies, but they succeed because they adopt tactics and strategies that offset their shortcomings. The counterinsurgent cannot evaluate the strength of the insurgent's capabilities by looking through the lens of the counterinsurgent's own paradigmatic strategic approach. The insurgent's approach is not weaker than that of the traditional U.S. military's, nor is it doomed to fail or guaranteed to succeed—it's just different. Next, students will review a typology of insurgent strategies [see McCormick, Marighella, and Lenin]. There are numerous kinds of strategies, and there are many ways that we can categorize them. In this program we will focus on two key distinctions that lead to four strategy types: outside-in (or rural-based) versus inside-out (urban-based), and high-profile versus low-profile. Finally, Robert Taber explains how and why insurgent strategies can be advantageous.

From there, students will examine the doctrinal prescriptions of U.S. Special Forces Unconventional Warfare (UW). Because of distribution restrictions, these readings are not available in *Chewing Sand*, but I will provide students copies in class. One of UW's key purposes is to foment U.S. sponsored insurgencies, and Special Forces doctrine provides the most comprehensive 'doctrinal template' for insurgencies that I have found. Additionally, Special Forces soldiers have validated their doctrine with decades of personal experience and meticulous research. These readings will not make students experts in insurgencies, but they will arm students with an operational clarity as well as a professional vocabulary of how insurgencies work, organize, develop, and function.

Because of their different strategic and operational roots, insurgents often develop and employ tactics that are very different from those of the U.S. military. Notwithstanding, insurgent tactics still comprise the same battlefield operating systems as the tactics of any other military. Using the guidance of historical guerrilla leaders, students will investigate examples of insurgent battlefield operating systems in order to understand the insurgent's tactical—and often idiosyncratic—methods [see Guevara and Marighella].

Finally, Leites and Wolf will synthesize theoretical, strategic, operational, and tactical understandings of insurgencies as they present a systemic view of these organizations to aid analysis at all levels.

In the second sub-course, *Counterinsurgency operations*, students will see how this systemic model also sets up a typology of counterinsurgency strategies. Leites and Wolf offer four strategy types that facilitate comprehensive offensive operations against an enemy organization that typically refuses to fight except on its own terms. Next, students review a critical fifth strategy found in U.S. military doctrine, Internal Defense and Development (IDAD). IDAD is a methodological strategy that attacks the non-military causes that provoke or propagate insurgencies.

Second, students will examine David Galula's theoretical presentations of counterinsurgency in what he terms both cold and hot revolutionary war phases. A review of historical, current, and imminent doctrine will follow. The seminar will encourage students to compare and contrast various doctrinal models that will highlight strengths and weaknesses and emphasize synchronization with Internal Defense and Development initiatives. Students will consider why different models are similar and why they are different given the ranking insurgent threats of their respective eras. Operationally, students will also examine the writings of three authors: Paret, Gann, and Kitson, each of whom presents unique operational prescriptions for operations against insurgencies. As before, students will tug, tear, pull, and chew on these ideas with respect to theoretical, strategic, and doctrinal schemes in order to enhance comprehension and to encourage critical thinking.

At the end, this sub-course examines a few tactics that are common among general purpose forces in counterinsurgency operations. More important than understanding the tactics themselves is the understanding of how these tactics support greater operational, strategic, and even theoretical ideas seen earlier in the course.

The final sub-course, *Case Studies*, presents students with three historical case studies in which students can apply all of the course's learning. Two of these cases, Malaya [see Komer] and the Philippines [see Greenberg], represent successes in counterinsurgency operations, whereas the final case, U.S. pacification efforts in Vietnam [see Blaufarb], represents a failed approach. I have chosen each of these cases very carefully: the insurgencies' strategy (low-profile, outside-in), ideology (Communism), era (post-WWII), and world region (the Far East) are identical. At the same time, tactical methods (and the successes and failures associated with each) varied greatly between cases. Juxtaposing each of these cases reveals the idiosyncrasies of every counterinsurgency operation, regardless of similarities between insurgent, counterinsurgent, and environmental factors. Students must rely on the analytical processes offered in this course, first for evaluating the insurgency and then for prescribing the counterinsurgency, to understand why certain tactics, methods, and procedures worked well or not so well.

In my opinion, there are two very general approaches to counterinsurgency that work: (1) The *Kill 'em all, let God sort 'em out* approach and (2) the *developmental* approach. I believe the former works. After all, it was how men like Saddam Hussein and Stalin, among others, quelled rebellion effectively within their borders. However, it is also my opinion that this approach is inconsistent with the values and culture of the United States. Obviously, it is inconsistent with Army values and the kind of leaders that Army is trying to produce.

On the other hand, not only can the developmental approach work, but it also embraces and cultivates the very values that are most representative of U.S. and Army cultures. In addition to Army values like duty, respect, selfless-service, and integrity, it also promotes a self-sufficient nation, creates representative (democratic) and responsive governments, and solves social, political, and economic problems. As a result, I believe that the second approach is not just more ethical, but also more effective over the long term. For example, you can defeat the ABC insurgency, but if you don't defeat the reasons why the ABC insurgency began, then you will soon have the DEF insurgency . . . and so on. . . .

I have designed this seminar to provide students with fundamental understandings as well as practical tools to assist counterinsurgents to victory. Unfortunately, though I think the developmental approach is more comprehensive, I also think it is much harder. A lot harder. Very very very much harder: time, money, lives, etc. Dropping nukes and turning an insurgent region into a parking lot is faster, cheaper, and easier than investing seven to fifteen years of blood, lives, and marriages at billions of dollars per year in order to create a bustling, developing, democratic, free-market economy. Nevertheless, choosing the harder right over the easier wrong is what leadership is all about, and I hope that readers of this book and students of this course find that the tools, concepts, and insights herein enable them to both leadership and victory.

Dean Nosorog
West Point, New York
May 2005

I humbly offer this book as a tribute to Archangel Michael for his defense in battle and his protections against evil, and as an affirmation to the one King whom he and I both serve.

The Revolution That Failed

Andrew F. Krepinevich, Jr.

THE KENNEDY ADMINISTRATION: REVOLUTION FROM ABOVE

Throughout the 1950s, neither the budding insurgency in South Vietnam nor the Eisenhower administration's focus on high-intensity conflict provided the U.S. Army with an incentive for thinking about wars of national liberation, let alone developing a capability to successfully combat them. With the coming Kennedy administration, however, the Army experienced strong pressure for change from the Commander-in-Chief himself. How the Army responded to Kennedy's efforts to engineer a "revolution from above" in its approach to war says a lot concerning how strongly the Army Concept was embedded in the organizational psyche.

The election of John Kennedy in 1960 brought about a change in administration and a change in national strategy as well, from Massive Retaliation to Flexible Response. In contrast to Eisenhower's Massive Retaliation, which threatened the use of U.S. nuclear forces in response to any act of Communist aggression, Flexible Response proposed to meet such aggression at the level of violence at which it was initiated.

Kennedy, and many defense experts, felt that Massive Retaliation had not provided the nation with a credible deterrent against Communist adventurism. As Soviet nuclear might grew throughout the 1950s, the costs that the United States would incur by resorting to nuclear war increased. These costs reached such a high level that they undermined the credibility of Massive Retaliation's nuclear threat in all but a few areas where America's vital interests were at stake. Thus, the Communist victory in Indochina, the shelling of Quemoy and Matsu by Communist China, and the Soviet suppression of Poland and Hungary were all effected without Massive Retaliation's being invoked.

And yet, containment of communism remained U.S. policy. The problem was imposing a credible deterrent against Communist expansionism, one where prospective American costs would be more in line with the anticipated benefit of communism restrained. The answer, Kennedy felt, was Flexible Response. The United States would maximize its options for responding to aggression and increase the credibility of its threats to employ force by generating forces capable of meeting the Communists at any level along the spectrum of conflict, from subversion and insurgency, up through conventional and tactical nuclear war, all the way to a full-scale nuclear confrontation.

Kennedy's philosophy found its roots in the writings of General Maxwell Taylor, Army Chief of Staff from 1955 to 1959. In *The Uncertain Trumpet* Taylor laid out the parameters for this new strategy and actually coined the term *flexible response*. As Taylor put it, Kennedy read *The Uncertain Trumpet* and made Flexible Response his slogan, "just as Ike had made Massive Retaliation his."[1]

Krepinevich, Andrew. (1986). "The Revolution that Failed." *The Army and Vietnam* (pp. 27–55). Baltimore: The Johns Hopkins University Press.

Taylor's interpretation of Flexible Response focused primarily on creating an army with the ability to wage a mid-intensity conflict, where the practitioners of the Army Concept would feel most at home. The new president would try to stretch Taylor's concept to cover low-intensity conflict as well. By and large, the Army welcomed Kennedy's commitment to Flexible Response as reprieve from the lean budget years of the Eisenhower administration.[2] However, Flexible Response also implied the generation of forces and doctrine capable of addressing threats to U.S. security at the lower end of the conflict spectrum—wars of insurgency. This strategy quickly ran into conflict with an Army bent on preparing for conventional war in Europe, not brushfire wars in the emerging nations of the Third World. The question soon became one of how quickly and to what degree of magnitude the president could get the Army to modify its operational concept.

John Kennedy came into office only a fortnight after Nikita Khrushchev proffered his country's support for "wars of national liberation." The president was so impressed by Khrushchev's hurling down the gauntlet before the new administration that he read excerpts from the speech at the first meeting of his National Security Council. Kennedy directed all members of his administration involved in the setting of national security policy to read and ponder the speech.

Of course, the president's concern regarding wars of national liberation predated the Khrushchev speech. As a congressman and senator, Kennedy had made several trips to Indochina during the Viet Minh insurgency. He had spoken out in the Congress on the shortcomings of French efforts to combat insurgency, both in Indochina and Algeria. To Kennedy, insurgencies—or wars of national liberation, as the Communists referred to them—were what the Chinese and Soviets were counting on as the wave of the future. Nuclear war was out of the question; even Khrushchev realized that. In Korea the United States had shown the Communists that limited wars of overt aggression did not pay. Thus the new approach—insurgency.

For the Army, which would have to bear the brunt of administration efforts to counter insurgencies, insurgency warfare implied dramatic changes in traditional military operations. The president said as much in an address to the graduating class at West Point in 1962: "This is another type of war, new in its intensity, ancient in its origins—war by guerrillas, subversives, insurgents, assassins; war by ambush instead of by combat; by infiltration, instead of aggression, seeking victory by eroding and exhausting the enemy instead of engaging him. . . . It requires in those situations where we must counter it . . . a whole new kind of strategy, a wholly different kind of force, and therefore a new wholly different kind of military training."[3] In the words of General Taylor, "It came through loud and clear that he saw a new kind of threat coming for which conventional armies, navies and air forces weren't ready to fight."[4] Kennedy's problem, and his challenge, was to effect a revolution in the Army's organizational perspectives, a revolution from above in which the service would be forced to stretch its limited resources to cover the counterinsurgency or war in Europe.

During his first year in office, the president made strong efforts to get the Army moving in this area. One of his first questions to his principal advisers after the inauguration was, "What are we doing about guerrilla warfare?" National Security Action Memorandum (NSAM) 2 instructed Secretary of Defense McNamara to look into the matter of "increasing the counterguerrilla resources." Kennedy also examined Special Forces equipment and manuals. Dissatisfied on both counts, he called a special meeting to confront the JCS. When the president queried General Taylor about the Army's efforts to develop a capability for low-intensity conflict, Taylor informed him, "We good soldiers are trained for all kinds of things. We don't have to worry about special situations." "That," Taylor later said, "didn't satisfy him a nickel's worth."[5]

Brig. Gen. William P. Yarborough, commander of the Special Warfare School at Fort Bragg, observed that Kennedy could not "find any military chain of command that was aware of this phenomenon in depth."[6] Despite his absence of concern over insurgency warfare, Taylor was held in high regard by the president, who saw him as a soldier-scholar who understood the nuances of this "new" form of conflict. Taylor was recalled to active duty shortly after the president took office and became Kennedy's

Special Military Representative, a duty that required the general to monitor the ongoing counterinsurgency programs.

Kennedy continued to push. He singled out the Special Forces for attention, authorizing them, over the objections of the Army brass, to wear the green beret as a mark of distinction, while approving a 5,000-man increase in the size of the force as well. His goal was to create a big enough shock in the Army that it would be forced into a revision of its priorities and a reorientation of its Concept. On 28 March 1961, in his special message to the Congress on the defense budget, the president argued that the nation needed "a greater ability to deal with guerrilla forces, insurrection, and subversion."[7] And in his State of the Union address to Congress on 25 May 1961, the president declared his intention to expand "rapidly and substantially" the existing forces for the conduct of "nonnuclear war, paramilitary operations and sublimited or unconventional wars."[8]

Kennedy pushed his approach through the national security structure. In NSAM 52, dated 11 May 1961, he directed the military to examine its force structure in light of a possible future commitment to Southeast Asia.[9] Yet the president realized that for all his prodding, and for all his authority, the Army could not be forced to adopt his concern for counterinsurgency. This led to an extraordinary session in the Oval Office on 30 November, when the president summoned in all the Army's major commanders. So far as anyone could determine, it was the first session of its kind.

Elvis Stahr, then secretary of the Army, was present. He found the president very much on a "counterinsurgency kick." Kennedy said, "I want you guys to get with it. I know that the Army is not going to develop in this counterinsurgency field and do the things that I think must be done unless the Army itself wants to do it."[10] This appeal had a minimal impact on the Army brass. The Army would do it if the president wanted, but the service itself was not behind it. Over a month later, many of the presidential queries concerning Army preparation for low-intensity conflict were still being ignored. Kennedy's frustration was evident in a memo to Robert McNamara in which the president bluntly informed his secretary of defense that he was "not satisfied that the Department of Defense, and it particular the Army, is according the necessary degree of attention and effort to the threat of insurgency and guerrilla war."[11] Responding quickly to the direct pressure exerted by the president, the JCS designated Marine Maj. Gen. Victor H. Krulak as Special Assistant for Counterinsurgency and Special Activities [SACSA]. The Army appointed Brig. Gen. William B. Rosson to be in charge of Special Operations.

That same month, on 18 January, Kennedy set up the Special Group, Counterinsurgency (SGCI), with General Taylor as its chairman. Other members included Robert Kennedy, the president's brother (and attorney general), U. Alexis Johnson (undersecretary of state), Roswell Gilpatric (undersecretary of defense), Gen. Lyman Lemnitzer (chairman of the JCS), John McCone (director of the CIA), McGeorge Bundy, and Edward R. Murrow (USIA). By placing in the group individuals who held positions of high responsibility in the administration, the president hoped to prod the Army on a more frequent basis than he himself had been able to do.

In addition to applying pressure from above, Kennedy sought to indoctrinate the Army from within. In his blistering note to McNamara, Kennedy informed the secretary of defense that he wanted counterinsurgency training added to the curricula of military schools at all levels, from West Point all the way up to the Army War College. The president also dropped a broad hint that future promotions to general officers would depend on the individual's demonstrated competence in the field of counterinsurgency. To get the indoctrination program moving, Kennedy directed that topnotch Army colonels and brigadier generals be sent to the Special Warfare Training Center at Fort Bragg for a course on counterinsurgency.[12]

PROBLEMS WITH THE KENNEDY APPROACH

Although the president felt that there was something special and out of the ordinary about wars of national liberation and the Communist insurgency threat, he did not have the time to oversee directly the administration's counterinsurgency program; nor did he have the time to become an expert himself on the nature of protracted conflict and counterinsurgency warfare. Like other presidents in postwar America, Kennedy relied heavily on his aides to carry out his directives and ensure that the bureaucracies complied with them. Unfortunately, the individuals chosen by Kennedy to perform this role were not well suited for the task. Their lack of expertise in the realm of low-intensity conflict hampered the ability of the administration to hold the Army's feet to the fire over counterinsurgency; thus the Army could give lip service to requirements placed on it by the administration or ignore them entirely. The Army was not intentionally frustrating the formulation of national security policy but was, rather, acting out of its convictions that its first priority was in Europe and that if you could win a big war, you could certainly win a little one.

One of the administration's leading "experts" on counterinsurgency was Walt W. Rostow, deputy to McGeorge Bundy, the president's special assistant for national security. Rostow, a graduate of Yale and a Rhodes scholar, had served in the Office of Strategic Services (OSS) during the war and was an economist long associated with the government. Rostow felt that "communism is best understood as a disease of the transition to modernization" and that "a guerrilla war must be fought primarily by those on the spot . . . [because] it is an intimate affair, fought not merely with weapons but . . . in the minds of men who live in the villages and in the hills."[13] Simply stated, insurgency was a threat to emerging Third World nations that revolved essentially around the need of the indigenous government to obtain the support and control of the population. Rostow also posited, quite correctly, that the best way to defeat insurgency was to nip it in the bud, before it had an opportunity to develop into its guerrilla warfare phase. Rostow felt, however, that once the guerrilla warfare phase had been reached, the vulnerable state might well have to "seek out and engage the ultimate source of aggression."[14] This Massive Retaliation mentality, rooted in his earlier World War II days, when he had served as a target selector during the bombing of Germany, led Rostow to conclude that strategic bombing of North Vietnam would provide a way out of counterinsurgency operations for the United States. This

great faith in air power led Rostow to focus more on the concept of a traditional state-to-state military confrontation between the United States and the DRV than on the insurgency in South Vietnam.

To a certain extent, Rostow was the protégé of General Taylor, perhaps *the* key individual involved in translating into action the president's anxieties over the Army's inertia on the counterinsurgency front. During the early 1960s, Taylor served as the president's special Military Representative, chairman of the SGCI, chairman of the JCS, and ambassador to South Vietnam. Kennedy also sent Taylor to South Vietnam on a number of special missions to get the facts on insurgency. The only problem with Taylor's serving in so many key positions was that he advocated preparing for limited war, not sublimited war (as counterinsurgency was then referred to). What Taylor had fought for in *The Uncertain Trumpet* was the regeneration of the Army's capability to wage mid-intensity conflicts in accordance with its Concept. Down the road, as U.S. involvement in Southeast Asia grew, Taylor's solution to the insurgency problem coincided with Rostow's: the execution of an American strategic bombing campaign against North Vietnam. Taylor could accept no more than most other generals the proposal that in order to deal effectively with the VC, the Army, which had fought to modernize and improve in terms of mobility and firepower, must become not more sophisticated but more primitive.[15] Ironically, the effect of placing Taylor at so many of the junction points between the political leadership and the Army was not so much the application of pressure from above on the military as it was the insulation of the service from the very pressure that the president was trying to generate.

Kennedy's secretary of defense, Robert McNamara, a graduate of the Harvard Business School and former president of the Ford Motor Company, possessed a background geared more to the managerial aspects of defense policy than to its doctrinal or operational elements. McNamara was indeed to effect a revolution at the Pentagon, but it was to be a managerial revolution inspired by the introduction of his Planning Programming Budgeting System (PPBS). PPBS, as implemented by the young, talented, civilian Whiz Kids that McNamara had brought to the

Pentagon with him, was to challenge the Army's procurement policies far more than its doctrine. Cost-effectiveness became the byword in the development of new forces. Thus, the battles waged between McNamara and the JCS were primarily over the technological and logistical elements of strategy. With few exceptions, the operational approach to counterinsurgency was left to the Army. McNamara was strictly out of his element when forced to look beyond the technical and managerial dimensions of the counterinsurgency problem and examine its operational nature. He felt more at ease referring to the "tremendous increases, percentagewise" in counterinsurgent force levels than he did when dealing with the strategy and tactics involved in such a conflict.[16] Finally, the secretary of defense was an extremely busy individual. The directive from the president to implement the strategy of Flexible Response, coupled with the introduction of PPBS into the Pentagon's procurement system, among other things, was enough to tax even a man of McNamara's energy. There just was not sufficient time for McNamara to become closely involved in the development of counterinsurgent forces.

In examining the men who sat on Kennedy's oversight board, the SGCI, one fairs no better in the search for someone versed in the field of low-intensity conflict. Indeed, one wonders why a president so intent on forcing the Army to develop a new approach to this form of warfare would opt for so conventional a group of men to bring about that change. It has been noted that the group's chairman, General Taylor, had his focus on the problems of limited war, not counterinsurgency. Robert Kennedy, the president's brother, was a member of the group primarily as JFK's watchdog. This notwithstanding, his knowledge of doctrinal and force structuring requirements was minuscule. Taylor recalls that the attorney general once asked, "Why can't we just make the entire Army into Special Forces?"[17] Roswell Gilpatric, representative for the Department of Defense (DOD), was an individual whose Air Force background was largely irrelevant to the problem at hand. U. Alexis Johnson, at the Department of State, was viewed by the president simply as a fellow "who gets things done."[18] Murrow, McCone, and Bundy represented agencies or organizations that

would be needed if a counterinsurgent capability were to be developed; none, however, came near to being an expert in counterinsurgency. Army Gen. Lyman Lemnitzer, chairman of the JCS, was not enthusiastic regarding the administration's push on low-intensity warfare.

Compounding the flaws within the membership of the group were structural defects. Despite the top-heavy nature of the SGCI, its staff was not sufficiently large to monitor the initiatives that it attempted to undertake. This was particularly crucial, since the senior composition of the membership offered little opportunity for personal follow-up. But the problem ran deeper. The record of the SGCI shows a good deal of activity dealing with organizational and programmatic detail but relatively little concerning the more profound problem of doctrine and the need for an integrated interagency approach. As in DOD, the emphasis was on the technical and logistical aspects of the problem rather than on development of a governmentwide approach to insurgency. When General Taylor departed in October 1962 to become chairman of the JCS, the SGCI declined. By 1966 its influence had so diminished that it was quietly absorbed into the NSC system of senior interdepartmental groups.

Ironically, such "experts" as the administration had were not at the center of the policy process but on the periphery. Roger Hilsman, initially director of intelligence and research at the State Department, had fought with guerrillas in Burma during World War II. He was a West Point graduate and had a close relationship with R. K. G. Thompson, the noted British expert on guerrilla warfare. Despite these credentials, Hilsman was never given a major role in the administration's counterinsurgency program. The same fate befell Air Force Brig. Gen. Edward Lansdale, who had worked with Magsaysay in the Philippines and in the special military mission in Saigon. Lansdale, not a favorite of Taylor's, quickly found himself relegated to a minor role in the policy process. Furthermore, the administration, while upgrading the status of the Special Forces, did not see fit to challenge the Army's designation of MAAG chiefs or, later, the commander of MACV, yet the officers assigned were quite ill-suited for supervising counterinsurgency operations. General officers with training in the field, such as Major General Rosson and

Brigadier General Yarborough, remained on the sidelines.

THE ARMY'S RESPONSE

The administration's emphasis on developing a counterinsurgency capability shook the Army brass. They were, in effect, being told to alter radically the Army's method of operation, a method that had been eminently successful in recent conflicts. The notion that a group of novice civilians (Kennedy, McNamara, and the Whiz Kids) should require the Army to de-emphasize its strong suits (heavy units, massed firepower, high technology) in favor of stripped-down light infantry was bound to encounter strong resistance from the Army leadership.

Attitudes with the Army hierarchy bore out both the service's disinterest in Kennedy's proposals and its conviction that the Army could handle any problems that might crop up at the lower end of the conflict spectrum. For instance, General Lemnitzer, chairman of the JCS from 1960 to 1962, stated that the new administration was "oversold" on the importance of guerrilla warfare. Gen. George H. Decker, Army Chief of Staff from 1960 to 1962, countered a presidential lecture to the JCS on counterinsurgency with the reply, "Any good soldier can handle guerrillas." Gen. Earle Wheeler, Army Chief of Staff from 1962 to 1964, stated that "the essence of the problem in Vietnam is military." At the time, General Taylor felt that counterinsurgency was "just a form of small war" and that "all this cloud of dust that's coming out of the White House really isn't necessary." Taylor later recalled the Army's reaction to Kennedy's program as being "something we have to satisfy. But not much heart went into [the] work."[19]

Indeed, in the Army's perception counterinsurgency operations were lumped with conventional-style military operations like those undertaken in the Korean War. A *Newsweek* interview with a Pentagon staffer reflected this sentiment. The United States, said the spokesman, ought to commit troops to the Asian mainland only on the conditions that no "privileged sanctuary" be granted the enemy, that U.S. power be applied "without any limitation" against the enemy's military resources, and that the United States not undertake a prolonged land war. This article noted that "many competent soldiers" believed in this approach. The prescription for victory in a limited war in Southeast Asia, he said, would center on a strategic bombing campaign and on mobile tank warfare on South Vietnam's "savannah grasslands and open plains, just like in Europe or west Texas."[20]

The Army's response to the administration's call for a reevaluation of its doctrine and force structure was a negative one. In the Army's thinking, there was scant difference between limited war and insurgency. The service's response was unidimensional, reflecting a traditional approach to the conflict, while ignoring its social and political dimensions. All would be solved if the president and his people would just let the Army alone. Unable to fit the president's prescriptions into its force structure, oriented on mid- and high-intensity conflict in Europe, the Army either ignored them or watered them down to prevent its superiors from infringing upon what the service felt were its proper priorities.

Doctrine, basically, is an authoritative, approved statement of how to perform a task. Current doctrine within the Army has often been described as what 51 percent of the Army thinks it is. In the Army, doctrine is developed in several ways. Service schools (such as the Command and General Staff College [C&GSC] and the Army War College), certain service commands (such as the United States Continental Army Command and the Combat Developments Command), and professional journals (such as *Parameters, Military Review,* and *Armor*) all contribute formally or informally in the production and dissemination of doctrine. The schools and commands are particularly important, since they contain the service's doctrinal memory and present the approved way of doing things to the Army's officer corps.

Service schools, through their instruction of officers, are of crucial importance in propagating doctrine. The higher the rank an officer achieves, the more times he will have returned to one of these schools to be "grounded" in the proper Army methods of war. Nearly all general officers have attended their respective branch's basic course (for newly commissioned officers) and advanced course (primarily for captains), as well as the C&GSC (for majors) and the Army War College (for colonels). Doctrine is also developed and disseminated through training given in field exercises and evaluations. This allows the doctrinal guidance presented in manuals and in the classroom to be put into practice, making "real" what had formerly been abstract. Finally, ideally, the actual employment of doctrine under wartime conditions provides the positive reinforcement necessary to validate the doctrine or negative feedback leading to modification in the Army's approach to the problem. Thus, the military reversals in Vietnam during the early 1960s ought to have resulted in the Army's modifying its approach to insurgency warfare.

DEVELOPMENT OF DOCTRINAL LITERATURE FOR COUNTERINSURGENCY

In the years following World War II, the Combat Developments Organization within the Army Field Forces proved inadequate for developing doctrine for future conflicts. Responding to this shortcoming, the G-3 (Operations) section of the Army Field Forces organized the Combat Development Group in October 1953. This arrangement was short-lived, however. In June 1954 an Army reorganization plan established the United States Continental Army Command (USCONARC), which replaced the Army Field Forces in February 1955. USCONARC was responsible for commanding all Army forces in the continental United States, as well as developing doctrine and material. Within this structure, the C&GSC was charged with "the development of doctrine for all of the combined arms and services."[21]

In 1961 the system was further restructured with the arrival of Robert McNamara as secretary defense. USCONARC was divided into three commands: the Continental Army Command (CONARC), which retained responsibility for training; the Army Material Command, responsible for procurement; and the Combat Development Command (CDC), charged with the development of doctrine. While this purportedly removed the service schools, particularly the C&GSC, from their primacy in the area of doctrinal development, they remained influenced in the doctrinal formation process. The new system, activated by General Decker on 7 March 1962, provided the basis for doctrinal development prior to U.S. intervention in Vietnam in 1965.

In spite of efforts to generate a forward-looking approach to doctrinal development through various changes and refinements in the organizations responsible for it, the Army failed to create a coherent body of doctrinal literature for counterinsurgency. An examination of Army field manuals (FMS) during the period reveals that counterinsurgency warfare was ignored almost entirely during the Eisenhower era. While this changed with the advent of the Kennedy administration, doctrinal literature on counterinsurgency during the early sixties was slow to materialize, and when it did, it reflected the service's tendency to fit all forms of conflict within the familiar framework of the Concept.

Any discussion of FMS must begin with FM 100-5, *Operations*, also referred to as the bible on how to fight. Editions of this manual were published in 1944, 1954, 1956, 1958, and 1962. Until the 1962 edition, there was no discussion in the manual concerning counterinsurgency warfare or how to organize guerrilla units in support of conventional operations (as was done in World War II and Korea).[22] As a result of the Kennedy administration's push in 1961, the 1962 edition contained two chapters relating to "counterinsurgency." Chapter 10, "Unconventional Warfare Operations," dealt basically with disrupting the enemy b organizing friendly guerrilla forces in a mid-intensity conflict environment. Chapter 11, "Military Operations against Irregular Forces," was fraught with overtones of the Concept. For example, the manual held that "operations to suppress and eliminate irregular forces are primarily *offensive in nature*. Thus, the *conventional force* must plan and seize the initiative at the outset."[23]

In addition to FM 100-5, the Army produced a number of manuals in the 31 series that were intended to address counterguerrilla operations. FM 31-20, *Operations against Guerrilla Forces*, published in 1951, called for conventional forces to deal with guerrilla or partisan forces. In 1953, FM 31-15, *Operations against Airborne Attack, Guerrilla Action and Infiltration*, discussed the provision of rear area security from partisan forces. Again, the framework for discussion was conventional war. Later published as *Operations against Irregular Forces*, the manual was adequate as an expression of general principles but did not provide guidance at the implementation level.[24] When the manual came out in 1964 retitled *Special Warfare Operations*, it included specific chapters on counterinsurgency operations. FM 31-21, *Guerrilla Warfare*, issued in 1955, called for the execution of counterguerrilla operations with conventional forces as part of a general war. Surprisingly enough, when the manual was revised in 1958, all mentions of counterguerrilla operations were deleted.[25] A 1963 edition, written by the Special Warfare Center, included a chapter on counterinsurgency, but only as it related to the Special Forces.[26] In 1963, FM 31-22, entitled *U.S. Army Counterinsurgency Forces*, was issued. Like FM 31-21, it was written by the Special Warfare Center and directed at Special Forces troops, *not* the Army as a whole.[27]

The result of this small but highly publicized surge in counterinsurgency doctrinal literature was not a little organizational confusion. In May 1962 Major General Rosson characterized the Army's progress in this area as "short term in nature, that is, designed to meet immediate requirements" (that is, pressure from the administration).[28] General Depuy, then a colonel serving as the director of special warfare at the Pentagon, recalled that "we were rather mechanistic about the whole thing" and that the doctrinal effort was perceived to be in response to a "fad" originating during the Kennedy administration.[29] By 1964 the Army had yet to publish a manual dealing specifically with counterinsurgency at the Army level. An Army evaluation of doctrinal literature for special warfare in January 1964 reported that "nowhere is there a definitive listing of doctrinal requirements for special warfare." The report observed that "except for some tips for individual advisors in FM 31-22, doctrine for the organization, employment, and support of an advisory organization, other than the Special Forces, does not exist."[30] Counterinsurgency doctrine was categorized overall as "defective" at the national level, the host country level, and the combined arms level.

As late as November 1964 the Army was still involved in a review and reevaluation of its role "in the entire field of counterinsurgency."[31] In February 1965, CDC was still working on an advisor handbook and on plans for the integration of counterinsurgency doctrine into the service schools and training programs of the Army.[32] Army doctrine, as reflected in its patchwork formulation, reflected the activity of the service going through the motions of churning out a response for a contingency that it did not really understand, out of a desire to satisfy the requirements of the civilian leadership. The result of this lack of motivation on the Army's part was that as late as 1966 most American unit commanders and division staff officers were not familiar with the standard doctrinal literature contained in Army field manuals.[33] Indeed, in 1967, CONARC would note that "there is insufficient doctrine on area warfare."[34]

Even if U.S. troop leaders had been familiar with counterinsurgency doctrine, there is strong evidence that the Army Concept persisted even after U.S. ground forces became involved in Vietnam. For example, the Army's, FM 31-16, *Counterguerrilla Operations*, published in 1967, framed counterinsurgency doctrine within the borders of the Concept. Counterinsurgency was a duty added to the regular combat mission of divisions and brigades; the Army prescribed no changes in organization nor any scaling down of the firepower to be used in fighting an insurgency.[35]

In addition to Army field manuals, the service's professional journals were being used to disseminate doctrine. These journals are, for the most part, associated with service schools and, as such, reflect the doctrinal emphasis given counterinsurgency by the school and the officers who attend it. By and large, the journals remained indifferent to the proliferation of insurgency warfare in the 1950s and early 1960s, exhibiting but a minor reaction to the counterinsurgency "fad" created by the Kennedy administration. For instance, in nineteen issues of *Army* magazine, from January 1959 through July 1960, there was not a single comment on insurgency in the letters section. One searches in vain for the professional strategists who might have conducted analyses of insurgencies that either were ongoing or had been recently concluded in Greece, the Philippines, Cuba, Malaysia, Indochina, and Algeria. A fall 1960 issue of *Military Affairs* devoted to unconventional warfare was as close as the professional journals were to come to a discussion of insurgency warfare prior to the Kennedy "revolution."

Kennedy's call for an Army counterinsurgency capability slowly created an increase in the journals' consideration of the subject. An examination of *Military Review* published by the

C&GSC revealed that despite a noticeable increase in 1962, as the administration's program began to impact on the Army, the overall share of insurgency-related articles quickly stabilized at slightly above 10 percent of the total, notwithstanding the increase in the American involvement in Vietnam and designation, in 1962, of counterinsurgency as a primary Army mission, coequal with nuclear and conventional war contingencies.

Given the general quality of the articles purporting to deal with counterinsurgency, it is just as well that the exposure remained low. One finds in many of them an author attempting to fit counterinsurgency doctrine into something approximating traditional Army operations. One contributor to *Armor* magazine, for example, assured his readers that if armored personnel carriers (APCS) and light tanks were substituted for heavy armor, "standard doctrine becomes applicable."[36] In fact, to fully develop Army counterinsurgency capabilities in Vietnam, the author concluded, what was necessary was the development of more APCS, to "kill more VC," or better yet, more light tanks, to "kill VC more efficiently." Another armor officer boldly stated armor's need to find a niche in counterinsurgency warfare lest the branch lose influence within the Army: "The future of armor lies in its officers and noncommissioned officers, developing new concepts for its employment in limited war counterguerrilla operations. If armor is not able to be deployed in this type of role, it will find itself becoming less and less 'THE COMBAT ARM OF DECISION.'"[37]

An artilleryman faced with much the same dilemma called for the employment of "lean" artillery in counterinsurgency operations, such as 105 mm howitzers. The use of artillery, said the contributor, was justified by its "tremendous killing power."[38] Articles such as these are disturbing not only in and of themselves but also as a reflection of the service schools that screened such articles and then offered them up as representative of new doctrinal development.

ARMY EFFORTS TO ADDRESS COUNTERINSURGENCY

Part of the Army's response to President Kennedy's directive to generate counterinsurgency forces was the proliferation of various conferences, boards, offices, and teams, ostensibly instituted to assist the leadership in coming up with an Army program of action. By March 1960 the insurgency in Vietnam had progressed to the point where the Army Chief of Staff, General Lemnitzer, recommended that MAAG in Saigon shift its emphasis to antiguerrilla warfare training. The JCS also began work on a Counterinsurgency Plan (CIP) for South Vietnam. The plan progressed slowly, however, and was not approved until after President Kennedy assumed office in January 1961. At Kennedy's prompting, the Army increased the resources devoted to the formation of counterinsurgency forces and doctrine. As previously mentioned, both the JCS and the Army set up special staff sections to oversee the development of the counterinsurgency program. A Remote Area Conflict Office (RACO) was established within the Army's Office of the Deputy Chief of Staff for Operations (ODCSOPS). RACO, which was to coordinate and expedite development of special warfare doctrine and material requirements, suffered from a lack of personnel familiar with special warfare, which minimized its effect on the development process.[39] Brigadier General Rosson, the Army's special assistant for special warfare, attempted to establish a special warfare program for the Army but received little encouragement or guidance from ODCSOPS. Despite the appearance of placing emphasis on the generation of a counterinsurgency capability, the effect was the creation of staff positions of high visibility but little real power.

Brigadier General Rosson's experience as head of the Special Warfare Directorate is a case in point. Rosson was intended to be Army Chief of Staff General Decker's eyes and ears on special warfare activities within the service and to recommend changes in doctrine and force structure as he saw fit.[40] General Decker, however, informed Rosson that he opposed the creation of Rosson's position as special assistant as an intrusion visited upon the Army by the Kennedy administration and the "New Frontiersmen."[41] Decker told Rosson that while he would have access to both the Chief of Staff and the Vice Chief of Staff, he would not be permitted to develop his own staff but would be required to work through the DCSOPS.[42] Rosson was to focus only on the Army's "special" assets—the

Green Berets and the Psychological and Civil Affair units, along with special warfare curricula at the service schools and work being done at test and development facilities. The bulk of the Army's forces were considered to be outside of Rosson's purview.[43] Decker told Rosson that he, Decker, and Lt. Gen. Barksdale Hamlett would handle special warfare requirements affecting Army main-force units, such as infantry and armor divisions, the implication being that the Army would retain the "purity" of these units and their orientation on the "big war" in Europe. That Rosson would control the Special Forces was bad enough; the Army leadership was not going to stand idly by while their standard units were engulfed by the president's counterinsurgency "fad." Thus, Rosson and his unwanted directorate were quickly crowded out of the picture, reinforcing the point that the Army leadership assessed its participation in developing a counterinsurgency capability in purely negative terms, that is, in terms of how much it would detract from optimum readiness for limited or general war.[44] Nonetheless, service efforts at doctrinal development were affected significantly by several internal reports, of which two became known as the Stilwell Reports, and another, the Report of the Howze Board on Special Warfare.

One Stilwell Report, entitled "Army Activities in Underdeveloped Areas Short of Declared War," was the product of Brig. Gen. Richard G. Stilwell, a brilliant officer serving on the Army staff. The report dealt with Army counterinsurgency capabilities and was highly critical of Army doctrine and force structuring. Submitted to the secretary of the Army and General Decker on 13 October 1961, the report stated that Army efforts to date had been marked by a "failure to evolve simple and dynamic doctrine." It went on to say that the average military man was not accustomed to thinking within the "conceptual framework" of counterinsurgency. Criticism of the JCS was strong. They were cited as having no in-house capability for generating doctrine or forces and being indifferent and sluggish in their response to directives from the administration to give such matters high priority.[45]

The report recommended upgrading the Special Warfare Division in DCSOPS to a directorate, establishing a direct command line between the Army Staff and the Special Warfare Center, and initiating a "comprehensive informational/education program throughout the Army." What was more important, the report called upon the Army *as a whole* to accept counterinsurgency as its mission rather than as a contingency limited to the Special Forces.

General Decker's response to the Stilwell Report and the queries that followed from Secretary Stahr consisted in adopting the report "as a primary reference" for use by the Army Staff.[46] The Chief of Staff dispatched briefing teams to provide senior officers with information on Army special warfare activities and developed a counterinsurgency course at the Special Warfare Center. The idea of a special warfare directorate would be "studied." There was, however, no commitment to make counterinsurgency an Army-wide responsibility. As Brigadier General Rosson had discovered, the Army leadership was in no hurry to implement any real changes, particularly changes that implied diverting appreciable resources away from standard Army operations.

Following on the heels of the Stilwell Report came the findings of the Howze Board on Special Warfare, issued on 28 January 1962. Formation of the board had been directed by General Powell, commanding general of USCONARC.[47] Although the board was not directed to examine the Army's doctrinal proficiency for counterinsurgency, it did address some doctrinal issues. The board concluded that the Army had "a latent potential" for counterinsurgency operations but that "neither its indoctrination nor training is now altogether satisfactory for this mission" and that "much of this concept is foreign to fundamental Army teaching and practice."[48]

Echoing the Stilwell Report's critique of Army doctrinal shortcomings, the Howze Board concluded that "the tactical doctrine for the employment of regular force against insurgent guerrilla forces as not been adequately developed, and the Army does not have a clear concept of the proper scale and type of equipment necessary for these operations."[49] The implications of the board's findings were best expressed by Lieutenant General Howze himself: "If the board's recommendations are approved the Army will experience a very considerable reorientation of its outlook and effort, particularly as respects training."[50] The question to be answered was whether the

Army was willing, or able, to effect these proposed changes.

Prompted in large measure by the findings of the Howze Board and the Silwell Report, as well as by a letter from the Chief of Staff, General Powell called a special conference on counterinsurgency in CONARC for 23–24 March 1962. The two-day conference produced a recognition that there was fragmentation in development of doctrinal manuals, with as many as three separate agencies developing field manuals on counterinsurgency.[51] It also produced USCONARC pamphlet 515-2, *Counterinsurgency*, published in April 1962. The pamphlet was compiled from presentations made at the conference and was intended to serve as a two-hour orientation course of instruction for Army personnel.[52] While it addressed, albeit briefly, the nature of protracted warfare and counterinsurgency, insurgency was still portrayed as an abnormal, or "special," situation for the Army. Counterinsurgency was viewed as something in which the Special Forces were involved, "in addition to their normal 'hot' war capability." The presentation itself, replete with lists of civilian needs, cold war weapons, and the like, characterized the Army's efforts as one to satisfy a requirement rather than effect a change in attitude and behavior. As a first step in a vigorous program of indoctrination it might have succeeded; by itself, it was just another slide show for the troops. Brigadier General Yarborough sensed that "the Army was getting tired of being booted from the highest level to get with the counterinsurgency bit," so the leadership directed that a film be made to explain to all Army personnel just what counterinsurgency was. According to Yarborough, the film was the Army's way of saying, "Everybody's going to understand this. You guys understand me, you're all going to understand counterinsurgency, every damn one of you." Ironically, Yarborough and the others at the Special Warfare Center quickly realized that because of such quick-fix efforts, the Army brass blithely assumed that everyone really did understand counterinsurgency and that therefore the problem was solved.[53]

On the surface, one had the impression that in terms of organizational commitment to the president's directives the Army was moving rapidly: studies were being done, boards were convening, the troops were being briefed, and staff sections were being created and/or expanded. Yet these actions represented simple, inexpensive responses requiring little diversion of time or resources. In fact, the Army was not taking the difficult and expensive steps to indoctrinate and train its soldiers to fight insurgents.

TRAINING FOR COUNTERINSURGENCY

Training is an important element of doctrinal development. Even if the Army managed to produce doctrinal literature (through FMS, professional journals, and so on) and even if it generated studies and conferences on what was to be done, there remained the task of training its officers and men in the new *modus operandi*, both in the classroom and in the field. Much of this classroom training is conducted at the Army's service schools, branch schools (such as the Infantry School at Fort Benning, Georgia), the C&GSC, and the Army War College. If the Army were going to adapt itself to counterinsurgency operations, it would have to orient its officers on a doctrine that was alien to standard Army operations. A look at the curricula at these schools, however, indicates that the Army modified its training only slightly, if at all.

Indeed, in the period prior to the Kennedy push on counterinsurgency the Army paid little attention to training for low-intensity conflict. The president's strong desire for increased training emphasis on counterinsurgency found the Army in a bit of a dither in its early efforts to respond to his orders. The result was a slapdash reaction, as was borne out in Lieutenant General Hamlett's June 1961 status report to the JCS. In the report, Hamlett noted that the Army's service schools had added from six to twelve hours of instruction on insurgency warfare under "common subjects"; furthermore, the Special Warfare School was sending an Unconventional Warfare Operations Traveling Team out to brief key personnel on the topic.[54] Unfortunately, most of the counterguerrilla warfare training was standard training redesignated to demonstrate the Army's "prompt" response to the president's interest. For instance, interior guard duty, map reading, organization of strong points, cross-training of individual and crew-served weapons, civil defense training, challenging, and the use of countersigns were all labeled "counterguerrilla operations."[55] Obviously, these subjects are part of military training for *any* kind of war. Counterguerrilla training, such as it was, focused on searching out and destroying guerrilla bands in situations more reminiscent of partisan warfare in World War II and Korea than of the protracted warfare of insurgency.

Responding to pressure generated by the SGCI, the Army directed its service schools to increase counterinsurgency instruction.[56] This directive was implemented on 30 March 1962 under the direction of CG CONARC, who also mandated an increase in unit training in counterinsurgency operations. The goal as advocated in the Stilwell Report was to give counterinsurgency "equal prominence" with other forms of warfare. Henceforth counterinsurgency training would no longer be considered "special" but would be a part of the Army's normal mission, on a par with conventional and nuclear warfare operations.[57]

One result of the Army's training program was the compilation of statistics showing how the Army had "accomplished" the mission. The data, it was hoped, would dispel any presidential misconceptions regarding the service's support for its low-intensity contingency. A JCS report to the NSC in July 1962 claimed dramatic increases in the hours devoted to counterinsurgency instruction at all the service schools.[58] Corresponding to the Army's counterinsurgency effort was its designation by the JCS as the organization responsible for the development of doctrine, tactics, and equipment for counterinsurgency to be employed by both the Army and the Marines.[59] Yet these actions were, in reality, only so much fluff. The real issue was how well the Army would translate its mandate for action into meaningful training programs for its troops. Predictably, the Army training program did not go much beyond the initial organizational drill of coughing up the data necessary to mollify its critics.

TRAINING TO DEFEAT GUERRILLAS

Just what was the Army teaching at its service schools? Was counterinsurgency being treated as a coequal with mid- and high-intensity conflict? How well were the courses on low-intensity conflict structured? Did they really address the problems facing the Army in developing an approach to combating insurgent forces? The best place to begin a search for the answers to such questions is in the schools that were highly focused on counterinsurgency, such as the Special Warfare Center at Fort Bragg.

The Special Warfare Center (SWC) was a newcomer to the Army school system. Established in 1952 as the Psychological Warfare Center, it was responsible for psychological warfare operations, as well as operations relating to unconventional warfare. The latter was a new role that reflected the creation of the Special Forces that same year. Indeed, unconventional warfare remained the "major objective" at the SWC up until the Kennedy administration.[60] The training conducted at the SWC was oriented overwhelmingly toward foreign nationals. As late as 1961, 95 percent of the students at the SWC were from foreign countries. With the administration's push to develop a counterinsurgency capability within the Army, the SWC quickly found itself with greatly increased resources and obligations. The center was charged with supporting the buildup of the Army's Special Forces and developing a senior officers' counterinsurgency and special warfare orientation course and a "national interdepartmental seminar."[61]

The SWC quickly ran into difficulty. By attempting to accommodate these requirements, the school became too big too fast.[62] This, combined with the short period of instruction involved, particularly in the senior officer's course, led to little in the way of productive instruction. As Brigadier General Yarborough remembered, the course "was obviously an attempt to give the president what he kept demanding of the military." The general felt that it "wasn't done properly" and that it was definitely "not a success."[63] The Seminar, very popular at first, proved to be too generalized to be of much use and was quietly shelved after the president's assassination.

Yet another "special" course conducted by the SWC was the Military Assistance Training Advisors (MATA) course, intended to provide officers and NCOs going to Vietnam with a working knowledge of what they could expect to encounter in their role as advisers. It was proposed by the Department of the Army and was approved by the Defense Department in January

1962. The program of instruction called for a four-week course including 25 to 30 hours of conversational Vietnamese, as well as the study of counterinsurgency operations in Greece and Malaya but, curiously enough, not Indochina. Students attending the course gave the program very low marks early on, citing as major shortcomings the absence of qualified instructors and the lack of any good definition of just what an adviser's duties were. The program was assembled so rapidly that CONARC had to authorize the school to hire Berlitz language instructors. Indeed, the lack of qualified language personnel was so acute that a conversational class in Vietnamese consisted in a single instructor's reciting phrases in front of an auditorium filled with students, who would then try to repeat them."[64]

The men sent to this school for training as advisers reflected the value that the service placed on its counterinsurgency contingency. Many of the early attendees were on their last duty assignment prior to retirement—which is evidence that men had to be pressured into accepting the assignment or were viewed as "expendable."[65] Many came from back-water assignments as ROTC or service school instructors or National Guard advisers. The course also remained too small—at the end of 1963, with roughly sixteen thousand servicemen in Vietnam, the Army had trained less than three thousand of its officers and NCOS in the MATA program.[66] Many key personnel, such as pilots, never attended the course, receiving waivers because of the shortage of such personnel in Vietnam.[67]

If the Army did not train its people in these courses on counter-insurgency, where, then, did they receive their training? One possibility is that they obtained it while attending the Army's branch schools. Since counterinsurgency is primarily a light infantry war, one would expect the instruction offered by the Infantry School at Fort Benning, Georgia, to have placed strong emphasis in this area. A look at the program of instruction, however, reveals that the infantry got into the counterinsurgency game late and departed early. In the Infantry Officer Basic Course (IOBC), the course given to new lieutenants in the branch, little instruction on counterinsurgency was given until 1963, when it jumped to 21 percent of the total. Of this, only *2 percent* of the instruction was directed *primarily* at counterinsurgency.[68]

The Infantry School remained basically indifferent to counterinsurgency until 1965, when it became evident that the Army was going to Vietnam. At that point, insurgency-related instruction jumped to 56 percent of the total, yet only 16 percent of the instruction focused primarily on counterinsurgency.

Nineteen sixty-five was the peak year for counterinsurgency training. As it became more and more evident that the Army was going to fight in Vietnam using only variations of its standard operational repertoire, interest in counterinsurgency quickly abated. By 1969 less than 28 percent of the instruction in IOBC concerned insurgency, a drop of over half the instruction presented four years earlier. Compounding this lack of effort was the fact that many hours of instruction supposedly dedicated to low-intensity conflict were actually more related to traditional infantry operations. For instance, over 20 percent of the "pure" counterinsurgency training given in 1965 concerned the infantry company in search-and-destroy operations.

The Infantry Officers Advanced Course (IOAC), given to Army captains, had more hours available for instruction but employed fewer hours teaching counterinsurgency doctrine. The pattern was the same as in the basic course, peaking in 1965 with 15 percent of the instruction being "counterinsurgency-related" and rapidly dropping off to 7 percent in 1969.[69] In no year was the level of purely counterinsurgency instruction above 6 percent. How the doctrinal instruction was weighted in favor of standard operations can be seen by examining the discussion devoted to big-unit operations (battalion and above) as opposed to small-unit, counterinsurgency operations. In 1964, on the eve of U.S. intervention, the former was given six times as much attention as the latter. Clearly, there was no great effort to dilute the doctrinal precepts of the Concept and provide counterinsurgency doctrine the coequal status called for by the administration.

An even more striking trend occurred at the Armor School at Fort Knox, Kentucky. Although the Army was to claim an ever-increasing need for armor units and armor officers in Vietnam, the school never took counterinsurgency seriously. Rather, it tried to fit its current operational doctrine into an insurgent conflict environment.

A study of the Armor Officer Basic Course (AOBC) for the years 1959-69 provides remarkable insight into the attitude of the armor branch toward low-intensity conflict. From 1959 to 1967 there was *no instruction* on counterinsurgency doctrine. In 1968 five hours of instruction were classified as pertaining to counterinsurgency, yet a closer examination reveals that none of the instruction directly addressed the topic.[70] The trends for the Armor Officer Advanced Course (AOAC) were much the same; insurgency related doctrine never exceeded 5 percent of the total course offering.[71] The armor branch simply rejected the notion that it should change its doctrine.[72] This notion was supported by Army Chief of Staff and later chairman of the Joint Chiefs of Staff Gen. Earle Wheeler. In addressing the 2d Armored Division, the general observed, "Our division is not a stranger to guerrilla-type warfare. In fact, some historians credit troops of the division with originating and perfecting the armored ambush—and the ambush is certainly basic to guerrilla warfare."[73]

Despite the armor branch's sanguine outlook concerning its ability to cope with the counterinsurgency mission, many of its junior officers did not feel that their indoctrination at Fort Knox prepared them for what they found in Vietnam. One young officer wrote back that the courses taught at the Armor School did not even "scratch the surface of the efforts, techniques and methods which can be directed towards the insurgency."[74] Another officer, citing his branch for "what I believe is the unbalanced thinking of armor and its preoccupation with fighting a nuclear war in Europe," charged the branch with "tying itself to a conventional war in the training of its officers."[75]

Perhaps even more important than the training being given the Army's junior officers was that imparted at the C&GSC. The C&GSC had been a prime influence in the formation of Army doctrine. Attendance at the college was not "automatic," as in the case of the branch schools for junior officers. Only the brightest young field grade officers (majors) attended. It was generally assumed that owing to its reputation as a doctrinal fount for the Army, the C&GSC would be "out in front" of the Army's counter-insurgency program. In reality the college remained a model of dedication to the Army Concept. Dr. Ivan Bir-

rer, a senior official at the C&GSC from 1948 to 1978, recalled that the Army brass showed little interest in whether the college modified its program of instruction or not, so long as it produced statistics showing that it was operating in compliance with Army directives. "All we had to do," said Birrer, "was certify that each officer had X number of hours of counterinsurgency. There were some efforts by the CONARC staff to at least review what was in our instruction, but we were too far from Washington for anyone to really come down and bother us. . . . For the most part, the tactical problems continued to be concerned with land warfare as we had customarily thought of it—on a large land mass."[76]

As with the programs of instruction offered at the Infantry and Armor schools, the C&GSC curriculum provided officers little in the way of a counterinsurgency education. Instruction ostensibly devoted to the topic was frequently skewed to reflect a conventional war environment. In any event, the attention given to counterinsurgency studies was paltry.[77] For example, in 1959–60 and 1960–61 the three hours of instruction devoted to insurgency warfare consisted of a class on how to defeat partisans in the Army's rear area during conventional operations. In 1961–62 this instruction was expanded, with an additional six hours being devoted to airborne unit operations against irregulars.

The impact of the administration's push on counterinsurgency started appearing at the C&GSC in 1962–63. Even so, twenty-seven of the forty-four hours devoted to insurgency that year dealt with corps- and division-level operations; the remainder included heavy doses of unconventional warfare doctrine. Such creative labeling of conventional topics as counterinsurgency-oriented continued in 1963–64. In one case, a counter-insurgency planning exercise called for the insertion of a two-division corps into a country resembling Ghana to clean out insurgents. The instruction was categorized as counterinsurgency training, yet in form and in substance it was right in step with conventional Army operations.

This form of labeling of course offerings continued throughout the war. According to Dr. Birrer, "It became expedient for Leavenworth to appear to be immersed with unconventional and insurgent warfare. We solved this problem . . . by a careful definition. Into the setting of our problems we would include a sentence or two suggesting that there might be the possibility of some irregular forces. . . . This permitted us to count the entire subject as unconventional warfare and it was by such a device that we ran the hours up to 437. But the point to be made is that at *no* time . . . did unconventional warfare really occupy any substantial place in the College Program." Thus the C&GSC "stridently supported the teaching of conventional warfare."[78]

Finally, a look at the Army War College—a school for "the best and the brightest" that the service has to offer—is in order. Here the Army trains its future general officers. During the Vietnam era the course of instruction ran approximately forty weeks and was divided into a series of seven to ten study blocks. These blocks of instruction reflected broad interest areas, such as "The United States and the North Atlantic Community" and "Management of United States Military Power." A rundown of the curricula throughout the 1960s finds the War College strikingly indifferent to insurgency conflict and to the growing conflict in Vietnam itself. From 1959 through 1964 *none* of the study blocks at the War College dealt with low-intensity conflict as either a primary or a related concern for the Army. Beginning in 1964–65 a one-month block of instruction on "The Developing Areas" was offered, yet it was not until 1968, *seven years* after President Kennedy's call for the Army to get moving on counterinsurgency and *three years* after the introduction of U.S. combat troops into Vietnam, that the War College adopted a short (three-week) block of instruction on "Army Internal Defense and Development Operations."[79]

Even in instances where the Army's senior leadership had the opportunity to acquire an understanding of insurgency warfare they balked. While the British sent their *senior* officers and NCOs to the British jungle warfare school in Malaya, the Americans persisted in sending their *junior* officers. To British officers this made no sense, since a junior officer who had attended the school was unlikely to have a great impact on his senior commander, who had not.[80]

In other service schools, Army indoctrination for counterinsurgency was also inadequate. Even while the schools ignored the directives of the political leadership, they dutifully compiled statistics showing that they were complying, in

form if not in substance. One civilian observing the events at the time recalled that "word went out from the Chief of Staff of the Army that every school in the Army would devote a minimum of 20 percent of its time to counterinsurgency. Well, this reached the Finance School and the Cooks and Bakers School, so they were talking about how to make typewriters explode . . . or how to make apple pies with hand grenades in them."[81]

The problems inherent in operating in an alien culture whose people spoke a strange language was, to a large extent, ignored by the Army. Only a few dozen soldiers a year received comprehensive training in Vietnamese; a six-week crash course in Vietnamese was given to a few hundred more men bound for Vietnam.[82] The vast majority received only a smattering of instruction; even the MATA course relied on contracted (Berlitz) instruction for its prospective advisers.[83] A number of internally generated reports during the early 1960s, including one by Major General Rosson, noted that the language barrier continued to present a major bar to optimum exploitation of U.S. assistance in this area.[84] Yet the Army failed to produce significant numbers of individuals whose understanding of the language and culture of Vietnam would have made them invaluable contributors to the success of the mission. One senses a belief within the Army hierarchy that if the Army were going to fight in Vietnam, it would fight as it had in Korea and as the war plans of the early sixties called for—with heavy units in a mid-intensity war not unlike that which they expected to find in Europe.

FIELD TRAINING

The Army's training exercises suffered from the same problems as did the instruction at its service schools: they were generally *pro forma* in nature, and even when serious attempts were made to train, they were often more a bastardized form of conventional operations than a reflection of counterinsurgency doctrine. Again, the statistics generated were impressive. By FY63 most enlisted men had received some form of counterinsurgency training. Many, however, had only been given the Army's two-hour slide show.[85] Beginning in FY64, the goal was to have battalion-sized units of all combat arms (infantry, armor, and artillery) conduct six weeks of counterinsurgency training, capped by a two-week field exercise, each year. Yet given the general lack of understanding in the Army of what counterinsurgency was, these efforts were bound to fail. For example, among the topics considered as part of counterinsurgency training were underwater demolition, air rescue operations, and guerrilla warfare.[86] The essence of counterinsurgency—long-term patrolling of a small area, the pervasive use of night operations, emphasis on intelligence pertaining to the insurgent's infrastructure rather than his guerrilla forces—proved both difficult to simulate and easy to ignore. Mock Vietnamese villages were set up but were of limited utility. Units were primarily taught how to enter a potentially hostile village, search it for booby traps and enemy hiding places, question the villagers about local enemy forces, and then move on.

A few examples of the training undergone by Army units highlight this confused and ineffectual approach. Of particular interest are the exercises conducted at Fort Bragg by the 82d Airborne Division and Special Forces units. The former performed the role of counterinsurgents, the latter that of the insurgents. The mission of the counterinsurgents was to search and destroy: to find, fix, and eliminate all guerrilla forces in the area. In these exercises, the heart of successful counterinsurgency operations was not population security but helicopter availability.[87] A large U.S. Strike Command (STRICOM) exercise in July and August 1963 purported to train participating forces in counterguerrilla operations; however, the exercise consisted in the U.S. XVIII Airborne Corps' going up against an enemy corps of two divisions. The role of U.S. "counterguerrilla" forces was not to combat insurgents but to *organize* them behind enemy lines, a useful unconventional warfare adjunct to mid-intensity conflict but of small relevance in counterinsurgency.[88]

Another special warfare exercise that year pitted a unit of the 82d Airborne against insurgent forces. The training consisted of an airdrop (a "counterguerrilla assault"), followed by the occupation of a town of one hundred Spanish-speaking individuals and the guarding of three supply dumps. Although short in duration, the exercise presented the unit with some real problems in population control. In summing up its experience, the battalion noted that during the operation, "it became increasingly obvious that a large gap exists in both doctrine and training concerning the handling of civilians and unarmed insurgents."[89]

Finally, let us look at an example of Army counterinsurgency training in Europe as described by Col. John K. Singlaub. The colonel reported that each American soldier received seven hours of instruction in counterguerrilla operations, while a ten-day orientation was provided for colonels and above.[90] In addition, the U.S. Seventh Army had dispatched several mobile training teams to units able to engage in some special tactical training. As in the United States, the "special warfare" instruction covered such conventional topics as "instinctive" firing, demolitions, combat in cities, and "ranger-type" (that is, commando) training. The most effective training provided, according to the colonel, occurred when Bundeswehr troops led by detachments of the U.S. 10th Special Forces acted as insurgents, opposed by Army regulars acting as the counterinsurgent force. In order to obtain intelligence on the guerrillas from the local population, Singlaub reported, U.S. commanders constructed a soccer field near one village, whereupon the entire population proceeded to abandon their support of the insurgents and come over to the government's side!

Even if the Army had achieved its goal of six weeks' training each year, and even if it had managed to make that training truly reflective of counterinsurgency operations, the time involved would have been relatively trivial compared with the overwhelming preponderance of time spent on "traditional" conflict contingencies (that is, Europe). Add to this the misplacement of training emphasis, the confusion over just what doctrine called for, and the frequent rotation of unit personnel, and it is easy to understand how the Army entered the war so unprepared in 1965.

The State-Centered Perspective on Revolutions
Strengths and Limitations

Jeff Goodwin

The basic question of every revolution is that of state power. . . . [T]hat "power" which is termed the state [is]...a power arising from society, but placing itself above it and becoming more and more separated from it. What does this power mainly consist of? It consists of special bodies of armed men who have at their disposal prisons, etc . . . A standing army and police are the chief instruments of state power. But can this be otherwise?

—*V. I. Lenin (1974 [1917]: 370; 1943 [1917]: 10)*

This chapter analyzes the strengths and limitations of the state-centered perspective on revolutions, which I briefly introduced in the previous chapter and which I deploy in the chapters that follow. As I noted earlier, the discussion here is primarily theoretical and somewhat abstract, although I do try to ground this discussion in a short case study of the Cuban Revolution, itself one of the major revolutionary conflicts of the Cold War era. Nonetheless, some readers may wish to forge straight ahead into the more empirical chapters on revolutionary movements in Southeast Asia and Central America in Parts 2 and 3, respectively.

I argue in this chapter that state-centered theoretical approaches comprise some of the most powerful analytic tools that are currently available to analysts of revolutions – more powerful (as I argued in the previous chapter) than the modernization and Marxist perspectives. Compared to state-centered approaches, furthermore, "poststructuralist" conceptions of power that are currently fashionable among some scholars simply beg too many fundamental questions. Certain types of cultural analysis as well as the recent turn to "civil society" are somewhat more helpful. But state-centered approaches are even more powerful for resolving the key puzzles that are distinctive to the study of revolutions. (Throughout, I refer to state-centered *approaches* in the plural, because – as I detail in this chapter – there is no single statist perspective or argument, but several overlapping ones.) State-centered analysis, like any theoretical tradition, has its blindspots and limitations, which I will also address. Fortunately, these limitations point the way toward the more powerful synthetic perspective on revolutions and political conflict more generally – a perspective, however, that I do not believe we have yet fully attained.

Goodwin, Jeff. (2001). "The State-Centered Perspective on Revolutions: Strengths and Limitations." *No Other Way Out: States and Revolutionary Movements, 1945–1991* (pp. 35–64). Cambridge: Cambridge University Press.

What is the statist theoretical tradition all about? All the state-centered approaches that I shall review emphasize or "center" a particular set of *causal mechanisms* – namely, those processes whereby states (foreign as well as domestic) shape, enable, or constrain economic, associational, cultural, and even social-psychological phenomena. State-centered theorists argue that these mechanisms are, for certain purposes, more powerful or causally important than (or at least complementary to) a range of alternative causal processes – for example, those emphasizing class conflict, civil society, culture, or social psychology. Statist perspectives, then, are intentionally one-sided.

And yet partly *because* of this very one-sidedness, state-centered approaches are exceptionally valuable for understanding revolutions. This follows, at least in part, from the fact that revolutions themselves are unusually state-centered phenomena, at least as most social scientists have conceptualized them. As Charles Tilly notes, "whatever else they involve, revolutions include forcible transfers of power over states, and therefore any useful account of revolutions must concern, among other things, how states and uses of force vary in time, space and social setting" (1993: 5).

I should emphasize that I do not write as an unbiased observer. My own previous empirical investigations into insurgencies and revolutions have found this state-centered perspective to be extremely illuminating (see Goodwin 1989, 1994a: Goodwin and Skocpol 1989; Foran and Goodwin 1993). At the same time, I will try to clarify the various limitations of this perspective (see also Goodwin 1994b; Emirbayer and Goodwin 1996). After discussing the considerable strengths of state-centered approaches to revolutions, accordingly, I will review the main weaknesses of statist analysis and suggest some of the theoretical resources that are available for redressing them.[1] I also examine how certain strengths and limitations of state-centered approaches are exemplified in a recent scholarly study of the Cuban Revolution (Pérez-Stable 1993)

Before discussing the analytic strengths of state-centered approaches to revolutions, let me begin by distinguishing the distinctive forms of state-centered analysis. Understanding the *variety*

of statist perspectives is important for appreciating both the strengths and limitations of this theoretical tradition.

FOUR TYPES OF STATE-CENTERED ANALYSIS

A good deal of confusion has resulted from the failure of proponents and critics alike to distinguish among – or even to note the existence of – four quite distinctive versions of statist analysis: the state-autonomy, state-capacity, political-opportunity, and "state-constructionist" approaches. Because individual states exist within an international state system, furthermore, each of these approaches has geopolitical or transnational as well as domestic dimensions.

The *state-autonomy perspective,* with which the other statist approaches are most often conflated, emphasizes the variable autonomy of state officials or "state managers" from the dominant social class, civil society more generally, or other states (see, e.g., Mann 1993, 1984; Skocpol 1979; Chorley 1943). According to this perspective – which derives in part from Max Weber's political sociology – politicians, bureaucrats, and military officers may develop identities, interests, ideologies, and (ultimately) lines of actions that are very different from those of organized groups in civil society or the officials of other states; state officials may not be usefully conceptualized, accordingly, as representatives of powerful capitalists, interest groups, the "popular will," or foreign potentates. In fact, the interests of state officials in accumulating resources (through taxes, for example) and mobilizing the population (for wars against other states, for example) may sometimes conflict with the interests of powerful social groups (including the dominant class), not to mention powerful foreign states. Overt conflicts between state officials, on the one hand, and economic elites, mobilized groups, and foreign officials, on the other, are typically adduced as evidence for this perspective.

A second statist approach – which may also be traced to Weber – emphasizes the actual material and organizational capacity (or lack thereof) of state officials to implement successfully their political agenda, even in the face of opposition from powerful actors in civil society or from other states. This perspective focuses on variations of states' fiscal resources, military power, and organizational reach (or "penetration") into civil society – what I referred to in the pervious chapter, following Michael Mann, as the "infrastructural power" of states. Infrastructural power refers, more specifically, to " the institutional capacity of a central state, despotic or not, to penetrate its territories and logistically implement decisions" (Mann 1993: 59; see also Evans 1995; Migdal 1988). Key determinants of such variations include the organizational or bureaucratic rationality of state institutions as well as the extent to which states confront threats, real or perceived, from other states that require war preparation. Some states also receive large infusions of resources from other states; a state's position in the international state system, in other words, may strongly shape its capacities (see, e.g., Collins 1995; Tilly 1992). While this second, *state-capacity approach* is typically utilized alongside the state-autonomy perspective, the two are analytically distinct; state officials, after all, may have very different aims than economic elites or other states and yet lack the capacity to actually implement their preferred policies. State autonomy, in other words, does not necessarily imply state capacity, or vice versa.

A third state-centered approach emphasizes how the apparent tolerance, permeability, or responsiveness of states or "politics" influences the ability of mobilized social groups to act collectively and/or to influence state policies.[2] More specifically, "political opportunities" have been deemed necessary – in addition to (for example) grievances and organization – for people to act collectively or to shape the agenda of state officials. Such opportunities, according to Sidney Tarrow (1994: 85), refer to "consistent - but not necessarily formal or permanent – dimensions of the political environment that provide incentives for people to undertake collective action by affecting their expectations for success and failure." At the very least, according to this *political-opportunity perspective*, the state must either lack the means (infrastructurally) or simply be unwilling to suppress such groups violently; it also helps if these groups can find powerful allies within a divided state or polity (see, e.g., Tarrow 1994; Kitschelt 1986). And geopolitics is again

important here. Some social groups, for example, may form alliances with, and receive significant resources from, foreign states; and international wars and imperial overextension have often produced political crises that have created unprecedented opportunities for political mobilization (see, e.g., Tilly 1992; Kennedy 1987; Collins 1993). In this sense, one may speak of "transnational political opportunities" (McCarthy 1997).

There exists, finally, what Theda Skocpol (1985: 21) calls a "Tocquevillian" approach, which emphasizes how states shape the very identities, goals, strategies, social ties, ideas, and even emotions of actors in civil society. This approach is so named because of Alexis de Tocqueville's masterful employment of it in *The Old Régime and the French Revolution* (1995) and in *Democracy in America* (1981). This is perhaps the most interesting and important statist approach of all, yet it is often elided in discussions of state-centered theory of else conflated with the political-opportunity perspective. I propose that we label this approach the *state-constructionist perspective*,[3] because it examines the ways in which states help to construct or constitute various social forces and institutions that are (falsely) conceptualized as wholly exterior to states.[4] In other words, the focus here – as against a political-opportunity approach – is not so much on whether a state or polity provides incentives or opportunities to act for *already existing* networks of like-minded people; rather, state constructionism emphasizes how the actions of foreign as well as domestic states help to make cognitively plausible and morally justifiable certain types of collective grievances, emotions, identities, ideologies, associational ties, and actions (but not others) in the first place (see, e.g., Birnbaum 1998; Wuthnow 1985).

A major thesis of this book is that states largely "construct" (in this specific sense) the revolutionary movements that challenge and sometimes overthrow them. Of course, this "construction" is never accomplished by states alone, or ex nihilo. Nor is state constructionism intended to slight the agency of revolutionaries themselves. The point is simply that revolutionaries cannot will revolutionary movements, let alone revolutions, into existence. Rather, as I suggested in the previous chapter, revolutionaries have been most successful when they have confronted states, and populations ruled in certain ways by those states, that exhibit certain determinate features and characteristic practices. But this claim stands or falls according to the adequacy of the empirical studies in subsequent chapters.

ANALYTIC STRENGTHS OF STATE-CENTERED APPROACHES TO REVOLUTIONS

Before turning to the weaknesses of the statist theoretical tradition, and of my state-constructionist thesis in particular, I want to emphasize how statist approaches help to resolve a series of key problems that are distinctive to the study of revolutions as a specific form of collective action and political conflict.

The Centrality of State Power and State Breakdowns

To begin with, consider this puzzle: *Why is revolution, unlike many other forms of social and political conflict, a peculiarly modern phenomenon?* Why, in other words, did revolutions occur with increasing frequency during the twentieth century, yet do not seem to have occurred at all before the seventeenth? This puzzle concerns the "conditions of existence" of revolutions – that is, the background conditions (which have only widely existed, evidently, for the past century or two) that are necessary for revolutions to occur. A state-centered perspective offers a compelling solution to this puzzle: the existence of the international state system itself. In other words, *no states, no revolutions.* This proposition follows tautologically, in fact, from the very definition of revolutions as involving, at the very least, the overthrow of national states or political regimes. Thus, there could be no revolutions, in the modern sense of the word, before there were states, and it follows that there cannot be revolutions if and when the international state system is replaced by some other mode (or modes) of governance. This simple yet profound proposition, frequently reiterated by Charles Tilly, is usually overlooked by analysts of revolutions; it is taken for granted by virtually all scholars or revolutions, including Marxists, cultural analysts, and many state-centered analysts themselves.

From a state-centered approach, it is much more than a convention or mere matter of convenience that scholars write books and articles about, for example, the "French," "Russian," and "Cuban" revolutions. In fact (as a state-capacity approach would suggest), prior to the emergence of modern national states,[5] revolutions as we now understand them – whether as radically transformative processes, a distinctive repertoire of contention, or a moral ideal – were simply impossible and generally unthinkable. Until the modern era, that is, no institution had sufficient infrastructural power – with the possible exception of the Catholic Church – to reform extensive social arrangements in more or less fundamental ways; the national state, however, made it possible to do – and to think of doing – just that. (Radical revolutionaries, in fact, have themselves often sought to consolidate national states precisely in order to remake societies.) Thus, while wars and political conflict may be old as humanity itself, the reality and ideal of reshaping a "political order," "society," "nation," or "people" – the political, economic, and/or cultural arrangements of a large population – are coeval with the modern state system as it originated in Europe and was then transported, imposed, and emulated around the globe.

This line of argument immediately suggests a solution to another puzzle: *Why are radical movements, unlike reformist movements and other forms of political conflict, typically concerned with "seizing" or "smashing" state power?* If the preceding analysis is correct, those who would "radically" transform modern societies must obviously concern themselves with the state. (If they don't, the state will certainly concern itself with them!) In other words, because the state enforces (through violence if necessary) the most fundamental "rules" of a society (whether these are codified as laws or exist as traditions or conventions) by virtue of its control of the principal means of coercion, and fundamental recasting of these rules requires access to, and indeed a thorough reorganization of, state power itself. Because of their actual and potential infrastructural power, in other words, states are necessarily the target (although not always the *only* target) of revolutionary movements.

This view of revolutions, I should note, is shared by state-centered and Marxist analysts alike, even though the latter are otherwise keen to emphasize how class struggles are supposedly the driving force behind revolutions. "The basic question of every revolution," wrote Lenin, "is that of state power. . . . The question of power cannot be evaded or brushed aside, because it is the key question determining *everything* in a revolution's development" (1974 [1917]: 370; emphasis in original). The task of revolutionaries, in Lenin's view, was not simply to change the structural characteristics of the state – to bring about "a gigantic replacement of one type of institution with others of a fundamentally different order" (1943 [1917]: 37) by means of which the social order as a whole could be radically reshaped. Perry Anderson (1974:11; emphasis in original) similarly notes that

> one of the basic axioms of historical materialism [is] that secular struggle between classes is ultimately resolved at the *political* – not at the economic or cultural – level of society. In other words, it is the construction and destruction of States which seal the basic shifts in the relations of production, so long as classes subsist.

It follows that successful revolutionary movements must, at the very least, secure or seize state power. And this implies, by definition, that the old state (especially its army) must collapse or surrender: for if it persists in the face of a revolutionary challenge, then the revolutionaries have obviously failed to attain the type of power that they need in order to change the political and/or social order as a whole in a more or less fundamental fashion.[6]

We now possess the solution to yet another conundrum: *Why must the state break down, collapse, or capitulate for a revolutionary movement, unlike many other forms of social protest, to succeed?* The fact that "state breakdowns," particularly the incapacitation of armies, create the possibility for full-fledged revolutionary change is one of the best-known ideas to emerge from statist analyses of revolution; it is a point that is central, for example, to Theda Skocpol's influential state-centered study, *States and Social Revolutions* (1979).[7] In fact, Skocpol not only implicitly utilizes a political-opportunity approach in order to explain why transformative, class-based revolts from below could occur in France, Russia, and China; she also employs a state-autonomy perspective in order to explain the political crises that

created such opportunities in the first place. Indeed, one of the more interesting claims of Skocpol's study is that the political crises that made revolutions possible in France, Russia, and China were *not* brought about by revolutionaries; rather, conflicts between dominant classes and autonomous state officials – conflicts, Skocpol emphasizes, that were produced or exacerbated by geopolitical competition – directly or indirectly brought about such crises, thereby opening up opportunities that rebellious lower classes and self-conscious revolutionaries seized, sometimes years later.

By illuminating the origins of, and the political opportunities created by, these sorts of state crises and breakdowns, sate-centered approaches help to resolve yet another classic puzzle: *Why do revolutions occur when and where they do?* It has become virtually obligatory for scholars to note that people are not often rebellious in the poorest of societies or during the hardest of times; and even where and when people are rebellious, and strong revolutionary movements form, they may not always be able to seize state power – *unless*, that is, they are able to exploit the political opportunities opened up by state breakdowns. "It is the state of the army, of competing armies," Barrington Moore, Jr., has noted, "not of the working class, that has determined the fate of twentieth-century revolutions" (1978: 375). Of course, revolutionaries need not wait for political opportunities to appear. They often topple states, especially infrastructurally weak states, through their own efforts.

The limited utility of poststructuralist conceptions of power (e.g., Foucault 1990), at least for the analysis of revolutions, follows from what has been said thus far. In fact, any view of power as "decentered," largely nonviolent, local, mobile, and ubiquitous fails to grasp the crucial difference that centralized state power (and its breakdown) makes for a variety of social processes, including but not limited to revolutions. Furthermore, the notion that the state itself is simply the "institutional crystallization" or "institutional integration of power relationships" that are fundamentally "local" in nature (Foucault 1990: 93, 96) fails to grasp the potential autonomy and distinctive capacities of states; it also underestimates the role of state power in constructing, or reconstructing, localized power relationships in the first place. It is precisely because not all forms of domination are "local" that revolutions are sometimes desired and even possible.

THE FORMATION OF REVOLUTIONARY MOVEMENTS

And yet, state power and its breakdown cannot alone explain (or predict) revolutions; analysts also need to explain why and how specifically revolutionary movements are able to take advantage of these crises – or *create* such crises – and actually seize power.[8] After all, an organized revolutionary movement simply may not exist or possess the sufficient leverage or "hegemony" within civil society that is necessary to take advantage of (or create its own) political opportunities. In such cases, state power will be reconsolidated – if it is reconsolidated at all – by surviving factions of the old regime or by political forces that eschew any significant transformation of the state or society.

Here again, a state-centered perspective provides us with some indispensable analytic tools. For although statist approaches (as we shall see) do not completely or adequately theorize collective action as such, they are particularly helpful in resolving the following puzzle: *Why are groups with a specifically revolutionary agenda or ideology, as well as a militant or "high-risk" strategy, sometimes able to attract broad popular support?*[9] State-centered approaches point to at least five distinctive state practices or characteristics that help to engender or "construct" hegemonic revolutionary movements; these practices and traits, moreover, are casually "cumulative," in the sense that a hegemonic revolutionary movement is more likely to develop the more they characterize a given state:

1. *State sponsorship or protection of unpopular economic and social arrangements or cultural institutions.* In certain societies, economic and social arrangements – particularly those involving people's work or livelihood or important cultural institutions – may be widely viewed as unjust (that is, as not simply unfortunate or inevitable). Yet unless state officials are seen to sponsor or protect those institutions – through legal codes, surveillance, taxation, conscription, and, ultimately, force – specifically *revolutionary*

movements are unlikely to emerge. People may blame their particular bosses or superiors for their plight, for example, or even whole classes of bosses, yet the state itself may not be challenged (even when the aggrieved are well organized and the political context is opportune) unless there exists a widely perceived symbiotic or dependent relationship between the state and these elites. Indeed, the fact that a despised state must actively protect certain institutions and groups will itself serve, in many instances, to delegitimate and stigmatize those institutions and groups.

For this reason, "ruling classes" that do not directly rule may be safer from revolutionaries than those which do; other things being equal, that is, some measure of state autonomy from the dominant economic class may act as a bulwark against revolution. In such contexts, contentious, anti-elite actions may be chronic, in such forms as pilfering, malingering, sabotage, riots, strikes, and demonstrations. Yet such actions are unlikely to escalate beyond a local or, at most, regional level in a way that would seriously and directly threaten a strong state.[10] But rebels are not revolutionaries, we have seen, unless they seriously contend for state power. Thus, if and when domination is widely perceived to be purely local and "decentered" (i.e., as poststructuralists conceptualize it), then revolution is unlikely, no matter how oppressive that domination is felt to be.

It follows that states that regulate, reform, or even abolish perceived economic and social injustices are less likely to become the target of political demands (revolutionary or otherwise) than those that are seen to cause or perpetuate such injustices. On the other hand, a state that suddenly attempts to reform unpopular institutions that it has long protected may not be able to preempt a revolutionary challenge; on the contrary, such reforms, or even attempted reforms, may be perceived as signs of the state's weakness and, accordingly, will simply serve to accelerate revolutionary mobilization. We might term this the "too-little-too-late syndrome." As Tocqueville argued, "the most perilous moment for a bad government is one when it seeks to mend its ways. . . . Patiently endured so long as it seemed beyond redress, a grievance comes to appear intolerable once the possibility of removing it crosses men's minds" (1955:177).

In sum, economic grievances and cultural resentments may only become "politicized" (that is, framed as resolvable only at the level of the state), and thereby a basis for specifically revolutionary movements, when the state sponsors or protects economic, social, or cultural arrangements that are widely viewed as grievous. Note that this is a "state-constructionist" argument: State practices, in this case, help to constitute both a distinctive *target* and *goal* or aggrieved groups in civil society – namely, the state itself and its overthrow (and reorganization), respectively.

2. *Repression and/or exclusion of mobilized groups from state power or resources.* Even if aggrieved groups direct their claims at the state, they are unlikely to seek its overthrow (or radical reorganization) if they manage to attain some significant share – or believe they *can* attain such a share – of state power or influence. Indeed, even if such groups view their political influence as unfairly limited, their access to state resources or inclusion in policy-making deliberations – unless palpably cosmetic – will likely prevent any radicalization of their guiding ideology or strategic repertoire. In fact, the political "incorporation" of mobilized groups – including the putatively revolutionary proletariat – has typically served to *deradicalize* them (see, e.g., Mann 1993: ch18; Bendix 1977 [1964]). Such groups often view this sort of inclusion as the first step in the accumulation of greater influence and resources; in any event, they are unlikely to jeopardize their relatively low-cost access to the state – unless that state itself is in deep crises – by engaging in "disloyal" or illegal activities.

Political inclusion also discourages the sense that the state is unreformable or an instrument of a narrow class or clique and, accordingly, needs to be fundamentally overhauled. Tocqueville emphasized how the exclusionary nature of French absolutism bred, by contrast, a political culture characterized by a utopian longing for total revolution – even though French social conditions were comparatively benign by European standards of the time (1955: pt. 3, ch. 1).[11]

Accordingly, neither liberal democratic polities nor authoritarian yet inclusionary (for example, "populist") regimes have generally been challenged by powerful revolutionary movements. By contrast, chronic repression and/or exclusion of mobilized groups from access to state power is likely to push them toward a specifically revolutionary strategy – that is, militant, extralegal, and even armed struggle aimed at overthrowing the state. Such repression, after all, serves as an object lesson in the futility of legalistic or constitutional politics (i.e., "playing by the rules"). A major claim of this book is that repressive and exclusionary authorization regimes – even those that stage competitive elections – tend to "incubate" or "construct" radical collective action: Those who specialize in revolution tend to prosper under such regimes, because they come to be viewed by politically repressed groups as more realistic and potentially effective than political moderates, who themselves come to be viewed as hopelessly ineffectual. Partly for this reason, virtually every powerful revolutionary movement of the present century – including those examined in this book – developed under a repressive and exclusionary regime, including the Bolsheviks in Russia, the Communists in China and in Southeast Asia (see Chapter 3), Castro's July Twenty-Sixth Movement in Cuba, the broad coalition that opposed the Shah in Iran, and the guerrilla movements of Central America (see chapter 5).

Note that this argument has both political-opportunity and state-constructionist aspects. In the former sense, it emphasizes how the *lack* of routine opportunities to influence state policy (or the contraction of such opportunities) tends to push certain groups and individuals toward radical politics; in the latter sense, emphasis falls on the ways in which repressive state practices reinforce the plausibility and justifiability of a radical political orientation of collective identity.

3. *Indiscriminate, but not overwhelming, state violence against mobilized groups and oppositional political figures.* Indiscriminate state violence against mobilized groups and oppositional figures is likely to reinforce the plausibility, justifiability, and (hence) diffusion of the idea that the state needs to be violently "smashed" and radically organized. For reasons of simple self-defense in fact, people who are literally targeted by the state may arm themselves or join or support groups that have access to arms. Unless state violence is simply overwhelming, then, indiscriminate coercion tends to backfire, producing an ever-growing popular mobilization by armed

movements and an even larger body of sympathizers (see, e.g., Mason and Krane 1989; Gurr 1986). Revolutionary groups may thus prosper not so much because of their ideology per se, but simply because they can offer people some protection from violent states. Many studies of revolutions (including this one) emphasize that groups have turned to militant strategies or armed struggle only after their previous efforts to secure change through legal means were violently repressed (see, e.g., Booth and Walker 1993; Walton 1984; Kerkvliet 1977).

Like political exclusion, indiscriminate state violence also reinforces the plausibility and diffusion of specifically revolutionary ideologies – that is, ideologies that envisage a radical reorganization not only of the state, but of society as well. After all, a society in which aggrieved people are routinely denied an opportunity to redress perceived injustices, and even murdered on the mere suspicion of political disloyalty, is unlikely to be viewed as requiring a few minor reforms; those people are more likely to view such a society as in need of a fundamental reorganization. In other words, violent, exclusionary regimes tend to foster unintentionally the hegemony or dominance of their most radical social critics – religious zealots, virtuous ascetics, socialist militants, and radical nationalists, for example, who view society as more or less totally corrupted, incapable of reform, and thus requiring a thorough and perhaps violent reconstruction (see McDaniel 1991: ch. 7).

Revolutionaries themselves, it must be noted, sometimes use violence against civilians and their political competitors, not just the state (see, e.g., Kriger 1992; Stoll 1993, 1999). Some revolutionaries coerce civilians or attack political moderates to ensure that they are seen as the only viable alternative to the state; some employ violence purposely to incite or provoke the state repression that will presumably expand their ranks. But this can easily become a self-defeating strategy since the targets of such violence are likely to blame the revolutionaries as much as the state for their travails. Indiscriminate counterstate violence can produce a popular backlash as easily as state violence. Perhaps the best example of this is the Shining Path insurgency in Peru, which I discuss in Chapter 7. Not surprisingly, the violence and abuses of the most popular and successful revolutionary movements pale in comparison to the crimes perpetrated by the states that they confront.

4. *Weak policing capacities and infrastructural power.* As the political-opportunity approach emphasizes, no matter how iniquitous or authoritarian a state may be – or the society that it rules – it can always retain power so long as it is capable of ruthlessly repressing its enemies. Such a state may in fact have many enemies (including revolutionaries), yet they will prove quite ineffective so long as the state's coercive might remains overwhelming.

Long before a state breakdown, however, revolutionaries may become numerous and well organized if the state's policing capacities and infrastructural power more generally are chronically weak or geographically uneven. Guerrilla movements, for example, have typically prospered in peripheral and especially mountainous areas where state control is weak or nonexistent: The Communist movement in China grew strong in the northwest periphery, Castro's movement in Cuba's Sierra Maestra, and El Salvador's guerrilla armies in that country's mountainous northern departments (see, e.g., Wolf 1969: ch. 6, on Cuba; Pearce 1986 on El Salvador). And revolutionaries are doubly fortunate if they confront states and armies that are ineffectual due to corruption or bureaucratic incoherence – traits that are often purposively fostered by ruling cliques or autocrats who fear palace coups. In such situations, revolutionaries themselves may bring about or accelerate state breakdowns not only through direct military pressure, but also by exacerbating conflicts between states (especially personalistic dictatorships) and dominant classes, and between states and their foreign sponsors. These types of conflicts, in addition to creating the general insecurity associated with revolutionary situations, may accelerate state breakdowns by creating economic downturns that bring on fiscal crises for states (see Foran 1992, 1997).

5. *Corrupt and arbitrary personalistic rule that alienates, weakens, or divides counterrevolutionary elites.* As these last remarks suggest, autocratic and so-called neopatrimonial (or "sultanistic") dictatorships are especially vulnerable to revolution (see, e.g., Dix 1984; Goldstone 1986; Goodwin and Skocpol 1989;

Wickham-Crowley 1992; Foran 1992; Snyder 1992; Chehabi and Linz 1998). In fact, such regimes not only tend to facilitate the formation of hegemonic revolutionary movements, but they also cannot easily defeat such movements once they have formed; examples of such regimes include the dictatorships of Diaz in Mexico, Chiang in China, Batista in Cuba (discussed later in this chapter), the Shah of Iran, Somoza in Nicaragua (see Chapter 6), and Ceausescu in Romania (see Chapter 8). As especially narrow and autonomous regimes, such dictatorships tend to have few fervid supporters; they also possess the discretionary power that may alienate certain state officials and military officers as well as vast sectors of society – including middle strata and even elites in addition to lower classes. In fact, because dictators often view economic and military elites as their chief foes, they may attempt to weaken and divide them in various ways, even though such groups share with dictators in counterrevolutionary orientation. By weakening counterrevolutionary elites, however, dictators may unwittingly play into the hands of the revolutionaries, since such elites may thereby become too weak either to oppose revolutionaries effectively or to oust the dictator and reform the regime, thereby preempting revolution. Some dictators have even driven elites, or segments thereof, into the camp of the revolutionaries.

Of course, not all dictators are equally adept at controlling their armed forces and rival elites; their incompetence or incapacity in this regard does not bode well for them personally, but it may prove decisive in preempting revolution. For if civilian and military elites can remove corrupt and repressive dictators, and perhaps institute democratic reforms, they thereby undermine much of the appeal or revolutionaries. In fact, this is precisely what happened in the Philippines in 1986 with the ouster of Ferdinand Marcos (Snyder 1992).

In sum, certain types of states are not only liable to break down and thereby to create the sort of political opportunities that strong revolutionary movements can exploit; certain states also unintentionally foster the very formation, and indeed "construct" the hegemony or dominance, of radical movements by politicizing popular grievances, foreclosing possibilities for peaceful reform, compelling people to take up arms in order to defend themselves, making radical ideologies and identities plausible, providing the minimal political space that revolutionaries require to organize disgruntled people, and weakening counterrevolutionary elites, including their own officer corps.

By thus illuminating both state breakdowns *and* processes of revolutionary mobilization, state-centered approaches provide us with some very powerful tools for explaining revolutions.

SOME COMMON CRITICISMS OF STATE-CENTERED APPROACHES

Like any theoretical tradition, the statist perspective has its share of critics. However, the various complaints that have been directed against this tradition are very uneven in their persuasiveness. Before turning to some of the more potent criticisms of statist analysis, I want to examine several that either rest upon unfounded assumptions or are simply unconvincing. Four such criticisms merit a brief response:

1. *"Societies affect states as much as, or possibly more than, states affect societies"* (Migdal, Kohli, and Shue 1994:2). This broad generalization challenges one combination of the state-autonomy and state-capacity approaches: the view that all states are autonomous from civil society and actually have the capacity to impose their preferred policies.[12] This is certainly a view worth challenging, but it is not clear that many state-centered theorists would defend it. In fact, state- centered theorists have generally emphasized that state autonomy and capacities are potential and *variable* rather than "given" a priori. As we have seen, moreover, statist analysts have emphasized precisely how state *breakdowns*, as well as infrastructurally *weak* states, have encouraged or made possible important social processes, including the formation of revolutionary movements.

This criticism also seems to confuse state-centered analysis with a sort of sweeping *political determinism* that robs "society" of any analytic autonomy whatsoever.[13] But a perspective that "centers" the state hardly implies that states are the *only* institutions that matter or that states themselves are not potentially shaped and constrained by a variety of socioeconomic and cultural forces. In fact, it is possible and sometimes desirable to combine or complement a state-centered analysis with, for example, class analysis (see, e.g., Skocpol 1979; Wickham-Crowley 1992).

2. *State officials are usually not autonomous actors; instead, they typically respond to the demands of the dominant class or (occasionally) of militant lower classes.* This criticism – the principal one expressed by Marxists (see, e.g., Cammack 1989) – is a narrower version of the preceding one, emphasizing how specifically class-based demands determine state policies. Like the previous criticism, this one also challenges one extreme version of the state-autonomy approach – namely, the idea that all states are autonomous from the demands of social classes (and, accordingly, are never influenced by such classes). Again, this is a claim that few if any statists would wish to make; it seems more reasonable, in fact, to assume that the relationship between states and classes is in fact quite variable over space and time.

Two other points about this criticism also need to be made. First, it has usually been raised in the context of complex, detailed debates about the relative importance of class and state actors in formulating specific state policies (e.g., Goldfield 1989; Skocpol and Finegold 1990). These debates, whichever side one finds most convincing, hinge upon the marshaling and interpretation of particular facts and sequences of events. Neither side, including that which emphasizes the importance of class actors, has suggested that its opponents *must* be wrong a priori, irrespective of the actual historical record. The *theoretical* grounds for believing that states *may* be autonomous from class forces, in other words, have not been convincingly challenged – or seriously challenged at all – in these debates; what is disputed is the relative autonomy of *particular* state actors in *specific* times and places (e.g., Democratic politicians in the U.S. Congress during the 1930's).

Second, even in those cases in which the class-biased character of state policies has been convincingly established, it would be quite unfortunate to dismiss or ignore state-centered perspectives on that account. In fact, state autonomy may very well explain why such policies were adopted in the first place. (For example, certain state officials may be in better position that particular capitalists to assess the interests of the capitalist class as a whole.[14]) The state-capacity approach, furthermore, may be helpful for understanding which, if any, class-based policies can actually be implemented. The political-opportunity perspective, furthermore, may be helpful for understanding whether other classes or groups can successfully mobilize *against* such policies. (In this regard, it may make a great deal of difference whether individual capitalists are simply acting in similar ways or the state is enforcing—with violence, if necessary—certain laws or policies at their behest.) And a state-constructionist analysis may be helping for understanding why specifically *class*-based actors are politically organized and influential in the first place.

3. *As a type of "structuralism," state-centered analysis necessarily neglects the purposive (including strategic) and cultural dimensions of social action.* The conflation of state-centered analysis with the sort of "structuralism" that denies the importance of purposive human agency would seem to rest upon an elementary confusion.[15] In fact, statist analysis may emphasize the actions and policies of state actors just as much as the impersonal "structural" characteristics of states (and both are undoubtedly important). For example, rationally calculating and acting state officials are the analytic pivot in some types of state-centered studies (see, e.g., Levi 1988).

The criticism that state-centered analysis fails to treat culture seriously is only partially correct (see, e.g., Friedland and Alford 1991). (I discuss the sense in which it *is* accurate in the next section.) While most statist analyses have in fact been "structuralist" or "instrumentalist" in the sense of neglecting the shared beliefs of politicians and state officials, this quality seems contingent rather than inherent to this perspective. So, for example, one important state-centered study, James M. Jasper's *Nuclear Politics: Energy and the State in the United States, Sweden, and France* (1990), emphasizes precisely the ways in which the ideologies and "policy styles" of state officials shape state policies. Jasper's study is no less state-centered for treating such officials as cultural actors rather than as rational calculators or as puppets of external forces. As Jasper's study emphasizes, moreover, state practices are "always already" cultural practices.

It is also possible, as Robert Wuthnow (1985) has convincingly shown, to explain the diffusion and institutionalization of ideologies from a state-centered perspective. As we have seen, in fact, a state-constructionist approach is indispensable for understanding how radical ideologies and strategic repertoires sometimes resonate with and diffuse among broad masses of people.

4. *Because they interpenetrate one another, the very distinction between "states" and "societies" is untenable and should be scrapped.* This criticism, which is perhaps the most radical that has been raised against statist approaches, has been elaborated most fully in a much-discussed article by Timothy Mitchell (1991). Mitchell notes that "the edges of the state are uncertain; social elements seem to penetrate it on all sides, and the resulting boundary between state and society is difficult to determine" (1991: 88). Mitchell terms this the "boundary problem." He points out, for example, that upper classes have sometimes controlled certain state institutions, making it difficult if not impossible to distinguish state power from the class or economic power of such groups. Mitchell concludes that, "The state should not be taken as. . . an agent, instrument, organization or structure, located apart from and opposed to another entity called society" (1991:95). But he goes even further, questioning the *analytic* utility of the conceptual distinction between states and societies.

This is a problematic argument. To begin with, upper-class control of certain state institutions does not remove the "statist" character of those institutions – the fact, that is, that they are buttressed (unlike most other organizations) by substantial means of violence. Indeed, this situation would seem to be precisely one in which state institutions are a virtual "instrument" of the upper classes.

The rejection of the state-society distinction exemplifies what Margaret Archer (1988) has termed, in a different context, the fallacy of "central conflation." Archer uses the term to characterize studies that, striving mightily to avoid either cultural or "structural" determinism, posit that ideas and social structures are so closely connected that "there is no way of 'untying' the constitutive elements. The intimacy of their interconnection denies even relative autonomy to the components involved" (1988: 80). Mitchell,

analogously, seems to assume that because states and societies are so closely bound together, it is impossible to speak of their interaction.

The "boundary problem" that Mitchell discusses is real enough, and social analysts do often reify the concepts of state and society in problematic ways (Goodwin 1994b). Yet it seems more helpful to recognize that concrete institutions and social forces (including, not least, revolutionary movements) may sometimes *share* certain analytic characteristics of both states *and* societies rather than to jettison these concepts completely. Throughout his article, in fact, Mitchell himself refers quite un-self-consciously to such things as "the French state," "state practices," and "state-society relations." His own language, in other words, would seem to testify to the unavoidable importance of the *conceptual* distinction between states and societies.[16] In sum, while states and societies can often (although certainly not always) become quite intertwined in the real world, the conceptual distinction between them is still worth preserving.

LIMITATIONS OF STATE-CENTERED APPROACHES

Although these general criticisms of state-centered perspectives are ultimately unhelpful, statist approaches do have their limitations. In this section, I examine some of the more serious theoretical gaps in state-centered analysis and point to some theoretical resources than can help to bridge them. A proper recognition of these gaps not only reveals the limits of what state-centered analyses can reasonably hope to explain, including the present study, but also helps to highlight more clearly what statist approaches to revolutions *can* explain.

For analysts of revolutionary movements (or collective action in any of its forms), the fundamental weakness of statist analysis is that it does not theorize the nonstate or nonpolitical sources – or the *independent* explanatory weight – of three general factors: (1) *associational networks* (including class formations and "civil society" more generally), (2) *material resources*, and (3) *collective beliefs, assumptions, and emotions* (including grievances, strategies and tactics, moral convictions, and identities). Needless to say, this is a significant problem indeed given the potentially crucial connection between social networks, resources, and culture, on the one hand, and collective action (revolutionary or otherwise), on the other. Fortunately, there are some powerful theoretical resources at hand that can help to make that connection.

For example, the role of social networks and interpersonal ties in mobilization processes has been powerfully addressed in recent years by so-called social-network analysts (see, e.g., Gould 1995; Bearman 1993; McAdam 1986). These scholars emphasize the crucial role of networks of social ties in recruiting people into, and then sustaining their collective identification with and commitment to, social movements and perhaps even larger political communities (thereby obviating a need, in some cases, for substantial material resources). Network analysts also stress how such social ties, sometimes in the shape of formal organizations, provide the "relational infrastructure" of actual collective actions. These insights have also been underscored by those who emphasize the importance of "civil society" – that is, voluntary associational activities – as a mechanism for democratic dialogue and as bulwark against state oppression; these insights may also be found in the work of Marxists who emphasize the importance of class-based collective action in particular.[17]

From all these perspectives, in fact, individuals with a strong inclination to pursue reformists or even revolutionary change, and who also find themselves in a political context that allows or even encourages such pursuits, will still be unable to act effectively unless they are connected to a sufficiently large social network of like-minded people. Seemingly "appropriate" political opportunity structures, in other words, will not give rise to collective action if such networks do not exist.

State-centered analysts can justly counter, on the other hand, that these associational networks are often politicized and radicalized, and even constructed in the first place, as a result of specific state structures and policies. Social networks, after all, do not simply fall from the sky. Network analysts, proponents of "civil society," and Marxists, unfortunately, often neglect the ways in which state actions shape the very formation (or prevent the formation) of voluntary organizations and revolutionary movements in

particular. Still, these associations are also typically rooted in class or ethnic relations, extended kinship networks, religious communities, urban neighborhoods, or rural villages – still other social networks, that is, that do not derive wholly or even in part from state practices. And associational networks and practices have their own dynamics and emergent properties that need to be taken seriously and analyzed in their own right. Revolutionaries themselves, for example, may act in ways that expand or corrode their ties to other people. For these reasons, a state-centered perspective on the associational networks of civil society is inherently limited.

The potentially autonomous influence of material resources on collective action, for its part, has been most carefully theorized by resource-mobilization and political-process theorists (e.g., McCarthy and Zald 1977; Tarrow 1994; McAdam 1982; Tilly 1978), as well as by certain rational-choice theorists (e.g., Popkin 1979; Olson 1965). All of these analysts point out (albeit in somewhat different ways) that even tightly knit groups may not be able to act collectively – at least not for long or with much effectiveness – if they do not have steady access to the resources, including infrastructure and technology (means of communication and transportation, weapons, safehouses, etc.) that are necessary to sustain their activities and (perhaps) motivate people to contribute to their cause. In other words, even tightly knit groups that would seem to have the opportunity as well as an interest in acting collectively may not be able to do so effectively without substantial material resources. So again, collective action (whether revolutionary or not) may depend on much more than the extant political context.

A group's access to material resources generally depends on how it is inserted into specific social networks and institutions; the class composition of such groups is of particular importance in this regard. Nonetheless, access to specifically state resources may also be quite important for political mobilization – even for would-be revolutionaries who are violently excluded from the state. Defectors from the state's armed forces, for example, often bring along their guns. Guerrilla armies, furthermore, usually build up their arsenals through raids on peripheral army garrisons or ambushes of government troops. And some revolutionary groups have access to the resources of foreign states – which is one of the ways in which the international state system (and geopolitical competition in particular) matters for revolutionary conflicts. While the extent of external aid to revolutionaries has often been exaggerated by their opponents (Wickham-Crowley 1992: ch. 5), such aid figured prominently (but not necessarily decisively) in the revolutionary conflicts in Mexico, Vietnam (see Chapter 4), Algeria, and Afghanistan.

Finally, the potentially independent role of beliefs, identities, and repertoires of contention in collective action has been powerfully underscored recently by theorists of "framing processes" and culture more generally (see, e.g., Jasper 1997; Selbin 1993, 1997a, 1997b; Snow and Benford 1992; Sewell 1985). Framing theorists, for example, drawing on Goffman's (1974) important study, argue that "objective" reality is recognized (or indeed recognizable) as unjust *and* alterable only when it is interpreted or "framed" as such by means of specific cultural systems or discourses. When extant collective frames do not allow such an interpretation— even of a reality that an external observer might find both unconscionable and easily rectified— then collective action aimed at altering that reality is obviously impossible. In fact, even resourceful groups that would seem to have the opportunity as well as a rational interest in changing their predicament will not (indeed, cannot) do so in the absence of an appropriate cognitive frame.[18]

As we have seen, a state-centered perspective would emphasize that specific state practices can strongly shape the plausibility, justifiability, and diffusion of a militant collective-action repertoire or a specifically revolutionary ideology or identity. In other words, revolutionary "frames," ideologies, strategies, and cultures no more drop from the sky than do social networks or material resources. Unfortunately, framing theory and other forms of cultural analysis often overlook the ways in which states shape the processes by which collective beliefs and norms are formulated and broadly diffused—typically as quite unintended outcomes of states' practices.

Still, like associational networks, revolutionary ideologies and strategic repertoires are also rooted in a variety of social relations and cultural systems that are not shaped wholly or much at all by state practices. Such ideologies have their own substantive properties that demand to be taken seriously and analyzed in their own right, and this has rightly become the focus of much recent scholarship on social movements and revolutions. (Revolutionary Marxism and Islamic "fundamentalism," for example, envisage the radical reconstruction of societies in very different and distinctive ways.) For these reasons, a state-centered perspective on culture and ideology—like that on social ties and resources—is inherently limited. Again, however, my goal in this book is not to present an exhaustive explanation of the revolutionary movements that I examine, if that were even possible, but a powerfully parsimonious one. And for that task a state-centered perspective is appropriate, or so I shall argue, despite its theoretical limitations.

THE CASE OF THE CUBAN REVOLUTION

The strengths and limitations of the statist approaches discussed in the preceding section are evident in several recent comparative studies of Latin American revolutions, including important works by Robert Dix (1984), Timothy Wickham-Crowley (1992), and John Booth and Thomas Walker (1993). All of these studies engage, if only implicitly, and often endorse different strands of state-centered theory (and sometimes other theoretical lenses) in their attempt to explain why radical revolutionary movements in the region have seized power only in Cuba and Nicaragua in recent decades. The strengths and limitations of statism are also evident in a recent case study of the Cuban Revolution—an exceptional historical study that does not explicitly draw upon or attempt to criticize a state-centered (or any other) theoretical perspective. I shall use Marifeli Pérez-Stable's *The Cuban Revolution: Origins, Course, and Legacy* (1993) to ground my main theoretical points about the strengths and weaknesses of state-centered analysis. (Pérez-Stable notes that while she has been influenced by both Theda Skocpol and Charles Tilly, she has "refrained from engaging the literature on revolutions" [1993: 184-5, fn16].) The Cuban Revolution is also interesting to examine in this context because of its intrinsic importance as well as its enormous influence on the revolutionary movements in Central America, which I analyze in Part 3.

Pérez-Stable develops a persuasive multicausal account of the Cuban Revolution, albeit one that especially "highlights the importance of social classes in the breakdown of the old Cuba and the making of the revolution" (1993: 8). In fact, two of the factors that, according to Pérez-Stable, "interacted to render Cuba susceptible to radical revolution" were the weakness of Cuba's *clases económicals* (i.e. the bourgeoisie) and the relative strength of the *clases populares,* or popular sectors, influenced in part by the ideology of radical nationalism (1993: 7).[19] Thus far, Pérez-Stable's account might seem like a purely Marxist or class-analytic interpretation of the Cuban Revolution. However, Pérez-Stable also draws attention to two other causal factors that implicate characteristics of the Cuban state: what she terms "mediated sovereignty" (i.e., the Cuban state's lack of autonomy from the U.S. government and U.S. corporations) and a near-chronic "crisis of political authority" that deepened with the dictatorship of General Fulgencio Batista during the 1950s (1993: 7).[20]

Pérez-Stable's account thus demonstrates both the necessity and the insufficiency of treating the prerevolutionary Cuban state as an independent causal factor in the revolution. She implies that the geopolitical subservience and weakness of that state, as well as the serious legitimation crisis that developed following Batista's coup of 1952, created a structural potential for some type of popular movement against the dictatorship; at the same time, she suggests that analysts also need to take into account the strength (and ideology) of Cuba's social classes in order to understand why a radical revolution actually occurred. Indeed, Pérez-Stable strongly suggests that the political crisis of the 1950s would not have resulted in revolution were it not for the weakness of the Cuban bourgeoisie and the strength of the radicalized popular sectors.

And yet the story that Pérez-Stable tells is even more interesting than this. For her account also suggests that the very weakness of conservative and moderate political forces in Cuba on the eve of the revolution, as well as the gradual attachment of the popular sectors to Fidel Castro, the July Twenty-Sixth Movement, and its Rebel Army, were themselves primarily a result of actions taken by the Batista dictatorship. In other words, Pérez-Stable makes a number of state-constructionist arguments, in my terminology, in her account of the fidelistas' rise to power: The dictatorship itself simultaneously created and pushed its opposition in a revolutionary direction.

Pérez-Stable repeatedly suggests, for example, that "Batista's resistance to calling elections undermined the moderate opposition and bolstered the July 26th Movement," and, more generally, "bolstered those who argued that armed struggle was the only way to challenge his rule" (1993: 9, 56; see also 57). Indeed, both the moderate opposition to Batista and Cuba's Communist Party—which at first viewed Castro as a "putschist" and "adventurist"—positively "endorsed armed rebellion when other avenues of struggle against Batista had all but disappeared" (1993: 69). Pérez-Stable further notes how broad sectors of the popular classes and even members of the clases económicas were disgusted by the harsh repression and undisguised corruption of the batistato. She notes that many wealthy Cubans supported the insurrection, contributing 5 to 10 million pesos to the rebels; indeed, Pérez-Stable suggests that "virtually all Cubans" backed Castro and the Rebel Army by January 1, 1959, when Batista fled the country: "the *clases económics* . . . joined in celebrating the revolution" (1993: 62-3).

At the same time, Pérez-Stable emphasizes that Batista might have preempted the revolution had he simply been less intransigent: "The general might have consented to free and honest elections and ushered in a provisional government in late 1955 when Cosme de la Torriente led the civic dialogue movement or early in 1958 when the Catholic church revived it" (1993: 58). Unfortunately, "Batista became more intransigent as momentum gathered against his rule" (1993: 57).

Revolution might also have been averted had the Cuban military replaced Batista with some sort of provisional government—as the United States government came to hope and scheme (see, e.g., Benjamin 1990: ch. 6)—or had the armed forces simply contained the guerrillas in the Sierra Maestra. But the corruption and politicization of the Cuban military under Batista divided and fatally weakened the institution. Pérez-Stable notes the unsuccessful coup attempt led by Colonel Ramon Barquin and the much more serious naval uprising against Batista at Cienfuegos (1993: 56).[21] She also refers to the failed government offensive against the rebels during the summer of 1958—an offensive that clearly demonstrated that the Cuban armed forces as a whole had neither the political will nor the capacity to fight an effective counterinsurgency war, thereby sealing Batista's fate. The commanding officer in northern Oriente province—a political appointee whose promotion rankled many professional officers – simply refused to engage the rebels (Bonachea and San Martín 1974: 231, 262). "By the end of the summer," Luis Pérez (1988: 309) has noted,

> The army simply ceased to fight. Desertions and defections reached epidemic proportions. Retreating units became easy prey for advancing guerrilla columns . . . . Local military commands surrendered, often without firing a shot. Some defected and joined the opposition.

"Military prowess," Pérez-Stable concludes, "did not ultimately defeat Batista" (1993: 57).

In sum, the facts that the army could not geographically contain the rebels and the state could not preempt popular support for them were primarily a consequence of the character and decisions of the Cuban armed forces and of the Batista dictatorship.

Pérez-Stable's analysis thus clearly demonstrates the utility of a state-centered perspective for understanding the Cuban Revolution. The Batista regime, she shows, was not only an ideal target for some type of mass movement in Cuba, but it also positively weakened the civilian and military enemies of a radical revolution and unwittingly enhanced the popular appeal of the fidelistas. In other words, the alignment (and ideology) of class forces in Cuba that Pérez-Stable highlights was itself very strongly shaped by the nature of the batistato. Thus, a state-centered perspective greatly illuminates the Cuban Revolution, although this is a case in which the regime and armed forces did not break down until they were beset by a powerful mass move-

ment. For the most part, that is, Cuban revolutionaries made their own political opportunities.

On the other hand, Pérez-Stable's account of the causes of the Cuban Revolution also points to some of the limitations of a purely statist perspective. The weakness of the Cuban bourgeoisie, for example, was not simply a result of state policies, but was also rooted in (among other factors) the historic division of interests between nascent industrialists and the sugar industry (1993: ch. 1). The oppositional hegemony of the fidelistas, moreover, was also a result of the astute political maneuvering of the rebels themselves and of their unswerving commitment to armed struggle and Cuban self-determination (1993: 58-9). Castro himself first "captured the popular imagination," as Pérez-Stable puts it, with his "integrity, compassion, and dignity, and . . . a political program of nationalist reform" (1993: 53). Radical nationalism itself, in fact, appealed to many Cubans not simply because their state was historically subservient to the United States, but also because the Cuban economy and class relations—which were strongly but not wholly shaped by that state—were widely viewed as exploitative and unjust (1993: 3-5) Pérez-Stable's study suggests, in sum, that an adequate explanation of the Cuban Revolution requires an examination not only of the pre-Revolutionary Cuban state and its effects on civil society; it also demands an analysis of the independent role of class relations, popular culture, and the nature and actions of the revolutionaries themselves as they built a vast network of active supporters and sympathizers.

CONCLUSION

Due to its various theoretical shortcomings, a state-centered perspective alone will not completely explain (nor accurately predict) the emergence or character of collective action, including the revolutionary movements discussed in this book. No theory can do this. These very shortcomings, however, point the way toward a more powerful synthetic perspective on revolutions and collective action. Clearly, such a perspective will necessarily highlight the roles of social ties, resource mobilization, and culture in addition to state structures and practices. Of course, these factors cannot simply be "tacked on" to a state-centered analysis in the guise of "independent variables." For, as the state-constructionist approach in particular emphasizes, all these factors are themselves more or less strongly shaped, influenced, or even induced by state-centered processes.

We still await the formulation of the sort of synthetic on revolutions and collective action that we clearly need.[22] Until that theory materializes, however, state-centered approaches will remain perhaps our single most powerful theoretical perspective on revolutions, and any superior perspective will need to incorporate the insights of this theoretical tradition. Indeed, this tradition's insights of this theoretical revolutionary mobilization tell us much that we need to know about revolutions, and they help to resolve some of the key puzzles that revolutions have raised for social analysts.

In adopting a state-centered perspective, however, including what I have called a "state-constructionist" standpoint, this book certainly does not pretend to offer a complete or full adequate account of the complex and multifaceted revolutionary movements that it examines. There are many interesting and important questions about these movements that I shall not even attempt to address (including questions about, for example, their "gendered" character.) Still, I want to push the statist perspective on revolutions as far as it can go, which I believe is quite far. And I shall make some bold claims in subsequent chapters about the power of the state-centered perspective to illuminate the revolutionary movements of the Cold War era. In particular, I shall argue that the statist approach goes a long way toward explaining both the emergence and differing ideological character of revolutionary movements in postwar Southeast Asia (Chapter 3); why those movements either succeeded or failed to seize state power (Chapter 4); the emergence (or reemergence) of popular revolutionary movements in some but not all of the countries of Central America during the 1970s and 1980s (Chapter 5); why those movements either succeeded or failed to seize state power (Chapter 6); why certain states failed to defeat revolutionary movements over the course of many years or even

decades (Chapter 7); and finally, the patterns of popular protest and revolutionary multifaceted (as well as important) issues, but I believe that a state-centered perspective shines the brightest light on them. In the end, however, the latter claim must be proven, not merely asserted, and that is the goal of the following chapters.

NOTES

1. This chapter discusses the relevance of state-centered analysis exclusively for understanding the origins or causes of revolutions, including the formation of strong revolutionary movements. I should note, however, that statist perspectives have also been employed to explain the long-term *outcomes* or achievements of revolutions. See, e.g., Skocpol 1979: part 2; Foran and Goodwin 1993.
2. This approach rests upon two important distinctions made by Charles Tilly: the distinction between "states," on the one hand (i.e., organizations that attempt to monopolize the principal means of coercion within a bounded population) and "polities," on the other (i.e., the state plus those "member" groups with routine access to it), and the distinction between the capacity to act collectively, which Tilly terms "mobilization" (i.e., the quantity of resources, including labor and skills, collectively controlled by a group) and actual collective action. See Tilly 1978: ch. 3.
3. As noted in Chapter 1, this label is modeled on the well-known idea of "cultural" or "social constructionism" that is, the notion that certain social phenomena—e.g., cultural assumptions, political grievances, and collective identities—are recognized, defined, or even produced (in whole or in part) through cultural and discursive practices. I do not limit the idea of state constructionism, however, to the cultural or discursive work of states; as I have suggested, the organization and practices of states—which are only partially discursive in nature—are equally if not more consequential for social life. See also Lieberman 1995 on "political construction."
4. For example, a "private" corporation cannot logically or temporally exist outside of a state-enforced legal order; the corporate form itself is legally defined and enforced, as are the property rights that attach to it. More generally, it makes little sense to view states as the dependent "super-structures" of economies, given that economic relations themselves are constituted through de

jure or de facto legal orders and, standing behind these, coercive state power. In some contexts, it would be more nearly correct to describe economies as the superstructures of states.

5. Tilly differentiates modern "consolidated" national states ("large, differentiated, [and] ruling heterogeneous territories directly, claiming to impose a unitary fiscal, monetary, judicial, legislative, military and cultural system on its citizens") from "segmented" states (for example, "a city-based bishopric and its immediate hinterland, or. . . a composite of different sorts of unit, each enjoying considerable distinctness and autonomy"). See Tilly 1993: 31, 35. Note that "national" states in this sense are *not* necessarily "nation-states," which rule peoples who share a homogeneous ethnic or religious identity. See Tilly 1992: 2-3.

6. This does not rule out the possibility, of course, that revolutionaries may institute radical changes in those territories of a national society that they effectively control or rule, even if the central government has not been toppled.

7. See also Skocpol 1994. State breakdowns are also emphasized in Goldstone 1991. Although Goldstone presents an explanation of these breakdowns that is very different from Skocpol's (one that emphasizes demographic pressures), he shares her view that revolts from below cannot succeed so long as states remain fiscally and militarily strong. See Collins 1993 and Chorley's (1943) classic study.

8. I thus disagree with Randall Collins to the extent that his writings sometimes seem to imply that state breakdowns themselves automatically induce revolutionary movements or popular mobilizations. See, e.g., Collins 1995: 1561; 1993: 119. To add to the confusion, Collins (following Goldstone) sometimes suggests that popular mobilization is a defining element of state breakdowns.

9. The concept of "high-risk" activism is borrowed from McAdam 1986.

10. As James C. Scott (1990) has emphasized, class struggles "from below" only very rarely break out of their localistic and necessarily disguised forms, even when inequalities, class identities, and oppositional subcultures are quite salient.

11. I argue in Chapter 8 that Tocqueville sheds considerable light on the gradual rejection by Eastern European dissidents of a reformed socialism or a "socialism with a human face"; by 1989 these dissidents generally rejected Communism in toto and were, with some exceptions, proponents of a Western-style, democratic capitalism.

12. Migdal, for example, emphasizes how state-centered theories "encounter. . . difficulties when they assume that the state organization is powerful and cohesive enough to drive society." This assumption, he notes, is especially problematic for students of African societies, such as Senegal, which has a conspicuously "weak" state (Migdal 1992: 20).

13. To be sure, a few state-centered theorists (e.g., Birnbaum 1988; Kitschelt 1986) sometimes lapse into a sort of political determinism, but this is hardly inherent to statist analysis as such.

14. This was Nicos Poulantzas's position in his famous debate with Ralph Miliband.

15. See, e.g., Cohen 1994: chs. 2-3. The confusion probably derives from Skocpol's polemic against "voluntaristic" accounts of revolutionary political crises. See Skocpol 1979: ch. 1. But this polemic was clearly directed against the view that such crises—as they arose in France, Russia, and China—were caused by the actions of self-conscious revolutionaries and/or revolts from below; for Skocpol, that argument stood the actual historical record on its head. Nowhere, in any event, did she question the potential importance of human agency as such. This simply is not what the statist perspective is all about.

16. Mitchell would have us focus on "disciplinary power," which he argues has produced the state-society distinction as a "metaphysical effect" (1991: 94). Yet this would simply re-create the "boundary problem" in a new form, since it is often difficult to distinguish disciplinary from other practices. (Is resistance to discipline itself disciplinary?) Here again, Mitchell seems to be talking about an *analytic* distinction that is often blurred in the real world, but should not be jettisoned for that reason.

17. Recent works on civil society include Putnam 1993 and Cohen and Arato 1992. The Marxist and class-analytic literature on revolution and collective action is of course vast. Among the more influential recent studies are Paige 1975, 1997; Wolf 1969; and Moore 1966.

18. The "cultural turn" in studies of political conflict remains overwhelmingly ideational or cognitive; emotions and affect, in other words, remain largely neglected. But see Jasper 1997; Goodwin 1997.

19. Although it reappears throughout her text, and she might have treated it as an analytically independent factor, Pérez-Stable does not consider radical nationalism an independent cause of the revolution.

20. Pérez-Stable also includes two other factors in her list of the causes of the revolution: "sugar-centered development" and "uneven development." These particular factors, however, seem only indirectly related to the revolution. They powerfully influenced both class and state formation in Cuba, to be sure, but because they characterized the island since the nineteenth century (at least), they do not tell us all that much about why a revolution occurred there in 1959. "Uneven development," furthermore, is a characteristic of virtually every capitalist country, including many that have never had anything remotely resembling a revolution.

21. See also Bonachea and San Martin 1974: 63-4, 147-52. The Cienfuegos revolt, they note, was led by "naval officers [who] felt frustrated at Batista's appointments of men who had not graduated from the Mariel Naval Academy to the highest ranks in the service" (1974: 147).

22. Tarrow's much-discussed *Power in Movement* (1994) certainly approaches such a synthesis (see also McAdam, Tarrow, and Tilly 1997), although I believe that it exaggerates the importance of political opportunities, on the one hand, and says too little about the cultural and social-psychological dynamics of collective action, on the other (see Goodwin and Jasper 1999). For rather different sketches of what such a theory might look like—ones that try to incorporate culture, social psychology, and biography—see Jasper 1997 and Emirbayer and Goodwin 1996.

Introduction

Opportunities, Mobilizing Structures, and Framing Processes—Toward a Synthetic, Comparative Perspective on Social Movements

Doug McAdam, John D. McCarthy, and Mayer N. Zald

In a widely read book published in 1960, the sociologist Daniel Bell pro-claimed the "end of ideology." As the 1960s dawned, a good many social scientists believed we had reached a stage in the development of society where ideological conflict would gradually be replaced by a more pluralistic, pragmatic consensus. Bell and his colleagues could not have been more mistaken. In the very year Bell's book was published, black students staged sit-in demonstrations throughout the American South. In turn the sit-ins revitalized both a moribund civil rights movement and the tradition of leftist activism dormant in America since the 1930s. During the ensuing decade the country was rent by urban riots, massive antiwar demonstrations, student strikes, and political assassinations. On a global level, student movements proliferated: in France, Mexico, Italy, Germany, Spain, Japan, Pakistan, and numerous other countries. In Czechoslovakia, an effort to reform and "humanize the face of communism" was brutally suppressed by Soviet forces.

In short, the 1960s witnessed a proliferation in the very kinds of social movements and revolutions that Bell had assumed were a thing of the past. The last twenty-five years have only served to underscore the poverty of Bell's argument. If anything, social movements and revolutions have, in recent decades, emerged as a common – if not always welcome – feature of the political landscape. In the 1970s Islamic fundamentalists wrest power from the Shah of Iran. The Sandinistas depose Somoza in Nicaragua. Terrorist groups in Germany and Italy step up their attacks on military installations, politicians, and symbols of "corporate hegemony."

The 1980s were witness to more of the same. In the Philippines, the 1984 assassination of Ferdinand Marcos's longtime political rival, Benigno Aquino, sparks a popular revolt that sweeps Marcos from office. In the United States, growing fear of the nuclear threat catalyzes a nationwide Nuclear Freeze campaign. In South Africa a revitalized antiapartheid movement forces the release of its longtime leader, Nelson Mandela. The decade comes to a stunning and improbable end as, one after another, the Warsaw Pact regimes collapse under the pressure of popular revolts.

Set in motion by the turbulence of the 1960s and fueled by the myriad movements of the last quarter century, the study of social movements

McAdam, Doug, et al. (1996). "Introduction: Opportunities, Mobilizing Structures, and Framing Processes—Toward a Synthetic, Comparative Perspective on Social Movements." In Doug McAdam et al. (Eds.), *Comparative Perspectives on Social Movements: Political Opportunities, Mobilizing Structures, and Cultural Framings* (pp. 1–22). Cambridge: Cambridge University Press.

and revolutions has clearly emerged as one of the scholarly "growth industries" in the social sciences, in both Europe and the United States. Working from a variety of perspectives, sociologists, political scientists, and historians have produced over the past twenty years a wealth of theoretical and empirical scholarship on social movements/revolutions. It is time to take stock of this mushrooming literature. Within this profusion of work we think it is possible to discern the clear outlines of a synthetic, comparative perspective on social movements that transcends the limits of any single theoretical approach to the topic. This book rests on that perspective, even as it seeks to extend and apply it comparatively.

THE EMERGING SYNTHESIS

Increasingly one finds movement scholars from various countries and nominally representing different theoretical traditions emphasizing the importance of the same three broad sets of factors in analyzing the emergence and development of social movements/revolutions. These three factors are (1) the structure of political opportunities and constraints confronting the movement; (2) the forms of organization (informal as well as formal), available to insurgents; and (3) the collective processes of interpretation, attribution, and social construction that mediate between opportunity and action. Or perhaps it will be easier to refer to these three factors by the conventional shorthand designations of *political opportunities, mobilizing structures,* and *framing processes.*

The emerging consensus among movement scholars regarding the importance of these three factors belies the very different and oftentimes antagonistic perspectives in which they developed. We begin by discussing each factor separately, with an eye to acknowledging the divergent intellectual streams that have influenced work on each.

Political opportunities

While it is now common for movement scholars to assert the importance of the broader political system in structuring the opportunities for collective action and the extent and form of same, the theoretical influences underpinning the insight are actually fairly recent. In the United States it was the work of such *political process*

theorists as Charles Tilly (1978), Doug McAdam (1982), and Sidney Tarrow (1983) that firmly established the link between institutionalized politics and social movements/revolutions. Drawing on these works, a number of European (or European trained) scholars schooled in the *new social movements* tradition brought a comparative dimension to the study of *political opportunity structures.* Among the Europeans who have explored the links between institutionalized and movement politics are Hanspeter Kriesi (1989), Herbert Kitschelt (1986), Ruud Koopmans (1992), and Jan Duyvendak (1992).

Though the work of all of these scholars betrays a common focus on the interaction of movement and institutionalized politics, this shared focus has nonetheless been motivated by a desire to answer two different research questions. Most of the early work by American scholars sought to explain the *emergence* of a particular social movement on the basis of *changes in the institutional structure or informal power relations of a given national political system.* More recently, European scholars have sought to account for *cross-national differences in the structure, extent, and success of comparable movements* on the basis of *differences in the political characteristics of the nation states in which they are embedded.* The first approach has tended to produce detailed historical case studies of single movements or protest cycles (i.e., McAdam, 1982; Costain, 1992; Tarrow, 1989a), while the second has inspired more cross-national research based on contemporaneous descriptions of the same movement in a number of different national contexts (i.e., Kriesi et al., 1992; Joppke, 1991; Ferree, 1987). In both cases, however, the researcher is guided by the same underlying conviction: that social movements and revolutions are shaped by the broader set of political constraints and opportunities unique to the national context in which they are embedded.

Mobilizing structures

If institutionalized political systems shape the prospects for collective action and the forms movements take, their influence is not independent of the various kinds of *mobilizing structures* through which groups seek to organize. By mobilizing structures we mean *those collective vehicles, informal as well as formal, through which people mobilize and engage in collective action.* This focus on the meso-level groups, organizations, and informal networks that comprise the collective building blocks of social movements and revolutions constitutes the second conceptual element in our synthesis of recent work in the field.

As was the case with the work on political opportunities, the recent spate of research and theorizing on the organizational dynamics of collective action has drawn its inspiration largely from two distinct theoretical perspectives. The most important of these has been resource mobilization theory. As formulated by its initial proponents (McCarthy and Zald, 1973, 1977), resource mobilization sought to break with grievance-based conceptions of social movements and to focus instead on *mobilization processes* and the formal organizational manifestations of these processes. For McCarthy and Zald social movements, while perhaps not synonymous with formal organizations, were nonetheless known by and became a force for social change primarily through the social movement organizations (SMOs) they spawned. In some ways, theirs was less a theory about the emergence or development of social movements than it was an attempt to describe and map a new social movement form – professional social movements – that they saw as increasingly dominant in contemporary America.

The second theoretical tradition to encourage work on the organizational dynamics of collective action has been the political process model. Indeed, one of the characteristics by which scholars in this tradition are known is their common dissent from the resource mobilization equation of social movements with formal organization. Charles Tilly and various of his colleagues (1975, 1978) laid the theoretical foundation for this second approach by documenting the critical role of various grassroots settings – work and neighborhood, in particular – in facilitating and structuring collective action. Drawing on Tilly's work, other scholars sought to apply his insights to more contemporary movements. For example, Aldon Morris (1981, 1984) and Doug McAdam (1982) analyzed the critical role played by local black institutions –

principally churches and colleges – in the emergence of the American civil rights movement. Similarly, Sara Evans's (1980) research clearly located the origins of the women's liberation movement within informal friendship networks which were forged by women who were active in the civil rights movement and in the American New Left. Even the more recent tradition of network studies of movement recruitment (Gould, 1991; Kriesi, 1988; McAdam, 1986; McAdam and Paulsen, 1993; Snow, Zurcher, and Ekland-Olson, 1980) would seem to betray an underlying theoretical affinity with the political process model's emphasis on informal, grassroots mobilizing structures.

While some proponents of these approaches initially treated the two models of movement organization as mutually exclusive, over time the profusion of empirical work inspired by both has led to a growing awareness among movement scholars of the diversity of collective settings in which movements develop and organizational forms to which they give rise. So instead of debating the relative merits of these "opposing" characterizations, movement scholars have increasingly turned their attention to other research agendas concerning the organizational dynamics of social movements. Among the more interesting of these agendas are (1) comparison of the "organizational infrastructures" of countries both to understand historic patterns of mobilization better and to predict where future movements are likely to arise, (2) specification of the relationship between organizational form and type of movement, and (3) assessment of the effect of both state structures and national "organizational cultures" on the form that movements take in a given country.

Framing processes

If the combination of political opportunities and mobilizing structures affords groups a certain structural potential for action, they remain, in the absence of one other factor, insufficient to account for collective action. Mediating between opportunity, organization, and action are the shared meanings and definitions that people bring to their situation. At a minimum people need to feel both aggrieved about some aspect of their lives and optimistic that, acting collectively, they can redress the problem. Lacking either one or both of these perceptions, it is highly unlikely that people will mobilize even when afforded the opportunity to do so. Conditioning the presence or absence of these perceptions is that complex of social psychological dynamics – collective attribution, social construction – that David Snow and various of his colleagues (Snow et al., 1986; Snow and Benford, 1988) have referred to as *framing processes*. Indeed, not only did Snow coin, or more accurately, modify and apply Erving Goffman's term, to the study of social movements, but in doing so helped to crystallize and articulate a growing discontent among movement scholars over how little significance proponents of the resource mobilization perspective attached to ideas and sentiments. In reasserting their importance, Snow and his colleagues drew not only on Goffman's work, but ironically on the collective behavior tradition which resource mobilization had sought to supplant as the dominant paradigm in the field. Within that older tradition, both Smelser (1962) and Turner and Killian (1987) had assigned to ideas a prominent place in their respective theories.

But Snow was not alone in asserting the importance of the more cognitive, or ideational dimensions of collective action. Two other streams of recent work have also called for further attention to the role of ideas or culture more generally in the emergence and development of social movements and revolutions. For many of the new social movement scholars it was the centrality of their cultural elements that marked the new social movements as discontinuous with the past. Small wonder then that the work of many of the most influential new social movements theorists focused primarily on the sources and functions of meaning and identity within social movements (Brand, 1985a, 1982; Inglehart, 1979, 1977; Melucci, 1988, 1985, 1980; Touraine, 1981).

The final theoretical perspective to emphasize the importance of shared and socially constructed ideas in collective action was the political process model. Though best known for their stress on the political structuring of social movements/revolutions, such theorists as Gamson (1992a), Tarrow (1989a, 1983), and Tilly (1978) also acknowledged the critical catalytic effect of new ideas as a spur to collective action. McAdam's (1982) discussion of the necessity for "cognitive liberation" as a prerequisite for mobi-

lization is only the most explicit acknowledgment of the importance of ideas within the political process tradition.

For all the convergence in these various theoretical perspectives little systematic work on framing processes (or the cultural dimensions of social movements) has yet been produced. To this point, the literature is long on ringing programmatic statements regarding the necessity for "bringing culture back in," but short on the kind of cumulative scholarship that we now have on the role of political opportunities or mobilizing structures in the emergence and development of movements. In part this lacunae may be a consequence of the ephemeral, amorphous nature of the subject matter. Studying political systems and various kinds of organization is inherently easier than trying to observe the social construction and dissemination of new ideas.

But it may also be that a lack of conceptual precision in defining what we mean by "framing processes" has handicapped efforts to study this important aspect of collective action. Though Snow and his colleagues meant something quite specific by their use of the term, recent writings have tended to equate the concept with any and all cultural dimensions of social movements. This usage threatens to rob the concept of its coherence and therefore its theoretical utility. In this volume we want to return to David Snow's original conception and define framing rather narrowly as referring to the *conscious strategic efforts by groups of people to fashion shared understandings of the world and of themselves that legitimate and motivate collective action.*

In undertaking this volume, we were guided by four aims. First, we wanted to abstract from the voluminous literature on social movements those three concepts that have emerged as the central analytic foci of most scholarship in the area. Second, by taking their theoretical measure we hoped to refine and sharpen our understanding of each of these concepts. We take up this second goal in the essays with which we introduce each of the book's three parts. Each essay focuses on one of the three concepts, sketching our current understanding of it, the limits of that conceptualization, and the modifications or conceptual refinements that might redress the limitations.

That leaves the third and fourth goals alluded to earlier. The third goal is to advance our understanding of the dynamic relations among opportunities, mobilizing structures, and framing processes. Whereas most scholarship has focused on one or another of these factors, we use this volume to sketch a broader analytic framework on social movements/revolutions that combines the insights gained from the study of all three factors. Finally, we wanted to explore the comparative uses of this emerging framework by discussing the concepts of political opportunities, mobilizing structures, and framing processes in cross-national perspective. In commissioning the chapters for this volume we sought to directly address these final two goals. Each author was asked to focus on the relationship between any two of our three concepts and, wherever possible, to do so in a way that furthered the comparative understanding of movement dynamics. But we would be remiss if we relied on the contributors alone to advance the final two goals of the volume. Accordingly, in the remaining two sections of this introductory essay, we will take up each of these topics in turn. We begin with some thoughts on the dynamic relationships among our three concepts.

LINKING OPPORTUNITIES, MOBILIZING STRUCTURES, AND FRAMING PROCESSES

Scholars have tended to study only one aspect of a movement – for example, the effect of expanding political opportunities or the organizational dynamics of collective action. The challenge, of course, is to sketch the relationships between these factors, thus yielding a fuller understanding of social movement dynamics.

The problem is there exist many relationships between our three factors. Which ones become relevant depends upon the research question of interest. We emphasize two such questions here. The first concerns the origins of social movements and revolutions; the second, the extent and form of the movement over time. In each case we are interested in understanding the factors and processes that shape the movement: its emergence on the one hand, and it ongoing development on the other.

The question of movement emergence

Understanding the mix of factors that give rise to a movement is the oldest, and arguably the most important, question in the field. More-

over, virtually all "theories" in the field are, first and foremost, theories of movement emergence. That includes the various perspectives touched on earlier. Proponents of collective behavior see strain, variably conceived, and the shared ideas it gives rise to, as the root cause of social movements. Though there is great diversity among those working in the new social movements tradition, most proponents of the perspective betray adherence to at least a broadly similar account of the movement emergence. That account highlights the role of the distinctive material and ideological contradictions in post-material society in helping to mobilize new political constituencies around either nonmaterial or previously private issues. Resource-mobilization theorists focus on the critical role of resources and formal organization in the rise of movements. The political process model stresses the crucial importance of expanding political opportunities as the ultimate spur to collective action.

In our view all of these theories have something to recommend them. Our starting point, however, reflects the underlying assumption of the political process model. We share with proponents of that perspective the conviction that most political movements and revolutions are set in motion by social changes that render the established political order more vulnerable or receptive to challenge. But these "political opportunities" are but a necessary prerequisite to action. In the absence of sufficient organization – whether formal or informal – such opportunities are not likely to be seized. Finally, mediating between the structural requirements of opportunity and organization are the emergent meanings and definitions – or frames – shared by the adherents of the burgeoning movement. As both collective behavior and new social movements theorists have long argued, the impetus to action is as much a cultural construction as it is a function of structural vulnerability.

Having stressed the significance of all three of our factors, it is important to add that their effects are interactive rather than independent. No matter how momentous a change appears in retrospect, it only becomes an "opportunity" when defined as such by a *group* of actors sufficiently well organized to act on this shared definition of the situation. Implicit in this description of the beginnings of collective action are two critically important interactive relationships. The first concerns the relationship between framing processes and the kinds of "objective" political changes thought to facilitate movement emergence. The point is, such changes encourage mobilization not only through the "objective" effects they have on power relations, but by setting in motion framing processes that further undermine the legitimacy of the system or its perceived mutability. So, it is pointless to ask whether Gorbachev's reforms encouraged the revolutions in Eastern Europe by changing the political structure of the former Warsaw Pact countries or by heightening people's subjective awareness of the system's illegitimacy and vulnerability. Clearly they had both effects. Gorbachev's stated unwillingness to intervene militarily in defense of the Warsaw Pact countries encouraged collective action both by objectively weakening the social control forces available to those regimes and by heightening public perception of their illegitimacy and vulnerability. Expanding political opportunities, then, derive their causal force from the interaction of those structural and perceptual changes they set in motion.

A similar reciprocal dynamic defines the relationship between organization and framing processes. Framing processes clearly encourage mobilization, as people seek to organize and act on their growing awareness of the system's illegitimacy and vulnerability. At the same time, the potential for the kind of system critical framing processes we have described here, is, we believe, conditioned by the population's access to various mobilizing structures. As Murray Edelman (1971: 32) has written, the perceptual roots of collective action are bound up with the "cuings among groups of people who jointly create the meanings they will read into current and anticipated events."

For us, the key phrase in the preceding sentence is "groups of people." That is, framing processes are held to be both more likely and of far greater consequence under conditions of strong rather than weak organization. The latter point should be intuitively apparent. Even in the unlikely event that system-critical framings were to emerge in the context of little or no organization, the absence of any real mobilizing structure would almost surely prevent their spread to the minimum number of people required to afford a basis for collective action. More to the point, however, is the suspicion that lacking organization these framings would never emerge in the first place.

This suspicion rests, in part, on the supposition that what Ross (1977) calls the "fundamental attribution error" – that is, the tendency of people to explain their situation as a function of individual deficiencies rather than features of the system – is more likely to occur under conditions of social isolation rather than organization. Lacking the information and perspective that others afford, isolated individuals would seem especially likely to explain their troubles on the basis of personal rather than system attributions. Only "system attributions" afford the necessary rationale for movement activity. For movement analysts, then, the key question becomes, What social circumstances are productive of system critical framing processes and the system attributions they yield? Following Ferree and Miller (1977: 34) the answer would appear to be: "among homogenous people who are in intense regular contact with each other." Their description speaks to the essence of what we have called mobilizing structures.

Besides defining the broad parameters of a model of movement emergence, our three factors can also be used to shed light on a second question concerning the beginnings of collective action. This is the critically important, yet woefully neglected, question of movement form. That is, under what conditions can we expect a given type of movement (e.g., grassroots reform movement, public interest lobby, revolution) to emerge? The important implication of the question is that the various types of movements are simply different forms of collective action rather than qualitatively different phenomena requiring distinct explanatory theories. This is most germane to the study of revolutions, a form of collective action that has, in recent years, come to be studied as a phenomenon distinct from other categories of movements. We demur. Rather than assuming difference, we need to treat movement type as a variable and seek to account for variation in type on the basis of particular combinations of opportunities, mobilizing structures, and collective action frames.

Space constraints and the complexity of the issue do not permit a full blown theory of movement type, but we can at least sketch our preliminary thinking on the topic and, in the process, illustrate the utility of our basic perspective for addressing this important question. Not surprisingly, we start by again stressing the central importance of political opportunities to an understanding of movement dynamics.

In our introduction to the "political opportunities" part of this volume, we take up an issue that has begun to be addressed by scholars in the political process and new social movements traditions. Concerned that the concept of political opportunities lacks conceptual precision, scholars such as Hanspeter Kriesi (1991) and Sidney Tarrow (1994: chap. 8) have sought to identify those specific dimensions of political systems that impact the structuring of collective action. We applaud these efforts and in the introduction to Part I offer our own schema for differentiating the relevant dimensions of "political opportunity structures." We leave the details of that scheme till then. For our present purposes, however, we need to at least list these dimensions. They are as follows:

1. The relative openness or closure of the institutionalized political system
2. The stability of that broad set of elite alignments that typically undergird a polity
3. The presence of elite allies
4. The state's capacity and propensity for repression

So, for example, scholars seeking to explain the emergence of collective action would be advised to analyze the ways in which *changes* in one (or more) of these dimensions rendered the political system more receptive or vulnerable to challenge by insurgent groups. But, apropos of our present discussion, it may be that the *form*, as much as the *timing*, of collective action is structured by the available political opportunity. That is, a change in any of the four dimensions may encourage mobilization, but the form the mobilization takes is very likely to be affected by the kind of opportunity presented.

In Chapter 5 of this volume, Elena Zdravomyslova provides two examples that nicely illustrate the argument, contrasting two movement groups that developed in Leningrad/St. Petersburg in the wake of Gorbachev's reforms. The first, the Democratic Union, was founded in 1988, largely in response to the Gorbachev-inspired thaw in public discourse and the attendant *relaxation of social control* by state authorities. In turn, in its form and practices, the Democratic Union clearly bore the imprint of these specific changes or opportunities. The group was oriented, almost exclusively, to disruptive public demonstrations aimed at exploiting and extending the state's more tolerant policy on public gatherings and political demonstrations.

In contrast, the second group Zdravomyslova analyzes, the Leningrad People's Front, emerged following passage of the Electoral Law of 1988. That law mandated popular elections to be held the following year, thus granting insurgents *new electoral access*. Consistent with the nature and "location" of the opportunity granted, the Leningrad People's Front mounted a broad-based *electoral campaign*.

In short, insurgents can be expected to mobilize in response to and in a manner consistent with the very specific changes that grant them more leverage. In the case of Zdravomyslova's two groups, insurgents were oriented to a relaxation in social control and the granting of electoral access respectively. But the same argument holds for the other two dimensions of political opportunities as well. The routine electoral transfer of institutional power from one group of incumbents to another can be expected to encourage the creation (or reactivation) of reform movements who interpret the transfer of power as granting them new elite allies. So, just as movements on the Left mobilized in the United States during the Kennedy and Johnson administrations, so too did the Reagan/Bush years see a marked increase in protest activity on the Right.

Finally, the broadest reform and revolutionary movements would seem to owe, not to the routine circulation of stable elite blocs but to those momentous, if rare, cleavages in previously stable governing alliances. So, the American civil rights movement recognized and successfully exploited the growing rift between two important partners in the New Deal Coalition: Southern Dixiecrats and Northern "labor liberals." As regards revolutions, virtually every major theorist of the form has stressed the critical importance of elite cleavages as a central impetus to mobilization (Goldstone, 1991; Skocpol, 1979).

The important implication in all this is that in both their timing and form social movements bear the imprint of the specific opportunities that give them life. But what was true of timing is no less the case with form; that mobilizing structures and framing processes mediate the effects of political opportunities. Once again, the American civil rights movement affords a nice example of these processes. The breadth and scope of the movement owed, first and foremost, to the significance of the political realignments and elite divisions that presaged it. At the same time, nothing about the type or "location" of this opportunity can account for the specific organizational form or ideological content of the movement. To understand that one must look to the particular mobilizing structures within which the movement emerged and to the framing processes that characterized the movement at the outset. Clearly these two factors are related. In the case of the civil rights movement, initial mobilization centered largely in the black church (McAdam, 1982; Morris, 1984). Given the church's institutional centrality in the early days of the struggle, it is hardly surprising that the initial "framings" coming out of the movement had a distinctly religious cast to them. On the contrary, the influence of this particular mobilizing structure was evident in any number of specific organizational features of the movement, from reliance on the mass meeting as a mobilizing device, to the disproportionate number of ministers in the ranks of early movement leaders.

Thus, type of opportunity may dictate the broad category of movement, but the formal and ideological properties of the movement are apt to be more directly influenced by the organizational forms and ideological templates available to insurgents. And these, in turn, are largely a product of the mobilizing structures in which insurgents are embedded on the eve of the movement.

The question of movement development and outcomes

Having used our three factors to analyze the timing and form of movement emergence, we turn our attention to the later stages of collective action. What can a perspective stressing the role of opportunities, mobilizing structures, and framing processes tell us about the dynamics of movement development? A great deal, we think. Indeed, we see a lot of continuity between the processes shaping movement emergence and those influencing the ongoing development and eventual decline of collective action. The similarities and differences between these two phases of collective action should become clearer as we discuss each of the three factors.

Political opportunities. Little needs to be added to our earlier discussion of this factor. Suffice it to say, the broad political environment in which the movement is embedded will continue to constitute a powerful set of constraints/opportunities affecting the latter's development. So, for example, cross-national differences in the more stable, institutional features of political systems should have significant effects on the trajectories of particular movements. For instance, the stark contrast between the American winner-take-all electoral system and West Germany's partially proportional system of representation probably accounts for the very different developmental histories of the American and West German environmental movements. While the restrictive structure of electoral politics in the United States foreclosed that as a viable developmental option for American environmentalists, the opposite was true in West Germany. Though no less "radical" than their American counterparts, the West German Greens found the ease of electoral access too alluring to pass up. As a consequence the West German – and now, German – environmental movement has long had a more electoral or institutional character than its American counterpart.

Besides helping to account for cross-national differences in the development of comparable movements, a focus on *changes* in the structure of political opportunities can contribute to our understanding of the shifting fortunes of a single movement. In accounting for the decline of the American civil rights movement one would want to mention a number of factors. But among the most important would have to be the redemocratization of voting rights in the South, the development of significant Republican strength in the region, and Nixon's recognition and exploitation of this development in his successful 1968 presidential campaign. The success of Nixon's "Southern strategy" in 1968 dealt a serious blow to the black struggle, by forcefully demonstrating the irrelevance of the "black vote" to Republican Party fortunes, thereby granting the movement little leverage over Nixon or any of his Republican successors.

So the structure of political opportunities, as defined by both the enduring and volatile features of a given political system, can be expected to continue to play a major role in shaping the ongoing fortunes of the movement. What is different from the emergent phase is the fact that, after the onset of protest activity, the broader set of environmental opportunities and constraints are no longer independent of the actions of movement groups. The structure of political opportunities is now more a product of the interaction of the movement with its environment than a simple reflection of changes occurring elsewhere. Thus to understand fully the impact of the environment on the developing movement we will need to look much more closely at the movement itself and specifically those of its features which appear to account for much of its capacity to reshape the broader political landscape.

The organizational structure of the movement

The relevant organizational question in regard to movement emergence is whether insurgents have available to them "mobilizing structures" of sufficient strength to get the movement off the ground. However, once collective action is underway, the nature of the organizational challenge confronting the movement changes significantly. It is no longer the simple availability of mobilizing structures, but the organizational profile of those groups purporting to represent the movement that becomes important. The nature of these groups is apt to change a great deal as well. While movements often develop within established institutions or informal associational networks, it is rare that they remain embedded in these *nonmovement* settings. For the movement to survive, insurgents must be able to create a more enduring organizational structure to sustain collective action. Efforts to do so usually entail the creation of the kinds of formal social movement organizations (SMOs) stressed as important by resource-mobilization theorists. Following the emergent phase of the movement,

then, it is these SMOs and their efforts to shape the broader political environment which influence the overall pace and outcome of the struggle. In turn, the empirical literature would seem to suggest that the success or failure of these efforts owes primarily to some combination of three organizational factors.

Disruptive tactics. Notwithstanding the pluralist's claim that political effectiveness depends on tactical restraint and respect for "proper channels," there is increasing empirical evidence to the contrary. McAdam (1983b) found that the pace and effectiveness of civil rights protest was largely a function of the movement's ability to devise innovative and disruptive tactics that temporarily broke the stalemate between civil rights forces and their segregationist opponents. Lacking sufficient power to defeat Southern segregationists in a local confrontation, insurgents sought, through use of new and provocative tactics – the sit-ins, freedom rides, the Freedom Summer project – to induce their opponents to disrupt public order to the point where supportive federal intervention was required.

In his study of fifty-four "challenging groups," William Gamson (1990) reports evidence consistent with the single case study cited above. Gamson finds that groups which used "force and violence" against their opponents tended to be "more successful" than groups that did not. These findings are not so counterintuitive as one might think. The successful use of "proper channels" would seem to depend upon control over precisely the kinds of conventional political resources – money, votes, influence with prominent others – that movement groups tend to lack. Lacking such resources, movements may have little choice but to use their ability to disrupt public order as a negative inducement to bargaining.

Finally, in his seminal synthesis of recent movement scholarship, Tarrow (1994) argues persuasively that it is disruption or the threat of same that grants to movements their improbable effectiveness as vehicles of social change.

"Radical flank effects." Besides the narrow function of disruptive tactics, movements would, in general, appear to benefit from the presence of a "radical" wing. Or, more precisely, movements that boast a number of groups spanning a wide tactical spectrum seem to benefit from what has

come to be known as the "radical flank effect" (Barkan, 1979; Haines, 1988). The term is used to describe one effect that often follows from the presence of "extremist" groups within the same movement with other more "moderate" SMOs. As Haines (1988) shows in his analysis of changes in the funding of the major civil rights organizations, such a situation is likely to redound to the benefit of the moderate SMOs. In effect, the presence of extremists encourages funding support for the moderates as a way of undercutting the influence of the radicals.

A similar dynamic may also characterize relations between the state and the movement. In the modern era, the demands of most movements are ultimately adjudicated by representatives of the state. To respond to a movement, state actors must focus on those movement leaders and organizations that seem to speak for the movement and yet who are perceived to be reliable negotiating partners. In such a situation, the presence of groups deemed extremist can actually help legitimate and strengthen the bargaining hand of more moderate SMOs. Ironically, pressure from the extremists may simultaneously push the moderates to adopt more radical positions themselves. The end result is often state support for legislative or policy changes once deemed far too radical, by both moderates and the state alike.

Goals. In their efforts to interact successfully with the broader political and organizational environment, SMOs rely heavily on their goals. That is, the reactions of other major parties to the conflict – the state, countermovement, the media, and so on – are shaped to a considerable degree by the group's stated goals. Encoded in those goals are perceived threats to the interests of some groups and opportunities for the realization of others. Thus, the mix of opposition and support enjoyed by a given SMO is conditioned by the perception of threat and opportunity embodied in the group's goals. Given this dynamic, another finding from Gamson's study of "challenging groups" makes intuitive sense. He found that groups whose goals required the "displacement" of their opponents were much less likely to be successful than those whose objectives were "nondisplacing" (Gamson, 1990: 41–44).

We close our discussion of the effect of goals on movement development by noting one additional finding from Gamson's study. Besides the substance of group goals, Gamson also looked at the sheer number of objectives pursued. Specifically, he distinguished groups based on their pursuit of "single" versus "multiple" goals. At first blush, there might appear to be a virtue in the second approach, promising as it does to draw more people into the movement based on its diverse set of goals. Then too a single-issue organization that succeeds in achieving its goal faces extinction. Not so with a group pursuing many goals.

On reflection, however, it seems clear that there are a number of dangers with the multiple-goal strategy as well. The pursuit of a number of goals promises to spread thin the already precious resources and energy of the SMO. Just as dangerous is the impetus to internal dissension and factionalism that may accompany the pursuit of multiple goals. Who gets to decide which goals will be accorded top priority and what resources will be expended for which purposes? If a group settles on a single goal, it immediately eliminates potentially divisive issues such as these. Consistent with this latter view, Gamson finds single-issue groups to be successful more often than those addressing multiple goals (Gamson, 1990: 44–46).

Our point in surveying the literature on these three factors was not to get us bogged down in the empirical details of movement studies. Rather it was to underscore the central point of our discussion of movement development: *Movements may largely be born of environmental opportunities, but their fate is heavily shaped by their own actions.* Specifically, it is the formal organizations who purport to speak for the movement, who increasingly dictate the course, content, and outcomes of the struggle. In terms of our three factors, this means that both political opportunities and framing processes are more the product of organizational dynamics than they were during the emergent phase of the movement. We have already said a good bit about the role of political opportunities in the later stages of collective action. We close this discussion, then, with a few words about framing processes and their increasing "organizational" character following the emergence of the movement.

Framing processes

As with political opportunities, framing processes remain just as important to the fate of the ongoing movement as they were in shaping the emergence of collective action. Movements are no less dependent on the shared understandings of their adherents during the later stages of insurgency than they were early on. The difference is that, in the mature movement, framing processes are far more likely (1) to be shaped by conscious, strategic decisions on the part of SMOs, and (2) to be the subject of intense contestation between collective actors representing the movement, the state, and any existing countermovements. We take up each of these issues in turn.

Framing is no less a collective process during the early days of the movement than it is later on. But the collective settings within which framing takes place and the nature of the framing process are apt to be very different at the two points in time. We can expect the initial framing processes to be less consciously strategic than later *efforts*. In fact, at the outset, participants may not even be fully aware that they are engaged in an interpretive process of any real significance. This is certainly not the case later on as various factions and figures within the movement struggle endlessly to determine the most compelling and effective way to bring the movement's "message" to the "people."

In the absence of such a strong strategic self-consciousness, the initial framing process also has a more emergent, inchoate quality to it than do later framing efforts. Accordingly, the outcome of the process is less predictable than it is later on, when insurgents are typically acting to reaffirm or, at most, extend an existing ideological consensus. That is, later framing efforts tend to be heavily constrained by the ideas, collective identities, and worldviews adopted previously (Moore, 1993).

Finally, and most important, later framing processes tend, far more than the earlier efforts, to be the exclusive "property" of formal SMOs. Established organizations or institutions may serve as the *settings* within which initial framings get fashioned, but typically they are not produced by the recognized leadership as a part of normal organizational procedures. This tends to change during the later periods of movement development. So just as the structure of political opportunities comes, in part, to be responsive to SMO actions, so do later framing efforts come to be the product of formal organizational processes.

Besides these changes in the *internal* character of movement framing processes, the broader *environmental* context in which framing takes place differs dramatically between the early and later stages of collective action. While the political establishment is apt to be either unaware or amused and unconcerned by initial framing *efforts,* their reaction is expected to change if and when the movement is able to establish itself as a serious force for social change. Assuming this happens, later framing *efforts* can be expected to devolve into intense "framing contests" between actors representing the movement, the state, and any countermovements that may have developed. To complicate matters further, these contests will not be waged directly but, rather, will be filtered through various news media. Thus the outcome of later framing *efforts* will turn, not only on the substantive merits of the competing frames, but on the independence, procedures, and sympathies of the media.

To summarize, then, we see the central analytic focus of movement research shifting over the life of the movement. While environmental opportunities would seem to play the critical determinant role during the emergent phase of collective action, thereafter the movement itself comes to occupy center stage. Specifically, the extent, character, and outcomes of collective action are expected to turn, in large part, on the interaction of the movement – or, more precisely, the SMOs that purport to speak for it – with other organized parties to the conflict.

USING THE PERSPECTIVE COMPARATIVELY

Unlike earlier theoretical approaches to the study of social movements, the perspective outlined has emerged out of a sustained dialogue between scholars working in a wide variety of national contexts. As a result the perspective has always had an implicit comparative focus. However, we aim to make this implicit focus more explicit. To do so we will again take up each of our three central concepts, suggesting how each can be used to illuminate cross-national differences and similarities in movement dynamics.

Political opportunities

As was noted earlier, most research on political opportunities has sought to show how *changes* in some aspect of a political system created new possibilities for collective action by a given challenger or set of challengers (Costain, 1992; McAdam, 1982; Tarrow, 1989a). Thus, the concept has typically been employed in case study fashion to help explain the emergence of a particular movement or "cycle of protest." Recently, however, the concept has informed a very different, and explicitly comparative, research agenda. Instead of focusing on the role of expanding political opportunities in facilitating the emergence of a single movement, scholars have begun to compare movements cross-nationally, seeking to explain variation in their size, form of organization, and degree of success by reference to cross-national differences in the formal structures of political power.

So, for example, Myra Marx Ferree (1987) has sought to understand the different character and form of the West German and U.S. women's movements, in part, by reference to differences in institutionalized politics in the two countries. Likewise, in his comparative account of the emergence and development of the U.S. and West German antinuclear movements, Christian Joppke (1991) has attributed many of the key differences between the two movements to the very different national political contexts in which they have developed. Dieter Rucht (1990) also studied the antinuclear movement, but broadened his list of cases to include France as well as the United States and West Germany. But in doing so he again accounts for variations in "the courses, strategies, organizations, action repertoires, and outcomes of these struggles" on the basis of an interpretive scheme "which focuses on [differences in] . . . political opportunity structures." Finally, in the most ambitious research effort to date regarding the relationship between national political context and the extent and nature of collective action, Hanspeter Kriesi and several of his colleagues (Kriesi et al., 1991, 1995) have studied the rise and subsequent development of new social movements in France, Switzerland, Germany, and the Netherlands.

Mobilizing structures

A similar comparative turn can be discerned in recent work by movement scholars on the origins and effects of various mobilizing structures.

Dieter Rucht, in Chapter 8 of this book, represents a prime example of this trend. Rucht seeks to describe and explain the different "social movement structures" exhibited by the so-called new social movements in France, Germany, and the United States. In an earlier article, John McCarthy (1987) compared rates of institutional affiliation cross-nationally to help explain the very different loci, form, and character of collective action in different countries. He sought, for example, to account for the religious roots and character of many American movements on the basis of significantly higher rates of church affiliation in the United States than in comparable Western democracies. Finally, Kim Voss is currently studying the historical fate of early labor movements in the United States and England to determine whether differences in their organizational forms might help to account for the demise of the American Knights of Labor and the ultimate success of its English counterparts. (See Chapter 10.)

The variety of these efforts suggests the rich potential for comparative work in this area. Taking only the three examples touched on here, researchers have sought to understand cross-national variation in (1) the likely institutional locations of mobilization, (2) the role of the political system in structuring the organizational profile of the movement, and (3) the effect of the organizational structure in facilitating or constraining movement survival.

Framing processes

Reflecting the recency of the framing concept and the somewhat underdeveloped nature of theory in this area, it is perhaps not surprising that our third concept has yet to yield much in the way of comparative research. We are convinced, however, that the potential for such research is as great with this concept as with the other two.

In the essay introducing the section on framing processes, we seek to refine our conceptual understanding of the concept by distinguishing between five related, but clearly distinct, topics. These are (1) the *cultural tool kits* (Swidler, 1986) available to would-be insurgents; (2) the *strategic framing efforts* of movement groups; (3) the *frame contests* between the movement and other collective actors — principally the state, and countermovement groups; (4) the *structure and role of the media* in mediating such contests; and (5) the *cultural impact* of the movement in modifying the available tool kit.

Besides sharpening our understanding of the basic framing concept, the preceding list is useful for the clear comparative lines of research it suggests. Indeed, all five topics lend themselves easily to cross-national research on framing dynamics. For example, as regards the first topic, one could imagine a comparative mapping of ideas and attitudes similar to McCarthy's (1987) cross-national work on "institutional affiliations." That is, instead of comparing countries in terms of their "infrastructural deficits and assets," one could seek to discern which ideational themes were especially resonant in which national contexts.

Our second topic suggests a narrower research agenda focusing on the similarities and differences in the framing strategies employed by movement groups in specified countries. Or by seeking to include as objects of study the framing efforts of the state and countermovement groups as well as the movement the researcher could well expand the empirical focus to address our third topic as well. Indeed, an ongoing collaborative research project by German and U.S. scholars is currently attempting to do just that for the American and German pro- and antiabortion movements. In a preliminary report of that research (see Gamson et al., 1993), project members seek to sketch the major "frame packages" advanced by proponents and opponents of abortion in the two countries.

Our fourth topic, the role of the media in shaping public and policymaker perception of the movement, would make for an interesting and important comparative study. To better understand the role of the media in movement dynamics one could study cross-national variation in media characteristics — for example, degree of autonomy from the state, operating procedures, editorial orientation, and so forth — and seek to link these differences to variation in movement outcomes. For example, impressionistically, at least, the failure of the Perot campaign in the 1992 presidential campaign and the success of Berlusconi in the 1994 Italian elections would seem to stem from significant differences in the media's ability to expose crucial policy weaknesses on the

part of the two candidates. In turn, this difference in outcomes would seem to owe much to variation in several key characteristics – independence and editorial orientation in particular – of the media in the two countries.

Finally, one could also make our fifth topic the object of systematic comparative research. The goal would be to assess the extent to which a given movement has managed, in a number of countries, to reshape the terms of public discourse. So, for example, one could imagine a comparative study of "the feminization of public discourse," designed to gauge the ideational impact of the women's movement in all Western industrial democracies. Or to take a much debated historical case, one could seek to determine whether "American exceptionalism" in its relative lack of class consciousness was as much the effect as the cause of a weak labor movement. That is, by assessing the shifting ideational content of public discourse throughout the West one might be able to determine whether America was always "exceptional" in its antagonism to labor, or whether class movements in other countries were more successful in encoding labor's interests into public discourse.

CONCLUSION

Reflecting the ambitious aims of this book, we have covered a lot of ground in this introductory essay. Specifically, we have tried to do four things here. First, we sought to sketch a broad analytic perspective on social movements that we see as having emerged among movement scholars over the past decade or so. This perspective stresses the determinant and interactive effects of *political opportunities, mobilizing structures,* and *framing processes* on movement dynamics. Second, we tried to identify the various intellectual influences that have contributed to our understanding of each of these three concepts. Third, we sought to infuse the perspective with a sense of dynamism by addressing two questions of long-standing interest to movement scholars and identifying the *relationships* between our three factors that we see as especially critical in shaping (1) the emergence or (2) the development or decline of collective action. Finally, we sketched what we see as the inherent comparative nature and empirical promise of the perspective.

It should be obvious how seriously we take the comparative agenda. Much of the richness of the perspective sketched here is owed to the cross-national discourse that informs it. This book is an attempt not only to synthesize the fruits of that discourse but to encourage and contribute to it as well. For only by abandoning the limits of the nationally specific case study approach to the study of social movements can we ever hope to advance our understanding of collective action.

Rationality and Revolutionary Collective Action

Michael Taylor*

In a much-praised book on *States and Social Revolutions,* Theda Skocpol announced her commitment to a strongly "nonvoluntarist, structural" methodological programme. Social revolutions are to be explained, she argued, as the product not of individual actions but of structural and situational conditions. In particular, "the sufficient distinctive causes" of the social-revolutionary situations commencing in France, 1789, Russia, 1917, and China, 1911 can be located in the relations of each of these states to other states and to its own domestic social classes (and I take a set of relations to be a structure) together with the country's "agrarian sociopolitical structure".[1] Skocpol's work on revolution is the most purely "structuralist" of the best recent work on revolution and peasant rebellion. Neither rational action nor any attitudes, interests, goals, beliefs, etc., are to have any explanatory role (at least in her statements of her methodological programme and general theoretical argument; they creep back in, as they have to, in her narrative histories of the three revolutions). Structural outcomes ("basic transformations of a society's state and class structures") are explained directly in terms of structural causes.

I shall take issue here with this one-sided structuralism, amongst other things, and try to show how rational-choice theory can contribute to our understanding of large-scale historical change. But although I share the view of those who believe that explanations of "macrophenomena" should be provided with "microfoundations", I do not believe that this is all that explanation should consist of and I wish to argue for a methodological perspective which is both individualist *and* structuralist (though not in the manner of Bhaskar and Giddens).

To this end, I first argue (in sections I-V) that peasant collective action in revolutions and rebellions was based on community (as many historians have argued) and this is mainly *why* the large numbers of people involved were able to overcome the free-rider problem familiar to students of collective action (which has *not* been recognized by the historians). In establishing this I will have shown that revolutionary and rebel collective action is the product of rational action and in fact is explained by what I will call the thin theory of collective action (since it rests on the thin theory or rationality). There are many who reject this theory—and who will therefore be sceptical about my argument on revolutionary collective action—on the grounds that there is much collective action which the theory cannot account for, including some participation in interest groups and other associations, which have largely replaced community as the vehicle

Taylor, Michael. (1988). "Rationality and Revolutionary Collective Action." *Rationality and Revolution* (pp. 63–97). Cambridge: Cambridge University Press.

of movements of social and political change. I comment on this in section VI and go on to examine briefly (in Section VII) some alternative accounts of individual rationality or motivation which might form the basis of a better theory of collective action. This will leave me convinced that no such theory is yet available while agreeing that there are indeed facts about collective action which the thin theory is unable to account for. It would therefore be useful to know when the thin theory is applicable to characterize the conditions in which it is likely to provide good explanations. I try to do this in section VIII. In the final section, after what may seem to have been a long detour, I connect this argument about the applicability of the thin theory to the question of explaining revolution, to Skocpol's "nonvoluntarist, structural" method in particular, and to social explanation in general.[2]

I

Social revolutions, whose origins and development it is Skocpol's aim to explain, are defined as "rapid, basic transformations of a society's state and class structures . . . accompanied and in part carried through by class-based revolts from below".[3] The revolts (which in the three historical cases Skocpol considers are agrarian revolts) can be successfully mounted only if certain structural preconditions are met, preconditions having to do with the social structure of the class in revolt and with its relations to other classes and to the state. It is also a condition of their success that the old regime's state repressive capacity has been weakened. The initial weakening of the state's repressive capacity, which provides the opening for peasant revolt, is the product of a political crisis whose causes lie in the state's relations to its own domestic classes and its position within international structures: finding itself under intensifying military pressure from more economically advanced and hence more powerful foreign nations, the state's attempt to cope by trying rapidly to extract extraordinary resources from its population and to carry out basic reforms was impeded by a backward agrarian economy and powerful landed upper class, with the result that the regime collapsed.

In the final section I shall return briefly to this question of the emergence of revolutionary situa-

tions, of breakdowns in the repressive apparatus which provide openings for sustained revolutionary collective action by the peasants. The image of a structure of competitive international relations in which a state is enmeshed and which compel it to behave in certain ways towards its own population may seem to offer especially persuasive support to Skocpol's structural position, though here to I shall argue the need for rational choice explanation. But my main concern in this essay is with the explanation of the sustained peasant revolts which took advantage of the collapse of state power and which are a central part of most social revolutions.[4]

At first blush it would appear that the participation of vast members of peasants in collective action contradicts the familiar "logic of collective action". But I shall argue that this is not so, if we take the "logic" to encompass (to put very loosely) the argument advanced by Mancur Olson in *The Logic of Collective Action*, as clarified, qualified and extended by a number of people (especially Russell Hardin in chapter 4 of his *Collective Action*); the theory of conditional cooperation;[5] and the implications which can be informally drawn from these two bodies of theory about the intervention of political entrepreneurs (which I will discuss in connection with collective action in the Chinese and Vietnamese revolutions).

I call this collection of arguments the thin theory of collective action to emphasize that it is founded on the thin theory of rationality. (There are, so far as I am aware, no other, elaborated, "thicker" theories of collective action founded on broader accounts of rationality. The alternative accounts of rationality which will be discussed briefly in section VII do not, in my view, provide foundations for superior explanations of collective action). By the "thin theory of rationality" I mean the familiar account of rationality which also provides the foundation for conventional neo-classical microeconomic theory. I emphasize (with no attempt at precision) three features of the thin theory: (i) Rationality is relative to *given* attitudes and beliefs (which are each assumed to be consistent) and the agent's actions are *instrumental* in achieving or advancing the given aims in the light of the given beliefs. It is for this reason alone that Jon Elster has called the theory "thin".[6] (ii) The agent is assumed to be egoistic. (iii) In applications of the thin theory the range of incentives assumed to affect the agent is limited. Olson, for example, limits them to the increase in the supply of the public good caused by the individual's action, the resources he must devote to the action, and "selective incentives" which themselves are limited to economic or material incentives and "social sanctions and social rewards".[2] Other theories limit them even more, for example to profit alone.[8] Without such limitation, a thin theory is liable to become a tautology. The ends which are limited in this way are not themselves assumed to be rational in any sense.

Action which is rational according to the thin theory of rationality will be said to be "thin-rational" and in the agent's "thin self-interest".

It is important to bear in mind that most successful collective action takes place in what Olson calls intermediate groups or succeeds in large groups because they are made up of intermediate subgroups. Olson provided no theory of strategic interaction in these groups. If agents are thin-rational and there are no selective incentives (unless tacit selective incentives are said to be entailed in conditional cooperation itself), successful collective action outside of privileged groups must result from some form of conditional cooperation. At a minimum, an individual would not contribute or participate if nobody else did.

For my purposes in this chapter, I need to emphasize certain properties of conditional cooperation. As intuitively we would expect and as we can prove in the case of the n-person Prisoners' Dilemma super game, conditional cooperation is more likely to be rational (before selective incentives are brought in) in small groups than in large ones. It is also more likely to succeed in conditions where relations between people are those characteristic of *community*—not just because individual behaviour can more easily be monitored, but because a strong community has at its disposal an array of powerful, positive and negative social sanctions which were highly effective in maintaining social order and in the provision of other public goods in all precapitalist societies and continued to play an important role subsequently, though sometimes in atrophied and attenuated forms.[9] An important point here is that these sanctions can be used as selective incentives, not only to induce individuals simply to contribute or participate, but

also to bolster conditional cooperation—which is always a precarious business. Political entrepreneurs also have an important role to play here. Usually thought of as "an innovator with selective incentives",[10] the political entrepreneur also organizes collective action by facilitating conditional cooperation.

It might be argued that a community member would not take the trouble to implement sanctions against a free rider (and hence that nobody would find the threats to use the sanctions credible), since punishing a free rider is itself a public good for the community and each individual would therefore prefer others to do the job. Against this I suggest that the cost of applying a sanction is typically slight, and if a general argument about thin rationality which I make in section VIII is right, it will follow that in making *this* choice (to participate in community sanctioning of free riders), the individual does not act thin-rationally.[11] This argument should hold for the cases I will be concerned with here.

One final preliminary: I take the core properties of *community* to be: (i) its members have beliefs and values in common; (ii) relations between members are direct and many-sided; and (iii) its members practise "generalized" as well as merely "balanced" reciprocity.[12] Each of these criteria can be satisfied in varying degrees, so that a collection of individuals may be more or less of a community, and I shall speak of "weak" and "strong" communities. One important way in which some of the peasant communities I shall discuss are "weak" is that relations between their members are in certain spheres not direct, as required by the second criterion, but mediated—for example through the intervention in community affairs of local landlords and state officials. To the extent that people do not deal with each other directly but pursue their common ends through the agency of such outside parties, to that extent (other things being equal) they are diminished as a community.

When the peasant community was sufficiently strong, then, it provided a social basis for collective action, including revolutionary collective action and rebellions and other popular mobilizations. Revolutionary or rebel mobilization built on and used the existing network of local communities. The individual participated as a member of a community. These communities provided conditions in which spontaneous conditional cooperation could succeed or, failing that, could provide and effectively use against most of their members all the sanctions which are characteristic of the traditional community. Sometimes, mobilization was assisted by a political entrepreneur. And in some cases, where the local community was less strong (because there was little cooperation amongst its members in the agricultural work which dominated their lives, for example, or relations between members were too much mediated by landlords or officials), revolutionary mobilization could not occur without entrepreneurs—who set about their work, however, by building or strengthening the local community through organizing mutual aid and undermining the dependence of the villages on local landlords.

In arguing that community facilitates revolutionary collective action by making conditional cooperation rational and the use of social sanctions effective, I am assuming that the peasant rebellion is, in effect, embedded in a larger iterated game. Participation in rebellion is conditional on others continuing to participate (rebellions are not instantaneous events), but the experience of conditional cooperation, the knowledge conditions which are necessary for successful conditional cooperation (e.g. knowing that others are cooperating) and the effectiveness of social sanctions used during a rebellion all derive from the fact that the participants in the rebellion are members of a pre-existing community and will continue to be members of the same community after the rebellion.[13]

Part of this argument about community and revolutionary collective action has been made by numerous historians and by Skocpol. They have correctly seen in the peasant community the social basis of revolutionary collective action, but have not recognized that it is precisely in virtue of the peasant's membership of a community that it is *rational* for him to participate. Skocpol is prevented from understanding fully this connection between community and revolution by her anti-voluntarist and structuralist methodological commitments, as we shall see later. The general argument that supplying the motivational link—in this case, explaining collective action in terms of individual motivations and these in terms of social structure—makes for better explanation will be made in the final section.

II

Skocpol argues that although there were widespread peasant revolts against landlords in the French, Russian *and* Chinese Revolutions—far transcending the localized revolts or disturbances which these countries had experienced previously and far more successful in bringing lasting radical transformations—there was nevertheless an important difference between the French and Russian cases on the one hand and the Chinese on the other. In the former cases, the peasant community was still strong and "the peasant village assembly, relatively autonomous as it was from outside control, provided the organizational basis for spontaneous and autonomous revolts" (p. 138). The peasantry of China, on the other hand, during the revolutionary interregnum between 1911 and 1949, "lacked the kind of structurally pre-existing solidarity and autonomy that allowed the agrarian revolution in France and Russia to emerge quickly and relatively spontaneously in reaction to the breakdown of the central governments of the Old Regimes" (p. 148). The consequence was that, compared with the French and Russian Revolutions, the Chinese Revolution was much more protracted and peasant collective action had in effect to be organized, village by village, by the Communists.

Let us put some flesh on the rather abstract skeleton of the arguments made in the last section by looking at these three cases in more detail.[14]

In FRANCE, all through the eighteenth century, there had been bread riots in town and country. But in *1789* the peasants went much further. Across the country, they launched an assault on the seigneurial system itself, refusing to pay seigneurial dues, tithes and royal taxes and often destroying the local seigneur's feudal records and sometimes his chateau too, as well as seizing local grain stores. The direct end result of their actions was the radical transformation of the class structure through the abolition of seigneurialism, and an indirect result, through the effects of the peasant revolts on the behaviour of the Constituent Assembly, was the emergence of a new type of state. Though the final outcome may not have been intended by them, the peasants made a social revolution.

That the peasant revolts issued in this successful outcome was due to conjunctural factors. But the peasants' collective action was made possible in the first place by the pre-existing framework of village communities, which provided a foundation of long experience of reciprocity and acting together in the collective control of their agricultural and pastoral activities and of their common property and public facilities.

Albert Soboul has emphasized how much the cohesion and unity of the pre-revolutionary peasant community owed to its universally shared opposition to the lord.[15] It is true that within the community, inequality—especially differentiation into possessors and non-possessors of a plough-team—was well developed by 1789. Peasants could freely sell or bequeath the land they possessed (more than a third of French soil was in this category; and more than another third owned by the lords was used by the peasants as sharecroppers or tenants). But the resulting differentiation amongst the peasants was overshadowed by their common subjection to the lord, who exercised with respect to peasant land tenures a right of overlordship marked by the peasant's payment of seigneurial dues (in addition to royal taxes, tithes, and rents or crop shares), a crippling burden that was actually worsened during the eighteenth century by the "feudal reaction". One effect of this seigneurial regime, then, was to produce a defensive unity of the rural community in the face of the lord's depredations.

This unity was enhanced by a measure of communal self-government, exercised through the assembly of the community's heads of households, which met in the church (parish and community usually coinciding) and was assisted by the local priest. "The assembly dealt with all that concerned the community: sale, purchase, exchange or leasing of communal property; the maintenance of the church, of public buildings, roads, and bridges; the election of the communal syndics, of the schoolmaster, the communal shepherd, the hayward, the collectors of tithes, the assessors and collectors of the taille."[16]

But, as Soboul and Marc Bloch before him emphasized, the real foundation of the rural community's unity was its economic system, and in particular its collective possession of important resources and its communal regulation of the use of certain private possessions and of access to collective possessions in the common interest of all the inhabitants. Individual villagers were restrained from enclosing their land, were obliged to conform to the communal pattern of crop rotation, and were constrained by communal rules concerning such things as harvest dates, use of woods, rights of gleaning, of pasturing on the fallow and on communal lands, and so on.

A dispersed settlement pattern—as in the forest areas of Normandy and Brittany—was not necessarily a barrier to communal cohesion (as some writers have maintained). Though there was less collective organization of agriculture in such areas than in the open-field country of the North and East, there was often more communal land, especially pasture land and woodland, to defend and regulate in the common interest, and mutual aid was practised amongst the peasants at key points of the agricultural cycle.

On the eve of the Revolution, then, the great majority of the French people lived in cohesive communities, long used to meeting together in their assemblies, regulating their life together and working together. It was as the member of such a community that each individual participated in the revolt against the seigneurial regime.

Skocpol's analysis of the peasant revolution in RUSSIA during 1917 is confirmed by the account given in Graeme Gill's *Peasants and Government in the Russian Revolution*, which was published at the same time as Skocpol's book and appears to be the fullest account of the peasant land seizures in English to date.[17] After the fall of the Tsar in March, the peasants at first supported the provisional government and were willing to have local government bodies work out a solution to the land question. But they were not impressed with the government's feeble tinkering with the existing system of government in the countryside and soon became impatient with its temporizing over the redistribution of land. "The widespread peasant rejection of the emerging administrative structure was linked with the strength throughout the countryside of traditionally-based peasant organizations rooted in the fabric of village society".[18] Before long the peasants began to meet in their village assemblies and proceeded to create organizations of their own to put in the place of the official structure. The local functionaries of the

old regime were driven from the villages and in
their place the village assemblies or the entire village elected committees at village and district levels. The unrest which followed, especially in the
first part of 1917, was usually organized by these
new bodies, propelled and radicalized in many
cases by outside agitators.

Attacks on landowners and seizures of land
were generally carried out by each village acting
separately, though sometimes there was collective action at district level involving coordination between neighbouring villages. The decision
to move against the local landowner was usually
taken at a meeting of the village assembly or the
new committees at village and district level.[19]

At first, in March, the peasant assaults on
landowners were typically destructive, with peasants arresting and sometimes killing the local
landowners, seizing grain, cutting down and carrying off timber, destroying grain-stores and
equipment. But from April to August, the peasants turned mainly to seizing and redistributing
land, which they began immediately to use. Private lands were integrated into the land already
controlled by the *obshchina,* their owners and
workers sometimes driven from the area. In some
cases landowners were compelled to surrender
land which was not being used or was already on
a short lease in exchange for low rents decreed by
peasant committees or assemblies.

In all this activity the individual participated
as a member of an *obshchina*—typically a territorial community corresponding to a village or
small settlement, exercising a considerable measure of self-government through the assembly of
heads of households *(skhod).* Politically, it was
the lowest-level local government authority, with
a wide range of administrative, fiscal and law-
enforcement responsibilities. Economically, it
was the legal owner of most of the peasant land.
It allotted portions of arable land to the peasant
households, keeping some land, especially pasture and forest, for collective use. Peasant households did, however, have small hereditary plots
around the house and could buy land for private
ownership from outside the commune. In many
areas, the *skhod* exercised the right to reallocate
the communal land periodically between households in order to re-establish a fairer distribution. Such repartitional communes were weakest
in the northwest, southwest and parts of the

southeast. But even in the hereditary communes
the work of the peasants was subject to extensive collective regulation. As in similar regimes
in other countries and at other times, "the prevailing open-field system, with its formal three-
field cycle of farming and the division of land
into strips, made agricultural cooperation of all
the members of the commune mandatory at
the major stages of the farming year".[20] Many
other economic functions were exercised by the
commune.

It is scarcely surprising that the peasants of
such a commune were able to act as one in the
assault on the landlords. The *obshchina* was a
genuine community, whose members would find
conditional cooperation rational, especially
when it was organized by the *skhod* or the new
committees, and if they did not they could be
subjected effectively to the selective incentives
which characterize peasant communities nearly
everywhere.[21]

It is interesting to note that the unrest was
greatest in the areas where the traditional repartitional commune was strongest. But it was also
in these areas—especially the Central Agricultural Region and the Middle Volga Region—that
the peasants owned least land and were therefore most obliged to rent non-peasant land in
exchange for money, labour or a share of the
crop.[22] So the firmest social foundation for collective action was combined here with the greatest need for it.

The situation of the peasants in CHINA at the
fall of the Manchus differed significantly from
that of the peasants of pre-revolutionary France
and Russia. In the first place, the Chinese peasant community was normally more "open" than
its French or Russian counterparts (in the sense
of Eric Wolf's well-known contrast between
open and closed communities): it was less self-
sufficient, more a part of a larger economic system, more exposed to alien ideas and values;
there was more mobility out of and into the
community. The peasant was in fact a member of
two "communities": his village and the market-
ing "community" composed of a market town
and its dependent area containing perhaps 15 to
25 villages.[23] It was the market "community"
which constituted the peasant's social world. Its
size alone would have made it weak as a community. It was, in addition, characterized by very

considerable social, economic and political stratification. In particular, the gentry took a leading role in these local "communities", organizing and managing clans, peasant associations and secret societies. They *mediated* relations between peasants.

Finally, the agricultural work of Chinese peasants involved much less cooperation than it did in France and Russia. Households worked independently; there was no collective regulation of the village agriculture and no common lands to manage; and there was only limited mutual aid between households—principally in connection with water storage and irrigation, which in any case gave rise to as much conflict as cooperation.

The Chinese peasant community, then, was far weaker than its counterpart in France and Russia, too weak in fact to provide a foundation for a spontaneous revolution in the countryside. It had to be mobilized by the patient efforts of political entrepreneurs.

There were, it is true, many peasant rebellions before the Chinese Revolution. Some were on a great scale and a few even succeeded in installing new regional governments for a time or causing the ruling dynasty itself to be replaced.[24] Skocpol recognizes this, but believes that even the most sustained of these rebellions could not have led to social revolution because they were all eventually infiltrated by non-peasants—local gentry or those, like merchants or would-be literati, who aspired to the gentry. The peasants, she concludes, "lacked the local community-based autonomy to render their resistance even potentially revolutionary" (p. 151), and certainly it is true that these rebellions, far from having revolutionary outcomes, invariably had the end result of strengthening or re-establishing the traditional system. Presumably, Skocpol's view must be that these peasant insurrections would have been doomed to terminate in non-revolutionary outcomes (because they were infiltrated and coopted by gentry, etc.) even if the conjunctural factors had been propitious. But since many of them were so massive and sustained (especially in the period 1850-70 when great waves of rebellions, including those of the Taipings and the Nien, involved millions of peasants and engulfed large areas of the country), the question arises of how the peasants managed to get so far as to mount them in the first place.

Some of them were, indeed, more successful in reaching their own goals than many of the European peasant insurrections which did not have revolutionary outcomes but which were nevertheless made possible by the existence of strong peasant communities.

Skocpol, in her discussion of "Agrarian Structures and Peasant Insurrections", has I think overstated the case against the Chinese community, as her own later discussion of the Communist Party's mobilization efforts itself suggests. There *was* a non-negligible degree of community, sufficient to provide a foundation for collective action. It would of course have been stronger if much of the cooperation amongst peasants had not been mediated by non-peasants; but there was *something* there, especially in the North, for the CP cadres to go to work on, when they had displaced the local gentry as political entrepreneurs. This slightly different emphasis finds support in the work of Elizabeth Perry and Philip Huang. Huang shows how in the 1930s villages on the North China plain were more closed, less integrated into wider trading networks and possessed of greater "communal solidarity" than is portrayed in the influential analysis by William Skinner which is accepted by Skocpol.[25] Perry, in her discussion of the massive Nien Rebellion (1851—63), for example, stresses the importance of communal connections and especially the success that clans sometimes had in coordinating their members from many villages: "families, clans, and lineage settlements were at the heart of Nien organizational strength". She writes of the Red Spear Society, which came to have three million followers and attempted takeovers of entire county administrations during the republican period, that it was a "community-based movement" and "although rural villages constituted the basic organizational unity of the Red Spears, in Honan the movement expanded to encompass a network of village alliances".[26]

But she goes on to say that the village chapters which were the cells of the Red Spear movement were organized at the initiative of village notables. Clans, too, and the secret societies which often played an important role in the organization of rebellions, were led by gentry or merchants; and Skocpol is undoubtedly right to argue that for this reason the peasant movements could not have been revolutionary. Nevertheless the Chinese Communist Party did succeed in making a revolution in part by building on what there was already to hand in the way of village communities. In the militarily secure base areas the Party's cadres immersed themselves in the life of the villages, extending traditional forms of mutual aid and introducing new ones, forming peasant associations, and putting these new practices and groups to work to bring tangible economic benefits to the peasants.[27] In order to do this, the CCP had to displace the existing village elite, taking over its role as political entrepreneur, though putting it to different uses of course. My point is that they could not have done this successfully unless there was already some degree of community amongst the peasant members of the village.[28]

III

It should be clear from this brief review that the account given by Skocpol and others of the social—structural preconditions for successful peasant insurrections in three great social revolutions is quite compatible with the rational choice theory of collective action if what I had to say earlier about community is accepted. But I am saying something stronger than this, namely that the thin theory of collective action provides part of the explanation of social revolution. This is not Skocpol's view. For her, as we have seen, a proper understanding of social revolutions requires the adoption of a "nonvoluntarist, structural perspective". In particular, she says (at p. 115), peasant insurrections were caused by "structural and situational conditions"—those I have discussed above together with others whose effect was a weakening of the state's control of the countryside. (I return to the second group below.)

We can accept Skocpol's view that "no successful revolution has ever been 'made' by a mass-mobilizing, avowedly revolutionary movement". The actions of revolutionary groups and of peasants (who may not have revolutionary aims) can produce a revolutionary outcome only in the right conditions. It is true that neither the revolutionaries nor the peasants produce these conjunctures (which are characterized especially by state crises); and it may be true that no one

intended or foresaw the outcomes. But it does not follow that what happens in these revolutionary situations is not in part explicable by rational choice theories. Nor does it follow that the conjunctures themselves were not in turn the products of rational choices.

Skocpol points to the correlation between pre-existing social structure and the behaviour of entire villages or local populations; without the intervening links showing the effect of social structure on the individuals and the interactions between the individuals, this is, I submit, at the very least an incomplete explanation.

In the case of China, the peasants did not rebel spontaneously, even though they were given the right sort of revolutionary "opening". But the explanation for this failure to rebel is in the first place that it was not rational for the individual peasant to participate in rebellion, and it was not rational because his relations to other potential rebels were not those of a strong community. The Chinese peasants' attacks on their landlords came only after the CCP had penetrated their villages and helped them to organize collective action. The CCP chose consciously to do this, to pursue "the Yenan Way". Why? And why did this strategy succeed? Certainly, as Skocpol in effect says, the Communists chose in circumstances which were not of their choosing; their options were conditioned, both limited and opened up for them—as by the Japanese invasion for example—but nothing she says proves that the CCP had to do what it in fact did. To argue that what the CCP chose to make of its opportunity is explicable without reference to its leaders' preferences and beliefs is implausible. But this is only Skocpol's methodological position; the detailed account she herself gives of the Chinese Revolution shows plainly the crucial role of the Communists' aims and beliefs in its making. It would be equally implausible to claim that the success of the Communists' strategy—which, as Selden, Perry and others have emphasized, required the use of selective material incentives in a reconstructed community setting—is explicable without reference to the peasants' preferences and beliefs.

It might be argued that this much can be conceded without damage to a "non-voluntarist, structural" position if it is reckoned that action is always mechanically caused by structural and situational factors and/or by preferences and beliefs which themselves have causes external to their possessor. In this case, the argument would go, the (thin) rational choice theorist as we know him is reduced to the minor supporting role of a technician and the serious part of the business is to explain the evolution of structures and situations and/or to find the causal origins of attitudes and beliefs; or, more strongly, that individuals are nothing more than bearers and transmitters of structural and other causal forces and therefore make no independent contribution to the explanation. I deal with these views in the final section below.

IV

I am aware of only one writer who, in methodological contrast to Skocpol, has taken a rational choice approach to peasant collective action. This is Samuel Popkin, in his extremely valuable book *The Rational Peasant*.[29] But he does not argue, as I wish to, that pre-existing rural *community* made it rational for the individual peasant to participate in revolutionary collective action; indeed, as part of his sustained attack on the "moral economy" approach to peasant society he argues that there was little community to be found in the Vietnamese countryside at the time of. the revolution. What he does do is to show that because peasants were (thin-) rational there was a problem about collective action, that the problem was overcome by political entrepreneurs, and that the ways in which they overcame it are consistent with the rational choice theory of collective action. So, while he makes no general argument about rationality and community, he provides the part of the argument (the part concerning individual motivation) which is missing in Skocpol's treatment of the Chinese Revolution—for, so far as peasant collective action is concerned, there are important similarities between the Chinese and Vietnamese cases.

In imperial times and even (but decreasingly) under French colonial rule, there was some degree of local community amongst the peasants, especially in the Northern and Central provinces of Tonkin and Annam. In these areas, peasants lived in nucleated villages which were closed corporate communities, though they lacked some of the communal features that characterized the closed corporate communities of, say, much of Eastern and Western Europe before the twentieth century, including the Russian *mir* described earlier. The village had *some* autonomy, with its own village council to manage local affairs, including the collection of taxes, the distribution of communal lands, the adjudication of disputes within the village, and the organization of religious rites and festivals; it possessed *some* communal land—more than a quarter of all agricultural land in precolonial times but a declining proportion under French rule; the villages engaged in *some* mutual aid, including cooperative labour, and collectively they maintained part of the local irrigation, flood control and drainage system.

But against these signs of community we have to set the facts of considerable stratification and mediation in the village: within each village there was a hierarchy of notables determined by education, wealth and age; the village council was made up of senior notables and a junior notable served as village "chief"; landholdings were very unequally distributed and there was intense competition for land with frequent boundary disputes; the communal lands, far from occasioning cooperation, produced conflict, as the notables, who controlled their periodical redistribution, used the distributions to enrich their relatives, their supporters and themselves; and most of the work of cultivation was carried out by individuals and families acting alone, with only limited cooperative labour restricted to small groups practising balanced reciprocity of well-defined specific tasks, despite the enormous scope for enhanced production through greater cooperation to improve irrigation systems.[30]

In the South, in Cochinchina, the peasant community was even weaker. The economy here was dominated by large estates, divided into small holdings worked by sharecroppers and tenants producing rice for export. The villages were open and less compact than in Annam and Tonkin; many of them were frontier settlements of recent foundation, with less ramified kinship links and a shallower tradition of cooperation.

There was, besides, an almost total absence of farm cooperatives, peasant associations or any other kind of supravillage formal organization or voluntary association in the Vietnamese countryside.[31]

In these circumstances, the Communists had to *build* a revolutionary movement village by village, and their approach was similar in some respects to the strategies pursued by the Chinese Communist Party. In this, they were of course assisted by the presence of an alien colonial power (though also impeded by its weakening of the village communities) and hugely assisted by the Japanese occupation of Vietnam in 1940, their displacement in March 1945 of French rule, and their own withdrawal in August 1945 paving the way for the Communists' "August Revolution".

The Communists were not alone in trying to build movements among the peasants during this period. The Catholic Church and two native politico-religious organizations—the Hoa Hao and Cao Dai—also had considerable success, using many of the methods adopted by the CP.[32]

In 1930-1 there had been large-scale peasant *jacqueries* against landlords and notables in Cochinchina (following a plunge in the price of rice caused by the world depression) and in Annam (following catastrophic famine). Both were organized by the recently formed Communist Party. In Cochinchina, the sporadic unrest was not coordinated over a large area and was quickly crushed. In Annam, the rebels actually took control of two provinces and held out for nine months. It seems clear that the leadership provided by the CP was crucial. In Cochinchina, the rapid defeat of the movement seems to have been partly due to the CP's failure to provide more coordinated leadership; while in Annam, in James Scott's view, "there is little doubt that the rebellion would not have taken on quite the dimensions of size and cohesiveness that it attained had it not been for the role of the Communist party", which was particularly strong in the affected provinces.[33] (An even worse famine at the turn of the century provoked little protest.) We should also recall that the village community was much stronger in Annam than in Cochinchina.

But it was not until after 1940 that the Communists really began to succeed in mobilizing the peasantry. After the destruction of their urban cells in 1940—undoing much of the rebuilding that had gone on since the French suppression following the uprisings of 1930—1—the CP under Ho Chi Minh's leadership began to embrace something like Mao's "Yenan Way".

From their mountain base near the Chinese border, the Viet Minh began to build peasant organizations in the villages first by taking advantage of the famine that Tonkin suffered in 1943-4: they alone brought help to the peasants by organizing bands to attack Japanese rice granaries, with participation in the attack bringing an immediate benefit in the form of a share of the rice that was seized. The support which the Viet Minh mobilized in the countryside after the August Revolution of 1945 enabled them to control large areas of all three regions (though less successfully in Cochinchina). As Popkin explains,[34] they did this by organizing the peasants in each village around pressing local problems, winning their support not in the first instance (or perhaps at all) for highly uncertain, large-scale, long-run goals but for less risky, small-scale goals whose achievement brought immediate concrete benefits. They subsidized and organized improvements in the local irrigation and water-storage system; they instituted popular literacy campaigns—using the classes to promote self-help and mutual aid as well; they made changes in the system of allocating communal land and of taxation, benefiting the poor and the village at the expense of the rich; they established village courts to arbitrate disputes, enabling the peasants to defend themselves against landowners in their own language; and they organized labour pools and enlarged the scope of mutual aid. In all this, the entrepreneurial role of the Communist cadres was crucial: by disaggregating the big overall goal of building a revolutionary movement into many smaller ones, by localizing the effort, by facilitating conditional cooperation, by enhancing the individual peasant's appreciation of the importance of his contribution and his valuation of the public good, and by the use of selective incentives, the Communists made it *rational* for the peasant to participate.

All this entrepreneurial organizing effort was in part made necessary by the relative weakness of the village community. But I want to argue—as I did in the case of China—that it would not have succeeded if there had been no community at all for the cadres of the CP to work on, once they had weakened the hold of the existing oligarchy of notables. Most peasant members of the village shared the same values and beliefs and had common enemies; they practised *some* reciprocity; they had lived and worked together in one place for many years. In this setting, the peasants of a single village were not so numerous and not such strangers to each other that conditional cooperation could not be made to work with a little help from political entrepreneurs; monitoring of participation and contributed effort was possible; and informal social sanctions could be effective.

V

Successful social revolutions have so far occurred only prior and during the transition to industrial capitalism. There have also been in this period countless peasant rebellions, some of them large-scale and sustained, which were not part of a revolution. The argument I have made about rationality and the role of community in revolutionary collective action applies also to these other forms of peasant collective action. Again, the historians of these rebellions have had a lot to say about community but nothing about rationality.

There seems to be wide agreement amongst historians that the local communities provide the social basis and organizational framework of peasant rebellion (and a variety of other kinds of popular disturbance as well). This is a refrain of Perez Zagorin's *Rebels and Rulers, 1500–1660*, for example. Writing generally of peasant rebellion in early modern Europe he says: "Agrarian rebellion almost invariably began in the mobilization of village communities, their members summoned to rise by the violent ringing of church bells in the parishes and then flowing together in growing crowds from all parts of the countryside... The village community contained the main potentiality of joint action. It was the elementary cell from whose coalescence with other similar cells peasant struggles, whether against the state or landlords, developed."[35]

For example, in the Croquant revolts in southwestern France in the 1590s and again in the 1630s and 1640s "the community in village and parish became the institutional cellule of revolt" and "Agrarian rebellion was thus sustained by the structure, action, and values of the peasant community."[36]

Of the biggest peasant rebellion of the early modern period, the German Peasant War of 1525-6, which was really a whole series of rebellions, Zagorin writes that "Mobilization followed communal lines as crowds of peasants belonging to a particular lordship, district, or jurisdiction streamed together carrying arms. Communities seem sometimes to have decided as a body to rebel. They then formed bands . . . which were organised and chose leaders paralleling the familiar *Dorf*, or village organisation."[37] The Peasant War was confined almost entirely to western Germany. This was one aspect of a broad divergence between Germany east and west of the Elbe in the later middle ages—the late development of serfdom in the east compared with its decline in the west as the peasants successfully struggled to limit the lords' powers—which was due, Robert Brenner has argued, to the great difference in the strength of the village community. Economic cooperation, village self-government and communal control of common resources were all much less developed in the east.[38]

The case of England is peculiar and controversial. Rodney Hilton seems to believe that the argument about community and rebellion applies to the medieval period in Europe in general and to the Great English rising of *1381* in particular.[39] Of Kett's rebellion of 1549, which was the biggest peasant rebellion of the early modern period in England, Zagorin again argues that the village community played an important role in the mobilization.[40] And even as late as the early nineteenth century, in the machine-breaking and rick-burning of "Captain Swing", in most of the actions, according to Hobsbawm and Rude, "the typical basic unit was a village group, composed of neighbours or bound by family ties, which took the initiative in organizing their own and neighbouring villages for common action by persuasion, the force of example, or impressment".[41] Nevertheless, Kett's rebellion was localized and short-lived and the Swing riots, though widespread, were not long sustained. More significantly, even when, during the English Revolution, political circumstances were more propitious for large-scale, sustained rebellion, there was none at all—only scattered, short-lived rioting. Even if we do not accept Alan Macfarlane's controversial judgment that the local community in England had already begun to decline (and the peasantry to disappear) by 1381,[42] it is nevertheless probably true that, after the sixteenth century, though there was *some* rural community, it was not sufficiently strong to provide the necessary basis for really sustained, large-scale revolutionary collective action, even when the repressive capacities of the state were temporarily weakened.[43]

VI

Some people may be skeptical about the argument I have made to the effect that revolutionary and rebel collective action has rational foundations and conforms to the thin theory of collective action. The sceptics presumably would include those (and there are many of them) who reject this theory on the grounds that "it's obvious" that there is in reality much participation in collective action which, if the theory were correct, ought not to occur, and this includes participation in interest groups and other associations, which have of course largely replaced community as the vehicles of movements for social and political change. A brief comment on this position will lead to an assessment of the applicability of the thin theory of rationality.

The first point is that in fact there is now a great deal of evidence on such associations which supports the thin theory of collective action (bearing in mind the modifications referred to in section I above): where large numbers of people share a common interest in a public good, relatively few do anything about it, and where an association or organization exists to further such an interest, of those who do join or participate or make donations, very many, perhaps most, are induced to do so by selective incentives admissible in Olson's theory, namely, "economic" and "social" incentives (or by a combination of these and the expected net subjective benefit arising from their contribution).[44] A number of studies have shown how important "social" incentives are in mobilizing people to contribute to collective action. An individual joins or contributes or participates because he is asked and tacitly or overtly pressured by friends, colleagues, workmates, or co-members of the association's local branch or cell. He cannot say "no" to them; he is afraid of losing their

approval, respect or cooperation. "Social" incentives of this kind are especially effective in relatively small and stable groups. Hence, many large associations have a federal structure and mobilize support through their local branches.[45] Often these local cells will be small enough for conditional cooperation to be rational for their members and the conditional cooperation will be bolstered by the operation of the informal social sanctions. Hence, too, an individual can more readily be mobilized in the first place if he works with others or has friends sharing the common interest, or is part of an existing social network linking him to members of the association in question. In other words, in the absence of genuine community, associations can sometimes mobilize people by trading on the remnants or surrogates of community.[46]

But associations are not communities, and only sometimes—and then only in highly attenuated forms—do they have available to them the positive and negative sanctions which a strong community can wield against its members with such extraordinary effectiveness. Failing these, an association must normally apply "economic" sanctions, for which (barring gifts like the state's backing for closed shops in trade unions) it must first gather the necessary resources, usually from its own members (though not of course at its founding and in its early days), and this puts a limit on the resources it can devote to producing the public good or on the resources it can devote to selective incentives to attract and retain supporters—a limit, either way, to its effectiveness in achieving its ends.

Although the evidence suggests that most collective action and failures of collective action are consistent with (thin) rational choice theory, there is clearly much collective action which is *not* explicable by the thin theory. People send dues to large associations without their contributions even being known to any one they know; they participate in massive demonstrations and movements *not* as members of a local branch or cell; they vote secretly in large constituencies; they contribute as isolated individuals to the provision of public goods by quietly refraining from various kinds of pollution without any social sanctions or pressure being applied or threatened; and so on. If these actions are not *thin*-rational, are they rational in some other sense, or are they simply not rational at all? If the latter, what explains them and why are people apparently sometimes thin-rational, sometimes not?

VII

In the thin theory, it will be recalled, rationality is relative to *given* aims and beliefs, and the agent's actions are *instrumental* in achieving or advancing the given aims in the light of the given beliefs; the agent is assumed to be egoistic; and the range of the agent's aims or the range of the incentives affecting the agent is limited, for without such limitation a thin theory is liable to become a tautology. It follows that, if a thin theory is to have much explanatory power, there are at least three general kinds of motivation which have little force. Since a thin theory requires action to be instrumental, it must be the case, first, that the pleasure or benefits of any kind which are got in the process of *doing* the action, as opposed to the value of the *consequences* of the action, must be unimportant; and second, that *expressive* motivations—the desire to be "true to one's self", to act consistently with one's deeply held commitments, and so on—play no important role. And since, in a thin theory, action must be instrumental in bringing about benefits to the agent himself, *altruistic* motivations must be relatively unimportant.

Each of these three kinds of motivation has been made the subject of alternative accounts of rationality or models of motivation. The authors of two of these models—Margolis's "new model of rational choice" incorporating altruism and Scitovsky's model of motivation incorporating in-process benefits[47]—believe that they have greater power than the thin theory to explain the whole range of facts about collective action; to explain, that is, both the facts which the thin theory seems able to account for (such as peasant revolutionary collective action, if my argument is correct) and those which it is not (such as those referred to at the end of the last section). If this were true, we would presumably have reason to abandon the thin theory of rationality and build an explanation of collective action on one of the alternative theories or a synthesis of them. Then we would have a unified theory of collective action consistent with community-based revolutionary collec-

tive action *and* with *all* forms of association-based revolutionary or reformist movements.

Unfortunately, neither Scitovsky's nor Margolis's theory (nor any other alternative to the thin theory that I am aware of) will do the job. I have set out elsewhere the reasons why in my view Margolis's theory (though it is the most interesting attempt to date to incorporate altruistic motivations systematically into a model of individual choice) is unusable[48] and I will not repeat them here. In Scitovsky's theory, contributing to the provision of a public good may not be a "cost", as it is in the thin theory of collective action; it may on the contrary bring what he calls "pleasure", which is derived essentially from stimulation, often the product of doing as opposed to *having*. This is true of the participatory or active forms of collective action—such as active participation in a political movement or in a protest demonstration. *These* kinds of collective action—some of which may not be consistent with the thin theory—are consistent with Scitovsky's theory. But it is hard to see how this can be claimed of non-participatory or non-active forms, such as charitable donations and subscription payments to associations. And of course the theory does not explain why someone would choose public rather than private forms of "pleasure"—political activity rather than mountaineering.

Both Margolis and Scitovsky's theories are incompletely specified, hence difficult to assess properly. Margolis's theory in particular is premised on the belief that the conventional model of rational choice is generally "unreliable in the context of public goods". Since in this context there *is* in fact very little participation in collective action (relative to the vast unrealized potential for collective action to provide public goods), it is doubtful that these two models can do better than the conventional theory. They would almost certainly predict *too much* collective action. As I suggested earlier, most cases of collective action that do occur can be explained by the conventional theory if we remember that it encompasses conditional cooperation and the use of selective social incentives, which are often ignored, as well as economic incentives. And if it turned out (as I think it would) that Margolis's and Scitovsky's theories were inferior to the simple thin theory in this vast majority of cases, then we should be wary of using them for the residue.

There is a more radical alternative to the thin theory, which claims to explain, or at least to understand or interpret, this residue—as well as much other collective action which its authors seem to believe is not explained by the thin theory (perhaps again because they neglect the possibility that it is explained by the theory of conditional cooperation together with the use of informal social sanctions in subgroups). This alternative bears on the issue of "structural" and "voluntarist" explanation with which I began and to which I will shortly return, so I will set it out more fully.

The approach differs radically from the thin theory (and also from Margolis's theory) in that it takes an *expressive* rather than an instrumentalist or consequentialist view of rationality. A relatively clear statement of one version is due to Stanley Benn.[49] "Action", he says, "is rational if it manifests attitudes, beliefs, or principles that it would be inconsistent in a person, under appropriate conditions, not to give expression to, given the character he is generally content to acknowledge as his own." This allows rationality to the expression of mere attitudes and beliefs as well as principles and appears to put little restriction on their content. But Benn later adds that the rational actor should be a "morally responsible person" who acts autonomously, that is, who has and uses standards which are "his own" in the sense that he subjects them to a continuing process of critical scrutiny. "In such ways he makes himself a person of some particular kind defined by the things he cares about." Action is rational, then, only if it is consistent with these autonomously derived *commitments* to the values, principles and ideals the individual cares about.

It is clear that rationality in this sense would often require the individual to do things which the thin theory would deem non-rational. If someone is deeply committed to, say, certain environmentalist ideals, and these commitments are part of the individual's "nature" or "identity" and it is the case in some particular time and place that all true environmentalists should join in a certain protest demonstration, then rationality as moral self-expression requires that he participate, even if the costs of participation are much greater than his likely benefits (but not, of course, if the individual's participation made no difference whatever).

A variant of this approach, sharing its general view that the thin theory provides a daft account of the concept of rationality, is due to Martin Hollis, who argues not that the thin theory of rationality does a relatively bad job of explaining the facts but that it is doing no explanatory work at all.[50] If I understand Hollis's elusive *Models of Man* at all, he too, like Benn, reckons that (fully) rational action has to be autonomous. But he arrives at this position from a different direction.

According to Hollis, the thin theory makes of the individual a *Plastic Man*. He is a causally determined automaton who (which?), faced with externally given opportunities and subject to externally given constraints, simply translates into action given preferences and beliefs which themselves have causal origins external to him. In which case, says Hollis, "rationality" is doing no explanatory work. (Presumably, the explaining is being done, if any is being done at all, by the causes of the constraints and opportunities and the individual's preferences and beliefs.)

The actions of *Autonomous Man,* on the other hand, "cannot be explained by causal laws and conditions". But in Hollis's view this does not make Autonomous Man's action altogether inexplicable, as some writers would have it, for Autonomous Man is "the explanation of his own actions". Unfortunately, the nature of this form of explanation is never made entirely clear.[51] Hollis's argument seems to be roughly as follows. By definition an autonomous man acts freely (his actions are not causally determined) and this he does only if he has good reasons for his actions; he has good reasons only if he acts in his "ultimate" or "real" interests and these are "bound up with" or "derive from" what he "essentially is". The "real interests" are never clearly defined but they come with the characters or roles which the individual autonomously chooses or affirms and which thereby give him his identity—give him a "self" which he expresses in his actions. Without autonomy, he would not be giving expression to a self but to external causal forces operating through him. On this account, then, to act *rationally* is to act in one's "real" or "ultimate" interests and this is to give expression to what one is. And it is this identity which in some sense *explains* its possessor's actions.

If an action is done just because it is required by a role or in some way expresses a "self" which is entirely determined by its bearer's social positions, then it is not of course autonomous, and on Benn's or Hollis's account it is not rational. Thus, an individual who is a roaring success as a capitalist entrepreneur, maximizing profit as (let us suppose) the role requires, cannot act rationally if he came to and performs this role uncritically and the role is not one he identifies with. Acting in this role cannot be *self*-expressive, for being a capitalist is not part of his identity.

A lot of collective action occurs precisely in situations where people act heteronomously. (The peasants whose revolutionary collective action I described earlier are surely in this category.) In such cases, I think Hollis would say, what explains the collective action are the causes determining the framework of opportunities and constraints in which the individuals act and the causes which move them to act. In these cases, I would at least agree, it is especially obvious that a theory of collective action which takes the individual's reasons for acting (his attitudes and beliefs) as unexplained givens is a radically incomplete explanation; but I want to insist that it is still a non-trivial *part* of the explanation.

In any case, there is, it seems to me, an analogous problem, if it is a problem, about explanations founded on a presumption of autonomy. Here, on Hollis's account, the explanatory buck, as it were, stops at the individuals' selves or identities. These are constituted by the characters or roles and the principles, ideals and projects which the individual has chosen to commit himself to or identify with. Without an explanation of how such commitments and identifications are made, this explanation of actions and their interaction is incomplete too.[52]

If I am not persuaded by Benn or Hollis to abandon the thin theory in favour of an expressive account of rationality, I do nevertheless take seriously the idea, or rather the range of ideas, of self-expression and I do believe that *expressive motivations* are important *in some contexts*. Undoubtedly some people are motivated to put their beliefs into practice; to act consistently with deeply held commitments to values, ideals and principles or simply to what is of central importance to them; not to be deterred from the pursuit of long-term projects; to make some-

thing coherent out of what remains of their lives; and to search for their "real selves" or even try to construct identities (however problematic the idea and however self-defeating the endeavour). All these (overlapping) things can come into conflict with what is rational on the thin theory, can require the individual sometimes to act against his or her narrow self-interest as it is defined by the thin theory in question.[53]

VIII

If we accept, then, that expressive motivations—as well as altruistic motivation and perhaps some Scitovskian pleasure-seeking—exist as well as the motivations of thin self-interest, we need, in the absence of an empirically well-founded or at least applicable general theory of motivation which incorporates all these sorts of motivation, to have some general idea of the conditions under which these other kinds of motivation are important relative to thin self-interest, or, equivalently, to be able to say when the thin theory of rationality alone is likely to provide a good foundation for explanatory theories.

I suggest, first, that behaviour is *most likely* to be thin-rational (and hence a thin theory is most applicable) where: (i) the options or courses of action available to the individual are limited; (ii) the thin incentives (or some of them at least) affecting the individual are to him well defined, clearly apparent and above all substantial; (iii) the individual's choice situation and the thin benefits and costs together are such that a lot (for him) turns on his choice, that is, there is a course of action available to him which if followed would bring him very much more (in thin terms) than at least one of the alternative available courses of action;[54] and finally, and more weakly and uncertainly, (iv) prior to the choice situation in question there have previously been many similar or analogous occasions.

These conditions are neither necessary nor collectively sufficient. I make only the weaker claim that, other things being equal, the more any one of them is met, the more purchase is a thin theory likely to get.

The final condition is the one I feel least sure of. The idea here is that, if this condition is satisfied, then non-rational behaviour is likely to have been selected out or filtered out (or both).[55]

But I would guess that this condition could readily be overridden by the other conditions.

A special case which satisfies both (ii) and (iii)—which are the most important conditions—is that of credible, substantial, explicit threats and offers (and throffers). Where selective incentives affect an individual's decision whether or not to participate in collective action, there are always at least tacit threats or offers (and this could also be argued of conditional cooperation). If these are explicit and substantial, they are even more likely to make the individual "think thin-rationally".

Of course, the extent to which the first three conditions are satisfied—the extent to which the agent's options are limited, or any of the incentives facing him are substantial, or a great deal turns on his choice—depends on the agent's resources of the relevant kinds. If the range of incentives specified in the thin theory is limited to monetary incentives, for example (or to any material things which money can buy), and the agent has already an abundant stock or supply of money, then he is less likely to be affected by threats and offers involving these incentives, and more likely not to act thin-rationally at all. In fact, thin theories invariably limit the incentives either to material incentives alone or (like the thin theory of collective action) to material incentives and "social" incentives based on the desire to avoid disapprobation. Now of course a person may be materially rich but not "rich" with respect to the "social" incentives, for there is a limit to how much approval, friendship, and so on, can be bought by money (or by food or other material goods), and approbation is not, like money, something of which one can accumulate a large stock that can then be spent over the rest of one's life; it has to be almost continuously earned. Furthermore, even in the sorts of societies in which these social incentives get most purchase, it seems likely that they are less fundamental motivators than the material incentives in the sense that they have much less force than material incentives when an individual is very poor materially.

So that, as long as material incentives are the only or the dominant motivators, it follows from conditions (i)—(iii) that the very poor are more likely to act thin-rationally than the relatively rich. Motivations *other* than those of thin self-interest will affect the rich more than the poor.

Among these other motivations I would include pleasure in the technical sense of Scitovsky, altruisim in Margolis's sense, and the expressive motivations mentioned at the end of the last section. Pleasure, altruism and "moral self-expression" are, as it were, luxuries.

It would of course be nice to have a general theory of motivation, with the thin theory dropping out as a special case applicable especially to zones of "scarcity" and "constraint" (see conditions (i)–(iii) above). But we do not have such a theory and I doubt if we ever will.

The relevance of all this to mobilization for revolutionary collective action—in community and association—should be apparent.

The situation of the poor peasant member of the traditional communities which provided a basis for peasant collective action in the revolutions and rebellions of the past was just the kind of structured, constrained and stable situation which, I have argued, tends to make the individual act thin-rationally. By "situation" I mean not just the peasant's poverty but also the effects on him of the community and of the social and political environment without which community could not flourish. Scarcity and the coercive potential of the community tend to put the peasant in mind of his narrow self-interest and to leave little scope for such motivations as pleasure, genuine altruism (as opposed to reciprocity) beyond the household, or moral self-expression.

The world of the traditional community gave way, as everyone knows, to a world of associations and organizations. It is especially the better-off members of such societies who are disproportionately most likely to make donations to, join or participate in voluntary associations of all kinds, and I am suggesting that this is *because* they tend not to act thin-rationally. The theory of collective action based on the thin theory of rationality should not be applied to them. Unfortunately we do not have a workable theory that *can* be applied to them. We have, as I have said, neither a general theory of motivation of which the thin theory is a special case, nor any alternative explanatory theory that is applicable to the residue of non-thin behaviour. It is quite likely that most of the cases of participation in collective action and other kinds of contribution to public goods provision that cannot be explained by the thin theory can be understood, *one by one*, as pleasure-seeking, altruism, or some form of self-expression, but the available theories that include these motivations are a long way from providing a foundation for a testable theory of collective action. And the prospects are not good, for pleasure-seeking and the search for self and its expression take myriad idiosyncratic forms, lacking any predictable regularity.

The destruction and decay of community in modern societies removes the most important social basis for collective action; it is also part of an historical process which makes non-thin-rational behaviour more common and the success of collective action less predictable.

IX

The argument made in the last section about the applicability of the thin theory of rationality seems to have returned us to the starting-point of Hollis's argument (section VII). For if the thin theory is applicable only in structured and con-strained situations of the sort I have indicated, then, it might be argued, it is precisely in these situations that the "structure" or situation is doing all the explaining because it limits the actors' options, provides or makes possible the use of non-trivial sanctions, and powerfully shapes the actors' attitudes and beliefs. If this is so, then, as I said earlier in discussing Skocpol's "anti-voluntarism", it would seem that the role of the rational-choice theorist is that of mere technician, the serious part of the business being left to those who can explain the causal origins of attitudes and beliefs and the situations in which they operate. This conclusion, I shall argue in this final section, is mistaken.

Let us go back to peasant rebellion (whether part of a successful social revolution or not). It is undeniably the product in the first place of indi-vidual actions. The actions are caused by atti-tudes and beliefs (including attitudes to and beliefs about structures) and these in their turn have causes. Amongst the causes of peasant atti-tudes and beliefs are surely *structures* (by which I mean sets of relations)—most obviously, the relations of production (the economic structure) whose terms are productive forces and persons, including peasants; the political relations between peasants and their landlords and the state; and other social relations amongst the peasants themselves, including aspects of the social structure of the village community not included in the economic or political structure. (I emphasize that I am not supposing that *abstract* structures—that is, sets of relations defined inde-pendently of specific relata—can be causes, even of attitudes to and beliefs about structures. But what can be causes, surely, are *specific* struc-tures, that is, structures with specific relata, or those parts of them which impinge on, say, the attitudes and beliefs in question.)

But the fact that individual actions, attitudes and beliefs are caused—by structures or by any-thing else—does not make them explanatorily irrelevant, any more than the fact that structures are in part the product of individual actions makes structures explanatorily irrelevant. We need, then, both individualist explanation of structures (and other macrophenomena) *and* structuralist explanation (amongst other kinds of explanation) of individual attitudes and beliefs. To deny either side of this supposition is to deny *any* causal force either to structures or to individuals, to attach *all* the explanatory power to one or the other. This is what is proposed by, on the one side, structuralists who would treat individuals as nothing other than the "effects" of structures or as mere "supports" or "bearers" of functions determined by structures, and history as "process without a subject"; and on the other side, those methodological individualists who suppose that all social phenomena can be reduced without residue to individual action and that explanation should always start with indi-viduals (or stop with them, depending on which direction you look in). Either attitude, it seems to me, rests on a dogma, an unproven assertion that flies in the face of common sense.

By *structuralist explanation* I simply mean causal explanation of social phenomena, or of attitudes and beliefs, in terms of social struc-tures—including economic and political struc-tures—or aspects or properties of such structures. Much structuralist "theory" or argument is or crucially relies upon some form of functionalist "explanation", and is therefore not a valid form of explanation.[56] But not all structural explanation is functional. Skocpol's explanation of social rev-olutions is not. Nor is the general theory proposed by Jeffery Paige in *Agrarian Revolution*, which gives us in effect a causal explanation of some of the attitudes, beliefs and options that would be relevant to an explanation of revolution, rebellion, etc., in terms of their bearers' locations in an economic-political structure.[57]

A pure individualist explanation would have the field to itself *only if* the causes of the attitudes and beliefs which cause action are themselves nothing but actions and properties of individuals. Certainly, individuals' actions and properties can be causes of attitudes and beliefs: a person's attitudes and beliefs can be caused (perhaps without his knowing it) by other attitudes and beliefs of his own; they can be produced directly by others' actions or behaviour; and they may even in part be *self*-made—the intentional products of the individual's own actions. But, as I have said, attitudes and beliefs, *including attitudes to and beliefs about structures,* can also be the products of the individual's situation or position in a social structure. So (if we set aside direct causation by the individual's physical environment) methodological individualism would have the explanatory field to itself only if structures (or all those aspects of them which could affect individuals' actions via their attitudes and beliefs) were *nothing but* individual (inter-) actions. Now a social structure might be, as Bhaskar and Giddens would say, the medium of action. And certainly, a structure typically emerges as a result of, and is maintained or transformed by, the actions of individuals. But it is not *the same thing as* these actions.

The methodological position I am here advocating (or supporting), though it involves attempting to supply causal links beginning and terminating at *individuals,* does not commit me to pure methodological individualism any more than it commits me to any version of methodological holism. To repeat: individuals—their actions or properties—are no more "rock-bottom" than (for example) structures. I am therefore not committed to certain views with which methodological individualists are customarily (though in most cases unjustly) saddled. Skocpol shares some of these misconceptions of methodological individualist practice. Most obviously, she seems to believe (as many sociologists persist in believing) that the position she attacks is destroyed by the obvious fact that outcomes are rarely the ones intended by the actors producing them. (In fact, of course, most rational choice theorizing outside of economics is centrally concerned with problems of unintended consequences.) A related misunderstanding, shared (I think) by Skocpol and very relevant to the argument of this essay, concerns the issue of the role of the individual in history, which is sometimes confounded or conflated with various other issues, including that of determinism. As Elster has argued,[58] the distinctive issue involved here is one of *stability*: whether a society, after any small "deviation" from its course brought about by the action of a single individual, will eventually resume the course it would have taken in the absence of the perturbation. But such stability entails nothing about how best to *explain* the course of history. (This, I *think*, is not Elster's view, but his brief discussion is unclear.) The historical path taken by a society may depend very much on what individuals do yet be immune to the effects of what is done by any individual, even (though I doubt it) an outstandingly creative or powerful or critically placed individual. Suppose that a rebellion is precipitated by a single act: a soldier fires on a crowd perhaps. It may be true (though impossible to prove) that the rebellion (or rather one like it) would have occurred even if this act had not been performed (indeed even if no act like this one had been performed), because there were underlying "social forces" which would (sooner or later) have produced the rebellion anyway. (Each of the clauses in parentheses in this sentence signals an obvious difficulty with specifying statements of this kind satisfactorily.) But it does not follow that the explanation of the rebellion and the historical path leading up to it must be non-individualist or that it cannot take the general form suggested earlier for good causal-cum-intentional explanation in the social sciences.[59]

Now it may be the case that, although the rebellion would *not* have occurred without the crucial precipitating act, this single act was sufficient to precipitate the rebellion only because of some underlying condition(s). Again, this does not oblige us to embrace purely structural explanation or some other form of holism.

Whichever of the two kinds of cause mentioned in the last two paragraphs—"unnecessary" or "necessary but superficial"—is the precipitating cause, the analysis of the *underlying* causes should in any case meet the criteria for good explanation. And I take it that good explanation should be, amongst other things, as *fine-grained* as possible: causal links connecting events distant in space-time should be replaced wherever possible by chains of "shorter" causal links.[60] This is an important reason for supplying explanations with causal links beginning and terminating at individuals. Structuralist and other holistic theories, where they take a causal form, are typically coarse-grained in this sense: they relate macrostates directly to macrostates without supplying a "mechanism" to show how the one brings about the other.

I have concentrated in this chapter (which is long enough as it is) on revolutionary collective action amongst peasants. But Skocpol's structuralist case may seem more persuasive when she argues that, whatever revolutionaries or peasants want, believe or do, they will not make a revolution unless the right sort of situation presents itself, and the production of such a situation is beyond their control, since it is in large part the consequence of the state's position in an international structure. I think we can accept this argument about the influence of international structures (at least in the cases of France and Russia) without, however, embracing Skocpol's resolute rejection of "voluntarist" and "purposive" explanation. For these structures, too, though they may have been intended or foreseen by no one, have to be explained in their turn and I see no reason why they should not in part be explained in terms of the rational actions of states (or state managers) and other actors. (There is no hint of *proof* in Skocpol's book that these were not the important proximate causes.) Indeed, I think there are more compelling reasons for believing that individuals in state managerial roles act (thin-) rationally, especially in response to economic and military competition and pressures from other states, than there are for believing that most other kinds of agents act rationally.[61] (This follows from the general argument about the applicability of the thin theory which I made in section VIII.) In fact, much of what Skocpol herself has to say about the historical behaviour of actual states seems to presuppose that they act rationally; and her general characterization of the state (pp. 29–32) attributes to it broad *aims*—above all in the maintenance of domestic order and defence against

other states—which give it specific *interests vis-à-vis* domestic actors, including both dominant and subordinate classes, as well as foreign actors, including states. Skocpol rightly emphasizes how revolutionaries, on seizing state power, themselves quickly adopt these basic interests of the state—and shows too how they also have other, ideologically inspired aims, not shared with the old regime managers, which seem to cause them to act in certain ways. Indeed, in her detailed historical accounts of the French, Russian and Chinese Revolutions—which are littered with statements about, or presupposing, intentional action—Skocpol fails quite generally to live up to her "nonvoluntarist, structural" methodological ideals.[62]

What of the other structural and situational conditions that Skocpol sees as necessary for social revolution? Like the state's international situation, these too have to be explained in their turn and again I see no reason why the explanation should not be at least partly intentional. Though intended by no one, these structures and situations are themselves in significant part the products of intentional actions. The peasant community, the relative power of the landed upper class and indeed the whole pre-revolutionary class structure, as well as the economic and military backwardness of the state relative to its competitors, and other characteristics of the international situation in which the state finds itself—*all* of these, as I hope to show in another place, are *precipitates* of past intentional actions.

NOTES

* I would like to thank the people who read and commented on, or listened to and discussed with me, the earlier versions of this paper which were presented at a seminar in 1982 at the Australian National University, Canberra, at the Western Political Science Association conference at Seattle in 1983, and at the Public Choice Institution at Halifax, Nova Scotia in 1984. They are Brian Barry, Stanley Benn, Alan Carling, Jon elster, Alan Gibbard, Bob Goodin, Russell Hardin, Margaret Levi, Daniel Little, Howard Margolis, Douglass North and Hugh Ward. I am also grateful to Yves-Marie Bercé for his help. I am sadly aware that I have not resolved all the problems raised by these people.

1. Theda Skocpol, *States and Social Revolution: A Comparative Analysis of France, Russia, and China* (Cambridge: Cambridge University Press, 1979), p. 154.

2. I begin and end this essay with discussion of Skocpol's outstanding work because I think that it does in fact provide an important part of the explanation of the French, Russian and Chinese Revolutions. But it does not provide the whole of the explanation even of these cases (as I shall argue) and its applicability to other revolutions is another matter.

3. Skocpol, *States and Social Revolutions*, p. 4.

4. "Peasant revolts have been the crucial insurrectionary ingredients in virtually all actual (i.e., successful) social revolutions to date" (cases like Cuba and Yugoslavia providing the exceptions, though not because urban workers played the crucial role), and certainly in the French, Russian, and Chinese cases "peasant revolts against landlords were a necessary ingredient . . . Whereas successful revolts by urban workers were not" (Skocpol, *States and Social Revolutions* pp. 112–13, and 318 n. 2). I shall not discuss urban collective action here; but it is worth noting an important contrast between urban workers and peasants. Communities of peasants—and the more their production is already geared to subsistence the more this is true—are, or can often quickly become, "self"-sufficient in food. They can thus survive for some time independently and often they can also support guerrillas and revolutionary armies (who may take advantage of, or strengthen, pre-existing community in order to expand subsistence food production). This is of course not possible for urban workers, who are necessarily parasitic on the countryside.

5. See Michael Taylor, *Anarchy and Cooperation* (London: Wiley, 1976). Robert Axelrod's work as reported most fully in *The Evolution of Cooperation* (New York: Basic Books, 1984), gives some support to the conclusion of this theory. It demonstrates the success of the "tit-for-tat" strategy which was shown in *Anarchy and Cooperation* to be the most rational strategy under certain conditions. But it must be borne in mind that Axelrod treats only tournaments in which players interact in pairs, so that his results have doubtful application to most public goods situations involving more than two people. On this and on the other work referred to in this paragraph, see my *The Possibility of Cooperation* (Cambridge: Cambridge University Press, 1987).

6. Jon Elster, *Sour Grapes: Studies in the Subversion of Rationality* (Cambridge: Cambridge University Press, 1983), p. 3. For a fuller discussion of the thin theory, see chapter 1 of *Sour Grapes* generally. In place of the usual "preferences" or "desires", I prefer "attitudes", a broader category including but not restricted to preferences, desires, goals, etc. (as in Donald Davidson's "Actions, Reasons and Causes", reprinted in his *Essays on Actions and Events*, Oxford: Clarendon Press, 1980).

7. Mancur Olson, *The Logic of Collective Action* (Cambridge, Mass.: Harvard University Press, 1965), pp. 60-1, n. 17 on p. 61 and n. 91 on p. 160.

8. In fact, *most* if not all explanatory rational choice theories assume agents to be motivated either by economic/material incentives alone or by these together with social incentives based on the desire to avoid disapprobation. They take for granted Harsanyi's "postulate" that "People's behavior can be largely explained in terms of two dominant interests: economic gain and social acceptance" (John C. Harsanyi, "Rational Choice Models of Behavior versus Functionalist and Conformist Theories", *World Politics*, 22 (1969), 513–38).

9. There is a detailed treatment of these and of their use in the provision of certain public goods—especially in "primitive" and peasant communities—in Michael Taylor, *Community, Anarchy and Liberty* (Cambridge: Cambridge University Press, 1982).

10. Olson, p. 177 of Appendix added in 1971 to *The Logic of Collective Action*.

11. Or as Olson (*The Logic of Collective Action*, p. 164 n. 102) says, "there is a 'threshold' above which costs and returns influence a person's actions, and below which they do not".

12. For a more detailed discussion of "community", see Taylor, *Community, Anarchy and Liberty*, section 1.4.

13. This is, I think, a good example of Russell Hardin's argument about "overlapping activities". See Hardin, *Collective Action* (Baltimore: Johns Hopkins Press for Resources for the Future, 1982), chapter 11.

14. On the peasant village community in the European cases generally (this section and sec. V), two articles by Jerome Blum are very useful: "The Internal Structure and Polity of the European Village Community from the Fifteenth to the Nineteenth Century", *Journal of Modern History*, 43 (1971), 541–76; and "The European Village as Community: Origins and Functions", *Agricultural History*, 45 (1971), 157–78.

15. Albert Soboul, "The French Rural Community in the Eighteenth and Nineteenth Centuries", *Past and Present*, no. 10 (1956), 78-95.

16. Ibid., p. 81.

17. Graeme J. Gill, *Peasants and Government in the Russian Revolution* (London: Macmillan, 1979).

18. Ibid., p. 29.

19. Ibid., pp. 149-50.

20. Teodor Shanin, *The Awkward Class: Political Sociology of Peasantry in a Developing Society: 1910–1925* (Oxford: Clarendon Press, 1972), p. 37.

21. For evidence on this from the 1905 revolution, see Maureen Perrie, "The Russian Peasant Movement of 1905-1907", *Past and Present*, no. 57 (1972), 123-55.

22. Gill, *Peasants and Government in the Russian Revolution*, pp. 157-69.

23. G. William Skinner, "Chinese Peasants and the Closed Community: an Open and Shut Case", *Comparative Studies in Society and History*, 13 (1971), 270-81.

24. See for example Jean Chesneaux, *Peasant Revolts in China, 1840–1949* (London: Thames and Hudson, 1973).

25. Philip C.C. Huang, *The Peasant Economy and Social Change in North China* (Stanford, California: Stanford University Press, 1985), Part 3.

26. Elizabeth Perry, *Rebels and Revolutionaries in North China, 1845–1945* (Stanford, California: Stanford University Press, 1980), pp. 128 and 155. See also her "Collective Violence in China, 1880-1980", *Theory and Society*, 13 (1984), 427–55.

27. See for example Perry, *Rebels and Revolutionaries*, chapter 6, and Mark Selden, *The Yenan Way in Revolutionary China* (Cambridge, Mass.: Harvard University Press, 1971).

28. This point is neglected by two earlier writers who recognize the importance of political entrepreneurs and the use of selective incentives, especially in the Chinese and Vietnamese revolutions: Jeffrey Race, "Toward an Exchange Theory of Revolution", in John Wilson Lewis (ed.), *Peasant Rebellion and Communist Revolution in Asia* (Stanford, California: Stanford University Press, 1974), and Joel S. Migdal, *Peasants, Politics, and Revolution* (Princeton, N.J.: Princeton University Press, 1974), chapter 10.

29. Samuel L. Popkin, *The Rational Peasant: The Political Economy of Rural Society in Vietnam* (Berkeley: University of California Press, 1979). An interesting forerunner of Popkin's analysis of political entrepreneurs and revolutionary mobilization is Jeffrey Race, "Toward an Exchange Theory of Revolution". But unlike Popkin, Race does not develop his argument systematically out of the free-rider problem.

30. Pierre Gourou, *The Peasants of the Tonkin Delta* (New Haven, Conn.: Human Relations Area Files, 1955); Popkin, *The Rational Peasant*, pp. 88–109.

31. Alexander B. Woodside, *Community and Revolution in Modern Vietnam* (Boston: Houghton Mifflin, 1976), pp. 142-7.

32. See Popkin, *The Rational Peasant*, chapter 5.

33. James C. Scott, *The Moral Economy of the Peasant: Rebellion and Subsistence in Southeast Asia* (New Haven: Yale University Press, 1976), p. 147.

34. Popkin, *The Rational Peasant*, chapters 5 and 6.

35. Perez Zagorin, *Rebels and Rulers, 1500-1660*, 2 vols. (Cambridge: Cambridge University Press, 1982), vol. 1, p. 86; see also p. 182.

36. Ibid., pp. 220 and 223. For a detailed treatment of the Croquants revolts, which establishes the community basis for rebellion and reproduces interesting documentary evidence of their organization and of the use of threats of sanctions against non-participants, see Yves-Marie Bercé, *Histoire des Croquants*, 2 vols. (Geneva and Paris: Droz, 1974).

37. Zagorin, *Rebels and Rulers*, vol. 1, p. 194.

38. Robert Brenner, "Agrarian Class Structure and Economic Development in Pre-Industrial Europe", *Past and Present*, no. 70 (1976), 30–75.

39. Rodney Hilton, *Bond Men Made Free: Medieval Peasant Movements and the English Rising of 1381* (London: Maurice Temple Smith, 1973), and "Peasant Society, Peasant Movements and Feudalism in Medieval Europe", in H.A. Landsberger (ed.), *Rural Protest* (London: Macmillan, 1974). In the latter (at p. 70) he writes of the peasants' "communal regulation of vital aspects of economic life" that "these necessary functions of economic life were the basis of the cohesion of the village community. The capacity for organisation in pursuit of social and political demands arose from the day-to-day experience of peasants" and peasants were thus "capable of tenacious common action".

40. Zagorin, *Rebels and Rulers*, vol. 1, p. 211.

41. E.J. Hobsbawm and George Rudé, *Captain Swing* (Harmondsworth: Penguin, 1973), p. 174.

42. Alan Macfarlane, *The Origins of English Individualism* (Oxford: Blackwell, 1978).

43. According to Craig Calhoun (*The Question of Class Struggle*, Oxford: Blackwell, 1982, especially p. 72), the potential of the English community for sustained collective action did not crumble until the early nineteenth century. He

argues that up to and including the Luddism of the 1810s, popular protest in England had been made possible by the small community—based on propinquity or, in the towns, on a common craft, or on a combination of these. But while community was the foundation of rebellious collective action it was also its limitation, since it provided no means of—was indeed an obstacle to—coordination over a large territory. What was needed was a combination of the small local communities and a national *organization* to coordinate them. Only then would revolution be possible. This combination made a brief appearance in England, beginning with the end of Luddism and fading already in the 1830s. This is Calhoun's argument.

Two comments on this argument are relevant here. First, revolutions can be made—and not only in the predominantly peasant societies I have considered here—without effective national organization or nation-wide coordination of local communities. Second, the period of about two decades, which on Calhoun's account had most revolutionary potential, was a very brief moment of time when artisans still lived or worked in quasi-communities *and* began to organize nationally, and this might indeed have been a potent mixture if only it could have developed and been sustained. But the rise of organizations on a national scale, and for that matter of formal organizations of all kinds, was precisely prompted and to some extent facilitated by the developing conditions which had undermined the village communities and the quasi-communities based on craft. The combination *could not* last long.

44. A good brief review of evidence on labour unions, farm groups and business associations is Terry M. Moe, *The Organization of Interests* (Chicago: Chicago University Press, 1980), chapter 7. There is also much interesting evidence scattered throughout James Q. Wilson, *Political Organisations* (New York: Basic Books, 1973), despite the author's disavowal of Olson's theory.

45. Olson himself pointed this out: *The Logic of Collective Action*, p. 68.

46. A number of studies showing this are discussed by Wilson in *Political Organisations*, though he fails to see that they give support to the thin theory of collective action. If some people join associations as a result of pressure brought to bear on them by existing friends and associates, it is also true, I would argue, that others join in part because of the prospect of *making* friends or having company. It also seems to me likely that *some* people, already sympathetic to a cause or to the goals of some association but not so strongly that they are prepared to do anything about it, join the association in order to put themselves in a position where they will be subject to the informal social sanctions exercised by their new associates and friends. There is in this bootstrapping operation a weaker version of the precommitment described by Jon Elster in *Ulysses and the Sirens* (Cambridge: Cambridge University Press, 1979): the precommitment does not actually eliminate options but makes the individual more vulnerable to pressure and coercion. The individual is committed to the cause enough to feel guilty about being a free rider but recognizes, in effect, that the commitment is too weak to overpower thin rationality. Another interesting possibility is that an individual with only a weak commitment joins in the hope that this will strengthen the commitment, out of a sense that he or she ought to have proper commitments, ones strong enough to issue in action. I will have more to say in a later section about commitment and problems of the "self". The decision to join in these last two cases is not of course rational on the thin theory.

47. Howard Margolis, *Selfishness, Altruism and Rationality* (Cambridge: Cambridge University Press, 1982); Tibor Scitovsky, *The Joyless Economy* (New York: Oxford University Press, 1976).

48. Michael Taylor, review of Margolis, *Selfishness, Altruism and Rationality*, Ethics, 94 (1983), 150-2.

49. Stanley Benn, "The problematic rationality of political participation", in P. Laslett and J. Fishkin (eds.), *Philosophy, Politics and Society*, 5th series (Oxford: Blackwell, 1979).

50. Martin Hollis, *Models of Man* (Cambridge: Cambridge University Press, 1977). See also Hollis's "Rational Man and Social Science", in Ross Harrison (ed.), *Rational Action* (Cambridge: Cambridge University Press, 1979).

51. Nor, likewise, is the idea of "agent causation", to which Hollis's notion bears a resemblance. See, for example, Roderick Chisholm, "Human freedom and the self", reprinted in G. Watson (ed.), *Free Will* (Oxford: Oxford University Press, 1982).

52. *Some* of these commitments may be *rationally* chosen, taken on in order to protect the individual from the temptations of short-run gain and bring him greater gain in the longer run.

53. My point here is analogous to Bernard Williams's well-known argument against Utilitarianism ('A Critique of Utilitarianism', in J.J.C. Smart and B. Williams, *Utilitarianism: For and Against* (Cambridge: Cambridge University Press, 1973)). The

good Utilitarian must act so as to maximize the sum of everyone's utilities, or at least of everyone who could be affected by the decisions available to him. This might require him to do something which conflicts with his projects or is inconsistent with his beliefs; to the Utilitarian it is enough that the utility of these things, which may be very great, has been entered into the aggregate utility calculation. But what if the right Utilitarian decision requires a man to turn aside from projects or ideals he is deeply committed to and identified with, that are part of what his life is about? (Such is the case, in Williams's example, of George, a chemist deeply opposed to chemical and biological warfare, who by taking a research job at a CBW laboratory could clearly increase the total utility of all those in any way affected by his choice, even after the great dis-utility attached to all the subsequent misery that would accrue to George if he took the job is taken into account.) To ask a man to do this, says Williams, is absurd; it is "to alienate him in a real sense from his actions and the source of his actions in his convictions"; it is "in the most literal sense, an attack on his integrity".

54. Harsanyi, "Rational Choice Models", makes a similar point. Something like this point is also made in connection with the decision to vote by Robert E. Goodin and K.W.S. Roberts in "The Ethical Voter", *American Political Science Review*, 69 (1975), 926-8.

55. On selection and filtering mechanisms, see Jon Elster, *Explaining Technical Change* (Cambridge: Cambridge University Press, 1983), p. 58 and chapter 6. The general idea can be found in several places in Joseph Schumpeter's writings; for example: *Capitalism, Socialism and Democracy*, 3rd edn (New York: Harper and Row, 1950), pp. 25 and 122-3; and *The Theory of Economic Development* (Cambridge, Mass.: Harvard University Press, 1934), p. 80. My attention was drawn to the last of these passages by the discus-

sion of it in Richard R. Nelson and Sidney G. Winter, *An Evolutionary Theory of Economic Change* (Cambridge, Mass.: The Belknap Press of Harvard University Press, 1982), at p. 40. The passage is also quoted by Elster, at p. 114 of *Explaining Technical Change*.

56. See Elster, *Explaining Technical Change*, part 1.

57. Jeffery M. Paige, *Agrarian Revolution* (New York: The Free Press, 1975).

58. Elster, *Explaining Technical Change*, pp. 32-3. My general methodological position is probably very close to that of Elster, to whose work I am indebted. I say "probably", because he apparently sees his approach as that of methodological individualism. See especially "Marxism, Functionalism, and Game Theory: the Case for Methodological Individualism", *Theory and Society*, 11 (1982), 453-82. See also *Making Sense of Marx* (Cambridge: Cambridge University Press, 1985).

59. The latest writer to draw this incorrect inference in support of holistic theorizing is Richard W. Miller in *Analyzing Marx: Morality, Power and History* (Princeton: Princeton University Press, 1984), p. 289.

60. Elster, *Explaining Technical Change*, pp. 24, 28-9.

61. For a stimulating discussion of the state's pursuit of its self-interest, see Anthony de Jasay, *The State* (Oxford: Blackwell, 1985). See also Fred Block, "Beyond Relative Autonomy: State Managers as Historical Subjects", in Ralph Miliband and John Saville (eds.), *The Socialist Register, 1980* (London: Merlin Press, 1980).

62. Something similar occurs in Paige's *Agrarian Revolution*, referred to earlier. Though not as coarse-grained as Skocpol's, Paige's general theory is similarly radically incomplete and ahistorical and cannot account for change, as it is supposed to do. But, as with Skocpol, history creeps back in, as it has to, when Paige turns to detailed study of cases.

Delbrück: The Military Historian

Gordon A. Craig

Hans Delbrück, whose active life coincided almost exactly with that of the Second German Empire, was at once military historian, interpreter of military affairs to the German people, and civilian critic of the general staff. In each of these roles his contribution to modern military thought was noteworthy. His *History of the Art of War* was not only a monument to German scholarship but also a mine of valuable information for the military theorists of his day. His commentaries on military affairs, written in the pages of the *Preussische Jahrbücher*, contributed to the military education of the German public and, during the First World War especially, helped them comprehend the underlying strategic problems that confronted the general staff. His criticisms of the High Command, written during the war and in the period following it, did much to stimulate a reappraisal of the type of strategical thinking that had ruled the German army since the days of Moltke.

The military leaders of Germany have always placed great emphasis upon the lessons that can be drawn from military history. This was especially true in the nineteenth century. I had been Clausewitz's ideal to teach war from purely historical examples; and both Moltke and Schlieffen had made the study of military history one of the responsibilities of the general staff. But if history was to serve the soldier, it was necessary that the military record be an accurate one and that past military events be divested of the mis-conceptions and myths that had grown up around them. Throughout the nineteenth century, thanks to the influence of Leopold von Ranke, German scholars were engaged in the task of clearing away the underbrush of legend that obscured historical truth. But it was not until Delbrück had written his *History of the Art of War* that the new scientific method was applied to the military records of the past, and it is this that constitutes Delbrück's major contribution to military thought.

It was not, however, his sole contribution. In the course of the nineteenth century the basis of government was broadened and in the Western world generally the voice of the people was felt increasingly in every branch of governmental administration. The control of military affairs could no longer remain the prerogative of a small ruling class. In Prussia, the embittered struggle over the military budget in 1862 was an indication that the wishes of the people and their representatives with regard to matters of military administration would have to be given serious consideration in the future. It seemed important therefore for the safety of the state and the maintenance of its military institutions that the general public should be educated to a proper appreciation of military problems. The military publications of the general staff were designed not only for use in the army but also for more general consumption. But the writings of

Craig, Gordon. (1986). "Delbrück: The Military Historian." In Peter Paret (Ed.), *Makers of Modern Strategy from Machiavelli to the Nuclear Age* (pp. 326–353). Princeton: Princeton University Press.

professional soldiers, devoted as they were to accounts of single wars and campaigns, were generally too technical to fulfill the latter function. There was a need for instruction in the elements of military affairs on a popular level, and Delbrück undertook to supply it.[1] In all of his writings, he thought of himself as a kind of military preceptor to the German people. This was most marked during the First World War, when in the pages of the *Preussische Jahrbücher*, he wrote monthly commentaries on the course of the war, explaining on the basis of available materials the strategy of the High Command and of Germany's opponents.

Finally, especially in his later years, Delbrück became a valuable critic of the military institutions and the strategical thinking of his time. His study of the military institutions of the past had shown him, in every age, the intimate relationship of war and politics, and had taught him that military and political strategy must go hand in hand. Clausewitz had already asserted that truth in his statement that "war admittedly has its own grammar, but not its own logic" and in his insistence that war is "the continuation of state policy by other means." But Clausewitz's dictum was too often forgotten by men who misinterpreted Clausewitz as having argued for the freedom of military leadership from political restrictions.[2] Delbrück returned to the Clausewitz doctrine and argued that the conduct of war and the planning of strategy must be conditioned by the aims of state policy and that once strategical thinking becomes inflexible and self-sufficient even the most brilliant tactical successes may lead to political disaster. In Delbrück's writings in the war years, the critic outgrew the historian. When he became convinced that the strategical thinking of the High Command had become antithetical to the political needs of the state, he became one of the foremost advocates of a negotiated peace. After the war, when the Reichstag undertook to investigate the causes of the German collapse in 1918, Delbrück was the most cogent critic of Ludendorff's strategy, and his criticism grew naturally from the precepts that he had drawn from history.

I

The details of Delbrück's life may be passed over quickly.[3] He himself summed them up tersely in 1920 with the words: "I derived from official and scholarly circles, on my mother's side from a Berlin family; I had war service and was a reserve officer; for five years I lived at the court of Emperor Frederick, when he was Crown Prince. I was a parliamentarian; as editor of the *Preussische Jahrbücher*, I belonged to the press; I became an academic teacher."

Delbrück was born in November 1848 in Bergen. His father was a district judge; his mother, the daughter of a professor of philosophy at the University of Berlin. Among his ancestors were theologians, jurists, and academicians. He received his education at a preparatory school in Greifswald and later at the universities of Heidelberg, Greifswald, and Bonn, showing an early interest in history and attending the lectures of Noorden, Schafer, and Sybel, all men deeply inspired by the new scientific tendency that was Ranke's contribution to scholarship. As a twenty-two-year-old Bonn student, he fought in the war against France, being invalided out as a result of an attack of typhus. After his recovery, he returned to the university and, in 1873, took his doctoral degree under Sybel with a dissertation on Lambert von Hersfeld, a German chronicler of the eleventh century, whose writings he subjected to a penetrating appraisal that revealed for the first time the critical acumen that was to distinguish all of his historical work.[4]

In 1874, with the assistance of the Badenese minister Franz von Roggenbach, Delbrück was appointed as tutor of Prince Waldemar of Prussia, the son of the crown prince, and his five years in this post not only gave him an insight into the political problems of his time but helped to turn his attention to military affairs. While he was performing his annual duties as a reserve officer, during the spring maneuvers in Württemberg in 1874, he read the History of the Infantry by Friedrich Wilhelm Rüstow, a former Prussian officer who had been forced to flee the country to escape punishment for political activity in 1848-1849, had served as Garibaldi's chief of staff in Sicily in 1860, and was one of the founders of the Swiss general staff system.[5] Delbrück later said that his reading of Rüstow had determined his choice of career, although it was not, in fact, until 1877, when he was given the opportunity to complete the edition of Gneisenau's memoirs and papers that had been begun by Georg Heinrich Pertz, that he began the study of war in a serious way. As he immersed himself in the history of the War of Liberation he was struck by what seemed to be a fundamental difference in the strategical thinking of Napoleon and Gneisenau on the one hand and Archduke Charles, Wellington, and Schwarzenberg on the other. As he carried his investigations further in the biography of Gneisenau with which he followed his editorial task,[6] the difference seemed more marked, and he sensed that nineteenth-century strategy in general was markedly different from that of the previous century. He read Clausewitz for the first time and held long conversations with the officers attached to Frederick's court. While he did so, his interest was heightened and he determined to seek the basic and determining elements of strategy and of military operations.

After the death of Prince Waldemar in 1879, Delbrück embarked upon his academic career, although not without difficulty. His *Habilitation* took place in 1881, but his first lectures in Berlin, on the campaign of 1866, aroused the objections of the university dean because of the contemporary nature of the theme and because Delbrück had not been authorized to teach military history. The young scholar persisted but shifted his attention to more remote periods of history, lecturing first on the history of the art of war from the beginning of the feudal system, and then pushing his researches even further back into the period between the Persian Wars and the decline of Rome. He began a systematic study of the sources in the ancient and medieval periods and published short studies of the Persian Wars, the strategy of Pericles and Cleon, and tactics of the Roman maniple, the military institutions of the early Germans, the wars between the Swiss and the Burgundians, and the strategy of Frederick the Great and Napoleon. Meanwhile, he encouraged his students to make equally detailed studies of special periods. Out of these lectures and monographs grew Delbrück's *History of the Art of War in the Framework of Political History,* the first volume of which appeared in 1900.[7]

Delbrück's preoccupation with a subject that was not highly regarded in academic circles, and his political and publicistic activities (from 1882 to 1885 he was a Free Conservative deputy in the Prussian Landtag and from 1884 to 1890 in the German Reichstag, and he was a member of the editorial board of the *Preussische Jahrbücher* from 1883 to 1890, and sole editor thereafter), which were often highly critical of imperial policy,[8] robbed him of much of the recognition that his scholarship normally would have received. He did not become a professor until 1895 when the official in charge of the university matters in the Prussian Kultus-ministerium, Friedrich Althoff, appointed him to a newly created *ausserordentliche Professur* at the University of Berlin. A year later he became *Ordinarius* when he succeeded Heinrich von Treitschke as Professor of Universal and World History, but he never became *Rektor* of his university and was never elected to the Prussian Academy of Sciences, although these distinctions fell to colleagues who never wrote or did anything comparable to the work for which he is chiefly remembered.[9]

II

From the date of the publication of the first volume, the *History of the Art of War* was the butt of angry critics. Classical scholars resented the way in which Delbrück manhandled Herodotus; medievalists attacked Delbrück's section on the origin of the feudal system; patriotic English scholars were furious at his slighting of the Wars of the Roses. Many of the resultant controversies have been written into the footnotes of the later editions of the work, where the fires of academic wrath still smolder. But in its main outlines the book stands unaffected by the attacks of the specialists and it has received its need of praise from such widely separated readers as General Wilhelm Groener, Reichswehr minister under the Weimar Republic, and Franz Mehring, the great socialist publicist. The former referred to it as "simply unique";[10] the latter as "the most significant work produced by the historical writing of bourgeois Germany in the new century," a comment repeated with less qualification ("by far the greatest work in this field in view not only of the colossal scope of the materials used but also of the seriousness of the undertaking") by K. Bocarov in his introduction to the first volume of the Soviet Defense Ministry's complete edition of the work in translation.[11]

Of the four volumes written by Delbrück, the first discusses the art of war from the period of the Persian Wars to the high point of Roman warfare under Julius Caesar. The second volume, which is largely concerned with the early Germans, treats also the decline of Roman military institutions, the military organization of the Byzantine Empire, and the origins of the feudal system. The third volume is devoted to the decline and near disappearance of tactics and strategy in the Middle Ages and concludes with an account of the revival of tactical bodies in the Swiss-Burgundian Wars. The fourth volume carries the story of the development of tactical methods and strategic thinking to the age of Napoleon.

In Proust's novel *The Guermantes Way*, a young officer remarks that "in the narrative of a military historian, the smallest facts, the most trivial happenings, are only the outward signs of an idea which has to be analyzed and which often brings to light other ideas, like a palimpsest." These words are a reasonably accurate description of Delbrück's conception of military history. He was interested in general ideas and tendencies rather than in the minutiae that had crowded the pages of earlier military histories. In his introduction to the first volume of his work, he specifically disclaimed any intention of writing a completely comprehensive history of the art of war. Such a work, he pointed out, would necessarily include such things as "details of drill with its commands, the technique of weapons and of the care of horses, and finally the whole subject of naval affairs—matters on which I have either nothing new to say or which I don't for a moment comprehend." The purpose of the history was stated in its title; it was to be a history of the art of war in the framework of political history.[12]

In the introduction to his fourth volume, Delbrück explained this in greater detail. The basic purpose of the work was to establish the connection between the constitution of the state, and tactics and strategy. The recognition of the interrelationship between tactics, strategy, the constitution of the state and policy reflects upon the relationship [between military history and] world history and has brought to light much that until now has been hidden in darkness or left without recognition. This work has been written not for the sake of the art of war, but for the sake of world history. If military men read it and are stimulated by it, I am pleased and regard that as an honor; but it was written for friends of history by a historian."[13]

At the same time, however, Delbrück realized that, before any general conclusions could be drawn from the wars of the past, the historian must determine as accurately as possible how those wars had been fought. It was precisely because he was intent on finding general ideas that would be of interest to other historians that Delbrück was forced to grapple with the "trivial happenings," "the smallest facts" of past campaigns, and, despite his own disclaimer, his reappraisal of those facts was of great value not to historians alone but to soldiers as well.

The "facts" were to be found in the great volume of source material that had been handed down by the past. But many of the sources of military history were obviously unreliable and were no better than "washroom prattle and adjutants' gossip."[14] How was the modern historian to check these ancient records?

Delbrück believed that this could be done in several ways. Provided the historian knew the terrain in which past battles were fought, he could use all of the resources of modern geographical science to check the reports that were handed down. Provided he knew the type of weapons and equipment used, he could reconstruct the tactics of the battle in a logical manner, since the laws to tactics for every kind of weapon could be ascertained. A study of modern warfare would supply the historian with further tools, for in modern campaigns he could judge the marching powers of the average soldier, the weight-carrying capacity of the average horse, the maneuverability of large masses of men. Finally, it was often possible to discover campaigns or battles, for which reliable reports existed, in which the conditions of earlier battles were reproduced almost exactly. Both the battles of the Swiss-Burgundian Wars, for which accurate records exist, and the battle of Marathon, for which Herodotus was the only source, were fought between mounted knights and bowmen on the one side and foot soldiers armed with weapons for hand-to-hand fighting on the other; in both cases, the foot soldiers were victorious. It should be possible, therefore, to draw conclusions from the battles of Granson, Murten, and Nancy that could be applied to the battle of Marathon.[15] The combination of all these methods, Delbrück called *Sachkritik*.[16]

Only a few applications of the *Sachkritik* need be mentioned. Delbrück's most startling results were attained by his investigations of the numbers of troops engaged in the wars of the past. According to Herodotus, the Persian army that Xerxes, son of Darius, led against Greece in 480 B.C. numbered 2,641,610 fighting men and at least as many crew members, servants, and camp followers.[17] Delbrück pointed out that this could not be considered reliable. "According to the German order of march, an army corps, that is 30,000 men, occupies about three miles, without the baggage trains. The marching column of the Persians would therefore have been 420 miles long and as the first troops were arriving before Thermopylae the last would have just marched out of Susa on the other side of the Tigrits."[18]

Even if this awkward fact could be explained away, none of the fields on which battles were fought was big enough to hold armies as large as those in Herodotus' accounts. The plain of Marathon, for instance, "is so small that some fifty years ago a Prussian staff officer who visited it wrote with some astonishment that a Prussian brigade would scarcely have room enough there for its exercises."[19] On the basis of modern studies of the population of ancient Greece, Delbrück estimated in 490 B.C. at about 12,000. Since Herodotus claimed that it was out-numbered (and, although not giving the size of the opposing army, estimated Persian casualties at 6,400),[20] this would mean that total troops engaged far exceeded the limits set by the Prussian observer.

Nor were these the only reasons for believing that Herodotus tended always to inflate Persian troop strength. The Greek army at Marathon was a citizen army trained to fight in a rude phalanx but incapable of tactical maneuver. The Persian army was a professional army, and the bravery of its soldiers was admitted even in the Greek account. "If both things were true, the size (of the Persian army) as well as its military bravery, then the ever-repeated victory of the Greeks would remain inexplicable. Only one of the two things can be true; hence, it is clear that the advantage of the Persians is to be sought not in numbers but in quality."[21] Delbrück concludes that, far from having the mass army described by Herodotus, the Persians were actually inferior in numbers to the Greeks throughout the Persian Wars.

The account of Herodotus had long been suspect, and Delbrück's criticism was by no means

wholly original. But his real contribution lay in the fact that he applied the same systematic methods to the numerical records of every war from the Persian Wars to those of Napoleon. Thus, in his discussion of Caesar's campaigns in Gaul, he clearly demonstrated reasons, grossly exaggerated. According to Caesar, the Helvetians, in their great trek, numbered 368,000 persons and carried three months provisions with them. To Delbrück the numerical estimate smacked of the fabulous; but it was Caesar's remarks on the Helvetian food supply that enabled him to prove it so. He pointed out that some 8,500 wagons would be required to carry such provisions and, in the condition of roads in Caesar's time, it would be quite impossible for such a column to move.[22] Again, in his discussion of the invasion of Europe by the Huns Delbrück effectively disposed of the belief that Attila had an army of 700,000 men, by describing the difficulties that Moltke experienced in maneuvering an army of 500,000 men in the campaign of 1870. "To direct such a mass unitedly is, even with railroads, roads, telegraphs and a general staff an exceedingly difficult task. . . . . How could Attila have led 700,000 men from Germany over the Rhine into France to the Plain of Chalons, if Moltke moved 500,000 with such difficulty over the same road? The one number acts as a check on the other."[23]

Delbrück's investigations of numbers have more than a mere antiquarian interest. At a time when the German army was being taught to seek lessons in history, the destroyer of myths helped it avoid the drawing of false conclusions. In war and the study of war, numbers were of the highest importance.[24] Delbrück himself pointed out that "a movement that a troop of 1,000 men executes without difficulty is a hard task for 10,000 men, a work of art for 50,000, an impossibility for 100,000."[25] No lessons can be drawn from past campaigns unless an accurate statement of the numbers involved is available.

Sachkritik had other uses. By means of it, Delbrück was able to reconstruct the details of single battles in a logical manner, and his success in doing so made a profound impression upon the historical section of the German general staff. General Groener has attested to the value of Delbrück's investigation of the origins of that oblique battle order that made flanking possible;[26] and it is well known that his scientific description of the encircling movement at Cannae strongly influenced the theories of Count Schlieffen.[27] But it is his account of the battle of Marathon that is perhaps the best example of the skill with which Delbrück reconstructed the details of past battles, the more so because it most clearly illustrates his belief that "if one knows the armament and the manner of fighting of the contending armies, then the terrain is such an important and eloquent authority for the character of a battle, that one may dare, provided there is no doubt as to the outcome, to reconstruct its course in general outline."[28]

The Greek army at Marathon was composed of heavily armed foot soldiers, formed in the primitive phalanx, the maneuverability of which was restricted to slow forward movement. It was opposed by an army inferior in numbers but made up of highly trained bowmen and cavalry. Herodotus had written that the Greeks had won the battle by charging across the plain of Marathon some 5,480 feet and crushing the center of the Persian line. Delbrück pointed out that this was a physical impossibility. According to the modern German drill book, soldiers with full pack could be expected to run for only two minutes, some 1,080 to 1,150 feet. The Athenians were no more lightly armored than the modern German soldier and they suffered from two additional disadvantages. They were not professional soldiers, but civilians, and many of them exceeded the age limit required in modern armies. Moreover, the phalanx was a closely massed body of men that made quick movement of any kind impossible. An attempted charge over such a distance would have reduced the phalanx to a disorganized mob that would have been cut down by the Persian professionals without difficulty.[29]

The tactics described by Herodotus were obviously impossible, the more so because the Greek phalanx was weak on the flanks and, in any encounter on an open field, could have been surrounded by Persian cavalry. It seemed obvious to Delbrück that the battle was not fought on the plain of Marathon proper but in a small valley to the southeast where the Greeks were protected by mountains and forest from any flanking movement. The fact that Herodotus speaks of the opposing armies delaying the engagement for days shows that Miltiades, the Athenian commander, had chosen a strong posi-

tion; given the tactical form of the Greek army, the position in the Brana Valley was the only one possible. Moreover, that position dominated the only road to Athens. To reach the city, the Persians were forced to dispose of Miltiades' army, or give up the whole campaign, and they chose the former alternative. The only logical explanation of the battle, then, is that the Persians, despite their numerical inferiority and inability to use flanking tactics, made the initial attack; and Miltiades, shifting at the crucial moment from the defensive to the offensive, crushed the Persian center and swept the field.[30]

To the casual reader, the *History of the Art of War*, like many a work before it, is a mere collection of such battle pieces. But the care with which Delbrück reconstructed battles was necessary to his main purpose. He felt that by the study of key battles the student could acquire a picture of the tactics of an age and from that could proceed to the investigation of broader problems.[31] For the key battles are important not only as typical manifestations of their age but as mileposts in the progressive development of military science. In a sense, Delbrück, like Proust's young officer, believed that past battles were "the literature, the learning, the etymology, the aristocracy of the battles of today." By reconstructing single battles he sought continuity in military history, and thus his *Sachkritik* enabled him to develop the three major themes which give his work a meaning and a unity found in no previous book on the subject: namely, the evolution of tactical forms from the Persians to Napoleon, the interrelationship of war and politics throughout history, and the division of all strategy into two basic forms.

Delbrück's description of the evolution of tactical bodies has been called one of his most significant contributions to military thought.[32] Convinced by his researchers that the military supremacy of the Romans was the direct result of the flexibility and articulated movement that resulted from the tactical organization of their forces he went on to argue that it was the gradual evolution of the primitive Greek phalanx into the skillfully coordinated tactical formations used by the Romans that comprised "the essential meaning of the ancient art of war,"[33] and that the revival of such formations in the Swiss-Burgundian Wars of the fifteenth century and their improvement and perfection in the period that ended with Napoleon's mastery of Europe was the salient development of modern military history.

The turning point in the history of ancient warfare was the battle of Cannae,[34] where the Carthaginians under Hannibal overwhelmed the Romans in the most perfect tactical battle ever fought. How were the Romans able to recover from that disaster, to defeat the Carthaginians and eventually to exercise military supremacy over the whole of the ancient world? The answer is to be found in the evolution of the phalanx. At Cannae the Roman infantry was ordered as the Greeks had been at Marathon, and this delivered them into Hannibal's arms, for their exposed flanks and the inability of their rear to maneuver independently of the mass of the army made it impossible for them to prevent the encircling tactics employed by the Carthaginian cavalry. But in the years following Cannae, striking changes were introduced into the Roman battle form. "The Romans first articulated the phalanx, then dived it into columns [*Treffen*] and finally split it up into a great number of small tactical bodies that were capable, now of closing together in a compact impenetrable union, now of changing the pattern with consummate flexibility, of separating one from the other and of turning in this or that direction."[35] To modern students of warfare this development seems so natural as to be hardly worthy of notice. To accomplish it, however, was extremely difficult and only the Romans, of all the ancient peoples, succeeded. In their case it was made possible only by hundred years experimentation—in the course of which the army changed from a civilian to a professional army—and by the emphasis upon military discipline that characterized the Roman system.[36]

The Romans conquered the world, then, not because their troops "were braver than all their opponents, but because, thanks to their discipline, they had stronger tactical bodies."[37] The only people who successfully avoided conquest by the Romans were the Germans, and their resistance was made possible by a natural discipline inherent in their political institutions, and by the fact that the German fighting column, the *Gevierthaufe*, was a tactical formation of great effectivemess.[38] Indeed, in the course of their wars with the Romans, the Germans learned to imitate the articulation of the Roman legion,

maneuvering their *Gevierthaufen* independently or in union as the occasion required.[39]

With the decline of the Roman state and the barbarization of the Empire, the tactical progress that had been made since the days of Miltiades came to an end. The political disorders of the age following the reign of the Severi weakened the discipline of the Roman army, and gradually undermined the excellence of its tactical forms.[40] At the same time, as large numbers of barbarians were admitted into the ranks, it was impossible to cling to the highly integrated battle order that had been devised over the course of centuries. History had shown that infantry was superior to cavalry only if the foot soldiers were organized in strong tactical bodies. Now, with the decline of the state and the consequent degeneration of tactics, there was a growing tendency in the new barbarian empires of the west and in Justinians's army as well, to replace infantry with heavily armed mounted soldiers.[41] As that tendency gained the upper hand, the days when battles were decided by infantry tactics died away and Europe entered a long period in which military history was dominated by the figure of the armed knight.[42]

Delbrück has been accused of maintaining that the development of military science stops with the decline of Rome and starts again with the Renaissance,[43] and the accusation is justified. The essential element in all warfare from the days of Charlemagne to the emergence of the Swiss infantry in the Burgundian Wars was the feudal army. This, in Delbrück's opinion, was no tactical body. It depended upon the fighting quality of the single warrior; there was no discipline, no unity of command, no effective differentiation of arms. In this whole period, no tactical progress was made, and Delbrück seems inclined to agree with Mark Twain's Connecticut Yankee, that "when you come to figure up results, you can't tell one fight from another, nor who whipped." It is true that at Crecy, the English knights dismounted and fought a defensive battle on foot and that, at Agincourt, dismounted knights actually took the offensive; but these were mere episodes and cannot be considered as forecasts of the development of modern infantry.[44]

It was among the Swiss in the fifteenth century that the independent infantry was reborn. "With the battles of Laupen and Sempach, Granson,

Murten and Nancy we have again a foot soldiery comparable to the phalanx and the legions."[45] The Swiss pikemen formed themselves in bodies similar to the German *Gevierthaufe*;[46] and, in the course of their wars against the Burgundians, they perfected the articulated tactics used by the Roman legions. At Sempach, for instance, the Swiss infantry was divided into two bodies, one holding a defensive position against the mounted enemy, the other delivering a decisive blow on the enemy's flank.[47]

The revival of tactical bodies was a military revolution comparable to that which followed Cannae. It was the revival, rather than the introduction of firearms, that brought feudal warfare to an end. At Murten, Granson, and Nancy the new weapons were employed by the knights, but had no effect upon the outcome of the battle.[48] With the restoration of the tactical body of infantry as the decisive one in warfare, the mounted soldiers became a mere cavalry, a highly useful but supplementary part of the army. In his fourth volume, Delbrück discussed this development and the evolution of the modern infantry to the age of the standing army and concluded with an account of the revolution in tactics made possible by the French Revolution.[49]

The attention that Delbrück pays to the emergence of tactical bodies serves not only to give a sense of continuity to his military history but also to illustrate the theme that he considered basic to his book, namely, the interrelationship of politics and war. In every period of history, he pointed out, the development of politics and the evolution of tactics were closely related. "The Hopliten-Phalanx developed in quite a different manner under the Macedonian kings than it did in the aristocratic Roman *Beamten-Republik*, and the tactics of the cohort were developed only in relationship with constitutional change. Again, according to their nature, the German *hunderts* fought quite differently from the Roman cohorts."[50]

The Roman army at Cannae, for example, was defeated because of the weakness of its tactics. But contributory to that weakness was the fact that the army was composed of untrained civilians rather than professional soldiers and the constitution of the state required that the high command alternate between the two consuls.[51] In the years following Cannae the necessity of a unified command was generally recognized. After

various political experiments were tried, P.C. Scipio was in the year 211 B.C. made general in chief of the Roman armies in Africa and assured of continued tenure for the duration of the war. The appointment was in direct violation of the state constitution and it marked the beginning of the decline of republican institutions. The interrelationship of politics and warfare is in this case apparent. "The importance of the Second Punic War in world history," Delbrück writes, "is that Rome effected an internal transformation that increase her military potentiality enormously,"[52] but at the same time changed the whole character of the state.

Just as the political element was predominant in the perfection of Roman tactics, so also the breakdown of tactical forms can be explained only by a careful study of the political institutions of the Jater Empire. The political and economic disorders of the third century had a direct effect upon Roman military institutions. "Permanent civil war destroyed the cement that till now had held the strong walls of the Roman army together, the discipline that constituted the military worth of the legions."[53]

In no part of the *History of the Art of War* does Delbrück include a general discussion of the relationship of politics and war. But, as he moves from one historical epoch to another, he fits the purely military into its general background, illustrating the close connection of political and military institutions and showing how changes in one sphere led of necessity to corresponding reactions in the other. He shows that the German *Gevierthaufe* was the military expression of the village organization of the German tribes and demonstrated the way in which the dissolution of German communal life led to the disappearance of the *Gevierthaufe* as a tactical body.[54] He shows how the victories of the Swiss in the fifteenth century were made possible by the fusion of the democratic and aristocratic elements in the various cantons, and the union of the urban nobility with the peasant masses.[55] and in the period of the French Revolution he describes the way in which the political factor, in this case "the new idea of defending the fatherland, inspired the mass [of the soldiers] with such an improved will, that new tactics could be developed."[56]

The most striking of all of Delbrück's military theories was that which held that all military strategy can be divided into two basic forms. This theory, formulated long before the publication of the *History of the Art of War*, is conveniently summarized in the first and fourth volumes of that work.[57]

The great majority of military thinkers in Delbrück's day believed the aim of war to be the annihilation of the enemy's forces and that, consequently, the battle that accomplishes this is the end of all strategy. Often they selectively cited Clausewitz to support their claim. Delbrück's first researches in military history convinced him that this type of strategical thinking had not always been generally accepted; and that there were long periods in history in which a completely different strategy ruled the field. He discovered, moreover, that Clausewitz himself had asserted the existence throughout history of more than one strategical system, suggesting in a note written in 1827 that there were two sharply distinct methods of conducting war: one which was bent solely on the annihilation of the enemy; the other, a limited warfare, in which such annihilation was impossible, either because the political arms or political tensions involved in the war were small or because the military means were inadequate to accomplish annihilation.[58]

Clausewitz began to revise *On War*, but died before he could complete his intended comprehensive analysis of the two forms. Delbrück determined to accept the distinction and expound the principles inherent in each. The first form of warfare he named *Niederwerfungsstrategie* (the strategy of annihilation). Its sole aim was the decisive battle, and the commanding general was called upon only to estimate the possibility of fighting such a battle in a given situation.

The second type of strategy Delbrück called variously *Ermattungsstrategie* (the strategy of exhaustion) and two-pole strategy. It was distinguished from the strategy of annihilation by the fact "that the *Niederwerfungsstrategie* has only one pole, the battle whereas the *Ermattungsstrategie* has two poles, battle and maneuver, between which the decisions of the general move." In *Ermattungsstrategie*, the battle is merely one of several equally effective means of attaining the political ends of the war and is essentially no more important than the occupation of territory, the destruction of crops or commerce, and the blockade. This second form of strategy is neither a mere variation of the first nor an inferior form. In certain periods of history, because of political factors or the smallness of armies, it has been the only form of strategy that could be employed. The task it imposes on the commander is quite as difficult as that required of the exponent of the strategy of annihilation. With limited resources at his disposal, the *Ermattungsstrategie* must decide which of several means of conducting war will best suit his purpose, when to fight and when to maneuver, when to obey the law of "daring" and when to obey that of "economy of forces." "The decision is therefore a subjective one, the more so because at no time are all circumstances and conditions, especially what is going on in the enemy camp, known completely and authoritatively. After a careful consideration of all circumstances—the aim of the war, the combat forces, the political repercussions, the individuality of the enemy commander, and of the government and people of the enemy, as well as his own—the general must decide whether a battle is advisable or not. He can reach the conclusion that any greater actions must be avoided at all cost; he can also determine to seek [battle] on every occasion so that there is no essential difference between his conduct and that of one-pole strategy."[59]

Among the great commanders of the past who had been strategists of annihilation were Alexander, Caesar, and Napoleon. But equally great generals had been exponents of *Ermattungsstrategie*. Among them, Delbrück listed Pericles, Belisarius, Wallenstein, Gustavus Adolphus, and Frederick the Great. The inclusion of the last name brought down upon the historian a flood of angry criticism. The most vocal of his critics were the historians of the general staff who, convinced that the strategy of annihilation was the only correct strategy, insisted that Frederick was a precursor of Napoleon. Delbrück answered that to hold this view was to do Frederick a grave disservice. If Frederick was a strategist of annihilation, how was one to explain away the fact that in 1741, with 60,000 men under his command, he refused to attack an already beaten army of only 25,000, or that, in 1745, after his great victory at Hohenfriedber, he preferred to resort again to a war of manever?[60] If the principles of *Niederwerfungsstrategie* were to be considered the sole criteria in judging the qualities of a general, Frederick would cut a very poor figure.[61] Yet Frederick's greatness lay in the fact that although he realized that his resources were not great enough to enable him to seek battle on every occasion he was nevertheless able to make effective use of other strategical principles in order to win his wars.

Delbrück's arguments did not convince his critics. Both Colmar von der Goltz and Friedrich von Bernhardi entered the lists against him, and a paper warfare ensued that lasted for over twenty years.[62] Delbrück, who loved controversy, was indefatigable in answering refutations of his theory. But his concept of *Ermattungsstrategie* was rejected by an officer corps trained in the tradition of Napoleon and Moltke and convinced of the feasibility of the short, decisive war.

Yet the military critics completely missed the deeper significance of Delbrück's strategic theory. History showed that there could be no single theory of strategy, correct for every age. Like all phases of warfare, strategy was intimately connected with politics, with the life and the strength of the state. In the Peloponnesian War, the political weakness of Athens in comparison with that of the League that faced it determined the kind of strategy which Pericles followed. Had he attempted to follow the principles of *Niederwerfungsstrategie*, as Cleon did later, disaster would have followed automatically.[63] The strategy of Belisarius' wars in Italy was determined by the uneasy political relations between the Byzantine Empire and the Persians. "Here as always it was politics that determined the administration of the war and that prescribed to strategy its course."[64] Again, "the strategy of the Thirty Years' War was determined by the extremely complicated, repeatedly changing political relationships," and generals like Gustavus Adolphus, whose personal bravery and inclination toward battle were unquestioned, were nevertheless compelled to make limited war.[65] It was not the battles won by Frederick the Great that made him a great general, but rather his political acumen and the conformity of his strategy with political reality. No strategic system can become self-sufficient; once an attempt is made to make it so, to divorce it from its political context, the strategist becomes a menace to the state.

The transition from dynastic to national war, the victories of 1864, 1866, and 1870, the immense increase in the war potential of the nation seemed to prove that *Niederwerfungsstrategie* was the natural form of war for the modern age. As late as 1890, Delbrück himself, despite his insistence on the relativity of strategy, seems to have believed that this was true.[66] Yet in the last years of the nineteenth century, the mass army of the 1860s was being transformed to the *Millionenheer* which fought in the First World War. Might not that transformation make impossible the application of the strategy of annihilation and herald a return to the principles of Pericles of Frederick? Was not the state in grave danger as long as the general staff refused to admit the existence of alternate systems of strategy? These questions, implicit in all of Delbrück's military writings, were constantly on his lips as Germany entered the First World War.

III

Since Delbrück was Germany's leading civilian expert on military affairs, his writings in the war years, 1914-1918, are of considerable interest. As a military commentator, his sources of information were in no way superior to those of other members of the newspaper and periodical press. Like them he was forced to rely on the communiqués issued by the general staff, the stories that appeared in the daily press, and reports from neutral countries. If his accounts of the war were distinguished by the breadth of vision and understanding not usually found in the lucubrations of civilian commentators, it was due to his technical knowledge of modern war and the sense of perspective he head gained from his study of history. In his monthly commentaries in the *Preussische Jahrbücher* one can find a further exposition of the principles delineated in his historical works and especially of his theory of strategy and his emphasis upon the interrelationship of war and politics.[67]

In accordance with the Schlieffen strategy, the German army swept into Belgium in 1914 with the purpose of crushing French resistance in short order and then bringing the full weight of its power against Russia. This was *Niederwerfungsstrategie* in its ultimate form, and Delbrück himself, in the first month of the war, felt that it was justified. Like most of his fellows, he had little fear of effective French opposition. The instability of French politics could not but have a deleterious effect upon France's military institutions. "It is impossible that an army that has had forty-two war ministers in forty-three years will be capable of an effectively functioning organization."[68] Nor did he feel that England was capable of continued resistance. Its past political development, he believed, would make it impossible for it to raise more than a token force. England had always relied on small professional armies; the institution of universal conscription would be psychologically and politically impossible. "Every people is the child of its history, its past, and can no more break away from it than a man can separate himself from his youth."[69]

When the first great German drive fell short of its goal, however, and the long period of trench warfare set in, Delbrück sensed a strategical revolution of the first importance. As the stalemate in the West continued, and especially after the failure of the Verdun offensive, he became increasingly convinced that the strategical thinking of the High Command would have to be modified. In the West at least, defensive warfare was the order of the day, a fact "the more significant since, before the war, the preeminence of the offensive was always proclaimed and expounded with quite exceptional partiality in the theory of strategy fostered in Germany."[70] Now, it was apparent that conditions on the western front approximated those of the age of *Ermattungsstrategie*. "Although this war has already brought us much that is new, nevertheless it is possible to find in it certain historical analogies: for example, the Frederician tillery, its field fortifications, its infrequent tactical decisions and its consequent long withdrawals presents unmistakable similarities with today's war of position and exhaustion (*Stellungs- und Ermattungskrieg*)."[71] In the West, reliance upon the decisive battle was no longer possible. Germany would have to find other means of imposing its will upon the enemy.

By December 1916 Delbrück was pointing out that "however favorable our military position is, the continuation of the war will scarcely bring us so far that we can simply dictate the peace."[72] A complete and crushing victory of German arms was unlikely, if not impossible.

That did not mean, however, that Germany could not "win the war." Its inner position not only separated its opponents but enabled it to retain the initiative. Its strength was so formidable that it should not be difficult to convince its opponents that Germany could not be defeated. While a firm defensive in the West was sapping the will of Allied troops, the High Command would be well advised to throw its strongest forces against the weakest links in the Allied coalition—against Russia and Italy. A concentrated offensive against Russia would complete the demoralization of the armies of the czar and might very well precipitate a revolution in St. Petersburg. A successful Austro-German offensive against Italy would not only have a tremendous moral effect in England and France but would threaten France's communications with North Africa.[73]

In Delbrück's opinion, then, Germany's strategy must be directed toward the destruction of the enemy coalition and the consequent isolation of England and France. In this connection, it was equally important that no measures be adopted that might bring new allies to the Western powers. Delbrück was always firmly opposed to the submarine campaign which he rightly feared would bring the United States into the war.[74]

But in the last analysis, if the war was to be won by Germany, the government would have to show a clear comprehension of the political realities implicit in the conflict. Since the war in the West had become an *Ermattungskrieg*, the political aspect of the conflict had increased in importance. "Politics is the ruling and limiting factor; military operations is only one of its means."[75] A political strategy must be devised to weaken the will of the people of France and England.

In the political field, Delbrück had felt from the beginning of the war that Germany suffered from a very real strategical weakness. Because of our narrow policy of Germanization in the Polish and Danish districts of Prussia, we have given ourselves the reputation in the world of being not the protectors but the oppressors of small nationalities. If this reputation were confirmed in the course of the war, it would give moral encouragement to Germany's enemies and would jeopardize the hope of ultimate victory. Turning to history, Delbrück argued that the example of Napoleon should serve as a warning to Germany's political leaders. The emperor's most overwhelming victories had served only to strengthen the will of his opponents and to pave the way for his ultimate defeat. "May God forbid that Germany enter upon the path of Napoleonic policy. . . . Europe stands united in this one conviction: it will never submit to a hegemony enforced upon it by a single state."[77]

Delbrück believed that the invasion of Belgium had been a strategical necessity;[78] but it was nonetheless an unfortunate move, for it seemed to confirm the suspicion that Germany was bent upon the subjugation and annexation of small states. From September 1914 until the end of the war, Delbrück continued to insist that the German government must issue a categorical disclaimer of any intention of annexing Belgium at the conclusion of hostilities. England, he argued, would never make peace as long as there was danger of German retention of the Flanders coast. The first step in weakening the resistance of Western powers was to state clearly that Germany had no territorial desires in the West and that its war aims would "prejudice in no way the freedom and honor of other people."[79]

Perhaps the best way to convince the Western powers that Germany was not seeking world domination was to make it apparent that Germany had no objection to a negotiated peace. Delbrück had favored such a peace ever since the successful Allied counteroffensive on the Marne in September 1914. He firmly believed that the war had been caused by Russian aggression and saw no reason why England and France should continue to fight the one power that was "guarding Europe and Asia from the domination of Moskowitertum."[80] As the war was prolonged, he was strengthened in his conviction that the sincere willingness to negotiate would win for Germany a victory that arms alone would be powerless to effect; and after the entrance of the United States into the war he openly predicted defeat unless Germany's leaders used that weapon. He was, therefore, enthusiastic about the passage by the Reichstag of the Peace Resolution of July 1917,[81] for he felt that it would do more to weaken the resistance of the Western powers than any possible new offensive upon the western front.

Delbrück never for a moment wavered in his belief that the German army was the best in the world, but he saw that best was not good enough. Throughout 1917 he hammered away at one constant theme: "We must look the facts in the face—that we have in a sense the whole world leagued against us—and we must not conceal from ourselves the fact that, if we try to penetrate to the basic reasons for this world coalition, we will ever and again stumble over the motive of fear of German world hegemony . . . . Fear of German despotism is one of the weightiest facts with which we have to reckon, one of the strongest factors in the enemy's power."[82] Until that fear was overcome, the war would continue. It could be overcome only by a political strategy based upon a disclaimer of territorial ambitions in the West and a willingness to negotiate.

Just as the conditions of the present war were, to Delbrück, comparable in some ways to those of the eighteenth century, so was this heightened emphasis upon the political aspects of the war in full accordance with the principles of *Ermattungsstrategie* as practiced by Frederick the Great. When the German army had taken the field in 1914 it had staked all on the decisive battle and had failed. Delbrück would now relegate military operations to a subordinate position. The battle was no longer an end in itself but a means. If Germany's political professions failed at first to convince the Western powers that peace was desirable, a new military offensive could be undertaken and would serve to break down that hesitation. But only such a coordination of the military effort with the political program would bring the war to a successful issue.

In his desire for a political strategy that would be effective in weakening the resistance of the enemy, Delbrück was bitterly disappointed. It became apparent as early as 1915 that strong sections of German public opinion regarded the war as a means of acquiring new territory not only in the East but in the West. When Delbrück called for a declaration of willingness to evacuate Belgium, he was greeted with abuse and was accused by the *Deutsche Tageszeitung* of being "subservient to our enemies in foreign countries."[83] The changing fortunes of war did not diminish the desire for booty and the powerful *Vaterlandspartei*, the most important of the annexationist groups, exercised a strong influence on national policy. Not only did the German government not make any declaration concerning Belgium but it never made its position clear on the question of a negotiated peace. When the Peace Resolution was being debated in 1917, Hindenburg and Lundendorff threatened to resign if the Reichstag adopted the measure. After the passage of the resolution, the influence of the High Command was exerted so effectively that the government did not dare to make the resolution the keystone of its policy. As a result of the so-called crisis of July 1917, the Western powers were encouraged to believe that the Reichstag's professions were insincere and that Germany's leaders were still bent on world domination.

To Delbrück the crises of July had a deeper significance. It showed within the government a dearth of political leadership and a growing tendency on the part of the military to dominate the formulation of policy. Germany's military leaders had never been known for their political acumen, but in the past they had followed the advice of the political head of the state. Gneisenau had willingly subordinated his views to those of Hardenberg; Moltke—although at time reluctantly—had bowed to Bismark's political judgment. Now, in the time of Germany's greatest crisis, the military were taking over completely and there was among them no man with a proper appreciation of the political necessities of the day. For all their military gifts, Hindenburg and Ludendorff still thought solely in terms of a decisive military victory over the Western powers, a *Niederwerfung* that would deliver western Europe into their hands. It was with a growing sense of despair that Delbrück wrote: "Athens went to her doom in the Peloponnesian War because Pericles had no successor. We have fiery Cleons enough in Germany. Whoever believes in the German people will be confident that it has not only great strategists among its sons but also that gifted statesman in whose hands the necessity of the time will place the reins for the direction of foreign policy."[84] But that gifted statesman never appeared; and the fiery Cleons prevailed.

It was, consequently, with little confidence that Delbrück watched the opening of the German offensive of 1918. "It is obvious," he wrote, "that no change can be made in the principles I have expounded here since the beginning of the war, and the dissension with regard to our western war aims remains."[85] Strategy, he insisted is not something in the abstract; it cannot be divorced from political considerations. "The great strategical offensive should have been accompanied and reinforced by a similar political offensive, which would have worked upon the home front of our enemies in the same way as Hindenburg and the men in field gray worked upon the front lines." If only the German government had announced, fourteen days before the opening of the offensive, that they firmly desired a negotiated peace and that, after such peace, Belgium would be evacuated, what would the result have been? Lloyd George and Clemenceau might have regarded these claims as signs of German weakness. But now, as the offensive rolled forward, "would Lloyd George and Clemenceau still be at the helm? I doubt it very much. We might even now be sitting at the conference table."[86]

Because of the failure to coordinate the military and political aspects of the war, Delbrück felt that the offensive, at most, would lead to mere tactical successes and would have not great strategical importance. But even he did not suspect that this was the last gamble of the strategists of annihilation, and the suddenness and completeness of the German collapse surprised him completely. In the November 1918 issue of the *Preussische Jahrbücher* he made a curious and revealing apology to his readers. "How greatly I have erred," he wrote. "However bad things looked four weeks ago, I still would not give up the hope that the front however wavering, would hold and would force the enemy to an armistice that would protect our boundaries." In a sentence that illustrates the responsibility that he felt as a military commentator to the German people, he added, "I admit that I often expressed myself more confidently than I felt at heart. On more than one occasion, I allowed myself to be deceived by the confident tone of the announcements and reports of the army and the navy." But despite these mistakes in judgment, he could, he said, be proud of the fact that he had always insisted that German people had a right to hear the truth even when it was bad and, in his constant preaching of political moderation, he had tried to show them the road to victory.[87]

It was in this spirit also that Delbrück made his most complete review and most searching criticism of the military operations of the last phase of the war. This was in the two reports which he made in 1922 before the Fourth Subcommittee of the commission set up by the Reichstag after the war to investigate the causes of the German collapse in 1918. In his testimony before the subcommittee, Delbrück repeated the arguments that he had made in the pages of the *Preussische Jahrbücher*, but the removal of censorship restrictions enabled him to give a much more detailed criticism of the military aspect of the 1918 offensive than been possible during the war.[88]

The main weight of Delbrück's criticism was directed against Ludendorff, who conceived and directed the 1918 offensive. In only one respect, he felt, had the general shown even military proficiency. He had "prepared the attack, as regards both the previous training of the troops and the moment for taking the enemy by surprise, in a masterly manner with the greatest energy and circumspection."[89] But the advantages of this preliminary preparation were outweighed by several fundamental weaknesses and by gross mistakes in strategical thinking. In the first place, the German army on the eve of the offensive was in no position to strike a knockout blow against the enemy. Its numerical superiority was slight and, in reserves, it was vastly inferior to the enemy. Its equipment was in many respects equally inferior, and it was greatly handicapped by a faulty supply system and by insufficient stocks of fuel for its motorized units. These disadvantages were apparent before the opening of the offensive but were disregarded by the High Command.[90]

Ludendorff was sufficiently aware of these weaknesses, however, to admit the impossibility of striking the enemy at that point where the greatest strategical success could have been won. In his own words, "tactics were to be valued more than pure strategy." That meant, in effect, that he attacked at those points where it was easiest to break through and not at those points where the announced aim of the offensive could best be served. The strategical goal of the campaign was the annihilation of the enemy. "In order to attain the strategical goal—the separation of the English army from the French and the consequent rolling-up of the former—the attack would have best been arranged so that it followed the course of the Somme. Ludendorff, however, had stretched the offensive front some four miles further to the south because the enemy seemed especially weak there."[91] The

defensive wing of the army under Hutier broke through at this point, but its very success handicapped the development of the offensive, for its advance outpaced the real offensive wing under Below which was operating against Arras. When Below's forces were checked "we were forced with a certain amount of compulsion to follow the line of [Hutier's] success . . . thereby the idea of the offensive was altered and the danger of dispersing our forces evoked."[92]

In short, by following the tactical line of least resistance Ludendorff began a disastrous policy of improvisation, violating the first principle of that *Niederwerfungsstrategie* that he professed to be following. "A strategy that is not predicated upon an absolute decision, upon the annihilation of the enemy, but is satisfied with single blows, may execute these now in this place, now in that. But a strategy which intends to force the decision, must do it where the first successful blow was struck." Far from obeying this percept, Ludendorff and Hindenburg operated on the principle that, when difficulties developed in one sector, new blows could be struck in another.[93] As a result, the grand offensive degenerated into a series of separate thrusts, uncoordinated and unproductive.

The cardinal fault was the failure of the High Command to see clearly what could be accomplished by the German army in 1918 and the failure to adapt its strategy to its potentialities. Here Delbrück returned to the major theme of all his work as historian and publicist. The relative strength of the opposing forces was such that the High Command should have realized that annihilation of the enemy was no longer possible. The aim of the 1918 offensive, therefore, should have been to make the enemy so tired that he would be willing to negotiate a peace. This in itself would have been possible only if the German government had expressed its own willingness to make such a peace. But once this declaration had been clearly made, the German army in opening its offensive would have won a great strategical advantage. Its offensive could now be geared to the strength at its disposal. It could safely attack at the points of tactical advantage—that is, where success was easiest—since even minor victories would now have a redoubled moral effect in the enemy capitals.[94] The High Command had failed in 1918 and had lost the war because it had disregarded the most important lesson of history, the interrelationship of politics and war. "To come back once more to that fundamental sentence of Clausewitz, no strategical idea can be considered completely without considering the political goal."[95]

IV

The military historian has generally been kind of misfit, regarded with suspicion both by his professional colleagues and by the military men whose activities he seeks to portray. The suspicion of the military is not difficult to explain. It springs in large part from the natural scorn of the professional for the amateur. But the distrust with which academicians have looked on the military historians in their midst had deeper roots. In democratic countries especially, it arises from the belief that war is an aberration in the historical process and that, consequently, the study of war is neither fruitful nor seemly. It is significant that in his general work *On the Writing of History,* the dean of military historians in the early twentieth century, Sir Charles Oman, should entitle the chapter dealing with his own field "A Plea for Military History." Sir Charles remarks that the civilian historian dabbing in military affairs has been an exceptional phenomenon, and he explains this by writing: "Both the medieval monastic chroniclers and the modern liberal historiographers had often no closer notion of the meaning of war than that it involves various horrors and is attended by a lamentable loss of life. Both classes strove to disguise their personal ignorance or dislike of military matters by deprecating their importance and significance in history."[96]

The prejudice that Oman resented was felt equally keenly, throughout his life, by Hans Delbrück. When, as a relatively young man, he turned his talents to the study of military history, he found that the members of his discipline regarded his specialty as not worth the energy he expended upon it. Ranke himself, when he learned after Delbrück's *Habilitation* that the young man intended to write a history of the art of war, expressed his disapproval of the project, and Theodor Mommsen, when Delbrück presented him with the first volume of the work, said rather ungraciously that "his time would

hardly permit him to read this book."[97] Few academic historians heeded Delbrück's plea in 1887 that there was a crying need for scholars "to turn not only an incidental but a professional interest to the history of war,"[98] and in his last years he was still complaining, as he did in the pages of his *Weltgeschichte,* about those who persisted in believing that "battles and wars can be regarded as unimportant by-products of world history."[99]

It may be that the passage of time has diminished interest in the discoveries of Delbrück's *Sachkritik* and that even the strategical controversies that he delighted in have become somewhat remote from our present concerns. But there is no doubt that the *History of the Art of War* will remain one of the finest examples of the application of modern science to the heritage of the past, and, however modified in detail, the bulk of the work stands unchallenged. Moreover, in an age in which war had become the concern of every man, the major theme of Delbrück's work as historian and publicist is at once a reminder and a warning. The coordination of politics and war is as important today as it was in the age of Pericles, and strategical thinking that becomes self-sufficient or neglects the political aspect of war can lead only to disaster.

NOTES

1. See Hans Delbrück, "Etwas Kriegsgeschichtliches," *Preussische Jahrbücher* 60 (1887), 607.
2. See the essays on Clausewitz and Moltke, above.
3. Delbrück himself has written brief autobiographical sketches in *Geschiechte der Kriegskunst im Rahmen der politischen Geschichte* (Berlin, 1900–20), I:vii f., and *Krieg und Politik* (Berlin, 1918–19), 3:225ff. See also J. Ziekursch in *Deutsches biographisches Jahrbuch* (1929). An excellent account of Delbrück's life is given in Richard H. Bauer's article on Delbrück in *Some Historians of Modern Europe,* ed. Bernadotte Schmitt (Chicago, 1942), 100-27.
4. Hans Delbrück, *Über die Glaubwürdigkeit Lamberts von Hersfeld* (Bonn, 1873). See Richard H. Bauer in *Some Historians of Modern Europe,* ed. Schmitt, 101f.
5. On Rüstow, see *Allegemeine Deutsche Biographie,* 30:34ff.; Marcel Herwegh, *Guillaume Rüstow* (Paris, 1935); and Georges Rapp, Viktor Hofer, and Rudolf Jaun, *Der schweizerische Generalstab,* 3 vols. (Basel, 1983), esp. vol. 3.

6. Hans Delbrück, *Das Leben des Feldmarschalls Grafen Neidhardt von Gneisenau* (Berlin, 1882).

7. *Geschichte der Kriegskunst im Rahmen der politischen Geschichte* (Berlin, 1900). The work is in seven volumes but only the first four can be considered Delbrück's own. The fifth volume (1928) and the sixth (1932) were written by Emil Daniels; a seventh volume (1936) was written by Daniels and Otto Haintz. The first four volumes will be treated here. All citations will be made from the first edition. A second edition of the first two volumes appeared in 1908 and a third edition of the first volume in 1920. None of the changes in these later editions made essential differences in the original work. The first four volumes were also repeated in 1962-64 (Berlin).

8. See especially Annelise Thimme, *Hans Delbrück als Kritiker der Welhelminischer Epoche* (Düsseldorf, 1955).

9. Andreas Hillgruber, "Hans Delbrück," in *Deutsche Historiker,* ed. Hans-Ulrich Wehler (Göttingen, 1972), 4:42.

10. Wilhelm Groener, "Delbrück und die Kriegswissenschaften," in *Am Webstuhl der Zeit, eine Erinnerungsgabe Hans Delbrück dem Achtzigjährigen . . . dargebracht,* ed. Emil Daniels and Paul Rühlmann (Berlin, 1928), 35

11. Franz Mehring, "Eine Geschichte der Kriegskunst," *Die Neue Zeit* (Erganzungsheft, no. 4, October 1908), 2, and *Gesammelte Schriften,* vol. I (Berlin, 1959). On the Soviet edition of the *Geshcichte der Kriegskunst,* see Otto Haintz, introduction to the first four volumes of the 1962 edition of the Delbrück work, p. 6.

12. *Geschichte der Kriegskunst,* I:xi.

13. Ibid., 4:preface.

14. Ibid., 1:377.

15. Delbrück used this last method in his first account of the Persian Wars, *Die Perserkriege und die Burgunderkriege: Zwei kombinierte kriegsgeschichtliche Studien* (Berlin, 1887).

16. *Geschichte der Kriegskunst,* 1: introduction

17. Herodotus, 7: 184-87.

18. *Geschichte der Kriegskunst,* 1:10

19. Hans Delbrück, *Numbers in History: Two Lectures Delivered before the University of London* (London, 1913), 24.

20. Herodotus, 6: 109-16

21. *Geschichte der Kriegskunst,* 1: 39

22. Ibid., 1: 427.

23. Delbrück, *Numbers in History,* 18.

24. General Groener made explicit acknowledgment of Delbrück's contribution. See "Delbrück und die Kriegswissenschaften," 38.

25. *Geschichte der Kriegskunst,* 1:7.

26. Groener, "Delbrück und die Kriegswissenschaften," 38. The oblique battle order, first used by Theban Epaminondas, bears a striking resemblance to that used by Frederick the Great at Leuthen in 1757. On Epaminondas, see *Geschichte der Kriegskunst,* 1: 130-35.

27. *Geschichte der Kriegskunst,* 1: 281-302. Graf Schlieffen, *Cannae* (Berlin, 1925), 3. See also the essays on Moltke, above.

28. *Geschichte der Kriegskunst,* 2: 80. Delbrück used the method not only for the battle of Marathon but also in his reconstruction of the battle of the Teutoburger Wald.

29. Delbrück's argument becomes weaker if one assumes that the Greeks would begin their charge only when they came within arrow range, but Herodotus says explicitly (6: 115) that they "advanced at a run towards the enemy, not less than a mile away." Ulrich von Wilamowitz defended Herodotus by arguing that the goddess Artemis gave the Greeks sufficient strength to make the charge and criticize scholarship that estimated the importance of divine, and other forms of, inspiration. He was supported by J. Kromayer, with whom Delbrück argued the point in the *Historische Zeitschrift* (95:Iff., 514f.) and the *Preussische Jahrbücher* (121:158f.)

30. *Geschichte der Kriegskunst,* 1:41-59.

31. Ibid., 1: 417.

32. F.J. Schmidt, Konrad Molinski, and Siegfried Mette, *Hans Delbrück: Der Historiker und Politiker* (Berlin, 1928), 96. Eugen von Frauenholz, *Entwicklungsgeschichte des deutschen Heerwesens* (Munich, 1940), 2: vii.

33. *Geschichte der Kriegskunst,* 2:43.

34. Ibid., I: 330ff.

35. Ibid., I: 380.

36. Ibid., I: 381. See also I: 253. "The meaning and power of discipline was first fully recognized and realized by the Romans."

37. Ibid., 2: 43.

38. Ibid., 2: 45ff.

39. Ibid., 2: 52f.

40. Ibid., 2: 205ff. This chapter, entitled "Niedergang und Auflösung des römischen Kriegswesens," is the key chapter of the second volume.

41. Ibid., 2: 424ff.

42. Ibid., 2: 433.

43. T.F. Tout in *English Historical Review* 22 (1907), 344-48.

44. *Geschichte der Kriegskunst,* 3:483. For a penetrating criticism of Delbrück's discussion of medieval warfare, see Tout, cited in note 43.

45. *Geschichte der Kriegskunst,* 3: 661. See essay on Machiavelli, above.
46. Ibid., 3: 609ff.
47. Ibid., 3: 594.
48. Ibid., 4: 55.
49. See essay on Frederick the Great, Guibert, and Bülow, above.
50. *Geschichte der Kriegskunst,* 2: 424.
51. Ibid., 1: 305.
52. Ibid., 1: 333.
53. Ibid., 2: 209.
54. Ibid., 2: 25-38, 424ff.
55. Ibid., 3: 614f.
56. Ibid., 4: 474.
57. Ibid., 1: 1000ff.; 4: 333-63, 426-44.
58. See the essay on Clausewitz, above.
59. Hans Delbrück, *Die Strategie des Perikles erläutert durch die Strategie Friedrichs des Grossen* (Berlin, 1890), 27-28. This work is Delbrück's most systematic exposition of the two forms of strategy.
60. *Preussische Jahrbücher,* 115 (1904), 348f.
61. In the *Strategie des Perikles,* Delbrück wrote a parody that showed that the application of such criteria to Frederick's campaigns would prove him a third-rate general. For this, Delbrück was accused in the Prussian Landtag of maligning a national hero.
62. A full account of the controversy, with bibliography, appears in *Geschichte der Kriegskunst,* 4: 439-44. See also Friedrich von Bernhardi, *Denkwürdigkeiten aus meinem Leben* (Berlin, 1927), 126, 133, 143. The most thorough and judicious criticism of Delbrück's strategical theory is that of Otto Hintze, "Delbrück, Clausewitz und die Strategie Friedrichs des Grossen," *Forschungen zur Brandenburgischen und Preussischen Geschichte 33* (1920), 131-77. Hintze objects to the sharp distinction that Delbrück draws between the strategy of Frederick's age and that of Napoleon and insists that Frederick was at once a *Niederwerfung* and an *Ermattung*-strategist. He also questions Delbrück's interpretation of Clausewitz's intentions, as does H. Rosinski in *Historissche Zeitschrift 151* (1938). See Delbrück's answer to Hintze, *Forschungen zur Brandenburgischen und Preussischen Geschichte 33* (1920), 412-17.
63. *Geschichte der Kriegskunst,* 1: 101f.
64. Ibid., 2: 394.
65. Ibid., 4: 341.
66. *Strategie des Perikles,* ch. 1.
67. The articles that Delbrück wrote in the *Preussische Jahrbücher* are collected in the three-volume work called *Krieg und Politik* (Berlin, 1918-19). To the articles as they originally appeared Delbrück has added occasional explanatory notes and a highly interesting summary statement. The best article on Delbrück's war writings is that by General Ernst Buchfinck, "Delbrücks Lehre, das Heer und der Weltkrieg," in *Am Webstuhl der Zeit,* ed. Schmitt, 41-49. See also Martin Hobohm, "Delbrück, Clausewitz and die Kritik des Weltkrieges," *Preussische Jahrbücher,* 181 (1920), 203-32.
68. *Krieg und Politik,* 1: 35.
69. Delbrück's views on England's weakness as a military power were most clearly developed in an article in April 1916. See *Krieg und Politik,* 1: 243ff.
70. Ibid., 2: 242.
71. Ibid., 2: 164. See also 2:17.
72. Ibid., 2: 97.
73. Buchfinck, "Delbrücks Lehre, das Heer und der Welkrieg," 48.
74. *Krieg und Politik,* 1: 90, 227ff., 261.
75. Ibid., 2: 95.
76. Ibid., 1: 3f.
77. See ibid., 1: 59 and the article entitled "Das Beispiel Napleons," in ibid., 2: 122ff.
78. *Krieg und Politik,* 1: 33.
79. Ibid., 2: 97.
80. Ibid., 1: 18.
81. The Peace Resolution, passed by the Reichstag by 212 votes to 126, stated in part: "The Reichstag strives for a peace of understanding and a lasting reconciliation among peoples. Violations of territory and political, economic and financial persecutions are incompatible with such a peace. The Reichstag rejects every scheme which has for its purpose the imposition of economic barriers or the perpetuation of national hatreds after the war. The freedom of the seas must be secured. Economic peace alone will prepare the ground for the friendly association of the peoples. The Reichstag will actively promote the creation of international organizations of justice. But so long as the enemy governments dissociate themselves from such a peace, so long as they threaten Germany and her allies with conquest and domination, then so long will the German people stand united and unshaken, and fight till their right and the right of their allies to live and grow is made secure. United the German people is unconquerable."
82. *Krieg und Politik,* 2: 187.
83. See R.H. Lutz, ed., *Fall of the German Empire,* Hoover War Library Publications, no. 1 (Stanford, Ca., 1932), 307
84. *Krieg und Politik,* 3: 123.
85. Ibid., 3: 63.
86. Ibid., 3: 73.

87. Ibid., 3: 203-206.

88. Delbrück's testimony is reproduced completely in *Das Werk des Untersuchungsaus schusses der Deutschen Verfassunggebenden Nationalversammlung und des Deutschen Reichstages 1919-1926. Die Ursachen des Deutschen Zusammenbruches im Jahre 1918* (Vierte Reihe im Werk des Untersuchungsausschusses), (Berlin, 1920-29), 3: 239-73. Elections from the Commission's report, but only a very small portion of the Delbrück testimony, may be found in *The Causes of the German Collapse in 1918,* ed. R.H. Lutz, Hoover War Library Publications., no. 4 (Stanford, 1934).

89. *Die Ursachen des Deutschen Zusammenbruches,* 3: 345. Lutz, ed., *Causes of the German Collapse,* 90.

90. *Die Ursachen des Deutschen Zusammenbruches,* 3: 246.

91. Ibid., 3: 247.

92. Ibid., 3: 346.

93. Ibid., 3: 250-51.

94. Ibid., 3: 253f.

95. Ibid., 3: 253.

96. Charles Oman, *On the Writing of History* (New York, n.d.), 159f.

97. Haintz, introduction to the 1962 edition of *Geschichte der Kriegskunst,* 9.

98. Delbrück , "Etwas Kriegsgeschichtliches," 610.

99. Hans Delbrück, *Weltgeschichte* (Berlin, 1924-28), 1: 321.

People's Wars

Gordon H. McCormick

What is meant by the term "people's war"? The concept that can be defined both narrowly and broadly. Defined narrowly, the team is used to denote the body of strategic thought on "protracted war" developed by Mao Zedong in the 1930s and the 1940s, during the period of the Chinese Civil War and the struggle against the Japanese. This definition is firmly rooted in the larger Marxist-Leninist theory of class struggle. Defined broadly, the concept of people's war is used generically to denote any form of guerrilla conflict or popular insurrection, regardless of its ideological roots. By this definition, the opening and middle stages of the Chinese Communist struggle against the Nationalist (Kuomintang) regime was an example of a people's war, as was the Afghan campaign against the Marxist regime in Kabul.

The definition of people's war used in this entry takes a middle course. The term, on the one hand, will be used to describe a body of ideas on population-based conflict or insurgency that goes beyond the specific concept of operations developed by Mao. At the same time, we will retain the ideological meaning of the term by referring to those forms of "popular warfare" based on the concept of class struggle. Defining the concept in this manner distinguishes it, on the one hand, from the type of conflict waged in Afghanistan, which would represent a more generalized form of guerilla warfare, as well as from the type of class-based revolutionary conflict envisioned by Lenin, which was based primarily on political rather than military forms of struggle. While the last act of revolutionary takeover, in Lenin's view, would be carried out by a popular insurrection, the months and years leading up to the insurrection would be characterized by careful, behind-the-scene political work, designed to place the revolutionary party in a position to catalyze a final uprising and seize power when the historical moment was deemed to be propitious. It would not be characterized by a period of revolutionary *war,* per se, in which the outcome of the struggle would be decided by a military interaction.

Although the concept of people's war, for definitional purposes, can be usefully distinguished from the larger concept of guerrilla warfare, we should not lose sight of the fact that the first is merely an ideological subset of the second. The defining operational problem, in each case, is the same: overcoming the conventional military superiority of the state (or occupying power) through an asymmetrical campaign based on the support (and resources) of a constituent population. While the leadership of a people's war will attempt to draw support from among a revolutionary class (classically, the peasantry), the non-Marxist insurgency will define its natural constituency along different lines (e.g., ethnicity, communal affiliation, or regional identity).

McCormick, G. (1999). "People's Wars." *Encyclopedia of Conflicts Since World War II* (pp. 23–34). New York: M. E. Sharp, Inc.

Where the first defines its popular base "horizontally" (according to class) across national or ethnic lines, the second defines its base of support "vertically" (according to some other group identifier) without regard to its class affiliation.

The underlying organizational tasks facing the leadership of a people's war are similar to those faced by that of any insurgency. We can define these as (1) *penetration,* which speaks to the revolutionary organization's need to "get inside" targeted social groupings as a prelude to "turning" them to the service of the organization's political and military objectives, (2) *transformation,* which speaks to the insurgency's need to consolidate its control over the targeted group and redirect some percentage of its resources to the organization's goals, and (3) *application,* which refers to the ways in which these resources are used to further develop an insurgent infrastructure, undermine the competing infrastructure of the state, and, ultimately, extend the insurgent's zone of control. Collectively, these tasks define the process of social mobilization. Every insurgent organization must address each of these operational tasks if it is to pose a viable challenge to the state. The manner in which it does so will define its theory of victory.

Revolutions and people's wars in the twentieth century have virtually all imitated or tried to imitate earlier revolutions. These successful cases of the past establish operational models that are adopted by latter-day revolutionaries who hope to repeat the success of those that preceded them by replicating their experience. While such cases have generally addressed the question of "why" one should revolt, as well as what revolutionary changes should be carried out in society at such time as one actually wins, the principal influence has been over *how* an armed revolt should be prosecuted in the first place. For those who come to the problem of overthrowing a standing regime with high ambition but little practical experience, a revolutionary paradigm offers an immediate (if often stylized) recipe for action.

The tradition of people's war, for its part, has been dominated by two original paradigms: the model of protracted conflict developed by Mao and the *foco* concept of guerrilla warfare developed by Ernesto "Che" Guevara. Most revolutionary insurgencies since the end of World War

II have sought to either directly apply or adapt and refine one or the other of these baseline concepts of operation to local circumstances. Each of these models can be usefully defined in contrast to the other. The concept of protracted conflict developed by Mao is designed to be prosecuted by a "low-profile" organization carrying out a "bottom-up" approach to insurgency. By contrast, it can be said that the theory of insurgency developed by Che Guevara is designed to be prosecuted by a "high-profile" organization from the "top down." In certain key respects, these two models represent operational opposites. In doing so, they bound the larger concept of people's war.

THE CHINESE MODEL OF PEOPLE'S WAR

Mao's assessment of the operational problem facing the Chinese Communist Party during its early struggles in the 1920s and 1930s rested on two essential considerations that bear on the general study of people's war. The first of these was the government's equally apparent political weakness. Deposing the old regime, in Mao's view, would require the party to overcome its material weaknesses by exploiting the opportunities provided by its comparative political advantage. As Mao observed at the time, "All guerrilla units start from nothing and grow." At the outset of this type of struggle, the standing regime represents a force in being. The guerrilla, by contrast, represents a force in development. The latter begins with little more than an idea. The guerrilla's one opening under these circumstances, according to the theory of class conflict, is provided by the inherent frailty of the regime's political base and the corresponding weakness of its institutional presence throughout the countryside. Exploiting this opening, Mao argued, will permit a guerrilla force to bridge the gap between its grand ends and limited means over the course of the struggle.

TIME, SPACE, AND INITIATIVE

The strategy designed by Mao to square the circle between ends and means rested on the calculated use of time and space. Buying time, Mao argued, was essential if the regime's strengths were to be turned into weaknesses and the guerrilla weaknesses were to be turned into strengths. The struggle, in its most abstract form, was envisioned to be an institutional contest between the developing architecture of the "new state" on the one hand and the declining institutions of the "old state" on the other. Building the new and dismantling the old, Mao recognized, would be a protracted undertaking. As this process unfolds, however, the relative balance between the guerrilla and the government would gradually shift. This shift, furthermore, could be expected to take on a dynamic quality over time. Guerrilla successes, he argued, would tend to be self-reinforcing, just as the regime's growing record of failure would tend to lead to the further erosion of the state and its administrative organs. While this process would ebb and flow, over the long run the decline of the state could be expected to accelerate, eventually at and increasing rate. The guerrillas' principal operational challenge, in this view, was not to end the war quickly, but to keep it going.

Unlimited time, in this strategy, required unlimited space. Space, in Mao's view, would provide the guerrillas with the room for maneuvers to buy the time necessary to win. All space, in this sense, is not created equal. For practical purposes, a distinction was made between territory that, in the opening stages of the engagement, was under the effective control of the regime, and that which was not. If the guerrillas' evaluation of the political environment facing each side was accurate, the regime's administrative control throughout the countryside would be imperfect. To survive their weak beginning, the guerrillas would open the struggle in those areas of the country in which the regime was weak and avoid making a stand in those areas of comparative regime strength. In pursuing such a strategy, the insurgency would give itself the best opportunity to gain the time it required to establish an institutional counterweight to the state. Revolutionary organization, in turn, would further extend the guerrillas' ability to establish effective spatial control.

These ideas formed the basis of Mao's concept of protracted war. According to this formula, the war will evolve via the dual mechanisms of "destruction and construction"—through the step-by-step destruction of the state and the associated construction of the new counterstate. The two, in Mao's view, are mutually dependent and must proceed in tandem. The erosion of the government's administrative architecture at the margin of its control will open additional opportunities for the insurgents to expand their own institutional presence, just as the organization's earlier (if still limited) institutional base provided the springboard to open its campaign against the state in the first place. This can be expected to take on an iterative quality over time, as each new advance by the guerrillas lays the groundwork for the next. The speed with which this campaign unfolds will be regulated by the strength of the state (which will tend to increase as the opposition pushes forward from the periphery to the state's center of gravity), the nature of the government's counter-strategy, the level of local resistance to the guerillas' efforts to establish their own institutional presence, the natural time limits associated with building an alternative set of political and military forms.

Expressed in geographical terms, this progression is intended to slowly result in an extension of guerrilla authority from peripheral areas of the countryside (or political margin), where state control will be comparatively weak, toward the cities (or political center) of the country where the position of the regime is traditionally much stronger. This process can be described as one of protracted encirclement, in which the urban regions of the country are encircled and eventually detached from the interior. The dynamic quality of this strategy is manifest in several ways. First, it calls for the guerrillas to push into areas of marginal control, even as they are being pulled into these areas by the political vacuum created by the retreat of the state. Second, as the opposition gains ground, it will naturally acquire the means to gain strength by gradually expanding its base of popular support. The inverse process, meanwhile, is occurring with the state, which is losing ground in a zero-sum contest for territorial control with the guerrillas. The result, in theory, is a compound shift in the relative balance of advantage as the guerrillas become absolutely stronger and the regime grows absolutely weaker at a more or less equivalent rate.

The nature of this encirclement strategy is somewhat different from that which typically characterizes Western military thought. For Mao, encirclement is not achieved by means of development, but through a process of "strategic convergence." Encirclement in the first sense, as one commentator noted some years ago refers to a process of "eccentric maneuver," in which the attacking force advances from a single point to surround and strike at the enemy's flanks. In the Maoist system, by contrast, encirclement has taken on a more subtle cast. It is not a single action, but complex "concentric maneuver" in which semi-autonomous forces converge on their target from multiple points in a protracted series of coordinated moves. Such an approach, if successful, will complicate the task facing the regime, which will be forced to counteract the guerrillas on multiple fronts, while simplifying the task facing the insurgents, who will be able to reduce their profile (and hence their vulnerability) to the enemy by not placing all of their eggs in a single (easily targeted) basket.

THE EVOLUTION OF THE ARMED STRUGGLE

A centerpiece of this strategy is the development of a series of rural bases from which the insurgents will attempt to extend their areas of control. "Political mobilization," Mao observed, is a fundamental condition for winning the war. Mobilization, in turn, will only be translated into effective insurgent support if it results in the creation of network strategic areas that are able to service the guerrillas' material needs. The base area, in this sense, provides a "protective shell" that provides the guerrillas with the opportunity "to organize, equip, and train." It is formed by bringing a large number of points of influence together under a common administrative center. This process is achieved by establishing a local military advantage, displacing (or neutralizing) the residual presence of the old regime, and creating an alternative set of governing and administrative institutions. This progression, once again, is a dynamic one. According to Abimael Guzman, on of Mao's recent imitators, "Base development, the [concomitant] development of [a] popular guerrilla army, and the resulting extension of the people's war [can be expected to take on a] momentum of their own, leading to

the greater unfolding of the revolutionary situation." One thing leads to the next.

In developing this view, Mao clearly distinguished between "guerrilla bases" and "guerrilla zones." The guerrilla base, as we have suggested, is a region that has already been incorporated into the emerging insurgent regime. While Mao acknowledged that there could be different types of bases, depending upon their location and relative vulnerability to government attack, each represents a guerrilla "stronghold." Such strongholds can be distinguished from guerrilla zones, which Mao defined as areas in which the insurgents were able to operate with relative freedom, but where the state still retained a meaningful political and military presence. The guerrilla zone, in this sense, is considered to be an area of transition (contested ground). The final conquest of the zone, according to Mao, will be achieved by using the established basing system as a springboard to converge on any remaining state presence within the target area. Bases, in this view, effectively "encircle" guerrilla zones, which, once captured, will be absorbed into an expanded base area.

The revolution, in Mao's concept, will unfold in a series of stages, moving from the "strategic defensive," through a period of "strategic equilibrium," on to the "strategic offensive." The initial defensive stage of the conflict can be characterized as a period of "preparation." The insurgents' overriding objective during this phase is to establish a secure political base in the interior from which they can subsequently branch out and expand their range of operations. This is a period of high vulnerability. Like a water course, the guerrillas must find their own level. Decisive battles, head-on engagements, and areas of regime strength must all be avoided as the opposition gradually lays down its roots. This view was summarized nicely by Mao in his argument that the "first principle of war is to preserve oneself, and destroy the enemy." The insurgents' primary concern during the defensive stage of the struggle, in this view, must be on preserving their core organization, form which the means to destroy the enemy will eventually develop. By the end of this period, much of the countryside will have been transformed into a political checkerboard. While the regime will still enjoy effective control at the center, large areas of the countryside will have been brought under guerrilla influence.

The second stage of the conflict, strategic equilibrium, will be reached when the insurgents feel they have achieved "equivalence" with the incumbent regime. Mao referred to this stage as a period of "stalemate." If the initial defensive struggle can be described as a period of preparation, this phase of the war can be characterized as one of "consolidation." While the overriding concern during phase one was to establish an initial series of base areas, the primary operational objective in stage two will be to geographically connect these bases in an effort to consolidate and further extend the guerrillas' zone of control. Over time, the regime's remaining positions of influence in the interior are to be restricted, isolated, and gradually disconnected from the center. The checkerboard or "jigsaw" pattern of influence that characterized the end of phase one will evolve into an increasingly continuous pattern of guerrilla control by the end of phase two. By the end of this period, the regime will find itself forced into a defensive posture, preoccupied with hanging on to what it was and decreasingly able to move offensively against the guerrillas.

In Maoist parlance, the final phase of the people's war is the period of "annihilation." It might also be thought of as a period of "exploitation," in which the institutional groundwork laid during the preparatory and consolidative phases of the struggle are brought to fruition. The guerrillas will enter this stage poised to transition to the strategic offensive. The early pattern of territorial dispersion that flagged the opening weakness of the guerrillas will have been transformed over time into a pattern of territorial control in which the insurgents will have surrounded all but the most important points of regime influence. This development, in Mao's view, should be matched by a reorganization of significant elements of the guerrilla "army," which can now be gradually reformed into units capable of carrying out fluid but increasingly conventional operations. Guerrilla warfare, according to Mao, is not a strategy of choice but of necessity, imposed by the initial material weakness of the opposition. Once the balance of advantage in the conflict has swung to the opposition, the guerrillas are in

position to come out of the shadows and confront the regime on its own terms.

THE CUBAN MODEL OF PEOPLE'S WAR

The Cuban model of people's war, codified by Che Guevara, was based on a highly stylized (and often inaccurate) interpretation of the Cuban insurrection (1956–1959). The baseline document outlining the key features of this model was written by Che Guevara and published by the Cuban Ministry of the Armed Forces in 1960 under the title *Guerrilla Warfare*. It was Che Guevara's first and most influential book. Guevara opened the monograph with the following observation: "The victory of the Cuban people over the Batista dictatorship . . . showed plainly the capacity of the people to free themselves by means of guerrilla warfare from a government that oppresses them." Three "fundamental lessons," he argued, could be drawn from this experience. First, that "popular forces can win a war against the army"; second, that "it is not necessary to wait until all conditions for making [a] revolution exist, the insurrection can create them"; and, third, that "in underdeveloped America the countryside is the basic area of fighting." The model of action that emerged from these "lessons" would shape or otherwise influence revolutionary efforts over the next thirty years.

Guevara's concept of operations was developed without reference to Mao's earlier writings on protracted war or a close understanding of the experiences of the Chinese Revolution. Guevara and Fidel Castro both claimed to have only been introduced to Mao's work in 1958, after the key features of the Cuban insurrection were already well defined. In their view and the view of others, this proved to be fortuitous, freeing them from the temptation to apply revolutionary lessons from a time and place that may have little to do with the particular challenges (and opportunities) faced by the Cuban guerrillas. The "university of experience," in Guevara's view, was a more useful instructor "than a million volumes of books." This perspective was echoed by Regis Debray, one of the chief interpreters of the Cuban insurrection, who suggested that it was a "stroke of good fortune that

Fidel had not read the writings of Mao Zedong before disembarking on the coast of Oriente: he could thus invent, on the spot and out of his own experience, principles of a military doctrine in conformity with the terrain."

Where Mao's concepts of protracted conflict may have been an appropriate model for the Far East, the new doctrine of people's war that emerged from the experience of the Cuban insurrection, it was argued, was the model of choice for the unique circumstances found in Latin America. "Revolutionaries in Latin America," Debray observed, were "reading Fidel's speeches and Che Guevara's writings with eyes that have already read Mao on the anti-Japanese war, Giap, and certain texts of Lenin—and they think they recognize the latter in the former." This, he argued, was both a distorted and dangerous "superimposition." The popular struggle in Latin America, according to Debray, possessed "highly special and profoundly distinct conditions of development, which [could] only be discovered through a particular experience." Prior "theoretical works on people's war," accordingly, could "do as much harm as good." While such writings, he suggested, "have been called the grammar books of war, . . . a foreign language is learned faster in a country where it is spoken than at home studying a language manual." The Cuban experience, in short, was believed to offer a new paradigm for action.

THE FOCO

The central instrument in Guevara's theory was the guerrilla *foco*. The foco or guerrilla band, in Guevara's view, was the nucleus of the insurrection. It would be comprised of a handful of dedicated men who would "jump start" the campaign to overthrow the standing government through the power of example. Over time, Guevara envisioned, the foco would naturally begin to attract recruits. As this occurred it would slowly grow until it reached some maximum (optimal) size, which Guevara defined as somewhere between thirty and fifty men. At this point, it would split in two, each foco working independently of the other to attract a following in different regions of the country. Over time, as this budding process continued, the number of operational guerrilla bands would grow until the

insurgents would eventually become a force to be reckoned with in the countryside. In Guevara's view this process was similar to that of a beehive "when at a given moment it releases a new queen, who goes to another region with a part of the swarm." The "mother hive," in this case, "with the most notable guerrilla chief will stay in the less dangerous places, while the new columns will penetrate other enemy territory [and repeat the earlier] cycle."

Guevara's concept of operations, to be sure, shared certain features with the theory of protracted war formulated by Mao. First and foremost was the assumption that the guerrillas' natural base of support would be found among the peasantry. It followed, in turn, that the natural locus of the insurgency should also be in the countryside. While Guevara, at least in theory, did not completely dismiss the supporting role that could be played by an urban underground, he clearly relegated the struggle in the cities to a subordinate position. The insurrection would turn on the rural guerrilla. Those who, "following dogma," still believed that a revolutionary action could only be carried out by urban workers, underrated, in his view, both the revolutionary sentiment of the peasantry on the one hand and the difficulties associated with operating in an urban environment on the other. "Illegal workers' movements," Guevara argued, faced "enormous dangers" (which were not similarly faced by their rural counterparts) because of their greater proximity to the regime's center of influence. To offset this greater risk, "They must function secretly without arms." The rural guerrilla, by contrast, is able to operate "beyond the reach of the oppressive forces," and is thus able to sidestep the state's opening advantage.

Like Mao, Guevara also believed that the insurgent struggle would evolve in stages. The first stage of the conflict was the "nomadic" phase, in which the initial guerrilla nucleus must continually remain on the move in order to survive. As the foco's relationship with the peasantry began to stabilize, the guerrillas would move into the second, "semi-nomadic" phase, in which the guerrillas, while still retaining a high level of fluidity, would be able to establish the first permanent base areas. The final phase of the conflict, Guevara argued, was the stage of "suburban guerrilla warfare." In language reminiscent of Mao, Guevara wrote that this stage would finally enable the guerrillas to "encircle fortified bases," engage in "mass action," and confront the army in open battle and win. "The enemy will fall," he suggested, when "the process of partial victories becomes transformed into final victories, that is to say, when the [army] is brought it accept the battle in conditions imposed by the guerrilla band; there he is annihilated and his surrender compelled." This, in turn, would ultimately result in an uprising of popular sentiment against the standing regime, sweeping it from power.

THE HEROIC GUERRILLA

While Guevara's writings on people's war share certain similarities to those of Mao, the strategic theory that underlies this work is, in the end, quite distinct. First, in contrast to Mao, Guevara gave primacy to what he referred to as the "subjective" rather than "objective" conditions for victory. A successful insurrection, in this view, did not require that the peasantry be already primed to revolt; the conditions for revolution could often be engineered by the guerrilla band. While Guevara gave a least passing reference to the necessary preconditions for revolution in his initial discussion of the problem in *Guerrilla Warfare*, this caveat was increasingly relaxed over time. Guerrilla conflicts, he argued in a later article, could be successfully prosecuted throughout Latin America. Once set in motion, the revolution would "make itself." While the "initial conditions" did not exist everywhere in the orthodox sense of the term, the desire for revolutionary change lay just below the surface of the popular consciousness. It was only necessary to define, release, and finally channel these sentiments.

In contrast to Mao, Guevara's theory of victory ultimately relied heavily on the spontaneity of the insurgent's natural allies to provide the guerrilla foco with the critical mass it required to win. Guevara assumed, implicitly, that Latin-America society was in an inherently unstable equilibrium. The task facing the guerrilla nucleus was to aggravate the tension that he believed defined every Latin-American society, kick out the props that held up the old regime, and stand back while the target government was

overcome in popular uprising. Once set in motion, the guerrillas would not so much control this event as ride it into power. What was required under these circumstances was not a grassroots, step-by-step program of local contact, indoctrination, and organization, but an action-oriented program designed to capture the popular imagination and inspire the peasantry "from above." The foco's operational challenge, in this respect, was to sharpen and accelerate the natural process of social polarization, raise the peasants' political consciousness, and embolden them to join the revolution.

While the Chinese model of people's war considered political organization to be a necessary precondition for social mobilization, the Cuban model argued that a high-profile "guerrilla outbreak" could be used to effectively bypass the organizational requirement and proceed directly to mobilization. The basis of the insurgency, in the first case, rests with the vitality of the guerrillas' interlocking, village-based associations. Collectively, these represent an institutional counterweight to the state and the foundation of the insurgency's political and military position. The basis of the insurgency, in the second case, rests squarely on the shoulders of the guerrilla combatant, and through him, the guerrilla foco. Success or failure in this case depends on the power of their example. The guerrilla foco, for its part, must be a "firefighter teacher," who "need know little more than what is required of a good man or soldier." The guerrilla foco, for its part, must be an "armed nucleus," able to employ its limited resources to move its would-be followers to action. Creating this effect would not depend on organization, but on courage, discipline, and a willingness to act.

As this discussion suggests, the Cuban model placed great importance on the psychological dimensions of a guerrilla conflict. The guerrilla combatant, we are told, must never lose faith. He must "see reasons for a favorable decision even in moments when the analysis of the adverse and favorable conditions does not show an appreciable positive balance." It is particularly important to continually generate the impression of impending victory. This can be achieved initially in small ways that have big effects. A small guerrilla force can enhance its offensive punch, for example, by "striking like a tornado" to "sow panic" within the enemy's ranks. The cumulative effects of small victories won in such a fashion can, in turn have higher-order effects on the general morale (and, hence, effectiveness) of the regime's military and political base, imbuing them with a sense of imminent doom. As these perceptions begin to take hold, the "objective conditions" of the conflict will gradually begin to shift to the insurgents' advantage, making it increasingly easy to sustain this momentum over time. The guerrillas will win when the enemy has finally come to believe that their own defeat is inevitable.

The theory of guerrilla warfare advanced by Che Guevara, in the end, had an uneven relationship to the underlying dynamics of the Cuban insurrection. Many aspects of the Cuban experience that proved to be critical to the ultimate success of the July 26 revolutionary movement were either left out or significantly downplayed in Guevara's concept of operations. Several of these should be noted here. First and foremost, perhaps, was Guevara's increasingly unrealistic view of the "revolutionary readiness" of Latin-American society. As noted above, Guevara gave little attention to the particular preconditions that must exist to bring even the best laid plan to seize power in the popular insurgency to fruition. Revolution for Che Guevara could effectively be created out of whole cloth. What was of critical importance was not the particular state of society, or even the competing institutional strength of the opposition, but the courage, fortitude, and determination of the guerrilla fighter. Winning, in his view, boiled down to an act of will. Weak, pre-existing objective conditions could be offset by the individual guerrilla's grim refusal to accept defeat.

Second, in focusing on the *rural* guerrilla, Guevara ignored the decisive role played by the urban underground during the Cuban insurrection. The latter provided significant assistance to Fidel's rural operations. During the early days of the war, in particular, support from the July 26 movement's pre-existing urban networks was critical to the very survival of the rural foco. Throughout the course of the war, the actions of the urban underground—often carried out in a coordinated and simultaneous manner across the country—served as a major source of the distraction, providing the guerrillas with the

breathing space they required to stay in the game. The army was continually faced with the need to divide its efforts between the countryside and the cities, which made it difficult to concentrate on finding, fixing, and finally destroying Fidel's small group of rural combatants. In these and other ways, the cities proved to be a key variable in the outcome of the war. Despite this fact, the role of the urban underground was effectively dismissed in Guevara's writings in favor of his naturally heroic country cousin.

Finally, as much as Guevara appreciated the inherently dynamic, interactive nature of warfare, in attempting to generalize from the Cuban experience he imposed a post facto order and associated determinism on the course of the Cuban insurrection that it did not possess. Under the best of circumstances, combat is an uncertain process. There is often a high level of uncertainty surrounding the thousands of individual events that might make up a battle, and the hundreds of battles, that might make up a war, which will often prove to be decisive in determining who is left standing at the end of the day. This was certainly the case in the Cuban insurrection, where except for happy chance, the guerrillas could have been defeated on any number of occasions during the course of the struggle. As the Duke of Wellington said of the Battle of Waterloo, "it was a close run thing." And yet, the problematic character of the conflict (and guerrilla warfare in general) is missing in Guevara's interpretive mode. The inherent uncertainty surrounding the problem of revolutionary action, in this case, is effectively replaced by a discussion of the guerrilla's fighting spirit. The guerrilla, in Guevara's view, will dominate events because of his superior determination.

The limits of this last assumption were demonstrated once and for all in Guevara's final action in Bolivia (1966-1967), where he was captured and killed attempting to put his theory into practice, one last time. The dramatic nature of his defeat proved to be the death knell for his model of guerrilla warfare. While the heroic quality of his death served to inspire those who came after him, subsequent guerrilla operations in Latin America would be defined by their efforts to correct the weaknesses inherent in his voluntarist theory of people's war.

SUMMARY: TWO MODELS OF GUERRILLA WARFARE

The Chinese and Cuban models of people's war represent competing views of the structure and dynamics of guerrilla warfare. While both theories acknowledge that the underlying basis of revolutionary change ultimately rests on long-run historical forces, the operational guidance given to revolutionary hopefuls attempting to tap into and harness these forces, in each case, is distinct. For the Maoist, this is ultimately a problem of organization. Organization, in this sense, means building a grassroots, village-based alternative to the state. It follows that the chief measure of performance—which in this case is provided not by the scope or intensity of one's military actions, but the scope, depth, and vitality of one's organizational forms. The guerrilla's ability to pose a political and military challenge to the state is believed to be a by-product of his slowly developing institutional base. There is nothing "willful," in this view, about revolutionary outcomes. Strength of the character and a pure heart are not considered to be effective substitutes for building and institutional counterweight to the state.

The opposite point of view, in many respects, defines the Cuban model of insurgency. Guerrilla actions, in this theory, are not a manifestation of popular support, but the source of such support in the first place. The target population, in this respect, is not "organized" but "impressed." Popular mobilization is less an iterative *process* than a catalytic *event*, in which the insurgents' natural constituency, spurred by the dramatic character of guerrilla actions, discovers its revolutionary identity and joins the rebellion. This shift, as noted, is expected to occur with little or no organizational investment by the insurgents. It will occur not as a result of a prior shift in local control, but in the wake of a general change in the sentiment of the revolutionary class. The guerrillas' primary task, then, is not institutional but psychological. Their goal is to capture the popular imagination in the expectation of generating a popular uprising against the state. Will, rather than numbers, can be expected to carry the day.

These two models of people's war, then, can be defined by a simple dichotomy. The Chinese model represents a bottom-up, low-profile approach to guerrilla conflict. For the low-profile challenger, insurgency is considered to be an institutional contest. The conflict will be pursued by undermining the institutional architecture of the state and replacing it with the guerrillas' own institutional alternative. Popular support is mobilized at the grassroots level (from the bottom up) in a staged process of organization building. The Cuban model, by contrast, can be defined as a top-down, high-profile approach to insurgency. For the high-profile challenger, a guerrilla conflict will not be prosecuted by undermining the state's institutional forms, but by attacking its perceptual foundations. The regime will not be slowly dismantled and replaced, but effectively taken by storm (from the top down) in a psychological convergence of popular sentiment away from the old regime and in favor of the opposition. The guerrilla's operational challenge is, first, to provide the spark that sets the conflict in motion and, second, to serve as a conduit to channel the population's revolutionary sentiments.

BIBLIOGRAPHY

Boorman, Scott A. *The Protracted Game: A Wei-chi Interpretation of Maoist Revolutionary Strategy.* London: Oxford University Press, 1969.

Childs, Matt D. "An Historical Critique of the Emergence and Evolution of Ernesto Che Guevara's Foco Theory." *Journal of Latin American Studies* (October 1995).

Connor, Walker. *The National Question in Marxist-Leninist Theory and Strategy.* Princeton: Princeton University Press, 1984.

Debray, Régis. *Revolution in the Revolution?* Westport: Greenwood Press, 1980.

Dunn, John. *Modern Revolutions.* Cambridge: Cambridge University Press, 1972.

Guevara, Che. *Guerrilla Warfare.* Lincoln: University of Nebraska Press, 1985.

———. "Guerrilla Warfare: A Method." In *Venceremos! The Speeches and Writings of Ernesto (Che) Guevara*, ed. John Gerassi. New York: Macmillan, 1968.

———. "Interview with Laura Berquist" (No. 1). In *Che: Selected Works of Ernesto Guevara*, ed.

Rolando E. Bonachea and Nelson P. Valdés. Cambridge: MIT Press, 1969.

Guzman, Abimael. "Interview." *El Diario,* July 24, 1988.

Johnson, Chalmers. *Autopsy on People's War.* Berkeley: University of California Press, 1973.

Katzenbach, Edward L., Jr., and Gene Hanrahan. "The Revolutionary Strategy of Mao Tse-tung." *Political Science Quarterly* (September 1955).

Mao Zedong (Mao Tse-tung). "Guerrilla Warfare." In *Mao Tse-tung on Guerrilla Warfare,* trans. and ed. Samual B. Griffith II. Baltimore: Nautical and Aviation Publishing Company of America, 1992.

———. "On Protracted War." In *Selected Military Writings of Mao Tse-tung.* Beijing: Foreign Languages Press, 1967.

———. "Problems of Strategy in Guerrilla War Against Japan." In *Selected Military Writings of Mao Tse-tung.* Beijing: Foreign Languages Press, 1967.

McCormick, Gordon H. "Che Guevara's Revolutionary Odyssey." *Queen's Quarterly* (Summer 1998).

———. *Peruvian Maoism: The Shining Path and the Theory of People's War.* Santa Monica: RAND, 1992.

———. *Sharp Dressed Men: Peru's Tupac Amaru Revolutionary Movement.* Santa Monica: RAND, 1993.

Tucker, Robert C. *The Marxian Revolutionary Idea.* New York: W.W. Norton, 1969.

Minimanual of the Urban Guerrilla

Carlos Marighella

I would like to make a two-fold dedication of this work; first, to the memories of Edson Souto, Marco Antonio Bras de Carvalho, Melson Jose de Almeida ("Escoteiro") and so many other heroic fighters and urban guerrillas who fell at the hands of the assassins of the Military Police, the Army, the Navy, the Air Force, and the DOPS, hated instruments of the repressive military dictatorship.

Second, to the brave comrades—men and women—imprisoned in the medieval dungeons of the Brazilian Government and subjected to tortures that even surpass the horrendous crimes carried out by the Nazis. Like those comrades whose memories we revere, as well as those taken prisoner in combat, what we must do is fight.

Each comrade who opposes the military dictatorship and wants to oppose it can do something, however small the task may seem. I urge all who read this minimanual and decide that they cannot remain inactive, to follow its instructions and join the struggle now. I ask this because, under any theory and under any circumstances, the duty of every revolutionary is to make the revolution.

Another important point is not merely to read this minimanual here and now, but to circulate its contents. This circulation will be possible if those who agree with its ideas make mimeographed copies or print it in a booklet, (although in this latter case, armed struggle itself will be necessary.)

Finally, the reason why this minimanual bears my signature is that the ideas expressed or systematized here reflect the personal experiences of a group of people engaged in armed struggle in Brazil, among whom I have the honor to be included. So that certain individuals will have no doubts about what this minimanual says, and can no longer deny the facts or continue to say that the conditions for armed struggle do not exist, it is necessary to assume responsibility for what is said and done. Therefore, anonymity becomes a problem in a work like this. The important fact is that there are patriots prepared to fight like soldiers, and the more there are the better.

The accusation of "violence" or "terrorism" no longer has the negative meaning it used to have. It has aquired new clothing; a new color. It does not divide, it does not discredit; on the contrary, it represents a center of attraction. Today, to be "violent" or a "terrorist" is a quality that ennobles any honorable person, because it is an act worthy of a revolutionary engaged in armed struggle against the shameful military dictatorship and its atrocities.

Carlos Marighella
1969

---

7 Marighella, Carlos. (2004). "Minimanual of the Urban Guerrilla." Retrieved from www.marxists.org/archive/marighella-carlos/1969/06/minimanual-urban-guerrilla/ on 14 SEP 04.

A DEFINITION OF THE URBAN GUERRILLA

The urban guerrilla is a person who fights the military dictatorship with weapons, using unconventional methods. A revolutionary and an ardent patriot, he is a fighter for his country's liberation, a friend of the people and of freedom. The area in which the urban guerrilla operates is in the large Brazilian cities. There are also criminals or outlaws who work in the big cities. Many times, actions by criminals are taken to be actions by urban guerrillas.

The urban guerrilla, however, differs radically from the criminal. The criminal benefits personally from his actions, and attacks indiscriminately without distinguishing between the exploiters and the exploited, which is why there are so many ordinary people among his victims. The urban guerrilla follows a political goal, and only attacks the government, the big businesses and the foreign imperialists.

Another element just as harmful to the guerrillas as the criminal, and also operating in the urban area, is the counterrevolutionary, who creates confusion, robs banks, throws bombs, kidnaps, assassinates, and commits the worst crimes imaginable against urban guerrillas, revolutionary priests, students, and citizens who oppose tyranny and seek liberty.

The urban guerrilla is an implacable enemy of the regime, and systematically inflicts damage on the authorities and on the people who dominate the country and exercise power. The primary task of the urban guerrilla is to distract, to wear down, to demoralize the military regime and its repressive forces, and also to attack and destroy the wealth and property of the foreign managers and the Brazilian upper class.

The urban guerrilla is not afraid to dismantle and destroy the present Brazilian economic, political and social system, for his aim is to aid the rural guerrillas and to help in the creation of a totally new and revolutionary social and political structure, with the armed population in power.

PERSONAL QUALITIES OF THE URBAN GUERRILLA

The urban guerrilla is characterized by his bravery and his decisive nature. He must be a good tactician, and a good marksman. The urban guerrilla must be a person of great cleverness to compensate for the fact that he is not sufficiently strong in weapons, ammunition and equipment.

The career military officers and the government police have modern weapons and transport, and can go about anywhere freely, using the force of their own strength. The urban guerrilla does not have such resources at his disposal, and leads a clandestine existence. The guerrilla may be a convicted person or one who is out on parole, and must then use false documents.

Nevertheless, the urban guerrilla has an advantage over the conventional military or the police. It is that, while the military and the police act on behalf of the enemy, whom the people hate, the urban guerrilla defends a just cause, which is the people's cause.

The urban guerrilla's weapons are inferior to the enemy's, but from the moral point of view, the urban guerrilla has an undeniable superiority. This moral superiority is what sustains the urban guerrilla. Thanks to it, the urban guerrilla can accomplish his principle duty, which is to attack and survive.

The urban guerrilla has to capture or steal weapons from the enemy to be able to fight. Because his weapons are not uniform—since what he has are expropriated or have fallen into his hands in various ways—the urban guerrilla faces the problem of a variety of weapons and a shortage of ammunition. Moreover, he has no place in which to practice shooting and marksmanship. These difficulties have to be overcome, forcing the urban guerrillas to be imaginative and creative—qualities without which it would be impossible for him to carry out his role as a revolutionary.

The urban guerrilla must possess initiative, mobility and flexibility, as well as versatility and a command of any situation. Initiative especially is an indispensible quality. It is not always possible to foresee everything, and the urban guerrilla cannot let himself become confused, or wait for instructions. His duty is to act, to find adequate solutions for each problem he faces, and to retreat. It is better to err acting than to do nothing for fear of making a mistake. Without initiative, there is no urban guerrilla warfare.

Other important qualities in the urban guerrilla are the following: to be a good walker, to be able to stand up against fatigue, hunger, rain or heat. To know how to hide, and how to be vigilant. To conquer the art of dissembling. Never to fear danger. To behave the same by day as by night. Not to act impetuously. To have unlimited patience. To remain calm and cool in the worst of conditions and situations. Never to leave a track or trail. Not to get discouraged.

In the face of the almost insurmountable difficulties in urban guerrilla warfare, sometimes comrades weaken and give up the fight.

The urban guerrilla is not a businessman in an urban company, nor is he an actor in a play. Urban guerrilla warfare, like rural guerrilla warfare, is a pledge which the guerrilla makes to himself. When he can no longer face the difficulties, or if he knows that he lacks the patience to wait, then it is better for him to relinquish his role before he betrays his pledge, for he clearly lacks the basic qualities necessary to be a guerrilla.

HOW THE URBAN GUERRILLA LIVES

The urban guerrilla must know how to live among the people, and he must be careful not to appear strange and different from ordinary city life. He should not wear clothes that are different from those that other people wear. Elaborate and high-fashion clothing for men or women may often be a handicap if the urban guerrilla's mission takes him into working class neighborhoods, or sections where such dress is uncommon. The same care has to be taken if the urban guerrilla must move from the South of the country to the North, and vice versa.

The urban guerrilla must make his living through his job or his professional activity. If he is known and sought by the police, he must go underground, and sometimes must live hidden. Under such circumstances, the urban guerrilla cannot reveal his activity to anyone, since this information is always and only the responsibility of the revolutionary organization in which he is participating.

The urban guerrilla must have a great ability for observation. He must be well-informed about everything, particularly about the enemy's movements, and he must be very inquisitive and knowledgable about the area in which he lives, operates, or travels through.

But the fundamental characteristic of the urban guerrilla is that he is a man who fights with weapons; given these circumstances, there is very little likelihood that he will be able to follow his normal profession for long without being identified by the police. The role of expropriation thus looms as clear as high noon. It is impossible for the urban guerrilla to exist and survive without fighting to expropriate.

Thus, the armed struggle of the urban guerrilla points towards two essential objectives:

1. the physical elimination of the leaders and assistants of the armed forces and of the police;
2. the expropriation of government resources and the wealth belonging to the rich businessmen, the large landowners and the imperialists, with small expropriations used for the sustenance of the individual guerrillas and large ones for the maintenance of the revolutionary organization itself.

It is clear that the armed struggle of the urban guerrilla also has other objectives. But here we are referring to the two basic objectives, above all expropriation. It is necessary for every urban guerrilla to always keep in mind that he can only maintain his existence if he is able to kill the police and those dedicated to repression, and if he is determined—truly determined—to expropriate the wealth of the rich businessmen, landowners and imperialists.

One of the fundamental characteristics of the Brazilian revolution is that, from the beginning, it developed around the expropriation of the wealth of the major business, imperialist and landowning interests, without excluding the largest and most powerful commercial elements engaged in the import-export business. And by expropriating the wealth of the principle enemies of the people, the Brazilian revolution was able to hit them at their vital center, with preferential and systematic attacks on the banking network—that is to say, the most telling blows were levelled at the businessman's nerve system.

The bank robberies carried out by the Brazilian urban guerrillas hurt big businesses and others, the foreign companies which insure and re-insure the banking capital, the imperialist companies, the federal and state governments—all of them are systematically expropriated as of now.

The fruit of these expropriations has been devoted to the tasks of learning and perfecting urban guerrilla techniques, the purchase, production and transportation of weapons and ammunition for the rural areas, the security precautions of the guerrillas, the daily maintenance of the fighters, those who have been liberated from prison by armed force, those who have been wounded, and those who are being persecuted by the police, and to any kind of problem concerning comrades liberated from jail or assassinated by the police and the military dictatorship.

The tremendous costs of the revolutionary war must fall upon the big businesses, on the imperialists, on the large landowners, and on the government too—both federal and state—since they are all exploiters and oppressors of the people. Men of the government, agents of the dictatorship and of foreign imperialism, especially, must pay with their lives for the crimes they have committed against the Brazilian people.

In Brazil, the number of violent actions carried out by urban guerrillas, including executions, explosions, seizures of weapons, ammunition and explosives, assaults on banks and prisons, etc., is significant enough to leave no room for doubt as to the actual aims of the revolutionaries; all are witnesses to the fact that we are in a full revolutionary war and that this war can be waged only by violent means.

This is the reason why the urban guerrilla uses armed struggle, and why he continues to concentrate his efforts on the physical extermination of the agents of repression, and to dedicate 24 hours a day to expropriations from the people's exploiters.

TECHNICAL PREPARATION OF THE URBAN GUERRILLA

No one can become an urban guerrilla without paying special attention to technical preparation.

The technical preparation of the urban guerrilla runs from a concern for his physical condition to a knowledge of and apprenticeship in professions and skills of all kinds, particularly manual skills.

The urban guerrilla can have a strong physical constitution only if he trains systematically. He cannot be a good fighter if he has not learned the art of fighting. For that reason, the urban guerrilla must learn and practice the various forms of unarmed fighting, of attack, and of personal defense. Other useful forms of physical preparation are hiking, camping, the practice of survival in the woods, mountain climbing, rowing, swimming, skin diving and training as a frogman, fishing, harpooning, and the hunting of birds and of small and big game.

It is very important to learn how to drive a car, pilot a plane, handle a motor boat and a sailboat, understand mechanics, radio, telephone, electricity and have some knowledge of electronics techniques. It is also important to have a knowledge of topographical information, to be able to determine one's position by instruments or other available resources, to calculate distances, make maps and plans, draw to scale, make timings, and work with an angle protractor, a compass, etc. A knowledge of chemistry, of color combination and of stamp-making, the mastery of the skills of calligraphy and the copying of letters, and other techniques are part of the technical preparation of the urban guerrilla, who is obliged to falsify documents in order to live within a society that he seeks to destroy. In the area of "makeshift" medicine, the urban guerrilla has the special role of being a doctor or understanding medicine, nursing, pharmacology, drugs, basic surgery and emergency first aid.

The basic question in the technical preparation of the urban guerrilla is, nevertheless, to know how to handle weapons such as the submachine gun, revolver, automatic pistol, FAL, various types of shotguns, carbines, mortars, bazookas, etc.

A knowledge of various types of ammunition and explosives is another aspect to consider. Among the explosives, dynamite must be well understood. The use of incendiary bombs, smoke bombs, and other types is also indispensible prior training. To know how to improvise and repair weapons, prepare Molotov cocktails, grenades, mines, homemade destructive devices, how to blow up bridges, tear up and put out of service railroads and railroad cars, these are necessities in the technical preparation of the urban guerrilla that can never be considered unimportant.

The highest level of preparation for the urban guerrilla is the training camp for technical training. But only the guerrilla who has already passed a preliminary examination can go to this school—that is to say, one who has passed the test of fire in revolutionary action, in actual combat against the enemy.

THE URBAN GUERRILLA'S WEAPONS

The urban guerrilla's weapons are light arms, easily obtained, usually captured from the enemy, purchased, or made on the spot. Light weapons have the advantage of fast handling and easy transport. In general, light weapons are characterized as being short-barrelled. This includes many automatic weapons. Automatic and semi-automatic weapons considerably increase the firepower of the urban guerrilla. The disadvantage of this type of weapon, for us, is the difficulty in controlling it, resulting in wasted rounds or a wasteful use of ammunition—corrected for only by a good aim and precision firing. Men who are poorly trained convert automatic weapons into an ammunition drain.

Experience has shown that the basic weapon of the urban guerrilla is the light submachine gun. This weapon, in addition to being efficient and easy to shoot in an urban area, has the advantage of being greatly respected by the enemy. The guerrilla must thoroughly know how to handle the submachine gun, now so popular and indispensible to the Brazilian urban guerrillas.

The ideal submachine gun for the urban guerrilla is the INA .45 caliber. Other types of submachine guns of different calibers can also be used—understanding of course, the problem of ammunition. Thus, it is preferable that the manufacturing capabilities of the urban guerrillas be used for the production of one type of submachine gun, so that the ammunition to be used can be standardized. Each firing group of urban guerrillas must have a submachine gun handled by a good marksman. The other members of the group must be armed with .38 revolvers, our standard weapon. The .32 is also useful for those who want to participate. But the .38 is preferable since its impact usually puts the enemy out of action.

Hand grenades and conventional smoke bombs can also be considered light weapons, with defensive power for cover and withdrawal.

Long-barrelled weapons are more difficult for the urban guerrilla to transport, and they attract much attention because of their size. Among the long-barrelled weapons are the FAL, the Mauser guns or rifles, hunting guns such as the Winchester, and others.

Shotguns can be useful if used at close range and point blank. They are useful even for a poor shot, especially at night when precision isn't much help. A pressure airgun can be useful for training in marksmanship. Bazookas and mortars can also be used in action, but the conditions for using them have to be prepared and the people who use them must be trained.

The urban guerrilla should not attempt to base his actions on the use of heavy weapons, which have major drawbacks in a type of fighting that demands lightweight weapons to insure mobility and speed.

Homemade weapons are often as efficient as the best weapons produced in conventional factories, and even a sawed-off shotgun is a good weapon for the urban guerrilla fighter.

The urban guerrilla's role as a gunsmith has a basic importance. As a gunsmith, he takes care of the weapons, knows how to repair them, and in many cases can set up a small shop for improvising and producing effective small arms.

Experience in metallurgy and on the mechanical lathe are basic skills the urban guerrilla should incorporate into his manufacturing plans for the construction of homemade weapons. This production, and courses in explosives and sabotage, must be organized. The primary materials for practice in these courses must be obtained ahead of time, to prevent an incomplete apprenticeship—that is to say, so as to leave no room for experimentation.

Molotov cocktails, gasoline, homemade contrivances such as catapaults and mortars for firing explosives, grenades made of pipes and cans, smoke bombs, mines, conventional explosives such as dynamite and potassium chlorate, plastic explosives, gelatine capsules, and ammunition of every kind are indispensable to the success of the urban guerrilla's mission.

The methods of obtaining the necessary materials and munitions will be to buy them or to take them by force in expropriation actions specially planned and carried out. The urban guerrillas will be careful not to keep explosives and other materials that can cause accidents around for very long, but will always try to use them immediately on their intended targets.

The urban guerrilla's weapons and his ability to maintain them constitute his firepower. By taking advantage of modern weapons and introducing innovations in his firepower and in the use of certain weapons, the urban guerrilla can improve many of the tactics of urban warfare. An example of this was the innovation made by the Brazilian urban guerrillas when they introduced the use of the submachine gun in their attacks on banks.

When the massive use of uniform submachine guns becomes possible, there will be new changes in urban guerrilla warfare tactics. The firing group that utilizes uniform weapons and corresponding ammunition, with reasonable care for their maintenance, will reach a considerable level of effectiveness.

The urban guerrilla increases his effectiveness as he increases his firepower.

THE SHOT; THE URBAN GUERRILLA'S REASON FOR EXISTENCE

The urban guerrilla's reason for existence, the basic condition in which he acts and survives, is to shoot. The urban guerrilla must know how to shoot well, because it is required by this type of combat.

In conventional warfare, combat is generally at a distance with long-range weapons. In unconventional warfare, in which urban guerrilla warfare is included, combat is at short range and often very close. To prevent his own death, the urban guerrilla must shoot first, and he cannot err in his shot. He cannot waste his ammunition because he does not possess large amounts, and so he must conserve it. Nor can he replace his ammunition quickly, since he is a part of a small team in which each guerrilla has to be able to look after himself. The urban guerrilla can lose no time, and thus has to be able to shoot at once.

One basic fact, which we want to emphasize completely, and whose importance cannot be overestimated, is that the urban guerrilla must not fire continuously, using up his ammunition. It may be that the enemy is responding to this fire precisely because he is waiting until the guerrilla's ammunition is all used up. At such a moment, without having the opportunity to replace his ammunition, the guerrilla faces a rain of enemy fire, and can be taken prisoner or killed.

In spite of the value of the surprise factor, which many times makes it unnecessary for the urban guerrilla to use his weapons, he cannot be allowed the luxury of entering combat without knowing how to shoot. And when face-to-face with the enemy, he must always be moving from one position to another, since to stay in one place makes him a fixed tarket and, as such, very vulnerable.

The urban guerrilla's life depends on shooting, on his ability to handle his weapons well and to avoid being hit. When we speak of shooting, we speak of accuracy as well. Shooting must be practiced until it becomes a reflex action on the part of the urban guerrilla. To learn how to shoot and have good aim, the urban guerrilla must train himself systematically, utilizing every practice method shooting at targets, even in amusement parks and at home.

Shooting and marksmanship are the urban guerrilla's water and air. His perfection of the art of shooting may make him a special type of urban guerrilla—that is, a sniper, a category of solitary combatant indispensible in isolated actions. The sniper knows how to shoot at close range and at long range, and his weapons are appropriate for either type of shooting.

THE FIRING GROUP

In order to function, the urban guerrillas must be organized into small groups. A team of no more than four or five is called a firing group. A minimum of two firing groups, separated and insulated from other firing groups, directed and coordinated by one or two persons, this is what makes a firing team.

Within the firing group, there must be complete confidence among the members. The best shot, and the one who knows best how to handle the submachine gun, is the person in charge of operations.

The firing group plans and executes urban guerrilla actions, obtains and stores weapons, and studies and corrects its own tactics.

When there are tasks planned by the strategic command, these tasks take preference. But there is no such thing as a firing group without its own initiative. For this reason, it is essential to avoid any rigidity in the guerrilla organization, in order to permit the greatest possible initiative on the part of the firing group. The old-type hierarchy, the style of the traditional revolutionaries, doesn't exist in our organization. This means that, except for the priority of the objectives set by the strategic command, any firing group can decide to raid a bank, to kidnap or execute an agent of the dictatorship, a figure identified with the reaction, or a foreign spy, and can carry out any type of propaganda or war of nerves against the enemy, without the need to consult with the general command.

No firing group can remain inactive waiting for orders from above. Its obligation is to act. Any single urban guerrilla who wants to establish a firing group and begin action can do so, and thus becomes a part of the organization.

This method of action eliminates the need for knowing who is carrying out which actions, since there is free initiative and the only important point is to greatly increase the volume of urban guerrilla activity in order to wear out the government and force it onto the defensive.

The firing group is the instrument of organized action. Within it, guerrilla operations and tactics are planned, launched and carried through to success. The general command counts on the firing groups to carry out objectives of a strategic nature, and to do so in any part of the country. For its part, the general command helps the firing groups with their difficulties and with carrying out objectives of a strategic nature, and to do so in any part of the country.

The organization is an indestructable network of firing groups, and of coordinations among them, that functions simply and practically within a general command that also participates in attacks—an organization that exists for no other purpose than that of pure and simple revolutionary action.

THE LOGISTICS OF THE URBAN GUERRILLA

Conventional logistics can be expressed with the formula FFEA:

F—food
F—fuel
E—equipment
A—ammunition

Conventional logistics refer to the maintenance problems for an army or a regular armed force, transported in vehicles, with fixed bases and supply lines. Urban guerrillas, on the contrary, are not an army but small armed groups, intentionally fragmented. They have neither vehicles nor rear areas. Their supply lines are precarious and insufficient, and they have no fixed bases except in the rudimentary sense of a weapons factory within a house. While the goal of conventional logistics is to supply the war needs of the "gorillas" who are used to repress rural and urban rebellion, urban guerrilla logistics aim at sustaining operations and tactics which have nothing in common with conventional warfare and are directed against the government and foreign domination of the country.

For the urban guerrilla, who starts from nothing and who has no support at the beginning, logistics are expressed by the formula MMWAE, which is:

M—mechanization
M—money
W—weapons
A—ammunition
E—explosives

Revolutionary logistics takes mechanization as one of its bases. Nevertheless, mechanization is inseperable from the driver. The urban guerrilla driver is as important as the urban guerrilla machine gunner. Without either, the machines do not work, and the automobile, as well as the submachine gun becomes a dead thing. An experienced driver is not made in one day, and apprenticeship must begin early. Every good urban guerrilla must be a driver. As to the vehicles, the urban guerrilla must expropriate what he needs. When he already has resources, the urban guerrilla can combine the expropriation of vehicles with his other methods of acquisition.

Money, weapons, ammunition and explosives, and automobiles as well, must be expropriated. The urban guerrilla must rob banks and armories, and seize explosives and ammunition wherever he finds them.

None of these operations is carried out for just one purpose. Even when the raid is to obtain money, the weapons that the guards carry must be taken as well.

Expropriation is the first step in organizing our logistics, which itself assumes an armed and permanently mobile character.

The second step is to reinforce and expand logistics, resorting to ambushes and traps in which the enemy is surprised and his weapons, ammunition, vehicles and other resources are captured.

Once he has weapons, ammunition and explosives, one of the most serious logistics problems facing the urban guerrilla is a hiding place in which to leave the material, and appropriate means of transporting it and assembling it where it is needed. This has to be accomplished even when the enemy is alerted and has the roads blocked.

The knowledge that the urban guerrilla possesses of the terrain, and the devices he uses or is capable of using, such as scouts specially prepared and recruited for this mission, are the basic elements in solving the eternal logistics problems faced by the guerrillas.

CHARACTERISTICS OF THE URBAN GUERRILLA'S TACTICS

The tactics of the urban guerrilla have the following characteristics:

1. It is an aggressive tactic, or, in other words, it has an offensive character. As is well known, defensive action means death for us. Since we are inferior to the enemy in firepower, and have neither his resources nor his power base, we cannot defend ourselves against an offensive or a concentrated attack by the "gorillas". That is the reason why our urban technique can never be permanent, can never defend a fixed

base nor remain in any one spot waiting to repel the circle of repression.
2. It is a tactic of attack and rapid withdrawal, by which we preserve our forces.
3. It is a tactic that aims at the development of urban guerrilla warfare, whose function will be to wear out, demoralize and distract the enemy forces, permitting the emergence and survival of rural guerrilla warfare, which is destined to play the decisive role in the revolutionary war.

THE INITIAL ADVANTAGES OF THE URBAN GUERRILLA

The dynamics of urban guerrilla warfare lie in the guerrilla's violent clash with the military and police forces of the dictatorship. In this conflict, the police have superiority. The urban guerrilla has inferior forces. The paradox is that the urban guerrilla is nevertheless the attacker.

The military and police forces, for their part, respond to the conflict by mobilizing and concentrating greatly superior forces in the pursuit and destruction of the urban guerrilla. The guerrilla can only avoid defeat if he depends on the initial advantages he has and knows how to exploit them to the end, to compensate for his weakness and lack of material.

The initial advantages are:

1. He must take the enemy by surprise.
2. He must know the terrain of the encounter.
3. He must have greater mobility and speed than the police and other repressive forces.
4. His information service must be better than the enemy's.
5. He must be in command of the situation, and demonstrate a decisiveness so great that everyone on our side is inspired and never thinks of hesitating, while on the other side the enemy is stunned and incapable of acting.

Surprise

To compensate for his general weakness and shortage of weapons compared to the enemy, the urban guerrilla uses surprise. The enemy has no way to combat surprise and becomes confused and is destroyed.

When urban guerrilla warfare broke out in Brazil, experience proved that surprise was essential to the success of any guerrilla operation. The technique of surprise is based upon four essential requirements :

1. We know the situation of the enemy we are going to attack, usually by means of precise information and meticulous observation, while the enemy does not know he is going to be attacked and knows nothing about the attackers.
2. We know the strength of the enemy we are going to attack, and the enemy knows nothing about our strength.
3. Attacking by surprise, we save and conserve our forces, while the enemy is unable to do the same, and is left at the mercy of events.
4. We determine the time and place of the attack, fix its duration and establish its objectives. The enemy remains ignorant of all of this information.

Knowledge of the Terrain

The urban guerrilla's best ally is the terrain, and because this is so he must know it like the palm of his hand. To have the terrain as an ally means to know how to use with intelligence its unevenness, its high and low points, its turns, its irregularities, its fixed and secret passages, its abandoned areas, its thickets, etc., taking maximum advantage of all of this for the success of armed actions, escapes, retreats, covers, and hiding places. Impasses and narrow spots, gorges, streets under repair, police checkpoints, military zones and closed-off streets, the entrances and exits to tunnels and those that the enemy can close off, corners controlled or watched by the police, traffic lights and signals; all this must be thoroughly known and studied in order to avoid fatal errors.

Our problem is to get through and to know where and how to hide, leaving the enemy bewildered in areas he doesn't know. Being familiar with the avenues, streets, alleys, ins and outs, the corners of the urban centers, its paths and shortcuts, its empty lots, its underground passages, its pipes and sewer systems, the urban guerrilla safely crosses through the irregular and difficult terrain unfamiliar to the police, where the police can be surprised in a fatal ambush or trap at any moment.

Because he knows the terrain, the urban guerrilla can pass through it on foot, on bicycle, in a car, jeep or small truck, and never be trapped. Acting in small groups with only a few people, the guerrillas can rendezvous at a time and place determined beforehand, following up the initial attack with new guerrilla operations, or evading the police cordon and disorienting the enemy with their unexpected audacity.

It is an impossible problem for the police, in the labrynthian terrain of the urban guerrilla, to catch someone they cannot see, to repress someone they cannot catch, and to close in on someone they cannot find.

Our experience is that the ideal guerrilla is one who operates in his own city and thoroughly knows its streets, its neighborhoods, its transit problems, and its other peculiarities. The guerrilla outsider, who comes to a city whose streets are unfamiliar to him, is a weak spot, and if he is assigned certain operations, he can endanger them. To avoid grave mistakes, it is necessary for him to get to know the layout of the streets.

Mobility and Speed

To insure a mobility and speed that the police cannot match, the urban guerrilla needs the following:

1. Mechanization
2. Knowledge of the terrain
3. A disruption or suspension of enemy transport and communications
4. Light weapons

By carefully carrying out operations that last only a few moments, and leaving the site in mechanized vehicles, the urban guerrilla beats a rapid retreat, escaping capture.

The urban guerrilla must know the way in detail, and, in this manner, must go through the schedule ahead of time as a training, to avoid entering alleyways that have no exit, or running into traffic jams, or being stopped by the Transit Department's traffic signals.

The police pursue the urban guerrilla blindly, without knowing which road he is using for his escape. While the urban guerrilla escapes quickly because he knows the terrain, the police lose the trail and give up the chase.

The urban guerrilla must launch his operations far from the logistical centers of the police. A primary advantage of this method of operation is that it places us at a reasonable distance from the possibility of capture, which facilitates our evasion.

In addition to this necessary precaution, the urban guerrilla must be concerned with the enemy's communication system. The telephone is the primary target in preventing the enemy from access to information, by knocking out his communications systems.

Even if he knows about the guerrilla operation, the enemy depends on modern transportation for his logistics support, and his vehicles necessarily lose time carrying him through the heavy traffic of the large cities. It is clear that the tangled and treacherous traffic is a disadvantage for the enemy, as it would be for us if we were not ahead of him.

If we want to have a safe margin of security and be certain to leave no tracks for the future, we can adopt the following methods:

1. Deliberately intercept the police with other vehicles, or by seemingly casual inconveniences and accidents; but in this case the vehicles in question should neither be legal nor have real license numbers
2. Obstruct the roads with fallen trees, rocks, ditches, false traffic signs, dead ends or detours, or other clever methods
3. Place homemade mines in the way of the police; use gasoline or throw Molotov cocktails to set their vehicles on fire
4. Set off a burst of submachine gun fire or weapons such as the FAL aimed at the motor and tires of the cars engaged in the pursuit

With the arrogance typical of the police and the military authorities, the enemy will come to fight us equipped with heavy guns and equipment, and with elaborate maneuvers by men armed to the teeth. The urban guerrilla must respond to this with light weapons that can be easily transported, so he can always escape with maximum speed without ever accepting open

fighting. The urban guerrilla has no mission other than to attack and quickly withdraw. We would leave ourselves open to the most crushing defeats if we burdened ourselves with heavy weapons and with the tremendous weight of the ammunition necessary to use them, at the same time losing our precious gift of mobility.

When our enemy fights against us with the cavalry, we are at no disadvantage as long as we are mechanized. The automobile goes faster than the horse. From within the car, we also have the target of the mounted police, knocking him down with submachine gun and revolver fire or with Molotov cocktails and hand grenades.

On the other hand, it is not so difficult for an urban guerrilla on foot to make a target of a policeman on horseback. Moreover, ropes across the street, marbles, and cork stoppers are very efficient methods of making them both fall. The great disadvantage faced by the mounted policeman is that he presents the urban guerrilla with two excellent targets—the horse and its rider.

Apart from being faster than the horseman, the helicopter has no better chance in pursuit. If the horse is too slow compared to the urban guerrilla's automobile, the helicopter is too fast. Moving at 200 kilometers an hour, it will never succeed in hitting from above a target that is lost among the crowds and street vehicles, nor can the helicopter land in public streets in order to capture someone. At the same time, whenever it flies too low, it will be excessively vulnerable to the fire of the urban guerrillas.

Information

The chances that the government has for discovering and destroying the urban guerrillas lessens as the power of the dictatorship's enemies becomes greater and more concentrated among the population.

This concentration of the opponents of the dictatorship plays a very important role in providing information about the actions of the police and government officials, as well as hiding the activities of the guerrillas. The enemy can also be thrown off with false information, which is worse for him because it is a tremendous waste.

By whatever means, the sources of information at the disposal of the urban guerrilla are potentially better than those of the police. The enemy is observed by the people, but he does not know who among the people transmits information to the urban guerrillas. The military and the police are hated by the people for the injustices and violence they have committed, and this facilitates obtaining information which is damaging to the activities of government agents.

Information, which is only a small segment of popular support, represents an extraordinary potential in the hands of the urban guerrilla.

The creation of an intelligence service, with an organized structure, is a basic need for us. The urban guerrilla has to have vital information about the plans and movements of the enemy; where they are, how they move, the resources of their banking network, their means of communication, and the secret activities they carry out. The reliable information passed on to the guerrillas represents a well-aimed blow at the dictatorship. The dictatorship has no way to defend itself in the face of an important leak which facilitates our destructive attacks.

The enemy also wants to know what actions we are planning so he can destroy us or prevent us from acting. In this sense, the danger of betrayal is present, and the enemy encourages betrayal and infiltrates spies into the guerrilla organization. The urban guerrilla's technique against this enemy tactic is to denounce publicly the spies, traitors, informers and provocateurs. Since our struggle takes place among the people and depends on their sympathy—while the government has a bad reputation because of its brutality, corruption and incompetence—the informers, spies, traitors and the police come to be enemies of the people, without supporters, denounced to the urban guerrillas and, in many cases, properly punished.

For his part, the urban guerrilla must not evade the duty—once he knows who the spy or informer is—of physically wiping him out. This is the proper method, approved by the people, and it minimizes considerably the incidence of infiltration or enemy spying.

For complete success in the battle against spies and informers, it is essential to organize a counter-espionage or counter-intelligence service. Nevertheless, as far as information is concerned, it cannot all be reduced to a matter of knowing the enemy's moves and avoiding the infiltration of spies. Intelligence information must be broad—it must embrace everything, including the most insignificant material. There is a technique of obtaining information, and the urban guerrilla must master it. Following this technique, intelligence information is obtained naturally, as a part of the life of the people.

The urban guerrilla, living in the midst of the population and moving about among them, must be attentive to all types of conversations and human relations, learning how to disguise his interest with great skill and judgement.

In places where people work, study, and live, it is easy to collect all kinds of information on payments, business, plans of all kinds, points of view, opinions, people's state of mind, trips, interior layout of buildings, offices and rooms, operations centers, etc.

Observation, investigation, reconnaissance, and exploration of the terrain are also excellent sources of information. The urban guerrilla never goes anywhere absentmindedly and without revolutionary precaution, always on the alert lest something occurs. Eyes and ears open, senses alert, his memory is engraved with everything necessary, now or in the future, to the continued activity of the guerrilla fighter.

Careful reading of the press with particular attention to the mass communication media, the research of accumulated data, the transmission of news and everything of note, a persistence in being informed and in informing others, all this makes up the intricate and immensely complicated question of information which gives the urban guerrilla a decisive advantage.

Decisiveness

It is not enough for the urban guerrilla to have in his favor surprise, speed, knowledge of the terrain, and information. He must also demonstrate his command of any situation and a capacity for decisiveness, without which all other advantages will prove to be useless.

It is impossible to carry out any action, however well-planned, if the urban guerrilla turns out to be indecisive, uncertain, irresolute. Even an action successfully begun can end in defeat if command of the situation and the capacity for decision falter in the middle of the execution of the plan. When this command of the situation and a capacity for decision are absent, the void is filled with hesitation and terror. The enemy takes advantage of this failure and is able to liquidate us.

The secret of the success of any operation, simple or complex, easy or difficult, is to rely on determined men. Strictly speaking, there are no simple operations: all must be carried out with the same care taken in the most difficult, beginning with the choice of the human elements—which means relying on leadership and the capacity for decision in every situation.

One can see ahead of time whether an action will be successfull or not by the way its participants act during the preparatory period. Those who fall behind, who fail to make designated contacts, are easily confused, forget things, fail to complete the basic tasks of the work, possibly are indecisive men and can be a danger. It is better not to include them.

Decisiveness means to put into practice the plan that has been devised with determination, with audacity, and with an absolute firmness. It takes only one person who hesitates to lose all.

OBJECTIVES OF THE GUERRILLA'S ACTIONS

With his tactics developed and established, the urban guerrilla trains himself in methods of action leading to attack, and, in Brazil, has the following objectives:

1. To threaten the triangle within which the Brazilian state and North American domination are maintained, a triangle whose points are Rio, Sao Paulo and Belo Horizonte, and whose base is the axis Rio—San Paulo, where the giant industrial, financial, economic, political, cultural, military, and police complex that holds the decisive power of the country is located.

2. To weaken the local militia and the security systems of the dictatorship, given the fact that we are attacking and the "gorillas" defending, which means catching the government in a defensive position with its troops immobilized in the defense of the entire complex of national maintenance, with its ever-present fears of an attack on its strategic nerve centers, and without ever knowing where, how or when the attack will come.

3. To attack every area with many different armed groups, small in size, each self-contained and operating independently, to disperse the government forces in their pursuit of a thoroughly fragmented organization, instead of offering the dictatorship the opportunity to concentrate its forces in the destruction of one tightly organized system operating throughout the country.

4. To give proof of its combatitivenes, decision, firmness, determination, and persistence in the attack on the military dictatorship, in order to allow all rebels to follow in our example and to fight with urban guerrilla tactics. Meanwhile, the government with all of its problems, incapable of halting guerrilla actions within the cities, will lose time and suffer endless attrition, and will finally be forced to pull back its repressive forces in order to mount guard over all the banks, industries, armories, military barracks, prisons, public offices, radio and television stations, North American firms, gas storage tanks, oil refineries, ships, airplanes, ports, airports, hospitals, health centers, blood banks, stores, garages, embassies, residences of high-ranking members of the regime such as ministers and generals, police stations, official organizations, etc.

5. To increase urban guerrilla actions gradually into an endless number of surprise raids, such that the government cannot leave the urban area to pursue guerrillas in the rural interior without running the risk of abandoning the cities and permitting rebellion to increase on the coast as well as the interior of the country.

6. To force the Army and the police, their commanders and their assistants, to give up the relative comfort and tranquility of their barracks and their usual rest, for a state of fear and growing tension in the expectation of attack, or in a search for trails which vanish without a trace.

7. To avoid open battle and decisive combat with the government, limiting the struggle to brief, rapid attacks with lightning results.
8. To insure for the urban guerrilla a maximum freedom of movement and of action, without ever relinquishing the use of armed action, remaining firmly oriented towards helping the formation of rural guerrilla warfare and supporting the construction of a revolutionary army for national liberation.

ON THE TYPES AND NATURE OF MISSIONS F OR THE URBAN GUERRILLA

In order to achieve the objectives previously listed, the urban guerrilla is obliged, in his tactics, to follow missions whose nature is as different or diversified as possible. The urban guerrilla does not arbitrarily choose this or that mission. Some actions are simple; others are complicated. The inexperienced guerrilla must be gradually introduced into actions and operations which run from the simple to the complex. He begins with small missions and tasks until he becomes completely experienced.

Before any action, the urban guerrilla must think of the methods and the personnel at his disposal to carry out the mission. Operations and actions that demand the urban guerrilla's technical preparation cannot be carried out by someone who lacks the technical skill. With these precautions, the missions which the urban guerrilla can undertake are the following:

1. assaults
2. raids and penetrations
3. occupations
4. ambushes
5. street tactics
6. strikes and work stoppages
7. desertions, diversions, seizures, expropriation of weapons, ammunition and explosives
8. liberation of prisoners
9. executions
10. kidnappings
11. sabotage
12. terrorism
13. armed propaganda
14. war of nerves

Assaults

Assaults are the armed attacks which we make to expropriate funds, liberate prisoners, capture explosives, submachine guns, and other types of weapons and ammunition.

Assaults can take place in broad daylight or at night. Daytime assaults are made when the objective cannot be achieved at any other hour, such as the transport of money by banks, which is not done at night. Night assault is usually the most advantageous for the guerrilla. The ideal is for all assaults to take place at night, when conditions for a surprise attack are most favorable and the darkness facilitates escape and hides the identity of the participants. The urban guerrilla must prepare himself, nevertheless, to act under all conditions, daytime as well as night.

The most vulnerable targets for assaults are the following:

1. credit establishments
2. commercial and industrial enterprises, including plants for the manufacture of weapons and explosives
3. military establishments
4. commissaries and police stations
5. jails
6. government property
7. mass communications media
8. North American firms and properties
9. government vehicles, including military and police vehicles, trucks, armored vehicles, money carriers, trains, ships, and airplanes.

The assaults on businesses use the same tactics, because in every case the buildings represent a fixed target. Assaults on buildings are planned as guerrilla operations, varied according to whether they are against banks, a commercial enterprise, industries, military bases, commissaries, prisons, radio stations, warehouses for foreign firms, etc.

The assault on vehicles—money-carriers, armored vehicles, trains, ships, airplanes—are of another nature, since they are moving targets. The nature of the operation varies according to the situation and the circumstances—that is, whether the vehicle is stationary or moving. Armored cars, including military vehicles, are not immune to mines. Roadblocks, traps, ruses, interception by other vehicles, Molotov cocktails, shooting with heavy weapons, are efficient methods of assaulting vehicles. Heavy vehicles, grounded airplaces and anchored ships can be seized and their crews and guards overcome. Airplanes in flight can be hijacked by guerrilla action or by one person. Ships and trains in motion can be assaulted or captured by guerrilla operations in order to obtain weapons and ammunition or to prevent troop movements.

The Bank Assault as Popular Mission

The most popular mission is the bank assault. In Brazil, the urban guerrillas have begun a type of organized assault on the banks as a guerrilla operation. Today, this type of assault is widely used, and has served as a sort of preliminary test for the urban guerrilla in his training in the tactics of urban guerrilla warfare.

Important innovations in the tactics of assaulting banks have developed, guaranteeing escape, the withdrawal of money, and the anonymity of those involved. Among these innovations, we cite the shooting of tires of cars to prevent pursuit, locking people in the bank bathroom, making them sit on the floor, immobilizing the bank guards and taking their weapons, forcing someone to open the safe or the strong box, and using disguises.

Attempts to install bank alarms, to use guards or electronic detection devices prove fruitless when the assault is political and is carried out according to urban guerrilla warfare techniques. This guerrilla method uses new techniques to meet the enemy's tactical changes, has access to firepower that is growing every day, becomes increasingly more experienced and more confident, and uses a larger number of guerrillas every time; all to guarantee the success of operations planned down to the last detail.

The bank assault is a typical expropriation. But, as is true with any kind of armed expropriatory action, the guerrilla is handicapped by a two-fold competition:

1. competition from the outlaw
2. competition from the right-wing counter-revolutionary

This competition produces confusion, which is reflected in the people's uncertainty. It is up to the urban guerrilla to prevent this from happening, and to accomplish this he must use two methods:

1. He must avoid the outlaw's technique, which is one of unnecessary violence and the expropriation of goods and possessions belonging to the people
2. He must use the assault for propaganda purposes at the very moment it is taking place, and later distribute material, leaflets—every possible means of explaining the objectives and the principles of the urban guerrillas, as expropriator of the government and the ruling elite.

Raids and Penetrations

Raids and penetrations are rapid attacks on establishments located in neighborhoods, or even in the center of the city, such as small military units, commissaries, hospitals, to cause trouble, seize weapons, punish and terrorize the enemy, take reprisals, or to rescue wounded prisoners or those hospitalized under police guard. Raids and penetrations are also made on garages and depots to destroy vehicles and damage installations, especially if they are North American firms and property.

When they take place on certain stretches of highway or in certain distant neighborhoods, these raids can serve to force the enemy to move great numbers of troops, a totally useless effort since when they get there they will find nobody to fight. When they are carried out on certain houses, offices, archives or public offices, their purpose is to capture or search for secret papers and documents with which to denounce deals, compromises and the corruption of men in government, their dirty deals and criminal transactions.

Raids and penetrations are most effective if they are carried out at night.

Occupations

Occupations are a type of attack carried out when the urban guerrilla stations himself in specific establishments and locations, for a temporary action against the enemy or for some propaganda purpose.

The occupation of factories and schools during strikes, or at other times, is a method of protest or of distracting the enemy's attention. The occupation of radio stations is for propaganda purposes.

Occupation is a highly effective model for action but, in order to prevent losses and material damage to our forces, it is always a good idea to plan on the possibility of a forced withdrawal. It must always be meticulously planned, and carried out at the opportune moment.

Occupations always have a time limit, and the swifter they are completed, the better.

Ambush

Ambushes are attacks, typified by surprise, when the enemy is trapped on the road or when he makes a police net surrounding a house or estate. A false alarm can bring the enemy to the spot, where he falls into a trap.

The principle object of the ambush is to capture enemy weapons and to punish him with death.

Ambushes to halt passenger trains are for propaganda purposes, and, when they are troop trains, the object is to annihilate the enemy and seize his weapons.

The urban guerrilla sniper is the kind of fighter specially suited for ambush, because he can hide easily in the irregularities of the terrain, on the roofs and the tops of buildings and apartments under construction. From windows and dark places, he can take careful aim at his chosen target.

Ambush has devestating effects on the enemy, leaving him unnerved, insecure and fearful.

Street Tactics

Street tactics are used to fight the enemy in the streets, utilizing the participation of the population against him.

In 1968, the Brazilian students used excellent street tactics against police troops, such as marching down streets against traffic and using slingshots and marbles against mounted police.

Other street tactics consist of constructing barricades; pulling up paving blocks and hurling them at the police; throwing bottles, bricks, paperweights and other projectiles at the police from the top of office and apartment buildings; using buildings and other structures for escape, for hiding and for supporting surprise attacks.

It is equally necessary to know how to respond to enemy tactics. When the police troops come wearing helmets to protect them against flying objects, we have to divide ourselves into two teams—one to attack the enemy from the front, the other to attack him in the rear—withdrawing one as the other goes into action to prevent the first from being struck by projectiles hurled by the second.

By the same token, it is important to know how to respond to the police net. When the police designate certain of their men to go into the crowd and arrest a demonstrator, a larger group of urban guerrillas must surround the police group, disarming and beating them and at the same time allowing the prisoner to escape. This urban guerrilla operation is called "the net within a net".

When the police net is formed at a school building, a factory, a place where demonstrators gather, or some other point, the urban guerrilla must not give up or allow himself to be taken by surprise. To make his net effective, the enemy is obliged to transport his troops in vehicles and special cars to occupy strategic points in the streets, in order to invade the building or chosen locale.

The urban guerrilla, for his part, must never clear a building or an area and meet in it without first knowing its exits, the way to break an encirclement, the strategic points that the police must occupy, and the roads that inevitably lead into the net, and he must hold other strategic points from which to strike at the enemy. The roads followed by police vehicles must be mined at key points along the way and at forced roadblocks. When the mines explode, the vehicles will be knocked into the air. The police will be caught in the trap and will suffer losses and be victims of an ambush.

The net must be broken by escape routes which are unknown to the police. The rigorous planning of a withdrawal is the best way to frustrate any encircling effort on the part of the enemy.

When there is no possibility of an escape plan, the urban guerrilla must not hold meetings, gatherings or do anything, since to do so will prevent him from breaking through the net which the enemy will surely try to throw around him.

Street tactics have revealed a new type of urban guerrilla who participates in mass protests. This is the type we designate as the "urban guerrilla demonstrator", who joins the crowds and participates in marches with specific and definate aims in mind. The urban guerrilla demonstrator must initiate the "net within the net", ransacking government vehicles, official cars and police vehicles before turning them over or setting fire to them, to see if any of them have money or weapons.

Snipers are very good for mass demonstrations, and along with the urban guerrilla demonstrator can play a valuable role. Hidden at strategic points, the snipers have complete success using shotguns or submachine guns, which can easily cause losses among the enemy.

Strikes and Work Interruptions

The strike is a model of action employed by the urban guerrilla in work centers and schools to damage the enemy by stopping work and study activities. Because it is one of the weapons most feared by the exploiters and oppressors, the enemy uses tremendous firepower and incredible violence against it. The strikers are taken to prison, suffer beatings, and many of them wind up killed.

The urban guerrilla must prepare the strike in such a way as to leave no track or clue that can identify the leaders of such an action. A strike is successful when it is organized by a small group, if it is carefully prepared in secret using the most clandestine methods. Weapons, ammunition, Molotov cocktails, homemade weapons of destruction and attack, all of these must be supplied beforehand in order to meet the enemy. So that the action can do the greatest possible amount of damage, it is a good idea to study and put into effect a sabotage plan.

Strikes and study interruptions, although they are of brief duration, cause severe damage to the enemy. It is enough for them to crop up at dif-ferent locations and in differing sections of the same area, disrupting daily life, occuring endlessly, one after the other, in true guerrilla fashion.

In strikes or in simple work interruptions, the urban guerrilla has recourse to the occupation or penetration of the site, or he can simply make a raid. In that case, his objective is to take captives, to capture prisoners, or to capture enemy agents and propose an exchange for arrested strikers.

In certain cases, strikes and brief work interruptions can offer an excellent opportunity for preparing ambushes or traps, whose aim is the physical destruction of the police. The basic fact is that the enemy suffers losses as well as material and moral damage, and is weakened by the action.

Desertions, Diversions, Seizures, Expropriation of Weapons, Ammunition and Explosives

Desertion and the diversion of weapons are actions carried out in military bases, ships, military hospitals, etc. The urban guerrilla soldier or officer must desert at the most opportune moment with modern weapons and ammunition, to hand them over to the guerrillas.

One of the most opportune moments is when the urban guerrilla soldier is called upon to pursue his guerrilla comrades outside the military base. Instead of following the orders of the "gorillas", the military urban guerrilla must join the ranks of the revolutionaries by handing over the weapons and ammunition he carries, or the military vehicle he operates. The advantage of this method is that the rebels receive weapons and ammunition from the army, navy, air force, military police, civilian guard or the police without any great work, since it reaches their hands by government transportation.

Other opportunities may occur in the barracks, and the military urban guerrilla must always be alert to this. In case of carelessness on the part of commanders or in other favorable conditions—such as bureaucratic attitudes or the relaxation of discipline on the part of lieutenants or other internal personnel—the military urban guerrilla must no longer wait but must try to inform the guerrillas and desert with as large a supply of weapons as possible.

When there is no possibility of deserting with weapons and ammunition, the military urban guerrilla must engage in sabotage, starting fires and explosions in munitions dumps.

This technique of deserting with weapons and of raiding and sabotaging the military centers is the best way of wearing out and demoralizing the enemy and leaving them confused.

The urban guerrilla's purpose in disarming an individual enemy is to capture his weapons. These weapons are usually in the hands of sentinels or others whose task is guard duty. The capture of weapons may be accomplished by violent means or by cleverness and tricks or traps. When the enemy is disarmed, he must be searched for weapons other than those already taken from him. If we are careless, he can use the weapons that were not seized to shoot the urban guerrilla.

The seizure of weapons is an efficient method of aquiring submachine guns, the urban guerrilla's most important weapon. When we carry out small operations or actions to seize weapons and ammunition, the materiel captured may be for personal use or for armaments and supplies for the firing teams.

The necessity to provide firepower for the urban guerrillas is so great that, in order to take off from the zero point, we often have to purchase one weapon, divert or capture a single gun. The basic point is to begin, and to begin with a spirit of decisiveness and boldness. The possession of a single submachine gun multiplies our forces.

In a bank assault, we must be careful to seize the weapons of the bank guard. The rest of the weapons will be found with the treasurer, the bank tellers or the manager, and must also be seized. Quite often, we succeed in capturing weapons in police stations, as a result of raids. The capture of weapons, ammunition and explosives is the urban guerrilla's goal in assaulting commercial businesses, industries and quarries.

Liberation of Prisoners

The liberation of prisoners is an armed action designed to free jailed urban guerrillas. In daily struggle against the enemy, the urban guerrilla is subject to arrest, and can be sentenced to unlimited years in jail.

This does not mean that the battle ends here. For the guerrilla, his experience is deepened by prison, and struggle continues even in the dungeons where he is held. The imprisoned guerrilla views the prisons of the enemy as a terrain which he must dominate and understand in order to free himself by a guerrilla operation. There is no jail, either on an island, in a city penitentiary, or on a farm, that is impregnable to the slyness, cleverness and firepower of the rebels.

The urban guerrilla who is free views the jails of the enemy as the inevitable site of guerrilla actions designed to liberate his ideological comrades from prison. It is this combination of the urban guerrilla in freedom and the urban guerrilla in jail that results in the armed operations we refer to as "liberation of prisoners".

The guerrilla operations that can be used in liberating prisoners are the following;

1. riots in penal establishments, in correctional colonies or camps, or on transport or prison ships;
2. assaults on urban or rural prisons, detention centers, prison camps, or any other permanent or temporary place where prisoners are held;
3. assaults on prisoner transport trains or convoys;
4. raids and penetrations of prisons;
5. ambushing of guards who move prisoners.

Executions

Execution is the killing of a foreign spy, of an agent of the dictatorship, of a police torturer, of a dictatorial personality in the government involved in crimes and persecutions against patriots, of a stool pigeon, informer, police agent or police provocateur. Those who go to the police of their own free will to make denunciations and accusations, who supply information and who finger people, must be executed when they are caught by the urban guerrillas.

Execution is a secret action, in which the least possible number of urban guerrillas are involved. In many cases, the execution can be carried out by a single sniper, patient, alone and unknown, and operating in absolute secrecy and in cold blood.

Kidnappings

Kidnapping is capturing and holding in a secret place a spy, political personality or a notorious and dangerous enemy of the revolutionary movement. Kidnapping is used to exchange or liberate imprisoned revolutionaries or to force the suspension of torture in jail by the military dictatorship.

The kidnapping of personalities who are well-known artists, sports figures or who are outstanding in some other field, but who have evidenced no political interest, can be a useful form of propaganda for the guerrillas, provided it occurs under special circumstances, and is handled so the public understands and sympathizes with it. The kidnappings of foreigners or visitors constitutes a form of protest against the penetration and domination of imperialism in our country.

Sabotage

Sabotage is a highly destructive type of attack using very few persons—and sometimes requiring only one—to accomplish the desired result. When the urban guerrilla uses sabotage, the first step is isolated sabotage. Then comes the step of dispersed and general sabotage, carried out by the population.

Well-executed sabotage demands study, planning and careful action. A characteristic form of sabotage is explosion, using dynamite, fire or the placing of mines. A little sand, a trickle of any kind of combustible, a poor lubrication job, a screw removed, a short circuit, inserted pieces of wood or iron, can cause irreparable damage.

The objective of sabotage is to hurt, to damage, to make useless and to destroy vital enemy points such as the following:

1. the economy of the country
2. agricultural or industrial production
3. transport and communication systems
4. military and police systems and their establishments and depots
5. the repressive military-police system
6. the firms and properties of exploiters in the country

The urban guerrilla should endanger the economy of the country, particularly its economic and financial aspects, such as its domestic and foreign banking network, its exchange and credit systems, its tax collection system, etc.

Public offices, centers of government and government depots are easy targets for sabotage. Nor will it be easy to prevent the sabotage of agricultural and industrial production by the urban guerrilla, with his thorough knowledge of the local situation.

Factory workers acting as urban guerrillas are excellent industrial saboteurs, since they, better than anyone, understand the industry, the factory, the machinery or the part most likely to destroy an entire operation, doing much more damage than a poorly-informed layman could do.

With respect to the enemy's transport and communications systems, beginning with railway traffic, it is necessary to attack them systematically with sabotage. The only caution is against causing death and injury to passengers, especially regular commuters on suburban and long-distance trains. Attacks on freight trains, rolling or stationary stock, stoppage of military transports and communciations systems, these are the major objectives in this area. Sleepers can be damaged and pulled up, as can rails. A tunnel blocked by a barrier of explosives, or an obstruction caused by a derailed car, causes enormous harm.

The derailment of a train carrying fuel is of major damage to the enemy. So is dynamiting a railroad bridge. In a system where the size and weight of the rolling equipment is enormous, it takes months for workers to repair or rebuild the destruction and damage.

As for highways, they can be obstructed with trees, stationary vehicles, ditches, dislocation of barriers by dynamite, and bridges destroyed by explosions.

Ships can be damaged at anchor in seaports or riverports, or in the shipyards. Aircraft can be destroyed or damaged on the ground.

Telephone and telegraph lines can be systematically damaged, their towers blown up, and their lines made useless. Transport and communications must be sabotaged immediately because the revolutionary movement has already begun in Brazil, and it is essential to impede the enemy's movement of troops and munitions.

Oil lines, fuel plants, depots for bombs and ammunition arsenals, military camps and bases must become targets for sabotage operations, while vehicles, army trucks and other military or police vehicles must be destroyed wherever they are found. The military and police repression centers and their specialized organs must also claim the attention of the guerrilla saboteur. Foreign firms and properties in the country, for their part, must become such frequent targets of sabotage that the volume of actions directed against them surpasses the total of all other actions against enemy vital points.

Terrorism

Terrorism is an action, usually involving the placement of an explosive or firebomb of great destructive power, which is capable of effecting irreparable loss against the enemy. Terrorism requires that the urban guerrilla should have adequate theoretical and practical knowledge of how to make explosives.

The terrorist act, apart from the apparent ease with which it can be carried out, is no different from other guerrilla acts and actions whose success depends on planning and determination. It is an action which the urban guerrilla must execute with the greatest calmness and determination.

Although terrorism generally involves an explosion, there are cases in which it may be carried out through executions or the systematic burning of installations, properties, plantations, etc. It is essential to point out the importance of fires and the construction of incendiary devices such as gasoline bombs in the technique of guerrilla terrorism.

Another thing is the importance of the material the urban guerrilla can persuade the people to expropriate in the moments of hunger and scarcity brought about by the greed of the big commercial interests.

Terrorism is a weapon the revolutionary can never relinquish.

Armed Propaganda

The coordination of urban guerrilla activities, including each armed action, is the primary way of making armed propaganda. These actions, carried out with specific objectives and aims in mind, inevitably become propaganda material for the mass communication system. Bank robberies, ambushes, desertions and the diverting of weapons, the rescue of prisoners, executions, kidnappings, sabotage, terrorism and the war of nerves are all cases in point.

Airplanes diverted in flight by guerrilla action, ships and trains assaulted and seized by armed guerrillas, can also be carried out solely for propaganda effect.

But the urban guerrilla must never fail to install a clandestine press, and must be able to turn out mimeographed copies using alcohol or electric plates and other duplicating apparatus, expropriating what he cannot buy in order to produce small clandestine newspapers, pamphlets, flyers and stamps for propaganda and agitation against the dictatorship.

The urban guerrilla engaged in clandestine printing facilitates enormously the incorporation of large numbers of people into the struggle, by opening a permanent work front for those willing to carry on propaganda, even when to do so means to act alone and risk their lives.

With the existence of clandestine propaganda and agitational material, the inventive spirit of the urban guerrilla expands and creates catapults, artifacts, mortars and other instruments with which to distribute the anti-government propaganda at a distance.

Tape recordings, the occupation of radio stations, the use of loudspeakers, graffiti on walls and other inaccessible places are other forms of propaganda. A consistent propaganda by letters sent to specific addresses, explaining the meaning of the urban guerrilla's armed actions, produces considerable results and is one method of influencing certain segments of the population.

Even this influence—exercised in the heart of the people by every possible propaganda device, revolving around the activity of the urban guerrilla—does not indicate that our forces have everyone's support. It is enough to win the support of a portion of the population, and this can be done by popularizing the motto, "Let he who does not wish to do anything for the guerrillas do nothing against them."

The War of Nerves

The war of nerves or psychological warfare is an aggressive technique, based on the direct or indirect use of mass media and rumors in order to demoralize the government.

In psychological warfare, the government is always at a disadvantage because it imposes censorship on the media and winds up in a defensive position by not allowing anything against it to filter through. At this point, it becomes desperate, is involved in greater contradictions and loss of prestige, and loses time and energy in an exhausting effort at control which is liable to be broken at any moment.

The objective of the war of nerves is to mislead, spreading lies among the authorities in which everyone can participate, thus creating an atmosphere of nervousness, discredit, insecurity, uncertainty and concern on the part of the government.

The best methods used by urban guerrillas in the war of nerves are the following:

1. Using the telephone and the mail to announce false clues to the police and government, including information on the planting of bombs and any other act of terrorism in public offices and other places—kidnapping and assassination plans, etc.—to force the authorities to wear themselves out by following up on the false information fed to them;
2. Letting false plans fall into the hands of the police to divert their attention;
3. Planting rumors to make the government uneasy;
4. Exploiting by every means possible the corruption, the mistakes and the failures of the government and its representatives, forcing them into demoralizing explanations and justifications in the very communication media they wish to maintain under censorship;
5. Presenting denunciations to foreign embassies, the United Nations, the papal nunciature, and the international commissions defending human rights or freedom of the press, exposing each concrete violation and each use of violence by the military dictatorship and making it known that the revolutionary war will continue with serious danger for the enemies of the population.

How to Carry Out the Action

The urban guerrilla who correctly carries through his apprenticeship and training must give the greatest possible importance to his method of carrying out actions, for in this he cannot commit the slightest error. Any carelessness in learning tactics and their use invites certain disaster, as experience teaches us every day.

Common criminals commit errors frequently because of their tactics, and this is one of the reasons why the urban guerrillas must be so insistently preoccupied with following revolutionary tactics, and not the tactics of bandits. And not only for that reason. There is no urban guerrilla worthy of the name who ignores the revolutionary method of action and fails to practice it rigorously in the planning and execution of his activities.

"The giant is known by his toe." The same can be said of the urban guerrilla, who is known from afar by his correct tactics and his absolute fidelity to principle.

The revolutionary method of carrying out actions is strongly and forcefully based on the knowledge and use of the following elements;

1. investigation and intelligence gathering
2. observation and vigilance
3. reconnaissance, or exploration of the terrain
4. study and timing of routes
5. mapping
6. mechanization
7. careful selection of personnel
8. selection of firepower
9. study and practice in success
10. success
11. use of cover
12. retreat
13. dispersal
14. the liberation or transfer of prisoners
15. the elimination of evidence
16. the rescue of wounded

Some Observations on Tactics

When there is no information, the point of departure for planning the action must be investigation, observation and vigilance. This method produces good results.

In any event, even when there is information, it is essential to make observations to see that information is not at odds with observation or vice versa. Reconnaissance or exploration of the terrain and the study and timing of routes are so important that to omit them is to make a stab in the dark.

Mechanization, in general, is an underestimated factor in the tactics of conducting an action. Frequently, mechanization is left to the end, on the eve of the action, before anything is done about it. This is a mistake. Mechanization must be seriously considered. It must be undertaken with considerable foresight and with careful planning, based on careful and precise information. The care, conservation, maintenance and camouflaging of stolen vehicles are very important details of mechanization. When transportation fails, the primary action fails, with serious material and morale problems for the urban guerrillas.

The selection of personnel requires great care in order to avoid the inclusion of indecisive or wavering persons who present the danger of contaminating others, a danger that must be avoided.

The withdrawal is equally or more important than the operation itself, to the point that it must be rigorously planned, including the possibility of defeat.

One must avoid rescue or transfer of prisoners with children present, or anything to attract the attention of people passing through the area. The best thing is to make the rescue appear as natural as possible, winding through different routes or narrow streets that scarcely permit passage on foot, in order to avoid an encounter between two cars. The elimination of tracks is obligatory and demands the greatest caution— also in removing fingerprints and any other sign that could give the enemy information. Lack of care in the elimination of evidence is a factor that increases nervousness in our ranks, which the enemy often exploits.

Rescue of the Wounded

The problem of the wounded in urban guerrilla warfare merits special attention. During guerrilla operations in the urban area, it may happen that some comrade is wounded by the police. When a guerrilla in the firing group has a knowledge of first aid, he can do something for the wounded comrade on the spot. Under no circumstances should the wounded guerrilla be abandoned at the site of the battle or left in the enemy's hands.

One of the precautions we must take is to set up first-aid courses for men and women, courses in which guerrillas can learn the rudiments of emergency medicine. The urban guerrilla who is a doctor, nurse, med student, pharmacist or who simply has had first aid training is a necessity in modern guerrilla struggle. A small manual of first aid for urban guerrillas, printed on mimeographed sheets, can also be produced by anyone who has enough knowledge.

In planning and carrying out an armed action, the urban guerrilla cannot forget the organization of medical support. This must be accomplished by means of a mobile or motorized clinic. You can also set up a mobile first aid station. Another solution is to utilize the skills of a medical comrade, who waits with his bag of equipment in a designated house to which the wounded are brought.

The ideal would be to have our own well-equipped clinic, but this is very expensive unless we expropriate all of our materials.

When all else fails, it is often necessary to resort to legal clinics, using armed force if necessary to force a doctor to treat our wounded.

In the eventuality that we fall back upon blood banks to purchase blood or plasma, we must not use legal addresses and certainly no addresses where the wounded can really be found, since they are under our care and protection. Nor should we supply the addresses of those involved in the guerrilla organization to the hospitals and health care clinics where we may take them. Such caution is indispensable to covering our tracks.

The houses in which the wounded stay cannot be known to anyone but the small group of comrades responsible for their care and transport. Sheets, bloody clothing, medicine and any other indications of treatment of comrades wounded in combat must be completely eliminated from any place they visit to receive treatment.

Guerrilla Security

The urban guerrilla lives in constant danger of the possibility of being discovered or denounced.

The primary security problem is to make certain that we are well-hidden and well-guarded, and that there are secure methods to keep the police from locating us.

The worst enemy of the urban guerrilla, and the major danger that we run into, is infiltration into our organization by a spy or informer. The spy trapped within the organization will be punished with death. The same goes for those who desert and inform to the police.

A well-laid security means there are no spies or agents infiltrated into our midst, and the enemy can receive no information about us even through indirect means. The fundamental way to insure this is to be strict and cautious in recruiting. Nor is it permissible for everyone to know everything and everyone. This rule is a fundamental ABC of urban guerrilla security.

The enemy wants to annihilate us and fights relentlessly to find us and destroy us, so our greatest weapon lies in hiding from him and attacking by surprise.

The danger to the urban guerrilla is that he may reveal himself through carelessness or allow himself to be discovered through a lack of vigilance. It is impermissible for the urban guerrilla to give out his own or any other clandestine address to the police, or to talk too much.

Notations in the margins of newspapers, lost documents, calling cards, letters or notes, all these are evidence that the police never underestimate. Address and telephone books must be destroyed, and one must not write or hold any documents. It is necessary to avoid keeping archives of legal or illegal names, biographical information, maps or plans. Contact numbers should not be written down, but simply committed to memory.

The urban guerrilla who violates these rules must be warned by the first one who notes this infraction and, if he repeats it, we must avoid working with him in the future.

The urban guerrilla's need to move about constantly with the police nearby—given the fact that the police net surrounds the city—forces him to adopt various security precautions depending upon the enemy's movements. For this reason, it is necessary to maintain a daily information service about what the enemy appears to be doing, where the police net is operating and what points are being watched. The daily reading of the police news in the newspapers is a fountain of information in these cases.

The most important lesson for guerrilla security is never, under any circumstances, to permit the slightest laxity in the maintenance of security measures and precautions within the organization.

Guerrilla security must also be maintained in the case of an arrest. The arrested guerrilla must reveal nothing to the police that will jeopardize the organization. he must say nothing that will lead, as a consequence, to the arrest of other comrades, the discovery of addresses or hiding places, or the loss of weapons and ammunition.

THE SEVEN SINS OF THE URBAN GUERRILLA

Even when the urban guerrilla applies proper tactics and abides by its security rules, he can still be vulnerable to errors. There is no perfect urban guerrilla. The most he can do is make every effort to diminish the margin of error, since he cannot be perfect. One of the means we should use to diminish the possibility of error is to know thoroughly the seven deadly sins of the urban guerrilla and try to avoid them.

The first sin of the guerrilla is inexperience. The urban guerrilla, blinded by this sin, thinks the enemy is stupid, underestimates the enemy's intelligence, thinks everything is easy and, as a result, leaves evidence that can lead to disaster.

Because of his inexperience, the urban guerrilla may also overestimate the forces of the enemy, believing them to be stronger than they really are. Allowing himself to be fooled by this presumption, the urban guerrilla becomes intimidated and remains insecure and indecisive, paralyzed and lacking in audacity.

The second sin of the urban guerrilla is to boast about the actions he has undertaken and to broadcast them to the four winds.

The third sin of the urban guerrilla is vanity. The guerrilla who suffers from this sin tries to solve the problems of the revolution by actions in the city, but without bothering about the beginnings and survival of other guerrillas in other areas. Blinded by success, he winds up organizing an action that he considers decisive and that puts into play the entire resources of the organization. Since we cannot afford to break the guerrilla struggle in the cities while rural guerrilla warfare has not yet erupted, we always run the risk of allowing the enemy to attack us with decisive blows.

The fourth sin of the urban guerrilla is to exaggerate his strength and to undertake actions for which he, as yet, lacks sufficient forces and the required infrastructure.

The fifth sin of the urban guerrilla is rash action. The guerrilla who commits this sin loses patience, suffers an attack of nerves, does not wait for anything, and impetuously throws himself into action, suffering untold defeats.

The sixth sin of the urban guerrilla is to attack the enemy when they are most angry.

The seventh sin of the urban guerrilla is to fail to plan things, and to act spontaneously.

POPULAR SUPPORT

One of the permanent concerns of the urban guerrilla is his identification with popular causes to win public support. Where government actions become inept and corrupt, the urban guerrilla should not hesitate to step in and show that he opposes the government, and thus gain popular sympathy. The present government, for example, imposes heavy financial burdens and excessively high taxes on the people. It is up to the urban guerrilla to attack the dictatorship's tax collection system and to obstruct its financial activities, throwing all the weight of armed action against it.

The urban guerrilla fights not only to upset the tax collection system—the weapon of armed action must also be directed against those government agencies that raise prices and those who direct them as well as against the wealthiest of the national and foreign profiteers and the important property owners. In short, against all those who accumulate huge fortunes out of the high cost of living, the wages of hunger, excessive prices and high rents.

Foreign industries, such as refrigeration and other North American plants that monopolize the market and the manufacture of general food supplies, must be systematically attacked by the urban guerrillas.

The rebellion of the urban guerrilla and his persistance in intervening in political questions is the best way of insuring popular support for the cause which we defend. We repeat and insist on repeating—it is the way of insuring popular support. As soon as a reasonable portion of the population begins to take seriously the actions of the urban guerrilla, his success is guaranteed.

The government has no alternative except to intensify its repression. The police networks, house searches, the arrest of suspects and innocent persons, and the closing off of streets make life in the city unbearable. The military dictatorship embarks on massive political persecution. Political assassinations and police terror become routine.

In spite of all this, the police systematically fail. The armed forces, the navy and the air force are mobilized to undertake routine police functions, but even so they can find no way to halt guerrilla operations or to wipe out the revolutionary organization, with its fragmented groups that move around and operate throughout the country.

The people refuse to collaborate with the government, and the general sentiment is that this government is unjust, incapable of solving problems, and that it resorts simply to the physical liquidation of its opponents. The political situation in the country is transformed into a military situation in which the "gorillas" appear more and more to be the ones responsible for violence, while the lives of the people grow worse.

When they see the military and the dictatorship on the brink of the abyss, and fearing the consequences of a civil war which is already well underway, the pacifiers (always to be found within the ruling elite) and the opportunists (partisans of nonviolent struggle) join hands and circulate rumors behind the scenes begging the hangmen for elections, "re-democratization", constitutional reforms, and other tripe designed to fool the people and make them stop the rebellion.

But, watching the guerrillas, the people now understand that it is a farce to vote in any elections which have as their sole objective guaranteeing the survival of the dictatorship and covering up its crimes. Attacking wholeheartedly this election farce and the so-called "political solution", which is so appealing to the opportunists, the urban guerrillas must become even more aggressive and active, resorting without pause to sabotage, terrorism, expropriations, assaults, kidnappings, executions, etc.

This action answers any attempt to fool the people with the opening of Congress and the reorganization of political parties—parties of the government and of the positions which the government allows—when all the time parliament and the so-called "parties" only function thanks to the permission of the military dictatorship, in a true spectacle of puppets or dogs on a leash.

The role of the urban guerrilla, in order to win the support of the population, is to continue fighting, keeping in mind the interests of the people and heightening the disastrous situation within which the government must act. These are the conditions, harmful to the dictatorship, which permit the guerrillas to open rural warfare in the middle of an uncontrollable urban rebellion.

The urban guerrilla is engaged in revolutionary action for the people, and with them seeks the participation of the people in the struggle against the dictatorship and the liberation of the country. Beginning with the city and the support of the people, the rural guerrilla war develops rapidly, establishing its infrastructure carefully while the urban area continues the rebellion.

A Militant Agreement for the Uprising

V. I. Lenin

Published: *Vperyod*, No. 7, February 21 (8), 1905. Published according to the text In *Vperyod*.

Source: *Lenin Collected Works*, Foreign Languages Publishing House, 1962, Moscow, Volume 8, pages 158-166.

Translated: Bernard Isaacs and The Late Isidor Lasker

Transcription\Markup: R. Cymbala

Other Formats: Text.

Revolutsionnaya Rossiya, No. 58, says: "May the spirit of fighting unity now at long last pervade the ranks of the revolutionary socialist groups, which are torn by fratricidal animosity, and may it revive the consciousness of socialist solidarity which has been so criminally sapped . . . . Let us spare the revolutionary forces as much as we can and increase their effectiveness by means of a concerted attack!"

We have often had occasion to protest against the tyranny of the phrase among the Socialists-Revolutionaries, and we must do so again. Why these frightful words, gentle men, about "fratricidal animosity" and so forth? Are they worthy of a revolutionary? Now of all times, when the real fight is on, when blood is flowing—the blood of which *Revolutsionnaya Rossiya* speaks in such flamboyant terms, these grotesque exaggerations about "fratricidal animosity" ring false than ever. Spare the forces, say you? But surely this is done by a united, welded organisation which is at one on questions of principle, and not by lumping together heterogeneous elements. Strength is not spared but wasted by such barren attempts at lumping. To achieve a "fighting unity" in deed and not merely in word, we must know clearly, definitely, and *from experience* exactly wherein and to what extent we *can* be united. *Without* this, all talk of fighting unity will be mere words, words, words; *this* knowledge, incidentally, comes from the very controversy, struggle, and animosity of which you speak in such "frightful" terms. Would it really be better if we hushed up the differences that divide vast sections of Russian public opinion and Russian socialist thought? Was it only the "cult of discord" that provoked the bitter struggle between Narodism, that nebulous ideology of the democratic bourgeoisie woven of socialistic dreams, and Marxism, the ideology of the proletariat? Nonsense, gentlemen; you only make your selves ridiculous by saying such things, by continuing to regard as an

Lenin, Vladimir. (2004). "A Militant Agreement for the Uprising" (1905); "Tactics of the Proletariat and Tasks of the Moment" (1906); "The Military Programme of the Proletarian Revolution" (1916). Retrieved from http://www.marxists.org/archive/lenin/by-title.htm on 12 SEP 04.

"insult" the Marxist view that Narodism and your "social-revolutionism" are essentially bourgeois-democratic. We shall inevitably argue, differ, and quarrel also in the future revolutionary committees in Russia, but surely we must learn from history. We must not have unexpected, unintelligible, and muddled disputes at a time when action is called for; we must be prepared to argue on fundamental issues, to know the points of departure of each trend, to anticipate possible unity or possible antagonism. The history of revolutionary epochs provides many, all too many, instances of tremendous harm caused by hasty and half-baked experiments in "fighting unity" that sought to lump together the most heterogeneous elements in the committees of the revolutionary people, but managed thereby to achieve *mutual friction and bitter disappointment.*

We want to profit by this lesson of history. Marxism, which to you seems a narrow dogma, is to us the quintessence of this historical lesson and guidance. We see in the *independent*, uncompromisingly Marxist party of the revolutionary proletariat the sole pledge of socialism's victory and the road to victory that is most free from vacillations. We shall never, therefore, not even at the most revolutionary moments, forego the complete independence of the Social-Democratic Party or the complete intransigence of our ideology.

You believe this *rules out* fighting unity? You are mistaken. You can see from the resolution of our Second Congress that we do not renounce agreements for the struggle and in the struggle. In *Vperyod*, No. 4, we stressed the fact that the beginning of the revolution in Russia undoubtedly brings closer the moment when such agreements can be practically implemented.[1] A joint struggle of the revolutionary Social-Democrats and the revolutionary elements of the democratic movement is inevitable and indispensable in the era of the fall of the autocracy. We think that we should serve the cause of future militant agreements better if, instead of indulging in bitter recriminations, we sanely and coolly weighed the conditions under which they would become possible and the likely limits of their "jurisdiction", if one may use the term. We began this work in *Vperyod*, No. 3, in which we undertook a study of the progress of the Socialist-Revolutionary Party from Narodism to Marxism.[2]

"The masses took to arms themselves," *Revolutsionnaya Rossiya* wrote in connection with the Ninth of January. "Sooner or later, without doubt, the question of arming the masses will be decided." "That is when the fusion between terrorism and the mass movement, to which we are striving by word and deed in accordance with the entire spirit of our Party tactics, will be manifested and realised in the most striking manner." (We would remark parenthetically that we would gladly put a question mark after the word "deed"; but let us proceed with the quotation.) "Not so long ago, before our own eyes, these two factors of the movement were separate, and this separateness deprived them of their full force."

What is true is true! Exactly! Intelligentsia terrorism and the mass movement of the working class *were separate, and this separateness deprived them of their full force.* That is precisely what the revolutionary Social-Democrats have been saying all along. For this very reason they have always been opposed to terrorism and to all the vacillations towards terrorism which members of the intellectualist wing of our Party have often displayed.[3] For this reason precisely the old *Iskra* took a position against terrorism when it wrote in issue No. 48: "The terrorist struggle of the *old type* was the riskiest form of revolutionary struggle, and those who engaged in it had the reputation of being resolute, self-sacrificing people. . . . Now, however, when demonstrations develop into acts of open resistance to the government, . . . the old terrorism ceases to be an exceptionally daring method of struggle . . . . Heroism has now come out into the open; the true heroes of our time are now the revolutionaries who lead the popular masses, which are rising against their oppressors. . . . The terrorism of the great French Revolution . . . began on July 14, 1789, with the storming of the Bastille. Its strength was the strength of the revolutionary movement of the people. . . . *That* terrorism was due, not to disappointment in the strength of the mass movement, but, on the contrary, to 'unshakable faith in its strength. . . . The history of *that* terrorism is exceedingly instructive for the Russian revolutionary."[4]

Yes, a thousand times yes! The history of *that* terrorism is instructive in the extreme. Instructive, too, are the quoted passages from *Iskra*, which refer to an epoch of eighteen months ago. These quotations show us, in their full stature, the ideas which even the Socialists-Revolutionaries, under the influence of the revolutionary lessons, would like to arrive at. They remind us of the importance of *faith* in the mass movement; they remind us of revolutionary tenacity, which comes only from high principles and which alone can safeguard us against the "disappointments" induced by a prolonged *apparent* standstill of the movement. Now, after the Ninth of January, there can be no question, on the face of it, of any "disappointments" in the mass movement. But only on the face of it. We should distinguish between the momentary "attraction" evoked by a striking display of mass heroism and the steadfast, reasoned convictions that link inseparably the entire activity of the Party with the movement of the masses, owing to the paramount importance which is attached to the principle of the class struggle. We should bear in mind that the revolutionary movement, however high its level since the Ninth of January, still has many stages to pass through before our socialist and democratic parties will be reconstructed on a new basis in a free Russia. And through all these stages, through all the vicissitudes of the struggle, we must maintain the ties between Social-Democracy and the class struggle of the proletariat unbroken, and we must see to it that they are continuously strengthened and made more secure.

It seems to us, therefore, a gross exaggeration for *Revolutsionnaya Rossiya* to assert that "the pioneers of the armed struggle were swallowed up in the ranks of the roused masses. . . ." This is the desirable future rather than the reality of the moment. The assassination of Sergei in Moscow on February 17 (4),[5] which has been reported by telegraph this very day, is obviously an act of terrorism of the old type. The pioneers of the armed struggle have *not yet* been swallowed up in the ranks of the roused masses. Pioneers with bombs evidently lay in wait for Sergei in Moscow while the masses (in St. Petersburg), without pioneers, without arms, without revolutionary officers, and without a revolutionary staff "flung themselves in implacable fury upon bristling bayonets", as this same *Revolutsionnaya Rossiya* expresses it. The separateness of which we spoke

above *still exists*, and the individual intellectualist terror shows all the more strikingly its inadequacy in face of the growing realisation that "the masses have risen to the stature of individual heroes, that mass heroism has been awakened in them" (*Revolutsionnaya Rossiya*, No. 58). The pioneers should submerge among the masses *in actual fact*, that is, exert their selfless energies in real inseparable connection with the insurgent masses, and proceed with them in the literal, not figurative, symbolical, sense of the word. That this is essential can hardly be open to doubt now. That it is possible has been proved by the Ninth of January and by the deep unrest which is still smouldering among the working-class masses. The fact that this is a new, higher, and more difficult task in comparison with the preceding ones cannot and should not stop us from meeting it at once in a practical way.

Fighting unity between the Social-Democratic Party and the revolutionary-democratic party—the Socialist-Revolutionary Party, might be one way of facilitating the solution of this problem. Such unity will be all the more practicable, the sooner the pioneers of the armed struggle are "swallowed up" in the ranks of the insurgent masses, the more firmly the Socialists-Revolutionaries follow the path which they themselves have charted in the words, "May these beginnings of fusion between revolutionary terrorism and the mass movement grow and strengthen, may the masses act as quickly as possible, armed cap-à-pie with terrorist methods of struggle!" With a view to bringing about speedily such a fighting unity, we take pleasure in publishing the following letter which we have received from Georgi Gapon:

An Open Letter to the Socialist Parties of Russia.

"The bloody January days in St. Petersburg and the rest of Russia have brought the oppressed working class face to face with the autocratic regime, headed by the blood-thirsty tsar. The great Russian revolution has begun. All to whom the people's freedom is really dear must either win or die. Realising the importance of the present historic moment, considering the present state of affairs, and being above all a revolutionary and a man of action, I call upon all the socialist parties of Russia to enter immediately into an agreement among themselves and to proceed to the armed uprising against tsarism. All the forces of every party should be mobilised. All should have a single technical plan of action. Bombs and dynamite, individual and mass terror—every thing that can help the popular uprising. The immediate aim is the over throw of the autocracy, a provisional revolutionary government which will at once amnesty all fighters for political and religious liberties, at once arm the people, and at once convoke a Constituent Assembly on the basis of universal, equal, and direct suffrage by secret ballot. To the task, comrades! Onward to the fight! Let us repeat the slogan of the St. Petersburg workers on the Ninth of January—Freedom or Death! Delay and disorder now are a crime against the people, whose interests you are defending. Having given all of myself to the service of the people, from whom I myself am sprung (the son of a peasant), and having thrown in my lot irrevocably with the struggle against the oppressors and exploiters of the working class, I shall naturally be heart and soul with those who will undertake the real business of actually liberating the proletariat and all the toiling masses from the capitalist yoke and political slavery.

"Georgi Gapon."

On our part, we consider it necessary to state our view of this letter as clearly and as definitely as possible. We consider that the "agreement" it proposes is possible, useful, and essential. We welcome the fact that Gapon speaks explicitly of an "agreement", since only through the preservation of complete independence by each separate party on points of principle and organisation can the efforts at a fighting unity of these parties rest on hope. We must be very careful, in making these endeavours, not to spoil things by vainly trying to lump together heterogeneous elements. We shall inevitably have to *getrennt marschieren* (march separately), but we can *vereint schlagen* (strike together) more than once and particularly now. It would be desirable, from our point of view, to have this agreement embrace the *revolutionary* as well as the socialist parties, for there is nothing socialistic in the immediate aim of the struggle, and we must not confound or allow anyone ever to confound the immediate democratic aims with our ultimate aims of socialist revolution. It would be desirable, and from our point of view *essential*, for the agreement that,

instead of a general call for "*individual* and mass terror", it should be stated openly and definitely that this joint action pursues the aim of a direct and actual *fusion* between terrorism and the uprising of the masses. True, by adding the words "everything that can help the popular uprising", Gapon clearly indicates his desire to make even individual terror subservient to this aim; but this desire, which suggests the idea that we noted in *Revolutsionnaya Rossiya*, No. 58, should be expressed more definitely and embodied in absolutely unequivocal practical decisions. We should like, finally, to point out, regardless of the realisability of the proposed agreement, that Gapon's extra-party stand seems to us to be another negative factor. Obviously, with so rapid a conversion from faith in the tsar and petitioning of the tsar to revolutionary aims, Gapon was not able to evolve for himself immediately a clear revolutionary outlook. This is inevitable, and the faster and broader the revolution develops, the more often will this kind of thing occur. Nevertheless, complete clarity and definiteness in the relations between parties, trends, and shades are absolutely necessary if a temporary agreement among them is to be in any way successful. Clarity and definiteness will be needed at every practical step; they will be the pre-condition for definiteness and the absence of vacillation in the real, *practical* work. The beginning of the revolution in Russia will probably lead to the emergence upon the political arena of many people and perhaps trends representing the view that the slogan "revolution" is, for "men of action", a quite adequate definition of their aims and their methods of operation. Nothing could be more fallacious than this opinion. The extra-party position, which seems higher, or more convenient, or more "diplomatic", is in actual fact *more vague*, more obscure, and inevitably fraught with inconsistencies and vacillations in practical activity. In the interests of the revolution our ideal should by no means be that all parties, all trends and shades of opinion fuse in a revolutionary chaos. On the contrary, the growth and spread of the revolutionary movement, its constantly deeper penetration among the various classes and strata of the people, will inevitably give rise (all to the good) to constantly newer trends and shades. Only full clarity and definiteness in their mutual relations and in their attitude towards the position of the revolutionary proletariat can guarantee maximum success for the revolutionary movement. Only full clarity in mutual relations can guarantee the success of an agreement to achieve a common immediate aim.

This immediate aim is *outlined* quite correctly, in our opinion, in Gapon's letter, namely: (1) the overthrow of the autocracy; (2) a provisional revolutionary government; (3) the immediate amnesty to all fighters for political and religious liberties, including, of course, the right to strike, etc.; (4) the immediate arming of the people; and (5) the immediate convocation of an All-Russian Constituent Assembly on the basis of universal, equal, and direct suffrage by secret ballot. The immediate translation into life by the revolutionary government of complete equality for all citizens and complete political freedom during elections is, of course, taken for granted by Gapon; but this might have been stated explicitly. It would be advisable also to include in the general policy of the provisional government the establishment everywhere of revolutionary peasant committees for the purpose of supporting the democratic revolution and putting into effect its various measures. The success of the revolution depends largely on the revolutionary activity of the peasantry itself, and the various socialist and revolutionary-democratic parties would probably agree on a slogan such as we have suggested.

It is to be hoped that Gapon, whose evolution from views shared by a politically unconscious people to revolutionary views proceeds from such profound personal experiences, will achieve the clear revolutionary outlook that is essential for a man of politics. It is to be hoped that his appeal for a militant agreement for the uprising will meet with success, and that the revolutionary proletariat, side by side with the revolutionary democrats, will strike at the autocracy and overthrow it all the more quickly and surely, and with the least sacrifices.

Endnotes

{1} See pp. 99-100 of this volume—*Ed.*
{2} See pp. 83-89 of this volume.—*Ed.*
{3} Krichevsky in *Rabocheye Dyelo*, No. 10. Martov and Zasulich concerning the shot fired by Lekert. The new-Iskrists generally in a leaflet in connection with the assassination of Plehve.[6]
{4} This article in *Iskra*, written by Plekhanov, dates back to the time when *Iskra* (Nos. 46-51) was edited by Plekhanov and Lenin. Plekhanov had at that time not begun to contemplate the new line of notorious compliance to opportunism.—*Lenin*
{5} The reference is to the assassination of Grand Duke Sergei, Governor-General of Moscow, by the Socialist-Revolutionary terrorists.
{6} On May 5 (18), 1902, the worker Hirsh Lekert made an attempt on the life of the Governor of Wilno, von Wal. Martov and Zasulich hailed this act of individual terror.

The leaflet on the assassination of Plehve mentioned by Lenin refers to leaflet No. 16 "To the Working People", signed by the Editorial Board of the Menshevik *Iskra*, which openly defended the Socialist-Revolutionary tactics of individual terror.

The Tactics of the Proletariat and the Tasks of the Moment

V. I. Lenin

Published: *Vperyod*, No. 4, May 30, 1906. Published according to the *Vperyod* text.

Source: *Lenin Collected Works*, Progress Publishers, 1965, Moscow, Volume 10, pages 490-493.

Translated:

Transcription\Markup: R. Cymbala

Other Formats: Text.

The report we published the other day of the resignation of the Goremykin Ministry is officially denied. But the newspapers which have some access to "reliable" sources of information do not believe this denial. The *Novoye Vremya* campaign in favour of a Cadet Ministry is now more cautious, but is going on. *Novoye Vremya* has discovered a Japanese diplomat who believes that "the Cadet Party is pursuing state aims". It even assures its readers, in an article by Mr. Rozanov, that "the Cadets will not relinquish civilisation even for the revolution", and that "this is all that can be expected at the moment". *Rech* believes that "the resignation of the Goremykin Cabinet can be considered a foregone conclusion, and the only question is, who is to be its successor". In short, the question of a Cadet Ministry is still on the order of the day.

The Cadets realise this, and perhaps something more. They have come to a dead stop and are "standing rigid" like setters. They are clutching with both hands at even the shadow of support from the left that would help them to execute their plans. It is significant that *Rech*, the chief organ of the Cadet Party, devoted the leading article in its last issue to the question of the Social-Democrats' attitude towards the idea of a Cadet Ministry. We publish elsewhere the full text of that article as a most instructive sign of the times.

The authors of the article sum up their main idea as follows: to create "common ground on which the liberation movement could take its stand with complete unanimity, *without distinction of shades*". This, in fact, is the principal aim of the Cadets' entire policy. Moreover, this, in fact, is the principal aim of all the liberal-bourgeois policy in the Russian revolution in general. To eliminate the "different shades" in the liberation movement means eliminating the difference

Lenin, Vladimir. (2004). "A Militant Agreement for the Uprising" (1905); "Tactics of the Proletariat and Tasks of the Moment" (1906); "The Military Programme of the Proletarian Revolution" (1916). Retrieved from http://www.marxists.org/archive/lenin/by-title.htm on 12 SEP 04.

in the democratic demands of the bourgeoisie, the peasantry and the proletariat. It means recognising with "complete unanimity" the liberal bourgeoisie as the medium of expression and champion of the aspirations of the whole liberation movement. It means converting the proletariat into a blind tool of the liberal bourgeoisie. But since everybody knows that the supreme political ideal of the liberal bourgeoisie—dictated by its most pro found class interests—is a deal with the old authority, we may formulate our last thesis differently. We can say that the bourgeois *Rech* wants to convert the proletariat into a blind accessory to the deal that the liberals want to make with the old authority. But the main target against which this deal will be directed will be the proletariat, and the next, of course, the revolutionary peasantry.

This is what a Cadet Ministry really means. The recent conflict in the State Duma over the question of instituting local land committees threw a glaring light on Cadet policy. The committees should have been the local authority, while the Ministry is to be the central authority; but in substance the Cadets' policy remains unchanged, always and everywhere. They are opposed to the election of local committees by universal suffrage: they are in favour of "equal representation of the landlords and the peasants, under the supervision of the old authorities". They have been *compelled* to admit this, against their own will, because for a long time they *concealed the truth*, tried to befog the issue and asserted that, "in general", they were whole heartedly in favour both of local land committees and of universal suffrage. Similarly, the Cadets are opposed to the convocation of a constituent assembly: they are in favour of a Cadet Ministry to be appointed by the supreme authority. Such a Ministry, as the instrument of central authority, will be quite on a par with local committees established on the vaunted principle of equal representation, etc.

The tactics the proletariat must adopt in face of this Cadet policy are clear. The proletariat must ruthlessly expose the true meaning of this policy, tolerating no ambiguities, no attempts to obscure the political consciousness of the workers and peasants. The proletariat must fully use all the vacillations in the policy of the "powers that be" and of the would-be "sharers of power" to enlarge and strengthen *its own* class organisation, and to strengthen its contacts with the revolutionary peasantry as the only class that is capable of carrying the liberation movement *beyond* the Cadet "darn", beyond a Cadet deal with the old authorities.

But should not the proletariat *support* the demand of the liberal bourgeoisie that the supreme authority should appoint a Cadet Ministry? Is it not the duty of the proletariat to do so since the appointment of a Cadet Ministry would facilitate the struggle for freedom and for socialism?

No, such a step would be a gross mistake, and *betrayal* of the interests of the proletariat. It would mean sacrificing the fundamental interests of the proletariat in the revolution for the sake of a momentary success. It would mean chasing a shadow and advising the proletariat to "lay down its arms", without even the slightest *real* guarantee that its struggle will *really* be facilitated. It would be the worst kind of opportunism.

The appointment of a Cadet Ministry by the supreme authority will not shake the foundations of the old authorities in the least. It will not necessarily change the real alignment of forces in favour of the truly revolutionary classes. Such a "reform" will not eliminate the struggle between the people and the old authorities in the least. There have been cases in the history of revolutions where such liberal Ministries appointed by the old authorities (for example, in Germany in 1848) served only as a screen for autocracy, and did more to stamp out the revolution than many a bureaucratic Ministry.

The Russian proletariat has no reason to fear a Cadet Ministry, which, at all events, will help the people to realise the true nature of the Cadets; but it must under no circumstances support the appointment of such a Ministry, for, in essence, this is a most ambiguous, sinister and treacherous measure.

Since the Duma was not swept away, it was to the proletariat's advantage that the Cadets obtained a majority in the elections. They will "exhaust" themselves much sooner than they would have done had they been in the minority. But the proletariat refused to render the Cadets any support during the elections, and the Unity

Congress of the R.S.D.L.P. endorsed this decision by prohibiting all blocs (agreements, alliances) with other parties. A Cadet Ministry will be to the proletariat's advantage *in the sense* that, if one were formed, the Cadets would the sooner "spend" themselves, become "played out", "winded", and reveal themselves in their true colours. But the proletariat will never support a *deal* between the bourgeoisie and Trepov for the purpose of carving up the people's freedom.

The only real way of "supporting" the liberation movement and really developing it is to stimulate the growth of the political and industrial organisations of the proletariat and to strengthen its ties with the revolutionary peasantry. This alone will really sap the strength of the old authority and prepare for its downfall. The bargaining of the Cadets is a dubious game. It would be both useless to support it, with a view to achieving some truly lasting gains for the revolution, and harmful to do so, because of the effect it would have on the development of the political consciousness, solidarity and organisation of the revolutionary classes.

The Military Programme of the Proletarian Revolution

V. I. Lenin

Written: September 1916

Source: *Collected Works*, Volume 23, p. 77-87

Publisher: Progress Publishers

First Published: *Jugend-Internationale* Magazine, Nos. 9 and 10, September and October 1917.

I

Among the Dutch, Scandinavian and Swiss revolutionary Social-Democrats who are combating the social-chauvinist lies about "defense of the fatherland" in the present imperialist war, there have been voices in favor of replacing the old Social-Democratic minimum-programme demand for a "militia", or "the armed nation," by a new demand: "disarmament." The *Jugend-Internationale* [1] has inaugurated a discussion on this issue and published, in No. 3, an editorial supporting disarmament. There is also, we regret to note, a concession to the "disarmament" idea in R. Grimm's latest theses. [2] Discussions have been started in the periodicals *Neue Leben* [3] and *Vorbote*.

Let us take a closer look at the position of the disarmament advocates.

I

Their principal argument is that the disarmament demand is the clearest, most decisive, most consistent expression of the struggle against all militarism and against all war.

But in this principal argument lies the disarmament advocates' principal error. Socialists cannot, without ceasing to be socialists, be opposed to all war.

> *Discussion presented by an unknown commentator from www.marxists.org:*
>
> This article (in a letter Lenin calls it "Entwaffnung"— "On Disarmament") was written in German and meant for publication in the Swiss, Swedish and Norwegian Left Social-Democratic press. However, it was not published at the time. Shortly afterwards Lenin re-edited it somewhat for publication in Russian.
>
> The original, German text appeared in *Jugend-Internationale*, organ of the International League of Socialist Youth Organisation, titled, "Das Militär programm der proletarischen Revolution".

Lenin, Vladimir. (2004). "A Militant Agreement for the Uprising" (1905); "Tactics of the Proletariat and Tasks of the Moment" (1906); "The Military Programme of the Proletarian Revolution" (1916). Retrieved from http://www.marxists.org/archive/lenin/by-title.htm on 12 SEP 04.

Firstly, socialists have never been, nor can they ever be, opposed to revolutionary wars. The bourgeoisie of the imperialist "Great" Powers has become thoroughly reactionary, and the war *this* bourgeoisie is now waging we regard as a reactionary, slave-owners' and criminal war. But what about a war *against* this bourgeoisie? A war, for instance, waged by peoples oppressed by and dependent upon this bourgeoisie, or by colonial peoples, for liberation? In Section 5 of the *Internationale* group these we read: "National wars are no longer possible in the era of this unbridled imperialism." That is obviously wrong.

The history of the 20th century, this century of "unbridled imperialism," is replete with colonial wars. But what we Europeans, the imperialist oppressors of the majority of the world's peoples, with our habitual, despicable European chauvinism, call "colonial wars" are often national wars, or national rebellions of these oppressed peoples. One of the main features of imperialism is that it accelerates capitalist development in the most backward countries, and thereby extends and intensifies the struggle against national oppression. That is a fact, and from it inevitably follows that imperialism must often give rise to national wars. *Junius*, who defends the above-quoted "theses" in her pamphlet, says that in the imperialist era every national war against an imperialist Great Power leads to intervention of a rival imperialist Great Power. Every national war is this turned into an imperialist war. But that argument is wrong, too. This *can* happen, but does not always happen. Many colonial wars between 1900 and 1914 did not follow that course. And it would be simply ridiculous to declare, for instance, that after the present war, if it ends in the utter exhaustion of all the belligerents, "there can be no" national, progress, revolutionary wars "of any kind", wages, say, by China in alliance with India, Persia, Siam, etc., against the Great Powers.

To deny all possibility of national wars under imperialism is wrong in theory, obviously mistaken historically, and tantamount to European chauvinism in practice: we who belong to nations that oppress hundreds of millions in Europe, Africa, Asia, etc., are invited to tell the oppressed peoples that it is "impossible" for them to wage war against "our" nations!

Secondly, civil war is just as much a war as any other. He who accepts the class struggle cannot fail to accept civil wars, which in every class society are the natural, and under certain conditions inevitable, continuation, development and intensification of the class struggle. That has been confirmed by every great revolution. To repudiate civil war, or to forget about it, is to fall into extreme opportunism and renounce the socialist revolution.

Thirdly, the victory of socialism in one country does not at one stroke eliminate all wars in general. On the contrary, it presupposes wars. The development of capitalism proceeds extremely unevenly in different countries. It cannot be otherwise under commodity production. From this it follows irrefutably that socialism cannot achieve victory simultaneously *in all* countries. It will achieve victory first in one or several countries, while the others will for some time remain bourgeois or pre-bourgeois. This is bound to create not only friction, but a direct attempt on the part of the bourgeoisie of other countries to crush the socialist state's victorious proletariat. In such cases, a war on our part would be a legitimate and just war. It would be a war for socialism, for the liberation of other nations from the bourgeoisie. Engels was perfectly right when, in his letter to Kautsky of September 12, 1882, he clearly stated that it was possible for *already victorious* socialism to wage "defensive wars". What he had in mind was defense of the victorious proletariat against the bourgeoisie of other countries.

Only after we have overthrown, finally vanquished and expropriated the bourgeoisie of the whole world, and not merely in one country, will wars become impossible. And from a scientific point of view it would be utterly wrong—and utterly unrevolutionary—for us to evade or gloss over the most important things: crushing the resistance of the bourgeoisie —the most difficult task, and one demanding the greatest amount of fighting, in the *transition* to socialism. The "social" parsons and opportunists are always ready to build dreams of future peaceful socialism. But the very thing that distinguishes them from revolutionary Social-Democrats is that they refuse to think about and reflect on the fierce class struggle and class *wars* needed to achieve that beautiful future.

We must not allow ourselves to be led astray by words. The term "defense of the fatherland", for instance, is hateful to many because both avowed opportunists and Kautskyites use it to cover up and gloss over the bourgeois lie about the *present* predatory war. This is a fact. But it does not follow that we must no longer see through to the meaning of political slogans. To accept "defense of the fatherland" in the present war is no more nor less than to accept it as a "just" war, a war in the interests of the proletariat—no more nor less, we repeat, because invasions may occur in any war. It would be sheer folly to repudiate "defense of the fatherland" *on the part* of oppressed nations in their wars *against* the imperialist Great Powers, or on the part of a victorious proletariat in *its* war against some Galliffet of a bourgeois state.

Theoretically, it would be absolutely wrong to forget that every war is but the continuation of policy by other means. The present imperialist war is the continuation of the imperialist policies of two groups of Great Powers, and these policies were engendered and fostered by the sum total of the relationships of the imperialist era. But this very era must also necessarily engender and foster policies of struggle against national oppression and of proletarian struggle against the bourgeoisie and, consequently, also the possibility and inevitability; first, of revolutionary national rebellions and wars; second, of proletarian wars and rebellions *against* the bourgeoisie; and, third, of a combination of both kinds of revolutionary war, etc.

Footnotes

[1] *Jugend-Internationale* (The Youth International) —Organ of the International League of Socialist Youth Organizations, which was associated with the Zimmerwald Left. It was published from September 1915 to May 1918 in Zurich.

[2] The reference is to Robert Grimm's these on the war question published in the *Grutlianer* Nos. 162 and 164, July 1916.

[3] *Neue Leben*(New Life)—A monthly journal of the Swiss Social-Democratic Party published in Berne from January 1915 to December 1917. It expressed the views of the Zimmerwald Right and early in 1917 took up a social-chauvinist position.

II

To this must be added the following general consideration.

An oppressed class which does not strive to learn to use arms, to acquire arms, only deserves to be treated like slaves. We cannot, unless we have become bourgeois pacifists or opportunists, forget that we are living in a class society from which there is no way out, nor can there be, save through the class struggle. In every class society, whether based on slavery, serfdom, or, as at present, wage-labor, the oppressor class is always armed. Not only the modern standing army, but even the modern militia—and even in the most democratic bourgeois republics, Switzerland, for instance—represent the bourgeoisie armed *against* the proletariat. That is such an elementary truth that it is hardly necessary to dwell upon it. Suffice it to point to the use of troops against strikers in all capitalist countries.

A bourgeoisie armed against the proletariat is one of the biggest fundamental and cardinal facts of modern capitalist society. And in face of this fact, revolutionary Social-Democrats are urged to "demand" "disarmament"! That is tantamount of complete abandonment of the class-struggle point of view, to renunciation of all thought of revolution. Our slogan must be: arming of the proletariat to defeat, expropriate and disarm the bourgeoisie. These are the only tactics possible for a revolutionary class, tactics that follow logically from, and are dictated by, the whole *objective development* of capitalist militarism. Only *after* the proletariat has disarmed the bourgeoisie will it be able, without betraying its world-historic mission, to consign all armaments to the scrap-heap. And the proletariat will undoubtedly do this, but *only when this condition has been fulfilled, certainly not before.*

If the present war rouses among the reactionary Christian socialists, among the whimpering petty bourgeoisie, *only* horror and fright, only aversion to all use of arms, to bloodshed, death, etc., then we must say: Capitalist society is and has always been *horror without end.* If this most reactionary of all wars is now preparing for that society an *end to horror*, we have no reason to fall into despair. But the disarmament "demand", or more correctly, the dream of disarmament, is, objectively, nothing but an expression of despair at a time when, as everyone can see, the bourgeoisie itself is paving the way for the only legitimate and revolutionary war—civil war against the imperialist bourgeoisie.

A lifeless theory, some might say, but we would remind them of two world-historical facts: the role of the trusts and the employment of women in industry, on the one hand, and the Paris Commune of 1871 and the December 1905 uprising in Russia, on the other.

The bourgeoisie makes it its business to promote trusts, drive women and children into the factories, subject them to corruption and suffering, condemn them to extreme poverty. We do not "demand" such development, we do not "support" it. We fight it. But *how* do we fight? We explain that trusts and the employment of women in industry are progressive. We do not want a return to the handicraft system, pre-monopoly capitalism, domestic drudgery for women. Forward through the trusts, etc., and beyond them to socialism!

With the necessary changes that arguments is applicable also to the present militarization of the population. Today the imperialist bourgeoisie militarizes the youth as well as the adults; tomorrow, it may begin militarizing the women. Our attitude should be: All the better! Full speed ahead! For the faster we move, the nearer shall we be to the armed uprising against capitalism. How can Social-Democrats give way to fear of the militarization of the youth, etc., if they have not forgotten the example of the Paris Commune? This is not a "lifeless theory" or a dream. It is a fact. And it would be a sorry state of affairs indeed if, all the economic and political facts notwithstanding, Social-Democrats began to doubt that the imperialist era and imperialist wars must inevitably bring about a repetition of such facts.

A certain bourgeois observer of the Paris Commune, writing to an English newspaper in May 1871, said: "If the French nation consisted entirely of women, what a terrible nation it would be!" Woman and teenage children fought in the Paris Commune side by side with the men. It will be no different in the coming battles for the overthrow of the bourgeoisie. Proletarian women will not look on passively as poorly armed or unarmed workers are shot down by the well-armed forces of the bourgeoisie. They will take to arms, as they did in 1871, and from the cowed nations of today—or more correctly, from the present-day labor movement, disorganized more by the opportunists than by the governments—there will undoubtedly arise, sooner or later, but with absolute certainty, an international league of the "terrible nations" of the revolutionary proletariat.

The whole of social life is now being militarized. Imperialism is a fierce struggle of the Great Powers for the division and redivision of the world. It is therefore bound to lead to further militarization in all countries, even in neutral and small ones. How will proletarian women oppose this? Only by cursing all war and everything military, only be demanding disarmament? The women of an oppressed and really revolutionary class will never accept that shameful role. They will say to their sons: "You will soon be grown up. You will be given a gun. Take it and learn the military art properly. The proletarians need this knowledge not to shoot your brothers, the workers of other countries, as is being done in the present war, and as the traitors to socialism are telling you to do. They need it to fight the bourgeoisie of their own country, to put an end to exploitation, poverty and war, and not by pious wishes, but by defeating and disarming the bourgeoisie."

If we are to shun such propaganda, precisely such propaganda, in connection with the present war, then we had better stop using fine words about international revolutionary Social-Democracy, the socialist revolution and war against war.

III

The disarmament advocates object to the "armed nation" clause in the programme also because it more easily leads, they allege, to concessions to opportunism. The cardinal point, namely, the relation of disarmament to the class struggle and to the social revolution, we have examined above. We shall now examine the relation between the disarmament demand and opportunism. One of the chief reasons why it is unacceptable is precisely that, together with the illusions it creates, it inevitably weakens and devitalizes our struggle against opportunism.

Undoubtedly, this struggle is the main, immediate question now confusing the International. Struggle against imperialism that is not closely linked with the struggle against opportunism is either an empty phrase or a fraud. One of the main defects of Zimmerwald and Kienthal [4]—on the main reasons why these embryos of the Third International may possibly end in a fiasco—is that the question of fighting opportunism was not even raised openly, let alone solved in the sense of proclaiming the need to break with the opportunists. Opportunism has triumphed—temporarily—in the European labor movement. Its two main shades are apparent in all the big countries: first, the avowed, cynical, and therefore less dangerous social-imperialism of Messrs. Plekhanov, Scheidemann, Legien, Albert Thomas and Sembat, Vandervelde, Hyndman, Henderson, et al,; second, the concealed, Kautskyite opportunism: Kautsky-Haase and the social-Democratic Labor Group in Germany [5]; Longuet, Pressemane, Mayeras, et al., in France; Ramsay MacDonald and the other leaders of the Independent Labor Party in England; Martov, Chkheidze, et al., in Russia; Treves and the other so-called Left reformists in Italy.

Avowed opportunism is openly and directly opposed to revolution and to incipient revolutionary movements and outbursts. It is in direct alliance with the governments, varied as the forms of this alliance may be—from accepting ministerial posts to participation in the war industries committees (in Russia). [6] The masked opportunists, the Kautskyites, are much more harmful and dangerous to the labor movement, because they hide their advocacy of alliance with the former under a cloak of plausible, pseudo-"Marxist" catchwords and pacifist slogans. The fight against both these forms of prevailing opportunism must be conducted in *all* fields of proletarian politics: parliament, the trade unions, strikes, the armed forces, etc. The main distinguishing feature of *both* these forms of prevailing opportunism is the concrete question of the *connection between the present war and revolution, and the other concrete questions of revolution*, are hushed up, concealed, or treated with an eye to police prohibitions. And this despite the fact that before the war the connection between *this* impending war and the proletarian revolution was empha-

sized innumerable times, both unofficially and officially in the Basle Manifesto. [7] The main defect of the disarmament demand is its evasion of all the concrete questions of revolution. Or do the advocates of disarmament stand for an altogether new kind of revolution, unarmed revolution?

To proceed. We are by no means opposed to the fight for reforms. And we do not wish to ignore the sad possibility—if the worst comes to the worst—of mankind going through a second imperialist war, if revolution does not come out of the present war, in spite of our efforts. We favor a programme of reforms directed *also* against the opportunists. They would be only too glad if we left the struggle for reforms entirely to them and sought escape from sad reality in a nebulous "disarmament" fantasy. "Disarmament" means simply running away from unpleasant reality, not fighting it.

In such a programme, we would say something like this: "To accept the defense of the fatherland slogan in the 1914-16 imperialist war is to corrupt the labor movement with the aid of a bourgeois lie." Such a concrete reply to a concrete question would be more correct theoretically, much more useful to the proletariat and more unbearable to the opportunists, than the disarmament demand and repudiation of "all and any" defense of the fatherland. And we would add: "The bourgeoisie of all the imperialist Great Powers—England, France, Germany, Austria, Russia, Japan, the United States—has become so reactionary and so intent on world domination, that *any* war waged by *the bourgeoisie of those* countries is bound to be reactionary. The proletariat must not only oppose all such wars, but must also wish for the defeat for revolutionary insurrection, if an insurrection to prevent the war proves unsuccessful."

On the question of a militia, we should say: We are not in favor of a bourgeois militia; we are in favor only of a proletarian militia. Therefore, "not a penny, not a man", not only for a standing army, but even for a bourgeois militia, even in countries like the United States, or Switzerland, Norway, etc. The more so that in the freest republican countries (e.g., Switzerland) we see that the militia is being increasingly Prussianized, particularly in 1907 and 1911, and prostituted by being used against strikers. We can demand popular election of officers, abolition of all military law, equal rights for foreign and native-born workers (a point particularly important for those imperialist states which, like Switzerland, are more and more blatantly exploiting larger numbers of foreign workers, while denying them all rights). Further, we can demand the right of every hundred, say, inhabitants of a given country to form voluntary military-training associations, with free election of instructors paid by the state, etc. Only under these conditions could the proletariat acquire military training for *itself* and not for its slaveowners; and the need for such training is imperatively dictated by the interests of the proletariat. The Russian revolution showed that every success of the revolutionary movement, even a partial success like the seizure of a certain city, a certain factory town, or winning over a certain section of the army, inevitably *compels* the victorious proletariat to carry out just such a programme.

Lastly, it stands to reason that opportunism can never be defeated by mere programmes; it can only be defeated by deeds. The greatest, and fatal, error of the bankrupt Second International was that its words did not correspond to its deeds, that it cultivated the habit of hypocritical and unscrupulous revolutionary phrase-mongering (note the present attitude of Kautsky and Co. towards the Basle Manifesto). Disarmament as a social idea—i.e., an idea that springs from, and can affect, a certain social environment, and is not the invention of some crackpot—springs, evidently, from the peculiar "tranquil" conditions prevailing, by way of exception, in certain small states, which have for a fairly long time stood aside from the world's path of war and bloodshed, and hope to remain in that way. To be convinced of this, we have only to consider the arguments advanced, for instance, by the Norwegian advocates of disarmament. "We are a small country," they say. "Our army is small; there is nothing we can do against the Great Powers [and, consequently, nothing we can do to resist forcible involvement in an imperialist *alliance* with one or the other Great Power group] .... We want to be left in peace in our backwoods and continue our backwoods politics, demand disarmament, compulsory arbitration, permanent neutrality, etc." ("permanent" after the Belgian fashion, no doubt?).

The petty striving of petty states to hold aloof, the petty-bourgeois desire to keep as far away as possible from the great battles of world history, to take advantage of one's relatively monopolistic position in order to remain in hidebound passivity—this is the *objective* social environment which may ensure the disarmament idea a certain degree of success and a certain degree of popularity in some small states. That striving is, of course, reactionary and is based entirely on illusions, for, in one way or another, imperialism draws the small states into the vortex of world economy and world politics.

In Switzerland, for instance, the imperialist environment objectively prescribes *two* courses to the labor movement: the opportunists, in alliance with the bourgeoisie, are seeking to turn the country into a republican-democratic monopolistic federation that would thrive on profits from imperialist bourgeois tourists, and to make this "tranquil" monopolistic position as profitable and as tranquil as possible.

The genuine Swiss Social-Democrats are striving to use Switzerland's relative freedom and her "international" position to help the victory of the close alliance of the revolutionary elements in the European workers' parties. Switzerland, than God, does not have "a separate language of her own", but uses three world languages, the three languages spoken in the adjacent belligerent countries.

If 20,000 Swiss party members were to pay a weekly levy of two centimes as a sort of "extra war tax", we would have 20,000 francs per annum, a sum more than sufficient periodically to publish in three languages and distribute among the workers and soldiers of the belligerent countries—in spite of the bans imposed by the general staffs—all the truthful evidence about the incipient revolt of the workers, their fraternizing in the trenches, their hope that the weapons will be used for revolutionary struggle against the imperialist bourgeoisie of their "own" countries, etc.

That is not new. It is being done by the best papers, like *La Sentinelle*, [8] *Volksrecht*, [9] and the *Berner Tagwacht*, [10] although, unfortunately, on an inadequate scale. Only through such activity can the splendid decision of the Aarau Party Congress [11] become something more than merely a splendid decision.

The question that interests us now is: Does the disarmament demand correspond to this revolutionary trend among the Swiss Social-Democrats? It obviously does not. Objectively, disarmament is an extremely national, a specifically national programme of small states. it is certainly not the international programme of international revolutionary Social-Democracy.

N. Lenin

Footnotes

[4] Lenin is referring to the international socialist conferences at Zimmerwald and Kienthal.

The first *Zimmerwald Conference* met on September 5-8 1915 and was attended by 38 delegates from 11 European countries. Lenin headed the RSDLP Central Committee delegation.

The Conference adopted the Manifesto "To the European Proletariat", in which, at the insistence of Lenin and the Left Social-Democrats, several basic propositions of revolutionary Marxism were included. It also adopted a joint declaration by the German and French delegations, a message of sympathy with war victims and fighters persecuted for their political activities, and elected the International Socialist Committee (ISC).

The Zimmerwald Left group was formed at this Conference. It included representatives of the RSDLP Central Committee headed by Lenin, the Regional Executives of the Social-Democratic Party of the Kingdom of Poland and Lithuania, the Central Committee of the Lettish Social Democratic Party, the Swedish Left (Karl Zeth Hoglund), the Norwegian Left (Ture Nerman), the Swiss Left (Fritz Platten), and the "International Socialists of Germany" group (Julius Borchardt). The Zimmerwald Left waged an active struggle against the Centrist majority at the Conference. But it was only the Bolsheviks among the Left who advocated a fully consistent policy.

The second *International Conference* was held at Kienthal, a village near Berne, between April 24 and 30 1916. It was attended by 43 delegates from 10 countries. The RSDLP Central Committee was represented by Lenin and two other delegates.

The Conference discussed the following questions:

1) the struggle to end the war;

2) attitude of the proletariat on the peace issue;
3) agitation and propaganda;
4) parliamentary activity;
5) mass struggle;
6) convocation of the International Socialist Bureau.

Led by Lenin, the Zimmerwald Left was much stronger at Kienthal than at the earlier Zimmerwald Conference. At Kienthal, it united 12 delegates and some of its proposals obtained as many as 20 votes, or nearly half the total. This was indicative of how the internationalism in the world labor movement had changed in favor of internationalism.

The Conference adopted a Manifesto "To the Peoples Suffering Ruination and Death" and a resolution criticizing pacifism and the International Socialist Bureau. Lenin regarded the Conference decisions as a further step in uniting the internationalist forces against the imperialist war.

The Zimmerwald and Kienthal conferences helped to unite the Left elements in the West-European Social-Democratic movement on the principles of Marxism-Leninism. Subsequently these Left elements took an active part in founding communist parties in their countries and in organizing the Third, Communist International.

[5] *The Social-Democratic Labor Group*—An organization of German Centrists founded in march 1916 by Reichstag members who had broken with the Social-Democratic Reichstag group. It had the support of the majority of the Berlin organization and became the backbone of the Independent Social-Democratic Party of Germany, founded in April 1917. The new party sought to justify avowed social-chauvinists and advocated preservation of unity with them.

[6] The *war industries committees* were established in Russia in May 1915 by the imperialist bourgeoisie to help the tsarist government in the prosecution of the war. The Central War Industry Committee was headed by one of Russia's biggest capitalists, Guchkov, leader of the Octobrists. In an attempt to bring the workers under their influence and foster chauvinist sentiments, the bourgeoisie decided to organize "workers' groups" in these committees, thereby creating the impression that a "class peace" had been achieved in Russia between the bourgeoisie and the proletariat. The Bolsheviks declared a boycott of the committees and successfully carried it out with the support of the majority of workers.

As a result of Bolshevik propaganda, elections to the "workers' groups" were held only in 70 out of a total of 239 regional and local committees, and workers' representatives were elected only in 36 of them.

[7] The *Basle Manifesto*—A manifesto on the war issue. Was adopted at the extraordinary International Socialist Congress held in Basle on November 24-25 1912.

[8] *La Sentinelle*—A Newspaper, organ of the Swiss Social-Democratic organization of Neuchatel Canton (Switzerland), published at La Chaux-de-Fonds from 1890 to 1906 and resumed in 1910. During the First World War it followed an internationalist policy.

[9] *Volksrecht* (People's Right)—A daily paper, organ of the Swiss Social-Democratic Party founded in Zurich in 1898. During the First World War it published articles by Left Zimmerwaldists.

[10] *Berner Tagwacht* (Berne Guardian)—A Social-Democratic newspaper founded in Berne in 1893. It published articles by Karl Liebknecht, Franz Mehrin and other Social-Democrats in the early days of the First World War. In 1917, it came out in open support of the social-chauvinists.

[11] The Aarau Congress of the Swiss Social-Democratic Party met on November 20-21 1915. The central issue was the party's attitude towards the Zimmerwald internationalist groups, and the struggle developed between the three following trends: 1) anti-Zimmerwaldists; 2) supporters of the Zimmerwald Right; and 3) supporters of the Zimmerwald Left.

Robert Grimm tabled a resolution urging the party to affiliate with the Zimmerwald group and endorse the political programme of the Zimmerwald Right. The Left forces, in an amendment moved by the Lausanne branch, called for mass revolutionary struggle against the war, declaring that only a victorious proletarian revolution could put an end to the imperialist war. Under Grimm's pressure, the amendment was withdrawn, but it was again proposed by M. M. Kharitonov, a Bolshevik with the right to vote delegated by one of the party's branches. Out of tactical considerations, Grimm and his supporters were obliged to approve the amendment and it was carried by 258 votes to 141.

The Wind of Revolution

Robert Taber

The wind of revolution. Popular will as the key to strategy. The confrontation of the haves and the have-nots. Fallacies of counter-insurgency. Guerrilla war as an extension of politics. Cracks in the armour of the modern state.

'They just lured us through a trap-door, closed it on our behinds, and let us have it,' [U.S. Army Lt. William Richter] later explained [an ambush in which 51 South Vietnamese Rangers were killed]. 'We were caught flat-footed and cut to pieces.'

'The same damn story,' a senior U.S. officer in Saigon grumbled. Different only in detail or degree, similar stories unfold week after week in South Vietnam. Posts are raided, officials assassinated, hamlets burned, towns assaulted. And they all add up to one gloomy conclusion: despite inferior fire power and strength, the communists are beating a South Vietnamese force of more than 400,000 soldiers backed up by 17,000 American advisors and nearly two million dollars a day in U.S. aid.

> Stanley Karnow, 'This is Our Enemy'
> *Saturday Evening Post,* 22 August 1964

Nationwide, the pacification program is at a standstill, and Viet Cong roam freely in areas once classed as secure . . . Even if another 40,000 to 50,000 troops were added to the 525,000 already planned, the U.S. still wouldn't have enough to dominate all of the South Vietnamese countryside, some military analysts claim.

A tough, veteran U.S. official working in a typical province in the Mekong Delta estimates it would take a full U.S. division (about 15,000 men) eight months to find and destroy the fewer than 4,000 Viet Cong thought to be operating there. Right now there is less than one full U.S. division to help police all 16 heavily populated provinces in the Delta. To do a proper job all over the country, this official thinks a million U.S. troops would be needed.

> *Wall Street Journal,* 8 March 1968

The excerpts above have been taken from typical reports nearly four years apart, the first in 1964, the second in 1968. The years pass, the investment in men and dollars mounts, but nothing changes, except the scale of the incredible destruction. The 'nearly two million dollars a day' of the 1964 report had become, by 1968, more than *three million an hour.* The 17,000 'advisers' had become more than half a million regular troops, with still more on the way. But journalists and military men, staring into the face of certain defeat, continued to talk about what it might take to 'do a *proper* job' in Vietnam.

NIXON SAYS WAR HURTS ECONOMY . . . DEFENCE PROFITS TOO HIGH, CONGRESS IS TOLD. . . . With each new crisis bringing a spate of headlines, reports,

---

Taber, Robert. (1970). "The Wind of Revolution." *The War of the Flea* (pp. 14-33). London: Paladin.

144 TABER

analyses, reappraisals, the American war in South-east Asia seemed likely to stand as the best-documented defeat in history. The nature of the dilemma confronting the United States in 1968, unchanged from the very inception of the war, was still only dimly perceived. Theodore Sorenson, adviser and aide to the assassinated President John F. Kennedy, defined it better than most when he likened the U.S. position to 'a six-sided box that we did not intend to make and cannot seem to break'. He described the 'six sides' in three sentences:

> Our worldwide military primacy cannot produce a victory, and our worldwide political primacy cannot permit a withdrawal. We are unable to transfer our will to the South Vietnamese and unable to break the will of the North Vietnamese. (Read: Viet Cong.)
> Any serious escalation would risk Chinese or Soviet intervention, and any serious negotiations would risk a Communist South Vietnam.*

That the United States was deep in a military-political morass had long been clear. '. . . this cruel and ugly war that nobody wants,' lamented the *New York Times;* and from *Newsweek:* 'Only the chronic optimist can now see the "light at the end of the tunnel" that used to illustrate the rhetoric of the military briefing officers.'

What continued to be lacking was any understanding of the *significance* of the defeat, of the true nature of its causes, and of the situation and strategy that had brought it about. Military and political analysts could continue to speak knowledgeably of the necessity of destroying the Viet Cong 'infrastructure' and of instilling in the South Vietnamese people 'the will to fight', a prescription relevant only to the Washington myth of a nation being somehow 'taken over' by aliens.

Unacknowledged, or perhaps not even understood, was the simple fact that the American adventure in South-east Asia had been *foredoomed.* And this is to say, condemned from the start by two principal factors that no insight or effect could remedy:

---

* *New York Times,* 4 March 1968.

1. Inherent contradictions – between stated U.S. war aims and actual goals, between necessary means and desired ends, between domestic political and economic realities and the international posture and ambitions of the United States (and these are to name only a few of the more obvious conflicts).
2. By an opposing strategy *based* on the exploitation of such contradictions, and by the existence of a strong and experienced adversary, ideally positioned to exploit them.

Analysis of the debacle brings us to a single central figure: not invaders, not armies, not the alien hordes of the State Department's imagination, but simply – the *guerrilla fighter.* When we discuss Vietnam we are studying the latest and most complete and detailed text existent on *la guerra de guerrillas,* the war of small bands, fought by Spanish partisans against Napoleon's invading armies, refined in our time to a politico-military science – part Marxist-Leninist social theory, part tactical innovation – that is changing the power relationships of the world we live in, and in the process has forced the professional military everywhere to revise their most fundamental concepts of the very nature of war.

Guerrilla war, *the strategy of contradictions,* has become the political phenomenon of the twentieth century, the visible wind of revolution, stirring hope and fear on three continents. At this writing, it is being waged in a score of countries, from Angola to Iraq and from Thailand to the Colombian and Guatemalan highlands. With the American involvement in Vietnam, it became the first concern of the Pentagon, the Central Intelligence Agency, the National Security Council, the White House. Yet little has been learned about it save that, in Mao's phrase, 'one spark can start a prairie fire'. The lesson of Cuba led to prompt military intervention in Santo Domingo: a stitch in time, but would it hold? Guerrilla war was strangled in its infancy and Che Guevara murdered there; but did he die? Fresh sparks are glowing, and Che dead proves even more potent than Che alive, a heroic figure giving vitality to unconquerable ideas, raising banners of insurrection even in the western capitals, where his portrait is lifted with the red and the black, behind him marching the cadres of the guerrilla wars to come. Fire-blackened cities showed that the United States itself, heartland of empire, is not immune. Yesterday military aircraft were bombing the slums of Saigon: tomorrow it could be Harlem, Newark, Chicago, Cincinnati, Cleveland, Watts.

In the world at large guerrilla war is destroying the last vestiges of feudalism and of the old colonialism, liberating the masses of the poor from the oppression of the privileged landowning and mercantile classes, from the oligarchies and the military juntas. Its full vigour now is turned against the new imperialism – the economic, political and military domination of the weak, industrially backward nations by the rich, the powerful, the technologically advanced, the grand alliance of industrial wealth and military might over which the United States of America holds hegemony.

Viewed from one standpoint, it is a potent weapon, a sword of national liberation and social justice; viewed from another, it is a subversive and sinister process, a plague of dragon's teeth, sown in confusion, nourished in the soil of social dissension, economic disruption, and political chaos, causing armed fanatics to spring up where peaceful peasants toiled.

In its total effect, it is creating new alignments and a new confrontation of powers that vitally relates to and yet transcends the Cold War. It is a confrontation, in its essence, of the world's *haves* and the world's *have-nots,* of the rich nations and the poor nations.

It is reshaping the world that we have known, and its outcome may well decide the form and substance of the foreseeable future, not only in the present theatres of war, which are vast and shadowy, but everywhere.

The questions then arise: What is it? What can be done about it – or with it? How to end it or to exploit it? Is it something that can be turned off and on at will, as an instrument of national policy or political expedience?

On the available evidence, most of it concentrated in a span of twenty years or so of what may be called the post-colonial period, a definition offers itself that will, in turn, suggest answers to other questions.

Guerrilla war, in the larger sense in which we have been discussing it, is *revolutionary* war, engaging a civilian population, or a significant part of such a population, against the military forces of established or usurpative governmental authority.

The circumstances may vary. In one instance – Israel and Algeria serve as examples – the authority may be alien, that is, colonial, and its opposition virtually the entire native population, led by a vanguard of militants.

In another set of circumstances – Cuba, for example – the authority may be a native, at least nominally independent government, and the insurgency initiated by a small faction, challenging the policies or legitimacy of the regime.

Again cases vary. The war of the Viet Cong was both ideological and intensely nationalistic. Led by communists, it appealed not only to the poor and exploited but also to a broad popular front made up of those who, regardless of class origin or interest, were unwilling longer to suffer foreign occupation or to accept the cruelty and corruption of military puppets installed by the foreigner. Social and ideological motives were only part of the picture. Patriotism (as the Americans would call it if speaking of themselves in a similar situation) played a large part. For a multitude of Vietnamese the war was simply the continuation of that earlier struggle against French colonialism, Americans replacing *légionnaires* and North African mercenaries in a twenty-year campaign of pillage and murder, calling it a crusade for liberty and democracy.

Where the war in South Vietnam has ideological and nationalistic roots, the revolution in Cuba had none that were visible. It began, rather, as the idealistic protest of a tiny faction of uncertain political orientation – vaguely 'liberal', vaguely socialistic, tinged with Spanish anarchism – against the corruption and oppression of the Batista regime. Class rivalries were not evident. Nationalism was not an apparent factor. The clash with foreign and feudal interests, the anti-Americanism, the militant proletarianism and Marxist slogans of the Cuban revolution were later developments, following rather than leading to the overthrow of Batista.

In Morocco (1952–6), the nationalists of the Istiqlal built their cause around the symbolic figure of the exiled sultan, Mohammed Sidi ben Yussef, and forced the abdication of the pretender and the dissolution of the French protectorate. In Israel powerful religious and ethnic drives gave the struggle for the Jewish national homeland the character of a holy war.

But ostensible causes can be misleading. Patriotism, race, religion, the cry for social justice: beneath all of these symbolic and abstract 'causes' that have inspired the revolutions of this century, one discovers a unifying principle, a common mainspring.

It is a revolutionary *impulse,* an upsurge of popular *will,* that really has very little to do with questions of national or ethnic identity, or self-determination, or forms of government, or social justice, the familiar shibboleths of political insurgency. It is not even certain that economic deprivation in itself is the decisive factor that it is widely assumed to be. Poverty and oppression are, after all, conditions of life on the planet that have been endured by countless generations with scarcely a murmur.

The *will to revolt,* so widespread as to be almost universal today, seems to be something more than a reaction to political circumstances or material conditions. What it seems to express is a newly awakened consciousness, not of 'causes' but of *potentiality.* It is a spreading awareness of the possibilities of human existence, coupled with a growing sense of the *causal* nature of the universe, that together inspire, first in individuals, then in communities and entire nations, *an entirely new attitude towards life.*

The effect of this sudden awareness, this sudden fruition of consciousness, is to produce in the so-called backward areas of the world, all at once, a pervasive and urgent desire for radical change, based on the new insight, startling in its simplicity, that the conditions of life that had seemed immutable *can,* after all, be changed.

Limitations that were formerly accepted all at once become intolerable. The hint of imminent change suggests opportunities that had not been glimpsed until now. The *will to act* is born. It is as though people everywhere were saying: *Look, here is something we can do, or have, or be, simply by acting. Then what have we been waiting for? Let us act!*

This, at any rate, describes the state of mind of the modern insurgent, the guerrilla fighter, whatever his slogans or his cause; and his secret weapon, above and beyond any question of strategy or tactics or techniques of irregular warfare, is nothing more than *the ability to inspire this state of mind in others.* The defeat of the military enemy, the overthrow of the government, are secondary tasks, in the sense that they come later. The primary effort of the guerrilla is to militate the population, without whose consent no government can stand for a day.

The guerrilla is subversive of the existing order in that he is the disseminator of revolutionary ideas; his actions lend force to his doctrine and show the way to radical change. Yet it would be an error to consider him as a being apart from the seed bed of revolution. He himself is created by the political climate in which revolution becomes possible, and is himself as much an expression as he is a catalyst of the popular will towards such change.

To understand this much is to avoid two great pitfalls, two serious areas of confusion, into which counter-insurgency specialists seem to fall.

One such pitfall is the *conspiracy theory:* the view that revolution is the (usually deformed) offspring of a process of artificial insemination, and that the guerrilla nucleus (the fertilizing agent, so to speak) is made up of outsiders, conspirators, political zombies – in other words, actual or spiritual aliens – who somehow stand separate from their social environment, while manipulating it to obscure and sinister ends.

The other is the *methods fallacy,* held – at least until very recently – by most American military men: the old-fashioned notion that guerrilla warfare is largely a matter of tactics and techniques, to be adopted by almost anyone who may have need of them, in almost any irregular warfare situation.

The first view is both naïve and cynical. Invariably expressed in the rhetoric of Western liberalism and urging political democracy (that is to say, multi-party elections) as the *desideratum,* it nevertheless lacks confidence in popular decisions; it tacitly assumes that people in the mass are simpletons, too ignorant, unsophisticated, and passive to think for themselves or to have either the will or the capacity to wage a revolutionary war.

Ergo, the revolution which in fact exists must be due to the machinations of interlopers. The guerrillas must be the dupes or the wily agents of an *alien* power or, at least, of an *alien* political philosophy.*

On the more naïve level, it seems to be assumed that people would scarcely choose the revolutionary path of their own accord; certainly not if the revolution in question were out of joint with the political traditions and ideals held dear by Americans. To quote former President Eisenhower in this connexion, relative to the war in South Vietnam:

> 'We must inform these people [the South Vietnamese] of what is happening and how important it is to them to get on our side. Then the will want to choose victory.'[†]

Alas! the victory they seem to have chosen is not General Eisenhower.

Most American foreign policy makers and experts of the new politico-military science of counter-insurgency (the theory and practice of counter-revolution) appear more cynical than General Eisenhower. It is manifest in their pronouncements that all modern revolutions are, or are likely to become, struggles between two world 'systems', the communist on one side, the Americans and their allies on the other, with the people most directly involved merely pawns, to be manipulated by one side or the other.

Since it is the United States that is, more often than not in this era, the interloper in almost any revolutionary situation that comes to mind (Vietnam, Cuba, Iran, Guatemala, Brazil, Congo, Venezuela, to name a few), it is not surprising that the Cold War psychology should lead us to look for our Russian or Chinese counterpart in the given area of contention, and, finding him, or thinking so, to assign to him a major role. To do so, however, is to succumb to a curious illogic, in which our powers of observation seem to fail us.

Can guerrilla tactics be employed successfully against guerrillas? The answer is negative. To suppose otherwise is to fall into the *methods fallacy*. Indian fighters do not become Indians by taking scalps. A spotted jungle suit does not make a United States marine a guerrilla.

The experience of the Second World War and of every conflict since then has made it clear that commando troops are not guerrillas. Nor can the so-called 'counter-insurgency' forces now being developed in a more sophisticated school be considered guerrillas, although they may employ some of the more obvious techniques of the guerrilla fighter – the night raid, the ambush, the roving patrol far from a military base, and so on.

Such techniques are as old as warfare itself. It is possible to conceive of their use by Cro-Magnon man, whoever *he* was, against the last of the Neanderthals; they were employed by the aboriginal Britons against Caesar's legionnaires, and they are the techniques of savages in the Colombian jungle and no doubt of a few surviving New Guinean headhunters to this day.

Headhunters are not guerrillas. The distinction is simple enough. When we speak of the guerrilla fighter we are speaking of the *political partisan*, an armed civilian whose principal weapon is not his rifle or his machete but his relationship to the community, the nation, in and for which he fights.

Insurgency, or guerrilla war, is the agency of radical social or political change; it is the face and the right arm of revolution. Counterinsurgency is a form of counter-revolution, the process by which revolution is resisted. The two are opposite sides of the coin, and it will not do to confuse them or their agents, despite superficial similarities.

Because of the political nature of the struggle, the disparity of the means at the disposal of the two forces, and, above all, the total opposition of their strategic aims, the most fundamental tactics of the guerrilla simply are not available to the army that opposes him, and are available only in the most limited way to the counter-insurgency specialist, the United States Special Forces officer, let us say, who may try to imitate him.

The reasons are clear.

First, the guerrilla has the initiative; it is he who begins the war, and he who decides when

---

* But what can this strange American word, 'alien', mean to the Vietnamese, to the Cubans, to the Congolese? Could it mean – shocking thought! – *American*?

† In a Republican political forum in Philadelphia, urging an 'intensive propaganda campaign' to create a clear unity of view between the South Vietnamese people and the United States'; quoted in the *New York Times*, 16 June 1964.

and where to strike. His military opponent must wait, and while waiting, he must be on guard *every-where*.

Both before and after the war has begun, the government army is in a *defensive* position, by reason of its role as policeman, which is to say, as the guardian of public and private property.

The military has extensive holdings to protect: cities, towns, villages, agricultural lands, communications, commerce, and usually some sort of industrial base to defend. There is also the purely military investment to consider: garrisons, outposts, supply lines, convoys, airfields, the troops themselves and their valuable weapons, which it will be the first tactical objective of the guerrillas to capture, so as to arm more guerrillas. Finally, there is a political system, already under severe strain if the point of open insurrection has been reached, to be preserved and strengthened.

In all of these areas, the incumbent regime and its military arm present highly vulnerable targets to an enemy who is himself as elusive and insubstantial as the wind.

For, while the army suffers from an embarrassment of wealth, and especially of expensive military hardware for which there is no employment, the guerrilla has the freedom of his poverty. He owns nothing but his rifle and the shirt on his back, has nothing to defend but his existence. He holds no territory, has no expensive and cumbersome military establishment to maintain, no tanks to risk in battle, no garrisons subject to siege, no transport vulnerable to air attack nor aircraft of his own to be shot down, no massed divisions to be bombarded, no motor columns to be ambushed, no bases or depots that he cannot abandon within the hour.

He can afford to run when he cannot stand and fight with good assurance of winning, and to disperse and hide when it is not safe to move. In the extremity, he can always sink back into the peaceful population – that sea, to use Mao Tse-tung's well-worn metaphor, in which the guerrilla swims like a fish.

The population, as should be clear by now, is the key to the entire struggle. Indeed, although Western analysts seem to dislike entertaining this idea, it is the population which is doing the struggling. The guerrilla, who is of the people in a way which the government soldier cannot be

(for if the regime were not alienated from the people, whence the revolution?), fights with the support of the non-combatant civilian populace: it is his camouflage, his quartermaster, his recruiting office, his communications network, and his efficient, all-seeing intelligence service.

Without the consent and active aid of the people, the guerrilla would be merely a bandit, and could not long survive. If, on the other hand, the counter-insurgent could claim this same support, the guerrilla would not exist, because there would be no war, no revolution. The cause would have evaporated, the popular impulse towards radical change – cause or no cause – would be dead.

Here again we come to the vital question of *aims*, on which the strategy and tactics of both sides are necessarily based.

The guerrilla fighter is primarily a propagandist, an agitator, a disseminator of the revolutionary idea, who uses the struggle itself – the actual physical conflict – as an instrument of agitation. His primary goal is to raise the level of revolutionary anticipation, and then of popular participation, to the crisis point at which the revolution becomes general throughout the country and the people in their masses carry out the final task – the destruction of the existing order and (often but not always) of the army that defends it.

By contrast, the purpose of the counterrevolutionary is negative and defensive. It is to restore order, to protect property, to preserve existing forms and interests by force of arms, *where persuasion has already failed*. His means may be political in so far as they involve the use of still more persuasion – the promise of social and economic reforms, bribes of a more localized sort, counter-propaganda of various kinds. But primarily the counter-insurgent's task must be *to destroy the revolution by destroying its promise* – that means by proving, militarily, that it cannot and will not succeed.

To do so will require the total defeat of the revolutionary vanguard and its piecemeal destruction wherever it exists. The alternatives will be to abdicate the military effort in favour of a political solution – for example, the partition of Vietnam after the French defeat at Dien Bien Phu, the Algerian solution, etc.; in other words, compromise or complete surrender.

That military victory against true guerrillas is possible seems doubtful on the basis of modern experience, barring the use of methods approaching genocide, as applied notably by the Germans in certain occupied countries during the Second World War.

The counter-insurgent cannot win by imitating the insurgent, because he is the alien in the revolutionary situation, and because his tasks are precisely the opposite of those of the guerrilla, where symmetry exists at all. The guerrilla's mere survival is a political victory: it encourages and raises the popular opposition to the incumbent regime. Thus he can afford to run and to hide. The counter-insurgent gains nothing by running and hiding. He surrenders everything. The guerrilla can disguise himself as – in fact he can be – a peaceful agrarian worker, and still spread his revolutionary message. In a similar role, the counter-insurgent would be merely a police spy, and would accomplish little, spread no message. The guerrilla can hit and run. Every successful raid gives him more arms and ammunition, and more favourable publicity. The counter-insurgent can gain nothing by such Red Indian tactics – even if similar targets were available to him – and they are not. His military campaign must be sweeping, continuous, and cumulative in its effects. Either he clears the country of guerrillas or he does not. If he does not, he continues to lose.

The distinction made here between guerrilla war as a politico-military technique and mere guerrilla-ism (banditry, on the one hand, or the application of irregular warfare techniques by regular military organizations, on the other) is by no means as arbitrary as it may at first appear.

Popular insurrections have occurred throughout history. They have usually failed, or in any case have produced only limited victories, because the techniques they can exploit today were then irrelevant to the historical situation. This is simply another way of saying that, until now, the popular majorities, the labouring, unspecialized masses of pre-industrial societies, were able to exert very little political or economic leverage.

The serfs of the medieval period, for example, were unable to resist the feudal military power not merely because they lacked arms and skills, political consciousness, and cohesion, but because they had no other means to affect the political and economic processes of their world.

Economically, they were manageable because they lived too close to the level of bare subsistence to be otherwise. They could not even think of withholding their labour – their only economic lever. Isolated by their brute condition and their ignorance, they lived below the level of politics. If they starved, or rebelled and were slaughtered, *there was no one to care,* no economically or politically potent class to whom it would make the slightest difference.

Subsequent revolutions, from the Renaissance to the Russian Revolution and not excluding Mexico, 1910–17, have been bourgeois in character, or have quickly been converted into bourgeois movements, after an initially populist period. Liberté, égalité, *fraternité* applied only to the great and petite bourgeoisie of France, after a brief Jacobin interval (significantly, all bourgeois historians loathe and fear the proletarianism of the Terror), because, in the end, only the bourgeoisie had the lever – wealth and the tools of production – to assume leadership in a confrontation with the landowning feudal aristocracy. Although there was now some class mobility and a greater need of democratic slogans, the landless, unspecialized masses remained submerged. They could remain idle and starve. All the better. It reduced beggary and banditry. Isolated, they could be slaughtered and *no one would care.*

History brings us to a pass in which (for a variety of reasons but principally because of the complexity of the productive processes, the fragmentation, specialization, and interlocking nature of the industrial society, and the importance of disciplined labour and huge consumer markets, relative to the profit system) the labouring masses assume political potency. Their new role in the industrial society – as producer, as distributor, as consumer – gives them a lever. If they withhold their work the economy collapses. If they cease to buy and to consume the same thing happens. If they are slaughtered there are worldwide repercussions, based, in the final analysis, on economic considerations.

The modern industrial society cannot function, and its government cannot govern, except with popular participation and by popular consent. What is true of the industrial states is also true, with minor qualification, of the nonindustrial states and colonies on which the former depend for the raw materials of their industry and, often, for their export markets.

For the best of economic reasons, modern governments must seem to be popular. They must make great concessions to popular notions of what is democratic and just, or be replaced by regimes that will do so. The governments of the dominant industrial states themselves, even more than those they dominate, are strapped politically by this factor of the domestic 'image'. They must use the liberal rhetoric and also pay something in the way of social compromise – schools, hospitals, decent concern for the well-being of all but the most isolated poor – if they are to retain power and keep the people to their accustomed, profit-producing tasks.

This fact makes such governments extremely vulnerable to a sort of war – guerrilla war with its psychological and economic weapons – that their predecessors could have ignored, had such a war been possible at all in the past.

They are vulnerable because they must, at all cost, keep the economy functioning and showing a profit or providing the materials and markets on which another, dominant economy depends. Again, they are vulnerable because they must maintain the appearance of normalcy; they can be *embarrassed* out *of* office. And they are triply vulnerable because they cannot be as ruthless as the situation demands. They cannot openly crush the opposition that embarrasses and harasses them. They must be wooers as well as doers.

These are modern weaknesses. They invite a distinctly modern development to exploit them, and that development is modern guerrilla warfare. The weaknesses peculiar to the modern, bourgeois–democratic, capitalistic state (but shared in some measure by all modern states)

make popular war possible, and give it its distinctive forms, which clearly cannot be imitated, except in the most superficial way, by the armies of the state itself.

Fundamentally, the guerrilla's tactics and those of the counter-insurgent differ because their roles differ. They are dissimilar forces, fighting dissimilar wars, for disparate objectives. The counter-insurgent seeks a military solution: to wipe out the guerrillas. He is hampered by a political and economic impediment: he cannot wipe out the populace, or any significant sector of it. The guerrilla, for his part, wishes to wear down his military opponent and will employ suitable tactics to that end, but his primary objective is political. It is to feed and fan the fires of revolution by his struggle, to raise the entire population against the regime, to discredit it, isolate it, wreck its credit, undermine its economy, over-extend its resources, and cause its disintegration.

Essentially, then, the guerrilla fighter's war is political and social, his means are at least as political as they are military, his purpose is almost entirely so. Thus we may paraphrase Clausewitz: *Guerrilla war is the extension of politics by means of armed conflict.* At a certain point in its development it becomes revolution itself – the dragon's teeth sprung to maturity.

Guerrilla war = revolutionary war: the extension of politics by means of armed conflict.

Until this much is properly understood by those who would oppose it, nothing else about it can be understood and no strategy or tactics devised to suppress it can prevail.

If, on the other hand, this much is understood by those who lead it, then it can scarcely fail in any circumstance – for the war will not even begin until all the conditions of its success are present.

Let us now begin to examine the mechanics of the revolutionary process called guerrilla warfare.

The War of the Flea

Robert Taber

The war of the flea. Political and military objectives. Creating 'the climate of collapse'. Organization of insurgent forces. Guevara on guerrilla war: the base.

The enemy advances, we retreat; the enemy camps, we harass; the enemy tires, we attack; the enemy retreats, we pursue.

Selected Military Writings of Mao Tse-tung

What Mao Tse-tung says of guerrilla tactics here is a key to communist thinking; it can be discerned in diplomacy as well as in war. The Soviet policy makers have mastered the Chinese lesson very well, and apply it to a wide variety of problems having nothing to do with guerrilla fighting. Berlin since the Second World War has been a prime example, and the establishment of Soviet missile bases in Cuba was another.

But then, why not? The policy of hitting the enemy when he is weak, evading him when he is strong, taking the offensive when he falls back, circling around when he advances – all of this is only common sense. There is no great novelty in it, nor can the Marxist–Leninist camp claim any special credit for it.

What *is* new – and Mao is the apostle and the long Chinese revolution the first proving ground – is the application of guerrilla activity, in a conscious and deliberate way, to specific political objectives, without immediate reference to the outcome of battles as such, provided only that the revolutionaries survive.

Oddly enough, however, it is the noncommunist Cubans rather than the Chinese who have provided the most clear-cut example of military activity producing political effects, in a war in which few of the battles would be described by military men as more than skirmishes, yet one in which the government came crashing down as surely as if an army had been destroyed on the battlefield.

The explanation seems to baffle military men, yet it is simple enough. Guerrillas who know their trade and have popular support cannot be eliminated by the means available to most governments. And on the other hand, few governments can stand the political, psychological, and economic stresses of guerrilla war, no matter how strong they may be militarily.

In general, all warfare involves the same basic problem: how to use one's strength to exploit the enemy's weaknesses and so to overcome him. In an internal war the government's strength is its powerful army, its arsenal, and its wealth of material means. Its weaknesses are social, political, and economic in the sense that the economy, while an asset, is vulnerable from several points of view. It provides both military and psychological targets.

Constitutional democracies, as I have already noted, are particularly exposed to the subversion that is the basic weapon of revolutionary war. The stratified class structure and the multi-party political systems of most such countries are sources of political and social dissension that can

---

Taber, Robert. (1970). "The War of the Flea." *The War of the Flea* (pp. 14-33). London: Paladin.

be exploited. Constitutional law is a further embarrassment, and sometimes may be a fatal impediment.

Fulgencio Batista fell not because he was a dictator but because his situation in a country with democratic institutions – moreover, a country almost entirely dependent on the favour of the United States with its similar institutions and traditions – did not permit him to be dictator *enough* to resolve the contradictions that confronted him. His hands were tied by conventions he could not break without losing his foreign support. His use of counterterrorism, that is, the *illegal* use of force, only increased his domestic opposition. Yet without it, he had no effective means to combat the disorder and subversion that threatened his regime. Similarly, the French in Indo-China were destroyed, in the final analysis, by the very ideas and institutions that they themselves had introduced. Franco, by way of contrast, probably stands because he has successfully stifled the very idea of political liberty in Spain, while putting enough bread on the table to satisfy the vocal majority.

This is to speak of legalistic – that is, social and political – difficulties.

On the military level, a regular army, under whatever political system, has disadvantages that are owing to the very size and complexity of the organization, and again to its defensive role, as the guardian of the national wealth and of the whole of the national territory.

The guerrilla, for his part, finds his strength in his freedom from territorial commitments, his mobility, and his relationship to a discontented people, as the spokesman of their grievances, the armed vanguard, as Che Guevara puts it, of militant social protest.

His weakness is merely – I use the word advisedly – *a military* weakness. He lacks the arms, and usually the manpower, to risk a military decision.

In the circumstances it is obvious what the guerrilla's tactics must be.

Politically, he must seek to aggravate such social and political dissension as exists and to raise the level of political consciousness and of revolutionary *will* among the people. It will also be part of his design, as well as the natural consequence of his actions, to bring about an intensification of the political regression that already exists, so deepening popular opposition to the regime and hastening the process of its dissolution.

Militarily, his tactics will be designed to wear the enemy down, by chipping away at the morale of the government troops and by inducing the maximum expenditure of funds, material, and manpower in the effort to suppress him. At the same time he will endeavour to build his own forces through the capture of government arms and by recruitment from an increasingly alienated populace, avoiding a military confrontation until the day – and it will come late – when an equalization of forces has been obtained.

An army deals from strength, seeking out the enemy's weaknesses in order to destroy him. The guerrilla is sometimes said to deal from weakness, but this is an absurdity. In fact, he exploits his own kind of strength, which lies in the extreme mobility of lightly armed forces without territorial or hardware investments, a bottomless well of manpower from which to recruit, and the fact that *time* – which is both money and political capital – works in his favour.

Analogically, the guerrilla fights the war of the flea, and his military enemy suffers the dog's disadvantages: too much to defend; too small, ubiquitous, and agile an enemy to come to grips with. If the war continues long enough – this is the theory – the dog succumbs to exhaustion and anaemia without ever having found anything on which to close his jaws or to rake with his claws.

But this may be to oversimplify for the sake of an analogy. In practice, the dog does not die of anaemia. He merely becomes too weakened – in military terms, over-extended; in political terms, too unpopular; in economic terms, too expensive – to defend himself. At this point, the flea, having multiplied to a veritable plague of fleas through long series of small victories, each drawing its drop of blood, each claiming the reward of a few more captured weapons to arm yet a few more partisans, concentrates his forces for a decisive series of powerful blows.

Time works for the guerrilla both in the field – where it costs the enemy a daily fortune to pursue him – and in the politico-economic arena.

Almost all modern governments are highly conscious of what journalism calls 'world opinion'. For sound reasons, mostly of an economic nature, they cannot afford to be condemned in the United Nations, they do not like to be visited by Human Rights Commissions or Freedom of the Press Committees; their need of foreign investment, foreign loans, foreign markets, satisfactory trade relationships, and so on requires that they be members in more or less good standing of a larger community of interests. Often, too, they are members of military alliances. Consequently, they must maintain some appearance of stability, in order to assure the other members of the community or of the alliance that contracts will continue to be honoured, that treaties will be upheld, that loans will be repaid with interest, that investments will continue to produce profits and be safe.

Protracted internal war threatens all of this, for no investor will wish to put his money where it is not safe and certain to produce a profit, no bank lends without guarantees, no ally wishes to treat with a government that is on the point of eviction.

It follows that it must be the business of the guerrilla, and of his clandestine political organization in the cities, to destroy the stable image of the government, and so to deny it credits, to dry up its sources of revenue, and to create dissension within the frightened owning classes, within the government bureaucracy (whose payrolls will be pinched), and within the military itself.

The outbreak of the insurgency is the first step – it is a body blow that in itself inflicts severe damage on the prestige of the regime. The survival of the guerrilla force over a period of time, demonstrating the impotence of the army, continues the process. As the guerrilla's support widens – and this will come automatically as the weakness of the government is revealed – political trouble is sure to follow, in the form of petitions, demonstrations, strikes. These in their turn will be followed by more serious developments – sabotage, terror, spreading insurrection.

In such circumstances it will be a remarkable government that will not be driven to stern repressive measures – curfews, the suspension of civil liberties, a ban on popular assembly, illegal acts that can only deepen the popular opposition, creating a vicious circle of rebellion and repression until the economy is undermined, the social fabric torn beyond redemption, and the regime tottering on the verge of collapse.

In the end, it will be a question whether the government falls before the military is destroyed in the field or whether the destruction of the military brings about the final deposition of the political regime. The two processes are complementary. Social and political dissolution bleeds the military, and the protracted and futile campaign in the field contributes to the process of social and political dissolution, creating what I have elsewhere called 'the climate' of collapse'.

This is the grand strategic objective of the guerrilla: to create the 'climate of collapse'. It may be taken as the key to everything he does.

Please note, I do not by any means wish to suggest that the train of events described above can be put into motion anywhere, at any time, by any agency, irrespective of objective and subjective conditions. Insurrections may be provoked or incited or may occur spontaneously as the expression of grievances or of frustrated aspirations or because of other factors: religious frenzy, blood feuds, mass hysteria induced by anything from a sports contest to a rape in Mississippi can lead to bloodshed and temporary anarchy. Guerrilla warfare does not necessarily follow. Insurrection is a phenomenon, revolution a process, which cannot begin until the historical stage has been set for it.

Since guerrilla war is, in our definition, a revolutionary process, it can only come out of a revolutionary situation. For this reason, I am inclined to agree with Che Guevara when he writes in *Guerrilla Warfare:*

Naturally, it is not to be thought that all conditions for revolution are going to be created through the impulse given to them by guerrilla activity. It must always be kept in mind that there is a necessary minimum without which the establishment and consolidation of the first centre [of rebellion] is not practicable. People must see clearly the futility of maintaining a fight for social goals within the framework of civil debate. When the forces of oppression come to maintain themselves in power against established law, peace is considered already broken.

In these conditions, popular discontent manifests itself in more active forms. An attitude of resistance crystallizes in an outbreak of fighting, provoked initially by the conduct of the authorities.

Where a government has come into power through some form of popular vote, fraudulent or not, and maintains at least an appearance of constitutional legality, the guerrilla outbreak cannot be promoted, since the possibilities of peaceful struggle have not yet been exhausted.

We have defined guerrilla war as the extension of politics by means of armed conflict. It follows that the extension cannot logically come until all acceptable peaceful solutions – appeals, legislative and judicial action, and the resources of the ballot box – have been proved worthless. Were it otherwise, there would be no hope of enlisting the popular support essential to revolutionary activity.

If people are to accept the risks and responsibilities of organized violence, they must believe first that there is no alternative; second, that the cause is compelling; third, that they have reasonable expectation of success. The last named is perhaps the most powerful of motives.

Where the cause appears just, the situation is intolerable, and oppression past all appeal, the way to action is clear.

Even then, however, much groundwork must be done before a guerrilla campaign will become feasible.

The experiences of Algeria, of Cuba, and of other successful revolutions indicate that, in most circumstances, guerrillas require the active support of a political organization outside of their own ranks but dedicated to their cause, an urban arm of the revolutionary movement that can provide assistance by means both legal and illicit, from placing bombs to defending accused revolutionaries in the courts of law (assuming that these still exist).

Isolation, military and political, is the great enemy of guerrilla movements. It is the task of the urban organization to prevent this isolation, to provide diversions and provocations when needed, to maintain contact, to keep the world aware of a revolution in progress even when there is no progress to report.

Usually the revolutionary political organization will have two branches: one subterranean and illegal, the other visible and quasi-legitimate.

On the one hand, there will be the activists – saboteurs, terrorists, arms runners, fabricators of explosive devices, operators of a clandestine press, distributors of political pamphlets, and couriers to carry messages from one guerrilla sector to another, using the towns as communications centres.

On the other hand, there will be sympathizers and fellow travellers, those not really *of* the underground, operating for the most part within the law, but sustaining the efforts of the activists, and, of themselves, accomplishing far more important tasks. The visible organization will, of course, have invisible links with the revolutionary underground, and, through it, with the guerrillas in the countryside. But its real work will be to serve as a respectable facade for the revolution, a civilian front, or, as the Cubans called it, *resistencia civica,* made up of intellectuals, tradesmen, clerks, students, professionals, and the like – above all, of women – capable of promoting funds, circulating petitions, organizing boycotts, raising popular demonstrations, informing friendly journalists, spreading rumours, and in every way conceivable waging a massive propaganda campaign aimed at two objectives: the strengthening and brightening of the rebel 'image', and the discrediting of the regime.

An Alternative Approach

Insurgency as a System

Nathan Leites and Charles Wolf, Jr.

The hearts-and-minds view of rebellion is that of the outsider looking in. In its stress on popular sympathies and economic condition, it concentrates on the environment that evokes R and causes it to emerge and grow, more or less spontaneously. Its emphasis is on the demand side of the problem. To transpose an analogy from economics, the hearts-and-minds view is a *demand-pull* version of the process, whereas the view we shall be presenting is more in the nature of a *cost-push* version. Our view will, to a greater extent, emphasize factors within the insurgent organization which influence its capabilities and growth. It will thus place somewhat greater emphasis on the supply (production) side of R's growth, and the bearing of supply considerations on the prevention or defeat of R.

Of course, behavior depends on interactions *between* supply and demand. Both need to be considered in understanding population behavior in the insurgency context, no less than consumer behavior in the marketplace. We offer two reasons for placing somewhat more emphasis on supply. One is that, while both demand and supply are important, we feel that in most discussions supply factors have either been neglected or misconstrued. In the theory of consumer behavior, to revert to the economic analogy, it is customary to distinguish between the effect of consumer prefer-ences (demand conditions) and the possibilities for buying different commodities as reflected by their relative costs (supply conditions). The interaction between them determines market behavior. By contrast, the hearts-and-minds analysis focuses principal attention on the preferences, attitudes, and sympathies of the populace (demand), to the neglect of the opportunities and costs required to indulge these preferences.[1] Similarly, in discussions of campus rebellions, principal attention is often focused on student demands and grievances, rather than on the actions (or inaction) of administrators and faculty that lower the costs and facilitate the organization and radicalization of student rebellion.

The second reason that supply conditions are probably more elastic (responsive)—at least in the short run—to programs and policies than are demand conditions, especially from A's point of view. Dealing with the demand conditions in the less developed countries involves the massive problems of modernization, and in the more developed countries the problems of reform that are only less massive in a relative sense. It is important and necessary to grapple with these problems (among other reasons, so that A can sustain its own sense of rectitude and purpose). Nevertheless, the problems are apt to be unyielding in the short run. The progress that can realistically be

Leites, Nathan, and Charles Wolf, Jr. (1970). *Rebellion and Authority: An Analytic Essay on Insurgent Conflicts.* Santa Monica, CA: Rand. Reproduction authorization obtained from RAND.

155

aimed for will probably leave the demand for R fairly strong, especially if—as seems likely—progress lags behind promises.[2] This prospect presents an asymmetrical advantage to R. It may be much easier for R to activate and enhance a potential demand for itself than for A to reduce this demand. Thus, demand may be harder to shift downward than upward. Hence, while *both* A and R must attend sharply to the supply or production side of the problem, A may have less leverage on the demand side than R. Hence, it may be efficient for R to allocate relatively more resources to influencing the demand side, and for A to allocate more to the supply side.

Fundamental to our analysis is the assumption that the population, as individuals or groups, behaves "rationally" that it calculates costs and benefits to the extent that they can be related to different courses of action, and makes choices accordingly. Apparent irrationalities can be explained by mistakes, uncertainties, misinformation, a shortage of information on the part of the population; or a misunderstanding on the observer's part of how the population weighs different things in its calculations. Consequently, influencing popular behavior requires neither sympathy nor mysticism, but rather a better understanding of what costs and benefits the individual or the group is concerned with, and how they are calculated. The rationality assumption is admittedly an oversimplification. Its justification hopefully lies in helping to analyze a subject that has often been treated in an obscure, if not obscurantist, way.

The following discussion will describe our alternative approach in terms of three elements: (1) the environment of the less developed countries, (2) the insurgency—R—as a system, and (3) the individual or group in relation to R. Finally, contrasts are drawn between the alternative approach and the hearts-and-minds view discussed in Chapter 2.

THE ENVIRONMENT

Traditional societies that have began to change provide, by the process of change itself, opportunities for insurgent movements.[3] (And societies in which the structure of traditional authority remains intact potentially provide the same opportunities, to the extent that change lies ahead

of them.) Endemic, if latent, cleavages and antagonisms tend to be inflamed once the transition to modernization has begun—antagonism between landlords and tenants; between urban and rural areas; among ethnic, racial, religious, and linguistic groups. Inequities in the distribution of wealth, income, education, and opportunity are chronic and widespread, and the pain that accompanies them is often felt more acutely as modernization begins to open up the possibility of remedies and evoke promises and aspirations that move ahead of the remedies. Resentment against the privilege and status enjoyed by foreigners as a colonial legacy, or by domestic elites as a legacy of traditional society, is often acute or easily aroused. Such patterns of bitterness and resentment are as much a part of the realities of transitional societies as are low income levels, and they are very likely to intensify as income levels rise—other things being equal—at least up to some threshold. As one experienced observer summarizes the point:

> Every insurgency . . . requires a cause. [But] there is always some issue which has an appeal to each section of the community, and, even if dominant, an inspired incident may easily revive it in an acute form. . . . All governments are vulnerable in criticism, and every grievance, shortcoming or abuse will be exploited.[4]

Although the preceding point applies with particular force in the less developed countries, it is relevant in the more developed countries, too. Thus Sidney Hook comments on disruption in university campuses in the United States.

> On every campus there are always some grievances. Instead of seeking peacefully to resolve them through existing channels of consultation and deliberation, the SDS [Students for a Democratic Society] seeks to inflame them. Where grievances don't exist, they can be created. In one piece of advice to chapter members, they were urged to sign up for certain courses in large numbers, and then denounce the University for its large classes![5]

Another characteristic of the less developed countries that enhances their vulnerability to insurgency is the mutual isolation of their component parts. Less developed countries are "plural" economic and social entities in the sense that they contain units that are physically, as well as functionally and technologically, remote from one another. Villages, districts, towns, provinces, and cities are in imperfect and intermittent contact. They are often in isolation from one another and particularly from the capital city and the institutions of the central government concentrated there. Thus, flows of commodities, information, and people from place to place are extremely limited. Because the links and contacts among these enclaves, and between them and the center, are meager, the ability of an A to maintain surveillance and establish control over an inchoate insurgency is accordingly limited. The difficulty (that is, the high cost) of obtaining reliable and timely information—which A needs more than does R—is highly correlated with many other structural characteristics of the less developed countries—for example, per capita income, urbanization, literacy, longevity, industrialization, and political participation. But from the standpoint of the circumstances that facilitate R's emergence, the high cost of information and communication may be considerably more significant than other typical attributes of the environment in less developed countries.[6]

Given these characteristics, it is a truism to say that transitional societies are vulnerable to insurgency. Changing the characteristics is complex and time-consuming. Moreover, the *process* of modernization itself by no means reduces the vulnerabilities in question, although that is more likely to be the *outcome* of modernization in the longer run. For these reasons, it is wise to separate the analysis of R from that of development and modernization in general. To analyze and understand R in the less developed countries, we need to factor it out of the wider set of modernization problems to which it is related. Focusing on R leads to viewing it as a system.

REBELLION AS A SYSTEM

What does it mean to view an insurgent movement as a system? The alternative approach to be explored here starts with the observation that insurgent movements, as operating systems, require that certain inputs—obtained from either internal or external sources—be converted into certain outputs, or activities. These activities characterize the stage to which R has progressed.

In general, insurgency requires inputs of recruits, information, shelter, and food—almost

always obtained from the internal environment (endogeny)—and cadres, publicity, material, and initial financing—often provided from external sources (exogeny).[7] The "mix" between endogeny and exogeny is variable: it differs between different Rs, and in the same R at different times. To obtain inputs from the local environment, R relies on various persuasive as well as coercive (damage-threatening or damage-inflicting) techniques.[8] In practice, both persuasion and coercion are important as well as intimately linked. Severe coercion is often combined with a considerable and effective persuasive effort by Rs.[9]

Persuasion may take many forms: ideological preparation, education, discrediting of established authority and practies,[10] and payment (rewards). Coercion may also take many forms: the threat and carrying out of kidnapping, assassination, torture, forcible tax collection, and destruction of confiscation of property, including crop and land seizure. Often coercion and persuasion are mixed, as, for example, in compulsory assemblies for group criticism and self-criticism. Again, the actual and the efficient combination between persuasion and coercion are important to study, in order to understand both the organization and operation of R and the problem of countering R. Certain hypotheses can be examined concerning mixes of coercion and persuasion that may be effective in influencing different types of individuals or groups. For example, coercion may be more effective in obtaining compliance from the "haves," who initially are relatively favored and hence have something appreciable to lose; while persuasion and inducements may be more effective in obtaining compliance from the disadvantaged, who have little to lose and may therefore tend to cherish, and perhaps magnify, any gains by comparison. Of course, a mixture of the two may be more effective than either alone, but the proportions in the mix will vary with the circumstances of the intended target.

The inputs acquired by combining persuasion and coercion are converted into outputs by the insurgent organization. As with many organizations, R tends to organize personnel, financial, logistics, intelligence, communications, and operations branches to manage the conversion of inputs into activities; and it uses a wide range of incentives (recognition, reward, promotion) and penalties (criticism, isolation, demotion, and physical punishment) to spur the operations of these branches.

The outputs or activities of R include acts of sabotage; violence against individuals, public demonstrations, small-scale attacks, and eventually larger attacks and mobile warfare, on the military side. But R's outputs also include the exercise of administrative and governmental jurisdiction (village aid projects, education and training, formation of youth and other organizations concerned with group action programs). The aim of R's activities is to demonstrate that A is immoral, incompetent, and impotent—that A is, in other words, undeserving and a loser.

The view of insurgency described here can be summarized in Figure 1.

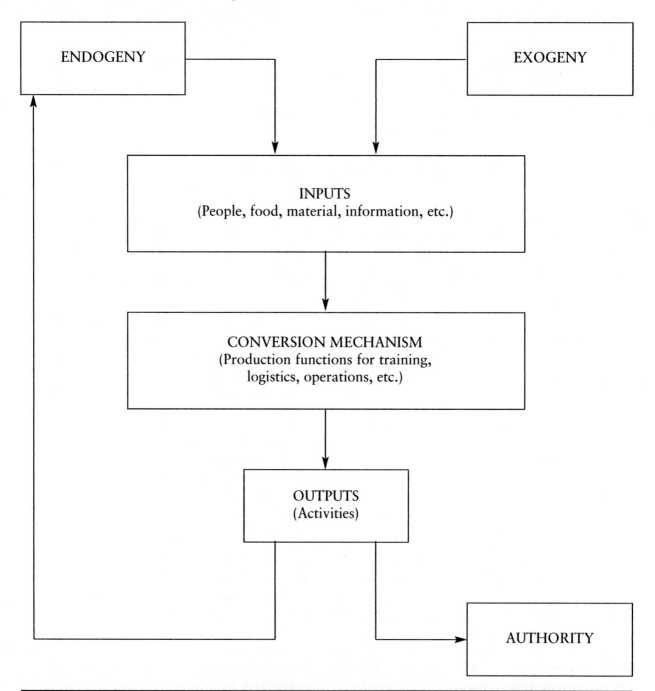

FIGURE 1

Insurgency as a system

The systems view of insurgency enables one to distinguish four methods of counterinsurgency which will be summarized here and elaborated later.[11] The first is to raise the cost to R of obtaining inputs, or reduce the inputs obtained for given costs: the aim is input-denial. The second is to impede the process by which R converts these inputs into activities—that is, to reduce the efficiency of R's production process. The third is to destroy R's outputs. And fourth is to blunt the effects of R's outputs on the population and on A—that is, to increase A's and the population's capacity to absorb R's activities.

The first two methods may be termed "counterproduction," which hinders R's production of activities by either denying inputs or changing the production coefficients so that smaller outputs are generated from given inputs.

Examples of the first method, input-denial, include interdiction by air, ground, or naval action; construction of barriers that impede the movement of people or supplies from a source to a destination; and preemptive buying programs that try to engage the available suppliers of particular inputs (such as rice) so that these goods are less readily available to R.

Efforts by A to reduce R's productive efficiency (the second method) include creating distrust and frictions within R's organization by planning rumors; attracting defectors (particularly those from the higher ranks in R's civil and military organization); disseminating credible misinformation about the behavior of R's leadership; and generally raising the noise level in R's information system.

The third method is the traditional counterforce role of military action. Besides the application of firepower from ground and air, it depends especially on accurate intelligence, so that targeting error in the use of such firepower is reduced. Otherwise, such error is likely to be high because targets are closely collocated with the people. (The importance of intelligence to reduce targeting error in counterforce operations can hardly be overemphasized, and we shall return to it later.)[12]

The fourth method, increasing A's and the population's capacity to absorb the outputs of R, is analogous to passive and active defense in strategic analysis.[13] Its passive-defensive aspects include such measures as building village fortifications ("hardening"), and relocating villagers so that they are less accessible to R (evacuation). Its active-defensive aspects involve creating or strengthening local paramilitary and police units with increased capacity to provide local defense against small unit actions by R. In the realm of political action, such capacity requires (1) A's adherence to law and order in contrast to R, and (2) its demonstrated ability to complete announced programs, thereby certifying that if *should* govern because it *is* governing.

How different is this approach from the one associated with the hearts-and-minds doctrine? Admittedly the differences are of degree rather than kind. But the differences of degree involve an important degree of difference. One contrast is to lay greater stress, in dealing with problems of counterinsurgency, on the supply side of insurgency (for example, on how the R system obtains its inputs, from what sources, in what quantities, in return for what persuasive, coercive, or inducement measures, how it manages these inputs and converts them into the system's outputs) rather than on the demand side (how receptive the feelings of the population are to an insurgency).

The supply side of the problem relates to the difficulty or cost of producing R's activities; the higher these costs, the lower the scale or the probability of R. The demand side of the problem relates to what people are willing to pay (or contribute) for R's activities. The more they want an insurgency, the higher the price they will pay for these activities; hence, the greater the scale or the probability or R.[14] But for given preference or desires, the price people will be willing to pay depends also on the resources they have available and the terms under which contributions toward an insurgency might be made (that is, the risks of damage or hopes of gain that enter into their calculations).

When counterrebellion operates on the supply side, the aim is to make the cost of R exceed the price that its internal or external supporters are willing to pay to support it, especially at high levels of activity. When counterrebellion operates on the demand side, it tries to reduce what people are willing to pay for R activities. Stressing the supply side means trying to raise the costs of producing R's activities, hence raising the costs of reaching a given scale or probability of rebellion. The analysis presented here places relatively greater emphasis on the supply than on the demand side, while the reverse applies to the hearts-and-minds orientation.[15]

While the demand-supply distinction helps clarify the contrasts between orientations, there are important interactions between demand and supply that should not be overlooked. The difficulty or cost of operating R and increasing its strength depends, as discussed earlier, on its access to various inputs provided by the population. The population's demand function influences that access and the terms on which it is obtained. For example, if demand rises, the costs of information and recruits may get lower (the supply function may fall). Conversely, if costs are increased, the demand function may fall. In effect, demand exercises an influence on supply, and vice versa.

This problem is also familiar in economies, although there too the usual demand-supply dichotomy often ignores interactions between the two.[16] But several particular points should be noted about the demand-supply interaction in the insurgency context. The demand that is operative in the sense of influencing R's supply function may, as discussed earlier, be confined to a small segment of the population. And the adroitness of R itself, as well as A's maladroitness, can activate and stimulate popular demand.[17] What is at work is a network of positive feedbacks: the population's effective demands influence the costs and effectiveness of R's activities, and R's activities influence (by the manipulation of both persuasion and coercion)[18] the population's demands. Conversely, clumsy reactions and overreactions by A to provocation from R can intensify popular demand. The discussion of provocation by R and "hot" violence by A, in Chapter 6, provides examples of this type of interaction.

Another contrast lies in the different view of endogeny and exogeny which emerges. Hearts-and-minds stresses nearly pure endogeny,[19] whereas the systems approach views the problem in terms of tradeoffs between the two. The inputs that the R system requires can be provided from internal or external sources, in combinations that may vary at different times in the same insurgency, and in different insurgencies. Internal sources can be primary, in the sense that they provide a larger (or more valuable) share of the total input than does exogeny, or they can be secondary.[20] Moreover, the value of external (or internal)

inputs cannot be inferred from their bulk, or their market prices. For example, external provision of leadership, money, intelligence, training, sanctuary, propaganda, and diplomatic pressure may have an importance in the emergence and growth of R which is not adequately measured by the flow of tons of supplies, or numbers of people, across a contiguous border.[21] Thus, while the problem of internal versus external sources is more likely to arise in terms of the mix between two sources of inputs, successful counterrebellion has always required either the absence of significant external support (for example, the Philippines and Malaya) or the shutting off of such support (Greece and Algeria). This is consistent with the fact that there have been cases of successful insurgency *without* such external support (Cuba), where the authority was weak and ineffectual. Curtailing exogeny in necessary but not sufficient for successful counterrebellion.

Even if one assumes the primacy of endogeny, the systems approach leads to different implications from those associated with the hearts-and-minds approach. The central questions include not only popular attitudes, but also R's operations: how R obtains its supplies; what forms of coercion and persuasion are used to influence the population; how R makes payments and raises revenues. Whether one wants to control R, or to strengthen or replicate it, the *inside* of R is what needs to be studied. While one wants to know something about the market within which R operates, under the systems approach one is especially concerned with how R operates within that environment, and with the difference between a successful and a less successful R in such operations (that is, an "interfirm" contrast).

Consider the analogy between two firms, F_1 and F_2, producing the same product in two non-competing markets, M_1 and M_2. If, at the end of a period, F_1 shows high output, low cost, and high profit, should we say that the explanation for its success relative to F_2 is due to differences in conditions *within the market* M_1, compared with M_2?

Sometimes this may be so, and if it is we would look principally to differences in demand conditions in the two markets—hence, in consumer preferences and income—for the explanation. But our analysis would be incomplete if we did not look as well to possible differences *within the firms*, F_1 and F_2, to account for their different degrees of success. For example, we might find that management in F_1 is superior to that in F_2, or that labor productivity in F_1 surpasses that in F_2, or that wage rates and labor incentives differ in the two firms, or that the speed of delivery or the quality of product differs. Market conditions may not differ at all, or not be enough to explain differences in performance.

In other words, even within the framework of a purely endogenous explanation (in the sense of *conditions within the country* rather than assistance from outside the country), we should make a distinction between factors accounting for R's success which are to be found *within* R itself and factors prevailing within the country but *outside* R.

Thus, endogeny needs to be further subdivided: endogenous with respect to the country, and endogenous with respect to the R movement itself. On this basis, one can accept pure endogeny without accepting the hearts-and-minds view that it is conditions prevailing in the country that explain successful R. It is possible to assert, on the one hand, that the success of R may be determined by factors inside its area of operation, and to deny, on the other, that its fortune depends decisively on the amount of sympathy for R and the extent of deprivation to which the bulk of the population is subjected. In this light, the subject of rebellion and counterrebellion should be considered as much a problem in organization and management as in political-economic development.

A comment very much in this spirit is made by George Kennan. Discussing the Bolshevik revolution's conquest of the Tsarist regime, he observes that the revolution's success depended on

> . . . the extraordinary discipline, compactness and conspiratorial tightness of the Communist Party; the magnificent political leadership . . . [of] Lenin; and the driving, unrelenting military leadership which the Party gave to the Red Army units in the civil war. . . . The cutting edge of these qualities was of far greater effectiveness than any of the shifting, undependable winds of popular sympathy.[22]

THE POPULATION BETWEEN R AND A

The basic importance of the population to R is as a principal—though not exclusive—source of inputs on which the insurgent system depends. This role is not necessarily less important than that ascribed to it in the hearts-and-minds view, but the role is different. What are some of the differences?

One difference is that the required size of the population that provides the needed inputs can be, as noted earlier, quite small.[23] Depending upon the size of the R system and the stage of its activities, the inputs of food, personnel, weapons, and information that it needs can be more or less limited, and consequently the subset of the population that is involved can be extremely limited. In other words, a small popular minority can be operationally a quite satisfactory underpinning for R, with a generalized impact that may be relatively large.

As a source of inputs, the important characteristic for scrutiny in this minority of the population is behavior or conduct, not sympathies or preferences. Conduct is, of course, affected by both preferences (goals) and opportunities (options). But there are at least two reasons that suggest the analysis of opportunities may be more rewarding than that of preferences. The first is that opportunities are more readily and reliably observable than preferences. Economy of effort would generally warrant seeking explanations that are readily available before looking for those that are elusive. The second reason is that the particular set of preferences to which the behavior of the population is relevant may have relatively little to do with sympathy for, or identification with, either contesting side—the insurgents or the authority. A pervasive, and probably frequent, passivity of feeling toward both sides is quite consonant with popular behavior that is highly beneficial to one side. As we have argued earlier, limiting damage or enhancing gain may be a sufficient explanation for the behavior of the population, without recourse to more elusive explanations concerning putative preferences or sympathies.

According to the alternative approach we are describing, it is appropriate to view an individual or group within the population as a rational decisionmaker who assesses opportunities and consequences of alternative actions.[24] The assessment involves a set of preference functions in which feeling for A or R may be relatively unimportant, or may even take a different direction from that obtained by attributing the burden of explanation for popular behavior to sympathetic feelings alone.

Moreover, the time horizon over which the calculations of this hypothetical and rational *decisionmaking* unit extends may be extremely short. The need to avoid today's damage may overwhelm considerations of long-run preference, or cumulative long-run gain, associated with a different course of action. (The time discount for the population, searching for a path to survival between pressures of R and A, may be extremely high.)

As an example of behavior from pure profit-maximization, note the following description by a Viet Cong defector of the reasons for his action:

> Question: What made you decide to rally [that is, defect]?
> Answer: . . . I thought that in fighting on the GVN side, a soldier may be happy because he has a good salary and even though he dies on the battlefield, he dies with a full stomach. On the contrary, a VC soldier usually eats at 3 p.m. a rice bowl as small as that [the subject describes it with his fingers] and he walks all night long to fight and to die with an empty stomach.[25]

Or again the following statement by a Viet Cong prisoner (or defector?):

> I do not know which side is winning . . . I did not think about which side was winning. I take the side which can do the most for me.[26]

Frequently, of course, pure profit-maximizing or damage-limiting influences may be less operative than a mixture of the two. For example, both influences may merge when the population is astute enough to comply, or seem to comply, with *both* A and R. Thus, in the Philippines during the Aguinaldo rebellion, a picture of jointly compliant behavior emerges in the following account by General Adna Chaffee:

> Throughout these islands, wherever a *presidente* of a *pueblo* or *cabeza* of a *barrio* was appointed or elected under America authority, he, with few exceptions . . . acted in the same capacity for the insurgents. . . . This dual form of government existed everywhere, in strongly garrisoned towns like Manila and in the small-est *barrio*. . . . [They] now commenced the difficult task of serving two masters. In all lawful matters, they served with due appearance of loyalty to the America government, while at the same time . . . they secretly levied and collected taxes . . . from the people. . . . They held communications with the enemy, and in all ways open to them gave the guerrilla bands aid and comfort.[27]

Notwithstanding the earlier point about the high time discount for the population and the probably overriding necessity of choosing today's safety at the cost of tomorrow's welfare, there is presumably a negative correlation between a population's belief in the eventual victory of a particular side (whether A or R) and the level of immediate threat required from that side to obtain a given degree of compliance. If I expect a particular side to lose—that is, myself to be ultimately at the mercy of its enemy—I will need a higher instant threat to offset the forecast of future damage at the hands of the other side.

Note that in the preceding discussion of the importance of profit-maximizing—in both the pure- and mixed-motivation examples—there would appear to be an inconsistency with the earlier discussion of the limited effectiveness of raising income and alleviating deprivation in securing compliant behavior. Resolution of the apparent inconsistency can be put in the following terms: considerations of gain have a more certain effect on income than on preferences; to the extent that a given side can manage the rate of exchange between gains and compliant behavior—that is, the substitution effect—its access to compliance is likely to be enhanced. But if the terms of exchange are not manipulated at the same time as income is raised, the benefactor may very well be himself adversely affected by the benefits he is providing, which may redound instead to the advantage of the other side.[28]

To recapitulate the main points of contrast between the role of the population in the approach we have been describing and its role in the hearts-and-minds view, let us set down four principle points:

1. As a source of critical inputs needed by R in its growth and progress, the proportion

of the population that is important can be a small minority, rather than a plurality or majority.

2. In discussing the population, emphasis should be placed on behavior, rather than on attitudes and sympathies. Attitudes, in the sense of preferences, affect behavior but are not identical with it; nor in most cases are they the primary influence on it.

3. In addition to attitudes and feelings, what influences behavior are the opportunities available to the population for choosing. In the population's calculations of the options available, *predictions* of the consequences of alternative actions may be crucial. Such predictions determine the estimates of profit (gain) or damage (loss) which influence behavior.

4. Moreover, the predictions within which profit-maximizing or damage-limiting calculations are made are very likely to give heavy weight to short-term as against long-term prospects—that is, to be accompanied by a high implicit time discount.

On each of these four points, the message usually conveyed by the hearts-and-minds view is distinctly different from, if not opposite to, that which we have been advancing. To be sure, our approach does not deny that there are those within R and A (and in the population, generally) who are disposed to disregard personal considerations on behalf of loyalty to a cause. Often R has an edge over A in this respect. But frequently feelings about a cause begin to merge with calculations of gain and lass. And where dissonance between them arises and endures, the result is often a change of feeling, rather than acceptance of repeated loss.

APPENDIX

Cost-Benefit Calculations and Behavior

The demand and supply formulation can also be described in terms of the costs and benefits of rebellion, as the population views them. Consider the following diagram in which costs (as calculated by an individual or group) are measured vertically, benefits horizontally.[1]

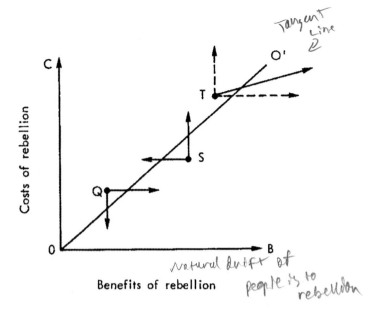

For all points lying along OO′, costs and benefits are equal. For A, the desirable region is above OO′, for R below OO′. At any given time, an individual's calculations may locate him at a particular point in the field. For example, an individual at Q is a supporter of A; or, more accurately, a nonsupporter of R. Toward such an individual, R's objective should be to shift him east or south; conversely, from A's point of view, it is desirable to shift an individual located at S west or north. When both R and A engage in such efforts, it is the resultant that matters. Resultant vectors that are flatter than OO′ will tend to strengthen R; those that are steeper will tend to strengthen A. The diagonal vector at T is an example of the former.

In demand-supply terms, eastward (westward) movements represent an upward (downward) shift in demand for R; northward (southward) movements represent increases (decreases) in costs, hence a fall (rise) in the supply of R.[2] Our prior discussion (and some of what follows in Chapter 5, below) suggests that A's efforts are perhaps more likely to be efficiently expended on raising costs than in lowering demand, while R's efforts, with nearly equal likelihood, may be efficiently expended on either. Yet, if concentration on raising costs causes A to overlook R's efforts to raise demand, the resultant may be flatter than OO′, to A's disadvantage. Indeed, if R is astute and A clumsy, R may turn A's efforts to raise costs into increased benefits instead. Various examples of this "judo" effect (provoking A to overreact, decoyed reprisals, coercion based on poor (or no) intelligence) are presented in Chapter 6.[3]

ENDNOTES

1. For clarification of the demand/supply distinction, and the important interactions between them, see pp. 37-39.
2. See this chapter, pp. 30-32.
3. That change exposes and intensifies vulnerabilities to insurgency is, of course, not confined to traditional societies. Thus, in the United States during the past decade, the most rapid improvements in civil rights since the Civil War have been followed or accompanied by the most violent resistance to the residual, if declining, discrimination. Eric Hoffer has eloquently and exhaustively examined the phenomenon in his various works. See, for example, **The True Believer** (New York: Harper & Bros., 1951); **The Passionate State of Mind** (New York: Harper & Row, 1955); and **The Ordeal of Change** (New York: Harper & Row, 1963). For another penetrating exposition, see Robert Waelder. **Progress and Revolution** (New York: International Universities Press, 1967).
4. Thompson, **op.cit.**, pp. 21-22.
5. In "The Prospects of Academe," **Encounter**, August, 1968, p. 62.
6. See Chapter 7, pp. 132-137. Although the characteristics we have been describing typify the less developed, transitional countries, they are not entirely excluded from the more developed countries. Watts and Appalachia are LDC pockets within an MDC garment. While opportunities for insurgency are more limited in the MDCs, they are not absent.
7. See Chapter 2, pp. 22-24.
8. Discussed more fully in Chapters 4 and 6.
9. R's effective use of persuasion is closely related to the asymmetrical quality of the demand for rebellion, alluded to earlier: such demand may be easier to shift upward than downward. See p. 29.
10. For any set of implementers of authority (officials, policemen, military personnel) there will always be a lower-performing segment whose discredit is easier and more appropriate for R to target.
11. See Chapter 5, pp. 76-83.

12.
13. Cf. Robert Levine, **The Arms Debate** (Cambridge: Harvard University Press, 1963), pp. 229-233, 240-243, 309; Herman Kahn, **On Thermonuclear War** (Princeton: Princeton University Press, 1960), pp. 126-144, 303-304, 518-521.
14. See the early discussion of income and substitution effects in Chapter 2, pp. 19-20. See also the Appendix to chapter 3, pp. 46-47.
15. In formal terms, the distinction between demand and supply relates to two functions:
$$D=D(p,x_i)$$
$$S=S(e,y_i)$$
D is the quantity of R activities that will be bought; p is the price per unit. S is the R activities produced; c is the cost per unit; x_i and y_i are other influences on demand and supply, respectively. (Both D and S can be disaggregated into endogenous and exogenous components.) The intersection between D and S determines the scale of R, or, from another standpoint, the probability or R.

    The demand curve is likely to be "kinked" at both high and low price levels (because of a shortage of wholly committed, ardent supporters at high levels, and the "bandwagon" effect at low levels), and hard to shift (inelastic with respect to policies and programs). The supply curve may have a negative second derivative and later an inflection point because of economics of scale and efficiencies for "learning-by-doing."
16. The interactions can operate both through the effects of **shifts** in demand on the supply function, and through **movements** along a given demand function. For example, shifting demand functions may stimulate (or discourage) research and development, and the emergence of technological change that influences supply. And movements along a given demand function can cause suppliers to accelerate (or decelerate) cost-reducing innovations. Where sellers and buyers are numerous and atomistic, the interaction are weakened.
17. See the statements by Thompson and Hook, footnote 4, this chapter.
18. See Chapter 6.
19. Fulbright, **op. cit.**; Hilsman, **op. cit.**; Halberstam, **op. cit.**
20. It is another question whether the level of, and changes in, the exogeny / endogeny ratio may not be highly important for U.S. policy. It may be the case that those Rs in which U.S. political

interests are most involved are likely to be cases in which the ratio is large, or is rising. However, one must be careful about imputing too much significance to this ratio, inasmuch as it can change over time. Furthermore, there are likely to be considerable lags between the achievement of a particular level and the flow and processing of information relating to it. Hence, what was at one time a high exogeny / endogeny ratio may have, by the time the relevant information reaches a decision point in A's bureaucracy, already become substantially lower.

21. See **New York Times,** January 10, 1967, p. 3; John Randolph article in **Los Angeles Times.** April 2, 1967; Richard I. Clutterbuck. **The Long, Long War** (New York: Praeger, 1966), p. 74.
22. **Foreign Affairs,** Vol. 46, No. 1, October, 1967, 7.
23. See Chapter 2, pp. 9-10.
24. The Appendix to this chapter extends this idealized view of the individual as a rational calculator in the insurgency context.
25. From a series of RAND interviews with former Viet Cong members.
26. **Ibid.**
27. Quoted by Leon Wolff in **Little Brown Brother** (Garden City: Doubleday, 1961), p. 334.
28. See the Appendix to Chapter 2.

Appendix

1. We assume (conveniently) that nonmaterial and probabilistic elements in benefits and costs can be handled through a Von Neumann-Morgenstern decision-theoretic process that individuals in the population engage in, or stimulate in an approximate way. Cf. Howard R. Raiffa, **Decision Analysis** (Reading, Mass Addison-Wesley. 1968).
2. The cost-benefit formulation can also be related to the discussion of preference effects, substitution effects, and income effects, mentioned in Chapter 2 (see Appendix to Chapter 2). The preference effect represents movements along the horizontal axis (from A's viewpoint, westward movements: from R's eastward). The substitution effect implies vertical movements (north, from A's viewpoint: south from R's). The income effect may move individuals southward, to R's advantage, because the costs of rebellion relative to income now seem lower than before. Or it may move them northward, to A's advantage, because they fear the loss of their increased income as a result of rebellion.
3. We are indebted to Daniel Ellsberg for this analogy. See also George K. Tanham and Dennis J. Duncanson. "Some Dilemmas of Countersurgency." Foreign Affairs Vol. 48, No. 1, October, 1969, pp. 119-121.

The Rebellion's Viewpoint

Structure, Operations, and Proclivities

Nathan Leites and Charles Wolf, Jr.

START AND STRUCTURE

An insurgent organization shares important characteristics with other modern organizations that operate in situations of conflicting interests: large corporations, trade unions, the military services, political parties. Like such organizations, R recruits, trains, and promotes its personnel; obtains and generates information, including information relating to immediate and potential adversaries; locates and procures other inputs that its operations require; raises and allocates funds; and produces and distributes services or products. It carries on these functions, moreover, in an environment of strong interaction between its own decisions and its anticipation of the vulnerabilities, defenses, and countermoves of an adversary. Knowing and preempting the adversary have an important influence on the choices that R makes. Like other organizations, R requires a reticulated structure to perform these functions, and to command and control them.

Yet R has distinctive attributes as well. Its goals include the erosion of existing law, order, and authority; rather than operate within them, it seeks to supplant them with a law, order, and authority of its own. (Of course, R's presump-

tion is that the supplanting order is better than the supplanted one.) R's means are distinguished by a readiness to use violence and terror to accomplish its aims. In this respect, R's distinctive characteristics may be shared by criminal organizations such as the Mafia, outlaw bands of the Western frontier, and the Ku Klux Klan. But its political aims serve to differentiate R from such organizations and place it closer to radical (if more peaceful) political parties.

The operations and proclivities of R, like those of other organizations, are likely to vary with its stage of development and rate of growth. Analysts have variously proposed three or five stages,[1] representing different levels of R's organization and activity. Whichever classification is used, the point is that R is a plural rather than a singular phenomenon, whose operational characteristics vary with its stage of development. An analogy with the process of economic development suggests itself.

One of the standard theories in the economic-development literature concerns the several stages of economic-development, the characteristics of each stage, and the values of key parameters that apply there. Rostow, for example,

Leites, Nathan, and Charles Wolf, Jr. (1970). *Rebellion and Authority: An Analytic Essay on Insurgent Conflicts.* Santa Monica, CA: Rand. Reproduction authorization obtained from RAND.

distinguishes a Stage I (traditional society), in which subsistence agriculture is dominant, investment and savings are low, and income is relatively stagnant; a Stage II (the "preconditions" stage), in which preconditions for growth are established in the form of a buildup of infrastructural investment; the beginnings of industry; the creation of a skilled labor supply; a rise in savings and investment; and a more rapid growth in gross national product than in population; and a Stage III (the "take-off" into self-sustaining growth), in which investment and savings rise (to exceed 12 percent of gross national product); industry expands; and national product grows substantially faster than population.[2]

It may be interesting to consider some of the relationships between these stages and the familiar stages in the R literature. One point of interest is that, while attention is given to attitudes, and changes in attitudes that occur over the different stages of economic development, generally the emphasis is placed on changes in key input parameters such as savings, investment, skills, and technology. The same emphasis might be applied to the analysis of insurgency (as we are suggesting in the systems approach discussed here). That is, one might look more closely at changes in key parameters that accompany the launching of R into a self-sustaining phase: for example, the ratio between persons with deep ideological conviction ("true believers") and cadres; between cadres and rank-and-file; between rank-and-file and active and passive supporters; and between supporters and the populace as a whole. Another interesting relationship—also the calculable and variable over the various stages of R—is the ratio discussed earlier between endogeny and exogeny. Moreover, some of the same reinforcement phenomena that apply to the successive stages of development also apply to the stages of R. As R manages, with increasing effectiveness, to disrupt law and order and undermine the functions of A, it becomes easier for R to acquire inputs (recruits, funds,[3] intelligence), which in turn increases the effectiveness of R's efforts to undermine the functions of A. A self-sustaining R—where the ratio of endogeny to exogeny approaches infinity—is the result.

Pursuing the analogy further, there may be a high correlation between parametric changes that accompany movement toward higher stages of economic development and those that accom-pany movement toward higher stages of insurgency. While environmental characteristics of less developed countries facilitate R, as noted earlier, the process of economic and social change in that environment may, within a certain range, contribute further to R's growth. A more skilled labor force, particularly if unemployed, may ease the recruitment and training of cadres. Growth of income may widen R's potential tax base. Development and technological progress may lead to increased unemployment for certain kinds of labor (rural as well as urban), to urban congestion, and to an intensification of frictions and tensions that make R's tasks easier and strain A's limited capacity to take preventive or countervailing action. Contrary to the usual belief, stages of development and stages of insurgency may therefore be positively associated with on another over a considerable range.[4]

It is important to distinguish the different stages of R, because the problems encountered in each—both from R's standpoint and from A's—are different. Indeed, the distinction between tactical nuclear war and conventional war is hardly greater than the distinction between an embryonic and a matured insurgency: between one in a formative stage, where the population is being organized, training and recruitment are underway, occasional acts of violence take place, and challenge to the established order is beginning; and one in an advanced stage, where the insurgent civil and military organization is already strong, guerrilla operations in small units are underway, and mobile warfare in larger units has begun.

Consequently, optimal strategies for counter-rebellion are likely to vary with the stage R has reached. For example, R's selection of targets for coercion and persuasion is likely to depend òn its level of development (one possible selection rule: target the "bad" early, the "good" later). On A's part, the relative importance of information and intelligence, compared with firepower and mobility, is also likely to vary with the stage of R's development, as we shall discuss later.[5]

Like other organizations, R starts small. Its long-term objectives are large, but its hard core of entrepreneurs and managers is small, and its initial program of preparation and activity is limited. At the start, it may face competition from other potential revolutionary movements (for example, Castro's initially competitive relationship with the Communist Party and other dissident groups in Cuba).[6] To pursue the economic analogy further, one might regard this competition as similar to that faced by a new firm from other firms in the same industry, as suggested earlier.[7] As it develops, R is likely to encounter, besides competition from the *same* side of the "market," opposition from *the other* side of the market: from A, depending on the sensitivity and effectiveness of A's detection system in the early stages of R's activities. Again, one may liken A's opposition to an emerging R to the opposition that a new firm encounters from trade unions or existing firms, which may raise the new firm's costs, or from uninterested consumers, who may resist the new firm's product.

Thus, an emerging R must surmount competition and opposition to achieve exclusiveness, or it may stagnate or regress toward failure. The analogous aim for the emergent firm is to achieve high profits, and if possible dominance, in the industry within the constraints of the antitrust laws—which is to say, as large a share of the market as is profitable and as the laws allow.

If one views insurgency in the terms we have been describing, it becomes relevant to ask what can be learned about R by examining the structure and operations of other organizations. Recognizing R's distinctive attributes, as well as those it shares, the organizations that may be particularly instructive to consider include enterprises that have in common with R a disposition toward violence and systematic violation of existing laws (although they may, in contrast, lack its dedication to a cause): criminal organizations such as the Mafia and the Chicago underworld of the 1920s. Some of our examples will be drawn from this context, as well as from certain familiar (and less familiar) rebellions of the past. In the following discussion, we present propositions about the operating characteristics and tactical doctrine of R, illustrating them with relevant references, quotations, and experience drawn from both R and non-R contests.

How Does R Get Started and Grow?

Our basic formulation of R's emergence and growth has already been presented[8] and needs only brief summary here. The environment of a typical less developed country[9] provides the market for R. The many deep grievances, frictions, and hostilities that pervade this environment, combined with its social and economic disjointedness and the resources available—including time and effort—for commitment by individuals and groups according to their preferences, determine the *demand* side of the market.[10] The terms on which such basic inputs as people, food, material, and information are obtained from various combinations of internal and external sources, and the efficiency with which they are organized and managed for conversion into the R's activities, constitute the *supply* side of the market. The intersection between demand and supply determines R's intensity at any point in time, and changes (shifts) in these factors account for R's development (growth or recession) over time.[11] (It should be evident that while communist management of the supply side of the market is a case that commands the particular attention of U.S. policymakers, in principle, in other contexts, entrepreneurship and management can be provided under auspices other than communism—such as the United States or its allies—perhaps for R within communist countries.)[11]

How Are Targets Selected?

Two aspects of the problem of target selection in the insurgency context should be distinguished: how an external supporter of R (exogeny) selects targets (countries) to encourage and support, and how R itself (endogeny) selects internal targets (individuals or institutions) to attack.

In divided countries such as North Korea and North Vietnam, target selection is simplified by the saliency of the "unliberated" half of the country—that is, by the very fact of division and the tradition of some degree of national unity.[12] But even in such cases, the selection may not be simple. There have, for example, been strong interdependencies between the insurgencies in Laos and South Vietnam. Even if liberation of South Vietnam through a successful R is the goal, how is the allocation of support between insurgency in Laos and that in South Vietnam determined? In this case, the answer has probably depended to a considerable extent on logistical considerations: the dependence of successful R in South Vietnam on a reasonably safe access route along the Annamite chain running down the eastern corridor of Laos to South Vietnam. Hence, it was efficient to support the Pathet Lao *before* shifting to the major effort in South Vietnam.

But in other cases, the decision process may be more complex. How valuable is it to the Soviet Union, for example, to increase the chances of a communist government's coming into power in on Latin America country rather than another? What are the chances for an insurgency to succeed in one country rather than another, and how sensitive is this outcome to various levels of external support? Does a potential endogenous movement have to establish its credentials for receiving external support by demonstrating performance in some way? Or does the external sponsor calculate its priority targets more or less independently of demonstrated performance by R? The questions have rarely been asked, probably because they are so hard to answer.

Perhaps the opportunities for emerging insurgencies to bargain one source of external support against another have grown because of fractures among the communist countries: Soviet support may be more readily forthcoming to avoid a possible Chinese monopoly, and vice versa. On the other hand, the extremely high cost of providing support for the communist regime in Cuba, after its acquisition of power, may have reduced the willingness of at least the Soviet Union to be drawn in as a potential source of support for R. Our ignorance of the external targeting process exceeds by a wide margin what we know.

Turning to the process by which R selects targets to attack within a country, we find that the result may be more predictable. In general, an efficient R is likely to start by picking, as targets for violent attack, resented, low-performing officials and landlords. In any set of officials or landlords, some must obviously be less good and more resented than others. There will always be a median performer, and exactly half the remaining officials will be worse. (The definition obviously also applies to municipal officials, policemen, and college administrators in more developed countries; and the same implications follow for targeting in urban and university rebellions.) Choosing the low-performers for attack enhances the probability of acceptance or endorsement by the population and minimizes the probability of denunciation, because the blame for the terror is extenuated by the offensiveness of the target itself. While ends do not necessarily justify means, it is only ends that *can* provide justification—in this case, by explaining the violence in terms of the target's own offensiveness. In some cases, the R may not choose to proceed against such targets itself; instead, it may settle for removing popular fears and compunctions about squaring old accounts. Members of the population may then freely perform the violence intended by the R (as with the "land reforms" in China after 1949 and in North Vietnam in 1956).

As R grows from small to large, and from weak to strong, the level and the quality of targets may rise. Executing a good official, or a generous landlord, may then evoke reactions of acceptance and nondenunciation from the population, not because the act can be extenuated as a deserved punishment, but rather because previous executions by R have excited general awe and fear. And execution of "good" targets later further strengthens R's claims to irresistible power and inevitable victory. Resignation rather than extenuation is then the principal characteristic of the population's response, though, of course, the two attitudes tend to be reinforcing rather than conflicting.

As R grows, it may thus move from the "bad" to the "good" targets, and from the low and relatively inconspicuous to the high and conspicuous targets.[13] In some cases, R may also *start* with an attack on a sector within the established order that is both effective and even relatively close to R's own goals. The aim may be to disrupt an effort that, by its accomplishments, is conceived as presenting the greatest dangers to those who claim favorable developments are not feasible within the existing structure. By all tokens of what is newfangled rather than old fashioned, the recently created campus at Nanterre, northwest of Paris, was one of the most advanced in the West (hence, in the world). It was there that the "Twenty Second of March Movement" arose in 1968, and the functioning of the university was made so difficult as to induce its closure—the occasion for the outbreak of the "May revolution."

OPERATING CHARACTERISTICS: DOCTRINE, ADAPTATION, LEARNING

Despite R's variability over time and place, several general characteristics usually identify its operations, as discussed in the following paragraphs.

Efficiency and Austerity

It is characteristic of R to preach and to practice austerity in individual behavior and efficiency in organizational activity. There is an obvious (though not logically tight) link between an affinity for puritanism in individual behavior and a concern with efficiency in organizational behavior. And both contribute to the belief, within R and the population, that R's victory is inevitable, a belief that, as we have see, is important in influencing calculations and predictions and enhancing support for R.

As formulated by Nasution:

> A guerrilla must fight with . . . economy . . . he must calculate his gains and losses like a good businessman.[14]

Pressed by penury and spurred by devotion to ultimate goals for which everything else should be but means, R typically rejects the professional military man's, or the romantic revolutionary's, idolatry of certain stances. As noted by Nasution:

> Guerrilla troops . . . should not defend or attack only to be putting up resistance or attacking [for its own sake]. . . . Acts of "letting people see that we are fighting . . ." must be stopped.[15]

The dedication—in doctrine, and frequently in action as well—to the "cost-effectiveness" calculus may come easier in a milieu at the ends of the military spectrum than in the conventional middle. In the conventional middle, innovation in calculus and conduct is not stimulated by sharp breaks in technique or organization, or by acute scarcity of resources (resulting from the typical poverty of R or the overwhelming magnitude of nuclear weapons costs).

In a sense, the initial pressure of inferiority and resource constraints impels R to discover those elementary principles of rationality and efficiency which it took much assistance and analysis, as well as very high weapons costs, to demonstrate to the wealthy establishments operating at either end of the military spectrum. When wealthy establishments regress to small wars, such as Vietnam, their concern for efficiency may undergo a dramatic lapse. Weapons costs are (individually) small, and the adversary seem, at first, to be inferior. Consequently, the spur to efficiency is lost, costs accumulate, and allocative choices are resolved by simply raising budget levels. A "small war," costing $25 billion annually, may be the result. Efficiency in small wars is evidently harder to learn by A's large establishment than by R's small one. Indeed, for R the learning is mandatory.[16]

Resisting Temptations to "Go Conventional"

Still, the efficiency that rebellions espouse as a matter of doctrine and achieve in practice has to be strenuously safeguarded against increasing enticements. As R grows, for example, it is likely to be tempted to accelerate its entrance into the circle of respectable powers by "going conventional." Mao, for example, affirms that it is precisely "during the progress of hostilities [that] guerrillas gradually develop into orthodox forces."[17] to lure R into making the change prematurely may be an objective of A, whose advantage in firepower makes this operational mode clearly preferable to it. In a remarkable manual on guerrilla wars written in the late nineteenth century, Major (later General) Charles Callwell observes:

> . . . at times it will be advisable to impress the hostile [guerrilla] forces with the belief that they are confronted by a less formidable opponent than is in fact the case, for it may be the only means of getting them to fight. . . . For general engagements are the object to be aimed at [by A].[18]

A possibly less astute A may seek the same objective not by stealth or deception, but by maneuver. Thus, after the appearance of conventional Viet Minh units in the fall of 1950,

> . . . the major objective which the French . . . [were] pursuing . . . [was] that of being able to maneuver the enemy's . . . regular divisions into a situation where they could be destroyed in one great battle. . . . This . . . search for the set-piece battle became an obsession of the successive French commanders-in-chief in Indochina until the end of the war.[19]

Of course, the temptation for R to go conventional prematurely is one that A abets at some nonnegligible risk to itself. By concentrating its efforts and attention on the set-piece conventional battle, A may divert resources and activities from the smaller-scale, unconventional operations that it success depends on.

Sometimes R succumbs to the temptation to go conventional with effects that are damaging (for example, Giap in the spring of 1951) or even disastrous (the Greek communists in the late 1940s). As General Grivas recalls:

> The rebellion . . . started with guerrilla bands operating over the whole of Greece from Cape Tainaron to Macedonia and Thrace. . . . [It] continually gained ground . . . [but then], obsessed by the idea that they ought to have under their complete control a strip of territory where they could set up a Government of "Free Greece," they chose an area in the Pindus mountains where they established a defensive line. There, however, their forces sustained a crushing defeat at the hands of the infinitely stronger National Army. . . .[20]

The operational requirement that a successful R forego conventionality complements the doctrinal stress on Puritanism and austerity in personal behavior. Thus, to survive and be successful, a rebellion must have the capacity to renounce the lures of modernity in military means, and even to regress to primitiveness—a lesson Rs have had to relearn repeatedly. For example, note this description of the Philippine rebels of 1899:

> All spring and summer, Aguinaldo toyed with the idea of abandoning Luna's concept of head-on, massed resistance to the United States. The Filipino could not match the American in tactics, marksmanship, artillery, naval support, ammunition and rifles; but there was another way . . . this was guerrilla warfare. . . .[21]

And again in the spring of 1946, although the Viet Minh had already created rather large, conventional units in the South, in the face of the French offensive in the fall and the winter,

> . . . the Viet Minh, renouncing open combat, dissolved its divisions and its regiments. . . .[22]

Similarly, the Algerian rebels dissolved their larger units and operations in response to the French offensives of 1959-1960.

Again, in Vietnam, after de Lattre defeated him in the north in the winter and spring of 1951, Giap refused to engage his conventional units again until the French gave him both a safe and promising opportunity at Dien-Bien-Phu three years later, and perhaps unexpectedly.

Striving for Flexibility

A rebellion of the puritan stamp is apt to shift back and forth between sharply diverging modes, as changing conditions appear to recommend it. One reason for such behavior is the precariousness of R's situation, as noted earlier. Another is its doctrinal fight against the human disposition toward creature worship (veneration of means) at the expense of glorifying God (adoration of the ultimate goal), which is at the ideological core of modern, puritan-minded R.

R's flexibility and mobility are noted in Callwell's manual:

> Restricted by no precedents, governed by no strategic code, embarrassed by no encumbrances, they come and go at will. . . . The enemy is untrammeled by the shackles which so limit the regular army's freedom of action. And this fact is of great strategical importance.[23]

However, Rs are rarely "ten feet tall," and their capacity to acquire and sustain such flexibility may be severely limited. If a high degree of centralization, as is often the case, is combined with a high degree of vulnerability both in the top command and in its downward communications, R's actual stance may be one of protracted rigidity, with belated and abrupt shifts of position. Commenting on the command and control structure in Malaya, for example, one observer recalls:

> The Communist high command convened only about twice a year to map out policy for the entire six-month period to come, and their communications were poor. As a result, the British gained . . . advantage over a considerable period if they could change the situation in such a way as to make the agreed policy inapplicable. [There was] at least one instance where the guerrillas recognized a certain method as bad, but were unable to change it until the next semi-annual meeting of their high command.[24]

In addition to the limits imposed by its imperfect technology of command, communication, and control, R's flexibility may be limited by the need to maintain some visible forward momentum. Thus, the prospect of de-escalating from larger to smaller unit actions in Vietnam, from main-force actions to guerrilla actions and sabotage, is one that the Viet Cong cannot view with relish. However, the hazard presented to R's organization and morale—particularly that of its marginal adherents—by a loss of momentum does not imply that an R once broken cannot be resumed again (as with the Hukbalahap in the Philippines), or that an R cannot be maintained at a low intensity for long (as in Burma since virtually the end of World War II). By subduing its impatience for total power and a new order, R may develop and sustain a consciously prized capacity for protracted conflict, with a slow rate of change in the balance of strength between itself and its enemy, as well as with a tolerance for long pauses, or—though not without hazard—even extended regressions. While it is irremediably inferior to A in total firepower, R may exceed A's staying power—particularly that part supported by a foreign prop. In fact, it is a prideful conviction of its own staying power which offers R a sustaining substitute for traditional victory.

Emphasis on Staying Power Rather than Victory

While no doubt often dreaming of "victory" over its enemy in that word's traditional meaning, R may steel itself to recognize that this is almost certainly beyond its means, and that the pursuit of such an objective might amount to suicide. Thus, commenting on the "Preliminary General Plan of Insurrectionary Action in Cyprus," General Grivas notes:

> . . . it should not be supposed that by these means we should expect to impose a total defeat on the British forces in Cyprus.[25]

Dien-Bien-Phu is the exception—and even that battle left the enemy with much of his force in the theater, and with a vast potential outside it (without, of course, the will to use the one or the other).

Staying power rather than traditional victory provides R with its main chance. R's aim is to aggravate and exploit its enemy's limited willingness to allocate resources to the fight. The aim is to degrade the cost-effectiveness of A's effort to such an extent, and to so erode A's prospects (particularly as they may relate to support from a foreign source) that withdrawal becomes indicated. Such an outcome is favored, of course, by the familiar prescription that subduing a given effort of the rebels requires A to commit a large multiple effort.[26]

The pattern is familiar from other rebellions at very different times and places. In the Philippine rebellion against the Americans, for example:

> The insurrectos had no hope of winning the war by guerrilla tactics. With their eyes fixed on the political future, when Bryan's victory would bring them . . . deliverance, they played a waiting game.[27]

In the Irish rebellion:

> In the early summer of 1921 . . . the strength of the British forces in Ireland amounted to about 50,000 . . . the Cabinet estimated that the only way to make sure of winning . . . was to raise an additional 100,000. . . . Lloyd George hesitated to call for the 100,000 men needed. . . .[28]

In another situation, R may aim not so much at leading A to consider the cost of combat excessive, as at weakening A in its conflict with another enemy, one more powerful than R. It is the *other* enemy who will defeat A, although he might not be able to do so if the power he confronts were not being reduced by R at the same time. (For example, the resistance in Axis-occupied counties during World War II in relation to the Allies, or that to Napoleon in Spain in relation to Wellington.)

"Playing it Safe": Surprise, Stealth, and Evasion

Linked with its emphasis on austerity, flexibility, and staying power is R's preoccupation with "playing it safe." The rule is to seek or accept contact with the enemy's forces only when you are certain of success.[29]

The doctrine is amplified by Nasution:

> An enemy target of one platoon must be attacked . . . by one company or more, a target of one company must be attacked by one battalion.[30]

Elaborating "the tactics of avoiding strength and striking at weakness," Mao teaches that

> . . . if we do not have a 100 percent guarantee of victory, we should not fight a battle; . . . when the enemy is well armed and his troops numerous and courageous, . . . we have to evade clashes.[31]

And Guevara, for all his reputation for audacity, displays tactical conservatism by noting:

"Even though surrounded, a well-dug-in enemy.
. . is poor prey."[32]

In its emphasis on "playing it safe," R stresses
the strength it acquires through elusiveness.
Retreat and withdrawal are not to be avoided;
they are in the nature of the struggle. Break off
contact immediately—the doctrine runs—when
the calculations that led you to engage in it are
revealed to have been wrong. Then the prime
objective should be instant disengagement, and
the only purpose in fighting should be to overcome the enemy's obstruction of the withdrawal.[33] Thus, when a Viet Minh unit was
surprised by the French, the French commander:

> . . . realized that the enemy, far from fighting to
> the death, was trying desperately to buy time to
> last until the evening in order to withdraw into
> the nearby hills. . . .[34]

Elusiveness and withdrawal are similarly emphasized in the tactical teaching of Guevara:

> . . . when [guerrilla] troops are encircled by the
> enemy . . . before darkness, pick out the best
> escape route. After nightfall, move out with
> stealth. . . .[35]

Surprise in the offensive is the counterpart to
stealth in the defensive. As Mao elaborates the
point:

> The peculiar quality of . . . [guerrilla] opera-
> tions . . . lies entirely in taking the enemy by
> surprise. . . . A guerrilla unit . . . should think
> frequently about the ways in which it can
> appear . . . where the enemy does not expect it.
> . . . Then, following the principle that "the
> thunderclap leaves no time to cover one's ears,"
> the unit can strike . . . and vanish . . . without a
> trace. . . .[36]

Emphasis is thus placed on hit and hide, a pre-
cept whose accomplishment is facilitated by the
fact that there is a negative relationship between
the level of a country's economic development
and the time required for reinforcements to
arrive.

Retreat, far from being a loss or a humiliation, is, properly used, glorious and rewarding.
Success in withdrawing against odds—foiling
the enemy's determination to annihilate R there
and then—may prove and foster R's sense of
strength.[37] R's weakness becomes its strength, in
a sense which the Cheyenne might readily have
understood. Although their "highest ideal was
war," they took pride in the fact that

> With their camp equipment, women, children,
> and aged . . . [they] could still show a clean set
> of heels to the best cavalry in the West.[38]

In such a fashion R may exhaust A by inducing it
to futile pursuits, in the process impressing the
population with R's superior agility and elusiveness. According to a participant observer describing the Algerian rebels:

> If we go through a village in the daytime,
> the rebels come there that night. If we camp in
> one for the night, they are back in it next
> morning, a few hours after we have left. All
> they want is to make fools of us and to prove
> to the Arabs that they can't be caught, and that
> even an army will never be able to force an
> engagement on them unless they want it. . . .
> Meantime the rebels are winning the savage
> hearts of the people.[39]

Non-attachment to Territory

It is a major tenet of insurgent doctrine that
acquisition and retention of territory should not
be an overwhelming consideration. As Mao
observes:

> To gain territory is no cause for joy, and to
> lose territory is no cause for sorrow.[40]

Progress is not indicated by location of the "forward edge of the battle area" (FEBA), as in conventional military conflicts. Instead, chunks of
real estate are to be regarded with indifference,
whether they are small or large, until the end of
the struggle when the insurgency will get it all.
Expressly because territory is everything in the
end, it must be nothing along the way. In Nasution's words:

> We are no longer acquainted with back and
> front . . . our moves are not cognizant of advance
> and retreat as in former times. . . . Often leaders
> who do not understand have pointed to it as a
> sign of weakness if a guerrilla was not able to
> defend "his" area. . . . [However], in guerrilla
> war the enemy is not prevented from entering
> any area . . . he is lured into such areas that are
> difficult to pass and that are some distance away,
> with the purpose of tiring him, lengthening his
> lines of supply, thus creating opportunities . . . to
> . . . destroy him.[41]

On the other hand, when R fails to recognize this "basic tenet of guerrilla strategy," in Valeriano's words, the consequences can be severe. When the Huk disregarded the basic tenet

> . . . [it] gave the Japanese their one major success against the Huk in the Philippines, when they launched an attack on the Huk Mount Arayat "redoubt" in 1943. The attack was successful . . . because the Huk foolishly sought to hold their ground.[42]

R's capacity to learn, from experience, the unimportance of real estate is reflected by the sequel to this incident. According to Valeriano:

> The Huk showed how well they had learned their lessons when Philippine [government] troops undertook an almost identical encirclement of Mount Arayat in 1947, with approximately the same number of well-trained troops, but with far more popular support than the Japanese had had. Reporters, ice cream and soft drink vendors, and sightseers accompanied the government troops, and all the while, horse-and-ox-drawn carts driven by guerrilla supporters carried away supplies of the Huk through gaps in the troop lines. . . . It appeared later that more casualties had probably been inflicted by government troops on unidentified friendly forces than on the Huk.[43]

The progress of technology has rendered a firm territorial base less valuable to R currently than in past rebellions. Thus, A's massive advantage in total firepower now makes the existence of a firm territorial base undesirable for R, while radio communication makes such a base unnecessary for R's command and control.

As a corollary to the unimportance of territory, retreat becomes magnified in importance as a tactical maneuver in R's operational doctrine. If territory is unimportance, then retreat becomes regularized, plausible, and central in the planning and conduct of operations. In the words of Truong Chinh:

> When we occupy a place, we must always have in mind the moment when we may have to leave it. When we defend a place, we must always have in mind the moment when we may have to abandon it.[44]

So unimportant is territory that R may defer seizing it, even when the opportunity and strength to do so lie at hand, preferring to exploit rather than to expel A, provided R's longer-term interests are thereby enhanced. Indeed, given the differential value that A and R place on territory, symbiotic arrangements between them are possible. A can (temporarily at least) retain territory without being attacked, under the proviso that it, in turn, allow the territory to provide inputs that R requires. As Sir Robert Thompson notes:

> In many district and provincial towns [of South Vietnam], government forces will be unable to go outside the perimeter, and there may even be a local gentlemen's agreement that, if they do not, they will not be attacked. . . . The insurgents do not yet want to capture and hold such towns. They are still a . . . source of supply while in government hands, and guerrillas do not want to be encumbered with the administrative and defense problems involved[45]

Imposing an "Air Defense" Requirement on A

By remaining flexible, mobile, and territorially unattached, R seeks to impose on its enemy an air defense type of requirement, which will attrite A's resources and resolution. Commenting on general war, rather than insurgency, Secretary McNamara described the air-defense problem in these terms:

> The requirement for air defense is more a function of the number of targets to be defended than of the number of attacking bombers. Since the enemy would not know in advance which targets our bombers would attack, he would have to continue to defend all of the targets. Accordingly, his expenditures for air defense are likely to be about the same regardless of whether we have a relatively small bomber force or a large one.[46]

The statement has its direct analogue in the insurgency context. Thus, T.E. Lawrence noted that if his relatively small numbers of Arab guerrillas were to operate not "as an army attacking with banners displayed" but as "an influence . . . without front or back, drifting about like a gas," they could create exorbitant resource requirements for the defending Turkish forces. According to Lawrence's rough cost-effectiveness analysis, in an area of perhaps 100,000 square miles, the Turks would need 600,000 men to defend against a relatively small Arab guerrilla force, although they possessed at most 100,000 men for the defensive task.[47] Nasution notes the same point:

> We can create disturbances with extremely few arms . . . so that the enemy cannot . . . have any sense of security.[48]

The Level of Development and R's Operating Modes

There is an intimate connection between the foregoing tenets of R's doctrine, and the structural characteristics of less-developed countries for which the tactical doctrine has been articulated. To be mobile, flexible, unattached to territory, prepared to retreat, and bent on maximizing staying power, R must retain a low degree of visibility when it chooses to. It seems likely that the visibility of insurgent organization and operations varies inversely with the level of economic development. Hence, under-developed countries may provide congenial conditions for propitiating R.

Technology and economic development steadily depress the overall degree to which successful hiding is feasible: consider the desert before and after aerial photography, or the night before and after flares, or the jungle before and after defoliation or before and after land-clearing.

It is worth noting that while visibility generally varies directly with technology and development, this is not equivalent to saying that R's visibility in urban areas is necessarily greater than in rural areas. For example, it was as difficult for the British to locate the Cypriot guerrillas in the towns as in the mountains.[49] And in Kenya:

> Looking for the enemy in the forest was . . . to seek a needle in a haystack: but looking for him in the Reserve . . . was like looking for a needle in a haystack of needles.[50]

Without being able to transform in a short time, or even in a generation, those characteristics of underdeveloped countries that enable R to achieve invisibility, A may find it advantageous to expand facilities and activities that enhance visibility. Lacking time to wait for visibility to emerge as a byproduct of generalized economic and technological development. A may instead concentrate on developing those particular facilities and activities—those attributes of moder-

nity—which extend its knowledge of who is where and when. Thus, for A, at least in the short run, "census" may be of equal or greater worth than "grievance"; photogrammetry may be more important than pharmaceuticals, and protected telecommunications more important than productive agriculture or modern industry, in reducing the invisibility that underdevelopment offers to R.

ENDNOTES

1. Mao distinguishes a preparatory stage, a stage of guerrilla warfare, and a final stage of mobile warfare. Cf. **Selected Works**, Vol. 11, 224 ff.; Vo Nguyen Giap. op. cit., 29-30, 49 ff., 101; George K. Tanham, op. cit., 10-11.
2. W. W. Rostow, **The Stages of Economic Growth** (Cambridge University Press, 1960), Chapter 2. Rostow proposes two further stages after the development take-off: technological maturity, and high mass-consumption.
3. Some of R's inputs may be obtained by sales of its outputs. During the spring of 1968, posters produced in the "occupied" **Ecole des Beaux-Arts** of Paris were quickly marketable at attractive prices in New York. While most of the stock was allotted for fund-raising at home, a fraction was devoted to fund-raising abroad: endogeny and exogeny need not be far apart.
4. Although probably **not** at the higher stages of development. Cf. Chapter 7, pp.
5. Concerning the point about R's activity in selecting targets and combining coercion and persuasion, see Chapter 4, pp., and Chapter 6. Concerning the information-firepower-mobility tradeoff question, see Chapter 7.
6. For accounts of this relationship, see Theodore Draper's **Castro's Revolution: Myths and Realities** (New York: Praeger, 1962), pp. 201-211: and his **Castroism: Theory and Practice** (New York: Praeger, 1965), pp. 39, 81-82. See also Albert and Roberta Wohlstetter, **Controlling the Risks in Cuba**, Adelphi Papers, No. 17, London, Institute for Strategic Studies, April, 1965.
7. See Chapter 3, pp.
8. See this chapter, and Chapter 3.
9. For a useful description of a "typical" less-developed-country profile, see the factor-analysis by Irma Adelman and Cynthia Taft Morris, "Factor Analysis of the Inter-relationships Between Social-Political Variables and Per Capita Gross National Product," **Quarterly Journal of Eco-**

nomics, Vol. 79, No. 4, November, 1965, 555-578.

10. See Chapter 3, pp. 28-32.

11. See Chapter 3, pp. 37-38.

12. Cf. Thomas C. Schelling, **The Strategy of Conflict** (Cambridge: Harvard University Press, 1960), pp. 74ff.

13. See the more extensive discussion of coercion and damage in Chapter 6.

14. Abdul Harris Nasution, **Fundamentals of Guerrilla Warfare** (New York: Praeger, 1965), p. 21.

15. **Ibid.**, pp. 39, 223. The second sentence is attributed by Nasution to an officer fighting under his orders during the conflict with the Dutch.

16. Cf. Chapter 6, pp. 94-95. The text commentary on efficiency may seem to conflict with certain examples of R's behavior: for example, the continuation of large unit actions by the Viet Cong against the overwhelming firepower of U.S. forces in Vietnam. Perhaps the exception, if it is one, weakness the rule. But it is by no means clear that the example is really an exception. To the extent that such large actions had the effect of diverting U.S. forces from the smaller actions (i.e., the guerrilla war) and from attacking the local infrastructure of the Viet Cong, as well as of raising the intensity of domestic political opposition to the war in the United States, the large unit actions may have been an efficient mode for the Viet Cong to follow, even if the rate of exchange in casualties was unfavorable.

17. Gen. Samuel B. Griffith, trans., **Mao Tse-tung on Guerrilla Warfare** (New York: Praeger, 1961), p. 42.

18. Charles E. Callwell, **Small Wars: Their Principles and Practice** (London: Her Majesty's Stationery Office, 1899), p. 78. The Callwell book is strikingly modern, dealing with mobility, intelligence, and crop destruction, among other subjects. In the filed of insurgency, it is analogous to Alfred Marshall's nineteenth century text on the principles of economics. One important difference is that the analysis of insurgency has not developed much since Callwell's book; his work is still among the best in the field.

19. Bernard Fall, **Street Without Joy**, 3rd rev. ed., (Harrisburg, Pa.: Stackpole, 1963), p. 102.

20. A. A. Pallis, trans., **General Grivas on Guerrilla Warfare** (New York: Praeger, 1962), p. 72

21. Wolff, **op. cit.**, p. 247

22. Philippe Devillers, **Histoire du Viet-Nam de 1940 à 1952** (Paris: Editions du Seuil, 1952), p. 166. Our translation.

23. Callwell, **op. cit.**, pp. 64-65.

24. Brigadier David Leonard Powell-Jones, in **Counterinsurgency: A Symposium**, The RAND Corporation, R-112-ARPA, January, 1963. Santa Monica, Calif., pp. 27-28.

25. Pallis, op. cit., p. 5. The point is typical of other rebellions as well, for example, the Spanish rebellion: "During more than five years the guerrillas . . . never obtained a complete victory over a French division and exercised no influence on strategic operations with [one] exception. . . ." J. Lucas-Dubreton, **Napoleon devant l'Espagne** (Paris: Librairie Artheme Fayard, 1946), pp. 327, 328, Our translation; and the Irish rebellion: "We have not been able to drive the enemy from anything but a fairly good-sized police barracks," according to the Irish Republican Army's Chief-of-Staff after the end of operations. Holt, **op. cit.**, pp. 256-257.

26. See discussion of force ratios in Chapter 5.

27. Wolff, **op. cit.**, p. 289.

28. Holt, **op. cit.**, pp. 251-252.

29. That there can be a conflict between this goal and that of attriting an adversary, particularly the foreign source of support for A, is evident. Where R's effort is devote to influencing the calculation of future costs so as to diminish the opponent's staying power, contact with the enemy's forces may be sought in circumstances where "success" is not anticipated.

30. Nasution, **op. cit.**, p. 45.

31. Mao, **Basic Tactics**, pp. 54, 56, 69.

32. Guevara, **op. cit.**, p. 36

33. Mao, **Basic Tactics**, pp. 83, 120.

34. Fall, **Street Without Joy**, pp. 151-152.

35. Guevara, **op. cit.**, pp. 42-43.

36. Mao, **Basic Tactics**, pp. 85-86.

37. Mao, **Basic Tactics**, pp. 141-142.

38. Paul Wellman, **Death on the Prairie** (New York: MacMillan, 1934), p. 89.

3. Pierre Leulliette, **Saint Michael and the Dragon** (New York: Houghton Mifflin, 1964), pp. 24, 64.

40. Mao, **Basic Tactics**, p. 67.

41. Nasution, **op. cit.**, pp. 44, 187.

42. Napoleon D. Valeriano and Charles T. R. Bohannan, **Counter-guerrilla Operations: The Philippine Experience** (New York: Praeger, 1962). p. 23.

43. Valeriano and Bohannan, **op. cit.**, p. 23.

44. Truong Chinh, **op. cit.**, p. 189. Guevara asserts the same principle: "No guerrilla leader worthy of the name will neglect the orderly withdrawal of his forces. A withdrawal must be well timed, quick, and permit the recovery of all the

wounded, of gear and ammunition. There can be no surprise attack against or encirclement of, withdrawing forces." Guevara, **op. cit.**, p. 46.

45. Sir Robert Thompson, op. cit., 44-42.

46. Statement of Secretary McNamara read by Deputy Secretary Cyrus R Vance before the House Armed Services Committee, February 5: **Hearings on Military Posture and H.R. 4016 Before the Committee on Armed Services,** Eighty-ninth Congress, First Session, 1965, p. 203.

47. See T. E. Lawrence, **Encyclopaedia Britannica** (1950), Vol. X, 951. An air-defense-type calculation can be formulated more precisely by the following simple model suggested by James Hayes: If G is the size of a guerrilla force, V_i the points to be defended by A, and e the relative effectiveness of A's forces compared with those of R, then A requires a total force, F, given by the equation:
$$F = e\ G \backslash \Sigma\ V_i.$$
F is large relative to G, because $\Sigma\ V_i$ is large relative to e.

48. Nasution, **op. cit.**, p. 204. For essentially the same point, see David Galula. **Counterinsurgency Warfare: Theory and Practice** (New York: Praeger, 1964), p. 11.

49. Pallis, **op. cit.**, p. 163.

50. Majdalany, **op. cit.**, p. 163.

The Authority's Viewpoint
Concepts and Conduct of Counterrebellion

Nathan Leites and Charles Wolf, Jr.

POLITICS AND FORCE IN COUNTERINSURGENCY

According to a frequent assertion, in successful counterinsurgency politics is primary and force is secondary. In this respect, counterinsurgency is supposed to differ from conventional war, where the order is reversed.

As noted earlier, belief in the primacy of politics over force characterizes the slogans and priorities of the hearts-and-minds view. But advocacy of the primacy of politics is not confined to civilians. Sometimes the views expressed by professional military men also stress the primacy of politics in counterrebellion, although the typical military view would have it otherwise.[1] While the view that politics is primary is both frequently expressed and widely accepted, is it true?

One difficulty in answering this question arises from the unclear meaning of "politics" and "force." Tautology often lurks behind such strongly drawn but loosely defined dichotomies, and this is a case in point. Frequently, perhaps usually, the political effectiveness of an A is judged by whether or not an R is suppressed (deterred), while the suppression (deterrence) of rebellion is construed to depend on the political effectiveness of A. Thus, if Magsaysay was indeed successful in suppressing the Huks, he was politically effective (thereby demonstrating the primacy of politics over force), and if Batista was notably *un*successful in suppressing Castro, it was because of his political ineffectiveness, thereby demonstrating the same point!

However, if an effort is made to define the concepts so that each can be observed *independently* of the other, it is highly questionable whether the commonplace assumption about what is primary and what is secondary is right. If politics is construed as the domain of nonviolence, persuasion, and consensus, and force as the domain of violence, coercion, and constraint, than the biggest contrast between counterinsurgency and other types of war probably lie *within* these categories, rather than between them. The main differences (and they are significant ones) between counterinsurgency and other wars should probably be put, not in terms of the commonplace view, but in other terms. The *types* of force, and the *types* of political actions that are most relevant in determining outcomes, are likely to differ significantly between counterinsurgency and other wars. Military techniques that work effectively in counterinsurgency are not likely to be effective in other wars, and political techniques and strategies that work in counterinsurgency are likely to differ from those that work in other kinds of wars.

Leites, Nathan, and Charles Wolf, Jr. (1970). *Rebellion and Authority: An Analytic Essay on Insurgent Conflicts.* Santa Monica, CA: Rand. Reproduction authorization obtained from RAND.

179

But politics is not necessarily more important in counterrebellion than in conventional wars—particularly, recent and future conventional wars. In its influence on the outcome of the Battle of Britain, for example, Churchill's political ingenuity played as decisive a role as that played by the Royal Air Force. To mobilize (maneuver) the British populace into such intense resolution that compromise became unthinkable was an act of great political dexterity, comparable in its influence on Britain's stamina and the outcome of the war with the military effectiveness of the RAF. The contrast with the role of domestic politics in influencing military outcome in the Battle of France is obvious and notable. The importance of Syngman Rhee's political ingenuity in freeing the North Korean prisoners-of-war in 1953, and thereby influencing the outcome of the Korean war is another case in point.

Moreover, politics does not seem to be less important in contingencies closer to the nuclear end of the spectrum. Thus, in the Suez crisis of 1956 and the Cuban missile crisis of 1962—in both of which nuclear threats arose, with differing degrees of imminence—political maneuvering was singularly important in influencing military outcomes. For example, recall the profound political importance of the military almost valueless Jupiter missiles in 1962.

Of course, politics is equally significant in insurgent conflicts. But the ingredients of effective political action are different from those suggested by the previous examples. From A's standpoint, effective politics requires that A demonstrate a growing capacity to govern—by adhering to and enforcing law and order; by maintaining discipline within and between its agencies; and by completing announced programs visibly and expeditiously. Demonstrating competence and acquiring a reputation for effective action constitute A's political task. Political actions that strengthen A are synonymous with political actions that expand A's capacity to absorb and offset harassment from R.[2] Elections, political organizing, governmental probity, and development programs may contribute to this end.

If, on the one hand, politics is important in conflict other than rebellions, so, on the other hand, is the use of force important in rebellions as well as in other wars. Thus, Magsaysay's reorganization of the Philippine Constabulary into smaller, more decentralized, and mobile units, combined with the altered incentive structure created for the Armed Forces of the Philippines to reward effective application of force against the Huks,[3] was not less important in suppressing the Huks than were the *political* moves (for example, the relatively free elections of 1953 and reduced corruption in the civil administration) instituted by Magsaysay at the same time.

The military measures, forces, and capabilities that are best suited for counterinsurgency are apt to differ from those that are best suited for other types of contingencies. Thus, if the forces of Asian countries are designed to meet major conventional invasion by China, North Vietnam, or North Korea, or if Latin America forces are designed for hemisphere defense, their capabilities for deterring or meeting insurgent threats may be considerably less (for a given budget) than if they were specifically designed to meet these lower-level threats. A capability to prevent R—that is, a deterrence capability—requires a highly developed intelligence system, enlarged and improved paramilitary and police forces, and expanded engineering and medical units for civic action in remote areas, rather than conventionally armed and trained military units with heavy firepower and armor. A capability to wage effective counterinsurgency warfare—that is, a "war-fighting" capability—is likely to require forces (as does nuclear war) with a high degree of surface mobility, airlift, and aerial reconnaissance, as well as a capacity for operating effectively in small units for long periods of time while retraining good communications with higher-echelon headquarters. On the other hand, forces to meet a major conventional aggression are likely to stress *not* these capabilities, but rather armor, artillery, fighter aircraft, and air defense, as well as highly centralized operations by large, division-level units. And the *use* of forces trained, commanded, and equipped for major conventional contingencies in unconventional, insurgent conflicts is likely to entail both high costs and low effectiveness. The war in Vietnam is the most obvious and glaring example.

Defense capabilities for deterring Rs, as well as for fighting them in their earliest stages, should emphasize police and militia forces rather than military ones. Such forces are apt to be more closely associated with civil than military administration because their primary mission is preserving law and order and protecting the population. Fulfilling these missions depends critically on an intimate knowledge of local happenings, people, and organizations—in other words, on police intelligence, rather than the order-of-battle, counterforce type of intelligence with which the military tends to be preoccupied.[4]

Thus, the requirements in an insurgency context for both deterrence and war-fighting capabilities are likely to differ sharply from the requirements for deterring or meeting large-scale conventional aggression. The ingredients of effective force in counterinsurgency are not less important than, just very different from, the ingredients of effective force in other contingencies. A decision to base force structures on one set of contingencies is thus likely to mean reducing capabilities for other contingencies.

In sum, politics typically plays a powerful and often undervalued role in military confrontations at the higher levels of the spectrum, including nuclear as well as conventional contingencies; and the use of force plays a highly important and often undervalued role in lower levels of conflict, including counterinsurgency. The differences between counterinsurgency and other conflicts relate to the content and conduct of political and coercive roles, not to their relative importance. In analyzing and specifying these roles, the systems view of counterinsurgency differs as sharply from the conventional military emphasis on counterforce (attrition) as it does from the hearts-and-minds emphasis on sympathy.

Waging Counterinsurgency

The systems view of counterinsurgency suggests four methods or tasks, which will be elaborated in this chapter.[5] Deterring insurgency, as distinct from waging counterinsurgency, requires attention to the same tasks, though they become more difficult to perform as the level of R's organizations and operations advances. Both political and military functions enter into the performance of each task, in proportions that are likely to reflect the particular division of labor between civilian and military administration prevailing in a particular country as well as the quality of the task in question. The four tasks involve intervention by A at different places in the R system—that is, moving successively down the diagram of R's operations as illustrated in Figure 1.

Reducing R's Resources: Controlling the Supply and Prices of R's Inputs

The central role of controlling the supply of inputs is summarized in a Vietnamese proverb that recalls a celebrated metaphor of Mao's: "Dry the river and catch the fish." The river must be cut off from replenishment by external, as well as internal, sources of supply. To the extent that internal sources (endogeny) operate, the task of control is likely to fall predominantly on the police establishment. The extent that external sources (exogeny) operate, input control is likely to depend mainly on customs and border-control agencies, and on border surveillance by the military—on the ground as well as in the air.

In the higher stages of R, the contribution of exogeny to R's logistics may be larger, but its importance in supporting R's buildup and operations at lower levels is not negligible. Even though R, in the early guerrilla mode, maintains or reverts to a primitive level of living, it retains an intense need for inputs of certain key resources, such as arms and medicine, and these are most likely to come from external sources.

Barrier devices to insulate a country from external sources of supply to R may become an important ingredient—though a costly on to A— in waging successful counterrebellion.[6] However, the ratio between potential suppliers of R (both external and internal) and members of R is usually very high, and the potential suppliers are widely dispersed. Hence, barriers may be easily circumvented. Concentrating and controlling the endogenous suppliers—the populace—may therefore also be necessary to achieve a satisfactory rate of return from intercepting external support for R. The importance of whether supply lines are protected or vulnerable is suggested by the contrast between the French in Indochina and the British in Malaya. Whereas the French supply lines (roads) were highly vulnerable to R's ambushes and demolitions, the Malayan R's supply lines (between jungle and villages) were highly vulnerable to A's hamlet control.

Successful resource control by A may divert, and may be intended to divert, R's effort from fighting to "production," thereby reducing R's mobility and increasing its vulnerability. As Lucian Pye noted in commenting on the Malayan insurgency:

> . . . approximately three out of every five people under the party's control have had to devote all their time and energies to the logistical problem; and increasingly in many areas all the people have had to concentrate on getting supplies.[7]

The importance of R's civil organization, apart from its influence on the population's attitudes and calculations, arises from its central role in locating supplies, collecting them, and forwarding them to the end users. So central is this logistic role that one experienced observer has advanced the theorem that as long as the organization remains intact, the rate of regeneration of R's armed forces (with respect to any given level of damage to them) tends toward unity, even for large damage and short time periods:

> The mere killing of insurgents, without the simultaneous destruction of their infrastructure, is a waste of effort because . . . all casualties will be made good by new recruits [sic].[8]

Although the rate at which R can regenerate its forces is high if the organization remains intact, the presumption is that the rate of regeneration of R's organization is low. It is, in other words, easier for R to reproduce forces if the organization is intact than to reproduce or repair the organization itself. The proposition has merit if most of those capable and willing to act as entrepreneurs and managers for R already exercise these functions, *or* if the costs of recruiting and training replacements are high. Hence, if those in the organization, or in its key positions, are eliminated, there is limited replacement. Without replacement, there is a weakened organization. Without the organization, the military force becomes ineffective.[9]

In some cases the *timing* of A's actions may have a major influence on an R's access to inputs. In May 1969, the University of California at Berkeley decided to oust student "squatters" from a piece of unused university land they had occupied. The squatters had some sympathizers among the rest of the student body, and when the forceable ouster led to severe and nonselective violence by state and local police, they acquired more. If the University had waited only one month to repossess "People's Park," the student population of the campus would by then diminished by 80 percent!

In sum, reducing R's access to inputs requires the interdiction of external sources by border surveillance, barriers, or coercive measures applied directly against the external source of supply, and the interdiction of internal sources by control of domestic resources and population. Waging successful counterinsurgency thus requires that attention be devoted to counterproduction efforts (including the next task, degrading R's production efforts), rather than counterforce efforts alone. R's armed forces are not *un*important for A's targeting, but they are *less* important than R's organization and logistic network in reducing R's effectiveness.[10] Of course, the exact mix between targets that is efficient for A to adopt will depend not only on the relative importance of the targets, but also on the cost to A of attacking them. Combining the two considerations is likely to make an optimal strategy one that emphasized counterproduction rather than counterforce.

Impeding R's Conversion Mechanism: Degrading R's Production Function

A related task of A's counterinsurgency efforts is to reduce R's efficiency in converting acquired inputs into the outputs of the insurgent system. To this end, A can use various measures to reduces the productivity of R's resources, as well as to force R to divert resources from producing offensive operations to more defensive, protective activities. Examples of the first sort are measures that cause R's forces to lose sleep, to be on the move at times and places of A's choosing. Large-scale B-52 attacks on Viet Cong areas have often been credited with this type of impact on enemy operations.

As for the second sort of measures, one way of degrading R's efficiency is by targeting the production mechanism directly—for example, by destroying crops that are relied on to provide food for R's forces. The difficulty of accomplishing this task springs, of course, from having to isolate R from readily available input sources and force it to undertake its own production. Once R has been obliged to start its own production, the production bases themselves become vulnerable to attack. For example, Valeriano notes:

> As they [the Huks] retreated further into the mountains, their food supply depended on what they could produce out of little clearings that they themselves made. . . . . We used aircraft to spot these "production bases." We . . . refrained from spraying the production bases with chemicals, as the British did [in Malaya]. We had chemicals available, but we preferred to fly agricultural experts over these areas so they could determine the approximate harvest time; then just before harvest we destroyed these bases by ground action.[11]

The timing of the strike against such intermediate inputs is a matter of some importance if A is to maximize the wastage of R's effort and the consequent degradation of R's production function.

Forcing R to devote more resources to survival can also contribute to degrading the efficiency of its production of militant outputs. As Thompson notes:

> It must be the aim of counterguerrilla forces to compel guerrilla forces to expend their money on mere existence.[12]

And according to another observer of the Malayan campaign, the goal of aerial bombing in Malaya was not so much destroying R's units directly as exactly an indirect penalty by keeping them on the move, and thereby causing the expenditure of energy that otherwise would have been available for offensive actions.[13]

Another way of impairing R's efficiency, at once diverting resources and directly lowering productivity, to attract defectors from R. If defectors can be attracted from (especially) the middle and higher levels in R's organization, the effects in reducing morale, increasing internal conflicts, and increasing R's anxiety and precautions against penetration of its system can be a major impairment to R's production process.[14]

The degradation of R's efficiency involves a combination of instruments and actions by civil as well as military agencies of A. Effective programs for attracting defectors (for example, the Economic Development Corps (EDCOR), in the Philippines, and, though less successful, the Chieu Hoi ["open arms"] program in Vietnam) involve both military pressures and civil inducements: making the life of a guerrilla appear short or hard to bear, and making the option to defect an attractive alternative in terms of employment, income, and status.

Intelligence is, of course, central to all efforts to degrade R's efficiency, whether they divert resources from militancy to subsistence, or directly impair R's productivity.[15] Information about what works and what does not, and who and what are vulnerable to what combination of measures, must be collected and fed back into A's plans and actions.

Reducing R's Forces: Destroying Outputs

The third aspect of counterrebellion is counterforce. The target is not R's inputs or their sources, nor its conversion mechanism. R's forces are targeted directly. This is the traditional military task; it is best understood, most familiar, and most typically preferred by the military. Emphasis on counterforce enables counterrebellion to be most readily related doctrinally to other wars. It is for these reasons the task to which most attention and resources are usually devoted—usually, from A's point of view, inexpediently.

Even though the counterforce task is primarily a military responsibility, there are apt to be important differences between doing it efficiently in the counterinsurgency context and in more conventional military environments. Recalling the point noted earlier, that it is more difficult for R to regenerate middle and higher levels of leadership than rank-and-file forces, it may be more expedient for A to select R's higher leadership as targets than would be the case in other types of conflict (or than it would be for R with respect to A). The underlying assumption here is that there are usually larger gaps in capability between the higher levels of R's leadership and the next level of organizers than there are in A, and that the capacity of the R system to replace these higher levels of organization and management is more limited.

A notable example of the successful targeting of R's leadership is provided by Magsaysay's seizure of a large fraction of the top Huk leadership at a clandestine meeting in Manila in 1951. Good intelligence and swift implementation lay behind the move, resulting in a substantial set-back to the movement, and in the increase effectiveness of Magsaysay's further measures against the Huks.[16] The incident provides an example of an important point: that the top leadership of an R may be relatively more important and perhaps more separable from the rest of the movement than is the leadership in conventional conflicts.

Another contrast between the roles of counterforce in insurgency and other conflicts is that indirect means of acquiring or reducing R's forces are likely to be relatively more important in the insurgency context. Thus, attracting defectors or obtaining information that enables key figures in the R movement to be seized or eliminated may be both more important and more feasible in counterinsurgency than in conventional conflicts. Hence, the design of reward systems for stimulating defection may be of greater importance to A than the expenditure of firepower. Preliminary studies (in both Malaya and the Philippines) of the relative efficiency of acquiring R forces and particularly key leaders or cadres through such indirect means, compared with the expenditure of firepower against R's forces, suggest that the indirect mode produces vastly greater yields.[17]

Reducing the Effectiveness of R's Actions

Whatever A's effectiveness in resource-denial, in degrading R's production of new forces, or in reducing R's forces after production, A can seek to increase its capacity and that of the population to withstand or absorb R's actions. One aspect of enhancing A's absorptive capacity can be likened to "passive defense" in nuclear warfare. This may involve relocating the population and fortifying the new living areas against surprise attacks by R. (The analogy to hardening, dispersal, and evacuation in the nuclear context is evident.) One example of measures to increase A's absorptive capacity is evacuation of the population from the Quang Tri area just below the demilitarized zone in Vietnam so the people would be less vulnerable to Viet Cong attack (and so the area could be declared a free bomb zone for aerial strikes by the United States). The strategic hamlets in Malaya and Vietnam, which entailed hardening, evacuation, and relocation provide another example.

Another aspect of the task of enhancing A's absorptive capacity is more closely analogous to active defense. It involves building up local defense capabilities, usually in the form of constabulary, paramilitary, or militia forces that can hold out defending a fortified hamlet until A's heavier military forces can provide assistance. This active defensive role may be enhanced, in addition, through aerial patrols that maintain round-the-clock surveillance and can apply a heavy concentration of ready firepower in the event of guerrilla attack. Small aircraft with long loiter times and enough weaponry to counter a light or moderately heavy guerrilla attack effectively may be an important component in this type of active defense system. The main purpose of such an aerial police would be to provide both the symbol and the reality of A's presence and protection, another example of the mixing of civil and military functions in insurgent conflicts.

Of course, the basic requirement for increasing absorptive capacity for R's output is to strengthen A itself: its capacity to be informed, undertake programs, control, protect, punish, and act and react vigorously, quickly, and intelligently. These are the ingredients of nation-building in the less developed countries generally, whether or not they are subjected to insurgent threats or pressure. The tasks of authority-building are manifestly more difficult in an insurgency or a potential insurgency. But this difficult, long-run task can, in turn, be set in motion by progress in the principal components of successful counterinsurgency—itself an intensified form of the larger task of building effective authority in the less developed countries.

CONTRASTS BETWEEN COUNTERINSURGENCY AND OTHER CONFLICTS

While it is, as we have suggested, expedient for A to join closely politics and force—civil and military instruments—in counterinsurgency, this point is hardly a distinguishing one. Still, there are important contrasts between counterinsurgencies and other conflicts as traditionally analyzed and practiced.

Traditionally, wars between As have been waged and analyzed as *counter*force and *pro-*

territory, aiming at the destruction of the enemy's forces and the occupation of his territory. Consequently, the location and movement of the "forward edge of the battle area" (FEBA) were viewed as providing a relatively clear indication of success. To a limited extent, what we previously called controlling inputs (for example, economic warfare or pre-emptive buying) and interfering with the conversion of inputs into forces and capabilities (the daytime strategic bombing in World War II) was also pursued in conventional wars. But their roles were minor in the light of the primary counterforce and pro-territory focus on such wars.

On the other hand, counterforce and pro-territory efforts are by no means irrelevant in counterinsurgency wars, particularly in the more advanced stages of R when the insurgency has established military base areas and territorial control. Nevertheless, the difference in emphasis is important. Counterinsurgency is primarily a counterproduction effort, rather than an effort to annihilate forces or acquire territory. The aim of successful counterinsurgency is to counter R's ability to produce and reproduce forces as well as "harden" the structure of government authority so it can withstand R's attacks while the essential counterproduction effort is gaining momentum.

In conventional war, destroying the enemy's forces (counterforce) is a means of acquiring his territory. Destroying his forces and acquiring his territory, in turn, provide the means of coercing the adversary to accept a desired outcome. In counterinsurgency, by contrast, the adversary may have no territory in the earlier and usually critical stages. (Indeed, as noted earlier, to eschew territory, retreat, evaporate, and accept local setbacks are fundamental attributes of R's operating doctrine.) Instead, A's aim should be to attack R's organization, that is, to attack the apparatus by which the forces and outputs of the system are produced. Counterforce is part of the process, but not the most important part. R's military forces are a part of the target system, but not necessarily the major part. In addition, A must target both the population and the exogenous sources of R's support: the former, in order to influence the population's behavior so as to limit the inputs available to R internally; and the latter, in order to restrict external resupply of key inputs.

Force Ratios in Counterinsurgency

An important point of contrast between counterinsurgency and conventional wars arises in connection with the much discussed "force ratios" between counterinsurgencies and insurgents. Sir Robert Thompson has properly characterized much writing on this matter as "nonsense," and "one of the myths of counterinsurgency."[18]

Part of the nonsense arises from the fact that the data are so ambiguous. It is never quite clear what is in the numerator and denominator of the ratios cited. Do they include only active combatants? And what about guerrillas who are only part-time combatants—should they be expressed in terms of some "full-time" equivalents? And should the counterinsurgents include the police, air, and naval patrol forces, or only active ground combat forces?

Although the familiar ration of ten counterinsurgencies to one insurgent has often been cited as prerequisite to successful counterinsurgency, two important qualifications need to be attached to this ratio, apart from the ambiguity (as noted) of the numerator and denominator. First, widely different rations have prevailed in different insurgencies: the range extends from one or two to one in the Philippines, to twenty or thirty to one in Kenya, and perhaps forty to one in Malaya, at least toward the *end* of the campaign. The second qualification is that the ratio itself is sensitive to the stage in the conflict at which it is computed, and to whether a given ratio comes about by a build-up of the counterinsurgents or by a reduction in the insurgency's ability to produce forces. To the extent that A is successful in its efforts to disrupt R's production mechanism, the ratio will be drastically raised by the decline in R's production capability toward the end of the counterinsurgency effort. A rising ratio brought about by the reduction of R's forces thus has quite a different meaning from (and from A's point of view a more auspicious significance than) one brought about by a rise in counterinsurgent forces.

Still, as noted earlier, an important contrast exists between force ratios in counterinsurgency and in conventional wars. The contrast arises from the fact that where there is a front line in the battle area, the defender generally has a strong advantage, one further strengthened by defensive fortifications. Consequently, although there are major exceptions—Israel's rout of much larger Arab forces in the six-day war of June 1967 is a striking example—the familiar planning factor of two or three to one in favor of the defender reflects this advantage. Where there is no front line, as in counterinsurgency, this model no longer applies, and it is more appropriate to use an air-defense model. The defender does not know where an attack may come. Hence, even if he is able to keep an advantage by maintaining a high-level alert at each of the targets, there are so many targets to defend that the aggregate force ratio becomes much larger than that of the attacking force.[19]

Putting the problem this way underscores an important influence on the force ratios needed by A. The better A's information about where and when an attack may come, and the shorter his response time[20] (as through aerial surveillance and lift), the smaller the force ratio he needs. Therefore, A's intelligence and information system will play a central role in influencing force ratios.[21]

Moreover, it is probably no less important to stress the *kinds* of forces that A needs than the *numbers*. As noted earlier,[22] A's mobility, weapon training, and communications are likely to be different from, and considerably less expensive on a unit cost basis than, those associated with military forces equipped for fighting large-scale conventional wars.

Indicators of Success in Counterinsurgency

One of the distinguishing characteristics of counterinsurgency is the difficulty and complexity of finding reliable indicators of success. After the fact, it is easy to put things in their places: to say that at such and such a time it became clear that the insurgency was going uphill or downhill, that the force ratios were decidedly moving in the right direction, or that a decisive turn was taken toward A's success or failure. But *during* a counterinsurgency campaign, it is hard to be clear about "winning" and "losing."

The difficulty of identifying reliable indicators of success is related to the previously noted points about the unsuitability of indicators normally used for evaluating success in conventional war: destruction of the enemy's military

forces, and acquisition of his territory (that is, casualties, and movement of the FEBA). Counterforce and pro-territory indicators are not appropriate in counterinsurgency.

Neither is measuring the warmth of popular support, and its shift from R to A, a reliable indicator of success, even if we had a good calorimeter for this purpose (which we do not). Genuine popular support to transitional societies is multifaceted and heterogeneous; perhaps more important, it is rare in any durable sense. And when it appears to be most genuine, it is as likely to be a manipulated appearance, as a deep-rooted conviction. (This is not to deny that genuine support is desirable in principle, or that successful manipulation of its appearance is an important quality to cultivate, whether by A or R.) Nevertheless, as we have suggested earlier, Rs or As can wax in the face of popular dislike, and wane in the midst of popular sympathy.

Rather, the difficulty of assessing successes and observing the process of winning and losing in counterinsurgency arises from the four political-military tasks of counterinsurgency previously discussed in this chapter. Observing each task accurately is difficult, and observation is complicated by the possibility that progress in one task may be accomplished by regress in another.

To be confident that the process of winning in counterinsurgency is actively underway, we need to know several things: that R's access to inputs is becoming more difficult (the prices at which inputs are available are rising, and the quantity available is diminishing); that R's organization is experiencing increased difficulties in converting its inputs into insurgent activities (there is growing evidence of lassitude, friction, and misunderstanding within the R organization); that R's forces are being destroyed (and faster than the conversion mechanism is producing new ones); and that A' efforts to strengthen local defense capabilities (by hardening, relocation, fortification and the build-up of a responsible and effective police force) are making progress.

That such an assessment is difficult, demanding an active and competent intelligence system, is evident. However, if there is a single indicator that is more reliable than any other probably is the rate at which middle- and higher-level officers and cadres in R's organization or acquired by A—

whether by defection or capture. Given the high regeneration coefficient of the intact infrastructure, this is the crux of R's strength and stamina. Depleting the core of the organization is the aim; acquiring cadres is the key to the core. In both Malaya and the Philippines, this indicator was—retrospectively—a good predictor. And it has never been deceptively high in counterinsurgencies that have been unsuccessful, probably because it is harder to falsify than other indicators.

The selection of approach indicators is further complicated by two problems which, though they also operate in conventional conflicts, play a more critical role in insurgent wars. One problem is possible distortions in the actions of members of A as a result of the selection of a particular indicator. If casualties inflicted on R's forces become accepted as an important indicator of success, incentives facing A's personnel are changed. Or the threshold of reliability for distinguishing R's forces from the general population may be lowered, so that a higher proportion of actual casualties may be imposed on the population than before.

A second problem is that accurate observation of success requires that the indicators relating to R's own behavior be known as well. For example, if one is concerned with judging the process of winning or losing, it would be useful to know how an external sponsor of R might be viewing the same process. If R is concerned with strengthening its control in one part of the country by executing local officials, then combat undertaken by R in other parts of the country may be considered successful even if R's casualties are high, because such combat diverts A's attention and resources from the area in which control by R is being strengthened. The first problem makes concentration on pure counterforce indicators of success unreliable and misleading, and the second makes the use of territorial indicators inapplicable.

Judging the process of counterinsurgency requires, in other words, intimate knowledge of R's organization and of the impact on that organization of various tasks and measures undertaken by A. What A must be after is suppression of R's *capacity* to undertake disruptive acts to some tolerable (to A)level, so that eventually the continued effort and sponsorship of the residual R will not seem worth the costs.

When a given package of measures (or costs) undertaken by A buys a greater current and expected future suppression of R's capacity, then the process of winning is underway.

Finally, it is important not to specify an unrealistically high suppression level in concluding that a win has been obtained. The normal level of dacoity, disorder, and illegal activity in less developed countries is usually high. Efforts to establish an unrealistically stringent suppression level may have the effect of vitiating relationships between A and its own external support, turning allies into suspicious and disaffected adversaries.

ENDNOTES

1. Despite frequent rhetoric to the contrary, a probably more typical, but not more accurate, military viewpoint was expressed by General Earle G. Wheeler in 1962, before he became Chairman of the Joint Chiefs of Staff:

   It is fashionable in some quarters to say that the problems in Southeast Asia are primarily political and economic rather than military. I do not agree. The essence of the problem in Vietnam is military.

   Quoted by Alastair Buchan, "Questions about Vietnam," **Encounter**, January, 1968, p. 7. The reason this formulation is no more accurate than the other is that it focuses on **the amount and the priority** of the force (the opposing view focuses on **the amount and the priority** of politics). Both views neglect what in our view are the more important questions concerning the **types** of force and politics, as discussed below.

2. See Chapter 3, pp. 37-38, and this chapter, pp. 82-83.

3. See Wolf, "Insurgency and Counterinsurgency: New Myths and Old Realities," **The Yale Review**, Vol. LVI, No. 2, Winter 1967, 225-241.

4. Cf. Chapter 7.

5. See also Chapter 3, especially Figure 1.

6. The problem of devising efficient barrier systems, through different combinations of barbed wire, lumber, steel and concrete, minefields, seismic and electronic detectors, ground forces and aerial reconnaissance, warrants more attention than it has received in the abundant literature on insurgency. Devising an efficient system is very likely to depend critically on local factors relating to terrain, weather, and the scope and composition of normal border traffic, as well as on political constraints. John Randolph has provided an excellent introduction to his problem in

a series of articles in the Los Angeles Times. See Los Angeles Times, April 16, 1967.

7. Lucian Pye, Lessons from the Malayan Struggle Against Communism, D/57-2, (Cambridge: Center for International Studies, Massachusetts Institute of Technology, 1957, p. 51.

8. Thompson, op. cit., p. 116. A milder, but probably more accurate, formulation is also advanced by the same author (p.119):

> ... 'fix-and-destroy' operations ... serve only the limited purpose of killing insurgents. They do not destroy their . . . infrastructure. They must, therefore, be regarded as secondary to those operations which are achieving the primary aim [of destroying infrastructure].

9. An interesting corollary is associated with the reversal of these propositions: if R's infrastructure grows, its potential force strength grows by a larger amount.

10. See pp. 83-84.

11. A. H. Peterson, G. C. Reinhardt, and E. E. Conger, eds., Symposium on the Role of Airpower in Counterinsurgency and Unconventional Warfare: The Philippine Huk Campaign, The RAND Corporation, RM-3652-PR, June, 1963, Santa Monica, Calif., p. 36. Valeriano's account shows an adroit combination of civil technology (that is, agricultural expertise) with military tactics.

12. Thompson, op. cit., p. 116.

13. Air Commander A. D. J Garrison in A. H. Peterson, G. C. Reinhardt, and E. E. Conger, eds., Symposium of the Role of Airpower in Counterinsurgency and Unconventional Warfare: The Malayan Emergency, The RAND Corporation, RM-3651-PR, June, 1963, Santa Monica, Calif., pp. 60-61.

14. These effects on R's production function can be distinguished from the direct subtraction of outputs that results from attracting defectors. In other words, attracting defectors has the joint effect of degrading R's production function, as well as reducing the outputs of R's system.

15. See Chapter 7.

16. To some extent, the special importance of top leadership in an insurgency is analogous to the importance of the top dozen or so leaders of the Mafia and other syndicates of organized crime.

17. See Chapter 7.

18. Thompson, op. cit., p. 48.

19. See the discussion in Chapter 4, p.

20. Below some threshold value. Unless the response time is at least quicker than some minimum value, it may make no difference.

21. See Chapter 7.

22. See Chapter 4.

Inflicting Damage

Nathan Leites and Charles Wolf, Jr.

In previous chapters we have attempted to show how the various factors pertinent to the outcome of the struggle between A and R are related to each other. Now we pass from general to partial analysis, to look at conditions, characteristics, and consequences of each of a few types of instruments employed in the conflict, first, in this chapter, force and coercion: then, in Chapter 7: intelligence and information. In both cases, shall put forward propositions about conduct frequently adopted by R and A, respectively; to be sure, there are instances of R acting in the way we suggest is typical of A, and vice versa. Castro's R was in many ways similar to the A described below, while Castro's A came closer, in many respects, to the R evoked in the pages to follow.

MOTIVES AND SEQUELS

"Hot" Violence Without Calculations

Commenting on the forces of order in Vietnam, a prominent participant-observer recalls:

> There was a constant tendency to mount large-scale operations, which [served] little purpose . . . merely to indicate that something aggressive was being done.

The rebels in question may have thoroughly learned that the weak (in firepower) must deny themselves as targets to the strong. But the forces of order may, in calculation or conduct, not always accept the bothersome fact of their opponents' elusiveness. While the professional military will not frivolously *declare* a limitation of interest in what they do to the enemy, still they may, less consciously, come to view their immediate obligation as maintaining a high level of action *on their own part,* without examining whether they thus enhance impact on the particular opponent they are now facing. That is, and advanced armed force may be more oriented (and may not always know it is) toward what would harm an enemy of its own class, rather than toward what would damage inferior military forces. The rebels, under threat of extinction and less burdened with tradition and pride, might find it easier to consider the situation on its merits.

Also, for A, the low risk of *flagrant* failure facilitates raising the scale of operations; in fact,

> the certainty of never running the risk of a clear defeat, such as an equally armed opponent could inflict upon us, enables any military commander to conduct some sort of operation.[2]

And the incentives facing A's forces are likely to leave this temptation weakly opposed, if opposed at all. As long as the most analytic minds in A's military establishment have not yet agreed on the indicators of "winning" and "losing" in this kind of war,[3] field officers may not

Leites, Nathan, and Charles Wolf, Jr. (1970). *Rebellion and Authority: An Analytic Essay on Insurgent Conflicts.* Santa Monica, CA: Rand. Reproduction authorization obtained from RAND.

feel too guilty about fulfilling the professional duty of spending ammunition. As an observer of the war in Algeria notes:

> The armored patrol that scoured the country in the evening had made a rule never to come back without "emptying its magazines."[4]

Such an aspiration may be pursued even at the expense of enunciated firing doctrine. A's forces may have permission to respond copiously if the insurgents fire first, but not to initiate an action that is bound to result in a high ratio of collateral over intended damage. However, if the other side does not oblige—or simply is not present where one suspects it—the destruction upon which A is intent may be wrought anyhow.[5]

Such a penchant for sheer action without regard for ultimate impact may be strengthened by various emotions that one can permit oneself to express in conduct, as long as reliable measures of effectiveness are lacking.

"It is only natural," judges Sir Robert Thompson, that in the trying conditions created by the rebels' refusal to fight according to other books, "troops will begin to lose their temper"—a reaction that their opponents may predict, welcome, and encourage.[6]

The war at large—a demeaning imposition on the forces of order!—may come to be the object of a rage (to be sure, not always a fully conscious one, for obvious reasons) that is least inconveniently taken out on handy rebels, or the proverbial sea in which they presumably swim. If drafters, in particular, are used against rebels ethnically foreign to them, they may come to hate all that involves the rebels, not only (or not so much) because they have had buddies killed, but simply because the war itself, with all its discomforts, sufferings, and dangers, appears to be the other people's fault. Sensing that one's side has no reliable knowledge how the rebels can be defeated makes one even more disposed to concentrate on harming anybody that seems connected with them.

If the rebels are viewed as criminals, any damage they inflict may appear as an atrocity justifying—even requiring—huge retaliation. An observer of the Algerian war recalls about his service as an officer, when approaching a village:

> If the whole line was ordered to advance, more of our men might be knocked out, and then nobody could prevent their creating havoc in all the houses.[7]

In other words, it is not a legitimate enemy that is hiding there (and he uses illegitimate devices, to boot).

Proper retribution wrought against rebels allows for strong sensations to alleviate the boredom of war, in which nothing may be happening for long stretches of time. A conscript in Algeria supposedly told a fellow sufferer:

> As for me, I strike and I kill, because my buddies are being killed and because I am bored to death (*je m'emmerde*) here. . . .[8]

In such trying conditions one may come to depend on regular doses of pleasure from inflicting damage. Frequently there was in Algeria, an observer alleges,

> rivalry for the distribution of the quarry: the only question was who would procure for themselves the pleasure of torturing, the buddies of the soldiers killed in an ambush or those specialized in the safe job of interrogation.[9]

Where the requirement to be "cool" (disciplined) in the act of inflicting damage is weak, the search for pleasure may distort even the application of measures inspired by plausible considerations of utility. "After several rebel chiefs are caught in women's clothes" during the so-called Battle of Algiers, 1956-1957, a former parachutist recalls,

> we make a point of searching Arab women . . . they are inspected from head to foot, more meticulously than the men—it's not hard to imagine in what manner.[10]

Personal feelings may induce those who inflict damage to violate the calculated precepts of their superiors, perhaps with disastrous effect on the enterprise. Thus, the *Organization de l'Armée Secrète* (OAS) in Algeria, 1961-1962, seems to have failed in large measure because of the refusal by the rank and file to apply the leadership's code on violence. While a great deal was allowed, or even requested, particularly in relation to the European rebels' French enemies, much was forbidden with regard (for example) to conscripts from the mainland, toward whom the rank and file's feelings were far from tender. An incident in which a French army patrol was killed in an OAS stronghold noticeably reduced the European rebels' changes to secure the complicity, or even the neutrality, of the armed forces.

Harming for a Purpose

In contrast to such casual or passionate conduct by many As stands the puritanical conduct aimed at by R. R is led by a tight organization devoted to a particular leadership and a general cause. Its active members usually have a sense of moving upward, rather than of suffering or being threatened with major losses (which is apt to induce despair and blind infliction of injury). Oriented toward victory and pursuing it in penury, R attempts to offset a lack of resources by a high efficiency in attempts to offset a lack of resources by a high efficiency in their use. Thus, R may strive to treat the infliction of damage as an instrument for future success rather than for immediate expression or enjoyment[11]—fearing also the dissolving impact of pleasure on skill. As T.E. Lawrence notes about the Arab army:

> The members had to keep always cool, for the excitement of a blood-lust would impair their science.[12]

Rebels, in addition, may obscurely share the contempt that A feels for them, say, on ethnic or class grounds; they may want to show that they are not savage, but civilized, and hence use violence with greater discrimination.

Engaging in violence for reasons other than its presumable contribution to ultimate victory may then appear, to the perfect rebel, to be a serious matter, conduct to which one would feel tempted only in extreme conditions and which may even— or especially—then be a grave sin. Firing impulsively when one's firepower is low and when the shot may furnish the enemy with precious intelligence about one's location (a well-known point from South Vietnam, 1965-1969) is a far from venial mistake in the eyes of the rebel leadership. On the contrary, that leadership typically worships coolness in the service of passion, and prides itself on having learned through "study" (a favorite word of the Viet Cong, for example) what efficiency dictates in the particular and changing situation at hand. "The opponents," notes Che Guevara,

> can be distinguished by the character of their fire. The enemy, well-supplied with ammunition, is characterized by impulsive fire in heavy volume. The guerrilla forces, not so favored, will fire sporadically—not one shot more-than absolutely necessary.[13]

Thus, when

> once one of our heroes . . . had to use his machine gun for almost five minutes, burst after burst . . . this caused . . . confusion in our forces, because the rhythm of fire led them to believe that this . . . position had fallen to the enemy.[14]

While the Cuban rebellion hardly lived up to this ideal to the degree implied by Guevara, the aspiration he evokes has been influential in many Rs.

Valuing the capacity to make strikes depend on calculations, R may also cultivate the ability to vary its impact on the enemy by a combination of firepower and less rude procedures—for example, negotiation. When the Vietnamese communists were negotiating with the French Government at Dalat shortly after the end of World War II, the leader of the Viet Minh in the South (Nguyen Binh) issued an order to his armed forces (April 19, 1946), to

> support the Dalat conference by a general offensive on all fronts and by sabotaging the agencies of the French sharks.[15]

Indiscriminate Destruction

One may inflict damage for the purpose of annihilation. One may not desire to leave a residue for coercion: destroying may be the "final solution." "They are nine million, and we are one," ran a popular saying among Europeans in wartime Algeria. "Everyone of us should kill off nine, and the problem is solved."[16]

Or one may proceed to annihilate for a given period a fraction of what may be presumed to be one's total target. When in the fall of 1901 a considerable number of American soldiers were horribly killed or wounded by Philippine rebels in a certain province, the U.S. general in charge ordered the area to be transformed into what later was to be called a "free-kill zone," after the inhabitants' removal into camps. He informed his men:

> I want no prisoners. I wish you to kill and to burn; the more you burn and kill, the better it will please me.

He directed that Samar be converted into "a howling wilderness."[17] Though the motive may have been backward-looking (retribution), such conduct could be a case of coercion if those spared are able to draw *practicable* lessons from it as to how their own destruction may be avoided.[18]

Partial annihilation, intended to convince the target population that one is resolved to go the whole way, may be effective in one wants to induce flight or staying-out-of-bounds. When the first Arab village (Dir Yassin) feel to Israeli forces in 1948 and the belief spread (with the assistance of the Arab leadership, who overestimated the ratio of anger over fear in the response of its people) that most of the inhabitants had been promptly killed, this event triggered the flight of the Arabs from Palestine: a windfall for the Israelis. By killing Muslims at random in the European quarters of the big cities in Algeria, the OAS aimed at a separation in space between the two "communities" of the country. Analogous to the calculations behind some of the Anglo-American bombing of Germany in the last war, the communists in Malaya intended to make production fall off by having laborers stay away from places of work made perilous, and leave places of residence (close to the former) also rendered unsafe. They may have calculated that the balance of strength between themselves and their opponents would be more favorably affected by a decline in rubber production than by their taxing the high total earnings of plantation workers—that inducing "paralysis" and "chaos" was more worthwhile than coercing. In addition, by curtailing the revenue that the British were drawing form Malaya the communists may have intended to affect their opponents' willingness to continue the battle—which may also have been a calculation behind the "indiscriminate terror" by the *Front de la Libération Nationale* against Europeans in Algeria.

In addition, of course, rendering the situation unbearable for those who cannot or will not leave has as its objective the acceptance of one's demands as, in the target's view, a necessary and sufficient condition for the cessation of their discomforts. When General J. Franklin Bell introduced military law in Batangas, Cebu, and Bohol early in the century, he explained that:

> . . . it is necessary to make the state of war as insupportable as possible . . . by keeping the minds of the people in such a state of anxiety . . . that living under such conditions will soon become unbearable. Little should be said. The less said the better. Let acts, not words, convey the intention.[19]

The total damage inflicted—if one embarks on such a course at all—may then be thought minimized, if the rate of infliction is high, not low. As General Lloyd V. Wheaton suggested early in the century about the Philippine rebels:

> The nearer we approach the methods found necessary by the other nations through centuries of experience in dealing with Asiatics . . . the fewer graves will be made.[20]

Halfway measures between precise coercive acts[21] and "countervalue" campaigns with high levels of destruction per time unit may perhaps run greater risks of being both bloody and vain—of stimulating rather than intimidating—than either of these two policies.

Of course, there remains also, in the case of massive infliction (not to speak of extreme levels of destruction which may make the entire target appear doomed), the possibility that the victims will react by supporting the enemies of those who plague them, rather than by being cowed. "Returnees," an observer says about the Viet Cong,

> reported that indoctrination sessions on the armed struggle cited the Malayan insurgency as a case where . . . *indiscriminate* terror . . . failed. "We were told," said one of them, "that in Singapore the rebels on certain days would dynamite every 67th streetcar that passed along a street, the next day it might me every 30th, and so on, but that this hardened the hearts of the people against the rebels."[22]

But then, this device may be adopted in desperation, after other and less risky procedures have proved unavailing, and when one's resources, or standards preclude making it every *third* streetcar.

Demonstrating Capability

"The OAS strikes whom it chooses, when it chooses, and where it chooses," ran a major slogan of the European rebellion in Algeria. Its selection of targets was probably influenced by the intent not only to draw attention to its existence, but also to heighten estimates of its capacity for destruction, and hence of its prospects.

Such estimates, needless to say, may contribute to their own verification.

A similar effect may be sought when an R, raising its own level of damage-infliction, foresees and desires that the authorities will respond by taking it (yet) more seriously. Unless the heightened countereffort on behalf of law and order appears to be rapidly and strikingly successful, the impact on estimates may be favorable to the rebels.

Inculcating Compliance

Beyond instilling useful beliefs about the outcome of the conflict, an R may attempt to establish proper habits of obedience to the future government even before its birth, and a spirit of loyalty (the faith may follow the act).

One way of doing this is by starting with small things, but being deadly serious about them. An observer of the Mau Mau in the fall of 1953 reported that

> . . . boycott had been imposed on smoking, the wearing of hats, drinking beer, and the use of buses, and it was more than an African's skin was worth to be caught by a Mau Mau in any of these easily detectable activities.[23]

If the Viet Cong insists on taxing buses traveling on the roads it controls, it is probably not only to collect revenue, but also to present itself as an obeyed-government-in-being.

Coercion

How can one, in the formulation of the Chinese proverb, "kill just one and frighten ten thousand others?" One mode is to cow by a combination of ferocity and capriciousness. The intention may be to evoke this reaction on the part of the population: while one will never be completely safe with *that* power, the least unsafe thing to do is to stay on the safe side with regard to its demands. (The capriciousness is intended to reinforce the impression of power, but it must not be *so* massive as to make compliance with demands seem as unsafe as noncompliance.)

Another, and probably more effective, mode for R is to take seriously the cliché that "force is the only language they understand," and to make its force a language—that is, a set of events (signs) related, with not too much variance, to

another such set (referents). R may then combine severity and regularity—may be draconian.[24]

As one observer notes:

> The FLN with one killing, would set an example strong enough to scare a large crowd into acquiescence and, once successful, would stop.[25]

What contributes to such an effect will be discussed below.

To be sure, when infliction of damage is justified by its coercive effect, the claim may be wrong and also a cloak for other motives. If during the Algerian war "the forces of order kill prisoners . . . ostensibly . . . because they hope to impede recruitment to the rebels,"[26] one wonders whether this obvious gain was thoughtfully compared with a plausible cost: impeding defection. The covert joke may become a flagrant one, as observed by another eyewitness in the same conflict:

> As we approach, two men flee from a hut. One of them . . . is wounded in the stomach. He is dying. The captain orders that he be left alone: "He should suffer before he croaks, that will teach him to flee."[27]

What contrast to a serious draconian stance, as it is described by a French officer talking about his opponents in Indochina (and probably making them a few—perhaps only a very few—feet taller than they actually were):

> The Viets spill rivers of blood . . . but always according to the precise line. The various penalties . . . are inflicted . . . with a definite aim in mind, and after an analysis of the situation. . . . The peasant . . . comes to believe that the Party is . . . omniscient. . . . The man who has a "correct" attitude . . . has nothing to fear. . . . The system of the Viets excludes all surprise. *Every peasant knows what is going to happen to him, he knows in advance the consequences of his attitude, whether he behaves "badly" or "well."* It is this forecast solidly implanted in the brains which is the greatest force of Ho Chi Minh's camp.[28]

The point is to be as implacable (in the case of disobedience) as one is restrained (in that of compliance), having rendered oneself, in the first place, well-informed about who has behaved how. "Above all it is important," explains a French officer analyzing the conduct of his Viet

Minh counterpart (a woman), "to administer constantly the proof that there is no violation . . . without heads rolling." Thus:

> once she had ordered a village to cut a road. To be sure, when night fell hundreds of peasants got busy. . . . But around daybreak [they] began to think of the trouble with the Foreign Legion . . . they were getting into. So they began filling up the ditch they had dug a few hours before. [A bit later], dozens of heads rolled. Since then, the Viet Minh securely enjoys the preference of the villagers, who zealously finish off wounded French soldiers.[29]

If both opponents follow similar lines in this regard, what will determine the outcome? It is an obviously crucial question on which extant knowledge or even reflection is meager. Sets of factors conveyed by such words as *resources*, *appeals*, and *stamina* will presumably then come into their own, in addition to severity and the accuracy of targeting.

The conditions of impunity offered by a draconian system must be such that they impose only a reasonable cost. If the cost of compliance is unreasonably high, even though lower than the extreme penalty threatened for disobedience, the targets' reactions, in feelings and longer-run conduct, are apt to be different from those of the reasonable-cost case. This is "extortion."

A side choosing coercion may genuinely want to convince its targets that it knows how to pick out all the guilty ones and only them, even when they are in close collocation with innocents. Recalling how the few obstinate collaborators with the French in the Casbah were liquidated, the head of the FLN's organization for violence in Algiers (Saadi Yacef) describes the end of one such cafe owner by the action of a famous specialist (Ali Lapointe):

> Ali intervened at the head of a small commando. Medjebri and two of his acolytes were the sole targets. At the moment when Ali entered that Muslim cafe, many customers were already present. . . . Ali directed his fire . . . so that only the three condemned men were hit, there was no innocent victim whatsoever.[30]

A draconian side will stress that its policy, in the expression of the Viet Cong, has "two faces": clemency and punishment. It may tend toward indicating that every target, even the worst enemy, always has it within his power, until the very moment of being sanctioned, to limit damage to himself by some known, feasible, and not too costly conduct. The enemy deterred may then also be the enemy changing sides.

A side oriented toward coercion may with to choose its examples among targets that are liked as little (disliked as much) as possible by the public that is to be influenced. If an unpopular district chief is publicly disemboweled by the Viet Cong, and his family's arms and legs broken, the message to the farmer may not be less impressive, and may perhaps be less revolting, than if the victims were taken from among his own group. And the chance of denunciation (informing) by the population will be reduced by the unpopularity of the target. On the other hand, a side may want to show—probably nearer to the successful completion of its campaign (that is, in the later stages of R)—that nothing will save even the otherwise most popular violator from his due punishment, thus adopting a stance which, the side hopes, is both morally impressive and conducive to prudence.

One step beyond the pure coercion just described, a side may hold targets responsible for the commission or prevention of acts that are neither definitely within, nor clearly outside, their control to perform or to impede. According to a German military order in the occupied Soviet Union:

> In case of sabotage of telephone lines, railway lines, etc., sentries will be posted, selected from the civilian population. In case of repetition, the sentry in whose area the sabotage was committed, will be shot.[31]

The effect may be to keep people on their toes to prevent their heads from being lost. Again, during the German occupation of the Soviet Union:

> In the villages of Byelorussia, it was only rarely that peasants attacked the Germans or German installations at night, and tilled the soil by day. . . . The inhibiting factor was that after such activity had become known in the village and thereby to the Germans, the whole village would probably be wiped out by the Germans. . . . Informers came forward to save the village by surrendering one person.[32]

But there are limits to be kept; perhaps less effective than the severity of the punishment threatened is the feasibility of avoiding it—particularly when the rule in question is an explicit one. According to an observer, a colonel of the South Vietnamese army acting as province chief

introduced his own land reform campaign. In Vinh Long, families with sons or husbands known to be fighting with the Viet Cong, or to have gone north in 1954 with the Viet Minh, were given three months to get them back. "I take half their land and say to them that if after three months they have not got their men back, I will take their homes and property," he told me. . . . "At the end of that time I give them another three months. If their men are not back then, they go to a concentration camp and lose their property, which we divide up among those who are for us." "How on earth do you expect them to get their relations back from North Vietnam?" I asked. "That's their business," replied the Colonel. "In this province the men who are willing to fight for us [and] their families . . . are those who will do well."[33]

But when the feasibility of compliance—crucial for the impact of such conduct, though the colonel does not quite seem to perceive that—appears to be low, as perhaps in this case, does not the demand itself become a mockery, a pretext for damaging which merely adds insult to injury? Still, the effect may also be one of cowing: if they punish me for even what is beyond me, I had at least better do all I can. Or there may be a mixture of both reactions, depending on the magnitudes of various factors: How free does the victim feel to condemn, oppose, or flee the side in question? How does he evaluate the cost and prospects of counteraction?

One further step beyond coercion-by-regularity consists in adding, to a full application of known and practicable norms, a striking but limited unit of damage that is grossly arbitrary. Having robbed their first bank in Liberty, Missouri, with a parsimony of violence, Jesse James' whole band galloped out of town.

At this moment George Wymore (or Wynmore), a 19-year-old student at the college, was hastening to his class. When the horsemen came thundering down the street towards him, he ran to get into a house. One of the riders wheeled his horse, drew a revolver and fired four times. When he was picked up later, quite dead, it was found that every one of the four shots had taken effect, and any one of them would have been fatal. . . . Jesse . . . wanted to establish . . . a *precedent of deadliness,* so that future towns, when he raided them, would know that he and his gang would kill on the slightest excuse or without excuse.[34]

Here compliance (or noninvolvement) ceases to guarantee impunity, but disobedience still spells punishment. The victim of torture-for-intelligence cannot be sure that the pain will subside if he talks; but he may be rather certain that in will not unless he does. Threatened with some damage from which there is no protection in any case, the target may be expected to develop a reaction already noted: better avoid all that I can predictably escape! Will he be less or more motivated in this sense than when compliance guarantees impunity? Again, there will be forces working in either direction: one may be stricken by terror in the face of such ferocity, or one may be impelled by rage as well as discouraged by the possible futility of compliance.

Coercion at large, as well as that variant of it called deterrence, requires unceasing effort to produce and maintain a favorable environment.

The serious coercer will strive for ever higher levels of intelligence,[35] aiming at a situation in which inflictions are consonant with norms (whether declared or inferable from conduct)—in which he damages most of the guilty and very few innocents. When it comes to choosing between substantial losses to the latter and a notably incomplete reaction to the former, the aversion against making a mistake will, in a person genuinely oriented toward coercion, be as strong as that against letting a violator enjoy impunity. The coercer disapproves of such practices as the following, from an allegation about Americas fighting Philippine rebels:

John T. McCutchen, a conservative reporter, told of what usually happened when the body of a mutilated American was found: ". . . a scouting party goes out to the scene of the killing . . . and they proceed to burn the village and kill every native *who looks as if* he had a bolo or a rifle."[36]

To enable itself to act on less uncertain evidence, the A—initially, probably much less well-informed about the rebels than the rebels are about A—must allocate a substantial fraction of its resources to intelligence.[37] This effort, however, may be thought doomed to failure (how does one distinguish the innocent form the guilty in a faceless mass?) or be unnecessary (are the population and the rebels not close to each other?). The situation then arises is described by a French officer in Indochina:

> We whites are, after all, lost in the yellow mass as in a fog. We see badly, we divine badly, we are groping. [Hence] the Viets are beating us in the war of atrocities.[38]

Thus R may have the basis of intelligence for correct targeting for massive infliction of extreme damage, while A, lacking that basis, may be incapable of coercion even if it aspired to such practices.

Not only must the coercer arrange to *be informed* about what the coercees do, he must also arrange to *inform them* about what they can expect from him, by warning and setting examples. Here again, effort is required to ensure that the target population be clear as to what precise lesson is to be learned from damage presented in support of a rule. Hence, damage-inflictors may spread the knowledge of their acts in overt ways, difficult to hide—as when the FLN cut off the noses and ears of people who had, say, smoked despite the prohibitions, and now were impressed into service as walking examples. During the Napoleonic war in Spain

> the Spaniard who had helped the Frenchman has his right ear cut off, and bears on his forehead, branded by red-hot iron, these words: 'Long Live Mina' [a guerrilla leader].[39]

Intending both to render their new laws familiar and to prove how correct and complete their intelligence is (how omniscient, hence how powerful, hence how destined to victory, hence how worthy of support on all grounds they are), rebels often leave with fresh corpses a summary of detailed charges. In the Irish revolution, which was notable for the rarity of informers,

> many dead bodies, often of Irishmen who had served in the British Army, were found by the roadside, shot by the IRA with a label attached to them bearing the words: 'Convicted as a spy. Spies and traitors beware.'[40]

To be sure, nothing prevents A from imitating its enemy. When "Tiger" Tam, Minister of the Interior, wins "the Battle of Saigon" in 1950:

> . . . one finds numerous corpses abandoned in the streets . . . with numerous wounds inflicted by a knife. Attached to them is a paper with the reasons for their condemnation. This is in the usual Viet Minh manner for the execution of "traitors"; but the grounds indicated are quite out of the ordinary. . . . "so-and-so is a communist assassin who has been executed for his crimes."[41]

Being outspoken about extreme damage inflicted may convey disregard for the decent opinions of local mankind, and thus may cow, if it does not do the opposite—but at least an intermediate reaction is less probable. In the case of an organization with a penchant for self-righteousness which it is capable of communicating, proclaimed ferocity may encourage the population to believe that here is the next legitimate authority, quasijudicial, quite judicious, and very fearsome.

Nontotalitarian authorities, on the other hand, who under the stress of conflict, resort to procedures greatly at variance with their usual standards may be too ashamed and afraid of world opinion to admit what they have done. Instead, they may trust that the population's, if not R's, own media (such as the "Arab Telephone") will bring the news to those to be deterred (which indeed happened, for instance, after the French repression in Setif, in the spring of 1945). Or they may simply prefer to risk wasting the coercion than to have its use publicized and possibly exaggerated.

It is often affirmed that being severe toward the population, or, worse, inflicting considerable amounts of damage on it, does not pay: one is more apt to arouse than intimidate. However that may be, certain characteristics of damaging behavior by either side—apart from the level and sum of damage inflicted—are apt to affect popular reactions.

1. *Compliance may vary directly with the degree to which the severity of the sanctions inflicted by one side is understandable*—that is, is seen to exist for reasons other than cowing. The population may be out of sympathy with R, but may also appreciate that, given its business, informing merits death. The population may even understand that the rebels, lacking facilities

for locking people up and fearful of escapees turning in formers, may have to punish severely or not at all. On the other hand, if, say, a minor lack of respect provokes one side to an extreme sanction, this is more likely to be resented in a way that in the long run reduces compliance[42]— unless that side maintains so overwhelming a threat towards its targets that awareness of misdeeds is obliterated form consciousness.

2. *The less complete the enforcement of a rule, but incapacity or discrimination, the lower the compliance*—not only because of the chance of impunity thus provided, but also, again, because of the impression of weakness and injustice thereby generated. To this extent, more damage, suitable allocated, might be better received than less damage randomly imposed.

3. *The less a side*—while insisting, with severe threats, on a certain kind of conduct—*is capable of protecting the compliant population from the other side's making good on its perhaps even severer threats, the more resentment, and in the long run the more resistance, that side is likely to provoke.* When "the peasant has his choice," proposes a participant-observer of As fighting Rs in less developed countries,

> the government must be ruthless. . . . When, however, an area is outside government control . . . the government has no right to be ruthless. [Yet] there was a tendency in Vietnam to get this the wrong way round.[43]

"In the past," recalls an eyewitness-actor about the treatment of the Huks before Magsaysay, "the farmer who gave food to the Huk, however unwillingly, had been treated as . . . [a] supporter of the enemy." With the new policy under which the rebellion was defeated, "the assumption was that if he was . . . in need because of taxes levied on him by the Huk, he was a person entitled to help from his government."[44] (However, to what extent would the gain from such a policy be offset by increased compliance with the other side's demands?)

4. *A side* (usually a nontotalitarian A) *may arouse unfavorable reactions among its targets,* reactions well beyond what they might have been *had a given amount of damage been administered in draconian fashion;* if it appears to be not only harsh but unintelligible and unpredictable as well. Its rationale, if such can be fath-

omed at all, may change erratically. Sharp deviations from the patters of strong coercion are apt to create in the population a belief in A's incompetence and destructiveness. On the first count, A may appear doomed, contemptible, and hateful (in its weakness, causing misery); on the second, again, hateful and doomed.

"As for myself," a Eurasian officer—lord of a semiautonomous domain in the Mekong Delta during the first war there—explains:

> I destroy the villages which must be destroyed. I kill those who have to be killed. But the French destroy and kill at random because they don't have the necessary information. . . . Of me the farmers say that I am just. But they fear the Expeditionary Corps because its conduct is unforeseeable.[45]

"It is not only their uselessness," says a French officer in Vietnam about the "unjust atrocities" that according to him were common in his army, "which is shocking, but above all the revelation, through them, of lack of discernment." The latter "causes both hate and contempt."[46]—and rage, though it may be inhibited by fear, about being put into a situation where, with the best of will, one is unable to limit damage to oneself to reasonable levels. "The peasants," this officer explains,

> simply can't divine what the Expeditionary Corps is going to do when it appears in a village; it may just as well set everything on fire as distribute medicine.[47]

An officer recalling the conflict in Algeria notes:

> Two or three times in a row we visited the same village, distributing candies . . . pamphlets . . . food and medicine. Then, for weeks, we abandoned the village to its fate. Or, the day after, we arrived as warriors . . . candies changed into grenades, pamphlets into lists of suspects, good words into threats. Now, acting on intelligence or caprice, we were going to perform population control. . . . Somebody looking suspect was just out of luck. A passerby, arousing suspicion, appearing at the wrong time or place . . . was apt to become . . . one "killed while escaping."[48]

Wile such conduct may cow its targets, it is more likely to work against compliance, even apart from the bad feelings it arouses. If those who obey often are penalized while, in other cases, those who disobey avoid punishment, the case for damage-limitation is weakened. So it may also be if the combination of much arbitrariness with high overall damage makes one suspect a campaign aimed at mere annihilation—in the face of which chances of survival may seem enhanced through resistance.

Reprisal

A side may inflict reprisals against damage done to it, both for punishment and deterrence—the latter frequently a pretext for the former, which in turn may cloak vengeance, which, on its part, may justify pleasure in hurting and wrecking.[49]

While in one major type of reprisal the victims are presumably members of the other side, in another situation—for instance, when As are impressed with R's dependence on support by the population—a contiguous (usually in space, but possibly in time) sector of the population may itself become the target. After all, it is easily at hand, in contrast to the infuriatingly elusive rebels, and suspect by opportunity as well as by a (not always fully conscious) equation in A's mind between R and the population.

Hence, "from the moment at which the French army has suffered heavy losses" in an encounter with the Algerian rebels, explains one of them, "the nearest village . . . should be considered as no long in existence."[50] And in another Algerian episode:

> We pursue them all day from one village to another, in helicopters, in jeeps, and on foot, without stopping, for they never stop. As we go along we set fire to all the [houses] where we find traces of them, and to a few others.[51]

No case is, or can be, made for the assertion that "traces" indicated the continued presence of the notoriously mobile enemy, or for the implicit contention that, had he been present, he had enjoyed complicity from the population whom he was otherwise supposed to "terrorize."

If survivors connected with such reprisals feel a sense of collective responsibility for the initial deed, perhaps because it happened close to them or was committed by members of a group of which they feel a part, and if the reprisal itself is not felt to be disproportionate, such conduct may seem acceptable to the population. But if the first condition is not met, and if it is not clear how the victims could have prevented the initial act at all—or, at any rate, at reasonable cost to themselves—there is little coercion: hardly a lesson to be learned for future conduct. If *any* member of the population may have to pay for *any* participant in an R whose cause has some measure of appeal (in contrast to that of a gang), the R may indeed come to seem to represent the population: one of its cardinal tenets is validated.

In addition, reprisals at random may hit persons whom a side may want to spare, in view of their contributions to its cause, or the shock produced by damage befalling them.

Still, if large enough numbers are killed in this way, random reprisals may be expedient for some time (here again it is the middle road that is apt to be inexpedient), partly because they inhibit the rebels themselves.[52] In 1945 the French, with rebellion in Algeria at a low level, reacted to the death of about 100 Europeans by killing about 15,000 Muslims in Setif; it may have worked. In 1955, with rebellion much higher, the French responded to similar damage by killing perhaps 5,000 in Philippeville; it didn't work. Would 50,000 have done it? The figure of 500,000— mentioned at the time on the mainland in oral and popular recommendations—would probably have produced a striking effect for a far from negligible time. But, apart from certain totalitarian regimes during certain periods, the regard for the public on which A depends, as well as its own conscience, may make it choose a middle level of violence, offering even less prospect of effectiveness than the low or high extreme. (Repugnance to the high level of violence on moral grounds is so strong that the mention of its possible effectiveness is largely avoided in public print. Our violation of this taboo makes us liable to being misinterpreted as advocating, retrospectively, the largest number of deaths mentioned in the above example concerning Algeria. We do not. If we were to advice an A having such an option, we should on moral grounds rule out even considering it. That does not change the shape of reality of which we spoke.)

Provocation

One may inflict damage for the purpose of provoking one's opponent to raise his level of counteraction: he will believe it will do him good, but I foresee that it will harm him (I may be mistaken, and fatally induce him to abandon the ineffectual middle ranges of violence to which he was accustomed for its devastating higher reaches.) In the first half of the sixties, violent actions by rebels in Latin America against civilian governments or against Americans (such as the kidnapping of a U.S. officer in Venezuela) were often suspected of aiming at a local *golpe*, or intervention, by the United States.

When the relations between my opponent and the population are not bad enough, to my taste, I may desire to make my enemy nastier by wounding him harder. Presumably, this was a motive behind the preference of communist elements, in the resistance against the German occupiers during World War II, for killing isolated German soldiers and then disappearing—confidently expecting that reprisals not only would seem disproportionately large in the population's judgment, but would also make victims far beyond the Party's immediate sphere. In the occupied Soviet Union

> the Germans had issued warnings that any damage to German installations or personnel would be punished by reprisals on the population living in the vicinity of the crime. The partisans would simply kill a German soldier in some safe place, and . . . leave his body in a village street. The Germans almost always . . . retaliated by burning down the village and killing its inhabitants, [though] often it was obvious that the body had been moved, because there was no blood on the ground.[53]

"Along the route of retreat of the paratroops," an observer reports about an episode of the first war in Vietnam,

> "the Viets had planted on bamboo spikes of the heads of the soldiers they had killed, like so many milestones. Some of the men went berserk from it, others cried hysterically when they recognized the head of somebody they had known; others just swore softly that they'd kill every Vietnamese they'd find as soon as they got to a Vietnamese village" . . . .They *did* burn down the first Vietnamese village they found.[54]

At the time of the conflict between the Zionists and the British in Palestine, "children in communal settlements were taught a 'spitting drill' to be used against British soldiers with the objective, sometimes achieved, of goading them into incidents."[55]

It may be particularly useful to induce an opponent to kill his own supporters. As the famous Eurasian officer who was operating on the French side in Indochina explains to an observer:

> The French are blind. They fall into all the traps laid by the enemy. Once they discovered the body of one of their men, frightfully tortured, at the entrance to a village. They set fire to the village, having no inkling of the fact that it was pro-French. The Viets had deposited the mutilated corpse there, warning the inhabitants not to touch it.[56]

Apart from modifying preferences, successful provocations may change the outcome of calculations (on limiting damage or maximizing advantages) in a sense welcome to the provoker. For instance, life in the forces of one or the other side may be refused by a villager so long as his normal environment endures, but may be accepted when it is destroyed.

What I want to provoke may not be enhanced pressure by my opponent against my potential allies, but enhanced intervention by a third party against him. One way of doing this is to cause my opponent to inflict such damage on me as will trigger the third party's intervention on my behalf—a calculation sometimes attributed, in another context, to nuclear-minded Frenchmen (interested in reducing the probability of being abandoned by Washington in case of a forward move by Moscow).

Or, I may myself damage what is of value to the third party whose intervention I want to bring about, finding an excuse to do so in the course of fighting my opponent. When the Cuban rebels of 1897 seemed to adopt a policy of burning cane fields owned by Americans, there arose "suspicion that these tactics were designed to coax us into extracting Cuban chestnuts from the Spanish fire."[57]

Should R start off with a bang—which has obvious advantages for its growth—or begin inconspicuously in order to delay A's reaction? Fearing a countervalue response by its opponent, a side (usually R) may abstain from inflicting counter-force damage that would otherwise be indicated—a reaction, as we noted above, contributing to the usefulness to A of *high* reprisal. For example, an American officer who had commanded U.S. Philippine guerrilla forces in central and southern Luzon admitted that

> . . . the Japanese, through brutality to the Philippine people, forced us to abandon harassment. We tried various means of keeping them from retaliating against the . . . civilians, but none worked.[58]

Similarly, an observer of the Southern Sudanese rebels in the mid-sixties noted:

> From time to time the Anya-Nya carry out . . . raids on administrative centers; but these have now diminished because the army's policy of massive retaliation has had some success. The rebels have decided that the consequences for the civilian population of the towns are too tragic to make such raids worthwhile.[59]

A similarly prudent behavior may be adopted if a side believes it is better off not to unleash a counterforce *exchange.* "To Jimmy's way of thinking," explains an observer about a Mau Mau general staying put in the jungle,

> he had but to bide his time and build up his food stocks . . . balancing his nuisance value against the effort it would take the Army to move him. The important thing was not to exceed the limit. He had an instinct for correctly interpreting his intelligence, which was good. . . . [60]

The student rebellions of the sixties in the MDCs occurred in conditions in which the provocation assumed a major role for both A and R, in view of the following circumstances:

1. The counterforce capability of R with regard to the establishment at large was low.
2. That of A, in relation to R, was high.
3. As long as violations of established rules and inflictions of damage by R were below a certain level (rising as the decade proceeded), they did not appear to justify the crushing counteraction which (2) rendered possible. The evolving pattern came to include intruding upon, molesting and insulting members of A chosen for "confrontation"; inspecting, throwing into disarray and even damaging objects in their offices; "occupying" premises.
4. But making itself suspected of having induced a coronary in a member of A (fatal to the President of Swarthmore, mild to the Dean of Harvard) was already too much of R, and might expediently be followed by cessation or reduction of attack: punishing itself, rather than suffering a retribution it had rendered acceptable, and thus wiping the slate clean with a view to resuming the offensive. Paving stones were an accepted weapon against the forces of order for a month in the Paris of 1968—on condition that they not kill. A single death clearly due to the rebels would have had a significant impact adverse to them.
5. Similarly, had even one rebel then been killed clearly by the defenders of the status quo, they would have incurred a notable disadvantage.
6. Not only was there a high sensitivity to the damage inflicted by A and R, the preoccupation with the human costs of the battle tended to prevail—with the exception of the upper levels of R and A—over interest in its outcome—in contrast, say, to a contest between landowners and peasant rebels aiming at their extinction, where the mutual infliction of extreme damage is apt to be taken for granted. When students confront academic authorities, demands concerning, say, student power or R.O.T.C. are soon likely to take second place to the insistence on, say, amnesty or the enforcement of discipline.
7. In such conditions, it is of major worth for R to provoke A into an inexpediently (for it) high level of "repression." University administrators or "pigs" may act on the sentiments aroused in them when hit by dirty words or substances: autonomously or uncontrollably (not that an *attempt* is always made on higher levels to restrain them) they may counterattack to a measure which splits A itself, and causes its desertion by needed elements of R. This is what happened when the forces of order reacted sharply (though their casualties may not have been below those of their opponents) in the "Battle of the *rue Gay-Lussac*" in Paris, during the night of May 10-11, 1968, inducing the government's capitulation to the rebels a day later.

8. A, in its turn, is equally interested in having R go beyond those levels or amounts of violating rules and inflicting damage which have come to be accepted as bordering on the permissible. Thus it was noted in Paris, during the spring just recalled, that the police, recurrently, did not use its capability for preventing, at low cost, the assemblage in the streets of large number of its opponents or the construction of barricades by them. It may have preferred—once having incurred the cost mentioned under (5)—offering television audiences repeated spectacles of masses surging through the city and barricades having to be overcome by bulldozers. One month after the first big battle, ordinary folk were still descending from many parts of the city upon the latest battleground to collar the rebels and ask them to stop.

Hitting the Worst—and the Best[61]

A side (usually R) may inflict damage for the purpose of arousing positive reactions toward it on the part of those unsympathetic to its victims. The Robin Hoods prefigure their future reign of justice by punishing oppressors and exploiters, employing some of the rituals customary in the established order for the corresponding acts. Helping underprivileged elements in the population to improve their lot in various ways, R may require strength which it can turn against its beneficiaries, now obtaining compliance inspired by the desire to limit damage. That is, first the rebels assist the population's effort to limit damage to itself from A; then, having grown by that campaign, they in turn threaten damage to the population, *unless* . . . The rebels may then begin to deplete the stock, not of the "bad," but of the "good" agents of A: those who are efficient without being obnoxious, and those who achieve unusually good relations with the population. As an observer noted about South Vietnam:

> . . . as early as 1957, the cream of village officialdom had been murdered by the Communists, who had correctly identified this group as a key element in the struggle.[62]

And in Algeria a participant-observer remarked about the rebels:

If they have to choose between liquidating a police officer who everyone knows is a monster and liquidating [an officer] who is trying to make contact [with the population], they will pick [the latter] without a moment's hesitation.[63]

Both kinds of targeting will spare agents of A who are neither here nor there. In 1960 in South Vietnam, there was

> . . . a period of . . . terror directed at . . . officials in the countryside who were either unjust administrators or who, by their good example, served the government well . . . the mediocre, those who saw and heard no evil [in the Viet Cong], survived.[64]

Indeed, they were encouraged in the trait that protected them: "the assassination pattern . . . stimulated mediocrity among civil servants"[65]—an effect which the rebels went so far as to foster by explicit, though discreet, suggestions:

> Especially to low-ranking civil servants, the National Liberation Front would convey the idea that it would not harm a Government of Vietnam representative providing he arranged that the programs for which he was responsible were not implemented in any effective way . . . A civil servant would imagine he could enjoy the best of both worlds: he could perform well enough not to arouse the suspicions of his superior, but not so well as to earn the hostility of the NLF. He might even be in contact with the NLF so as to be certain they understood his position.[66]

Being Generous

Just as an R may seek to please by making itself the secular arm of natural law against a perverted order, it may desire to impress by unexpected generosity—to abstain from inflicting *expected* damage on enemies so as to foster their disaffection from A, or even their conversion to itself. This device is likely, however, to be productive only to the extent that A does not inflict extreme damage on any agent whose loyalty is open to even marginal doubt. If it does not, it may, for instance, be to the rebels' advantage to be nice to prisoners. In 1947, a participant-observer's colleague

> visited a camp in central China where the Nationalists kept five thousand Communist

prisoners. "Where were they caught?" he asked the Nationalist general in charge of the camp. "Between you and me, we have no more than ten real Communist soldiers among these prisoners." "Who are the others, then?" "Nationalist soldiers caught and released by the Communists. We don't want them to contaminate our army."[67]

On the other hand, here are the musings of a French officer who has captured an Algerian rebel:

> If I set him free . . . either he mends his ways and will have his throat cut by his brothers . . . or he doesn't, and then, in order to prove that we have not contaminated him, his first gesture will be to cut a throat.[68]

The other side's ferocity may thus counter the device of being humane.

Insulting

Whatever its motive, an act of inflicting injury may also insult the victim, making compliance (in that be desired) less likely. This is especially apt to happen to a side (usually A) associated with ethnic or class strata that hold in contempt the groups with which the other side (ordinarily R) appears to be connected.

The latter's insulting behavior is often a leaning-over-backward against an obscure temptation to accept their superior's sentiments about them. When lower orders maltreat their betters, they unwillingly acknowledge, through tier very rage, the formidable stature of their victims—who may sense this and then find their treatment more bearable.

But the insults heaped upon the injuries administered by masters to their inferiors are likely to express a more serene conviction that the latter are low in all senses of the word: such insults are harder to take "lying down." For instance, in Algiers:

> One day, a sergeant got a bit high and then scoured the neighborhood in a truck, picking up all the Arabs he came across wearing good European clothes—without even bothering to ask for their papers. He came back with his truck completely full. After assembling his captives in the muddy courtyard, he first made them do a few squats and pushups. Then, because he saw they were trying not to get their clothes dirty, he continued with more and more strenuous exercises.

> "Stand up! Lie down! On your back! On your stomach! Move your legs, your arms, your head . . . " When one would collapse, completely out of breath, a good jab with a bayonet brought him to order again. We were at the windows, laughing, jostling to get a better view.

> Since then, it has become an unwritten rule to make a particular search for well-dressed Arabs. Heaven help the suspect caught with a necktie on and with his shoes shined.[69]

Insult may be harder to take than injury: its presence interferes with the determination of conduct by calculations of limiting damage or enhancing gain. The very fact of continuing to calculate in the presence of insult may somehow be associated with the particular loss to be avoided: by taking it lying down (as my tormenter is confident I will), I prove the correctness of his assertions about me. In sharp opposition to this reaction, as noted above, one of the major motives of an R connected with lower groups is precisely to demonstrate the falsity of one's masters' unfavorable conceptions about oneself, just because these conceptions have an obscure and powerful hold on one.

Combining *little* injury with *much* insult is the least expedient combination, where rage is least impeded by pain and fear. It is also one to which nontotalitarian. As, as shown by some of the incidents already noted, are particularly drawn.

Assimilating the Population to the Enemy

If R is associated in A's eyes with inferior ethnic or class groupings, A may, as noted, find it impracticable to distinguish between the guilty and the innocent in the faceless mass (or not useful to do so, if one wants to produce impressive body-counts), and regard it as sound practice to presume that any member of the appropriate sector of the population is a rebel. According to a historian reconstructing the mood of Napoleon's soldiers in Spain:

> The prevalent opinion in the Army is this: the more Spaniards who perish, the fewer enemies we will have.[70]

"Most of my buddies," a conscript reports about Algeria, "were convinced that all their troubles were the fault of the *bougnoules*. They wanted to kill as many as they could as soon as feasible, so as to go home as quickly as possible."[71]

DEVICES FOR COMPLIANCE

Modes of Threatening and Promising

Enunciating a demand, a side may immediately execute anticipatory punishment against likely offenders. During the first war in Vietnam, recalls an observer,

> an agent of a French intelligence service was in the habit of taking his 'clients' up in a plane. He'd throw two or three out of the plane, and then tell the others: "now you'll talk, or suffer the same fate."[72]

Consider a French intelligence officer's comments on the rebel leadership of the 'Autonomous Zone of Algiers.'

> When one or several members of the Council wanted to install themselves in a house in the Casbah, they first sent a team of masons to construct a hiding place there. The masons immediately gathered together the people in the building and told them, in substance: You are soon to receive important personages. You will be responsible for their security with your lives. And sometimes, to indicate that this was no idle threat, a burst of gunfire cut down on the spot the residents who seemed . . . most suspect.[73]

Thus one may relinquish a strict connection between actual conduct and incurred damage for the present, so as to confer maximum credibility on a new and vital connection of that very kind.

Attempting to make a violator desist, a side may acquaint him with his thickening file or with his current classification-for-punishment. In South Vietnam, according to one observer:

> . . . village heads are classified according to their cooperation with the Viet-Cong, their non-cooperation with the Viet-Cong and support of the government, or their non-cooperation with both. The Viet-Cong communicate this classification to the individual concerned. He then knows that cooperation with the government gives him a classification . . . sharply decreasing his life expectancy.[74]

(The implicit condition, of course, is that he recognize his actions in what purports to be his record. Intelligence must be good).

The full execution of a threat may be preceded by a graded series of warnings, perhaps in the guise of symbolic or limited damage recalling vividly what is to come. The Mafia employed a

> . . . system of graded warnings from the cutting down of a vine and the maiming of an ass or mule, to the depositing at a man's door of his beheaded dog or a sheep with its throat cut . . . .[75]

The Binh-Xuyen used to

> take small pieces from the bodies of those they had kidnapped, which were then sent by parcel post to families addicted to haggling.[76]

The demands made by an R on the population usually entail, in themselves, only limited loss to the latter. Thus, if the demands are backed up by extreme threats, the probable loss from noncompliance may exceed that from obedience, even if one is aware of a good chance that recalcitrance will remain unobserved. It then needs a stern and discerning A to balance the resulting pull toward behavior demanded by the rebels.

A "totalitarian" side is apt to threaten a target with extreme damage not only to itself—damage which it may be willing to assume but hopes to escape—but also to others closely connected with the target. The target may believe it has little right to impose such loss on others, but that it will not avoid doing so, unless it complies.[77] As recalled by the American general officer who had commanded U.S. Philippine forces in the Islands while they were occupied:

> If there was one informer in a village that the guerrillas contacted for support, information would be relayed to the Japanese. The would round up all the inhabitants, usually behead the head man or several of the leaders, and often burn their homes and destroy their crops. This put tremendous pressure on civilians to refuse to support us.[78]

Presumably the pressure could be increased even further by sharpening the specificity and certainty of the opponent's forecast of who will have to pay for his deed and how. A preferred procedure of the Viet Minh to induce a Vietnamese soldier serving under a French officer in an isolated post to betray it, was to

> . . . have his mother come to tell her son that she would die if he did not deliver the post over to the Viet Minh. She would bring with her the order for her execution signed by the secretary of the local executive committee.[79]

Beyond this there is a double blackmail with regard to, say, a soldier of the other side and his family: threatening each with damage to the other. Attempting to forestall the use of this device by its opponent, a side may take potential hostages for its members out of the other side's reach.[80] As a counterpart to threats of future damage, a side may encourage forecasts that the current level of injury which it inflicts will sink if conduct desired by it is chosen. The population in a "black" or "grey" area may be stimulated thereby to contribute to a color change in the direction of white.

Fashions in Compromising

A side may compromise persons by using their concern for the undoing of a loss that it has itself imposed on them: their only hope of restitution is made to depend on that side's success. If the former owner of property confiscated by the rebels wants payment, the rebels give him bonds, Che Guevara explains—documents that become " 'bonds of hope' . . . [to] bind old and new owners to . . . the success of the cause."[81]

Or a side may bestow a gain (say, land) on the population, expecting that the latter will foresee the undoing of that gain if the other side succeeds or if disobedience is shown to the bestowing side.

Finally, a side can maneuver a target into a situation where he believes he is threatened by the other side and can minimize damage by moving toward the side that put him in this spot. Thus, a side may in effect give a target its name, expecting that he will thereupon calculate, or can be persuaded, to play its game.

One might acquire (or be led to believe that one has acquired) the reputation of being partisan to the side in question by being forced to commit a compromising act ("entrapment"). This may be done by luring a target in search of advantage; he does not fathom that he will soon be concerned only with limiting damage to himself. Or force may be employed against the person to be compromised, as in certain variants of the Viet Cong's drafting and abducting persons for "re-education courses." Or coercion may occur, as in the case of "forced oathing" by the Mau Mau, compromising one with regard to supernatural entities.

But what seems to the interested side to be a compromising act may, because of a countermaneuver on the part of its opponent, turn out otherwise. As the Viet Minh tried to plant its men within the small posts manned largely by Vietnamese, the French multiplied various tasks:

> The chief of the post [usually a French NCO] . . . might submit his recruits to strange tests. For example, he makes them kill Viet Minh prisoners in public . . . That precaution does not always suffice. The Viets may instruct their men thus: If the French sergeant orders you to kill party members, do it unhesitatingly . . . Volunteer for execution![82]

Instead of forcing the target to perform a compromising act, the interested side may commit one toward him—for example, by treating him surprisingly well, say, if he is a prisoner. One recruitment device of the Viet Cong was

> to release a captured prisoner almost immediately . . . and without any explanation; the soldier returning to his unit would find his officers highly skeptical of his story. . . . He would be treated as . . . [a] spy . . . whereupon the NLF would find him receptive to its recruitment efforts.[83]

The target's life may be manipulated in more complicated fashion so as to raise the level of threat to him from one's opponent. Having asked villagers whether they receive visits from the other side and having got an (untruthful) "no" for an answer, a side may arrange an ambush near the village which will damage the other side, or at least be noted by them. Thereupon the first side may re-enter the village and say to the villagers (as in the campaign against the Huks):

> You people have been . . . foolish. . . . Our soldiers came here to see if you needed any help. You lied to them. You said there were no Huk here. They knew you lied, and so they waited for the Huk to come. They killed some, and captured some, but others got away. You know what those Huk are thinking now—the ones who got away? They are thinking that somebody here betrayed them.[84]

The villagers, agreeing with this estimate, change sides. "I don't need to kill Viet cadres," the boss of the Hué during much of the first war in Vietnam confides to an observer:

> When I suspect somebody . . . I put him into prison on whatever charge, [and] then I release him without apparent reason. Suspected by the

Party, he is eager to clear himself by the excellence of his work. I pass false information to him which he transmits to the Viets, who will liquidate him when they find out. If he is valuable, I call him and demonstrate to him that he is irremediably "burned" with his side. I save him by recruiting him. It is thus that I have acquired my best officials.[85]

THE POPULATION UNDER CROSS-FIRE

The Dominance of Damage-Limiting

As noted earlier, the effort to limit damage may prevail over aspirations to better one's condition or act according to one's ideals; the more so, the fiercer and longer the conflict. "The villagers," guesses a French officer in Algeria

aren't going to vote for those who build schools for them nor for those who promise independence; they are going to vote for the one who can hold the threat of death over them.[86]

What may be mistaken by a side for an expression of the population's antipathy toward it may simply be fear of the damage foreseen to result from the other side's reacting to the first side's approach (for example, by recruitment in a village). And, as noted earlier,[87] a side may be prepared to recruit persons for rather high levels of participation under duress.

As an analyst observed about the occupied Soviet Union during World War II:

Even though the peasant knew who was going to win the war, in many cases where the Germans had . . . adequate forces . . . [he] might decide that it was safer to submit to the Germans and be hostile to the Partisans. [Although] he jeopardized his future by working with the Germans, he could not afford the luxury of making long-range estimates. . . . He tried to survive in the immediate future.[88]

That is, as observed before,[89] calculations of damage that may befall one during the conflict may dwarf estimates of injury derived from the combination of a particular war record with a particular war outcome.

Members of the population may desire to stay with one side as long, and only as long, as it is profitable or prudent to do so, veering toward its

opponent when assessments against these criteria begin to point in the opposite direction—that is, when a change of rule impends, or day is about to break (night to fall). Or the population may—a frequently noted maneuver—attempt to satisfy both contenders at the same time.[90]

If one can plead with a side that one's compliance with its opponent's demands was due to duress, perhaps the sanction will be lightened or lifted. Hence, if a side does not insist strongly enough on compliance, one should wait until it does (and probably make it do so by an initial refusal). "One of the first steps," a French officer recalls about his civic action programs in Algeria

was to open a first-aid station. . . . When the population failed to respond to an invitation to use the station, for fear of being seen making contact with the enemy, it was necessary to resort to forced treatment. Twice a week the battalion doctor would make a tour. . . . Another . . . step was to open, or reopen, schools. Again, parents and children did not respond to the first request for attendance; but on being told that, as of a given date, they would be fined for their childrens' truancy, the parents decide to cooperate.[91]

How Does a Side Make Itself Stronger Toward Those in the Middle?

One limits damage by veering toward (1) the more predictable side, (2) the side imposing a lesser cost on impunity, (3) the more severe side. Preferences with regard to these three "goods"—or to the latter two adjusted for expectations—vary. There are, for instance, those individuals who are little tempted to transgress and are hence mostly interested in a low cost of impunity; those who are much tempted to transgress and are hence interested in a side's severity (mildness); and those who especially dislike uncertainty and are hence interested in a side's predictability.

"Severity" refers, of course, both to the level of threats and enforcement, including the chances of concealment and escape. To be stronger with regard to the population may thus also mean, as we already noted,[92] to be harsher toward it. As recounted by a French paratroopers' chaplain:

An old Muslim, arrested for having sawed off telegraph poles, explains to a captain who expresses surprise about his deed: "Sir, the

French come and tell me: you musn't saw off poles; if you do, you go to prison. I say to myself: I don't want to go to prison, I won't do it. The French leave. At night, the rebel comes and says: saw off the poles from here to there. I answer: no, the French would put me into prison. The rebel tells me: You cut the poles or I cut your throat. I calculate: If I don't cut the poles, he'll surely cut my throat; he has done it to others, in the next village. I prefer going to prison. So, Sir, I cut the poles, you caught me; put me in prison!"[93]

A population beset by both rebels and forces of order may feel there is much to choose, where observers accustomed to less uncomfortable situations fail to perceive the difference. One may strongly prefer a high probability of death to its certainty, if that appears to be one's alternative. We shall surely kill you unless you kill so-and-so, R may say to a person approached. The other side, to be sure, may kill you for doing it. But also, they may not find out, or not find you; even if they do, their legality may enable you to survive.

Or one may choose the side threatening a merciful death against the side promising a painful one. "At the time of the last elections," recalls a French officer serving in Algeria

> Muslims came to me and said: We are coming to see you, but we shall not vote. If we did, we would have our throats cut. You can kill us with your gun; it's more agreeable to die that way than by the knife.[94]

Reactions to Unintended Damage

So far we have dealt with damage to the population which is intended to by a side. But what about the flies who got crushed when elephants fight? On what factors does a population's reaction to collateral damage from the conflict between A and R depend?

Sometimes the population will be hostile to a side in the measure in which that side's fire, though directed at the opponent, makes it suffer. Thus, hostile reactions by moderate student groups against university authorities occurred frequently in the late nineteen sixties (at Harvard, Columbia, and Berkeley), when those authorities called upon the police to oust militant students who had occupied university prop-

erty, and the police in energetic pursuit of their mission struck against bystanders, as well as occupiers.

But, clearly, rage—and particular rage against the directly inflicting side—is not the only possible response, as the reaction of occupied Europeans showed during World War II. (Also, of the population's major reaction does conform to the hypothesis previously mentioned, the cost of this to the inflicting side, directly and indirectly, may or may not be higher than the immediate tactical gain from the strikes in question.) In some cases, elements of the population may be sufficiently hostile to the side against which the attacks were intended, to nourish their aversion with this very suffering (as, to some extent, in the situations during World War II previously referred to). Or they may at least be willing to pay a certain— possibly a substantial—price for a preferred outcome of the war. And their reaction is apt to be influenced not only by the amounts of injury produced, but also by their estimate of each side's eagerness and skill in avoiding "unnecessary" damage to the population, directly and indirectly. Once again. ruthlessness, negligence, and clumsiness may be attributed either to the inflicting side or to its opponent who provoked such reactions or gave it no choice; the attributions are, as in the campus disorders noted above, likely to be based on matters of fact, as well as of rumor and sentiment. Finally, the entire dimension of the legitimacy of damage may be dwarfed by the search for, and the execution of, maneuvers to limit it.

If a side imposes a certain conduct on the population for which the other side then punishes it, the population's reaction will depend on a variety of factors: its assessment of the utility of the conduct for the side that imposed it (being much harmed for little is galling); the degree to which that side promised protection from its opponent and yet did not deliver it; the degree to which it assumes some responsibility for the misery it has provoked. These considerations would seem hard to overlook. That they *are* overlooked is suggested by an incident related by an observer of the first war in Vietnam:

> Luong Ha is a Catholic village . . . to the southeast of the Plain of Reeds, at about 20 kilometers from RC-16 [a highway]. It was

obeying the Viet Minh peacefully. Then, in Saigon, a program for extending pacification was prepared. And so a column [of the Expeditionary Corps] went to Luong Ha. The priest and his peasants were drawn in, a militia constituted . . . a post and towers built for defense. Then the column left again, leaving behind it a platoon commanded by a French captain. As a result the village was massacred at night. . . . The Viets immobilized the soldiers by mortar and machine gun fire. They passed between the post and the towers, and killed a good part of the population.

When the French returned shortly afterwards, the vicar reported:

> Nobody is working in the fields anymore, nobody is reconstructing his house. The Viet Minh cadre has told us . . . that this was just a warning: next time all the men will be shot. We ask of the French to leave important forces in the village, to send us rice and medicine.

The observer in question (Lucien Bodard) concludes his account of the incident as told to him by the French officer in charge:

> But he raised his arms to heaven and remarked to me, "These people are insatiable. I'm not God, after all. I can't put troops everywhere. And I've no budget for rice.[95]

Yet the officer attempted compensation for these incapacities before leaving the village, he distributed a substantial number of military decorations.[96]

ENDNOTES

1. Thompson, **op. cit.**, p. 165.
2. Roger Trinquier, **Modern Warfare** (New York : Praeger, 1964), p. 59.
3. See Chapter 5.
4. Jean-Jacques Servan-Schreiber, **Lieutenant in Algeria** (New York: Knopf, 1957), p. 33.
5. For an instance from the war in Algeria, see Leulliette, **op. cit.**, p. 24.
6. Thompson, **op. cit.**, p. 34 ff.
7. Servan-Schreiber, **op. cit.**, p. 41.
8. Jacques Tissier, **Le Gâchis** (Paris: Editeurs Francais Réunis, 1960), p. 73. Our translation.
9. Robert Bonnaud, **Itineraire** (Paris: Editions de Minuit, 1962), p. 49. Our translation.
10. Leulliette, **op. cit.**, p. 284. Our translation.
11. See Chapter 4, pp. 56-60.
12. **Encyclopaedia Brittanica**, Vol. X, 1950, 953.
13. Guevara, **op. cit.**, p. 45.
14. **Ibid.**, p. 16.
15. Quoted by Devillers, **op. cit.**, p. 238.
16. Morland, Barangé, and Martinez, **Histoire de l'O.A.S.** (Paris: Julliard, 1964), p. 470. Our translation.
17. See Wolff, **op. cit.**, p. 307.
18. See this chapter, pp. 103-104
19. Quoted by Wolff, **op. cit.**, p. 349.
20. Quoted by Wolff, **op. cit.**, p. 350.
21. See pp. 100-103.
22. Douglas Pike, **Viet Cong: The Organization and Techniques of the National Liberation Front of South Vietnam** (Cambridge: M.I.T. Press, 1966), p. 251. Emphasis added.
23. Majdalany, **op. cit.**, pp. 190-191.
24. When popular discontent was on the increase in Athens around 620 B.C. Draeon, while not proceeding to a reform of the laws,

    > . . . met . . . the demand for publication of the laws, in writing, so that men might know . . . what penalties a magistrate or court had the right to impose.

    A. R. Burn, **The Lyric Age of Greece** (London: Edward Arnold, 1960), p. 287.
25. David Galula in **Counterinsurgency: A Symposium**, The RAND Corporation, R-412-ARPA, p. 27.
26. Bonnard, **op. cit.**, p. 45.
27. Benoist Rey, **Les Egorgeurs** (Paris: Editions de Minuit, 1961), p. 57. Our translation.
28. Lucien Bodard, **La Guerre d'Indochine: I, 1'Enlisement** (Paris: Editions Gallimard, 1963), pp. 445-446. Emphasis added. Our translation.
29. **Ibid.**, pp. 252-253.
30. Saadi Yacef, **Souvenirs de la Bataille d'Alger** (Paris: René Julliard, 1962), p. 83. Our translation.
31. Quoted by Aubrey Dixon and Otto Heilbrunn, **Communist Guerrilla Warfare** (London: Allen and Unwin, 1954), p. 142.
32. Herbert Dinerstein, unpublished manuscript, p. 34.
33. Denis Warner, **The Last Confucian** (Baltimore: Penguin Books, 1964), p. 31.
34. Paul I. Wellman, **A Dynasty of Western Outlaws** (Garden City: Double-day, 1961), pp. 71, 73. Emphasis added.
35. Cf. Chapter 7, pp. 140-141.
36. Wolff, **op. cit.**, p. 318. Emphasis added.
37. Cf. Chapter 7.
38. Bodard, **l'Enlisement**, **op. cit.**, p. 452.
39. Lucas-Dubreton, **op. cit.**, p. 346.
40. Holt, **op. cit.**, p. 205.

41. Bodard, **l'Humiliation**, p. 269, Our translation.
42. See pp. 119-121, concerning sequels to insults.
43. Thompson, **op. cit.**, pp. 146-147.
44. Valeriano, RM-3652-PR, p. 209.
45. Bodard, **l'Enlisement**, p. 287.
46. **Ibid.**, p. 444.
47. **Ibid.**, p 446.
48. Philippe Héduy, **Au Lieutenant des Taglaits** (Paris: Editions de la Table Ronde, 1960), p. 133. Our translation.
49. See pp. 90-94.
50. Quoted by Robert Davezies, **Le Front** (Paris: Editions de Minuit, 1959), p. 155.
51. Leulliette, **op. cit.**, p. 153.
52. See pp.
53. Dinerstein, **op. cit.**, p. 39.
54. Fall, **Street Without Joy**, p. 268.
55. Christopher Sykes, **Crossroads to Israel** (Cleveland: World, 1965), p. 285.
56. Bodard, **l'Enlisement**, p. 287.
57. Wolff, **op. cit.**, p. 39.
58. Colonel B. L. Anderson in A. H. Peterson, G.C. Reinhardt, and E. E. Conger, eds., **Symposium on the Role of Airpower in Counterinsurgency and Unconventional Warfare: Allied Resistance to the Japanese on Luzon, World War II**, The RAND Corporation, RM-3655-PR, June, 1963, Santa Monica, Calif., p. 27.
59. **The Economist**, April 23, 1966, p. 348.
60. Dennis Holman, **Bwana Drum** (London: W. H. Allen, 1964), p. 108.
61. Cf. Chapter 4, pp. 54-55.
62. Fall, **The Two Vietnams**, p. 281.
63. Servan-Schreiber, **op.cit.**, p. 70.
64. Warner, **The Last Confucian**, pp. 160-161.
65. Pike, **op. cit.**, p. 248.
66. **Ibid.**, pp. 257-258.
67. Galula, **op. cit.**, p. 52.
68. Quoted by Héduy, **op. cit.**, p. 293.
69. Leulliette, **op.cit.**, pp. 288-289.
70. Lucas-Dubreton, **op. cit.**, p. 364.
71. Tissier, **op. cit.**, p. 57.
72. Bodard, **op. cit.**, p. 436.
73. Trinquier, **op. cit.**, p. 15.
74. James Farmer, **Counterinsurgency: Principles and Practices in Viet-Nam**, The RAND Corporation, P-3039, December, 1964, Santa Monica, Calif., p. 27.
75. Norman Lewis, **The Honored Society: A Searching Look at the Mafia** (New York: Putnam's Sons, 1964), p. 31.
76. Bodard, **l'Humiliation**, p. 125.
77. See the earlier discussion (pp. 110-112) about reprisals and (pp. 108-110) about the other side's inhibited, unaffected, or provoking response.
78. Brigadier General R. W. Volckmann (Ret.), quoted in A. H. Peterson, G. C. Reinhardt, and E. E. Conger, eds., **Symposium on the Role of Airpower in Counterinsurgency and Unconventional Warfare: Allied Resistance to the Japanese on Luzon, World War II**, The RAND Corporation, RM-3655-PR, July, 1963, Santa Monica, Calif., p. 6.
79. Bodard, **l'Enlisement**, p. 88.
80. Thus, in Vietnam in 1954 ". . . the repatriates going North included the dependents of the hard-core fighters who were ordered to go underground in the South. . . . The population exchange enabled the hard-core regulars who stayed behind in the South to engage in mobile warfare, without having to worry about reprisals against their relatives, who, during the earlier Indochina war, were often the first victims of their operations." Fall, **The Two Vietnams**, pp. 358-359.
81. Guevara, **op. cit.**, p. 31.
82. Bodard, **l'Enlisement**, pp. 87-88.
83. Pike, **op. cit.**, p. 260.
84. Quoted in Valeriano and Bohannon, **op. cit.**, p. 171.
85. Bodard, **l'Humiliation**, p. 365.
86. Héduy, **op. cit.**, p. 267.
87. See Chapter 2, pp. 11-12.
88. Dinerstein, **op. cit.**, p. 39.
89. See Chapter 3, pp. 43-45.
90. Ibid, Chapter 3.
91. Galula, R-412-ARPA, p. 77.
92. See Chapter 2, pp. 12-14
93. Louis Delarue, **Avec les Paras du 1er R.E.P. et du 2e R.P./Ma.** (Paris: Nouvelles Editions Latines, 1961), pp. 24-25. Our translation.
94. Quoted by Claude Dufresnoy, **Des Officiers Parlent** (Paris: Rene Julliard, 1961), p. 124. Our translation.
95. **l'Enlisement**, pp. 302-305.
96. **Ibid.**, p. 306.

Intelligence and Information

Nathan Leites and Charles Wolf, Jr.

Efficient action requires information, as we have stressed before. To this extent R and A face a similar problem. But it is much easier for R to obtain information about A than vice versa. For A is large, visible, usually loosely organized, and easy to penetrate, while R is small, "invisible" (by training and doctrine),[1] tightly organized, highly security-conscious, and hard to penetrate. Hence, this chapter will be more concerned with the operations of A than those of R.

INFORMATION COSTS AND AVAILABILITIES

As discussed earlier, many current views of insurgent conflicts—the ones we have called "hearts-and-minds" views—stress those characteristics of the less developed countries (LDCs) that influence the *demand* for rebellion.[2] At the same time, these views often neglect the characteristics of the LDC environment that influence the *supply* of rebellion: that make it easier for R to get started, and harder for A to detect until it has reached a stage of organizational firmness where the chance of aborting it is lost, and the costs of controlling it have risen.

Perhaps the most significant characteristic of the LDCs, in this connection, is the high cost of information. In the LDCs, the cost of "finding out" is usually high (almost regardless of what it is that is being investigated); the time required to obtain information is long; and the reliability of what is obtained is low. Analyzing "opportunities for organization" of the Chinese Communist Party's armed forces in the late thirties, Mao observes:

> When we are devoting ourselves to warfare in an open region, it is the . . . areas with a low cultural level, where communications are difficult and facilities for transmitting correspondence are inadequate, that are advantageous.[3]

Less developed countries are usually "plural" economies and societies, as we have noted earlier.[4] Linkages among the component parts are much less reticulated than in the more developed countries (MDCs). Flows of information, as well as of commodities and people, across the component units are relatively limited, and reliable and timely information about activities in the disparate units is scarce and expensive. From the standpoint of facilitating R, the infrequency and unreliability of contact and communication are no less important, but are usually given much less emphasis than popular grievances and discontents.

The contrast afforded by the quality, timeliness, and availability of information in the MDCs is striking. Information is abundantly available: information concerning people, products, prices, traffic flows, purchases and sales, borrowing and lending, payments and receipts, and so on and on.

Leites, Nathan, and Charles Wolf, Jr. (1970). *Rebellion and Authority: An Analytic Essay on Insurgent Conflicts*. Santa Monica, CA: Rand. Reproduction authorization obtained from RAND.

Easy and rapid checks can be made of residence, credit standing, schooling, family background, fingerprints, and, with slightly more difficulty, employment, occupation, and income. The freedom of choice available to people in the more developed noncommunist countries is enhanced by an abundance of accessible information on the possible choices, as well as on the options chosen. And the wide assortment of channels for tracing people and activities, through private as well as government sources, provides information that increases the effectiveness of preventing, as well as punishing, violation of the law.[5]

This easy access to extensive, timely, and reliable information in the MDCs means that A is likely to have warning of potential threats against it. This is particularly true where the potential threats are accompanied by organization and by political purposiveness, which implies prior planning and hence greater exposure to tracing. Violence, indeed even quite large-scale violence, can still occur in the MDCs. Events in various American cities, as well as in Paris and Rome, in recent years make this point clear. Nevertheless, while the magnitude of such violence can be large, its quality is likely to differ from that which constitutes the grit of the rebellion. Violence in the MDC environment is more likely to be of the "hot" kind that erupts quickly, without the organization, planning, and purposiveness that the "cool" violence of R requires. Cool violence involves premeditation and calculation, which increase the risk of detection and prevention in the MDC environment.[6]

Some exceptions to these points must be made for the university campuses of MDCs. As the experience of the late nineteen sixties in the United States and most other MDCs has shown, campus authorities sometimes were ill-informed about preparatory efforts that were underway to disrupt them. More often, and increasingly, A's information improved, but it remained exceedingly reluctant to react with preventive severity against the student rebels under the circumstances and for the reasons described earlier.[7]

In the plural environment of the LDCs, where information is expensive, unreliable, and usually delayed, cool violence is more feasible. R can organize and move from preparation to direction action (from a "preconditions" stage to a "take-off" stage, to use the earlier analogy from the economic growth literature) with relatively little advance warning, awareness, and preparation by A. Thus, the supply of R is facilitated by the inaccessibility (or high costs) of reliable and timely information. By the same token, effective counterrebellion requires that A improve its capacity to collect, store, collate, evaluate, retrieve, and use information. That is, A must seek to surmount the barriers that the LDC environment normally presents to improved performance in these activities. Contrary to the hearts-and-minds view, improved information-handling probably has a higher value for A than conferring benefits or widening suffrage; while for R, interdicting the flow of accurate and timely information to A is as important as, in the LDC environment, it is feasible.

Each of the four tasks into which we have previously divided counterinsurgency[8] depends critically on information. To restrict R's access to inputs, A must know where the inputs come from, how they are distributed, how transactions are consummated, and what the nodes or choke points in the distribution system are. Impending the conversion of inputs into R's activities and forces depends on actions by A which require much improved intelligence about R: infiltrating R's own organization, spreading misinformation within it, attracting wavering (and preferably leading) figures away from it and the like.[9] Conducting counterforce operations against R is also more sensitive to reliable and timely intelligence than in other conflict situations because, as noted earlier, R's forces eschew a territorial base and are more mobile, dispersed, and immersed in the population.

Finally, strengthening A's capacity to absorb R's pressure, while A grows stronger or at least grows no weaker, is likely to depend on how well A can improve its ability to handle and use intelligence information. In trying to "harden" rural hamlets and build up local defensive militia with the proper training and equipment, A can do better if it has more information on such subjects as how R operates, when it is likely to attack, in units of what size, and, above all, whether A can adapt its own behavior to variations in these tactics. Moreover, in eliciting behavior from the population which will increase the manning and improve the performance of local defensive paramilitary forces, A needs an active counterintelligence effort to meet R's anticipated efforts to infiltrate and disrupt these forces.

Perhaps more valuable to A than any of these kinds of information about R is A's possession of a capability to discriminate between those who cooperate with A and those who do not, and to apply this knowledge accurately in its targeting. Information-handling is crucial for such discrimination. To be effective, however, the information must be closely coupled with technologies for delivering penalties that minimize error. When the Berkeley police in May 1969 employed tear gas sprayed (in a strong breeze!) from a helicopter, and fired buckshot to disperse student militants, they struck the innocent (killing one of them) as well as the offenders. Weaponry, non information, was the source of targeting error, and its effect was to weaken A's position and strengthen support for the student rebels. Similarly, when the police moved to clear a university building that militant students had occupied at Harvard in April 1969, lack of precision in targeting and delivery damaged the respect accorded the Administration, and temporarily radicalized much of the student body. Compared with approximately 140 occupants of the building who were arrested, 20 bystanders outside were injured by the police, 10 non-occupants were arrested by mistake, and about 70 occupants got away!

There is perhaps nothing more likely to enhance A's legitimacy and respect than a demonstrated capacity to locate its proper target accurately, and to make the punishment (as well as the reward) fit the crime, both in severity and timeliness.[10] On the other hand, "legitimacy" is likely to be short-lived if it lacks such a capacity to discriminate. To increase A's capacity to absorb R's output requires that A demonstrate a capacity for selective and discriminating action, and this depends heavily on A's ability to collect and profit from information about the behavior of the population. The same holds for R, but usually (as noted above) the acquisition of such a capability is less difficult for it—and often R is more aware than A of the value of such efforts.

TRADE-OFFS AMONG INFORMATION, FIREPOWER, AND MOBILITY

Information, then, is more important in insurgent and counterinsurgent conflicts than in other forms of conflict. If, for example, one defines a side's capabilities in terms of intelligence information (measured as the probability of observing or locating some activity or target), firepower (tons of ordnance deliverable per unit of time), and mobility (cargo or personnel lift capability per unit of time), improvements in intelligence are likely to be more important (productive) than increases in mobility or firepower.[11]

The reasons for the relatively greater importance of intelligence follow from the previous discussion of the four component tasks of counterinsurgency. Controlling R's inputs, interdicting R's conversion mechanism, and strengthening A's absorptive capacity all acquire enhanced importance in counterinsurgency, as compared with other forms of conflict; and intelligence information is, in turn, of relatively greater importance in these tasks than is firepower or mobility. Even the counterforce component depends more on detailed information, in counterinsurgency, than on the other ingredients, because of the non-territorial characteristic of R's forces. The adversary's forces are more mobile and harder to locate than in other forms of conflict, so detailed information about them will be needed. With good information, modest firepower can be very effective in counterforce operations against R; without it, firepower will be wasted or even harmful to A, due to mistargeting.

Moreover, in counterinsurgency, the relatively greater importance of R's leadership, compared with its rank and file, means that capturing or killing a key leader is worth many units of R's forces. And this form of micro-targeting is highly dependent on intelligence. Recall the earlier reference to Magsaysay's strategy of "targeting." R's leadership, and his singular success in acquiring a large proportion of the Huks' top leadership in a Manila raid in 1954, as a result of good information. Desmond Palmer makes the same point about Malaya:

> Successful elimination of one well-known leader whose name conjures up terror to the inhabitants of an area, may well be more effective than the elimination of two-thirds of a guerrilla squad.[12]

If information is more important to A when fighting R than in other types of conflict, its usefulness to A also varies inversely with the level attained by R: the earlier stage of R, the greater the chance that timely information will enable A to make it fail. As R moves toward higher levels, the conflict begins to resemble a conventional one, and the trade-offs alluded to become more similar to those in conventional conflicts. While intelligence is relatively more important in all stages of counterinsurgency than in other types of conflict, its primacy—in relationship to firepower and mobility—is more pronounced, the earlier the stage of R. These points on the several comparisons we have been discussing (between intelligence and other ingredients of conflict, and between insurgent conflicts and other forms of conflict) can be made more precise with the aid of a simple descriptive model, as set forth in the Appendix to this chapter.

Possibly, too, the indirect payoffs from the improved intelligence are also higher in counterinsurgency than in other conflicts. Accordingly, intelligence may provide a means by which an escalating process of increased effectiveness is apt to result from an initial improvement of A's intelligence capability. Positive feedbacks are numerous and strong in the chain that connects intelligence to progress in counterinsurgency. As Thompson puts it:

> Good intelligence leads to more frequent . . . contacts. More contacts lead to more kills. These in turn lead to greater confidence in the population, resulting in better intelligence and still more contacts and kills.[13]

Imbedded in this positive feedback chain, and probably largely accounting for it, is the response of the population to a changing environment. As improved intelligence makes the conflict go more favorably for a certain side, giving information to that side appears less dangerous because its capacity for providing protection against reprisals from the other side rises. Furthermore, contributing information may itself be sensed as an effective act rather than a vain gesture: intelligence and assistance is provided to the side which now appears more likely to win (and is then also more likely viewed as deserving to do so).

Yet, this tendency, of course, may be offset by a countervailing penchant to "let George do it," particularly to the extent that the other side— though losing—increases penalties on the population's hostile behavior. Indeed, a losing side may even overcompensate by shifting its declining resources more toward such "micro-damage" activities intended to control the population, and away from guerrilla combat.

TECHNIQUES AND OPERATIONS

Hearts-and-minds views of counterinsurgency often recognize the importance of information, but they view the process by which it is acquired as simple if popular support is on one's side, and impossible, as well as repugnant, if the population is either hostile or *attentiste*. The notion that intelligence is a complex technical problem that can be handled efficiently or inefficiently, responsibly or irresponsibly, and that these differences require careful study and analysis is usually odious to those holding these views.

One effect of these attitudes is that when the United States gets involved in counterinsurgency conflicts, intelligence planning and operations do not receive the allocation of attention, brains, and resources their importance warrants. These attitudes and the priorities they generate need to be reversed. The analysis and understanding of intelligence should be made as respectable as its central importance in counterinsurgency requires. Thompson reflects this orientation:

> If subversion is the main threat, starting as it does well before an open insurgency and continuing through it and even afterwards, it follows that within the government the intelligence organization is of paramount importance. In fact, I would go so far as to say that no government can hope to defeat a communist insurgent movement unless it gives top priority to, and is successful in building up such an organization.[14]

The ingredients of effective organization and operations are numerous and complex. An effective system requires not just collection of information from multiple sources (some degree of redundancy is essential) but also processing classifying, evaluating, storing, and retrieving information. Indeed, modern technological progress in information processing and handling is probably more important for counterinsurgency than are changes in weapons technology.

As a part of intelligence operations, A must be able to communicate information to the population and the rebels. When the population is the audience, the aim of communicating is to identify the kind of behavior that is sought and the kind of behavior that is discouraged, with clear indication of the consequences attached to each behavior: the carrot and the stick, each adequately publicized. When R is the audience, A needs to communicate information relating to the structure of rewards for defection, the speed and reliability with which such rewards will be paid, and the protection that will accompany payment.

Once having communicated to the population, A must be in a position to observe their behavior, distinguish compliant from noncompliant behavior, and control resources for applying rewards or punishments, accordingly. The demands thereby placed on the intelligence system require that it be closely linked to the command and control of A's entire operations. For this reason, as well as others, A's intelligence operations must be strong and unified. The role of the Special Branch in the British command structure in Malaya is a model: standing astride all intelligence and counterintelligence activities (both police and military), and with its direction tightly linked with the top-command structure under Sir Gerald Templar.[15] This central and crucial role contrasts rather strikingly with the overlapping, muzzy organizational separation of intelligence and command functions in operations against the Viet Cong in Vietnam.[16]

In conducting intelligence operations, A must be able to acquire information *about* R, as well as cause misinformation *within* R. A's ability to increase its formation about R depends fundamentally on being able to provide security and protection to the population, or at least to selected components of the population, in combination with rewards and penalties. What is not usually recognized, however, is that the provision of protection and security is not an all-or-nothing affair, that it can be done in various ways, and that the various ways depend as much (or more) on dexterity and ingenuity as on force.

One means of providing protection is by preserving anonymity. An example is the familiar device of the "little booth" into which everybody in a village is compelled to pass. The point is to coerce everyone into the role of *possible* informer; the informer is rendered untargetable because he is anonymously immersed in a sea of non-informers. Universality confers anonymity, and anonymity confers security. Thus in Malaya

> . . . the police would surround a village during curfew and leave a piece of blank paper at every house; in the morning they would let [require?] each villager [to] drop his paper [unmarked except for the information itself] into a . . . box, which was later opened at police headquarters, with the anonymity of the informants thus . . . protected.[17]

In another variant, A arrests a large number of people, among whom the informer (already known to A) finds himself, and then releases them all together.

Informers may be protected by rendering them unidentifiable to the adversary in other ways. Thus in Kenya

> . . . [through] the use of hooded men. These were captured Mau-Mau willing to . . . identify their informer associates . . . A dozen or more of them were . . . seated in a line of canvas booths and suspects were slowly led past them. If a hooded man recognized a suspect as a member of Mau-Mau, he merely held up his hand and when the escorting officer walked across to him he gave him details in a whisper. . . . Men frequently broke out in a sweat or trembled uncontrollably as they faced the line of informers . . . many of them broke down.[18]

An alternative means for providing protection is simply to render an informer inaccessible to R by evacuating the informer and his family to a geographically remote area, or to a fortified settlement.[19]

Either side obviously can benefit from causing misinformation to circulate within the opponent's organization — for example, by arousing false suspicions about the reliability of its members. Valeriano recounts how the location of a Huk unit in the Philippines was sometimes accompanied by a simple ruse: an L-5 plane would fly over the unit, and, though under fire, the pilot, using an electric megaphone, would say (to the supposed informer) as a parting sally:

> Thank you very much, friend down below. By your information we have been able to contact your friends. Be very careful, I hope you have not exposed yourself unnecessarily![20]

Edward Lansdale has observed that this tactic

> . . . frequently caused many casualties to the enemy as a fire fight. As the enemy withdrew, he would hold kangaroo courts.[21]

Compromising members of R by acknowledging (falsely) their help can also be used to reach R's civil infrastructure. Valeriano, for example, recounts how he was able to dislodge a village mayor whom he knew to be a Huk sympathizer, but who had political influence in Manila which made his removal difficult. After an accidental and successful encounter outside the village, come of the Huk dead were brought into the village:

> When a large crowd had assembled and the mayor was about to inspect the bodies, Colonel Valeriano stepped up and loudly thanked him 'for the information that led to the killing of these two men.' . . . the mayor fled to Manila the next day[22]

Another technique for causing misinformation within the opponent's organization is, of course, the use of infiltrators whose task may be eased by causing false confidence within the other side which enables its guard to be penetrated. Where R's communications are primitive, as is usually the case, any operation that results in scattering the guerrillas affords A an increased opportunity for infiltrating them. Their lack of good local communication systems puts them:

> . . . at a loss to tell the difference between an unknown guerrilla unit that is genuine and one that is a plant.[23]

Infiltration can be facilitated by fabricating a highly plausible record for the penetrators. One means of doing so is by according them the same severs treatment that the opponent's genuine members receive. For example, in the Philippines

> Colonel Valeriano . . . staged sham battles in front of local villages between uniformed forces and some of his men dressed in Huk clothes. After tying them up and manhandling them a little, the soldiers would turn the pseudo-Huks over to the police for safekeeping . . . when they finally came out of prison, the men had a great deal of information. . . .[24]

Once a side becomes aware that infiltration has occurred, the false suspicion and unjust punishments that may be provoked may have a more deleterious effect than the infiltration itself: that is, the second-order impact of the infiltrators may be greater than the first-order impact.[25]

In collecting accurate information, as distinct from causing the circulation of misinformation, what we have discussed earlier is in the realm of "micro" tactics and operations: mainly those concerned with specific tricks, devices, stratagems. At the broader, "macro" level, probably the main requisite is to set up a structured and protected *market* for the kind of information that A wants. While sources of information need tight protection — through anonymity, as well as direct protection, as described earlier — the structure of the market itself (that is, the prices to be paid for different types of information, a system for quickly cross-checking new information against previously available data, quick and reliable payments, and the like) needs to be highly publicized and reliably implemented. The returns from this form of endeavor can be extremely high to A. From some empirical work on Malaya, it appears that the returns (in terms of communist guerrillas "acquired" by capture, surrender, or elimination) per dollar expended on information exceeded by more than tenfold the returns per dollar expended on firepower in the Malayan emergency.[26]

The more one shifts emphasis from the demand side of R to its supply, to the factors influencing the ease or difficulty of R's start and growth, the more important does intelligence become. In the conduct of an effective counterrebellion, intelligence operations demand the highest priority in resources, people, and ingenuity. Indeed, for counterrebellion to be waged at budget levels that make the prospects look more encouraging to A (including its external sources of support) than to potential Rs (including their external sources of support), the relative allocation of scarce resources to intelligence is likely to be high.

It should be evident that the problem of intelligence and information in the "third world" — the LDCs— is exceedingly complex, and deeply imbedded in the characteristics of these societies. The difficulty (or, put another way, the high cost) of obtaining reliable information is highly correlated with many other structural characteristics of these societies. But the fact that cost of information is correlated (negatively) with per capita income, urbanization, longevity, literacy, industrialization, political participation, and the like does not necessarily mean that improving information flows must be merged with these other major problems. To some extent, the information and intelligence problem can be approached, and solutions found, *separately* from many of the other problems of modernization in the third world. Improved intelligence, like improved counterinsurgency more generally, is related to but by no means identical with the solution of the basic structural problems of development. To say that the latter must be solved before the former is to establish goals that are unreasonably and unrealistically ambitious.

It may be worthwhile to conclude with some cautionary observations about the impact of programs directed specifically toward improving information acquisition and dissemination in the third world. Improved informational capabilities are likely to be crucial, if vulnerability to and incidence of insurgency are to be reduced. At the same time, improvements in these capabilities provide instruments with which more efficiently repressive dictatorships can be developed. This is another example of the general propositions that programs and techniques that may be supported in the underdeveloped countries with *one* set of intended objectives (for example, deterring or meeting communist insurgencies), may turn out to be used for quite *different* purposes in practice. Precautions can and should be taken, and some degree of control and leverage can be maintained to reduce the risk of misuse, particularly where U.S. support is involved. But a fundamental dilemma remains: reducing the risk of effective insurgency may — under certain circumstances — increase the risk of oppressive abuse of the capabilities created with this aim in mind. Efforts to solve one problem may lead to other, perhaps worse problems — a danger to be kept well in mind. Forewarning is, to some extent, forearming — but *only* to some extent.

ENDNOTES

1. See Chapter 4, pp. 63-68.
2. See Chapters 2 and 3.
3. Mao, **Basic Tactics**, p. 69.
4. See Chapter 3, pp. 30-32.

5. The following incident provides a suggestive example of how the private sector participates actively in linking information collection and dissemination with law enforcement by public authorities. When one of the authors made a purchase at a local store, he observed that the charging of the purchase to his account was accompanied by a call from the salesman to the store's credit bureau. In response to his question as to what the call was intended to accomplish, the salesman said it provided an opportunity to check whether the credit card had been stolen. The salesman related an incident that had occurred a few weeks before when a man came in and made a credit purchase. The salesman called the credit bureau, which advised him that the credit card had been stolen during a burglary several weeks earlier. He delayed the customer a few minutes; the store detective appeared and arrested him.

In this case, a private for-profit corporation finds it to its own advantage to maintain a service which collates information from various sources, including the police, and operates as a complement to established law-enforcement agencies. This kind of function and service is nonexistent in most LDCs. The usual measures of the cost of information (in terms of message units, or telephone or teletype service) within the LDCs drastically underestimate the extent to which the real costs of obtaining, storing, and using information exceed those prevailing in the MDCs. This is because a considerable part of the **social** costs of obtaining information in the MDCs is diffused throughout the society, and is borne by **private** institutions, as in the incident just described, as well as by public agencies. As a result, the costs of obtaining information in particular cases and for particular purposes are substantially reduced.

In considering information and intelligence in the LDCs, local law-enforcement agencies can perhaps make better use than they normally do of the services of private economic organizations—whose main aim is **not** law enforcement—to improve the collection and utilization of information that would assist in strengthening law and order.

6. This is not to say that "cool" violence cannot occur (it does), only that it is less likely; nor that A, in MDCs, cannot be disrupted by hot violence. It can be. However, the quantity of violence that is needed is probably greater where the violence is hot than where it is cool, and cer-

tainly is greater in the MDCs where the authority structure is firmer.

7. See Chapter 6, pp. 115-117.
8. See Chapter 5.
9. See this chapter, pp. 142-144.
10. See the extensive discussion of coercion and countercoercion, and the role of discrimination in such efforts, Chapter 6.
11. Given certain assumptions about the costs of obtaining such improvements in intelligence compared with the costs of incremental firepower and mobility, it follows that incremental resources devoted to improvement in intelligence would be more efficiently used than elsewhere.
12. Desmond Palmer. **The Counterintelligence Organization in an Insurgency,** unpublished paper, July, 1966, p. 26.
13. Thompson, op.cit., p. 89.
14. Thompson op. cit., p. 84.
15. See Thompson, **op. cit.,** pp. 81-83, 85; and Clutterbuck, **op. cit.,** pp. 56-59, 100. The Head of Special Branch was the No. 3 man in the entire command structure in the Malayan counterinsurgency operation.
16. Desmond Palmer also stresses the importance of centralized intelligence operations in counterinsurgency. For example, "To be able to act with the speed required means that all collateral intelligence must be available in one place and ready for quick use." Palmer, **op. cit.,** p. 29.
17. Statement by Captain Anthony S. Jeapes, R-412-ARPA, p. 108.
18. Majdalany, **op. cit.,** p. 208.
19. The French made use of this technique in Algeria, combined with heavy emphasis on punishment for noninformers. It is hard to see how the French practice of evacuating informers from their native villages to the city of Algiers could have elicited confidence on the part of a would-be informer that he would be inaccessible to the Liberation Front! Patrick Kessel and Giovanni Pirelli, **Le Peuple Algerien et La Guerre** (Paris: Francois Maspers, 1962), p. 386. Our translation.
20. Valeriano, RM-3652-PR, pp. 49-50. The ruse was accompanied by calling out the names of the Huk leaders in the unit that had been located, using individual names drawn from the government's own intelligence files, though imputed to the "friend down below."
21. **Ibid.,** p.50.
22. R-412-ARPA, p. 76.
23. Galula, R-412-ARPA, p. 47.
24. R-412-ARPA, p. 48.
25. For an illustration of this pattern, see the American reaction to the infiltration of Otto Skorzeny's Special Troops among separated American units in the Ardennes in 1944: **Reading in Guerrilla Warfare,** U.S. Army Special Warfare School, Fort Bragg, N.C., December, 1960, pp. 29-30.
26. Cf. RM-3651-PR; G. J. Pauker, **Notes on Nonmilitary Measures in Control of Insurgency,** The RAND Corporation, P-2642, October, 1962, Santa Monica, California; H. Speier, **Revolutionary War,** P-3445, September, 1966. Other work on the Philippines, although based on even less complete data, suggests similar results.

Counterinsurgency in the Cold Revolutionary War

David Galula

From the counterinsurgent's point of view, a revolutionary war can be divided into two periods:

1. The "cold revolutionary war," when the insurgent's activity remains on the whole legal and nonviolent (as in Steps 1 and 2 in the orthodox pattern).
2. The "hot revolutionary war," when the insurgent's activity becomes openly illegal and violent (as in the other steps in the orthodox pattern and in the entire process of the shortcut pattern).

The transitions from "peace" to "war," as we have seen, can be very gradual and confusing. Even when the insurgent follows the shortcut pattern, violence is always preceded by a short period of stirrings. In Algeria, for instance, the police, the administration, and the government suspected that something was brewing during the summer of 1954. For analytical purposes, we shall choose as a dividing line between the two periods the moment when the counterinsurgent armed forces are ordered to step in, and we shall approach the study of counterinsurgency warfare in chronological order, starting with the "cold revolutionary war."

The situation at this stage is characterized by the fact that the insurgent operates largely on the legal side, and only partly on the fringe of legality, through his subversion tactics. He may or may not have been recognized as an insurgent; if he has been identified as such, only the police and a few people in the government generally realize what is looming.

The essential problem for the counterinsurgent stems from the fact that the actual danger will always appear to the nation as out of proportion to the demands made by an adequate response. The potential danger is enormous, but how to prove it on the basis of available, objective facts? How to justify the efforts and sacrifices needed to smother the incipient insurgency? The insurgent, if he knows how to conduct his war, is banking on precisely this situation, and will see to it that the transition from peace to war is very gradual indeed. The case of Algeria gives an excellent illustration of the counterinsurgent's dilemma because the insurgent made an effort to start with a big "bang," and yet the dilemma persisted. The Algerian rebels, with publicity foremost in their minds, set November 1, 1954, as their D day. Seventy separate actions took place, scattered all over the territory—bomb throwings, assassinations, sabotage, minor harassments of isolated military posts—all largely ineffectual. And then nothing.

Galula, David. (1966). "Counterinsurgency in the Cold Revolutionary War," *Counterinsurgency Warfare: Theory and Practice*. New York: Praeger.

According to Mohamed Boudiaf, one of the chief planners of the insurgency, the results were "disastrous in a large part of Algeria. In the Oran region, notably, the repression was extremely brutal and efficient. . . . It was impossible for me during the first two months even to establish a liaison between the Rif [in Spanish Morocco] and the Oran region."* Was it enough to warrant a mobilization of French resources and energy, a disruption of the economy, the imposition of a war status on the country?

Four general courses of action are open to the counterinsurgent under these circumstances, and they are not mutually exclusive:

1. He may act directly on the insurgent leaders.
2. He may act indirectly on the conditions that are propitious to an insurgency.
3. He may infiltrate the insurgent movement and try to make it ineffective.
4. He may build up or reinforce his political machine.

DIRECT ACTION AGAINST THE INSURGENT

The direct approach consists of depriving the insurgent of any physical possibility of building up his movement. At this stage, the insurgent's movement generally has no life of its own; everything depends on its leaders, who are, consequently, the key elements. By arresting them or by restricting their ability to contact people, by impeaching them in the courts, by banning their organizations and publications if necessary, the counterinsurgent may nip the insurgency in the bud.

Such a method is easy, of course, in totalitarian countries, but it is hardly feasible in democracies. One of two situations may arise: Either the counterinsurgent government may already have equipped itself as a precautionary measure (even in the absence of pressure) with special powers and laws designed to cope with insurgencies. In this case, the main problem is to act without giving undue publicity to the insurgent,

an important matter particularly if the insurgent's cause has a wide popular appeal.

The other possibility is that the counterinsurgent may not have provided himself in advance with the necessary powers. Thus when he attempts to act directly against the insurgent, he opens a Pandora's box. Arrests have to be justified. On what basis? Where is the limit to be drawn between normal political opposition, on the one hand, and subversion, which is difficult to define under the best circumstances? The arrested insurgent can count almost automatically on some support from the legitimate opposition parties and groups. Referred to the courts, he will take refuge in chicanery, exploit to the utmost every advantage provided by the existing laws. Worse yet, the trial itself will serve as a sounding board for his cause. The banned organizations will spring up again under other labels, and the counterinsurgent will bear the onus of proving their ties to the old ones.

The counterinsurgent will inevitably be impelled to amend normal procedures, but this time under pressure. The difficulty can be assessed easily when one recalls that it took some ten years in the United States to ban the Communist Party, which did not even have any significant appeal to the population. (Some contend, and they have a point, that it would have taken less time had the Party actually appeared dangerous.)

Since legal changes are slow, the counterinsurgent may be tempted to go a step further and to act beyond the borders of legality. A succession of arbitrary restrictive measures will be started, the nation will soon find itself under constraint, opposition will increase, and the insurgent will thank his opponent for having played into his hands.

It can be therefore concluded with relative safety that the direct approach works well if:

1. The insurgent's cause has little appeal (but we have assumed that no wise insurgent would launch an insurgency unless the prerequisite of a good cause had been fulfilled).
2. The counterinsurgent has the legal power to act.
3. The counterinsurgent can prevent the insurgent from gaining publicity.

---

* *Le Monde* (Paris), November 2, 1962.

INDIRECT ACTION AGAINST THE INSURGENT

We have seen in Chapter 2 that insurgency cannot normally develop unless two essential prerequisites are met: the insurgent's having a cause, and his being helped initially by the weakness of his opponent. Two other conditions, although not absolutely necessary, are also helpful to the insurgent: geographic factors, and outside support. By acting on these conditions, a counterinsurgent could hope to frustrate the growth of an insurgent movement.

Geographic factors are what they are and cannot be significantly changed or influenced except by displacing the population—an absurdity in peacetime—or by building artificial fences, which is also too costly in peacetime. The question of outside support offers more leeway but rests largely outside the counterinsurgent's reach.

To deprive the insurgent of a good cause amounts to solving the country's basic problems. If this is possible, well and good, but we know now that a good cause for the insurgent is one that his opponent cannot adopt without losing his power in the process. And there are problems that, although providing a good cause to an insurgent, are not susceptible of solution. Is there an intelligent solution to the racial problem in South Africa? It will continue to exist as long as two different races continue to live in the same territory.

Alleviating the weaknesses in the counterinsurgent's rule seems more promising. Adapting the judicial system to the threat, strengthening the bureaucracy, reinforcing the police and the armed forces may discourage insurgency attempts, if the counterinsurgent leadership is resolute and vigilant.

INFILTRATION OF THE INSURGENT MOVEMENT

An insurgent movement in its infancy is necessarily small; hence, the views and attitudes of its members have a greater importance at the early period than at any other time. They are all, so to speak, generals with no privates to command. History is full of cases of obscure political movements that floundered and vanished soon after they were created because the founders did not agree and split the movement.

A young insurgent movement is necessarily inexperienced and should be relatively easy to infiltrate with agents who will help to disintegrate it from within and to derail it. If they do not succeed in this, they can at least report its activity.

Two famous cases of infiltration may be mentioned. In Czarist Russia, the Okhrana had succeeded in infiltrating the Bolshevik Party to such an extent and with such zeal that it was sometimes difficult to tell whether the agents were acting as Bolsheviks or as agents. A Grand Duke was assassinated in a provocation engineered by the Okhrana. When the triumphant Bolsheviks seized the Okhrana records, Lenin discovered that some of his most trusted companions had been in the pay of the Czar's police.

This attempt was ultimately unsuccessful, but another case has shown better results so far. It is well known that the American Communist Party has been so infiltrated by the FBI as to have become innocuous.

There is much merit in this idea, but it should be remembered that the longer the insurgent movement lasts, the better will be its chances to survive its infantile diseases and to take root. It may of course dwindle by itself, without outside intervention. Relying on luck, however, does not constitute a policy.

Strengthening the Political Machine

Most of the counterinsurgent's efforts in the "hot" revolutionary war, as we shall show, tend to build a political machine at the grass roots in order to isolate the insurgent from the population forever.

This strategy, on which we shall not elaborate now, is just as valid in the cold revolutionary war, and it should be easier to implement preventively than when the insurgent has already seized control of the population. Such a strategy, to us, represents the principal course of action for the counterinsurgent because it leaves the least to chance and makes full use of the counterinsurgent's possibilities.

It may be useful to remember that a peacetime political machine is built essentially on patronage.

Counterinsurgency in the Hot Revolutionary War

David Galula

Force, when it comes into play in a revolutionary war, has the singular virtue of clearing away many difficulties for the counterinsurgent, notably the matter of the issue. The moral fog dissipates sooner or later, the enemy stands out more conspicuously, repressive measures are easier to justify. But force adds, of course, its own difficulties.

At our point of departure in the study of the hot revolutionary war—that is, the moment when the armed forces have been ordered to step in—the situation usually conforms to the following pattern:

The insurgent has succeeded in building his political organization. He directs either an elite party leading a united front, or a large revolutionary movement bound to the cause. Although his actions other than subversion are overt, he operates clandestinely.

The country's map reveals three sorts of areas:

The "red" areas, where the insurgent effectively controls the population and carries out guerrilla warfare.

The "pink" areas, in which he attempts to expand; there are some efforts at organizing the population and some guerrilla activity.

The "white" areas, not yet affected but nevertheless threatened; they are subjected to the insurgent's subversion but all seems quiet.

Confusion is prevalent in the counterinsurgent's camp. There is a realization that an emergency exists, but the feeling of crisis is more widely spread in government circles than among the population of the white and even the pink areas. The true allegiance of every citizen is open to doubt. The leadership and its policy are questioned. The political, the judicial, the military structures geared for ordinary days have not yet been adapted to the requirements of the situation. The economy is rapidly deteriorating; the government's expenses are rising while its income is declining. In the psychological field, the insurgent has the edge since he exploits a cause without which he would not have been able to develop so far as to engage in guerrilla warfare or terrorism. The counterinsurgent forces are torn between the necessity of guarding key areas and fixed installations, of protecting lives and property, and the urge to track the insurgent forces.

With this general picture in mind, we shall now discuss the various avenues open to the counterinsurgent.

Galula, David. (1966). "Counterinsurgency in the Hot Revolutionary War," *Counterinsurgency Warfare: Theory and Practice*. New York: Praeger.

LAWS AND PRINCIPLES OF COUNTERINSURGENCY WARFARE

Limits of Conventional Warfare

Let us assume that the political and economic difficulties have been magically solved or have proved manageable,* and that only one problem remains, the military one—how to suppress the insurgent forces. It is not a problem of means since the counterinsurgent forces are still largely superior to the insurgent's, even though they may be dispersed. It is primarily a problem of strategy and tactics, of methods and organization.

The strategy of conventional warfare prescribes the conquest of the enemy's territory, the destruction of his forces. The trouble here is that the enemy holds no territory and refuses to fight for it. He is everywhere and nowhere. By concentrating sufficient forces, the counterinsurgent can at any time penetrate and garrison a red area. Such an operation, if well sustained, may reduce guerrilla activity, but if the situation becomes untenable for the guerrillas, they will transfer their activity to another area and the problem remains unsolved. It may even be aggravated if the counterinsurgent's concentration was made at too great risk for the other areas.

The destruction of the insurgent forces requires that they be localized and immediately encircled. But they are too small to be spotted easily by the counterinsurgent's direct means of observation. Intelligence is the principal source of information on guerrillas, and intelligence has to come from the population, but the population will not talk unless it feels safe, and it does not feel safe until the insurgent's power has been broken.

The insurgent forces are also too mobile to be encircled and annihilated easily. If the counterinsurgent, on receiving news that guerrillas have been spotted, uses his ready forces immediately, chances are they will be too small for the task. If he gathers larger forces, he will have lost time and probably the benefit of surprise.

True, modern means of transportation—particularly helicopters, when available—allow the counterinsurgent to combine strength with swiftness. True, systematic large-scale operations, because of their very size, alleviate somewhat the intelligence and mobility deficiency of the counterinsurgent. Nevertheless, conventional operations by themselves have at best no more effect than a fly swatter. Some guerrillas are bound to be caught, but new recruits will replace them as fast as they are lost. If the counterinsurgent operations are sustained over a period of months, the guerrilla losses may not be so easily replaced. The question is, can the counterinsurgent operations be so sustained?

If the counterinsurgent is so strong as to be able to saturate the entire country with garrisons, military operations along conventional lines will, of course, work. The insurgent, unable to grow beyond a certain level, will slowly wither away. But saturation can seldom be afforded.

Why Insurgency Warfare Does Not Work for the Counterinsurgent

Insurgency warfare is specifically designed to allow the camp afflicted with congenital weakness to acquire strength progressively while fighting. The counterinsurgent is endowed with congenital strength; for him to adopt the insurgent's warfare would be the same as for a giant to try to fit into a dwarf's clothing. How, against whom, for instance, could he use his enemy's tactics? He alone offers targets for guerrilla operations. Were he to operate as a guerrilla, he would have to have the effective support of the population guaranteed by his own political organization among the masses; if so, then the insurgent would not have it and consequently could not exist; there would be no need for the counterinsurgent's guerrilla operations. This is not to say that there is no place in counterinsurgency warfare for small commando-type operations. They cannot, however, represent the main form of the counterinsurgent's warfare.

Is it possible for the counterinsurgent to organize a clandestine force able to defeat the insurgent on his own terms? Clandestinity seems to be another of those obligations-turned-into-

---

* Except, of course, the psychological handicap, which can be alleviated only by the protraction of the war. To solve it would require that the counterinsurgent espouse the insurgent's cause without losing his power at the same time. If it were possible to do so, then the insurgent's cause was a bad one to start with, tactically speaking.

assets of the insurgent. How could the counterinsurgent, whose strength derives precisely from his open physical assets, build up a clandestine force except as a minor and secondary adjunct? Furthermore, room for clandestine organizations is very limited in revolutionary war. Experience shows that no rival—not to speak of hostile—clandestine movements can coexist for long; one is always absorbed by the other. The Chinese Communist maquis succeeded in suppressing almost entirely their Nationalist counterparts in the Japanese-occupied areas of north and central China. Later on, during the final round of the revolutionary war in China, ordinary bandits (almost a regular and codified profession in some parts of China) disappeared as soon as Communist guerrillas came. Tito eliminated Mikhailovitch. If the Greek Communist ELAS did not eliminate the Nationalist resistance groups, it was due to the restraint they had to show since they were entirely dependent on the Western Allies' support. More recently, the FLN in Algeria eliminated, for all practical purposes, the rival and older MNA group. Because the insurgent has first occupied the available room, attempts to introduce another clandestine movement have little chance to succeed.

Can the counterinsurgent use terrorism too? It would be self-defeating since terrorism is a source of disorder, which is precisely what the counterinsurgent aims to stop.

If conventional warfare does not work, if insurgency war-fare cannot work, the inescapable conclusion is that the counterinsurgent must apply a warfare of his own that takes into account not only the nature and characteristics of the revolutionary war, but also the laws that are peculiar to counterinsurgency and the principles deriving from them.

The First Law: The Support of the Population Is as Necessary for the Counterinsurgent as for the Insurgent

What is the crux of the problem for the counterinsurgent? It is not how to clean an area. We have seen that he can always concentrate enough forces to do it, even if he has to take some risk in order to achieve the necessary concentration. The problem is, how to keep an area clean so that the counterinsurgent forces will be free to operate elsewhere.

This can be achieved only with the support of the population. If it is relatively easy to disperse and to expel the insurgent forces from a given area by purely military action, if it is possible to destroy the insurgent political organizations by intensive police action, it is impossible to prevent the return of the guerrilla units and the rebuilding of the political cells unless the population cooperates.

The population, therefore, becomes the objective for the counterinsurgent as it was for his enemy. Its tacit support, its submission to law and order, its consensus—taken for granted in normal times—have been undermined by the insurgent's activity. And the truth is that the insurgent, with his organization at the grass roots, is tactically the strongest of opponents where it counts, at the population level.

This is where the fight has to be conducted, in spite of the counterinsurgent's ideological handicap and in spite of the head start gained by the insurgent in organizing the population.

The Second Law: Support Is Gained Through an Active Minority

The original problem becomes now: how to obtain the support of the population—support not only in the form of sympathy and approval but also in active participation in the fight against the insurgent.

The answer lies in the following proposition, which simply expresses the basic tenet of the exercise of political power:

In any situation, whatever the cause, there will be an active minority for the cause, a neutral majority, and an active minority against the cause.

The technique of power consists in relying on the favorable minority in order to rally the neutral majority and to neutralize or eliminate the hostile minority.

In extreme cases, when the cause and the circumstances are extraordinarily good or bad, one of the minorities disappears or becomes negligible, and there may even be a solid unanimity for or against among the population. But such cases are obviously rare.

This holds true for every political regime, from the harshest dictatorship to the mildest democracy. What varies is the degree and the purpose to which it is applied. Mores and the constitution may impose limitations, the purpose may be good or bad, but the law remains essentially valid whatever the variations, and they can indeed be great, for the law is applied unconsciously in most countries.

It can no longer be ignored or applied unconsciously in a country beset by a revolutionary war, when what is at stake is precisely the counterinsurgent's power directly challenged by an active minority through the use of subversion and force. The counterinsurgent who refuses to use this law for his own purposes, who is bound by its peacetime limitations, tends to drag the war out without getting closer to victory.

How far to extend the limitations is a matter of ethics, and a very serious one, but no more so than bombing the civilian population in a conventional war. All wars are cruel, the revolutionary war perhaps most of all because every citizen, whatever his wish, is or will be directly and actively involved in it by the insurgent who needs him and cannot afford to let him remain neutral. The cruelty of the revolutionary war is not a mass, anonymous cruelty but a highly personalized, individual one. No greater crime can be committed by the counterinsurgent than accepting, or resigning himself to, the protraction of the war. He would do as well to give up early.

The strategic problem of the counterinsurgent may be defined now as follows: "To find the favorable minority, to organize it in order to mobilize the population against the insurgent minority." Every operation, whether in the military field or in the political, social, economic, and psychological fields, must be geared to that end.

To be sure, the better the cause and the situation, the larger will be the active minority favorable to the counterinsurgent and the easier its task. This truism dictates the main goal of the propaganda—to show that the cause and the situation of the counterinsurgent are better than the insurgent's. More important, it underlines the necessity for the counterinsurgent to come out with an acceptable countercause.

Victory in Counterinsurgency Warfare

We can now define negatively and positively what is a victory for the counterinsurgent.

A victory is not the destruction in a given area of the insurgent's forces and his political organization. If one is destroyed, it will be locally re-created by the other; if both are destroyed, they will both be re-created by a new fusion of insurgents from the outside. A negative example: the numerous mopping-up operations by the French in the Plain of Reeds in Cochinchina all through the Indochina War.

A victory is that plus the permanent isolation of the insurgent from the population, isolation not enforced upon the population but maintained by and with the population. A positive example: the defeat of the FLN in the Oran region in Algeria in 1959-60. In this region, which covers at least a third of the Algerian territory, FLN actions—counting everything from a grenade thrown in a café to cutting a telephone pole—had dwindled to an average of two a day.

Such a victory may be indirect; it is nonetheless decisive (unless of course, as in Algeria, the political goal of the counterinsurgent government changes).

The Third Law: Support from the Population Is Conditional

Once the insurgent has established his hold over the population, the minority that was hostile to him becomes invisible. Some of its members have been eliminated physically, thereby providing an example to the others; others have escaped abroad; most have been cowed into hiding their true feelings and have thus melted within the majority of the population; a few are even making a show of their support for the insurgency. The population, watched by the active supporters of the insurgency, lives under the threat of denunciation to the political cells and prompt punishment by the guerrilla units.

The minority hostile to the insurgent will not and cannot emerge as long as the threat has not been lifted to a reasonable extent. Furthermore, even after the threat has been lifted, the emerging counterinsurgent supporters will not be able to rally the bulk of the population so long as the population is not convinced that the counterinsurgent has the will, the means, and the ability to win. When a man's life is at stake, it takes more than propaganda to budge him.

Four deductions can be made from this law. Effective political action on the population must be preceded by military and police operations against the guerrilla units and the insurgent political organizations.

Political, social, economic, and other reforms, however much they ought to be wanted and popular, are inoperative when offered while the insurgent still controls the population. An attempt at land reform in Algeria in 1957 fell flat when the FLN assassinated some Moslem peasants who had received land.

The counterinsurgent needs a convincing success as early as possible in order to demonstrate that he has the will, the means, and the ability to win.

The counterinsurgent cannot safely enter into negotiations except from a position of strength, or his potential supporters will flock to the insurgent side.

In conventional warfare, strength is assessed according to military or other tangible criteria, such as the number of divisions, the positions they hold, the industrial resources, etc. In revolutionary warfare, strength must be assessed by the extent of support from the population as measured in terms of political organization at the grass roots. The counterinsurgent reaches a position of strength when his power is embodied in a political organization issuing from, and firmly supported by, the population.

The Fourth Law: Intensity of Efforts and Vastness of Means Are Essential

The operations needed to relieve the population from the insurgent's threat and to convince it that the counterinsurgent will ultimately win are necessarily of an intensive nature and of long duration. They require a large concentration of efforts, resources, and personnel.

This means that the efforts cannot be diluted all over the country but must be applied successively area by area.

STRATEGY OF THE COUNTERINSURGENCY

Translated into a general strategy, the principles derived from these few laws suggest the following step-by-step procedure:

In a Selected Area

1. Concentrate enough armed forces to destroy or to expel the main body of armed insurgents.

2. Detach for the area sufficient troops to oppose an insurgent's comeback in strength, install these troops in the hamlets, villages, and towns where the population lives.
3. Establish contact with the population, control its movements in order to cut off its links with the guerrillas.
4. Destroy the local insurgent political organizations.
5. Set up, by means of elections, new provisional local authorities.
6. Test these authorities by assigning them various concrete tasks. Replace the softs and the incompetents, give full support to the active leaders. Organize self-defense units.
7. Group and educate the leaders in a national political movement.
8. Win over or suppress the last insurgent remnants.

Order having been re-established in the area, the process may be repeated elsewhere. It is not necessary, for that matter, to wait until the last point has been completed.

The operations outlined above will be studied in more detail, but let us first discuss this strategy. Like every similar concept, this one may be sound in theory but dangerous when applied rigidly to a specific case. It is difficult, however, to deny its logic because the laws—or shall we say the facts—on which it is based can be easily recognized in everyday political life and in every recent revolutionary war.

This strategy is also designed to cope with the worst case that can confront a counterinsurgent, i.e., suppressing an insurgency in what we have called a "red" area, where the insurgent is already in full control of the population. Some of the operations suggested can obviously be skipped in the "pink" areas, most can be skipped in the "white" ones. However, the general order in which they must be conducted cannot be tampered with under normal conditions without violating the principles of counterinsurgency warfare and of plain common sense. For instance, small detachments of troops cannot be installed in villages so long as the insurgent is able to gather a superior force and to overpower a detachment in a surprise attack; Step 2 obviously has to come after Step 1. Nor can elections be staged when the insurgent cells still exist, for the elections would most likely bring forth the insurgent's stooges.

Economy of Forces

Because these operations are spread in time, they can be spread in space. This strategy thus conforms to the principle of economy of forces, a vital one in a war where the insurgent needs so little to achieve so much whereas the counterinsurgent needs so much to achieve so little.

While a main effort is made in the selected area, necessarily at some risk to the other areas, what results can the counterinsurgent legitimately expect from his operations in these other areas? To prevent the insurgent from developing into a higher form of warfare, that is to say, from organizing a regular army. This objective is fulfilled when the insurgent is denied safe bases, and it can be achieved by purely conventional raids that do not tie down large counterinsurgent forces.

Through this strategy, insurgency can be rolled back with increased strength and momentum, for as soon as an area has been made safe, important forces can be withdrawn and transferred to the neighboring areas, swollen with locally recruited loyal and tested personnel. The transfer of troops can begin as soon as the first step is concluded.

Irreversibility

The myth of Sisyphus is a recurrent nightmare for the counterinsurgent. By following the strategy just outlined, the counterinsurgent introduces some measure of irreversibility in his operations. When troops live among the population and give it protection until the population is able to protect itself with a minimum of outside support, the insurgent's power cannot easily be rebuilt, and this in itself is no mean achievement. But the turning point really comes when leaders have emerged from the population and have committed themselves on the side of the counterinsurgent. They can be counted upon because they have proved their loyalty in deeds and not in words, and because they have everything to lose from a return of the insurgents.

Initiative

This is an offensive strategy, and it inevitably aims at regaining the initiative from the insurgent. On the national scale, this is so because the counterinsurgent is free to select the area of main effort; as soon as he does it, he no longer submits himself to the insurgent's will. It is so equally on the local scale because he confronts the insurgent with a dilemma: accepting the challenge, and thus a defensive posture, or leaving the area and being powerless to oppose the counterinsurgent's action on the population.

In conventional warfare, when the Blues attack the Reds on Point A, the Reds can relieve the pressure by attacking the Blues on Point B and the Blues cannot escape the counterpressure. In revolutionary warfare, when the insurgent exerts pressure in Area A, the counterinsurgent cannot relieve the pressure by attacking the insurgent in Area B. The insurgent simply refuses to accept the fight, and he can refuse because of his fluidity. The Chinese Nationalists' offensive against Yenan in 1947 is an example; when the Vietminh started pressing against Dien Bien Phu in northeastern Indochina, the French command launched Operation Atlante against the Vietminh areas in Central Vietnam; Atlante had no effect on the other battle.

However, when the counterinsurgent applies pressure not on the insurgent directly but on the population, which is the insurgent's real source of strength, the insurgent cannot so freely refuse the fight because he courts defeat.

Full Utilization of the Counterinsurgent's Assets

If the insurgent is fluid, the population is not. By concentrating his efforts on the population, the counterinsurgent minimizes his rigidity and makes full use of his assets. His administrative capabilities, his economic resources, his information and propaganda media, his military superiority due to heavy weapons and large units, all of which are cumbersome and relatively useless against the elusive insurgent, recover their full value when applied to the task of obtaining the support of a static population. What does it matter if the counterinsurgent is unable on the whole to run as fast as the insurgent? What counts is the fact that the insurgent cannot dislodge a better-armed detachment of counterinsurgents from a village, or cannot harass it enough to make the counterinsurgent unable to devote most of his energy to the population.

Simplicity

Why is there so little intellectual confusion in conventional warfare while there has been so much in the past counterinsurgencies? Two explanations may be advanced: When a conventional war starts, the abrupt transition from peace to war and the very nature of the war clarify most of the problems for the contending sides, particularly for the defender. The issue, whatever it was, becomes now a matter of defeating the enemy. The objective, insofar as it is essentially military, is the destruction of his forces and the occupation of his territory; such an objective provides clear-cut criteria to assess gains, stagnation, or losses. The way to reach it is by military action supported by diplomacy and economic blockade. The national organization for war is simple: The government directs, the military executes, the nation provides the tools.

We have seen that this cannot be the case in counterinsurgency warfare. Transition from peace to war is very gradual, the issue is never clear, the objective is the population, military and political actions cannot be separated, and military action—essential though it is—cannot be the main form of action.

Conventional warfare has been thoroughly analyzed in the course of centuries—indeed for almost the entire extent of recorded history—and the process of battle has been sliced into distinct phases: march toward the enemy, contact with the enemy, test of the enemy's strength, attack, exploitation of success, eventual retreat, etc. The student learns in military schools what he has to do in each phase, according to the latest doctrine. Field games are staged to give him practical training in the maneuvers he may have to conduct. When he is in the field under actual war conditions, his intellectual problem amounts to determining which phase of the battle he finds himself in; then he applies to his particular situation the general rules governing the phase. His talent, his judgment come into play only here.

This has not yet been done for counterinsurgency warfare. Who indeed has heard of field games involving the task of winning the support of the population when such a task, which, in any event, requires months of continuous effort, has no clear built-in criteria to assess the results of the games? And who is going to play the part of the population?

Simplicity in concept and in execution is an important requirement for any counterinsurgency doctrine. The proposed strategy appears to meet this. For it is not enough to give a broad definition of the goal (to get the support of the population); it is just as necessary to show how to reach it (by finding and organizing the people who are actively in favor of the counterinsurgent), and in such a way as to allow a margin of initiative to the counterinsurgent personnel who implement the strategy—and they are a widely mixed group of politicians, civil servants, economists, social workers, soldiers—yet with enough precision to channel their efforts in a single direction. The division of the over-all action into successive steps following each other in logical order facilitates the tactical tasks of the agents; they know at each step what the intermediate objective is and what they have to do to reach it.

To Command Is to Control

With the step-by-step approach, the counterinsurgent provides himself with a way of assessing at any time the situation and the progress made. He can thus exert his control and conduct the war by switching means from an advanced area to a retarded one, by giving larger responsibilities to the subordinate leaders who have proved successful, and by removing those who have failed. In other words, he can command because he can verify.

What could happen in default of control? The general counterinsurgency effort would produce an *accidental* mosaic, a patchwork of pieces with one well pacified, next to it another one not so pacified or perhaps even under the effective insurgent's control: an ideal situation for the insurgent, who will be able to maneuver at will among the pieces, concentrating on some, temporarily vanishing from others. The *intentional* mosaic created by necessity when the counterinsurgent concentrates his efforts in a selected area is in itself a great enough source of difficulties without adding to it in the selected area.

From Strategy to Tactics

David Galula

COMMAND PROBLEMS

Single Direction

Destroying or expelling from an area the main body of the guerrilla forces, preventing their return, installing garrisons to protect the population, tracking the guerrilla remnants—these are predominantly military operations.

Identifying, arresting, interrogating the insurgent political agents, judging them, rehabilitating those who can be won over—these are police and judicial tasks.

Establishing contact with the population, imposing and enforcing control measures, organizing local elections, testing the new leaders, organizing them into a party, doing 'all the constructive work needed to win the whole-hearted support of the population—these are primarily political operations.

The expected result—final defeat of the insurgents—is not an addition but a multiplication of these various operations; they all are essential and if one is nil, the product will be zero. Clearly, more than any other kind of warfare, counterinsurgency must respect the principle of a single direction. A single boss must direct the operations from the beginning to the end.

The problem, unfortunately, is not simple. Tasks and responsibilities cannot be neatly divided between the civilian and the soldier, for their operations overlap each other too much. The soldier does not stay in his garrison with nothing to do, once the early large-scale operations have been concluded; he constantly patrols, ambushes, combs out; at some time in the process, he will have to organize, equip, train, and lead self-defense units. The policeman starts gathering intelligence right from the beginning; his role does not end when the political cells have been destroyed, because the insurgent will keep trying to build new ones. The civil servant does not wait to start his work until the army has cleared away the guerrillas.

Furthermore, no operation can be strictly military or political, if only because they each have psychological effects that alter the over-all situation for better or for worse. For instance, if the judge prematurely releases unrepentent insurgents, the effects will soon be felt by the policeman, the civil servant, and the soldier.

Another fact complicates the situation. However developed the civil administration may be in peacetime, it is never up to the personnel requirements of a counterinsurgency. When the broad objective of winning the support of the population is translated into concrete field tasks, each multiplied by the given number of villages, towns, and districts, the number of reliable personnel needed is staggering. Usually, only the armed forces can supply them promptly. As a

Galula, David. (1966). "From Strategy to Tactics," *Counterinsurgency Warfare: Theory and Practice*. New York: Praeger.

result, the counterinsurgent government is exposed to a dual temptation: to assign political, police, and other tasks to the armed forces; to let the military direct the entire process—if not in the whole country, at least in some areas.

The first one cannot be avoided. To confine soldiers to purely military functions while urgent and vital tasks have to be done, and nobody else is available to undertake them, would be senseless. The soldier must then be prepared to become a propagandist, a social worker, a civil engineer, a schoolteacher, a nurse, a boy scout. But only for as long as he cannot be replaced, for it is better to entrust civilian tasks to civilians. This, incidentally, is what the Chinese Communists have always tended to do. During the spring and summer of 1949, on the eve of their drive into south China, they recruited and trained in special schools more than 50,000 students whose mission was to follow the army and assist it by taking over "army servicing, publicity work, education and mobilization of the masses."* To imitate this example is not easy for the counterinsurgent. Where does one find such a large group of reliable civilians when the loyalty of almost everyone is open to question? But it will have to be done eventually. The second temptation—to let the military direct the entire process—on the other hand, is so dangerous that it must be resisted at all costs.

Primacy of the Political over the Military Power

That the political power is the undisputed boss is a matter of both principle and practicality. What is at stake is the country's political regime, and to defend it is a political affair. Even if this requires military action, the action is constantly directed toward a political goal. Essential though it is, the military action is secondary to the political one, its primary purpose being to afford the political power enough freedom to work safely with the population.

The armed forces are but one of the many instruments of the counterinsurgent, and what is

better than the political power to harness the nonmilitary instruments, to see that appropriations come at the right time to consolidate the military work, that political and social reforms follow through?

"A revolutionary war is 20 percent military action and 80 percent political" is a formula that reflects the truth. Giving the soldier authority over the civilian would thus contradict one of the major characteristics of this type of war. In practice, it would inevitably tend to reverse the relative importance of military versus political action and move the counterinsurgent's warfare closer to a conventional one. Were the armed forces the instrument of a party and their leaders high-ranking members of the party, controlled and assisted by political commissars having their own direct channel to the party's central direction, then giving complete authority to the military might work; however, this describes the general situation of the insurgent, not of his opponent.

It would also be self-defeating, for it would mean that the counterinsurgent government had acknowledged a signal defeat: Unable to cope with the insurgency through normal government structures, it would have abdicated in favor of the military who, at once, become the prime and easy target of the insurgent propaganda. It would be a miracle if, under these circumstances, the insurgent did not succeed in divorcing the soldier from the nation.

The inescapable conclusion is that the over-all responsibility should stay with the civilian power at every possible level. If there is a shortage of trusted officials, nothing prevents filling the gap with military personnel serving in a civilian capacity. If the worst comes to the worst, the fiction, at least, should be preserved.

Coordination of Efforts

The counterinsurgent leader, whom we now assume to be a civilian, has to take into account the problems of the various civilian and military components of his forces before reaching a decision, especially when their actions interrelate intricately and when their demands often conflict with each other. He also has to coordinate and to channel their efforts in a single direction. How can he do it? Among the theoretical solutions in terms of organization, two are obvious: (1) the

---

*General Chang Ting-chen, chief of the South China Service Corps, member of the Central Committee, as quoted in *The New York Times*, July 4, 1949.

committee, as in Malaya, for example, where control of an area at district level was invested in a committee under the chairmanship of the district officer, with the members drawn from the police, local civilians (European planters and representative Chinese and Malayans), and the soldiers; (2) or the integrated civilian-military staff, where the soldier is directly subordinated to the local civil authority (the author knows of no example of this setup, but the opposite case—with the civil authority directly subordinated to the local military one—is easy to find, as in the Philippines, where army officers took the place of a nonexistent civil administration, or in Algeria, where all powers were invested in the military for a brief period in 1958-59).

Each formula has its merits and its defects. A committee* is flexible, affords more freedom to its members, and can be kept small, but it is slow. An integrated staff allows a more direct line of command and is speedier, but it is more rigid and prone to bureaucratism. There seems to be room for both in counterinsurgency warfare. The committee is better for the higher echelons concerned with long- and medium-range affairs, the integrated staff for the lower echelons, where speed is essential. For counterinsurgency, at the bottom levels, is a very small-scale war, with small-scale and fugitive opportunities that must be seized upon instantly.

At the higher echelons, where the committee system prevails and where the civilian and military components retain their separate structures, they should each be organized in such a way as to promote their cooperation still more. In conventional warfare, the staff of a large military unit is composed roughly of two main branches—"intelligence/operations" and "logistics." In counterinsurgency warfare, there is a desperate need for a third branch—the "political" one—which would have the same weight as the others. The officer in charge of it would follow the developments in all matters pertaining to political and civic action, advise his chief, make

his voice heard when operations are in the planning stage and not have to wait until they are too advanced to be altered. Similarly, the civilian staff, which in conventional warfare usually has little to do with military affairs, should have its military branch, with a corresponding role toward the civilian chief. With these two organic branches working closely together, the danger of divergent efforts by the civilian and the military might be reduced.

Whatever system is chosen, however, the best organization is only as good as its members. Even with the best conceivable organization, personality conflicts are more than likely to be the order of the day. Although the wrong member can sometimes be fired and replaced, this will not solve the problem for all committees or integrated staff.

The question, then, is how to make these mixed organizations work at their maximum effectiveness in a counterinsurgency, regardless of the personality factors. Assuming that each of these organizations works more or less with its own over-all personality, how is the disjointed, mosaic effect of their operations to be avoided? If the individual members of the organizations were of the same mind, if every organization worked according to a standard pattern, the problem would be solved. Is this not precisely what a coherent, well-understood, and accepted doctrine would tend to achieve? More than anything else, a doctrine appears to be the practical answer to the problem of how to channel efforts in a single direction.

Primacy of the Territorial Command

The counterinsurgent's armed forces have to fulfill two different missions: to break the military power of the insurgent and to ensure the safety of the territory in each area. It seems natural that the counterinsurgent's forces should be organized into two types of units, the mobile ones fighting in a rather conventional fashion, and the static ones staying with the population in order to protect it and to supplement the political efforts.

The static units are obviously those that know best the local situation, the population, the local problems; if a mistake is made, they are the ones who will bear the consequences. It follows that

---

*After the above stress on the necessity for a boss at every level in counterinsurgency warfare, a committee must be seen in this case not as an organization where decisions are reached by vote, but merely as a convenient place to air problems for the benefit of the boss.

when a mobile unit is sent to operate temporarily in an area, it must come under the territorial command, even if the military commander of the area is the junior officer. In the same way as the U.S. ambassador is the boss of every U.S. organization operating in the country to which he is accredited, the territorial military commander must be the boss of all military forces operating in his area.

Adaptation of the Armed Forces to Counterinsurgency Warfare

As long as the insurgent has failed to build a powerful regular army, the counterinsurgent has little use for heavy, sophisticated forces designed for conventional warfare. For his ground forces, he needs infantry and more infantry, highly mobile and lightly armed; some field artillery for occasional support; armored cavalry, and if terrain conditions are favorable, horse cavalry for road surveillance and patrolling. For his air force, he wants ground support and observation planes of slow speed, high endurance, great firepower, protected against small-arms ground fire; plus short-takeoff transport planes and helicopters, which play a vital role in counterinsurgency operations. The navy's mission, if any, is to enforce a blockade, a conventional type of operation that does not require elaboration here. In addition, the counterinsurgent needs an extremely dense signal network.

The counterinsurgent, therefore, has to proceed to a first transformation of his existing forces along these lines, notably to convert into infantry units as many unneeded specialized units as possible.

The adaptation, however, must go deeper than that. At some point in the counterinsurgency process, the static units that took part initially in large-scale military operations in their area will find themselves confronted with a huge variety of nonmilitary tasks which have to be performed in order to get the support of the population, and which can be performed only by military personnel, because of the shortage of reliable civilian political and administrative personnel. Making a thorough census, enforcing new regulations on movements of persons and goods, informing the population, conducting person-to-person propaganda, gathering intelligence on the insurgent's political agents, imple-

menting the various economic and social reforms, etc.—all these will become their primary activity. They have to be organized, equipped, and supported accordingly. Thus, a mimeograph machine may turn out to be more useful than a machine gun, a soldier trained as a pediatrician more important than a mortar expert, cement more wanted than barbed wire, clerks more in demand than riflemen.

Adaptation of Minds

If the forces have to be adapted to their new missions, it is just as important that the minds of the leaders and men—and this includes the civilian as well as the military—be adapted also to the special demands of counterinsurgency warfare.

Reflexes and decisions that would be considered appropriate for the soldier in conventional warfare and for the civil servant in normal times are not necessarily the right ones in counterinsurgency situations. A soldier fired upon in conventional war who does not fire back with every available weapon would be guilty of a dereliction of his duty; the reverse would be the case in counterinsurgency warfare, where the rule is to apply the minimum of fire. "No politics" is an ingrained reaction for the conventional soldier, whose job is solely to defeat the enemy; yet in counterinsurgency warfare, the soldier's job is to help win the support of the population, and in so doing, he has to engage in practical politics. A system of military awards and promotion, such as that in conventional warfare, which would encourage soldiers to kill or capture the largest number of enemies, and thus induce him to increase the scope and the frequency of his military operations, may well be disastrous in counterinsurgency warfare.

The administrator in peacetime has to preserve a politically neutral attitude toward the population, has to let "a hundred flowers bloom, a hundred schools of thought contend," but not in counterinsurgency, where his duty is to see that only the right flower blooms and not the weed, at least until the situation becomes normal again.

The counterinsurgent government clearly needs leaders who understand the nature of the war. There are two possible ways to get them: by indoctrination and training in the technique of counterinsurgency warfare, and by a priori or natural selection.

The theory of counterinsurgency warfare can be taught like that of any other type of war, and of course, the counterinsurgent must see that it is taught to the entire personnel of his military and civilian forces. The difficulty arises in connection with giving practical training to the students. It is easy to stage exercises and games related to the military operations required in counterinsurgency warfare, but it is hardly possible to duplicate in a realistic way the setting for the nonmilitary operations. For one thing, the population with its behavior and its mood is the major factor in these operations. How can this be introduced in the game? Also, decisions taken in the nonmilitary operations seldom produce immediate effects, whereas the soundness of a military decision in the field can be assessed almost immediately. Most of the training will have to be done on the job. More will be said on this question in the next chapter.

Indoctrination and training, however, are slow processes, and the need for able leaders is immediate. There are no easy criteria enabling one to determine in advance whether a man who has not been previously involved in a counterinsurgency will be a good leader. A workable solution is to identify those who readily accept the new concepts of counterinsurgency warfare and give them responsibility. Those who then prove themselves in action should be pushed upward.

There is room in the armed forces, but not in the civilian component of the counterinsurgent force, for the cadres who cannot shed their conventional-warfare thinking. They can be assigned to the mobile units.

Needless to say, if political reliability is a problem, as it may well be in a revolutionary war, it is the most reliable cadres who should be assigned to work with the population.

SELECTION OF THE AREA OF EFFORTS

The Strategic Problem

Two opposite approaches are open to the counterinsurgent, and a third which is a compromise between the others. According to the first approach, one proceeds from the difficult to the easy. Efforts are concentrated initially in the red areas and progressively extended to the pink and white ones. It is the fastest way, if it succeeds. The other approach, from the easy to the difficult, requires fewer means at the outset, but it is slower and gives more opportunity for the insurgent to develop and to consolidate in the red areas. The choice between the approaches depends essentially on the relative strength of the opponents.

During the Greek War, the Nationalists chose initially a compromise heavily accented toward the first approach. They started by tackling the region of Thessaly in central Greece; immediately after that, they moved east and north against the Communist strongholds established along the borders. The Communists withdrew safely into satellites' territories and reappeared elsewhere. The first Nationalist offensive failed. In their second attempt, in 1949-50, the Nationalists adopted the opposite strategy: They eliminated the Communists from the Peloponnesus, then operated in greater strength in Thessaly, and finally cleaned the bolder regions. This time they succeeded, thanks in part to the defection of Tito from the Soviet bloc, which prevented the Greek Communists from playing hide and seek on his territory.

When the revolutionary war resumed in China after the Japanese surrender, the Nationalists had the choice between three courses of action:

1. Concentrating their efforts in Manchuria, the area most remote from the Nationalists' center of power, and where the Communist forces, armed with Japanese equipment, were the strongest.
2. Cleaning up central China, then north China, and finally Manchuria.
3. Operating everywhere.

Wide in theory, the choice was narrow in fact, because the Nationalists could not afford to let their opponents develop safely in Manchuria, the richest industrial part of China, where Communists were in direct contact with the Soviet Union. And as Manchuria had been occupied by Soviet troops in the last days of World War II, the Nationalist Government had to reassert its sovereignty over it. The Nationalists felt compelled to invest their best units in Manchuria.

Whether the Nationalists would have won had they acted otherwise is rather doubtful, for the Chinese Communists were a formidable opponent by 1945. But their chances might have been better if they had adopted the second course of action.

In Algeria, where the French, as of 1956, enjoyed an overwhelming military superiority over the FLN, their efforts were spread initially all over the territory, with larger concentrations along the borders with Tunisia and Morocco and in Kabylia, a rugged, heavily populated mountain area. The FLN forces were soon broken up, but lack of doctrine and experience in what to do after military operations, among other things, precluded a clear-cut French success. In 1959–60, the French strategy proceeded from west to east, starting with the Oran region, then to the Ouarsenis Mountains, to Kabylia, and finally, to the Constantine region. This time, there was enough experience; the period of muddling through was over. By the end of 1960, when the French Government policy had switched from "defeating the insurgency" to "disengaging France from Algeria," the FLN forces in Algeria were reduced to between 8,000 and 9,000 men well isolated from the population, broken into tiny, ineffective bands, with 6,500 weapons, most of which had been buried for lack of ammunition; not a single *wilaya* (region) boss in Algeria was in contact with the FLN organization abroad, not even by radio; purges were devastating their ranks, and some of the high-ranking FLN chiefs in Algeria made overtures of surrender. The borders were closed to infiltration, except very occasionally by one or two men. The French forces included 150,000 Moslems, not counting self-defense groups in almost every village. All that would have remained to do, if the policy had not changed, was to eliminate the diehard insurgent remnants, a long task at best, considering the size of Algeria and its terrain. In Malaya, this final phase of the counterinsurgency lasted at least five years.

The selection of the first area of efforts must obviously be influenced first of all by the strategic approach chosen. It is well to remember, in any case, that the counterinsurgent needs a clear-cut, even if geographically limited, success as soon as possible. In terms of psychological benefit to the course of the revolutionary war, it is worth taking this risk even if it means letting the insurgent develop in some other area.

The counterinsurgent, who usually has no practical experience in the nonmilitary operations required in counterinsurgency warfare, must acquire it fast.

These two considerations indicate that the choice of the first area should promise an easy tactical victory at the price of a strategic risk. In other words, it seems better to go from the easy to the difficult unless the counterinsurgent is so strong that he can afford the opposite strategy.

The Tactical Factors

In selecting the area, factors customarily taken into account in conventional warfare, such as terrain, transportation facilities, climate, remain valid. In this respect, the counterinsurgent must pay particular attention to whether the area can be easily isolated and compartmented by taking advantage of natural obstacles, sea, rivers, plains. It may seem strange that plains should be considered as natural obstacles in war, but the fact is that mountains, forests, and swamps are not obstacles for the insurgent, but rather his favorite ground. Nor are international boundaries barriers; usually, these have restricted only the counterinsurgent. If natural obstacles are lacking, consideration must be given to building artificial ones, as the French did along the Tunisian and Moroccan borders. This solution may be expensive, but it results in so much security and such a saving in manpower that it may be worth it.

However, since the population is the objective, factors pertaining to it acquire a particular importance. There are objective factors. How large is the population? The larger it is, the higher the stakes. Is the population concentrated in towns and villages, or dispersed all over the terrain? A concentrated population is easier to protect and control; thus an infantry company can easily control a small town of 10,000-20,000 inhabitants—short of a general uprising—but it would take a much larger unit if the same population were spread over the countryside. How dependent is the population on outside supplies and on economic facilities provided by the counterinsurgent administration? Does it have to import food and other material? Is trade important, or can it live in an autarchic economy?

Above all, there are subjective factors. How does the population view the respective opponents? What are the proportions of potential friends, neutrals, enemies? Can these categories be defined in advance? Can it, for instance, be assumed that the bourgeoisie, the rich farmers, the small farmers, etc., will take this attitude or that? Is there any leverage over them? Are there any divisive factors by which any of these categories can further be dissociated by either of the opponents? This sort of political analysis is as important in counterinsurgency warfare as map study is in conventional warfare, for it will determine, however roughly, whether the area considered will be easy or difficult to work on. In Algeria, for instance, it was automatically assumed that Moslem veterans who received a pension from the French Government would be hostile to the FLN, that Moslem women living in slavery under Islamic customs would welcome their emancipation. In spite of partial setbacks, these assumptions proved generally true.

There is an optimum dimension for the size of both the area and the population. Above it, isolation would be difficult to maintain and the efforts would be too diluted. Below it, insurgent influence would keep penetrating too easily from the outside, and the population, conscious of its small number and feeling too exposed and too conspicuous, would be reluctant to lean on the counterinsurgent side.

The right size cannot be determined in the abstract it varies too much from case to case. The fact that the insurgent usually moves on foot provides, however, a rough yardstick. The minimum diameter of the area should be equal to no less than three days' march so that outside guerrillas trying to infiltrate deeply would be forced to march more than one night. This would give the counterinsurgent more chance to catch them.

Political Preparation

On the eve of embarking on a major effort, the counterinsurgent faces what is probably the most difficult problem of the war: He has to arm himself with a competing cause.

Let us first eliminate the easy cases—easy as analytical problems—briefly described as follows:

1. The insurgent has really no cause at all; he is exploiting the counterinsurgent's weaknesses and mistakes. Such seems to be the situation in South Vietnam today. The Vietcong cannot clamor for land, which is plentiful in South Vietnam; nor raise the banner of anticolonialism, for South Vietnam is no longer a colony; nor offer Communism, which does not appear to be very popular with the North Vietnamese population. The insurgent's program is simply: "Throw the rascals out." If the "rascals" (whoever is in power in Saigon) amend their ways, the insurgent would lose his cause.

2. The insurgent has a cause that the counterinsurgent can espouse without unduly endangering his power. This was, as we have seen, the situation in the Philippines during the Huks' insurgency. All the counterinsurgent has to do is to promise the necessary reforms and prove that he means it.

We are left with the general case when the insurgent has the monopoly of a dynamic cause. What can the counterinsurgent do? Knowing that his ideological handicap will somewhat subside as the war itself becomes the main issue is no consolation because he has to last until then, and the time to launch a counteroffensive is at the start.

It would be a mistake to believe that a counterinsurgent cannot get the population's support unless he concedes political reforms. However unpopular he may be, if he is sufficiently strong-willed and powerful, if he can rely on a small but active core of supporters who remain loyal to him because they would lose everything including their lives if the insurgent wins, he can maintain himself in power. He may very well withdraw whatever benefits the population receives from the mere existence of his regime— a measure of law and order, a more-or-less running economy, functioning public works and services, etc.—and restore them gradually as a premium for the population's cooperation. He may, for instance, ration food and see that only those who cooperate receive ration cards. He may, at the same time, utilize to the utmost those who are willing to support him actively, giving them increased privileges and power, and ruling through them, however disliked they may be. This is the way the Kadar regime in Hungary and others, no doubt, keep themselves in power. But such a policy of pure force could bring at best a precarious return to the *status quo ante,* a state of perpetual tension, not a lasting peace.

In default of liberal inclinations and of a sense of justice—if there is some justice in the insurgent's demands—wisdom and expediency demand that the counterinsurgent equip himself with a political program designed to take as much wind as possible out of the insurgent's sails. This raises serious questions of substance and timing.

When looking for a countercause, the counterinsurgent is left with a narrow choice of secondary issues that appeal almost invariably to reason at a time when passion is the prime mover. And how far can he go in the way of reforms without endangering his power, which, after all, is what he—right or wrong—is fighting to retain? When the insurgent's cause is an all-or-nothing proposition, as in most anticolonial or Communist-led insurgencies, the margin for political maneuver is extremely limited. The insurgent wants independence today, speaks of revolution, promotes class struggle and the dictatorship of the proletariat; his opponent can offer only internal autonomy or some variation of it, insist on evolution, stress fraternity of all classes.

Yet, knowing that his program will have no or little immediate appeal, the counterinsurgent must somehow find a set of reforms, even if secondary, even if minor. He has to gamble that reason, in the long run, will prevail over passion.

He would be wise also to ascertain whether what he offers is really wanted by the people. Reforms conceived in the abstract at a high level may often sound promising on paper but do not always correspond to the popular wish. A practical method, therefore, would consist in investigating objectively the people's demands, making a list of them; crossing out those that cannot be granted safely and promoting the rest.

The counterinsurgent must also decide when to publicize his program. If he does this too early, it could be taken for a sign of weakness, raise the insurgent's demands, even encourage the population into supporting the insurgent in the hope of more concessions; and as the war lasts, the impact of the program would blur. If the announcement is unduly delayed, the task of winning the support of the population would become more difficult. Appreciating the right time is a matter of judgment based on circumstances, and no solution can be suggested in advance. It seems possible and judicious, however, to separate the political program from the specific concrete reforms. The program could be announced early in general terms. The reforms, since they are meaningless unless they can safely be implemented, could be publicized locally as soon as the preliminary military operations have been concluded; they should be publicized nationally when local experience has shown their value.

In any case, nothing could be worse than promising reforms and being unwilling or unable to implement them.

THE FIRST AREA AS A TEST AREA

However prepared, trained, and indoctrinated the counterinsurgent forces may be, reality will always differ from theory. Mistakes are bound to happen, but it would be inexcusable not to learn from them. This is why the first area selected must be considered a test area. The value of the operations conducted there lies just as much in what they teach as in their intrinsic results.

Testing means experimenting, being intent on watching objectively what takes place, being prompt and willing to alter what goes wrong. And learning implies drawing the proper lessons from the events and spreading the experience among others. All this cannot be left to chance and personal initiative; it must be organized carefully and deliberately.

The Chinese Communists, who used to be well aware of the importance of learning and combining theory with practice, seem to have applied in the early 1950's a method that owes little to Marxism and much to experimental science and plain common sense. They never explicitly explained their method, so what follows is a reconstruction based on observation of facts and on some logical guessing.

Whenever the top Chinese Communist leadership, i.e., the ten or twelve members of the standing group of the Central Committee, considered a major reform—for instance, the establishment of semisocialist agricultural cooperatives—the idea was first discussed thoroughly within the group. If it was not rejected there, a preliminary draft, Project No. 1, would be submitted next to the Central Committee with its seventy or so regular members, again thoroughly discussed, amended, or perhaps even discarded.

Out of the discussion would come a Project No. 2, which would be submitted then to a vertical slice of the Party composed of members selected from every level and every area of China. In typical Chinese Communist fashion, open and sincere discussion would be compulsory; one could not just approve without giving personal and convincing reasons. Such a broadening of viewpoints would, of course, produce further modifications of the project, or again reveal its impracticality. Out of this would come Project No. 3.

The Chinese Communists had early designated certain areas of every size as test areas. Thus, Manchuria as a whole was a test region because it was considered the vanguard for the industrialization of China; a province here and there, one or several districts in each province, one or several villages in each district had been selected for various reasons: because they were ideologically advanced, or average, or backward; because they were close to a large city or were populated by ethnic minorities. Project No. 3 would be implemented secretly in the test areas, with a minimum of local publicity. The operations would be watched by cadres of every level coming from the nontest areas.

At the end of the experiment, a thorough critique would be made and the project rejected altogether or modified according to the lessons of the experiment. If kept, it would be now announced as an official decision and applied with fanfare all over the country. The observers would return to their posts, not to carry out the reform by themselves but to serve as teachers and inspectors at their respective levels for the mass of local cadres.

This is how Peking was able to conduct in a few weeks the first relatively thorough census of China,* or impose within a month a tight rationing of grain. The fact that the Communist regime literally ran amuck in the subsequent period of the "Great Leap Forward" does not destroy the validity of the principle. And although the above example is not drawn from a counterinsurgency situation, the principle could indeed be used with profit in any counterinsurgency.

---

* If the thoroughness of the census cannot be doubted, the veracity of the published results is another affair. Only the Red Chinese know the exact truth.

The Operations

David Galula

We shall study here the tactical problems normally arising with the implementation of the strategy outlined in Chapter 4. Dealing with, and in, the abstract, we shall, of course, be more concerned with principles than with actual recipes.

THE FIRST STEP: DESTRUCTION OR EXPULSION OF THE INSURGENT FORCES

The destruction of the guerrilla forces in the selected area is, obviously, highly desirable, and this is what the counterinsurgent must strive for. One thing should be clear, however: This operation is not an end in itself, for guerrillas, like the heads of the legendary hydra, have the special ability to grow again if not all destroyed at the same time. The real purpose of the first operation, then, is to prepare the stage for the further development of the counterinsurgent action.

The goal is reached when static units left to garrison the area can safely deploy to the extent necessary. Consequently, if most of the guerrillas are merely expelled, the result is still good. If they disband into very small groups and stay hidden in the area, the situation is still acceptable as long as the counterinsurgent sees to it that they cannot regroup. To this effect, in this case, some

of the counterinsurgent mobile forces will have to remain in the area until the static units, having become well established and having imposed enough physical control over the population, are in a position to cope with the dispersed guerrillas and to prevent their regrouping into larger, more dangerous gangs.

The first step in the counterinsurgent's operations should not be allowed to drag on for the sake of achieving better military results.

Tactics for this operation are simple in essence.

1. Mobile units, plus units earmarked to stay in the area in order to reinforce whatever static units were originally there, are suddenly concentrated around the area. They start operating from the outside in, aiming at catching the guerrillas in a ring. At the same time, units garrisoning the adjoining areas are ordered to intensify their activity on the periphery of the selected area.
2. The sweep is next conducted from the inside out, aiming at least at expelling the guerrillas.
3. The over-all operation is finally broken down into several small-scale ones. All the static units, the original as well as the new ones, are assigned to their permanent sectors. A part of the mobile units operates as

Galula, David. (1966). "Operations." *Counterinsurgency Warfare: Theory and Practice*. New York: Praeger.

a body, centrally controlled; the rest is lent to the sectors. All the forces work on what is left of the guerrillas after the two earlier sweeps.

The operations are supplemented during this step—as in all the others—by tactical information and psychological warfare directed at the insurgent, the counterinsurgent's own forces, and the population.

Propaganda Directed at the Counterinsurgent Forces

The operations during this step, being predominantly of a military nature, will inevitably cause some damage and destruction. The insurgent on his part will strive to provoke clashes between the population and the counterinsurgent forces.

Since antagonizing the population will not help, it is imperative that hardships for it and rash actions on the part of the forces be kept to a minimum. The units participating in the operations should be thoroughly indoctrinated to that effect, the misdeeds punished severely and even publicly if this can serve to impress the population. Any damage done should be immediately compensated without red tape.

Propaganda Directed at the Population

To ask the local people to cooperate en masse and openly at this stage would be useless and even self-defeating, for they cannot do it, being still under the insurgent's control. Promoting such a line would expose the counterinsurgent to a public failure. Furthermore, if some local civilians were to cooperate prematurely and be punished for it by the insurgent, the psychological setback would be disastrous.

The counterinsurgent would be wiser to limit his goal to obtaining the neutrality of the population, i.e., its passivity toward both sides. The general line could be: "Stay neutral and peace will soon return to the area. Help the insurgent, and we will be obliged to carry on more military operations and thus inflict more destruction."

Propaganda Directed at the Insurgent

The insurgent's worst mistake at this stage would be to accept the fight, to remain active while the counterinsurgent is very strong. The goal of psychological warfare is to prod him into it.

Once the counterinsurgent has lost the benefit of surprise—if any—achieved during the concentration and after the first operations, if he then proclaims his intention to remain in the area in order to work with the population and to win its support, the insurgent, fearing the loss of face as well as the eventual loss of genuine strength, may be incited to accept the challenge.

THE SECOND STEP: DEPLOYMENT OF THE STATIC UNIT

Complete elimination of the guerrillas by military action being practically impossible at this stage, remnants will always manage to stay in the area, and new recruits will join their ranks so long as the political cells have not been destroyed. They can be conclusively wiped out only with the active cooperation of the population, cooperation which will be available to the counterinsurgent in the later steps of the process, if all goes well. This is why the counterinsurgent forces must now switch their attention from the guerrillas to the population.

This does not mean that military activity will stop. On the contrary, the static units will continue tracking the guerrillas, but now through small-scale operations and ambushes, with the understanding that this activity must never distract them from their primary mission, which is to win the support of the population.

The counterinsurgent also has to see that guerrilla forces do not come back in strength from the outside. Opposing such incursions will be the main task of the area's own mobile forces.

The purpose in deploying static units is to establish a grid of troops so that the population and the counterinsurgent political teams are reasonably well protected, and so that the troops can participate in civic action at the lowest level, just where civilian political personnel is insufficient in number. The area will be divided into sectors and sub-sectors, each with its own static unit.

The subdivision should be carried out down to the level of the "basic unit of counterinsurgency warfare": the largest unit whose leader is in direct and continuous contact with the population. This is the most important unit in counterinsurgency operations, the level where most of the practical problems arise, where the war is won or lost. The size varies from case to case, and in each case with the situation; the basic unit may be a battalion or a company initially, a squad or even a rural policeman at the end of the process.

Certain points require particular attention in the deployment of static units.

The administrative and the military limits should coincide at every level even if the resulting borders seem nonsensical from a strictly military point of view. Failure to observe this principle would result in confusion that would benefit the insurgent.

It seems logical that the grid be initially tighter in the center of the area than at the periphery, where the counterinsurgent forces will necessarily devote a greater part of their activity to military operations.

The units must be deployed where the population actually lives and not in positions deemed to possess a military value. A military unit can spend the entire war in so-called strategic positions without contributing anything to the insurgent's defeat. This does not mean that bridges, communication centers, and other vulnerable installations should not be protected, of course, but rather that counterinsurgent forces should not be wasted in traditionally commanding positions, for in revolutionary warfare, these positions generally command nothing.

If the rural population is too dispersed to allow the stationing of a military detachment with every group, the counterinsurgent faces the decision of resettling it, as was done in Malaya, Cambodia, and Algeria, and is being done today in South Vietnam. Such a radical measure is complicated and dangerous. Complicated because the population has to be moved, housed, and given facilities to retain its old, or to find new, independent means of living. Dangerous because nobody likes to be uprooted and the operation is bound to antagonize the population seriously at a critical time; a well-planned and well-conducted resettlement may ultimately offer the population economic and social advantages, but they will not become apparent immediately. Moreover, regrouping the population is basically a defensive-minded action. It gives the insurgent a large measure of freedom of the countryside, at least at night, and it is hardly compatible with the ultimate goal of actively using the population, both as a source of intelligence and as a widespread militia, against the guerrillas. A curious illustration of the effects of resettling the population is provided by the Algerian War. When the French sealed off the Tunisian border, they actually built the fence at some distance from it. By removing the local population in some sectors between the fence and the border, they created a no man's land. In 1959, when the situation had improved greatly, they resettled the population in its original dwellings between the fence and the border. Then the FLN, in turn, forcibly removed the population to Tunisia because the French were getting too much intelligence on FLN movements from it.

Resettlement clearly is a last-resort measure, born out of the counterinsurgent's weakness. It should be undertaken only if the trend of the war definitely shows no prospect for the counterinsurgent forces to deploy safely to the required level. If such is the case, resettlement must first be carefully tested in a limited way in order to detect the problems arising with the operation and to get the necessary experience. It should be preceded by intensive psychological and logistical preparation. Finally, the sizes of the various resettlements should correspond to the maximum possible deployment of the counterinsurgent forces; if, for instance, in a given area, a battalion can safely deploy its companies, 4 settlements of 2,000 persons each seem preferable to a single settlement of 8,000.

Areas very sparsely populated and difficult of access because of terrain may be turned into forbidden zones where trespassers can be arrested or eventually shot on sight by ground or air fire.

At every level, the territorial command must have its own mobile reserves. The more dispersed the static units, the more important the mobile reserves are. However, they should not be allowed to remain idle between military operations; they can and should also participate in the civic-action program. In other words, these local mobile reserves are static units on which the local command has an operational option with a specified warning time of one, two, or more hours.

The deployment must not follow a set pattern, such as a company or a platoon for every village. It must be flexible because, as the counterinsurgent work progresses and security increases in the area, the static units will have to spread out more and more, until only a few men will be left to provide the core for self-defense units. Consequently, heavy, expensive constructions for housing the troops should be prohibited, not so much for the cost involved as for psychological reasons. It is only human that soldiers would become attached to their barracks and thus be reluctant to move to less comfortable billets. It is also human that soldiers living in barracks would always appear to the population as outsiders, as people apart. If no construction other than what is strictly necessary is allowed, the counterinsurgent forces will be forced to live like the population, in shacks if necessary, and this will help to create common bonds.

The principle of the test area applies at every level. Until some practical experience has been acquired, it would be best for the basic unit not to spread at once all over its territory, even if it is safe to do so, but instead to concentrate its work first on one village so that the soldiers, when they occupy other villages, will know what to do and what to avoid.

During this step, the following objectives may be assigned to the information and psychological-warfare program.

Propaganda Directed at the Counterinsurgent Forces

As their main efforts will switch hereafter from military to other activities, the counterinsurgent forces need to be told the reasons for the change and to have their future tasks explained to them in general terms. This information program, if conducted in an atmosphere of free discussion, should and could be used for a practical purpose: According to the reactions of the participants, the leader can spot the officers and men who seem best fitted to work closely with the population and those who, on the contrary, are more attracted to the military side of the counterinsurgent work.

Propaganda Directed at the Population

The deployment of static units marks the beginning of a long campaign to shake the population from its neutral, if not hostile, stand. The deployment is a convincing argument to show that the counterinsurgents are there to stay, for they would not spread out if they contemplated leaving the area after an extensive but one-shot operation. This should naturally be the line to exploit, and perhaps the best way might be the indirect one, by letting the population make its own deductions from facts and rumors. For instance, negotiating a two- or three-year contract for billets or land with a villager would surely produce the right effect.

Propaganda Directed at the Insurgent

The deployment cannot be instantaneous or even simultaneous in all the selected area because the situation will inevitably show differences from sector to sector. During this period, the counterinsurgent's concentration of forces is still heavy due to the presence of mobile units operating in the area and to the fact that static units are not yet dispersed into small detachments.

It is still in the counterinsurgent's interest to pursue the same policy as in the preceding step and to incite the guerrillas to react at the worst possible time for them. The point should be stressed, therefore, that they will be lost once they have been cut off from the population. Calling on them to leave the area or to surrender may induce their leaders to do the very opposite, i.e., to fight.

THE THIRD STEP: CONTACT WITH AND CONTROL OF THE POPULATION

Three main objectives are pursued in this step:

1. To re-establish the counterinsurgent's authority over the population.
2. To isolate the population as much as possible, by physical means, from the guerrillas.
3. To gather the necessary intelligence leading to the next step—elimination of the insurgent political cells.

This is the most critical step in the process because of its transitional character, moving from emphasis on military operations to emphasis on political ones, and because it combines a heavy burden of both.

The main center of interest switches now to the level of the basic unit of work, where the real battle takes place.

1. *Contact with the population.* This particular operation, contact with the population, is actually the first confrontation between the two camps for power over the population. The future attitude of the population, hence the probable outcome of the war, is at stake. The counterinsurgent cannot afford to lose this battle.

The battle occurs because the population, which was until recently under the insurgent's open control and probably still is under his hidden control through the existing political cells, cannot cooperate spontaneously even if there is every reason to believe that a majority is sympathetic to the counterinsurgent. The inhabitants will usually avoid any contact with him. There is a barrier between them and the counterinsurgent that has to be broken and can be broken only by force. Whatever the counterinsurgent wants the population to do will have to be imposed. Yet the population must not be treated as an enemy.

The solution is first to request, and next to order, the population to perform a certain number of collective and individual tasks that will be paid for. By giving orders, the counterinsurgent provides the alibi that the population needs vis-à-vis the insurgent. A terrible error would be, of course, to issue orders and be unable to enforce them; the counterinsurgent must be careful to issue orders sparingly and only after making sure that the population can humanly comply with them.

Starting with tasks directly benefiting the population—such as cleaning the village or repairing the streets—the counterinsurgent leads the inhabitants gradually, if only in a passive way, to participate in the fight against the insurgent by such work as building roads of military interest, helping in the construction of the village's defensive installations, carrying supplies to military detachments, providing guides and sentries.

2. *Control of the population.* Control of the population begins obviously with a thorough census. Every inhabitant must be registered and given a foolproof identity card. Family booklets should be issued to each household in order to facilitate house-to-house control, and family heads made responsible for reporting any change as it occurs. This last measure is useful not only because it is essential to keep the census up to date, but also because the responsibility placed on the family head makes him participate willy-nilly in the struggle.

The insurgent cannot ignore the census and can guess only too well its implications. He will surely attempt to sabotage it. One way is to force villagers to destroy their new identity cards; since a civilian *sans* identity card is in for much trouble in a revolutionary war, this tactic will soon raise such an outcry among the population that the insurgent will be forced to discard it. He may instead try to register his own personnel, counting on the ignorance of the local counterinsurgent and on the solidarity or silence of the population. To oppose this more insidious tactic, the counterinsurgent can request that every able-bodied man subject to the census be vouched for by two guarantors from in outside his family who would be responsible under severe penalty for the veracity of his statements, which should be checked anyway before the identity card is issued. This measure also will contribute to turn the population against the insurgent.

A census, if properly made and exploited, is a basic source of intelligence. It would show, for instance, who is related to whom, an important piece of information in counterinsurgency warfare because insurgent recruiting at the village level is generally based initially on family ties; or who owns property or who works outside of the village and has, therefore, legitimate reasons to travel; or what is each man's source and amount of income, which would immediately separate those who can afford to indulge in abnormal activities from those who cannot. The census should, consequently, be well planned, and conducted in a systematic fashion so that the format and the results do not vary from sector to sector.

The aim of the control is to cut off, or at least reduce significantly, the contacts between the population and the guerrillas. This is done by watching the population's activities; after a while, when the counterinsurgent personnel has become acquainted with the population and knows each inhabitant, unusual behavior can be spotted easily. The process of getting acquainted with the population may be speeded up if the occupied villages are divided into sections, and each assigned to a group of soldiers who will always work there.

Control is also achieved by enforcing a curfew and two simple rules concerning movements of persons: Nobody may leave his village for more than twenty-four hours without a pass, and nobody may receive a stranger from outside the village without permission. The purpose is not to prevent movement—unless there are specific reasons for doing so—but to check on it. By making unchecked travel more difficult, the counterinsurgent again provides the population with a necessary alibi for not helping the insurgent.

These rules, however, have no value unless they can be strictly and systematically enforced. As they are bound to create offenders, a fast and summary system of fines has to be devised and announced to the population. The problem of fines is one that merits consideration at the highest level of the counterinsurgent hierarchy because it is a serious one, and because its solution cannot be left to the initiative of local leaders, which would lead to too light or too heavy punishment and, in any case, to chaos.

The guerrillas who remain in the selected area at the end of the first step will be few and scattered. They need very little in the way of supplies in order to survive. Cutting them off from their sources would require great effort to produce little result. If control of goods appears necessary, it should be restricted to items that are both scarce and very useful to the guerrillas, such as canned food, radio batteries, shoes. One case when food control is effective at little cost is when the guerrillas are geographically isolated from the population, as in Malaya, where they lived in the jungle while the population had been resettled outside.

3. *Protection of the population.* Just as the counterinsurgent, by forcibly imposing his will on the population, gives it an excuse for not cooperating with the insurgent, the opposite is true. By threatening the population, the insurgent gives the population an excuse, if not a

reason, to refuse or refrain from cooperating with the counterinsurgent.

The counterinsurgent cannot achieve much if the population is not, and does not feel, protected against the insurgent. The counterinsurgent needs, therefore, to step up his military activity, to multiply patrols and small-scale operations by day and ambushes by night. Above all, he must avoid the classic situation where he rules during the day and his opponent during the night.

Plans for rapid reaction against any insurgent move should be devised, involving counterinsurgent forces that can be ready at a moment's notice.

4. *Intelligence collection.* Whenever an organization is set up to collect intelligence, intelligence is bound to flow in, either because informers come spontaneously to the organization or because it goes after informers. The only real problem is how to prime the pump and hasten the flow.

Spontaneous information is hard to come by at this stage because of the population's fear of the insurgent and because of its lack of confidence in the counterinsurgent. To overcome this attitude, would-be informers should be given a safe, anonymous way to convey information. Many systems can be devised for the purpose, but the simplest one is to multiply opportunities for individual contacts between the population and the counterinsurgent personnel, every one of whom must participate in intelligence collection (not just the specialists). The census, the issuing of passes, the remuneration of workers, etc., are such opportunities.

When seeking informers, the counterinsurgent will have better results if he concentrates his efforts on those inhabitants who, by definition, ought to be his potential allies, i.e., those who would have least to win and most to lose through the insurgent's victory. The insurgent's program usually indicates who they may be.

If intelligence is still slow in coming, pressure may be applied. No citizen, even in a primitive country, can withstand for long the pressure from an uncooperative bureaucracy; insurgency conditions naturally increase the number of regulations that have to be complied with in daily life. Bureaucracy can be a powerful weapon in the hand of the counterinsurgent, provided it is used with moderation and restraint and never against a community as a whole but only against a few individuals.

In still tougher cases, visits to the inhabitants by pseudo insurgents are another way to get intelligence and to sow suspicion at the same time between the real guerrillas and the population.

5. *Starting to win the support of the population.* Implementing political reforms—if they have been conceived and announced by the government—would be premature at this stage. The time will be right when the insurgent political cells have been destroyed and when local leaders have emerged. In the political field, the task of the counterinsurgent leader is to discover what reforms are really wanted and to inform the higher echelons, or to determine whether the announced reforms conform with the popular wish.

On the other hand, the counterinsurgent can at once start working on various projects in the economic, social, cultural, and medical fields, where results are not entirely dependent on active cooperation from the population. If these projects are deemed useful a priori for the population, they may even be imposed on it; the accusation of paternalism will soon be forgotten when results speak for themselves.

The counterinsurgent should also seize every opportunity to help the population with his own resources in personnel and equipment. Lack of ostentation is the best attitude, as his actions, good or bad, will always be commented upon and amplified by public rumor.

In the field of information and psychological warfare, the problems and the tasks are numerous during this third step.

Propaganda Directed at the Counterinsurgent Forces

When forces are scattered among, and living with, the population, they need not be told any longer that they have to win its support. Being more vulnerable, they realize instinctively that their own safety depends on good relations with the local people. Good, friendly behavior will come about naturally on their part. The problem now is rather how to impress the counterinsurgent personnel with the necessity of remaining inwardly on guard while being outwardly friendly.

Another problem is how to make an active and efficient agent out of every member of the counterinsurgent forces, regardless of his rank and capacity. Where strict obedience to orders was sufficient in the preceding steps, initiative now becomes a must. Yet every individual effort must be channeled toward the same goal, deviations or honest mistakes kept to a minimum. This is the time when the local commander must assign specific tasks to his men every day, patiently brief them on their purposes, outline a way to fulfill them, anticipate the difficulties likely to arise, and propose a proper solution. After each particular operation, he must hold a meeting with his men, listen to their comments, draw the lessons, and spread the experience to other groups. If there is any way to teach initiative, this should do it.

Propaganda Directed at the Population

Three major goals are pursued during this step in regard to the population:

1. To get from it some measure of approval—or at least understanding—for the various actions taken by the counterinsurgent that affect the population (census, control of movements, imposition of tasks, etc.).
2. To lay the groundwork for the eventual dissociation of the population and the insurgent.
3. To prepare the commitment of sympathetic, but still neutral, elements.

The first point raises no great problem. It is just a matter of the counterinsurgent's telling the population what he proposes to do and why. The difficulty comes with the other points. Propaganda, like terrorism, has an unfortunate tendency to backfire; of all the instruments of warfare, it is the most delicate, and its use requires caution, adherence to reality, and much advance planning. Yet if the target is a rural population, propaganda is most effective when its substance deals with local events, with problems with which the population is directly concerned, and when it is conducted on a person-to-person basis or addressed to specific groups (the men, the women, the youth, the elderly, etc.), rather than to the whole.

It is hardly possible to "precook" this sort of propaganda at a high level. One can easily see that the responsibilities placed upon the local commander are extremely heavy, especially when he has just begun to contact the population and has not yet assessed its reactions in a general way. How can he fulfill his role if the higher echelons do not come to his aid?

He should, at least, be relieved of any responsibility in the execution of the strategic-propaganda campaign, which should be the task of specialized mobile personnel. He should be assisted at all times by a deputy who can relieve him of most of the command routines. He should be provided with up-to-date guidelines for his tactical propaganda, conceived at the first- or second-higher echelon above him where authorities are still close enough to the local situation. He should also be reinforced by psychological-warfare personnel whenever necessary.

Propaganda Directed at the Insurgent

Among guerrillas, as among any human group, can be found a variety of thoughts, feelings, and degrees of commitment to the insurgent's cause. Treating them as a bloc would surely cement their solidarity. From now on, the goal of the counterinsurgent's psychological warfare should be, on the contrary, to divide their ranks, to stir up opposition between the mass and the leaders, to win over the dissidents.

This is a task that usually exceeds the possibilities of the local commander, for he has only an indirect channel of communication with the guerrillas—through the population—and the scattered guerrillas are usually roving over a territory larger than his own. Thus he can participate in, but not conduct, the campaign, which should be directed from a higher level.

THE FOURTH STEP: DESTRUCTION OF THE INSURGENT POLITICAL ORGANIZATION

The necessity for eradicating the insurgent political agents from the population is evident. The question is how to do it rapidly and efficiently, with a minimum of errors and bitterness.

This is, in essence, a police operation directed not against common criminals but against men whose motivations, even if the counterinsurgent disapproves of them, may be perfectly honorable. Furthermore, they do not participate directly, as a rule, in direct terrorism or guerrilla action and, technically, have no blood on their hands.

As these men are local people, with family ties and connections, and are hunted by outsiders, a certain feeling of solidarity and sympathy automatically exists toward them on the part of the population. Under the best circumstances, the police action cannot fail to have unpleasant aspects both for the population and for the counterinsurgent personnel living with it. This is why elimination of the agents must be achieved quickly and decisively.

But who can ever guarantee that mistakes will not be made and innocent people wrongly arrested? One of the insurgent's favorite tricks, indeed, is to mislead the counterinsurgent into arresting people who are hostile to the insurgency. Assuming that only the right men have been arrested, it would be dangerous and inefficient to let them be handled and interrogated by amateurs. All these reasons demand that the operation be conducted by professionals, by an organization that must in no way be confused with the counterinsurgent personnel working to win the support of the population. If the existing police cannot be trusted, then a special police force must be created for the purpose.

Whereas all the counterinsurgent personnel participates in intelligence acquisition, only the police should deal with the suspected agents. The police work, however, does not relieve the local counterinsurgent commander of his overall responsibility; the operation is conducted under his guidance and he must remain in constant liaison with the police during the "purge." When to purge is his decision, which should be based on two factors:

1. Whether enough intelligence is available to make the purge successful.
2. Whether the purge can be followed through.

In the red areas, the intelligence situation with regard to the insurgent political organization conforms usually to the following pattern. The boss and the top cell members are too heavily committed in the insurgency to be expected to change their attitude readily and to talk freely when arrested. Minor suspects, when arrested singly or in small groups, do not talk, either, because they fear that the subsequent counterinsurgent moves against the political agents would be traced to their disclosures. Yet every villager normally knows who the cell members are, or at least knows who is screening them. This suggests that an indirect approach could be easier and more certain than the direct one.

The procedure would be:

1. To arrest simultaneously a large group of minor suspects.
2. On the basis of their disclosures, to arrest the cell members.

There is, of course, a risk that the cell members, alerted by the first move, would vanish. The risk is small, however, for what could they do? If they join the guerrilla remnants, they would place an additional burden on them without substantially increasing their effectiveness, for a few more guerrillas do not change the situation much, while a political cell eliminated means a great change. If they move to another area where they would be outsiders, their value to the insurgent as agents would greatly decrease, and they would also be easily spotted and arrested. Thus, in the same way as expulsion of the guerrillas was a satisfactory result in the first step, the expulsion of the political agents is equally acceptable.

The moment to initiate the purge, then, is not when the cell members have been positively identified—a process that would take much time and leaves much to chance—but instead, when enough information has been gathered on a number of suspected villagers.

The operation would have little usefulness if the purged village were not now, or soon to be, occupied by counterinsurgent forces, for the guerrilla remnants would probably succeed in forcing a relatively unprotected population to create another cell, and the purge would have to be repeated all over again. The counterinsurgent should not hesitate to take risks in providing a detachment to occupy a purged village, but if he is absolutely unable to do so, it would be better to do nothing and wait for a better time.

The arrested cell members normally ought to be punished according to laws, since they have taken part in a conspiracy against the government. Nothing, however, is normal in a revolutionary war. If the counterinsurgent wishes to bring a quicker end to the war, he must discard some of the legal concepts that would be applicable to ordinary conditions. Automatic and rigid application of the law would flood the courts with minor and major cases, fill the jails and prison camps with people who could be won over, as well as with dangerous insurgents.

Leniency seems in this case a good practical policy, but not blind leniency. Although insurgent agents who repent sincerely can be released immediately, with no danger to the counterinsurgent's war effort, those who do not should be punished. Two criteria may serve to test their sincerity: a full confession of their past activity and a willingness to participate actively in the counterinsurgent's struggle. Another advantage of a policy of leniency is to facilitate the subsequent purges, for suspects who have previously seen arrested agents set free will be more inclined to talk.

The main concern of the counterinsurgent in his propaganda during this step is to minimize the possible adverse effects produced on the population by the arrests. He will have to explain frankly why it is necessary to destroy the insurgent political cells, and stress the policy of leniency to those who recognize their error. It does not matter if he is not believed, for the population's shock will be that much greater when the repentant agents are actually released.

THE FIFTH STEP: LOCAL ELECTIONS

Now begins the constructive part of the counterinsurgent program. What was done so far was to remove from the population the direct threat of the armed insurgents and the indirect threat of the political agents. Henceforth, the objective of the counterinsurgent's effort is to obtain the active support of the population, without which the insurgency cannot be liquidated.

The population's attitude immediately after the purge gives a fair indication of the difficulty of the task ahead. If the previous work was well conducted, the population should no longer have excuses for refusing its cooperation. The destruction of the political cells should normally bring about a sudden and dramatic change for the better in the climate; people will cease avoiding contact with counterinsurgent personnel and will no longer obey the various taboos ordered by the insurgent; the friendly elements will spontaneously come forward.

If the post-purge behavior remains what it was, it means:

1. That the purge was not complete, and this can easily be corrected.
2. That the population is not yet fully convinced of the counterinsurgent's will and ability to win, and reality will sooner or later overcome the people's reticence.
3. That the population is deeply and genuinely attached to the insurgent's cause. This is far more serious, for it shows the extent of the ideological handicap and how far the counterinsurgent must go in the way of reforms if he wants to win the support of the population. It does not mean, however, that the counterinsurgent is certain to lose the war, for he can still get (rather than win) the needed support. If his energy matches his unpopularity, he may wait until peace becomes the key issue, and he can rely to a greater extent on his own strength and on his small minority of supporters.

Whichever the case, the problem is to start organizing the participation of the population in the struggle. The way to do this is by placing local leaders in positions of responsibility and power.

Two opposite approaches may be considered. One is to designate men who have been previously identified as supporters, thus imposing them on the population. This should be a last-resort approach because the power and influence of these men will always be dependent on the counterinsurgent's strength. They will be regarded as puppets; the population will never feel any real responsibility toward them.

A better approach would be to call for absolutely free elections for local provisional self-government, thus letting leaders emerge naturally from the population, which will feel more bound to them since they are the product of its choice. The danger that neutrals or even undetected insurgent supporters could be elected is small because the population will realize that the counterinsurgent knows by now who was for

whom, especially if he has spread the rumor that this was part of the information he sought for from the arrested agents. Chances are that the population will elect people known or suspected to be counterinsurgent supporters.

There is a far greater danger that the population will elect not natural leaders but men chosen for their presumed ability to placate the counterinsurgent. An obvious sign of this would be the absence of young men among the local leaders elected.

Whatever the results of the elections, the counterinsurgent must accept them with the publicly announced proviso that these new local leaders are temporarily in office until definitive elections when peace has been restored all over the country.

The propaganda directed toward the population during this step should stress four points: the importance of the elections, complete freedom for the voters, the necessity of voting, and the provisional nature of the elected local government.

THE SIXTH STEP: TESTING THE LOCAL LEADERS

The ultimate results of the counterinsurgent's efforts in regard to the population depend on the effectiveness of the men who have just been elected. If they are worthless, the counterinsurgent will have to count only on himself; he will thus remain an outsider vis-à-vis the population and be unable to reduce substantially his strength in the selected area in order to apply it elsewhere.

The first thing to do, therefore, is to test these new local leaders. The principle of the test is simple: They are given concrete tasks and they are judged on their ability to fulfill them. There are, at this stage, any number of tasks that can be assigned: running the local government, undertaking local projects in the social and economic field, taking over some police functions, levying volunteers for self defense units, propagandizing, etc.

The counterinsurgent will soon find which leaders are living up to expectations. His action will tend to consolidate their position and to build them up, using for this purpose all the available assets and the power of the counterinsurgent regime. As for those who failed in the test, his action will tend to eliminate or to shunt them away with the support, or at least the consent, of the population.

It may happen in a few local elections that the men elected are all worthless, and no better candidates are available. This would plainly be a case of bad luck, against which little can be done on the local scale except gerrymandering the constituency to merge it with a neighboring one where better men are available. This problem is less serious when it is a matter of discovering hundreds of local leaders than when it involves finding the best counterinsurgent leader on a national scale.

The various tasks entrusted to the local leaders have, of course, more than a test value. Most are also designed to win the support of the population through these leaders. Some tasks are conceived to make the population take an active part in the struggle against the insurgent: organizing self-defense units, recruiting full-time auxiliaries for the regular forces, organizing intelligence and control nets and propaganda teams.

Three of the many problems confronting the counterinsurgent during this step require particular attention.

The elected leaders are conspicuous targets for the insurgent and they should be protected, yet not in such a way that they rely entirely on the counterinsurgent's protection. They should be told, on the contrary, that the support of the population is their best protection and it is up to them to get it.

A certain degree of paternalism cannot be avoided initially since the elected leaders are both unknown and untrained, but a paternalistic attitude on the part of the counterinsurgent is self-defeating, for it will promote only passive yes-men, a plague in counterinsurgency situations. Paternalism must, therefore, be discarded as soon as possible, even if this involves risks.

The tasks to be done require logistical support in the form of funds, equipment, and qualified personnel. These should be made readily available and given with a minimum of red tape. Moreover, the manipulation of this logistical support is a political act, and it must be allocated with a priority in favor of villages or districts where the population is most active on the side of the counterinsurgent. A weapon that has such a stimulating value must not be utilized indiscriminately.

When in a part of the selected area, the situation has reached the stage where the population actively helps the counterinsurgent, it means that a breakthrough has been achieved, and it should be exploited at once to influence the less-advanced sectors. To do so is the main goal of the propaganda during this step.

As propaganda is much more convincing when it emanates from the population instead of coming from the counterinsurgent personnel, local inhabitants should be persuaded to act as propagandists not only in their own area but outside. When they do so, the way is virtually won in the selected area.

Another certain sign that a breakthrough has occurred is when spontaneous intelligence increases sharply.

THE SEVENTH STEP: ORGANIZING A PARTY

As the work proceeds in the area, test leaders will finally appear in each village and town. They will eventually have to be grouped and organized within a national counterinsurgent political party. There are several reasons for this:

1. A party is the instrument of politics, particularly in revolutionary war where politics counts for so much. The best policy may be worthless for the counterinsurgent so long as he does not possess the necessary instrument to implement it.
2. The newly found leaders who emerge locally operate within their own local sphere, isolated from their neighbors. They are able at best to oppose local resistance to the insurgent who, on his part, is organized not only on the local but also on the national scale, with all the intermediate levels. Thus, the insurgent retains a considerable political advantage, which cannot be tolerated.
3. The new leaders' powers over the population are mostly of an administrative nature. If their leadership is to extend to the political field, it can do so only through a party.

4. Their links with the population are based on a single, official ballot. They are fragile as long as the leaders are not backed by a political machine solidly rooted in the population. Just as the counterinsurgent himself has worked to discover the leaders, these must in turn find militants among the population; to keep the militants together, the leaders need the framework, the support, and the guidance of a political party.

Is it best to group the local leaders and the militants within an existing party or to create a new one? The answer depends obviously on the particular circumstances, the prestige of the existing party, the quality of its leadership, and the appeal of its platform.

The creation of a new party raises the problem of its political program. It cannot be undertaken as long as the counterinsurgent has not decided what political reforms he intends to accomplish.

Although in peacetime most political parties—with the notable exception of the Communists—aim at expanding their membership with little or no regard to the candidates' aptitudes, insurgency conditions impose more caution. The counterinsurgent political party should select its members carefully, and rely more on quality than on quantity.

The creation of a party is neither an easy nor a quick undertaking. The fact remains, nevertheless, that the local leaders have to be grouped in some kind of national organization as soon as a sufficient number of them has emerged. At the beginning, regional associations can serve temporarily for the purpose.

THE EIGHTH STEP: WINNING OVER OR SUPPRESSING THE LAST GUERRILLAS

The counterinsurgent, while concentrating on the tasks necessary for winning the support of the population, has not neglected to continue tracking the guerrillas left in the selected area after the intensive operation described in the first step. He may even have liquidated them completely. If not, he still has to finish with the last remnants.

The tactical problem results from their dilution; from their feeble offensive activity; from their avoidance of contact with the population, which dries up sources of intelligence; in some cases, from terrain difficulties. Under these conditions, hunting the guerrillas with the usual ambushes, patrols, and small-scale operations could be time-consuming and not very productive. This is why it would be more profitable for the counterinsurgent to revert now to the same massive military effort that characterized the first step, but this time with the important added asset of the population participating effectively in the operations.

The main difficulty is a psychological one and it originates in the counterinsurgent's own camp. Responsible people will question why it is necessary to make such an effort at this stage, when everything seems to be going so well. Arguments are not lacking against this line of reasoning. The fact is that guerrillas who still roam the area are certain to be a hard core, a breed produced by natural selection, and they can hardly be left behind for the population and a skeleton garrison to cope with. Thorough final operations will show the counterinsurgent's determination to smash his opponent and should bring valuable political benefits both within and without the selected area, on the population, on the insurgents, and on the counterinsurgent's own forces.

The basic operational principle to eliminate guerrillas who are few in number and isolated from the population is to force them to move, to become "roving bandits," and to catch them as they attempt to cross successive nets of counterinsurgent forces. Such were, in essence, the tactics followed with great success by the Chinese Communists themselves in south China in 1950-52, when they liquidated the Nationalist remnants.

The troop requirements are great, but since the guerrillas are operating in very small groups of a few men each, and are feebly armed besides, the net may be entrusted to the population which is temporarily mobilized and armed, and led by professional cadres drawn from the static units. Mobile reserves assigned to the area for the occasion will be used to flush out the guerrillas.

How long this effort can or should be maintained is a matter of local circumstances, the main factor being the disruption of the population's life. The best time, obviously, is when farming is at a standstill.

The military efforts need to be supplemented by an intensive psychological offensive against the guerrillas; the trump card here is an amnesty offer. This presents some danger but less than at any other time because the counterinsurgent has reached now a real position of strength in the selected area, based on the effective support of the population.

Even such a large effort, however, cannot be expected to bring a complete end to the insurgency in the area; a few guerrillas will still manage to survive. It may be interesting to note in this respect that in September, 1962, fourteen years after the start of the insurgency in Malaya, 20 to 30 Communist guerrillas were still holding out in the deep jungle inside Malaya, not counting 300 more operating on the Malaya-Thailand border.

These survivors may give up one day if the insurgency collapses, or they may leave the area for good, or they may hold out. In this last case, they should no longer be a problem.

CONCLUDING REMARKS

Such is, in the author's view, the basic mechanism of counterinsurgency warfare. Whether in the cold or in the hot revolutionary war, its essence can be summed up in a single sentence: Build (or rebuild) a political machine from the population upward. The idea is simple. How difficult it may be to implement it can be gathered from the following observations, written in a context utterly alien to a revolutionary situation, in a peaceful and well-developed country, and precisely for this reason the more relevant to our problem:

> Public indifference to politics is disheartening. On that snowy February morning when I started ringing doorbells, the first four families visited said bluntly, "We never vote." In my congressional district there are about 334,000 adults eligible to vote, but of these, 92,000 do not even bother to register.

> Of the 334,000 only 217,000 voted in the Kennedy-Nixon election.

> A recent study at the University of Michigan shows that of 100 registered adults, only seven attend political meetings of any kind, only four have ever given money to a campaign, only three have ever worked for a candidate and only two actually serve as working members of any political party.

> The burden of ruling our nation falls on the shoulders of an appallingly small number of people. As I campaign, month after month, I see these same people again and again. The others I never touch.*

Napoleon remarked that "War is a simple art, all a matter of execution."

What would happen, the reader may ask, if the party created by the counterinsurgent eventually adopts the original insurgent's program? A simple answer is, that would be a different story. The Allies won the war in 1918, "the war to end all wars." What they did with their victory is another story. There are no final solutions in human affairs. The risk that a specially created counterinsurgent party may later espouse the very cause of the insurgent does indeed exist, particularly when the insurgency was based essentially on ethnic or national differences, as, for instance, in the current conflict between the Kurds and Iraqi If this happens, all the counterinsurgent has really won is a respite, which is in itself a precious commodity. He can hope that the leaders of the new party, instead of embarking on a new insurgency, will choose to follow a more peaceful path. He can concede to them reforms he was forced to refuse to an intransigent insurgent party born out of terror and violence. Is this not, in fact, what occurred in Malaya where the British granted to others what they had refused to the Communist insurgents? As long as the revolutionary situation exists, even in a dormant form, as long as the problem that gave rise to the insurgency has not been eliminated, the

---

* James A. Michener, "What Every New Candidate Should Know," *The New York Times Magazine*, September 23, 1962.

danger persists and will require a variable degree of vigilance from the counterinsurgent.

Is it always possible to defeat an insurgency? This work, through a common intellectual accident, may have given the impression that the answer is a strong affirmative. When one learns in military schools about the offensive, one gets the impression that nothing can resist a well-mounted attack, which appears as the "irresistible force." Then one learns about the defensive and gets the impression that nothing can break through a well-conceived defense, "the immovable mass." (Let us disregard the nuclear-armed missile against which no defense has yet been devised.)

Obviously, it is not always possible to defeat an insurgency. The Greek insurgency was doomed from the start. So was the French counterinsurgency in Indochina. Except for these clear cases, victory in most of the other recent revolutionary wars could possibly have gone to either camp. The outcome was not decided in advance for Mao Tse-tung or for Chiang Kai-shek, for Batista or for Castro, for the FLN or for the French in Algeria.

Insurgencies in the recent past have stemmed from two major causes: (1) the rise of nationalism in colonial territories, and (2) Communist pressure, the latter sometimes inspiring and directing the insurgency alone, sometimes combining with the former, but always present and active.

Colonialism is dead now except for a few isolated instances against which the "wind of change" concentrates with fury. One would expect the issue to die with it. Unfortunately, this has not happened, for after colonialism comes "neocolonialism," which is not merely a Communist slogan. There are no colonies in Latin America apart from the Guianas, British Honduras, and other insignificant places. Yet the whole continent is seething with unrest. The revolutionary war in Cuba—which was not a colony—was but a sign. "As things are going now, the greatest outburst in history is brewing in Latin America," warned Eduardo Santos, the former President of Colombia.* The issue of

* As quoted in William Benton, "The Voice of Latin America," in *Britannica Book of the Year, 1961*.

neocolonialism is not confined to Latin America. Sincere and not so sincere complaints against economic exploitation by the West can also be heard in Africa and Asia. Few among the newly emancipated nations have been able to recover from the inevitable disorders that, even under the best circumstances, have marked the departure of the former rulers. Fewer still have been able to demonstrate that independence meant immediate progress for the masses, as they were led to believe. It would be a miracle if the perils and difficulties of the transition from colonial to national rule, actively fanned by the Communists, failed to result in scattered unrest, uprisings—and insurgencies.

There is no evidence that Communist pressure has abated, that the Communist apparatus for spreading revolution has been dismantled. Soviet Russia's line may change now, but it may switch again, as it has in the past, before Stalin, under Stalin, and after Stalin. Whatever the latest Soviet stand, Red China clearly intends to capitalize on her chief asset, to continue exporting her chief product—a coherent doctrine for revolution in "colonial and semicolonial countries where similar conditions prevail," as Liu Shao-ch'i said. She claimed leadership over these countries as early as 1951. On July 1 of that year, when the Chinese Communist Party celebrated its thirtieth anniversary, all the major speeches made on that occasion insisted on the world-wide importance of the Chinese Revolution. One of the orators in Peking, Lu Ting-yi, then head of the propaganda department of the Central Committee, said explicitly:

The prototype of the revolution in capitalist countries is the October Revolution.

The prototype of the revolution in colonial and semicolonial countries is the Chinese Revolution, the experience of which is invaluable for the people of these countries.

An ideological map of the world, also issued in 1951 in China, translates vividly the implications of this new, if perhaps unilateral, version of the Treaty of Tordesillas, by which Pope Alexander VI in 1494 gave Spain all lands discovered more than 370 leagues west of the Cape Verde Islands, and Portugal the right to explore and annex all lands in Africa and east of the Spanish sphere. In this 1951 map, Canada and Australia were rigidly considered by the Chinese as colonial countries, Latin America and Japan as capitalist territories. Subsequent statements by Chinese Communists indicate that all Latin America and Japan—this last an "American semicolony"—are within the Chinese sphere of influence, while Australia and Canada fall within the Soviet sphere.

The world is thus divided neatly into three major blocs, roughly equal in size and population, if not in stage of economic development:

The friends, the "sister countries," i.e., the Communist states.

The potential allies, i.e., the "colonial and semicolonial" countries.

The enemy, i.e., the "capitalist" countries.

Hence, the Chinese Communist strategy, the principal of which—if not the leadership role of China—seems to have been accepted by Soviet Russia: As a first step, deny the colonial bloc to the capitalists; as a second step, grab control of it. Then the Communists will have a two-to-one superiority over the capitalists in area and population; by the mere closing of markets and disruption of trade channels, they can hope to bring the capitalists to their knees, at minimum risk, progressively. The Communist military strength will serve to protect revolutionary gains and to deter or overcome any last-minute reaction to this strategy on the part of the capitalists.

How the advent of nuclear weapons and the danger of accidental collision or how the current Sino-Soviet dispute has affected the chances for success of this strategy can be endlessly argued.

The fact remains, nevertheless, that even if the Russian bear is turning suddenly into a horse—strong but peaceful—the Chinese, whose determination can leave no doubt in the mind of those who have watched how they operate on their own territory, are certain to keep plugging their line and thus to attract extremists, the very people who usually spark insurgencies.

There is, finally, a further reason to assume that the list of revolutionary wars is not closed. It is certainly easier to launch an insurgency than to repress it. We have seen how much disorder the Greek Communists were able to occasion, even though the essential prerequisites for their success were not met. With so many successful insurgencies in recent years, the temptation will always be great for a discontented group, anywhere, to start the operations. They may gamble on the inherent weakness of the counterinsurgent (inherent because of the asymmetry between one camp and the other), they may gamble on support from one side of the world or the other. Above all, they may gamble on the effectiveness of an insurgency-warfare doctrine so easy to grasp, so widely disseminated today that almost anybody can enter the business.

It is safe to assume that the West, almost automatically, will be involved directly or indirectly in the coming revolutionary wars. With the Communists pulling one way, chances are that the West will probably be involved on the side of order, i.e., on the side of the counterinsurgent.

That is why this book has been written.

Guerrillas in the 1960's

Peter Paret and John W. Shy

GUERRILLAS AND COUNTERGUERRILLAS

Guevara and the Dilemmas of the Guerrilla Leadership

The Castro revolution has produced the latest theorist of guerrilla warfare, Ernesto (Che) Guevara. The principles stated in his *La Guerra de Guerrillas* are interesting though hardly original; they are timeless tactical truths understood by all successful guerrilla leaders.[1] But Guevara does demonstrate how these principles were adapted to Cuban conditions. Of greater interest is that he suggests, perhaps unwittingly, some inherent weaknesses or limitations in irregular warfare—they may be called the dilemmas of the guerrilla leader—limitations not well understood by either guerrilla or regular. These dilemmas narrow the area where successful action is possible and, under some circumstances, may eliminate it altogether.

In accord with Clausewitz and Mao, Guevara declares that the guerrilla leader must be continually aggressive but must never risk defeat. Defeat not only hurts his small, poorly equipped forces but also carries the special penalty of weakening his hold on the minds of his supporters, both fighters and civilians. But a guerrilla leader who allows offensive activity to slacken likewise runs the risk of weakening confidence and morale, as well as giving his opponent the chance to regain the military initiative.

Second, guerrillas are most secure in comparatively difficult terrain, but in such areas, they rarely find ample supplies, profitable targets, and the civilian leaders who must be won over to their cause. Even the rural regions, the proper political and military base for a guerrilla movement, often comprise what Guevara calls "unfavorable terrain" for irregular operations. He recognizes, indeed, that the most sensitive sections of a country are its areas of highest population density, and that these must be the eventual objective of guerrilla attack and indoctrination. But he admits that operations in these areas are extremely dangerous, perhaps impossible except in the form of sporadic terrorism and sabotage, and may cost more than they are worth.

Guevara agrees with most other writers on guerrilla warfare when he asserts that partisans fight not because they are forced to but because they want to. This, however, does not blind him to the extraordinary physical and emotional demands placed upon the irregular fighter, and the fact that guerrilla discipline must be extremely severe. In Cuba, one method of solving this conflict between ideological motive and discipline was to entrust certain judicial functions to "committee[s] chosen from the most meritorious revolutionaries." Nevertheless, such self-imposed discipline cannot tolerate any chinks in the ideological armor and cannot long survive any weakening or motive.

---

12 Paret, Peter and John Shy. (1962). "Guerrillas and Counter-guerrillas." *Guerrillas in the 1960s* (pp. 31–51). New York: Praeger.

If the guerrilla leader can negotiate the dilemmas presented by the need to be active without being defeated, by terrain and targets, and by desire and discipline, he faces a further dilemma in dealing with the civilian population. It may be taken for grated that in the underdeveloped countries of the world, large parts of the population are dissatisfied with their social and economic lot, but that is not the same thing as supporting guerrilla warfare. Generally, such support is won by political persuasion and maintained by military success. It may also be necessary to use coercion. The question then arises whether coercion will intimidate or alienate the civilian population.

Obviously it will do both; the crucial question is which will preponderate. Guevara is not altogether clear on this point, although he returns to it repeatedly. He admits that when early sympathizers with the guerillas begin to have second thoughts, "treason" must be "justly punished." Attacking guerrillas display "absolute implacability" toward "contemptible persons." And precisely in those areas where propaganda is most important, the "unfavorable terrain" of thickly settled farmland or suburbs, the guerrillas must eliminate "recalcitrant enemies . . . without leniency when they constitute a danger. . . . There can be no enemies in vital positions within the area of operation." On the other hand, he insists that terrorism "is a negative weapon which produces in no way the desired effects, which can turn a people against a given revolutionary movement, and which brings with it a loss of lives among those taking part that is much greater than the return." The rejection of terror is thus a practical, not a moral decision.

Terror, less violent forms of coercion, and even sabotage, if it destroys the livelihood of the poor, may backlash and repel rather than attract popular support. Clearly, these techniques must at times be employed by any guerrilla force, but the problems of when and how to use them, and how to keep them under control, are extremely difficult ones. Widespread use of terror worked rather well for the Greek Communist rebels in the late 1940's; nevertheless, it finally drove over a half-million of what should have been their strongest supporters into the cities and contributed to the eventual Communist defeat. Terror was effective in Cyprus against a British

government without sufficient political strength or will; it failed in Malaya against a British government determined and able to resist and to wait.

The last, and perhaps the gravest, dilemma confronting the guerrilla commander is that of pushing the war to a victorious conclusion. Guevara orthodoxly states that partisans must eventually regularize their operations if they are to win. Unconventional warfare becomes conventional as guerrillas grow stronger and their opponents weaker. Since the vicious but inept Batista regime made the problem almost academic for the Cuban revolutionaries, Guevara's general assertion of the problem is backed by little specific advice on how to achieve regularization. But if the incumbent power has military strength combined with the will and the intelligence to use it, then the guerrilla leader will have to recognize that irregular warfare alone will not succeed, but is simply the means of converting popular support into an army sufficient for the climactic military encounters.

The guerrilla leader's principal difficulty will then be to time the transition to regular forces and conventional tactics. Mao warns of guerrillaism, of overlong attachment to irregular organization and methods; regularization unduly delayed exhausts the popular base of the struggle. Historically, the opposite error seems more common, as guerrillas succumb to the lure of uniforms, of heavy weapons, of being able to sleep at night, and of conventional, orderly battle. Often a diplomatic factor is also at work, since foreign governments seem to see in the existence of a regular army a tangible guarantee of the movement's eventual success. The step of regularization may then be taken to help obtain diplomatic recognition, and thus achieve an important political goal. Taken prematurely, however, it grants a strong incumbent the opportunity that guerrilla tactics deny him: to hit an enemy that cannot melt away. Both the FLN, in Algeria, and the Vietminh appear to have committed this error, although they recovered from their defeats; the Greek Communists made the mistake and did not recover.[2]

One prerequisite of regularization is the establishment of territorial base areas. As Guevara points out, even in the early stages of guerrilla war such bases offer the considerable advantage of rest, training, supply, and medical care. But a base area provides the sort of fixed target that increases the danger of a crippling blow. Rough terrain is useful but cannot in itself make a base area inaccessible to a competent modern force. Mao describes the development of "flexible bases," but these would seem to require both an area of operations and a sophistication of civilian underground organization that must be considered exceptional. Guevara discusses the value of a "secure" base; how to render it secure against a strong opponent without resorting to disadvantageous positional warfare he does not make clear.

External sanctuaries, such as Tunisia has provided for the FLN, are a partial alternative to internal base areas. In fact, there is little historical evidence to support the proposition that without outside help, guerrillas can win against an incumbent who is politically and militarily strong, unless, that is, the incumbent decides the game is not worth the candle. To a large extent, as Guevara notes, guerrilla warfare can and must be self-sustaining: The people provide food and shelter; the enemy furnishes small arms and ammunition. Both Guevara and the FLN leadership have emphasized the logistical and even morale advantages that accrue if guerrillas use the weapons of the enemy rather than foreign calibers, which, incidentally, suggests one reason for the surprising coolness of the Algerian rebels toward Communist aid. But some foreign assistance appears to be crucial for eventual success, and in particular for the transition to regular operations. It may happen, however, that foreign aid dampens the emotions that provide the fuel for guerrilla warfare, and renders the ideological struggle more difficult. Inevitably there will be some conflict between the aims of indigenous guerrillas and their foreign benefactors and it would be unrealistic to assume that this conflict can be permanently ignored or concealed. If there is a racial difference as well, or if the guerrilla movement itself is a nationalistic insurrection, then friction between what have been called the internal and the external fronts may be a major obstacle to success. The incumbent power will always try to exploit the facts or legends of foreign support, and thus attack the very basis of the insurgents' motives.

In all these dilemmas, the guerrilla leader must display exceptional judgment. Too much boldness can be as fatal as too much caution. The distance between the two is less than in conventional warfare, and a shrewd opponent will act so as to make it narrower still. There are many ways for the guerrilla leader to be wrong, but only one way for him to be right.

What Cyprus and Cuba were in miniature, the seven-year-long war in Algeria has been on a larger and bloodier scale. The military effort of the Algerian nationalists has consisted of guerrilla operations, backed by a small force of regulars, and of terror. Terror is employed both against the French and as a means of keeping their own adherents in line. Foreign support provides equipment, diplomatic assistance, and bases for organizing and training. The whole makes up a perfect example of what the French have come to call "revolutionary" or "subversive" warfare.

In the doctrine of *guerre révolutionnaire,* certain groups in the French army have attempted to collect and synthesize the whole range of modern unconventional warfare. Briefly, the basic characteristics of the doctrine have been expressed by them in an equation: *guerrilla warfare + psychological warfare = revolutionary warfare.* The terms should of course be taken in their broadest sense. "Guerrilla warfare" emphasizes the importance of actions by individuals and small groups— sabotage, terror, ambushes and raids—without denigrating the use of large formations. "Psychological warfare" defines all violent and nonviolent measures undertaken *primarily* to influence the opponent rather than to annihilate him. This may mean anything from a local rumor to clandestine indoctrination of civilians and full-scale diplomatic action. The doctrine's salient point is the complete interdependence between violence and nonviolence, not alone in the methods used but also in the targets chosen. "Revolutionary warfare" postulates insurgents who will direct their efforts at least as much at the inhabitants of the territory whose control is at stake as against the armed forces of the incumbent.[3]

Against such an opponent, conventional military methods are obviously insufficient. The French theorists have grasped the operational significance of the political factor, and have attempted to integrate it into their own weapons systems, in the form of psychological warfare, re-education, indoctrination of their own cadres, and shaping of government policy. But they have not been able to formulate a political alternative that would appeal as strongly to the Algerians as it did to themselves, and in the process they have gone far toward disrupting the army and the nation. Their example of copying the enemy's methods too closely is one for U.S. military forces to avoid.

THE TASKS OF COUNTERGUERRILLA ACTION

What are the conditions for successful counterguerrilla action? Combating guerrillas is both a military and a political problem. Much depends on the stage of development of the guerrillas. Different tactics must be used against them depending on whether they are well established, closely identified with the population, or just beginning the process of indoctrination and organization. But in no case will military or political measures by themselves solve the problem.

Counterguerrilla action may be separated into three major tasks. Generally, these must be pursued simultaneously since success in one area depends on progress in the others. In a very real sense, it is only for purposes of analysis that they can be discussed separately. The tasks are:

1. The military defeat of the guerrilla forces.
2. The separation of the guerrilla from the population.
3. The re-establishment of governmental authority and the development of a viable social order.

It is erroneous to think that military defeat pure and simple will be a final solution. Unless the population has been weaned away from the guerrilla and his cause, unless reforms and re-education have attacked the psychological base of guerrilla action, unless the political network backing him up has been destroyed, military defeat is only a pause and fighting can easily erupt again.

The worst military mistake in fighting guerrillas is to treat them as if they were conventional opponents. In the long run, the ability to control certain pieces of ground, or to mount periodic expeditions into and out of a particular area, means little in this sort of warfare. Instead, the security of one's own base and rear is essential;

the strategic offensive must be deliberately cautious and carefully coordinated, although tactical movement can be rapid, even daring. The French during much of the Indochinese war seem to have reversed these principles; strategically audacious, their tactics were marked by road-bound movements and hedgehog defense. On more than one occasion, they struck deep into the Vietminh base area without previously or even simultaneously taking elementary precautions to protect their own lines of communication and supply.

All successful counterguerrilla operations—in Greece, South Korea, the Philippines, and Malaya—have combined mobile striking forces with close territorial control. Territorial control has always been achieved by dividing the combat zone into areas and assigning to each more or less stationary units that act as both defenders and police. The striking forces, on the other hand, are more centrally located and directed, and must have maximum mobility.

There has been some confusion over the types of forces involved in counterguerrilla action and their respective roles. The territorial units are regulars, reservists, militia, or augmented police. The mobile striking forces require the very best regulars, organized and trained to fight unorthodoxly but exploiting all their inherent advantages. It is dangerous to rely too heavily on the technological means available to modern regular troops, but the imaginative combination of these means with unconventional tactics may very well be decisive. The mobile striking forces thus cannot consist of hastily recruited and trained progovernment civilians; on the contrary, they must be tough, disciplined, and thoroughly professional.

Just how professional forces may learn and employ irregular tactics is not so easily answered, and a solution may be more difficult than most soldiers realize; certainly the roots of the problem go deeper than their own alleged conservatism when face to face with a new situation. There are crucial differences between tactical operations against a conventional opponent and those against guerrillas; against the latter, for instance, physical destruction of the enemy becomes relatively more important, control of key terrain less. Not only must doctrine, training, and organization shift when dealing with a different kind of opponent, but effective counter-guerrilla tactics seem to require a different combat style, perhaps the harder to achieve because style is so much a matter of attitude and is usually taken for granted. Here it may be noted that the FLN claims that the previous regular experience of many of their fighters has often proved a disadvantage in irregular combat, while one British battalion commander in Malaya found recent conscripts better suited to certain unorthodox tasks than long-service regulars.[4] At the same time, it is most unlikely that military amateurism in itself can ever be a virtue.

In an important sense, guerrillas fight in a natural manner, their organization and tactics reflecting the popular, extralegal base from which they operate. Regular troops, on the other hand, even when employing irregular tactics, operate from a governmental, legal base, and appear to suffer from attitudinal and structural inhibitions that must first be recognized if they are to be overcome.[5] A simple diagram may clarify this point, which is too often insufficiently appreciated:

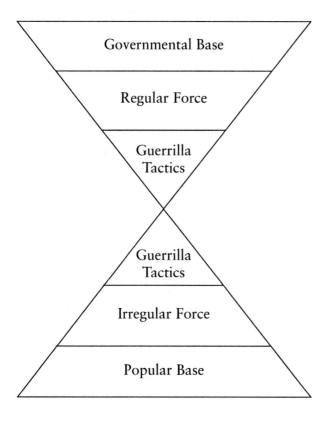

Although there may be a limited role for counter-guerrilla guerrillas, the great weakness of the mobile striking forces—imperfect tactical intelligence—is better corrected by the creation of local militia. But neither pro-government guerrillas nor militia can be effective without firm popular support.[6] And this leads to the second concern of counterguerrilla forces: Good troops employing proper tactics cannot make up for an unsound governmental and political base. The sound antipartisan tactical doctrine conceived and employed by the Germans in Russia and Yugoslavia could not compensate for a criminal political and administrative policy.

How deny the guerrilla his popular base? He must lose his hold over the people, and be isolated from them. Various techniques are available, and probably all of them would have to be used against a strong guerrilla movement.

Military defeat of the guerrilla forces, widely and persuasively publicized, is among the strongest ways of convincing people that support of the guerrillas is unwise. But such defeat is unlikely in the early stages of the conflict. A more comprehensive psychological warfare program is an obvious necessity. The program, however, must be sophisticated—as such programs have seldom been—since it must operate on the premise that the target of the program probably has more accurate information concerning the guerrillas than does the government.

To make untrue or distorted assertions to the people can be fatal. Indeed, it might be better to think of the program as public information rather than psychological warfare, because its second requirement is not to confuse people who are potentially sympathetic to the guerrillas with the guerrillas themselves (who should be attacked in a separate, tailor-made program). As Lucian Pye pointed out in his study of guerrilla Communism in Malaya, the temptation to treat *all* Malayan Chinese as potential guerrillas or Communists was very great.[7] To have succumbed to it, however, would have meant establishing the very link the government had to break. Finally, public information will have little permanent effect, without a long-term program of education or re-education, but this is more properly a part of the government's third task.

A standard technique in denying the guerrilla his popular base is the resettlement of populations. Resettlement has been successful with the Chinese squatters in Malaya, and partially so with the Arabs in Algeria and the Boers in South Africa. But when calculating the military advantages of resettlement and planning the details of the program, full weight must be given to its political, economic, and social effects.[8]

Rarely can guerrillas be isolated from the people without the use of unusually harsh coercive measures. Nevertheless, counterguerrillas must comprehend that their mission is essentially conservative, while that of the guerrillas is destructive. Unless harsh measures are employed rationally and with the clear understanding by all that they are emergency measures, to be stopped as soon as possible, they may actually break down the sense of security with which the legitimacy of any nontotalitarian government is inextricably linked.

The conduct of troops and police in the field can easily undo governmental propaganda or policy, however wise in conception these may be. To cite two cases among many, police brutality—tardily stopped—in South Korea and the Philippines was of considerable benefit to the Communists.[9] The history of the Indochinese war is replete with incidents that show not French ruthlessness, but rather the failure of French leaders to make a determined effort to curb the usual roughness with which troops on active duty treat sullen, uncommunicative civilians—and, at times, innocent bystanders. A cargo plane receives antiaircraft fire; in consequence, two fighters napalm a nearby village, not knowing whether the village is pro-Communist or not. Infantrymen, after a sweltering all-day crawl in the mud, spring a trap on a suspected village but find no guerrillas; they shoot down an unarmed young man who acts suspiciously, and compensate themselves for their trouble by liberating any poultry within reach. Legionnaires decide to flatten three "sassy" villages by calling for an air strike on them."[10]

Such conduct is understandable, and to prevent it requires unusual self-restraint as well as discipline, which in turn will be possible only when commanders themselves are convinced that fair dealing with the population is as much a part of

effective military action as aggressive patrolling. Correct treatment of civilians who seem to have done nothing to merit it is perhaps no more unnatural than combat itself, and it needs to be incorporated into the framework of military thought. Results in the field may not be immediately apparent, but without such behavior, there is little hope of redressing, in Guevara's words, "the notable difference that exists between the information which the rebel forces possess and the information which the enemies possess."

Even under the most extreme provocation, the same principle applies. The pressure to meet terror with counterterror will at times seem irresistible, but to do so is to play the guerrilla's game without his particular advantages. Brutality, fear, and the resultant social disorganization can work only for the guerrillas, no matter who initiates them. By forcing the legitimate power to adopt their own methods, the guerrillas gain a vital point. All government is based on the discriminating application of power; its indiscriminate use over extended periods implies a surrender both of policy and of ethics, and releases the kind of internal conflict that frequently destroys the capacity of a political and social organism to defend itself.

The ultimate technique in isolating guerrillas from the people is to persuade the people to defend themselves. Militia-type local defense units help in the military defeat of the guerrillas. They may gradually replace the garrison forces, freeing regulars for mobile operations. They protect their communities, ambush raiders, and furnish intelligence and security to mobile forces in the vicinity. But at least as important is their political function: Once a substantial number of members of a community commit violence on behalf of the government, they have gone far to break permanently the tie between that community and the guerrillas.

The third and final task of counterguerrilla action is the re-establishment of authority and the creation of a more stable society. The obvious first step is a program to allay the grievances that originally permitted the outbreak of violence. But, again drawing on Pye's study of Malaya, reform is not as easy as it may seem. By itself, economic aid is not enough. Reform must have at least two aspects if it is to be effective.

First, the administration of reform must be reasonably honest; not only must it not be compromised by corruption, but it must not seem to be simply responding to the program of the guerrillas. Economic and social problems must be attacked on their own merits, and not as if the government were itself a political party. Ramón Magsaysay, who defeated the Huk rebellion, demonstrated that the link between guerrilla warfare and social reform was as much one of credibility as of action.

Second, and even more difficult, is the fostering of political activity, including political groups critical of government policy. Despite certain obvious disadvantages, legal political activity provides a third choice for discontented persons otherwise forced to choose between supporting the government or the guerrillas. It also keeps the government in touch with the sources of discontent.

In re-establishing their authority, can governments hope to substitute a counterideology for any ideology the guerrilla movement may have? The answer is probably no. The current assumption that the popular mind, especially in illiterate, unsophisticated societies, can be manipulated at will is false. Unlike machine-gun bolts, ideologies are not easily interchangeable. The French tried it with little success in Algeria; nationalism was too strong for them. Communism takes hold because it exploits real aspirations and convictions, not through any magic power. And the exploitation is a long-term process. Non-Communist governments should recognize that developing a counterideology is also a long-term process, and that probably the best they can hope for in fighting guerrillas is to neutralize their ideological appeal by undercutting it rather than by complete substitution.[11]

Thus the tasks of counterguerrilla warfare are as much political as military—or even more so; the two continually interact. As with the guerrillas themselves, political considerations may often have to override military considerations if permanent success is to be achieved. Tactical victories are of little value if they compromise the strategic objective. Because the true objective of guerrilla warfare is control of the people, this is one type of war in which friend-or-foe thinking is inapplicable. The greatest danger for the counterguerrilla is to succumb to the lure of a shallow opportunism: To employ the troops of a politically discredited faction or of an unpopular foreign power simply because they are available is to sacrifice ultimate prospects for immediate convenience. The hard way is often the best way.

NOTES

1. Our quotations are from a translation prepared for the Department of the Army and from *Che Guevara on Guerrilla Warfare* (New York, 1961). Condensed translations previously published have important omissions.
2. Colonel T. Papathanasiades, "The Bandits' Last Stand in Greece," *Military Review*, XXX (February, 1951), 24–26.
3. See Peter Paret, "The French Army and la Guerre Révolutionnaire," *Journal of the Royal United Service Institution*, CIV (February, 1959), 59–69; reprinted in *Survival*, I (March–April, 1959), 25–32.
4. Chanderli, interview March 2 and 3, 1961.
5. Stanislaw Andrzejewski touches on these problems in *Military Organization and* Society (London, 1954).
6. Examples for this abound. To cite only one instance: On one of the few occasions when French counterguerrilla guerrillas in Indochina enjoyed some success against the Vietminh forces, a Communist political commissar reported: "The reason for the great extension of the [pro-French] rebel movement and why it succeeds in holding out against us stems from the fact that we are not supported by public opinion." Quoted in Bernard Fall, *Street Without Joy* (Harrisburg, Pa., 1961). 247.
7. *Guerrilla Communism in Malaya: Its Social and Political Meaning* (Princeton, N.J., 1956). See also his "Lessons from the Malayan Struggle Against Communism" and "The Policy Implications of Social Change in Non-Western Societies" (Communist Bloc Program Parts 17 and 18 [mimeographed], Center for International Studies, Massachusetts Institute of Technology [1957]).
8. For an account of the mishandling of resettlement in South Vietnam, see Stanley Karnow, "Diem Defeats His Own Best Troops," *The Reporter*, January 19, 1961, p. 26.
9. Lieutenant Colonel John E. Beebe, "Beating the Guerrillas in South Korea," *Military Review*, XXXV (December, 1955), 16; Major K. M.

Hammer, "Huks in the Philippines," *ibid.,* XXXVI (April, 1956), 50–54; Brian Crozier, *The Rebels* (Boston, 1960), p. 217.

10. Fall, *op. cit.,* pp. 105, 108, 254–55.

11. In its efforts to present the Moslems with an acceptable political alternative to independence, the French army has generally overemphasized the role of effective techniques, while the actual content of the proposals has seemed of secondary importance. See Peter Paret, "A Total Weapon of Limited War," *Journal of the Royal United Service Institution,* CV (February, 1960), 67.

Guerrillas in History

Lewis H. Gann

THE PLACE OF PARTISAN WARFARE IN HISTORY

Can anything by learned from this array of revolutionary wars and guerrilla actions? At first sight all these operations seem to have nothing in common. The art of small wars is as old as the history of warfare itself. The technique of partisan warfare cannot be labeled either reactionary or progressive. It is based essentially on the precepts of common sense, and requires no particular mystique for its elucidation. Revolutionary struggles had been waged untold centuries before Mao Tse-tung and other modern practitioners of this form of combat. "Bourgeois" nationalists, revolutionary socialists, clerically-minded peasants, and secular-minded peasants have all, at some time or another, excelled in the guerrilla's craft. Some revolutionaries have sought to put their trust in a "future-directed" program; others have tried to restore the past. Some, like the FLN and the Mau Mau, have used terror and torture as a matter of policy; others, like the Irgun Zvai Leumi, have been relatively restrained in their methods. Swamps, jungles, and inaccessible mountain country have traditionally provided the guerrillas' most favorable habitat; yet gangs have also operated successfully in cities.

Methods of suppressing partisans have also varied in the extreme. The Chinese in Tibet and the Russians in Hungary won by massive terror; yet frightfulness failed to yield results when employed by the Germans against Russian and Yugoslav partisans. The more diplomatic methods used by the British, restrained as they were in most instances by a humanitarian tradition, by Parliamentary inquiries and debates, by newspaper publicity, and generally by the continued operation of civilian courts, have also known their victories and defeats. In Malaya the British introduced social and political reforms to gain the support of the people. Yet in Cyprus the British came very near to victory without having converted the Greek-speaking Cypriots to their cause. The success won by revolutionary guerrilla campaigns in the postwar period can in fact easily be overestimated. Victories in China, in North Vietnam, and in Cuba, for instance, are balanced by an impressive list of failures in Malaya and the Philippines, in Kenya and in Angola (where the Portuguese have to operate against guerrillas operating from "privileged sanctuaries abroad"). In Algeria the French finally withdrew for political and financial reasons, but they had not in any sense suffered a military defeat.

Yet historians can arrive at a few tentative generalizations. From the technical point of view, partisan operations on their own remain subject to severe limitations. They tend to be at their most effective when carried out in direct concert

13 Gann, Lewis. (1971). "The Place of Partisan Warfare in History." *Guerrillas in History* (pp. 78–93). Stanford: Hoover Institution Press.

with regular forces, as, for instance, during the Peninsular War. For all the glamour with which partisan warfare has been endowed by rhetoricians, it always exacts a grim price from all the combatants, especially from the side that resists the invader. During the eighteenth century Spain and its Latin American colonies alike had steadily increased in wealth and prosperity. The partisan campaign against Napoleon had a disastrous effect on the economy of the Iberian Peninsula. The long-drawn-out war of independence waged by the Spanish American colonies against the motherland, a conflict set off in the first instance by Napoleon's invasion of Spain, set back the progress of Latin America for untold decades. The cost of partisan warfare moreover cannot be assessed merely in terms of limbs shattered and lives lost. From the standpoint of a statistician, a guerrilla operation may be much less destructive than an air raid or a rocket attack. But its moral and psychological effect are likely to be greater. An air raid has an impersonal quality about it. Sirens wail; planes drone overhead; searchlights pierce the sky; flak thunders; bombs whistle; walls shake; houses collapse. But no one knows the name of the pilot who drops the blockbusters. An air raid in some ways appears like a catastrophe of nature. Guerrilla warfare, on the other hand, entails personal violence. Partisan operations usually entail reprisals; reprisals lead to counterreprisals. Terror becomes commonplace until it takes a Goya to paint *Los Desastres de la Guerra*. Guerrilla warfare thus leaves a heritage of hate that may endure for generations, and may continue when the memories of conventional war have grown dim.

As regards the more technical side of guerrilla warfare, historians can likewise discern certain regular patterns. Partisans require a geological base. This is best established in regions with a difficult terrain, in rugged mountain country, in swamp and jungle land. But guerrillas also need a social environment conducive to unrest. Guerrillas are likely to make most progress in countries where the administration is weak, or where there has been a breakdown, or at any rate a partial breakdown, of the machinery for law enforcement. Such a collapse may come about in various ways. Foreign invasion may destroy the existing state machinery. The police forces may become subverted by infiltration. They may be

weakened by the rulers' unwillingness to make adequate use of the coercive machinery at their disposal. Such unwillingness, whether derived from fear or from legal formalism, is liable to sap morale of the police, and provide a moral dividend to the revolutionary. As Aristotle wrote more than two thousand years ago:

> In all well-attempted governments there is nothing which should be more jealously maintained than the spirit of obedience to law, more especially in small matters; for transgression creeps in unperceived and at last ruins the state, just as the constant recurrence of small expenses in time eats up a fortune. The expense does not take place all at once, and therefore is not observed; the mind is deceived, as in the fallacy which says that "if each part is little, then the whole is little." And this is true in one way, but not in another, for the whole and the all are not little, although they are made up of littles.[53]

Guerrilla movements can derive valuable support from sympathizers in cities. But urban risings such as those staged by the Paris Communards in 1871, by the white workers of Johannesburg in 1922, or by the Viennese Social Democrats in 1934, can never succeed without support in the country at large. Neither can urban warfare of the gangster variety destroy a state unless the rebels have the mass of the population behind them, and unless they can rely on at least the passive support of the regular armed forces.

Many political theoreticians have come to disagree with this assessment, and urban guerrilla warfare is being widely praised as a new form of insurrectionary action. Urban guerrilla warfare, in present-day revolutionary terminology, comprises many different activities, ranging from mass demonstrations to sabotage and political assassinations. Many advocates of urban guerrilla warfare moreover put special trust in an armed alliance between marginal intellectuals and marginal men of the slums. They overlook, however, the extreme difficulties of enforcing discipline among two groups which, by their very nature, resist disciplines in its various forms. During the Spanish Civil War volunteers from many parts of Europe and America joined the International Brigades. These became élite units, capable of tackling the most difficult military tasks and willing to sustain terrific casualty rates without flinching. The radical movements that developed in Europe and in the United States during the late 1960s did not succeed in creating comparable bodies. Western European or American students may condemn Ian Smith and his fellow-fascists. But they do not travel to Southern Africa to fight against the Rhodesian Light Infantry in the bush. The failure of the new radicalism to create the counterpart of the Lincoln Brigade or the Attlee Brigade is by no means fortuitous. Military organization requires planning, discipline, and respect for leadership. These do not go well with a cult of Bohemian libertinage, romantic rhetoric, or a publicity-conscious cult of self-fulfillment.

Urban guerrillas have other problems of a more practical kind. What is possibly an overcautious assessment derives from Che Guevara, who considered that guerrillas in built-up areas should always act under the direct command of superiors outside the city. Town-bred partisan bands should be small; they should not act independently, but should merely carry out their allotted share in a wider strategic plan.

This is important because the suburban guerrilla is working in an exceptionally unfavorable terrain, where the risks and consequences of exposure are tremendous. There is only little distance between the guerrilla's point of action and his refuge, so night action must predominate. He does not emerge into the open until the insurgents besiege the city.[54]

Guevara is essentially correct, even though he perhaps underestimates the military potential of modern megalopolis. The rise of great conurbations, the development of an affluent working class and of a relatively well-to-do intelligentsia able to buy motor cars, trucks, and walkie-talkie sets has made the terrorist's task easier in certain respects. A modern industrial city contains large numbers of technicians and do-it-yourself amateurs, who can serve complicated weapons, repair radios, and even produce home-made automatic guns and similar implements of war. Gasoline is cheap and easily available; so are a great variety of chemicals. Modern means of communication make the mobilization of huge crowds for the purpose of demonstration a simple matter. The television camera and other means of publicity drawn from the armory of entertainers, advertisers, and clerics facilitate the task of making propaganda. The old-fashioned European city rebel of the past thought like an infantryman and fought like an infantryman. The modern urban guerrilla may, however, take a leaf from the book of the gangster. The modern bandit has adapted himself to an age of motorization. He can escape swiftly in his automobile. He has an extensive amount of space in which he can operate. His activities are harder to check in many ways than those of the criminal living in the pre-automobile age because the policeman in a car does not know his beat as well as his colleague on foot. Urban guerrilla warfare still looks for its Guderian, who will mechanize big-city partisan warfare by the use of motorized demolition squads and assault units concealed in delivery vans, repair trucks, and similar vehicles that can merge into ordinary traffic at night.

Modern cities depend on certain essential services such as water and electricity supplies. A well-trained, well-disciplined guerrilla unit might conceivably reduce a city to temporary havoc by striking at the right time in the right places. In communities like Singapore and Hong Kong, where the population is confined largely within the boundaries of a single city, sabotage linked to civil disobedience might be extremely effective. It is therefore essential for communities threatened with urban guerrilla warfare to protect workers in essential services and their families, and to plan relief measures before a community has actually been assaulted.

Urban guerrilla warfare is nevertheless subject to severe limitations. In large countries with extensive industrial resources, the economic and political effects of disorganizing a city quarter or even a whole city will not be permanent. Stricken areas can quickly be helped by areas that have remained unscathed. Attacks on essential services or on enterprises that provide people with their livelihood alienate the mass of the population. Hence the guerrillas soon face betrayal and liquidation. Townsmen moreover are a hardy breed no matter what their nationality. In countries as far afield as Great Britain and Poland, Germany and Japan, even the most heavily bombed towns showed the most amazing resilience during the Second World War. The authorities always managed to restore essential services with surprising speed after the most devastating air raids.

A "first-strike" capacity is not therefore sufficient. The urban guerrilla must follow up his initial successes by further action in order to keep his quarry off-balance. At this point he will meet his greatest difficulty. Even determined and ruthless urban guerrillas, such as the OAS (*Organisation de l'Armée Secrète*), the armed underground force of the French settlers in Algeria, never succeeded in forcing its will upon the country despite the fact that the OAS had come support from the French army, at least at certain times and in certain places. The settlers were mainly an urban group, who numbered only some ten percent of Algeria's population. They had no support among the mass of Muslims. The OAS had little power outside the towns. The OAS could control the bulk of Europeans, but the settlers' underground army could not intimidate the country at large. The Muslim insurgents who battled against French suzerainty met with similar difficulties in the towns. The Algerian Arab quarters, with their attics and back alleys, provided excellent hiding places for urban guerrillas. Yet General Massu did gain almost complete success in clearing Algiers, even though the Algerians were as tough and ruthless as any guerrillas who ever handled a gun.

Terror, in other words, proved no substitute for victory. Back-alley killing may depress morale and weaken the waverers for a time. But terror must be transmuted into political power. As long as the people remain convinced that the government will win in the end, violence of the gangster type is apt to yield diminishing returns. Most men are optimists at heart. They believe that misfortune will strike someone else. Englishmen and Germans during World War II became accustomed to adapting their lives to air raids. Nowadays people accept traffic accidents as an inconvenience or as a misfortune, but certainly not as an unacceptable risk.

The use of bandit-like methods moreover can never endow its practitioners with the glamour that may be acquired in large-scale urban risings where the rebel banner waves over the barricades to inspire doubters and followers alike. Terrorists can, at best, levy illegal taxes by means of persuasion or political rackets. They may even succeed to some extent in setting up an armed lobby which for a time extorts concessions from a weak opponent. But sooner or later the terrorists must broaden the base of their support, must merge their struggle into a wider rising, or must pay the price for their miscalculations. Helicopters confer a tremendous advantage to the incumbent power in urban as well as in rural guerrilla fighting. Isolated quarters occupied by rebel forces can easily be deprived of water, electricity, and other essential services. They are liable to be surrounded, searched, and cleaned up piecemeal.

The successful guerrilla must be resigned to waging a long drawn-out war. In such a protracted struggle, much will depend on the combatants' will to win and on their ability to present a united front to the outside world. Western democratic countries intent on the suppression of a revolutionary campaign are subject to the contradictory pressures exercised by public opinion. Hence they have to be concerned over the peace-singer with her guitar as well as over the guerrilla with his Tommy gun. Partisans and counterpartisans alike must thus build up mass organizations to back their respective causes. Here, too, success breeds success. The people at large are swayed by the likelihood of victory as much as by hopes for a better world. Small determined groups of fighters may be willing to throw away their lives in a magnificent gesture that aims glory rather than victory. The great majority of men, however, are more prosaic in their calculations. Hence the Germans, for instance, had relatively little trouble with underground movements after their first great victories in 1940. Underground warfare only became serious when the *Endsieg* no longer seemed assured. Similarly, the revolt in Algeria began only after the French had given up in Indochina, and the uprising in Hungary followed the withdrawal of Soviet troops from neighboring Austria. For the same reason, successful anti-communist outbreaks are not to be expected in Eastern Europe at the present moment. The position might, however, well change if the Russian regime should weaken from within or become involved in a war against China.

Above all counterguerrilla forces must convince their opponents that resistance is hopeless, that the guerrilla leadership is selfish, incompetent, corrupt, and divided, that surrender will bring neither dishonor, torture, nor death, and that capitulation is the only rational policy. This task is essential in the battle for the minds of the civilian population. The government forces should, at the same time, attempt to sow dissension among the enemy and should not disdain bribery where necessary. In the War of the Spanish Succession the merciless terror let loose upon the rebellious Camisards was of little avail to the king. The royalists made headway, however, when they began to use more politic methods. Jean Cavalier, the Camisards' most audacious leader, was won over by personal concessions and ended his career, by a strange combination of circumstances, as George II's Governor of Jersey and a British major-general.

Guerrillas and counterguerrillas alike, resembling hostile brothers, must be masters in the art of organizational infiltration. They must be trained to fight in the style of city gangsters, as mobile military units, as demolition squads, and as "pseudo gangs" in the countryside. Planned assassinations of key administrators and "prophylactic executions" of possible opponents now represent an important element of Viet Cong guerrilla strategy in Vietnam. This mode of warfare is not, of course, a communist invention. The *sicarius*, the Jewish Zealot who resorted to street-corner knifings to expel the Romans from Judea, was already a well-known problem to the occupation authorities who served the Caesars in the Holy Land. In the twentieth century, such killings have become a characteristic form of totalitarian warfare, of both the Nazi and the communist variety. The Chinese communists and their pupils have used all these techniques, and have incorporated them as an essential component of their guerrilla strategy. Planned murders, including preemptive liquidations, serve the three-fold purpose of removing potential leaders of the opposition, disrupting the enemy administration, and terrorizing the waverers. As the Viet Cong have shown, prophylactic assassination is a formidable weapon in the insurrectionary's armory.

The employment of terror against large numbers of medium-rank functionaries moreover seems to pay bigger dividends than assaults a few highly placed men in the governmental hierarchy of the kind carried out by nineteenth-century anarchists. Nevertheless, terror has serious limitations. It may easily alienate public opinion. And, historically speaking, a strategy of assassination has never been successful on its own. Proponents of physical force among adherents of the "People's Will" group performed prodigious feats of ingenuity and courage in attacking high dignitaries of the tsarist regime. Yet these terrorists never managed to reach the Russian masses or to destroy the Russian monarchy. Subversion of the elitist kind reached even higher perfection among the Oriental sect known as Assassins which flourished many centuries earlier. The Assassins achieved an incredible degree of discipline and self-sacrifice among their adherents. Operating from well-secured bases, they carried out political murders with an astonishing degree or precision. Yet, lacking great armies or extensive guerrilla forces, they could effect nothing of permanent value.[55]

Guerrillas, like counterguerrillas, are lost, however, if they do not also have a constructive civilian program. The most effective partisans will look to the pursuits of peace as well as to those of war. They will act in the spirit of the ancient Jews mentioned in the book of Nehemiah, who rebuilt the walls of Jerusalem in the teeth of the enemy while, according to their leader, "half of my servants wrought in the work, and the other half held both the spears, the shields, and the bows and the habergeons."[56] Guerrillas and government forces alike need an effective civilian program. But the best programs are worthless, unless they can be effectively administered, and unless the administration is efficiently run. Guerrillas and counterguerrillas alike must therefore heed the lessons taught by colonial conqueror, such as Gallieni, that victory on the battlefield is useless without thoroughgoing governance of the civilian population. Effective administration, properly coordinated with military action, is indeed an essential condition of victory. The Viet Minh as well as the FLN displayed a sound understanding of this principle. So did the Irish, who built up an effective system of law courts while at the same time gunning down policemen of the Royal Irish Constabulary. No incumbent authority can win a guerrilla war, if it cannot provide effective protection to its subjects. Similarly, no guerrilla leader can effect a revolution if he cannot also govern, or if he remains a prisoner to the mindless revolutionary militarism that insists on the principle of "bomb now – rule later."

Sound government helps to win mass support. Mass support is vital; yet masses on their own can never win. Spontaneous risings like those which broke out against the communist régime in Eastern Germany stand little chance of success. Guerrillas require cadres. Even in the actual conduct of operations, quality counts for more than quantity; surprise and strategems may help to neutralize superior numbers. Modern guerrilla leaders in this respect can still learn from the military lessons embodied in the Old testament. When Gideon, an outstanding Hebrew military chief, was preparing for battle against the Midianites, the Lord said to Gideon, "Now therefore go to, proclaim in the ears of the people, saying, Whosoever is fearful and afraid, let him return and depart early from Mount Gilead. And there returned of the people twenty and two thousand; and there remained ten thousand." From these Gideon, by a curious method of personnel selection, picked out three hundred chosen warriors. Gideon then "divided the three hundred men into three companies, and he put a trumpet into every man's hand, with empty pitchers, and lamps within the pitchers." The three commando companies then delivered a surprise attack on the enemy camp at night. "And the three companies blew the trumpets, and brake the pitchers, and held the lamps in their left hands and the trumpets in their right hands to blow withal: and they cried, The sword of the Lord and of Gideon. And they stood every man in his place round about the camp: and all the host ran, and cried and fled. And the three hundred blew the trumpets, and the Lord set every man's sword against his fellow, even throughout all the host: and the host fled to Beth-shittah in Zererath, and to the border of Abdel-meholah, unto Tabbath."[57]

The use of unconventional methods and of surprise may be applied on the psychological as well as on the tactical level. Guerrillas and counterguerrillas alike require a knowledge of the background and culture of the enemy in order to understand his thinking.

Guerrilla and counterguerrilla warfare alike can benefit, therefore, not merely from a mass basis but also from trained élite formations. Both partisan and anti-partisan warfare have become a highly specialized art. Military planners would thus do well to prepare "small wars" in advance. There is much to be said for developing unconventional forces as a permanent part of the existing armed forces. For guerrilla wars to some extent represent a regression to "limited" warfare. They also enable weaker powers to harry stronger states. The Egyptians thus were able to force the British out of the Suez Canal Zone. Yet the conflict over the evacuation of the Canal Zone might well have taken a different turn if the British had been able to rely on professional guerrilla units, operating in civilian clothes and capable of striking both within and outside the Canal Zone. In addition, however, guerrillas may have their part to play in conventional and even in nuclear warfare, for if atomic weapons are ever used on the battlefield, the enemy's rear may conceivably be the safest place for the defender's own forces.

At the same time, special emphasis must be given to the question of supply. Guerrillas depend on their ability to live off the land. They cannot afford big supply trains. They must be inured to austerity. If guerrillas learn this lesson, they will enjoy tremendous advantages over heavy, ponderous armies, slowed down by big administrative "tails." Yet partisans also require ammunition, food, and water. Though guerrillas may be disciplined into making do with simple food, their physiological needs are roughly the same as those of conventional soldiers. The image of the Asian guerrilla able to subsist forever on a handful of rice and a sip of water is as much of a mythological figure as the Indian trader who—in the imagination of many a white settler in Africa—can live "on the smell of an oil rag." Guerrillas can usually obtain food and clothing in their operational areas. But areas, ammunition, communication equipment, and medical supplies must either be captured or supplied by an outside power through underground channels.

The suppression of guerrillas thus depends to a very considerable extent on the ability of the occupying power to prevent supplies from falling into guerrilla hands. In Soviet-occupied Europe a centralized state machinery controls supplies effectively, and can therefore stifle guerrilla movements in disaffected areas. (In Malaya the British solved their problem by resettling villages in centralized locations that could be effectively protected. The British also instituted a stringent system of food rationing, and sometimes even central kitchens, thereby starving out the guerrillas.) This type of civilian support forms an essential complement to anti-partisan strategy. Counterguerrilla forces moreover must improve their own efficiency by adjusting their equipment to the areas of operation and by using helicopters for logistic as well as tactical purposes. The helicopter, in fact, promises to be the anti-guerrillas' maid-of-all-work. Unfortunately there are never enough of these air-borne trucks and gunboats.

Military action, however, should never be pursued for its own sake. Counterguerrilla warfare, like conventional wars, is politics by other means. Armed action must therefore correspond to its political objectives. "Butcher and bolt" actions are useless unless victories are consolidated by maneuvers designed to "clear and hold." The "clear and hold" strategy in turn must influence the way in which the enemy is assaulted on the battlefield. There is no point in attacks that inflict huge losses on the civilian population. Intelligence, preferably gathered by local agents, is worth more than the best equipment. Firepower can never be a substitute for brains. The most brilliant victories on the battlefield will avail little in the long run unless the enemy's underground political organization can be destroyed. The political cadres must be captured or killed; otherwise the enemy's armed formations can always return in good time. On its own, the strategy of "search and destroy" is likely to be as inadequate as eighteenth-century British tactics of riot control, which entailed waiting for an outbreak, calling out the Guards, firing into the mob, and marching the troops back to barracks until the next outbreak. As we have previously seen, the old police tactics of repression gave place in nineteenth-century England to the strategy of prevention. This in turn depended on the constable's doing his beat. Anti-guerrilla strategy likewise requires adequate prevention, which in turn hinges on the quality of the political and administrative personnel in the field.

Once an area has been cleared, civilian administrators must therefore immediately step in with resettlement and food supply programs, with publicity and—where necessary—with agricultural reform. The authorities must build up administrative cadres that are in touch with the people and that can gather intelligence, in order that military measures and civilian programs may complement one another. (In Malaya, for instance, British officials encouraged the supplying of information by promising complete anonymity for the informer. Ordinary people could mail unsigned letters about communist troop movements. Before sending off their letters, informers would tear off a strip at the edge. At the end of the emergency, they could claim the reward offered for the information by matching their strip of paper against the document dispatched to the administration.) Information need not be extorted; information—like most other things—can be bought, provided always that the population is convinced that the war is going against the guerrillas and that governmental promises will be honored.

All these measures take time, and counterguerrilla operations are therefore an extraordinarily expensive kind of warfare for the suppressing forces. Partisans can choose the time and place of their attacks, while government forces have to defend the civilian population and also must wage war against the enemy. Over and over again, partisans have been able to pin down troops ten or twenty times their own strength. Providing that adequate forces are committed from the beginning, victory over a guerrilla force need not necessarily be too costly in terms of casualties. But with a policy of too-little-and-too-late or even barely-enough, such operations can exhaust the regular forces. The French never sent conscripts to Indochina, and by 1954 they were losing each year the equivalent of half the graduating class at St. Cyr, the French West point. Similarly, the United States Regular Army in the thirty years following the Civil War lost a considerable portion of its strength in Indian wars. Guerrilla warfare can thus be extremely effective. Partisan operations have therefore captured the imagination of many nonmilitary intellectuals and have acquired an aura of invincibility.

Yet, when all is said and done, "small wars" remain the weapon of the weak, and history only stresses the lesson. Thus the Boers only resorted to guerrilla warfare in the South African War (1899-1902) after their main armies had been defeated in the field. The Yugoslavs only took to the mountains after their regular army had been swiftly crushed by the Germans in 1941. Guerrillas cannot win against a determined enemy unless they are supported by a foreign regular force (such as Wellington's expeditionary force in Spain), or unless they solve the difficult task of creating regular units of their own. Partisan tactics on their own can only succeed under certain circumstances. They need a secure source of supplies; the enemy must be disunited; his will to resist must be broken; or war must be waged over an issue which the incumbent power does not consider worth a protracted war. After prolonged fighting the French finally abandoned Algeria, even though their army remained undefeated. But the French would never have abandoned Alsace-Lorraine, whatever the provocation, for they considered Alsace an inalienable part of their national patrimony. The Israelis may consider guerrilla irruptions to be a serious threat, but they will never consent to liquidate their state for fear of partisans.

Regarding revolutions in general, nothing can be more dangerous to insurrectionary planners than the romantic notion that virtuous peoples—rightly struggling to be free—must be necessarily win in their struggle against tyrants. This interpretation is based on a misconceived idea of revolutionary wars that many textbooks still help to perpetuate. According to the old version, the Americans won the War of Independence because the British Redcoats were no match against the liberty-loving farmers sniping from behind cover against the over-disciplined regulars. The French revolutionary forces are said to have been invincible because the revolutionaries alone were able to enforce conscription and to develop the tactics of the massed column. But the American War of Independence was not mainly won by guerrillas but by regular soldiers and sailors. British soldiers were perfectly capable of becoming as skilled in skirmishing as their American opponents. The French revolutionary generals merely perfected methods of impressment already used by Louis XIV in the War of the Spanish Succession and by Gustavus Adolphus in the Thirty Years' War. French revolutionary tacticians drew heavily on the work of military theoreticians of the later Bourbon period, just as revolutionary civilian administrators continued and perfected the work accomplished by the statesmen of the *ancien régime.*

Many revolutions moreover have come to grief. The German Spartakists (later known as Communists) could not seize power after World War I. Many nationalities never succeeded in creating independent states of their own. The Basques, Georgians, Catalonians, and Flemings are not likely ever to achieve representation in the United Nations as sovereign states. There is nothing inevitable about revolutionary success. Besides, many of the most successful revolutionaries would have failed but for foreign aid. Neither the Yugoslav partisans nor the Chinese communists, for instance, could win by their own efforts alone. Without British help, Tito could hardly have survived during World War II. When his forces finally entered Belgrade, he also had the indispensable support of the Soviet Army. The Long March of the Chinese communists in the 1930s was a long fight. Had Chiang Kai-shek, in 1937, been able to use his best units against the communists rather than the Japanese, Mao Tse-tung today might well be living as an exile in Moscow.

Military planners in the past have often made the mistake of underestimating the guerrilla. The danger now exists that the pendulum may swing too far the other way, and that partisan warfare will be overrated and come to looked upon as a military panacea. Truth, however, lies with neither extreme; "revolutionary wars" fought by guerrilla actions still remain only one of many forms of human conflict.

NOTES

53. *The Student's Oxford Aristotle;* Vol. VI, *Politics and Poetics,* trans. into English under the editorship of W. D. Ross...(London, Oxford University Press, 1942), p. 1307b.
54. Ernesto Guevara, *Che Guevara on Guerrilla Warfare* (New York, Frederick A. Praeger, 1961), p. 28.
55. The Assassins were adherents of the Ismaili doctrine of Islam. In 1090 Hasanibu-al-Sabbah seized the castle of Alamut, where he established his headquarters. He controlled an extensive network of agents and of trained terrorists who operated all over Persia and Iraq, subject to an extremely strict discipline. The Assassins struggled against the reigning Caliphate and, to a lesser extent, against the Caliphate of Cairo and the Christian Crusaders. The Assassins were extirpated in the thirteenth century by the invading Mongols.
56. Nehemiah 4:16.
57. Judges 7:3, 16, 20, 21, 22.

Framework

Frank Kitson

As Secretary of State for Defence, Denis Healey became known as an innovator and one of his ideas was to establish Defence Fellowships. Each year six or eight middle-aged officers were selected from the three services and sent off to a university to study some aspect of defence in the widest sense. Having failed to read the relevant Defence Council Instruction, I knew nothing of this until told to volunteer for a Defence Fellowship at the end of my tour of duty as a battalion commander. After filling in a few forms, I duly appeared in front of a distinguished board of senior officers and civil servants. Somewhat to my surprise I was selected to carry out an examination into the steps which should be taken in order to make the army ready to deal with subversion, insurrection and peace-keeping operations during the second half of the 1970s. My study was to last for one year and in October 1969 I duly took up residence at University College, Oxford, thanks to the kindness of the Master and Fellows. My work was to be supervised by Professor Norman Gibbs, Chichele Professor of the History of War.

It might be supposed that any person capable of handling an infantry battalion would have little trouble in preparing such a straightforward report, but that is not how it appeared to me at the time. One major problem was that the second half of the 1970s was still six years away

and it was difficult to know what sort of counter-insurgency and peace-keeping operations would be likely to confront the army so far ahead. Another problem was to relate the experience which I had gained in Kenya, Malaya, Muscat and Cyprus to the business of preparing the army for future eventualities. On reflection, preparation in this context seemed to mean education and training on the one hand, and organization on the other, but before breaking the subject down in this way it would obviously be necessary to isolate the essentials of countering insurgency and of peace-keeping.

There has never been much doubt that the main characteristic which distinguishes campaigns of insurgency from other forms of war is that they are primarily concerned with the struggle for men's minds, since only by succeeding in such a struggle with a large enough number of people can the rule of law be undermined and constitutional institutions overthrown. Violence may play a greater or lesser part in the campaign, but it should be used very largely in support of ideas. In a conventional war the reverse is more usually the case and propaganda is normally deployed in support of armed might.

Although the ultimate aim of an insurgent organization is to overthrow a government, or force it to do something it does not want to do, it will first have to get the backing of a proportion

Kitson, Frank. (1977). "Framework" *Bunch of Five* (pp. 281–298). London: Faber and Faber.

of the population, if it is to stay in being and to fight: insurgents are bound to rely to a considerable extent on the people for money, shelter, food and information. Insurgents therefore need to build up a programme in which violence is carefully balanced by political, psychological and economic measures, if it is to be effective, and the population as a whole, rather than the government, is likely to be the target, especially in the early stages of the struggle. Often insurgents do things which seem pointless or even damaging to their own cause when viewed in the context of harming the government, but in fact the actions in question may be solely concerned with achieving support from the population by coercion or persuasion. In this connection there is little doubt that terrorism is a potent form of persuasion; it is sometimes described as armed propaganda.

The particular form which an insurgent campaign takes is likely to depend on the surroundings. If a country contains mountains or large forested regions, it may be possible for insurgents to build up the sort of revolutionary army which can ultimately take on the forces of the government in battle. If, on the other hand, there is inadequate cover in the countryside, but large areas of urban development, a campaign relying mainly on political and economic attrition brought about by propaganda, sabotage and a low level of violence is likely to be more effective. Cities are particularly well suited to this form of struggle because they provide a large reservoir of people who can be manipulated into producing propaganda in the form of riots or marches, and because journalists and television teams are quickly on the scene to report it. Furthermore there is a heavy concentration of targets for sabotage around a city and plenty of prominent people such as politicians, diplomats and judges to murder. Where a country combines large areas of cover together with cities, revolutionary armies can be built up in the countryside whilst the cities can be used as a supply and recruiting base for the insurgent movement, for making propaganda, and for diverting government forces away from the country at critical moments in order to guard against sabotage or demonstrations.

The first thing that must be apparent when contemplating the sort of action which a government facing insurgency should take, is that there can be no such thing as a purely military solution because insurgency is not primarily a military activity. At the same time there is no such thing as a wholly political solution either, short of surrender, because the very fact that a state of insurgency exists implies that violence is involved which will have to be countered to some extent at least by the use of legal force. Political measures alone might have prevented the insurgency from occurring in the first place, but once it has taken hold, politics and force, backed up by economic measures will have to be harnessed together for the purpose of restoring peaceful conditions.

And this brings me to a most important point. It is fatally easy to underestimate the ability of a small number of armed men to exact support from exposed sections of the population by threats. There is always a temptation to delay using the forces of the law against subversive elements because of the danger that it will drive uncommitted people into supporting them. But neither government pronouncements, nor the natural loyalty of a people, will avail if terrorists are allowed to build up their organization unchecked. Over and over again in Kenya, Malaya, Cyprus and in many other countries it has been seen that members of the public cannot stand up to terrorism unprotected. Anyone who has looked on the miserable heaps of human wreckage left behind by execution squads knows why this is so. Certainly the use of force against terrorists must be carefully worked out in conjunction with measures designed to mitigate any unfavourable impact which it may have on people's attitudes, but it cannot be avoided altogether and a certain risk of polarization may have to be accepted in order that people should feel that something is being done to protect them.

It can be seen therefore that an effective counter-insurgency campaign should consist of a mixture of political and economic measures combined with the operations of the forces of the law. It can also be seen that the relative importance of the various different sorts of measures will have to be tailored to the situation, in the same way as insurgents tailor their campaign to the surroundings. In practice, if the insurgency represents anything more than a very minor disturbance, it is probably fair to say that the sum of the political and economic measures necessary to combat it will involve the whole business of government in one form or another. In other words, the overall plan of campaign should not be regarded as an operational matter, but primarily as a major function of government, and the form which the plan takes will result from consideration of the insurgents, aims, strengths, weaknesses and the opportunities which present themselves to both sides in relation to such factors as terrain and urban development.

But although these are the factors which determine the sort of struggle which will be waged, and although these are the considerations which journalists and other commentators naturally concentrate on describing, there is little point in examining them closely except in the context of a particular campaign. What it is both desirable and possible to do, is to identify certain areas in which decisions have to be made in order that an adequate framework can be set up. To my mind there are four such areas and they can be likened to the top, the bottom and the two sides of a frame. If the frame is well constructed, as was the case in Kenya and also ultimately in Malaya, the campaign can be expected to work.

The first requirement for a workable campaign is good co-ordinating machinery. It is no good having an overall plan composed of various measures unless they can be co-ordinated in such a way that measures of one kind do not cut across measures of another kind. To take a much over-simplified example, it might be felt that unemployment in certain areas is contributing to the support which the insurgents are getting, and that a good plan of economic development should be instituted to try and rectify the situation. But unless properly co-ordinated with other measures, this project might do more harm than good, since the money required might only be available at the expense of a more important project – say the enlargement of the police. To undertake both projects might overstrain the economy and produce conditions which would play into the insurgents' hands. Furthermore even if co-ordination at the top is correctly achieved, the results could still be disastrous for a different reason, if a similar degree of co-ordination is not realized at the lower levels. To continue with the example, even if in national terms the economic development programme does not cut across other measures, the resultant new building in a particular region, if not properly co-ordinated, might lead to a population shift and thereby to a security situation which was beyond the power of available forces to control. In short, co-ordination of measures across the board is not only necessary at the national level, but must be repeated at lower levels as well, right down to the bottom.

This is an easy principle to enunciate, but a difficult one to put into practice, particularly in a complex democratic society. Despite the reams of paper which have been written on the subject, it seldom happens that arrangements which have worked in one place will fit another place because patterns of civil administration seldom reproduce themselves sufficiently exactly. In particular the very simple system which used to operate in our Colonies, where a Provincial or District Commissioner wielded authority over a wide range of activities, is not likely to be met with again, so that the methods of co-ordinating political, economic and security measures which were so effective in Kenya and Malaya would be quite impracticable in the modern world. On the other hand, it is usually possible to devise a workable system without too much trouble. The difficulty lies in getting it accepted because of the price which has to be paid in political, economic, and personal terms. A political price has to be paid for example, whenever a locally-elected body has to give up some of its authority to the central government or to a civilian or military representative of it. The price is economic whenever boundaries change or new offices are set up with all that this implies in terms of accommodation and communications. The price is personal when one man has his little bit of power or freedom curtailed to fit in with other people. In the early days of an insurgency campaign those in authority usually hope that the situation will not become sufficiently serious to warrant payments of this kind. Later on, they may feel that the end is in sight and delay paying up for that reason. It is never easy to get the price paid.

The second requirement of a workable campaign propoganda is just as important as setting up co-ordinating machinery and is even more difficult to produce. It concerns the business of establishing the sort of political atmosphere within which the government measures can be introduced with the maximum likelihood of success. Almost always at the outset of an insurgency the government will be at a disadvantage because the insurgents will have expended a lot of time and effort on whipping up hostile opinion in order to get the trouble started. Although the government may have been trying to influence public opinion in the opposite direction, it is usual for some time to elapse before waverers start coming down on the government's side and longer still before enemy supporters start to change sides. Furthermore the struggle once joined can go one way and then the other, and must be kept up until the end, which is merely another way of repeating that insurgency is largely a battle for men's minds. In order to show why it is so difficult to get this part of the campaign going well, it is necessary to look at the sort of things which can be done, at the same time highlighting the difficulties and dangers involved in doing them. At this point it is worth noticing that the propaganda battle has not only got to be won within the country in which the insurgency is taking place, but also in other places throughout the world where governments or individuals are in a position to give moral or material support to the enemy.

There are really two separate aspects to the business of developing a frame of mind which rejects unconstitutional activity. The first part of the problem is to devise a system which ensures that the effect it will have on people's opinion and attitudes is considered at all stages during the formulation and execution of policy. This depends primarily on making all those involved in devising and carrying out the government's campaign aware of the possible public attitudes to their ideas, statements and actions. It applies to people working out programmes of economic development and to soldiers on patrol. It applies to the highest and to the lowest in all sorts of different spheres of employment. Making people aware of their responsibilities in this field is an important function of direction and as such it can only be achieved if co-ordinating machinery exists. But more is needed than co-ordinating machinery and it would seem that special staff advisers are required at every level to ensure on the one hand that policy-making groups are briefed on the consequences of their plans and on the other that ways of educating public opinion are considered and implemented.

The second part of the problem could perhaps be described as the mechanics of the business and involves the provision of people to monitor the enemy's propaganda and prepare and disseminate material required for countering it and putting across the government's point of view. It can be achieved either by direct action, as for example by the provision of leaflets, or the setting-up of an official wireless or television network, or by trying to inform and influence the existing news media.

Neither the working out of the sort of organization required, nor the provision of men and equipment is likely to prove particularly difficult. So far as men are concerned, they can be drawn from the army, the police, the civil service or direct from civilian life, subject to availability and time needed for training: equipment likewise is easy enough to get. The real difficulty lies in the political price which a democratic country pays in order to influence the way in which its people think. An information service, such as the one described here, represents the erosion of a basic freedom and its very existence in the hands of the government could in the long term prove a greater danger than the insurgents themselves, since it could be misused. So important is this consideration, that it may even be necessary to conduct the campaign within a framework which is knowingly left weak in this respect. If so, there should be no doubt in anyone's mind about the serious consequences of opting out of the propaganda war. In practice of course it might be possible to compromise and provide a limited propaganda capability at a low risk to the country's freedom of thought, but it is an extremely delicate matter.

The third part of the framework is intelligence. Clearly an adequate supply of the right sort of information is needed at the top to enable the government to work out a sensible policy for countering the insurgents. Information of a slightly different kind is also necessary at every level for the successful conduct of operations. Establishing an effective intelligence organization is therefore a matter of the first importance.

The problem about establishing the sort of organization needed, is that in normal times the requirement can best be met by a small, highly centralized and highly secure system which produces a relatively small amount of precise top-level information, whereas once an insurgent organization builds up, the operational requirement is for a mass of lower level information which must of necessity be less reliable. At the same time the government continues to require the sort of information which it has always had. Somehow therefore the intelligence organization must enlarge itself rapidly, must decentralize in order to give security force commanders at every level access to it, and must change its methods of working so as to produce the different sort of information that operational forces need.

There are many ways in which an intelligence organization can set about adapting itself to the needs of the moment and as with co-ordinating machinery the exact system can only be related to the circumstances of a particular campaign. It is none the less probable that a reorganization on the required scale will only be achieved at a considerable price. The most common difficulty derives from the fact that the head of the government in a democratic country is normally responsible for the conduct of the intelligence organization and can best keep control of it if it is highly centralized. Expansion, decentralization and contact with the outside world in the form of junior military commanders all bring in their train the possibility of the odd indiscretion. At the very least, if direct access is afforded to army officers it will inevitably increase the power of the military which may be politically unwelcome in itself, quite apart from any question of abuse. The problem will be greatly accentuated if part or all of the military contribution comes from an ally or is provided by a higher echelon of government than the one responsible for handling the insurgency and the intelligence organization. It is surprising how often this happens. For example, in most of our colonial Emergencies the bulk of the armed forces were controlled by Whitehall, although the responsibility for handling the insurgency and for the conduct of the intelligence service remained with colonial Government. A very similar situation prevailed in Northern Ireland until March 1972 and in countries with a federal constitution the same sort of problem could easily arise.

A major difficulty to reinforcing and decentralizing the intelligence service comes from the speed at which it has to be done, if it is to keep up with the rate of expansion of the insurgents' organization. The actual business of finding and training the right people is hard enough, but the security risk involved in bringing a large number of outsiders into such a sensitive sphere of activity at short notice is even harder. Intelligence services are always worried about their security and although this is sometimes used as an excuse for not taking action which is unpopular for one reason or another, it is none the less necessary to realize that the danger does exist. However, in all insurgency situations an effective intelligence organization has to be established, and established quickly. Somehow the government has to ensure that essential risks are accepted and that the necessary action is taken.

The fourth part of the framework concerns the law. No country which relies on the law of the land to regulate the lives of its citizens can afford to see that law flouted by its own government, even in an insurgency situation. In other words everything done by a government and its agents in combating insurgency must be legal. But this does not mean that the government must work within exactly the same set of laws during an insurgency as existed beforehand, because it is a function of government to make new laws when necessary. It does not even mean that the law must be administered in exactly the same way during an uprising as it was in more peaceful times, because once again a government has the power to modify the way in which the law is administered if necessary, for the wellbeing of the people, although the exercise of such power is usually — and rightly — subject to considerable constitutional restraint. It is therefore perfectly normal for governments not only to introduce Emergency Regulations as an insurgency progresses, but also to counter advantages which the insurgents may derive from, for example, the intimidation of juries and witnesses, by altering the way in which the law is administered. Ways by which the legal system can be amended range from changing rules governing the giving of evidence to dispensing with juries altogether, or even to introducing some form of internment without proper trial. It is a dangerous path to tread, and one that is justified only by the peril in which constitutional government and democracy are placed by insurgency.

In practice the constant interplay of action by insurgents trying to take advantage of loopholes in the law with counter-action by the government trying to block up the loopholes, constitutes one of the most intricate and important parts of an insurgency campaign. The difficulty, from the government's point of view, is that the loopholes themselves were probably built into the system to safeguard individual freedom so that blocking them up not only provides opportunities for enemy propaganda, but also genuinely endangers the liberty of the people. There is a parallel here to the countering of enemy propaganda by the setting up of an effective government information service. The extent and way in which the government should intervene in legal matters can only be discussed in the context of particular circumstances, but it must be accepted that this is an intensely political matter and one in which military commanders cannot expect to have anything like the last word. On the other hand it is their duty to ensure that they are not required to undertake operations which are incompatible with existing law, and a government which takes insufficient notice of this duty would be failing in its own constitutional duty as well as playing into the hands of the insurgents.

Before leaving the subject of the law there is one specific matter to which allusion must be made because it is fundamental to the whole business of dealing with insurgency. This concerns the way in which members of the insurgent organization should be treated on capture. In this connection four separate and sometimes contradictory requirements have to be met and it is important that the law should take account of them. The first requirement is that the captured insurgent should be prevented from doing further damage to the government's cause. The second is that he should be given every encouragement to change sides. The third is that maximum advantage should be taken of his ability to help the government, either through giving information, or in other ways. The fourth is that his treatment should be such as to influence others to return to their proper allegiance.

The key to the whole business lies in persuading the prisoner to change sides and all of his treatment, including his interrogation, should be carried out with this in mind. There must certainly be no brutality and the best results are usually achieved by holding prisoners in well-segregated compounds in small camps close to where they have been operating. This enables interrogation to be carried out by people in close touch with the operational situation, and it avoids the control which hard-core prisoners are likely to exercise over their fellows in large prisoner-of-war-type camps. This system is however expensive in terms of manpower and facilities and is likely to attract every sort of inhibiting propaganda assault from the insurgents who well realize the danger which it poses to their cause.

To summarize this chapter I would just say that in my opinion the first requirement for the successful conduct of a counter-insurgency campaign is for the government to set up a sound framework within which it can take place. This should consist of co-ordinating machinery at every level for the direction of the campaign, arrangements for ensuring that the insurgents do not win the war for the minds of the people, an intelligence organization suited to the circumstances, and a legal system adequate to the needs of the moment. I have no doubt that a system can be devised in each of these four spheres which will be capable of achieving the aim, but I am equally sure that such systems can only be implemented with great difficulty on most occasions, and it may even happen that sometimes the best system can only be obtained by the payment of too high a price. It would then be safer for the government to accept a less good one and endure a prolongation of the troubles. This is naturally a political decision and providing that it is made by the government in the full knowledge of the likely consequences then it is up to all concerned to accept it.

Of course my analogy of a picture-frame with its top, bottom and sides is artificial and would be misleading if carried too far. In particular it is worth noticing that the sort of decisions needed for establishing the framework are similar in kind to those needed for running the campaign as a whole. Indeed that is precisely what they are and in practical terms the framework evolves as the campaign progresses. This is true because decisions regarding the setting up of one part of the frame are often dependent on the existence of other parts of it. For example, it would not be sensible to make a radical alteration to the legal system unless an effective information service existed to keep enemy counter-propaganda in check, but such an information service could itself only work after a system of co-ordinated direction had been established at every level, which in turn might only be possible if the law was amended to permit it. There is therefore a chicken and egg aspect to building the frame which has little to do with carpentry. The evolving nature of the framework is also due to the fact that it must change to take account of changing circumstances. It cannot be set up and left alone thereafter.

So much for the framework. In the next chapter I discuss the essentials of carrying out operations against insurgents, but before doing so would like once more to stress the importance of the background against which they take place. Anyone who has previously been involved in such operations can quickly sense whether an effective framework exists. As crisis succeeds crisis, it is easy to tell which way the tide is flowing and it is reassuring to know that one is not swimming against it.

Operations

Frank Kitson

Interlocking political and economic restraints encountered by those trying to establish a sensible counter-insurgency framework usually give rise to intense frustration and to a series of confusing compromises. But those who turn with relief towards the subject of Security Force operations expecting to find easily-defined problems and clear-cut solutions will be disappointed. Political and economic restraints relentlessly weave their way through the fabric of operations as well. In this chapter I will try to outline the part that operations play in a counter-insurgency campaign and show how closely they are bound up with other aspects of the government's plan.

At this point it may be convenient to group operations under one of two headings. Firstly there are defensive operations, which are those designed to prevent insurgents from disrupting the government's programme. Secondly there are offensive operations, which are those designed to root out the insurgents themselves. Before discussing each in turn it is worth noticing how important it is to strike a balance between them. If too little emphasis is placed on defensive measures in order to concentrate resources on the offensive, the insurgents are offered an opportunity to achieve easy successes, which they can use to embarrass the government and thereby undermine its support. If, on the other hand, too little emphasis is placed on offensive operations, the insurgent organization gets bigger and bigger and an ever-increasing proportion of the country's resources has to be devoted to the Security Forces for defensive countermeasures, so that eventually the insurgents achieve their aim by making it appear that the price of further resistance is too high.

It is perhaps worth highlighting the ways in which political considerations affect the achievement of a good balance between defensive and offensive operations. There is almost always political pressure on Security Force commanders to devote more resources towards defensive operations because of the short-term difficulties which the government faces after every spectacular insurgent success. Furthermore, if the operational commander is insensitive to this political pressure, he stands to find himself suddenly confronted by an unnecessarily large number of specific political demands for defensive measures designed to restore confidence among the population. Those demands might easily be big enough to disrupt the offensive plan altogether and thereby upset the balance in the opposite direction. Undoubtedly the insurgent leadership will do all in its power to ensure that the balance of the Security Force's plan is upset, both by planning their own operations with this in mind, and by the use of propaganda designed to inhibit offensive action on the part of the government's forces.

Kitson, Frank. (1977). "Operations." *Bunch of Five* (pp. 281–298). London: Faber and Faber.

It is particularly important to understand the extent to which insurgents use propaganda when defending themselves against government offensive action. Anyone at home or abroad who can be persuaded to write, or broadcast or otherwise influence public opinion will be pressed into service. The aim is usually to try and get debilitating restraints imposed on the Security Forces, and a particularly effective line is to say that offensive Security Force action is driving uncommitted people into supporting the insurgents. Like all good propaganda this line is likely to contain at least an element of truth. What the insurgent propagandist naturally fails to point out, and what the writer or broadcaster often does not understand, is that the offensive action may be the lesser of two evils, in that failure to take it will result in a far greater increase of support for the insurgents as their organization grows unchecked and their power to coerce and persuade correspondingly increases. Of course the right level of offensive action depends on prevailing circumstances. The point which has to be understood is that a good balance between offensive and defensive action is difficult to achieve because of all the pressures which operate against it.

As already stated, the purpose of defensive operations is to prevent the insurgents from disrupting the government's programme and a number of different activities can be grouped under this heading. But although such a wide variety of operations can be described as defensive, and although many of them are far from being passive, there is one characteristic which is common to most of them: they are very expensive in manpower with all that this implies in economic terms. To understand why this is the case it is necessary to look briefly at some of the various types of operation which come under this heading.

Guarding and protection are the bread and butter of defensive operations. In any counter-insurgency situation there is bound to be a heavy commitment for the establishing of static guards on such things as military and police bases, power stations, broadcasting installations, docks, factories and commercial centres. In certain circumstances it may also be necessary to guard prominent people like judges and politicians. It is likely that there will be a requirement to protect exposed places where civilians are living, such as isolated villages or parts of cities which are particularly vulnerable to the enemy. It is often necessary to protect crops and stock in the countryside and shopping areas in the towns. Protection can sometimes be carried out satisfactorily by mobile patrols which is much less wasteful in manpower than the mounting of a guard.

A further extension of the business of protecting relates to the task of ensuring that legal assemblies, demonstrations and processions take place peacefully. Although such operations are of relatively short duration, they are immensely expensive in terms of manpower because they involve the gathering together of large numbers of people. It is fatally easy for violence to erupt under such circumstances and if there are too few members of the Security Forces available to control it, they will have to use undesirably severe measures or let the situation get out of hand.

Another form of defensive operation concerns the dispersal of illegal assemblies and riots. This is a subject for study in itself and involves a whole range of minor tactics and an understanding of the complete armoury of anti-riot gear and weapons. Perhaps the most important thing to realize is that riots are a symptom, rather than a disease in themselves. Some riots result from high spirits whilst others evolve spontaneously from legal gatherings. Some come about because factions of a divided community collide, whereas others represent deliberately engineered confrontations with the Security Forces to cause a diversion, to polarize feeling, or to make propaganda. Obviously different tactics should be used by the Security Forces in each case. For example, the aim when factions clash is to part them and get the contestants home as quickly as possible. The aim when insurgents deliberately activate a riot is to arrest a number of rioters and get them punished, so as to dissuade people from giving similar help to the insurgents in the future. Although it may seem odd to classify such an energetic pursuit as the handling of riots as a defensive operation, it is none the less correct to do so. Insurgents engineer riots to promote their cause and disrupt the government's programme;

the purpose of controlling them is therefore preventative. Furthermore few opportunities exist for capturing insurgents themselves during riots as they seldom take a direct part.

One final group of defensive operations deserving mention covers activities of the Security Forces designed to prevent the insurgents from gaining an influence over the population. Such activities may amount to little more than keeping close contact with the civilian population day by day, but it can be extended to the provision of a link between the people and the civil authorities where this has broken down. A more ambitious scheme for aiding the civil community, known as a hearts and minds campaign, or a community relations programme can also be included. Occasionally government forces have gone even further and organized a complete set of committees amongst the civilian community, parallel to the network normally set up by the insurgents, with each committee chaired or attended by a representative of the army or police. This system for influencing people's opinions and attitudes can be most effective under certain conditions, providing the requisite legal hacking is available.

This brief outline of defensive operations shows why so many men can get sucked in so quickly. An insurgent organization only has to stay in existence to the extent necessary for posing a relatively minor threat for the manpower bill to become almost unbearable. As indicated earlier, the main counter to the insurgents must come from offensive operations designed to destroy their organization and thereby remove the threat. But this may take years to become fully effective. Meanwhile two important palliatives can help to bridge the gap. The first is to make every possible use of technical developments to save men. A large number of gadgets now exist for carrying out all sorts of tasks: these range from surveillance devices, to information storage and sorting equipment and anti-riot gear. The second is to raise auxiliary forces from amongst the population wherever possible who can carry out the less skilled functions, particularly those related to guarding. There may be great risks involved in arming such people, especially when they are drawn from a heavily penetrated community, but the risks are usually worth taking. It may even happen that the

process of involving a man whose loyalty is in doubt will bring him down on the right side of the fence and give a lead to others in the neighbourhood.

It is now time to look at offensive operations. The purpose of offensive operations is to identify and neutralize members of an insurgent organization by apprehending them under conditions which enable them to be held in custody. Normally the problem resolves itself into one of providing adequate resources at the right place and of obtaining the requisite information.

A large part of this book has already been devoted to describing how this process can be carried out and at this point it is only necessary to summarize in the broadest outline. Suffice it to say, that for many years the question of providing the required information was regarded as being primarily the responsibility of the intelligence organization. The basic idea was that from time to time the intelligence organization would produce the sort of information which would enable units of the Security Forces to make contact with insurgents and for the rest of the time these units would occupy themselves with their defensive tasks or by conducting hit-or-miss offensive action such as systematic patrolling in likely areas. By the very nature of things this system cannot work effectively because from the start of the campaign the insurgent organization is always likely to expand faster than the intelligence organization, with the result that insufficient pinpoint information will be available for the Security Forces to fulfill their commitment.

A more practical system, and the one which I tried to apply in Malaya, is to make the tactical commander, rather than the intelligence organization, responsible for getting the pinpoint or contact information which he needs. This can be done by what is best described as a chain reaction of analysis alternating with action designed to get information. In other words a company or battalion commander starts by analysing all the information which he can get from records, the intelligence organization, the outgoing company commander, and discussion with anyone who can help, and then gets further information by using his own men. He adds this to what he had before, and to any further information which he may get from outside sources, and then sends out his men to get further information designed to confirm his ideas and extend them. The system is designed to narrow down the probability of success to points in time and space of sufficient exactitude for available troops to exploit.

A number of conditions have to be fulfilled if this system is to work well. In the first place it requires a high degree of understanding on the part of the troops and their commanders, including training in methods of storing large amounts of information at a low level in such a way that it can be found. It also requires the company commander to have access to an expanded and decentralized intelligence organization geared to collecting and passing on many scraps of unrelated bits of information. Finally the system only works if the tactical commander can be left in comparative peace from outside interference, and if he can be left in one place for a good long time. If he is constantly being obliged to divert extra resources to defensive tasks, or if he is suddenly moved while building up his chain reaction process the system falls down.

With all these conditions to meet it might be wondered whether the new system has any advantage to offer over the old one and in this respect it is only necessary to point out that at least it can be made to work, whereas the old one was bound to fail for the reasons discussed earlier. In passing, it might just be worth saying that the system often proves unpopular from a political point of view because it involves investing comparatively junior operational commanders with the power which comes from the accumulation of information, especially the sensitive information which they are likely to pick up by being in direct and constant touch with the intelligence organization. There is of course no reason why a company commander should misuse power any more than members of the intelligence organization, but it is none the less true that many people become nervous when they see this sort of power in the hands of relatively junior officers. Insurgent propaganda may then fan the flames of nervousness in order to inhibit what, from their point of view, is a very dangerous threat to their existence. This is not an argument for devolving control, but for ensuring that political control is always effective, and seen to be effective.

Before leaving the subject of the offensive it is necessary to mention special operations which are almost always valuable for identifying and apprehending members of an insurgent organization, although naturally the form of operation used has to be carefully tailored to the prevailing circumstances. In general, it is probably fair to say that successful special operations are usually those which base themselves on the chain reaction system for developing background information into contact information, but with the difference that the men employed are specially selected, trained and equipped to take advantage of some particular system. In Kenya, for example, we were using ex-Mau Mau gang members, posing as current gang members, to develop background information collected by normal intelligence methods.

Special Forces can be organized to develop information to the point where contact with the enemy can be made by normal military or police units or they can be organized to take action on their own information when it is fully developed. In either case it is worth making two points. The first one is that there is absolutely no need for special operations to be carried out in an illegal or immoral way and indeed there is every reason to ensure that they are not because they are just as much part of the government's programme as any of its other measures and the government must be prepared to take responsibility for them. The second point is that special operations must be organized and implemented under the auspices of the normal machine for directing the campaign and the advantages to be gained from them weighed against the psychological implications of their becoming known. Furthermore normal Security Force units should be informed as to the nature and purpose of special operations as far as is consistent with the requirements of security so that they come to regard Special Forces as helpful colleagues and not as wild, irresponsible people whose one purpose is to steal the credit from those who carry out more humdrum, but necessary, roles.

The Malayan Emergency
in Retrospect

Organization of A Successful
Counterinsurgency Effort

R. W. Komer

A Report prepared for
ADVANCED RESEARCH PROJECTS AGENCY

PREFACE

This Report, done under the sponsorship of the Advanced Research Projects Agency of the Department of Defense, is one of several case studies on the organization and management of counterinsurgency efforts in Southeast Asia. It does not attempt to give a full historical review or rounded treatment of its subject. Rather, it focuses on the structure and control — and their effect on policy and performance — of an actual counterinsurgency effort. Its purpose is to determine what lessons of future value the U.S. military establishment may learn from that effort.

Why another look at the Malayan insurgency? The case of Malaya, in which the United States did not play a role, is instructive as an example of how another Western power dealt with a serious insurgency, quite successfully as it turned out. Despite some notable differences, the similarities between Malaya and other Southeast Asian insurgencies are sufficient to make a comparative analysis worthwhile. Indeed, with the wisdom of hindsight, the Malayan experience seems even more relevant in the light of our own more costly and dubious experience in Vietnam. Also, as Sir Robert Thompson has aptly said, "Many Americans made studies of the British experience in Malaya, but these were largely superficial and confined to particular aspects of the campaign. It was never comprehended as a whole. . . ."[*]

A briefing based on this study has been given to the Assistant Secretary of Defense (Systems Analysis) and other OSD officials, and to CINC-PAC staff, at the Army War College, at the Armed Forces Staff College, at the Command and General Staff School, etc. Lessons from the

_____

[*]*No Exit from Vietnam*, Chatto and Windus, London, 1969, p. 131.

This research is supported by the Advanced Research Projects Agency under Contract No. DAHC15 67 C 0142: Views or conclusions contained in this study should not be interpreted as representing the official opinion or policy of Rand or of ARPA.

Komer, R. W. (1972). *The Malayan Emergency in Retrospect: Organization of a Successful Counterinsurgency Effort*. Santa Monica, CA: Rand.

study have been widely discussed with other Defense officials and State officials.

A related Rand study is Douglas S. Blaufarb's R-919-ARPA, *Organizing and Managing Unconventional War in Laos, 1962-1970* (U), January 1972, Secret.

SUMMARY

What seems most striking in retrospect about the experience of the British and Malayan governments in containing and ultimately defeating the Communist insurgency in Malaya is the wide range of civil and military programs tied together by unified management into a successful counterinsurgency (C-I) response. Though many mistakes were made in the early years and the whole process took from 1948 to 1960, the United Kingdom and the Government of Malaya (U.K./GOM) gradually evolved what stands out as an almost classic "long-haul low-cost" strategy well adapted to the problem they confronted.

Of course, such an approach was made feasible by several weaknesses of the insurgency, not least the fact that it was confined to the ethnic Chinese element of Malaya's polyglot population and even unable to gain popular support from more than part of this minority group. Also, it lacked any external aid. In coping with the insurgency the U.K./GOM had several advantages on which they shrewdly capitalized — among them a viable politico-administrative structure and close British/Malayan ties. But in the early years (1948-1952) the contest was by no means so unequal as all this might suggest; the U.K./GOM response was quite inadequate, and it looked as though they were losing. By 1954, however, the insurgency was clearly on the wane, and the next six years were mainly a painstaking mopping up.

Notably, the Malayan C-I approach was *not* primarily military. Instead, the U.K./GOM employed a mixed strategy encompassing civil, police, military, and psychological warfare programs, all within the context of a firm rule of law and steady progress toward self-government and independence, which robbed the insurgency of much political appeal. At all times the police and the paramilitary forces under their aegis far outnumbered the military and took more casualties. There was comparatively little use of airpower and artillery (which cost so much in Vietnam). Intelligence was provided mostly by Police Special Branch, whose signal contribution to the C-I success was out of all proportion to its small size.

Through a process of trial and error, the U.K./GOM came to put primary emphasis on breaking the guerrillas' links to their popular base. While offensive small-unit operations to destroy or drive back the guerrilla bands into the deep jungle played an indispensable role, the great bulk of U.K./GOM resources (even much of the military effort) at any given time was devoted to protecting the populated areas and clamping down on the flow of supplies and recruits to the guerrillas. Crucial to this end were the extensive resettlement of half a million ethnic Chinese squatters, pervasive food controls and food-denial operations, and tough population controls. As the other side of a carrot-and-stick approach the U.K./GOM undertook a variety of political, economic, and social measures, accompanied by an information campaign, to win "hearts and minds."

All this was pulled together, once the need was realized, by an unusual, unified civil-military command structure. Using the well-known British "committee" system, the war was managed by a network of war executive committees extending from the top down to district level. Territorially organized, this system paralleled — indeed was part of — the existing civil administrative structure. It was headed by civilians, even though military men often played dual roles in the top slots. It was also a combined British-Malayan structure from the outset and became progressively more Malayanized, although the British held most of the top jobs until 1956. An important feature from 1950 on was a single Director of Operations who had operational control over the C-I effort.

The British and Malayans also deserve high marks for flexibility and adaptiveness over time. When the initial C-I effort of 1948-1950 proved inadequate, confused, and undermanaged, they brought in General Briggs as single Director of Operations; this reorganization under the "Briggs Plan" became the chief blueprint for victory. They then further unified the top management under General Templer's dynamic leadership in 1952-1954. Meanwhile the whole command structure was being Malayanized in anticipation of independence. By 1956, there were only 1,800 Europeans in a civil service of over 160,000.

Among the many C-I innovations introduced in Malaya were the widely publicized reward-for-surrender programs, imaginative exploitation of surrendered insurgents, use of police jungle squads, and food-denial operations.

By utilizing local civil and police resources as much as possible, and through effective administration and unified management, the British and Malayans were able to achieve success at remarkably low cost. It took twelve years, but it cost less than $800 million in all, and could mostly be funded from Malaya's own tin and rubber export revenues. Of course, U.K./GOM success in containing the insurgency's growth by 1951-1952 facilitated this type of long-haul response. But its cost effectiveness also resulted from the integrated use of a wide range of relatively cheap nonmilitary resources.

It is instructive to compare the Malayan C-I effort with the U.S. approach in Vietnam, although numerous differences make for a very imperfect analogy, particularly as the Vietnamese insurgency grew to massive proportions and had superimposed upon it a quasi-conventional war. Among the notable differences between the two insurgencies were the level of outside support, the use of external sanctuaries, and the fact that the British controlled Malaya during 1948-1957 whereas the United States has been allied to a xenophobic foreign regime. Thus the most valid comparison would be between Malaya 1948-1954 and Vietnam 1958-1962 (when the latter was still essentially a rural-based insurgency).

Yet the way in which the U.K./GOM learned from their mistakes and gradually evolved a mixed civil-military counterinsurgency strategy well adapted to the threat offers lessons of wider applicability — even to Vietnam. In particular, Malaya has much to offer in showing how to pull together multinational and multifaceted civil-military programs for an optimum counterinsurgency response. Unified management made a crucial difference in Malaya. Lack of it — granted that the obstacles were far greater — was a serious handicap in Vietnam.

I. THE INSURGENT MOVEMENT

Like many other insurgent movements in Asian colonies of the Western powers, the Malayan insurgency grew out of one of those anticolonial movements of the 1920s which took the Russian Revolution as their source of inspiration. But from the outset the Communist movement in Malaya was almost exclusively drawn from the ethnic Chinese minority. It never gained much support from the Malay or Indian elements of Malaya's polyglot society, which critically limited its appeal.

A. The Seeds of Conflict: 1925-1941

A South Seas (Nanyang) Communist Party, described as "the overseas branch of the Chinese Communist Party," was formed in 1925, and a parallel labor organization was formed one year later. However, these two groups made little progress in winning popular support, and their seeming ineffectiveness prompted the Comintern to reorganize them in April 1930 as the *Malayan Communist Party* (MCP) and *Malayan General Labor Union* (MGLU). The Comintern was represented in the conference by a Nguyen Ai Quoc, who later became known as Ho Chi Minh. His role in the proceedings was reported to have been decisive.[1]

The newly founded party soon suffered a serious setback. In 1933 at least two of its leaders were arrested and the Comintern organization which supported it was destroyed.[2] But within a few years the party revived, particularly among Chinese students. The MGLU became the most powerful labor organization in the country and led a successful series of strikes in 1936 and 1937. MGLU-led strikes at the Batu Arang coal mines in 1937, which led to the temporary establishment of a "Soviet" government of workers, constituted "the most serious crisis" to date in the colony's history.[3]

After 1937 the rising threat from Japan brought about a gradual shift in MCP policies. Since it drew almost all of its support from the Chinese community in Singapore, its policies became increasingly shaped by the deepening Japanese penetration of China. Unlike some other Asian Communist parties (notably those of Indochina and the Philippines), the MCP did not carry its anti-Japanese policy to the point of open collaboration with the Western colonial administrators. But it inevitably became increasingly involved in national, as opposed to exclusively labor, issues. As early as June 1940 it shifted its stance to support Britain's aid to China. The MCP's new "united front" policy paid off handsomely in terms of popularity. According to one British estimate, its following more than quadrupled between 1934 and 1940 to a total of more than 50,000 (including 1,700 MCP members), giving it a formidable base for its wartime operations.

After the German attack on the USSR, the MCP — like other Communist parties — quickly abandoned its overtly anti-British position, and went so far as to offer its assistance to the colonial administration — an offer which the British rejected. According to Government of Malaya (GOM) records, however, the MCP's support of a "united front" against the Japanese was only one prong of a two-pronged policy. In secret documents circulated among its higher leadership, it reaffirmed its objective of expelling the British as soon as possible or, if the Japanese invaded the country, supporting an anti-Japanese front only as a means of extending its influence.[4]

B. Between Hammer and Anvil: 1941-1945

With the Japanese invasion of Malaya, the MCP found its prospects being rapidly transformed. It proposed that the Chinese community be permitted to form a military force — armed by the British — to fight the Japanese. The Governor of Malaya initially rejected this offer. But as the military situation deteriorated, he reversed his decision and even sanctioned the release from jail of those political prisoners whom the MCP chose to name. A few days later the first class of Chinese students began to study guerrilla warfare at the 101 Special Training School.[5]

The period of collaboration lasted no more than two months. With the surrender of the British Forces in Singapore on February 15, 1942, all active resistance in Malaya ended for the time being. The MCP's top leadership narrowly escaped from Singapore after its fall and set up headquarters in nearby Johore; some of its members were captured by Japanese forces late in 1942, but its senior leadership remained substantially intact. Long before the British were able to place their stay-behind operations on an organized basis, the MCP formed the Malayan Peoples' Anti-Japanese Army (MPAJA). It later won official U.K. and U.S. recognition as the foremost resistance organization behind the Japanese lines.

In 1943 the MCP Central Committee drew up its first wartime statement of policy, favoring such traditional objectives as the guarantee of civil liberties and free vernacular education. It ended with a call for Malayans to "unite with Soviet Russia and China to support the independence of the weak and small races in the Far East, and to aid the people of Japan in their anti-Fascist struggle." The restoration of British rule clearly had no part in the MCP's agenda, but this was soft-pedaled for the time being.

In 1943 the MPAJA established liaison with Force 136, the component of the British Special Operations Executive responsible for clandestine operations. In 1944, when new Liberator bombers brought Malaya within range of Allied support, supplies and personnel were parachuted into MPAJA bases in increasing quantities.[6] According to one estimate, "over 500 liaison personnel and more than a million and a half pounds of equipment were flown into Malaya during the last eight months of the war."[7] Many drops went astray and much equipment apparently disappeared into secret caches for postwar use. Supreme Allied Command South-East Asia was fully aware of the probable consequences of the military buildup of a highly politicized army under Communist or pro-Communist control. But as British planners expected heavy fighting to precede the liberation of Malaya, military considerations were accorded precedence in the shaping of high policy.[8] However, Japan's capitulation brought an end to the war without large-scale fighting.

Predictably, estimates of the MPAJA's actual military efforts vary widely. One Soviet source estimates the combined strength of the MCP and MPAJA at 10,000 in 1945; another Soviet source states that 10,000 Japanese troops were killed by the guerrillas. Malayan government sources, however, estimated the size of the guerrilla force at only 6,500, while their chief, Loi Tek, claimed no more than 2,000 MCP members at the end of 1946 — a figure only marginally higher than the prewar estimates. Whatever truth there may be in these figures, it is clear that compared to other guerrilla movements in both Europe and Asia, the MPAJA did not rank very high in offensive action.[9] The simplest explanation of its relative inactivity may be that it was confident that the issue of Japan's defeat would be decided in other theaters of the war, and that it could best serve its long-term interests by husbanding its strength for the power struggle which would inevitably follow the Japanese surrender.

C. Rising Tide of Violence: 1945-1948

In late 1945 Malaya was "somewhat of a shambles."[10] The end of the war came far more swiftly than anyone expected. On September 5, 1945, thirty days after the dropping of the first atomic bomb on Hiroshima, the British East Indies Fleet landed British-Indian forces at Singapore. The British then moved to reestablish their control of the country. Finding that the MPAJA had established *de facto* control of many areas, they decided to accord the guerrillas official military status, place them under military command, clothe and ration them — and pay them $30 (Malayan) per month. To cast the net as wide as possible, these arrangements were offered not only to known members of the MPAJA but to anyone who could plausibly claim to have joined it.[11] Impressive ceremonies were held in which the MPAJA marched alongside Commonwealth troops, and its members were awarded medals; one of its outstanding leaders, Chin Peng, was invited to London to participate in the victory celebrations, and awarded the Order of the British Empire.[12]

The British Military Government than began negotiations aimed at convincing the MPAJA leaders that negotiations, disbandment, and disarmament on agreed terms offered them a better future than returning to the jungle to continue their guerrilla war. The MPAJA leaders, on the other hand, clearly hoped to win such concessions from the British as would accord their army either *de jure* or *de facto* status as a permanent military force to augment (or replace) the Malaya Regiment. However, they soon realized that this objective was beyond their reach, and that hard bargaining over the terms of disbandment offered better prospects than did a renewal of insurgent warfare.

While the British were eager to collect all weapons dropped to the guerrillas, their required surrender was not too painful to the MPAJA. The country by then was saturated with a great variety of arms, and those turned in could be readily replaced by others. In some areas the MPAJA turned in more arms than had been issued to them. But more popular weapons, such as Sten guns, carbines, pistols, and revolvers were undoubtedly held back.[13] As soon as the MPAJA officially disbanded, the MCP replaced it with a number of front organizations of a traditional Communist character.

During 1945-1948 the MCP — now legalized and its prestige grown from its wartime role — switched its effort to labor agitation and strikes in an attempt to bring down the government. By gaining control of the Pan-Malayan Federation of Trade Unions and affiliated federations, it won substantial domination over the burgeoning Malayan trade union movement. By the end of 1945 there were 90 registered unions, and 291 more applications on file. A year later, they had grown to 289 unions, with 101 more applying.[14] Strikes became both more bitter and more frequent. In 1947 there were 291, involving 69,000 men and the loss of nearly 700,000 man-days.[15] In May 1948 alone, the number of man-days lost rose to 178,500 (or an annual rate of more than two million), while 117 of the 289 registered unions were officially regarded as controlled by the Pan-Malayan Federation of Trade Unions (or the MCP), leaving 86 independent of such control, and 86 doubtful.[16] It seemed that the day was not far off when the MCP would be able to extend its control to the other unions and command a position of overriding power in the economy.

The MCP also turned its attention to terror. During the twenty-seven months between October 1945 and December 1947, there were 191 murders and abductions by insurgents; during only the first six months of 1948, there were 107.[17] In the first week of June 1948, 7 persons were killed and 10 wounded in a riot involving only 200 people. An atmosphere of bitterness and defiance grew rapidly.[18] The challenge could not be postponed for long.

The exact date when the MCP decided to move to open insurgency may never be known. Having failed to seize power in 1945, its leaders were no doubt anxious to recover lost ground. Certainly their actions suggest that from early or mid-1947 on they were doing all they could to force the crisis. But in February 1948 they either received new instructions or had older ones confirmed. It is now widely assumed that a Cominform conference which brought together in Calcutta representatives of most Asian Communist parties served as the forum in which plans were laid for the insurrections that broke out soon afterward, notably in Burma (March), Malaya (June), the Philippines (August), and Indochina (September). Whether or not this interpretation is correct, the decision for insurrection was soon ratified by the MCP Central Executive Committee in March.[19] On June 19, under considerable pressure from the planters — after three of them were killed in one incident — the Federation in turn declared a "State of Emergency."[20] Captured documents showed later that the MCP leaders hoped to declare a Communist Republic of Malaya on August 3, 1948.[21]

D. Factors Favoring the Insurgency

Continuing postwar disruption had created a climate conducive to insurgency. Neither the government nor the economy had yet recovered from the harsh effects of wartime occupation. The political future of Malaya was uncertain, the administrative structure was still undermanned, the security forces were weak and understrength. Crime and banditry were rife, and some rural areas still under virtual MCP control.

Equally important, the insurgents had a popular base among Malaya's large and unassimilated ethnic Chinese minority (some 38 percent of its population). Most of these Chinese were apolitical in the Western sense. They lived as a group apart, and were not even represented in Malaya's exclusively Malayan political structure, though this had been attempted in the short-lived Malayan Union of 1946-1948 (see Section VIII). Few Chinese had entered government service or the security forces; for example, in 1948 there were only 228 Chinese in the 10,000-man police force.[22] Chinese merchants dominated Malayan commercial life, though most of the rural Chinese worked as rubber tappers or tin miners in Malaya's two chief industries. However, the MCP by no means enjoyed the backing of the whole Chinese community.

Most were probably fence sitters, whereas others actively supported the rival Nationalist Chinese Kuomintang.

But the MCP could draw on one group in particular. Severe wartime and postwar economic dislocation, especially unemployment and food shortages (Malaya had long been a food deficit area), had led about half a million Chinese to become "squatters" on fallow land along the jungle fringe in the countryside. Here they grew their own food so that they could survive. These squatters lived largely outside the ambit of slowly reviving GOM administration. In the postwar confusion, MCP power had flowed into this vacuum. The squatters became a main source of insurgent recruitment (along with students from the Chinese private schools), and the source of most of its logistic support. Some 70 percent of total guerrilla strength — especially as the old wartime resistance fighters were killed off — reportedly came from the laborers and squatters along the jungle fringe.

Last among the insurgent advantages was that Malaya was about 80 percent thick jungle. Even many of the rubber estates had become disused and overgrown during the war. Thus the guerrillas could find relatively secure jungle bases close to the population for the type of Maoist rural insurgency the MCP now launched. It was the jungle's protection which permitted the guerrillas to survive so long after their hopes of a takeover had vanished.

E. The Pattern of Insurgent Operations

In typical Communist style, the insurgent organization consisted of far more than the guerrilla/terrorists who were its cutting edge. An elaborate organization pattern evolved on a territorial basis, largely paralleling that of the GOM. Directing the insurgency was the clandestine Malayan Communist Party (it had been outlawed again in 1948). Its structure included a Federation-level central committee, three regional bureaus, ten state committees, and fifty district committees, each of which controlled about four branch committees. This territorial pattern was doubly significant because it helped shape the U.K./GOM response.

The party structure controlled the guerrilla "army"; normally the same key people served as both party leaders and guerrilla officers, especially as attrition took its toll. A state committee usually provided the command and staff for a guerrilla regiment, of which ten existed by 1950. They operated not as regiments, however, but typically as district companies and branch platoons (and later in much smaller groups).

The size of these active forces was badly underestimated in the early years; the best guess is that they numbered about 12,000 in 1948. British intelligence believed that about 60 percent of the old wartime guerrillas, many of whom had stayed in the jungle, rejoined what later was renamed the "Malayan Races Liberation Army" (MRLA), and provided most of its officers. The insurgents were equipped mostly with rifles, pistols, and light automatic weapons, largely from wartime British supply drops. Few mortars were ever found. They also lacked radio, which made them highly dependent on very slow courier communication — a crucial handicap as time passed because the security forces could react much more quickly than the guerrillas could coordinate.

Supporting the guerrillas was the *Min Yuen* (or People's Movement) organized clandestinely cell by cell, largely in the Chinese squatter villages. It provided the link between the guerrillas and their popular base, supplying food, drugs, information, recruits, and money — largely by coercion and extortion among the Chinese community. The Min Yuen was not composed of Communist Party members, and was linked to the MCP only through the lowest echelon branch committee. The British estimated in 1952 that active working members of this separate logistic structure numbered about 11,000 (of whom 3,500 to 4,000 were armed).[23] By this time a more specialized group of ten-man "Armed Work Force" sections had been formed from the guerrillas themselves as well as from the Min Yuen to handle the increasingly difficult task of linking the guerrillas with their sympathizers. They worked for the district committees.

The Min Yuen, and related groups such as the Armed Work Force, Self-Protection Corps, and later the Masses Executives, played a crucial role. Gradually these support groups became larger than the guerrilla force itself; indeed, the latter eventually had to be drained to stiffen up the former so that the guerrillas might survive. Without them the guerrillas could not have survived for so long, since relatively little aid was even received from outside Malaya and Singapore.

Over time it was U.K./GOM success in separating the active insurgents from this support which reduced the insurgency to minor proportions.[24]

F. Course of the Insurgent Movement, 1948-1960

By the time the GOM declared an Emergency in June 1948, the terrorist campaign was already in full swing. The wartime guerrillas had been recalled and regrouped in the jungle to operate largely against the rubber estates along the jungle fringe and the tin mines. Apparently the insurgents hoped to disrupt the key rubber and tin industries on which Malaya's whole economy depended. Administrative dislocation and the sheer terrorization of the population were other aims.* Incidents rose rapidly. The MRLA initially organized eight regiments, but operated in these early days largely in company groups of about one hundred. The MCP seemed prepared for an early mass uprising.

When it did not occur and the opposing security forces grew, a lull set in 1949 while the insurgents withdrew to the deep jungle to regroup and rethink. Recognizing that an early mass revolt was no longer in the cards, their leadership decided on a more systematic strategy of classic Maoist pattern. It was to gain control of selected rural "liberated" areas by destroying the local government structure village by village through terrorism and attacks on local police posts.[25] The people in these areas would then be used to flesh out an organized guerrilla army, which in the final phase would move out of the liberated areas to take over progressively the whole country. Insurgent "incidents" again rose sharply in late 1949 and 1950. They reached their highest intensity between July 1950 and the end of December 1951. Perhaps their symbolic high point was the assassination of British High Commissioner Sir Henry Gurney in October 1951.

---

*That terror was a major technique is shown by the fact that the 4,668 civilian casualties in 1948-1960 exceeded the number of security force casualties (4,425). Some 1,055 civilians were killed or wounded in the peak year of 1950 alone.

But the gathering U.K./GOM response, reflected in a steep rise in security force contacts and kills after July 1951, was already forcing the insurgent hand. In October, even before Gurney's death, the MCP leaders directed an end to indiscriminate terror against civilians, which they found was alienating the very people on whom they depended for support, in favor of much more selective targeting. This MCP Politburo directive of October 1951 (not captured by the British until late 1952) was a tacit admission that the 1948 policy of quick takeover had failed.[26]

By this time, however, the insurgency had passed its peak, as reflected in the estimated decline in guerrilla strength from 12,000 in 1948 to something over 7,000 in 1951 and to only about 2,000 in 1957. Insurgent-created incidents dropped sharply from 450-500 a month in the period July 1950-December 1951 to around 100 a month by early 1953. Guerrilla casualties also told the tale, rising sharply to 70-100 a month by December 1950 and staying there till December 1953.

That the MCP knew the insurgency to be hopeless was evident when in late 1955 MCP leader Chin Peng made overtures for peace. The GOM, now led by Tungku Abdul Rahman as Chief Minister, offered full amnesty, but involved negotiations foundered on the GOM's refusal to accept Chin Pen's bedrock condition of legal status for the MCP. However, continued pressures and GOM amnesty offers produced some substantial mass surrenders in 1957-1958. By 1960 guerrilla strength and activity had declined so much that in July the Emergency was declared officially over. During the twelve years 1948-1960 the insurgents had lost 6,710 killed, 1,287 captured, and 2,702 surrendered — a total of 10,699.

II. MAIN LINES OF THE BRITISH/ MALAYAN RESPONSE

Though Britain and Malaya had been slow to appreciate the purpose behind the rising tide of violence in 1947-1948 and their initial response was confused and inadequate, they gradually evolved a long-haul, relatively low-cost strategy which proved successful over time. Through a process of trial and error, they slowly managed to separate the guerrillas from their support among the people and eventually to reduce the guerrillas themselves to a remnant. Such a response was facilitated by the insurgency's limited scope and lack of external support. But it was also as much a product of necessity as of design — severe financial limitations almost dictated a low-cost approach.

What makes the U.K./GOM response most notable is the multifaceted techniques employed — utilizing all available civil and military assets — and the degree of flexibility in its adaptation to the nature of the insurgent threat. It was not primarily a military effort but rather one in which the military played only a limited though indispensable role. Even in its security aspects, it was as much a police as a military operation.

A. Factors Shaping the Response

We have already noted several factors tending to favor the insurgency. Another was the *initial weakness of the security forces*. In March 1948 there were 30,000 troops in Malaya and Singapore, but only 11,500 in Malaya itself, of which but 5,800 were combat troops. The understrength police numbered only 10,000. Hence, police and troops together were not much stronger than the 12,000 guerrillas plus their Min Yuen support organization, especially when one considers that most policemen and many troops were tied down on static defense or routine law-and-order tasks. Also, almost no intelligence network directed at the insurgents existed at the time.

On the other hand, the British had several important factors working for them from the outset, on which they shrewdly capitalized. All were factors notably lacking in the U.S. experience in South Vietnam:

1. British-Malayan Ties

Not least among them were the long experience of the British in Malaya, their knowledge of the country, their control or influence over the local government, and traditional local respect for impartial justice under rule of law — a strong suit of British-trained local administrations. But as Sunderland remarks, "this was not a situation . . . in which British administrators were giving orders to a subservient oriental population." Rather, "persuasion and negotiation were the order of the day,"[1] while the Federation was headed by a U.K. High Commissioner assisted by an appointed Legislative Council, much power was reserved to the sultans of the nine semisovereign Malay states, which had mostly Malayan administrations. Only the two "straits settlements" of Penang and Malacca were directly U.K.-governed.

2. A Viable Administrative Structure

Also important was the framework of accepted civil administration which existed, though unwieldy and decentralized because of the mixture of quasi-autonomous Malay states and settlements. The federal administration handled defense, foreign affairs, commerce, communications, finance, and the judiciary. All else was administered by the states and settlements. Under them came 71 districts.[2] All levels were jointly staffed by British and Malays, with an increasing proportion of the latter as time passed. However, both army and police had mostly British officers.

A tiny elite, the Malayan Civil Service of 300-320 highly selected senior members (36 of them Malayan in 1948), held the key administrative posts, including that of District Officer. Below it came the Malayan Public Service, consisting of a senior cadre of about 2,500 in the government departments (of whom all but 587 were British) and a much larger junior cadre which was mostly local. Most senior British personnel were permanent career officers, which facilitated institutional memory. In sum, a well-organized territorial machinery with long tradition was in place before the insurgency, and the British had a pool of experienced talent to draw upon.

Depleted by the long Japanese occupation, however, this administration was weaker than it looked. As late as 1949, most of the technical departments were estimated to be 40 percent understrength. Many remoter areas were virtually unadministered, especially the Chinese squatter locales that lacked even police posts. Relatively few officials or policemen spoke Chinese.

3. Malay Loyalty

That the insurgency failed to make any headway among multiracial Malaya's 49 percent Malay population or even among its large (12 per-cent) Indian community crucially weakened its popular appeal. On the contrary, the Malays firmly supported the government and enlisted heavily in the security forces. Indeed, much anti-Chinese sentiment existed among them.

4. Anticolonialism Not a Major Issue

Closely related was the fact that Malaya had never been ruled in the classic colonial manner. In fact, as part of the decolonization process after World War II, the U.K. Labour government created in 1946 a short-lived Malayan Union, designed to enfranchise the entire population — including the ethnic Chinese — and to reduce the rulers' autocratic powers. It aimed at facilitating eventual independence for Malaya as a unitary state. But growing Malay resentment forced reversion to a federation in early 1948. Nonetheless, early independence was hardly in doubt, which robbed the insurgent movement of this element of appeal. Not only was the GOM in 1948 being Malayanized, but it was clear that the transition to full self-government would not be long delayed (see Section VIII).

5. Economic Constraints

One key factor that almost forced the U.K./GOM to opt for a long-haul, low-cost counterinsurgency strategy with maximum use of locally available assets was the United Kingdom's postwar economic straits. Britain had emerged from World War II almost bankrupt, needing vast aid infusions from the United States for its own postwar recovery. Moreover, the Malayan Emergency spanned a period of often acute competing demands for limited U.K. resources: the 1948-1949 Berlin Blockade, the Korean War, threats to Hong Kong, Middle East trouble before and after Suez, Cyprus, the Mau Mau troubles in Kenya, and NATO force commitments. Malaya was only one of many problems confronting Britain. Hence, London was able to contribute only modestly to Malaya, and required the latter to finance the C-I effort mostly from its own resources. The U.K. paid only for the British military units used and for some equipment, plus some modest grants for development projects.

But the GOM too was in sore economic straits from the wartime Japanese occupation and its aftermath. Of its two chief revenue sources, tin mining had come to a virtual standstill during the war, while rubber production was way down and prices were depressed. Long a food deficit area, Malaya was forced to use its slender reserves to purchase rice. Until 1950 the GOM was so short of funds that it had to calculate each month "whether there was enough to pay even the next month's salaries."[3] On the other hand, Malaya's natural wealth proved a longer-term boon. The Korean War brought a temporary boom in rubber prices, none too soon. They so swelled GOM coffers that the government was able to meet its whole cost of the Emergency in 1950 and 1951 from current revenues.[4] But rubber slumped again in 1952-1953, bringing a recession and forcing retrenchment, especially in the police and paramilitary forces.[5]

B. U.K./GOM Policy and Strategy

It is easier to pick out the main lines of U.K./GOM counterinsurgency policy and strategy in retrospect than it was at the time. But after an initial period of confusion, the local leadership settled on and gradually developed an effective C-I strategy. Its main features were:

1. Balanced, Multifaceted Response

For many reasons — the limited scope of the insurgency itself, existence of a sound administrative structure, competing local demands, and financial stringency — the U.K./GOM opted from the outset for a balanced civil/police/military response. It was designed to capitalize as much as possible on all available local resources rather than bring in large forces from outside. It relied even more on the civil arm than on the military; for example, full-time police strength (including special constables) was always far greater than that of the military. And all measures were carried out within the framework of an impartial rule of law, which was carefully modulated though firmly enforced (see Section IV).

2. Territorial Framework

Owing to the relatively small number and wide dispersion of the guerrillas and the existence of a viable civil structure, the U.K./GOM response could be organized on an essentially territorial basis. War management followed existing administrative lines from village to district to state to Federation level. The police were already organized in this manner. Though the pattern varied, troops were usually assigned on a similar basis, a brigade to each state and a battalion to each district. Stress was laid on working through the existing local administration. This also permitted minimum disruption of normal activities and socioeconomic life.

3. Unified Management

Rather than create a separate C-I command chain, the U.K./GOM managed the campaign via a British-style committee system, which essentially followed and fleshed out the existing civil administrative structure at each level and linked closely together at all times the military, police, and other civil aspects of the effort. The principle of civilian supremacy was maintained throughout, even when military men occupied civilian posts. Though top policy direction became increasingly centralized, execution was decentralized to state and district level or even below (see Section III).

4. Reliance on Intelligence

Though good intelligence on the insurgents was badly lacking at the outset, the U.K./GOM came to emphasize it as crucial to success. Instead of building up a big new military intelligence structure, they opted for expansion of the Police Special Branch as by far the best-suited to the purpose (see Section V). Major reliance was placed on inducing defections (a key source of intelligence) and on other forms of psychological warfare (see Section IX).

5. Separating the Insurgents from the People

Correctly appreciating after a while that the jungle guerrillas would be decisively weakened if they could be cut off from their sources of support among the population, the U.K./GOM launched a series of major programs — chiefly registration, resettlement, and food control — to deny men and resources to the guerrillas (see Sections IV and VII). Perry Robinson calls resettlement "the operational turning point of the Emergency" and food control what "hit the bandits hardest. . . ."[6]

6. Satisfying Popular Aspirations

Wisely, the U.K./GOM sought to temper the adverse impact of such tough control measures by parallel efforts at improved economic and social services. Popular support was seen as essential to victory. A major rural development program was undertaken (**see** Section VII). At the same time, the British made every effort to bring the ethnic Chinese fully into Malayan political life, as a viable alternative to revolt. Phased steps toward independence further undercut the MCP contention that revolt was the only road to this goal (see Section VIII). In the second half of the Emergency, after the U.K./GOM had gained the upper hand, these efforts became their main preoccupation.[7]

C. High Points of the C-I Response

But all of the above evolved only over time, out of the U.K./GOM's growing realization that their initial C-I response was wholly inadequate — as became evident during 1948-1950:

1. Initial Steps and Mis-steps, 1948-1950

When the rising tide of violence finally forced the U.K. High Commissioner to declare an Emergency in June 1948, the military was called on to support the civil power. Tough Emergency regulations were promptly issued, especially registration of all adults and permission for preventive detention without trial (see Section IV). Malcolm MacDonald, representing the British Cabinet as Commissioner General in Southeast Asia, played a dynamic role in galvanizing the federal authorities and having priority given to protecting rubber plantations and tin mines. [8]

Since the security forces were very thin on the ground, their buildup became an urgent need. First emphasis was placed on rapidly expanding the police and paramilitary forces. Various local guard forces organized by the rubber plantations and tin mines were put under police control as "special constables" or auxiliary police. By the end of 1949 their strength had risen to almost 18,000 regular police, 30,000 special constables, and 47,000 auxiliaries (see Section V). This helped free the military from static security missions for offensive jungle probes. Arrival of three Guards battalions from England helped beef up army strength in Malaya and Singapore to 32,000 by March 1950 (though not all was available for Emergency use).

There is little doubt, however, that in the early years both the top Federation authorities and the British Labour government underestimated the extent of the threat and took inadequate steps to meet it. In mid-1940 Major General Boucher, the General Officer Commanding Malaya District, told the Federal Legislative Council that "this is by far the easiest problem I have ever tackled. In spite of the appalling country and the ease with which he can hide, the enemy is far weaker in technique and courage than either the Greek or Indian Reds."[9] Two years later, the tide still had not yet turned. Though the mass uprising had fizzled, Harry Miller in his perceptive book grants that "the first three years of the war were largely three years of failure in the field."[10] Clutterbuck gives this description of the early years:

> By the spring of 1950, though we had survived two dangerous years, we were undoubtedly losing the war. The soldiers and police were killing guerrillas at a steady 50 or 60 a month, and getting 20 or 30 surrenders, but the Communists were more than making up for this by good recruiting. The soldiers were killing about six guerrillas for every man they lost in the jungle, but the hard-pressed police posts were losing more men than the Communists. The guerrillas were murdering more than 100 men a month, and the police seemed powerless to prevent it. There was a growing danger that the police and the civilian population would lose confidence in the government and conclude that the guerrillas in the end must win. The main reason why we were losing was that the guerrillas could get all the support they needed — food, clothing, information, and recruits — from the squatters. It was quite impossible to police and protect them. The squatter areas, insofar as they were governed at all, were ruled by the Communist parallel hierarchy, which the squatters accepted . . . the squatters had little to lose from a collapse of the established order and economy; and besides, they had no option but to pay "taxes" and provide food for the guerrillas. Thus, the Communists were fast building up their strength and their support, and at the same time, stocking up arms and ammunition by raiding or corrupting the village police posts.[11]

Other problems abounded. The GOM had not yet geared up fully from a peacetime tempo. Unified top-level command was lacking, little good intelligence was yet forthcoming, and guerrilla contacts were largely a hit-or-miss affair. Coordination between military and police was still poor in many respects (see Section VI).

2. The Briggs Plan of 1950

Recognizing the deterioration, the U.K./GOM agreed that someone had to be put in charge. London nominated Lieutenant General Sir Harold Briggs, who had retired in 1949 as commanding general in Burma and had much antiguerrilla experience, to be Director of Operations. Briggs proved an inspired choice. Both the organization he firmed up and the plans he developed were crucial to later success.

Having arrived in April 1950, Briggs developed what is known as the "Briggs Plan," a framework for C-I management and operations which, with later modifications, lasted throughout the Emergency. It was not a "plan" in the formal sense, but rather a series of programs laid out by Briggs shortly after his arrival to:

a) *Separate the guerrillas from the people.* To this end, Briggs gave first priority to a massive scheme for resettling the 400-500,000 Chinese squatters in "new villages" where they could be better protected, more closely watched, and far better cared for (see Section VII).

b) *Formalize and strengthen the C-I management system.* He rationalized and gave formal sanction to the pyramid of informal "directing committees which had grown up at various levels."

c) *Strengthen intelligence as the key to antiguerrilla operations.* This role was given to the Police Special Branch (see Section V).

d) *Deploy the security forces on a primarily territorial basis.* Briggs favored distributing a brigade to each state and a company or so per district for small-unit operations instead of the heavy emphasis on large troop sweeps. He also built up the local plantation, mine, and village defense militia. In September 1950, for example, he directed that every village form a Home Guard (see Section V).

The efforts set in train by General Briggs marked the turning point in the Emergency, although many results did not show until after he retired in November 1951. The bulk of the resettlement was completed by 1952. Guerrilla-initiated incidents began a permanent decline in the second half of 1951, while security force contacts rose greatly by 1951 and kills equally so. But the war was still far from over. Life in the countryside remained largely disrupted, and the guerrillas were still a potent force. Their assassination of Sir Henry Gurney in October 1951 — the symbolic high point of the insurgency — brought under new scrutiny the whole question of how the war was being handled.[12] It galvanized the U.K./GOM into fresh efforts.

3. Turning of the Tide, 1952-1954

Spurred by the assassination, Winston Churchill (just elected Prime Minister again) sent his new Minister of Colonies, Oliver Lyttelton, to Malaya. Lyttelton's six chief recommendations were (a) unified control of civil and military forces; (b) reorganization and training of the police; (c) increased educational effort, especially in the primary school, to help win the war of ideas; (d) improved protection of the resettlement areas; (e) an enlarged Home Guard, to include more Chinese; and (f) review of the Civil Service to insure that the best men were recruited.[13] General Sir Gerald Templer was appointed both High Commissioner and Director of Operations with in effect proconsular powers (see Section III).

Another step was to beef up the security forces even more. By the end of March 1952, army strength in Malaya alone (excluding Singapore) had reached 28,000, of whom 22,200 were fighting troops. It stabilized at around this level. By the end of 1951, police regular strength numbered 26,154, special constables 39,870, and part-time auxiliaries some 99,000. The special constables stabilized at about this level, but police expansion continued, and the Home Guard auxiliaries increased to a peak of about 200,000.

Until the end of 1951 U.K./GOM strategy had necessarily been defensive; in 1952 it swung over to the offensive. Jungle operations were intensified. Resettlement of the squatters had deprived the guerrillas of their main source of food and facilitated population control. Controls over food and other supplies were tightened. Indeed, by 1953 special food control operations in suspect areas became the dominant operational technique. Special efforts were made to improve the lot of the people in the "new villages" (see Section VII).

During 1952-1954 the backbone of the insurgency was effectively broken. Two-thirds of the guerrillas were wiped out. Terror incidents fell from 500 a month in 1951 to fewer than 100 by 1953, and total friendly casualties went down from 200 monthly to under 40. But the key to success was less the patrols and ambushes in the jungle than the tightening clamp on the MCP and its Min Yuen political and support organization, which forced the MCP to milk its guerrilla units to keep that organization going.[14] While the pervasive pattern of controls was hardly popular, major efforts were made to explain their impact and purpose. Indeed, strong incentives were provided to the people to avoid contact with the insurgents. Templer strengthened these in 1953 by instituting a policy of declaring "white areas," from which the Emergency Regulations were lifted once insurgency in them had died down. Malacca was declared the first "white area" in September 1953.

4. Mopping Up, 1954-1960

By mid-1954 the new Director of Operations, General Bourne, saw the problem as one of preventing a stalemate in which — if the guerrillas "lay low and kept their political and supply organization intact, the Emergency Regulations and military pressure would be relaxed, leaving the surviving guerrillas free to rebuild their offensive capacity."[15] Since the Briggs-Templer strategy of rolling up the insurgents from south to north had not proved too successful, Bourne modified it to one of destroying the insurgent organization in the weakest areas first, so that these could be declared "white" and troops could then be concentrated against the toughest "black" areas in western Malaya.

This strategy gradually worked, although subject to many complaints from planters and mine owners now chafing under the Emergency Regulations in black areas. By mid-1955, a third of Malaya's population lived in cleared "white" areas, and the security forces were gradually being phased down. Mass surrenders, triggered largely by two key defectors in 1957-1958, permitted overwhelming concentration on the few

tough black areas left. None of these was finally cleared until 1958-1959.[16]

When the Emergency was officially terminated in July 1960, twelve years after it began, there were no more than 20 or 30 guerrillas left in Malaya itself. The Emergency Regulations were lifted everywhere, except for a few needed to guard against subversion.[17] To this day, however, Chin Peng and a group of diehard guerrillas still lurk across the Thai border, and are even beginning to operate in northern Malaya again.

The human toll over the twelve years was surprisingly low, though this reflects more the peculiar nature of the insurgency — with its notable lack of large-scale engagements — than its low intensity. Police and paramilitary casualties were almost double those of the military. Though civilian casualties were as high as both combined, their modest total reflects both U.K./GOM self-discipline in controlling the use of firepower, and the ultimate ineffectiveness of the insurgent terror campaign. Two-thirds of them were incurred in 1948-1951 (see Table 1).

D. Financial Costs of the Emergency

A remarkable feature of the U.K./GOM effort was its relatively low incremental cost of under U.S.$800 million over the twelve-year span. Though complete figures are hard to come by and it is difficult to separate some Emergency costs from other outlays, enough is available to give the order of magnitude involved.

Malaya itself bore the lion's share of the costs — almost three-fourths. This was a heavy burden, taking for example 40 percent of GOM outlays in 1952, 32 percent in 1953, 23 percent in 1954, and 17 percent in 1956, after the insurgency had declined. Emergency needs also had to compete with growing demands for reconstruction, improved social services, and economic development — which further stimulated pressures for a low cost C-I strategy. Fortunately, Malaya's tin and rubber exports brought it a favorable trade balance every year of the Emergency. Through such good fortune, plus the careful management which helped hold down Emergency outlays, inflation was kept under control and the GOM was able to cope with Emergency as well as other demands.[18]

Fortunately, most annual incremental costs beyond normal GOM expenditures were carefully

TABLE 1

* CASUALTIES DURING THE EMERGENCY
(June 16, 1948 - July 31, 1960)

Insurgents	
Killed	6,710
Captured	1,287
Surrendered	2,702
Wounded	2,810
Total	13,509
Malayan police	
Regular police killed	511
Regular police wounded	701
Special constables killed	593
Special constables wounded	746
Auxiliary police killed	242
Auxiliary police wounded	154
Total	2,947
Military Forces	
Killed	519
Wounded	959
Total	1,478
Civilian Population	
Killed	2,473
Wounded	1,385
Missing	810
Total	4,668

*Source: Edgar O'Ballance, *Malaya: The Communist Insurgent War, 1948-1960*, Archon Books, Hamden, Connecticut, 1966, Appendix 'A', pp. 177-178.

TABLE 2

ANNUAL GOM EMERGENCY EXPENDITURES
(in U.S. dollars)

Cost of Emergency to GOM, 1948-1956		$373,980,000
1948 -	4,620,000	
1949 -	16,500,000	
1950 -	19,890,000	
1951 -	51,150,000	
1952 -	69,300,000	
1953 -	89,100,000	
1954 -	48,180,000	
1955 -	40,260,000	
1956 -	34,980,000	
Cost of Emergency to GOM, 1957-1960		$112,722,428
1957 -	40,194,388	
1958 -	34,919,424	
1959 -	23,828,826	
1960 -	13,779,790	
Cost of Emergency to U.K. Treasury, 1948-1960		$235,200,000
Total:		$721,902,428

Annual figures are from GOM *Weekly Press Summary*, August 15, 1953; GOM *Annual Reports*, 1953-1956; and from GOM *Annual Estimates*, 1959-1962. All above figures are actual costs, however; estimates give the actual expenditures for the most recent year (e.g., the annual estimate for 1959, prepared in 1958, will use the actual emergency expenditures for 1957). Conversion is on the basis of Malayan $1.00 = U.S.$0.33.

segregated as *Emergency expenditures,* especially after 1950. For the twelve-year period these add up to U.S.$486,702,428, which corresponds rather well to a *Straits Times* figure of $556,750,000.[19] GOM outlays rose gradually to a 1953 peak of about U.S.$89 million, then dropped to some $48 million in 1954, and declined gradually thereafter (see Table 2). These figures do not include the costs of economic and social development programs of more general benefit, which were carried in the regular federal budget.

Costs to the British Treasury have been given as £84 million, or U.S.$235 million. Of this, £68 million represented the incremental cost of maintaining troops in Malaya over normal cost at their home stations, and £16 million repre-

sented special U.K. grants to the GOM.[20] Most of these costs were incurred prior to 1955.[21] Australia and New Zealand probably paid for their own forces and gave other aid as well.

It is more difficult to break out U.K./GOM civil from military costs, but the former (including police and paramilitary forces) appear to have been at least twice as high as the latter. Indeed, on an incremental basis, total police and paramilitary costs alone appear to have been about as high as military costs.[22]

III. MANAGING THE C-I EFFORT

A special premium was placed on effective management by the very nature of a C-I response which required pulling together a wide range of civil and military efforts while avoiding more than minimum administrative disruption and facilitating a shift from U.K. to GOM leadership during the insurgency itself. This need — like many others — was not immediately recognized. But after a few years of floundering, the U.K. and the GOM found an answer notably different from that attempted in Vietnam. What they gradually developed — first at lower levels and then at the top — was an unusual civil/military form of unified management by committee. By all accounts, it played a key role in Malaya's successful counterinsurgency response.

Rather than exclusively British, it was a combined U.K./GOM conflict management, which became progressively Malayanized as Malaya moved toward independence — in a remarkably smooth transition. True, such factors as the long and intimate U.K./GOM relationship, the existence of a viable civil-administrative structure, and the limited extent of the insurgency made evolution of such a management structure far more practical than it would have been in South Vietnam. It is interesting to speculate whether, if the insurgents had been able to mount a greater military threat (as happened in Vietnam), a more military chain of command would have been established.

A. Weakness of Initial Command Structure

Inherent in the Malayan C-I effort from the outset was an apparent understanding that its direction would remain under the civil government structure at every level and would not be delegated to any special command. With some modification, this principle remained in effect throughout the Emergency. In keeping with traditional British practice, the military was subordinated to the civil power.[1] When the Federation declared an Emergency, the military was called on in effect to support the police. At no time during the Emergency did the senior British military hierarchy in the Far East — or in Malaya itself — have directing authority over operations (see Section VI).

On the other hand, when the Emergency first arose, there was no central planning or directing organization to deal with it. After Sir Henry Gurney became High Commissioner in October 1948, he put in direct charge of the Emergency effort the senior GOM civil servant, Chief Secretary M. V. del Tufo. In July 1948 Mr. W. N. Gray, a senior policy officer who had been Inspector General of the Palestine Police, had been brought in to direct the police and auxiliary forces. Presumably the police were in charge. But the task of expanding the police many-fold turned out to be a full-time job for Gray,[2] and the military commanders took the lead in operations. Informal directing committees rapidly developed at state level, usually composed of the chief police officer, the British adviser to the local sultan, the sultan's prime minister, and the local army commander.[3] Similar civil-military "committees" emerged at district level, usually with the civilian District Officer in the chair.

This system did not work well initially. As noted, the police and other civil elements were often too thin to shoulder the burden until they had been considerably beefed up. Police-military cooperation left a good deal to be desired in 1948-1950.[4] Intelligence was weak or wholly lacking. Funds were also scarce, since tin and rubber export prices were depressed. By 1950 these obvious weaknesses and the rise in terrorist incidents led the British Defence Coordinating Committee (Far East) to find the overall C-I direction unsatisfactory and to recommend that a civil coordinating officer directly under the High Commissioner be put in charge. It is significant that the committee focused at once on the management problem, something to which the United States has devoted far less attention during its long involvement in Vietnam.

B. The Briggs Reorganization

In order to maintain the principle of civil control, the GOM asked London for someone who was at least nominally a civilian, and London nominated the recently retired Lieutenant General Sir Harold Briggs to the unusual post of Director of Operations (DO) under the High Commissioner. Briggs' role was to be not one of command but rather a form of operational control. He was "to plan, to coordinate, and direct the anti-bandit operations of the police and fighting forces."[5] The police and armed forces could still appeal his decisions to the top civil or military authorities.

The unusual management structure which Briggs set up or strengthened to integrate C-I direction reflected what was practical at the time. One observer says that he brought what might be called "joint thinking" into the direction of the Emergency effort.[6] Another notes how:

> . . . he saw that what was wanted to deal with the peculiar nature of the Malayan Emergency was a new alignment, a new integration of the Army, and the Police with the civil administration. This was not a new idea but the credit is due to Briggs for picking it up and giving it a local habitation and a name. . .
>
> To my mind, the integration of these three services — an experiment in which Malaya has been a pioneer — has a significance which goes far beyond the Malayan Emergency in which it has proved its success. I think it contains the secret, not only of the successful conduct of this sort of semi-civil war, but also the secret of the defence of communities — especially of under-developed communities — against penetration, against subversion.[7]

C. The War Executive Committee System

As formalized by Briggs, the war executive committees were the operational nerve centers controlling and coordinating all facets of C-I operations at state and local level. This system reflected not only the particular needs of the Malayan situation but the oft-remarked British ability to run things by committee, in which coequal representatives of different services or departments have displayed an unusual capacity to reach firm policy decisions.

At the top of the Malayan committee pyramid, Briggs created in April 1950 the *Federal War Council,* which formulated overall policy and allocated resources. Briggs initially presided, but soon the High Commissioner himself took over to give the Council more authority. It also included the Chief Secretary, the Federation Secretary of Defense, the Police Commissioner, the General Officer Commanding (GOC) Malaya, and the Air Officer Commanding (AOC) Malaya. Later others were added. But Briggs, with a small staff, played the key role. To underline his civilian status, he wore civilian clothes.

Each of the nine Malay states had a counterpart *State War Executive Committee* (SWEC). Its chairman (always a civilian) was the Mentri Besar, the Malay grand vizier or prime minister to the local sultan. It included the senior civil servant (usually the British adviser to the state government), senior police officer, and senior soldier (usually a brigade commander), plus an executive secretary seconded from the MCS. The Special Branch head and the Home Guard Officer were usually present. Others often attended, such as deputies, staff officers, civil officials, planters, and other local community representatives. Thus most important operations of government were represented, reflecting Templer's later dictum that the regular operations of government could not be separated from those of the Emergency. The SWECs met weekly or biweekly, but each had a smaller *operations subcommittee* which met more frequently. It usually included at least the chairman, the senior military and police officers, and the local Special Branch head.

At district level a similar *District War Executive Committee* (DWEC) was formalized, chaired by the District Officer — the senior civilian. The senior police officer and the battalion commander or his deputy were members. The Special Branch officer and later the local information officer were added. Other officials attended as needed, and eventually prominent local leaders became unofficial members. At the lowest level, a company commander normally would establish his command post in the local headquarters of the police to facilitate coordination.

At Briggs' direction, each SWEC and DWEC created as its nerve center an *operations room,* manned by the military and the police on a 24-hour basis to bring together and display relevant intelligence and operational data. Each morning the key members of the SWEC or DWEC would gather at the operations room for what was known as "morning prayers" to review the situation and direct any action required.

It is significant that the SWECs and DWECs were action bodies, composed of commanders and executives, not staff officers. They took a wide range of civil as well as military decisions, which were recorded in minutes and disseminated up and down. SWECs and DWECs ordered police and military operations, controlled food supplies, set curfews, handled resettlement decisions, laid on information and psychological warfare operations, and the like. They also served as a device for prompt coordination among a variety of agencies and interests, which facilitated quick response. Equally significant, these committees served as vehicles for the review and exchange, on a regular and continuing basis, of all available information from all civil and military agencies concerned with the Emergency. As a means of keeping everyone fully informed at each key operating level, they proved an invaluable device. Lastly, they forced top civilian officials to participate in counterinsurgency direction instead of confining themselves mostly to normal administration. This also meant that military and police decisions were constantly subject to review by senior civil officials who were aware of any political implications they might entail.

Yet there were still many flaws in the 1950-1951 organization, especially at the top:

> No important decision could be carried out until it had been ratified by eleven state and settlement governments, the federal government, and the government of Great Britain — thirteen in all. The military director of operations had too limited an authority and was hampered by the civil officials. They had a "business as usual" tendency to carry on their normal work as if the revolt did not exist, and only assist the Director of Operations as they feel disposed to.[8]

Briggs' lack of command authority over military and police also created problems, particularly vis-á-vis the Commissioner of Police.[9] In his own final report, he apparently stressed how these limitations on his powers affected his ability to get particularly the police to move. Indeed, in a farewell interview he publicly declared that he had not been wholly satisfied with his powers and that this had led the GOM to promise that his successor would be given greater ones).[10] Briggs furthermore had to refer decisions to the High Commissioner through the civilian Chief Secretary. Additional delays and confusion were caused by the fact that the armed services and other agencies often issued separate instructions to their SWEC representatives. Bureaucratic habits, civil and military, died hard. As the *Straits Times* summed up the situation:

> The original problem was that there was no Director of Operations, and even no conception of the strength of the Communist challenge. It was a long time before there was effective cooperation between the police and the military, and a longer time still before the Government could bring itself to appoint a

Director of Operations. When General Briggs came out there was reason to believe that the war at last would be fought as it should be fought. Yet when General Briggs left Malaya just over a month ago, he revealed that he too had never had the authority he needed.[11]

D. Templer's Management Changes

The assassination of Sir Henry Gurney and Winston Churchill's election victory — both in October 1951 — set the stage for the next major management changes. Churchill thought that the loss of Malaya in 1942 had been partly due to divided control.[12] When he sent Minister of Colonies Lyttelton to Malaya, the latter's first recommendation on his return was to unify civil-military control under one man.[13] Chosen was General Sir Gerald Templer, the former Vice Chief of the Imperial General Staff. Churchill told him, "Ask for power, go on asking for it, and then — never use it."[14] In February 1952 Templer was appointed to the merged posts of High Commissioner and Director of Operations, with strengthened powers. As High Commissioner he was in charge of the civil authorities, while as senior military officer he was empowered to issue direct operational orders to the armed forces in Malaya. Divided command at the top was thus unified.

Templer reorganized his office under two deputies. General Sir Rob Lockhart (who had briefly replaced Briggs as DO) became Deputy Director of Operations and in effect his chief of staff. D. C. McGillivray, a veteran Colonial Office official, was named Deputy High Commissioner to assist Templer on the civil side. A clean sweep of other senior personnel also took place. Police Commissioner Gray had retired at the end of 1951; to replace him, Templer borrowed A. E. Young, the Commissioner of Police of the City of London. Chief Secretary del Tufo also retired, apparently since his position had been drastically changed by Templer's new powers. The Director of Intelligence resigned as well, and his post was reorganized (see Section V).

One of Templer's first acts was to issue a thirty-four-word directive:

> Any idea that the business of normal civil government and the business of the Emergency are two separate entities must be killed for good and for all. The two activities are completely and utterly interrelated.[15]

To reinforce his point, he then merged the Federal War Council with the Federal Executive Council (the High Commissioner's "cabinet"). This further integrated the civil-military direction. A smaller group of members met more frequently — usually weekly — and was called the Director of Operations Committee. Chaired by the DO, it included the senior service commander, the police commissioner, and the Director of Intelligence, as well as the Secretary of Defense and Chief Secretary of the GOM.[16]

However, Templer's chief contribution was in dynamic leadership and driving energy rather than in his management changes. He merely improved upon the basic structure already created by Briggs. But he fully used his unique powers to galvanize the C-I response, transferring officials or officers who didn't measure up. He was constantly on the move around the countryside, leaving much of the day-to-day management to his two deputies. In his capacity as Director of Operations Templer used a remarkably small staff (as had Briggs). It never exceeded nine officers: a brigadier, four officers of lieutenant-colonel rank (soldier, airman, policeman, and civil servant), and their four assistants. Four or five of them were usually with him when he traveled.[17]

E. Transfer of Power: 1954-1957

By mid-1954 it was clear that the GOM had gained the upper hand, and Templer was able to return home. Since the improved situation made it unnecessary to continue his unique post as both civilian and military proconsul, normal Commonwealth practice was resumed. His civilian deputy, Sir Donald McGillivray, became High Commissioner, and Lieutenant General Sir Geoffrey Bourne became Director of Operations subordinate to McGillivray. Bourne retained more operational power than Briggs had had, however; he was made clearly senior to the army and air commanders in Malaya (indeed he prepared their efficiency reports).

To conform to Malaya's transition toward independence, Bourne expanded the now effectively functioning SWEC/DWEC by adding local civilian officials and dignitaries. In October 1954 he added five important politicians to his Director of Operations Committee. In January 1955 this widening of membership was extended to the SWECs and DWECs. Such Malayanization was also deemed essential to prevent the new political leadership then emerging in Malaya from being able to escape responsibility for tough counterinsurgency decisions. Thus the SWECs and DWECs became important instruments in the gradual transfer of power to local leadership.

Also to this end, the top-level Director of Operations Committee was revamped in March 1956 as an *Emergency Operations Council*, and placed under the chairmanship of Tungku Abdul Rahman (Malaya's top political figure) in his new capacity as Minister of Internal Defense and Security. The DO became its executive officer, responsible to it for the day-to-day conduct of operations and with operational control over all security forces allotted to them.

Though the Emergency dragged on for three years after independence, few more management changes were made except for further Malayanization. All war executive committees had Malayan chairmen. Most senior Malayan army and police officers remained British, but they were now servants of (and paid by) the GOM. As one such officer has noted, all were "responsible to elected Malayan ministers, with no channel at all, either open or secret, to London."[18] They served as executives or commanders, not as advisers, but subject to the direction of the Malayan government at all levels. Of course, British and Commonwealth forces, while under the operational control of the DO, were financed by their own governments. They had a right of appeal from the DO's orders to their own higher authorities, but this was never used.

At times during the latter phases of the Emergency, the DO actually commanded troops. When in June 1956 the Federation Army was created, the DO doubled in brass as its first commander.[19] When Malaya became independent, however, the two jobs were again separated, so that the head of the new army could concentrate on building it up. But in 1959 the then DO (General Sir James Cassells) suggested that there was no further need for separation, and they were once more joined.[20]

In sum, the highest direction and operational conduct of counterinsurgency throughout the 1948-1960 Malayan Emergency were on both a joint civil-military and a combined British-Malayan basis. Call it war direction by committee if you will, but the fact is that it worked. It provided a viable managerial device for integrating U.K./Commonwealth and Malayan efforts and for pulling together all the multiple strands of C-I operations.

IV. ENFORCING THE RULE OF LAW

Of great value to the counterinsurgency effort was the British reputation for impartial administration and fair-minded justice. While the U.K./GOM enforced strict controls and occasionally took ruthless measures, it was done within a recognized framework of rule of law and subject to frequent public debate. Throughout the Emergency the U.K./ GOM acted under a clear legal mandate, for the most part scrupulously observed, which carefully spelled out what the security forces could and could not do.

"A state of emergency is quite different from martial law," by which the military takes over governing powers.[1] This never occurred in Malaya, even locally. The civil authorities retained power, and civil courts retained jurisdiction. There were no military courts. When the Emergency was declared in June 1948, it was given force and effect by a series of drastic special laws (Emergency Regulations) promulgated by the federal legislature. "As revised in 1949 and amended in 1953, they ran to 149 pages, covering subjects as diverse as possession of firearms, powers of arrest and detention, control of food supplies, and clearing of undergrowth."[2] They provided the legal framework for the whole C-I effort, and helped greatly in breaking the links between the insurgents and the people.

A. Registration of the Population—ID Cards

Perhaps most important among the special laws was a nationwide program to register everyone over twelve years old. (The MCP made considerable use of children as couriers and spies.) The program got off to a slow start, but by March 1949 some form of identity card had been issued to everyone registered — some 3,220,000 persons. Originally each Malay state or settlement had its own registration form, but in June 1950 a uniform ID card for the Federation was decided upon, and a Federal Registra-

tion Department created to carry out the scheme.[3] Each ID card bore the holder's photograph and thumbprint plus other data.[4] The scale of the effort is apparent from the fact that from 1950 (the first year that full statistics were reported) through 1956 some 1,059,956 new cards and 1,855,865 replacement cards were issued. Every time a person moved, his ID card had to be changed (as happened 1,887,136 times in the period 1953-1956).[5] Cancellations because of death, departure from Malaya, etc. were also meticulously handled. To provide citizens with incentive to protect their ID cards, they were required for a variety of purposes — such as food rations, space in a "new village," and building permits.

This registration/ID card program proved highly effective over time in helping to separate the insurgents from the population, especially in the squatter villages. It facilitated frequent police identity checks, often by having an early morning cordon thrown around an entire squatter settlement. The insurgents tried to disrupt the system by terror, forgery, and destruction of ID cards (in 1950 and 1951, for example, 151,450 cards were seized or destroyed).[6] When the insurgents made workers in the rubber plantations and rice paddies a special target and took away their cards, the GOM frustrated this by collecting the cards at the village gate when the workers went out into the fields and issuing tallies until they returned. Most important, the system made it very difficult for the guerrillas to live in the villages or even to circulate freely outside the jungle.[7]

B. Other Key Emergency Regulation

Other important provisions permitted detention without trial; the right to search and arrest without a warrant; imposition of curfews; imprisonment up to ten years for knowingly possessing MCP documents or assisting MCP propaganda; a ban on the MCP itself; the right to shoot on sight in specified "black areas;" resettlement from and to specified places; and food control. All these powers, adequately enforced, played a key role in forcing the insurgents into the jungle, weakening their links to the people, and impeding their activities.

But not all were equally wise. Perry Robinson sees as one of the "major mistakes" the early

1949 Emergency Regulation imposing up to the death penalty for "consorting" with terrorists. He points out that many Chinese could hardly avoid consorting in a sense when protection was inadequate.[8] This regulation was suspended in August 1952. The Regulations were applied, however, within the limits of widely publicized and careful safeguards, including judicial review and appeal. For example, a Public Review Board of independent citizens examined each case of detention-without-trial (at first once a year and later every six months) and heard appeals.[9] As an area was declared "white," certain Emergency Regulations were suspended.

Another severe law allowed levying collective punishment against people of an uncooperative village or town, though this was done only a few times. After Gurney's assassination, the GOM closed the nearby small town of Tras and incarcerated all its two thousand inhabitants.[10] In 1952, after a nearby ambush had killed the British district officer and eleven others, Templer himself imposed a strict twenty-hour house curfew and reduction of the adult rice ration by more than half on the town of Tanjong Malim. This lasted two weeks, till information was forthcoming from the people.[11] The regulation was repealed in 1953 as unfair to innocent members of the population.

The MCP, its front organizations, and the MCP-dominated labor union federation were declared illegal in July 1948, and some 600 party members were arrested in an initial police sweep. MCP control over the trade unions has been undermined earlier in 1948, when the Trade Union Ordinance was amended to require all union officers to have served at least three years in the industry which the union represented. Union federations were limited to those within a single industry. This effectively quashed the MCP-dominated Pan-Malayan Trade Union Federation. Many unions collapsed when their erstwhile leaders decamped to the jungle with union funds.

C. Detention and Banishment

Two of the most powerful and most controversial control measures were Emergency Regulations 17-D and 17-C, permitting detention of suspect persons and the deportation of noncitizens. During the early days, when it was especially difficult to distinguish ordinary civilians from MCP terrorists or Min Yuen members, large numbers of suspect Chinese were incarcerated in inadequate detention facilities under Regulation 17-D. The process of sorting them out through interrogation took a long time. By the end of 1948 some 5,100 people were being held on detention orders; by end-1949 the total had risen to 8,500.[13] It peaked in 1951 at 11,000. But by mid-1955 there were only 1,200 hard-core persons under detention. Rehabilitation camps were established, including a special one at Taiping in Perak for those who were not hard-core cadre but merely supporters. They were taught civilian trades, and few if any ever regressed.[14] By 1957 some 34,000 people had been detained at one time or another.

Even more dreaded was Emergency Regulation 17-C, which allowed the GOM to deport noncitizens to their country of origin. It was a powerful weapon because few Chinese were citizens. According to one account, 26,000 were deported to Mainland China before the Communist takeover there put an end to the practice.[15] During 1950 alone 3,773 detainees (and 3,324 dependents) were repatriated to China and 73 to India.[16] This regulation also was repealed in 1953.

V. KEY ROLE OF THE POLICE IN SECURITY AND INTELLIGENCE

A notable feature of the U.K./GOM counterinsurgency effort was the primary role assigned from the outset to the police. Their importance was stressed by both Briggs and Templer, the two senior military officers who were the chief architects of this effort. In fact, the police and the paramilitary forces under their aegis fielded far more men and had a far larger hand than the military in providing local security, thus helping to free the troops for the offensive role (in which the police participated). The police also played a key role in enforcing the rule of law so essential to separating the insurgents from the people. Policemen suffered far more total casualties (2,947) than did soldiers (1,478) during the Emergency; of the regular police alone, almost as many were killed (511) as military men (519).

But perhaps the greatest single police contribution was the gradual development of a police intelligence system which became the eyes and ears of the entire C-I effort. Brigadier Clutterbuck terms the police "the decisive element" in dealing with the Malayan insurgency; they provided the "security and intelligence" for which "the army was a support but not a substitute."[1]

A. Buildup of the Regular Police

The 10,000 regular federal police were weak and 2,000 understrength in 1948; the force had not yet been rebuilt to its prewar standards. Moreover, despite the polyglot nature of Malaya's population, the police were mostly Malay with a small number of British officers. Chinese speakers were sadly lacking; in 1947 the force had only 24 Chinese inspectors and 204 policemen.[2]

When the Emergency was declared in 1948, among the first major steps was to expand the police force rapidly and to create large paramilitary forces. But quantity was easier to get than quality, and it took some time before training and equipment could catch up. By end-1948 regular strength had reached over 15,000; by the end of 1952 it had risen to some 28,000 — including 2,488 Chinese. To create an effective communications network, the army provided the police with radios, etc., while trainers and operators were lent by the army, navy, and RAF.[3]

Numerous problems persisted, however, so that, when Templer brought in Young as Police Commissioner in 1952, the force was completely reorganized. An extensive new training program was developed, with emphasis on basic civil police duties and good relations with the populace. A new Police Training College opened in October 1952.[4] Full-time regular police and special constables were cut back in 1953, when falling rubber prices forced a GOM fiscal retrenchment, and stabilized at around 20,000. By 1959 only about 7,000 were regarded as engaged in Emergency duties.[5]

B. Police Role in Local Security and Antiguerrilla Operations

Though the police played the major role in local area security from the outset, initially they were woefully ill-equipped for a task of this magnitude. The main task of the police was, of course, in the populated areas. In the early days the weakly manned village police post became a favorite target of guerrilla groups. But these posts were to be quickly strengthened. Gradually the local security force in each Chinese village came to be a police post of ten to twelve Malay constables, supported by a part-time Home Guard of about thirty-five men, of whom normally five were on duty patrolling the perimeter at night (see below). Most villages also had a Chinese Special Branch sergeant.[6] By 1951 the police had become able to take over many local security roles from the army.

In 1949 the police also formed their own platoon-size "jungle squads" for jungle patrolling — a total of 253 by the end of that year.[7] These men later were organized into a Police Field Force of about three thousand, specially trained to man posts in the deep jungle. The police conducted a significant proportion of total patrols and ambushes, perhaps as many as a third of the total. Their effectiveness was comparable to that of the army; in 1955 their kill/contact ratio of 0.65 was equal to that of the Malay infantry battalions and compared to the 0.85 average of all infantry battalions. In 1954 all regular police except the Field Force and Special Branch reverted to mostly normal police duties.[8]

1. The Special Constables

To reinforce the police in their local security role, two major paramilitary forces were raised. In 1947-1948 tin mines and rubber plantations had organized their own local guard forces. These were regularized as special constables under the police force and increased to 29,700 by end-1948. But training was a serious problem. It was largely done at first by mobile army teams, but then was taken over by some five hundred British police sergeants from the recently demobilized Palestine Police. The number of special constables rose to 40,000 by end-1951.[9] Templer stabilized them at about this level and greatly improved their training. Their chief role was local protection of mines and plantations. As security improved, many of the special constables were later organized into *Area Security Units* of twenty-one men whose primary task was enforcing food control, and *Police Special Squads* whose role was reconnaissance and patrol for the District Special Branch Officer. By 1958 special constables had been reduced to 22,000 —including 894 women searchers. They were completely phased out in 1960.

2. *The Home Guard*

In the early days, many exposed Malay villages (kampongs) had formed their own part-time village guards. Other groups were formed to guard plantation compounds. Under police auspices, they were furnished with old weapons; they were called auxiliary police. By the end of 1948 they numbered about 17,000 and by end-1949 about 47,000. In September 1950 General Briggs created the volunteer, part-time Home Guard as part of his squatter resettlement program, as much as a political move to commit the ethnic Chinese to the government as to get them to help protect their own homes. It was unarmed, and was put under a Federal Civil Defense Commissioner.

In late 1951 the Home Guard was further formalized and its role expanded. By the end of the year it had reached 99,000 men, of whom three-fourths were kampong guards and other auxiliaries who had been absorbed. A retired major general was made Inspector General; each state also had its Home Guard Officer. The District Officer in each district was put in overall charge, and given an inspector, under police discipline and paid from police funds, to supervise the local Home Guard. But it operated under the police; the Home Guard Officer dealt only with recruiting, training, and administration. A three-phase training program was launched, in the final phase of which the guards could be armed — usually with shotguns.

Apparently the Home Guard was regarded as increasingly useful, especially as guerrilla strength decreased. By 1953 some 50,000 Chinese were serving in it, mostly in the new villages, in addition to about 100,000 Malays and aborigines protecting some 2,200 of their own villages. Their performance was apparently such that Templer thought they could begin relieving the police of purely defensive duties. They were reorganized into a *static* and an *operational* Home Guard. The former had arms for one-third of its men, and was eventually to replace the police in village defense (the normal pattern was around thirty-five men in each village, five of them on duty each night). The latter was uniformed and organized into twelve-man armed sections for part-time use in a more active role. [10] Weapons and other training was provided by mobile instructor teams.

By the end of 1955 some 152,000 Home Guard members had become fully responsible for local defense of 173 out of the 410 "new villages" as well as for other villages. By 1956 there were 450 "operational sections," while overall strength began to be phased down. In 1958 the full-time Home Guard professional staff from Federation down to district level, including instructors, numbered only 419 out of a total reduced by then to 68,000 men. By end-1959 the situation had so improved that the Home Guard could be demobilized.

C. Development of Police Intelligence— The Role of Special Branch

Usable, timely C-I intelligence is hard to come by, and the experience in Malaya proved no exception. In the early period the counterinsurgency effort was largely flying blind. There also seems to have been a failure to appreciate the significance of intelligence and how to go about getting it. [11] For example, all too often insurgencies tend to be measured by their external manifestations — incidents, attacks, terrorism, and sabotage — at the expense of the less obvious and far more complex evidence as to organization and key personnel. This is particularly true of military intelligence, and understandably so, since it is enemy activity with which the military have to deal. Thus, a lull in insurgent activity has often been misinterpreted as reflecting a decline in insurgent capabilities when, in fact, it may only have meant regrouping for a new phase.

Since in Malaya the C-I effort was regarded as primarily a civil one, the intelligence role was assigned to the police. In the British colonial tradition, the task of keeping tabs on potential subversives at local as well as national level had long been a function of Police Special Branch — usually a small, elite professional group. A Federation-wide Special Branch had been established in Malaya as long ago as 1919. [12]

But in 1947-1948 Special Branch was in as bad shape as the rest of the police. During the short-lived Malayan Union, it had even been taken out of the police and put in the new Malayan Security Service as its local political intelligence arm; only the Criminal Investigation Division (CID) was left in the police. But the two functions could not be separated in an insurgency where criminal terrorism and political subversion were part of the same problem. So in August 1948 a Malayan Special Branch was reestablished under the Deputy Commissioner of Police as one of two branches of the CID.[13]

In the early days of the Emergency good intelligence was a sometime thing. The military had to rely largely on their own resources. Guerrilla contacts were mostly hit-or-miss affairs. Information was still lacking on suspect Chinese, and the clandestinely organized MCP made a special effort to keep its activities secret. Little was known about the MRLA order of battle or command structure. A critical weakness was the lack of competent Chinese linguists who could develop information in the clannish and self-isolated Chinese community, and a special effort was made to recruit more talent. (The lowest rank in Special Branch was sergeant; most members were senior NCOs, warrant officers, or commissioned officers.) A Chinese contingent was created in Special Branch. But routine surveys and patrols, not targeted operations, were the best source of kills and captures in 1948-1950.

Briggs noted the lack of intelligence as a key weakness and stressed improvement. Resettlement and other measures taken under his aegis also helped develop intelligence leads. The Special Branch staff was strengthened at all levels. SWECs and DWECs always had the local Special Branch officer as an unofficial member, which greatly facilitated coordination of operations with intelligence. But in 1950-1951 "the difficulty was mainly the creation and training of adequate staff to handle intelligence."[14]

It remained for Templer to give intelligence first priority and to reorganize its direction for this purpose. Prior to this time the head of Special Branch apparently doubled in brass as chief intelligence officer on Briggs' staff, and so was heavily weighed down with line duties. In April 1952 Templer made the post of Director of Intelligence a purely staff post, in which the Director was responsible to Templer for coordination and supervision of both police and army intelligence. To handle this job Templer brought in Mr. John Morton, an experienced civilian who was chief of MI-5 in Singapore. A small combined intelligence staff was created to assist him.

Morton clearly delimited the respective intelligence functions of the military and the police. Special Branch was given primary responsibility for intelligence on the insurgents. All military-generated raw intelligence such as captured documents, and any prisoners or defectors, were sent to Special Branch for exploitation. The military handled only local and immediate combat intelligence for their troops in the field (aside from aerial photography and other air reconnaissance). The regular British secret intelligence agencies, MI-5 and MI-6, played no significant role. In recognition of its enhanced function, Special Branch was separated from the CID in April 1952. But it always remained a comparatively small elite group; in 1954, for example, it had only 459 men on Emergency duties.

Under this system the military did not develop a separate major intelligence structure but rather satellited on the police. To help provide the necessary linkage, some thirty "special military intelligence officers" were attached to Special Branch at various levels. They worked as liaison officers and expediters, collecting operational intelligence as it passed through Special Branch channels, putting it in militarily useful form, and seeing that it reached the troops promptly. Another link was provided by having the operations room of the SWECs and DWECs manned jointly by police and by intelligence sections of the brigades and battalions operating at state and district levels.

Several authorities have noted the problems involved in coordinating the police and military intelligence roles. Perry Robinson says, "it was very difficult in the early years for the Police to present the results of their Intelligence in a form the Army could use, and very difficult for the Army to appreciate the value of what the Police called Intelligence. . . . It was not easy; no subject has caused so much exasperation or so many major rows as the problem of getting the right sort of Intelligence and making the right sort of use of it."[15] But the point is that the system worked. As Brigadier Clutterbuck put it, "this was essentially a Special Branch war, and . . . they did win it."[16]

That British senior officers absorbed this lesson is also evident from remarks by the Director of Operations in the later Borneo confrontation with Indonesia, Lieutenant General Sir Walter Walker:

I am a great believer and a very strong supporter of Special Branch. When a properly established and fully manned special branch is on the ground then, in my view, military intelligence should be the servant and not the master of special branch. Why is this? It is for the simple reason that special branch officers and their staffs, and their agents, live in the country, speak the language and know the people. Indeed, they are of the people, whereas army intelligence staffs are here today and gone tomorrow and are continually rotating. To my mind it is a cardinal principle that reliable intelligence depends entirely on continuity at every level.[17]

Indeed, reflecting the peculiar nature of the Malayan insurgency problem, penetrating and building up intelligence on the insurgent structure became the predominant goal. Security force operations were frequently designed primarily to facilitate such penetrations. Sometimes operations were laid on to drive the guerrillas into areas where Special Branch already had established agents. Its weekly Intelligence Summaries grew steadily more detailed. Looking back on 1948-1957, the Director of Operations reported that the great majority of successful contacts with the guerrillas came to be brought about as a result of Special Branch work.[18] By 1957 Special Branch had a dossier on almost every individual guerrilla who was left.

Great stress was laid on captured or defecting insurgents, to exploit them for intelligence and psychological operations. Morton created an interrogation center staffed largely with ex-insurgents. As other measures took effect, the flow of intelligence from the ethnic Chinese population gradually increased and permitted much better targeting of security force operations. Many surrendered enemy personnel (SEPs) were successfully turned into agents and informers (see Section IX). In 1953 a Special Operational Volunteer Force was formed of SEPs, to go out on operations along with police or army units. It came to have about 300 SEPs in fifteen squads.[19]

VI. THE ROLE OF THE MILITARY

While the very nature of the Malayan conflict, the impact of British tradition and practice, and political-economic constraints all placed limits on the military's role in countering MCP insurgency, even this limited role was nonetheless essential to success. Especially in the early years, the police and paramilitary forces were wholly incapable of coping with the guerrillas unaided. During this period the military largely had to substitute for them in static security missions. But as these uncongenial tasks were gradually taken over by police and auxiliaries, the military could turn increasingly to offensive pressures on the guerrillas in the jungle.

Even so, the most striking feature of the military role in the Malayan Emergency is its atypical character. Instead of being a full-scale multiservice effort, it was mostly an army show. Instead of operating as a cohesive, integrated military force under their own high command, units were dispersed and used in support (and under the overall direction) of civil authority. Tactically, they never operated as divisions, and infrequently even as brigades or even battalions, but mostly in dispersed company and smaller units. Instead of having their own intelligence, they depended mostly on that from the police. While many problems and frictions occurred, it is impressive that the military proved so adaptable. Equally striking was their eventual mastery of jungle warfare; in a small-unit war of patrol and ambush they beat the guerrillas at their own game.[1]

A. Size of the U.K./GOM Forces

The small size of the regular military forces involved is also notable. Up through 1951 the army alone probably had fewer fighting men than the insurgents. When the Emergency began, there were only 5,784 combat troops in Malaya, plus 5,660 service troops. Their backbone was eleven understrength infantry battalions — six Gurkha, three British, and two Malay. These forces were on peacetime T/O, and not until early 1951 were they allowed war strength (around 800 men per battalion).[2] Combat reinforcements were quickly brought in from the adjacent Singapore base area, which throughout the Emergency also provided essential logistic support.

In early 1952 the number of fighting troops in Malaya reached over 22,000 — including twenty-three infantry battalions — out of a total of under 30,000. They stabilized at around this level — at end-March 1956 there were 22,500 combat troops in Malaya out of a 31,400 total. They were then phased down, until by 1960 strength had declined again to under 20,000 (of which 14,000 were combat troops).[3]

Of the combat units involved, perhaps the workhorses were the six Gurkha battalions which stayed throughout. British battalions rotated in and out; the three in Malaya in 1948 grew to seven by end-1949 and to a dozen in 1952. The Commonwealth was represented by Australian and East African battalions, a Fiji battalion, and a New Zealand SAS unit. A Royal Marine commando brigade (battalion equivalent), an SAS regiment, and part of a parachute regiment served at various times. Dyak and Iban tribesmen from Borneo — recruited after 1948 to serve primarily as jungle trackers with infantry patrols — were organized in 1953 into the Sarawak Rangers.[4]

A special effort was made to build a Malayan army. The two Malay Regiment battalions existing in 1948 were gradually increased to nine in 1956. Parts of them were formed into a new Federation Regiment on a multiracial basis (unfortunately few Chinese volunteered). Cadets and officers were sent to the United Kingdom for training. A Federation Army was formed in 1956. Also created were a Royal Malayan Navy and an RAF Regiment (Malaya). All three formed the nuclei for Malaya's armed forces after independence. By the end of the Emergency, the Malayan army's nine battalions provided roughly half the infantry still deployed.

B. Control of Military Forces

It is noteworthy that at no time during 1948-1960 did the higher military echelons in Malaya (division and above) formally control military operations through the military chain of command. The highest British military authorities in the Far East (located in Singapore) were the three commanders-in-chief of the land, sea, and air forces. Together they formed the Chiefs of Staff Committee (FE). Under Far East Land Forces (FARELF) were *inter alia* a Singapore Base District and a Malaya District, both administrative commands. An RAF command parallel to Malaya District also existed. The largest tactical formation was the 17th Gurkha Division. After 1952 the 1st Federation Division was formed to provide a nucleus for the new army of Malaya after independence, and in 1956 the Federation Army became an administrative entity.

But the primary role of all these headquarters was to train, administer, and support the forces allocated to the Emergency, and to plan and prepare for possible wartime contingencies in which the divisions would be reassembled. In the early days, when Federation police headquarters had primary responsibility for Emergency operations but were not up to overall management, GHQ FARELF and GOC Malaya played an informal operational role. But this changed when Briggs and especially when Templer took over. In U.S. parlance, the military retained command of troops and were responsible for their administration, training, and support. But operational control was in the hands of the elaborate network of war executive committees. Military resources were allocated by the military commands at the request of these civil/military directing bodies. Of course, GOC and AOC Malaya participated in these decisions as members of the Federal War Council, as did brigade commanders at SWEC level, and battalion or often company commanders at DWEC level.

The intermediate division commands almost never played a tactical role. Two abortive attempts to give such a role to a division commander by making him Deputy Director of Operations were abandoned because a division-level headquarters simply did not fit into the SWEC/DWEC territorial command system. A British major general, when asked about the role of a division commander in Malaya, replied that "As far as I can see, the only thing a divisional commander has to do in this sort of war is to go around seeing that the troops have got their beer!"[5] Only on the air side did the AOC Malaya in fact retain operation control over his assets, because of the need to allocate and supervise them centrally. He exercised this control through a Joint Operations Center.

As might be expected, difficulties arose at various times from such a command structure. Police and military modes of operation are quite different, to say the least, which produced complex problems of coordination and often friction. Miller cites how as of 1950,

> Coordination between the Army, the police, and the administrative officers was not as close as it should have been. The Army had never felt comfortable in their role of supporting the civil power; they were soldiers, many of them said,

fighting with one hand tied behind their backs. They were irritated by the slow, methodical tactics of the police. For their own part, the police were becoming irritated with the Army's superior attitude.

Operations were carried out on a basis of compromise between police and military methods. There was always divided authority on any large-scale operation involving troops and police. There was the inevitable clash between the soldier trained to deal with the enemy by all means within his power in the quickest possible time, and the policeman trained to act only after the fullest investigation and after convincing himself that he had got the right person.[6]

Also, as one brigadier observed of the early days, "no soldier wants to play second fiddle to a police force indefinitely that has demonstrated its inability to maintain law and order. . . ."[7] Despite these strains and stresses, police-military collaboration eventually worked out surprisingly well.

One unusual British military contribution was the creation under GHQ FARELF of a British Operations Research Section (FE) which between 1953 and 1957 produced some exceptionally valuable analyses of operational patterns. Among other things, these demonstrated that battalions which did well in marksmanship competitions also did well in ambushes, that advance information was crucial to the success of patrols and ambushes, and that jungle firing was ineffective at more than 100-yard range and was best done at no more than 20 yards.[8]

C. Tactical Employment of Army Units

While many problems were encountered, what stands out about the tactical employment of military forces in Malaya is the extent to which, though organized World War II-style for conventional operations, they for the most part adapted quickly to the atypical demands of small-scale jungle war.[9] Luckily a high proportion of commanders and troops had had jungle warfare experience in Burma in World War II, which stood them in good stead.

From the outset the army in Malaya was offensive-minded and sought to avoid being tied down. The first years must have been quite frustrating for military forces that were tied down partly to police-type local security work under civilian control and partly to tactical formations broken up and allocated territorially, and were mostly dependent on inadequate police intelligence for their eyes and ears.

But even when they were freer to operate offensively, their dominant mode of employment was atypical. They never were deployed as divisions and only infrequently as brigades or even battalions, but operated rather from "company bases" in platoon-sized or even smaller units. Small patrols and ambushes were the dominant, and certainly the most successful, tactical mode, especially after the MRLA guerrillas broke up into small units. Platoons or sections were normally rotated on the basis of twenty days in the jungle and ten days out.

Early emphasis was placed on systematic training for jungle operations. Marksmanship, junglecraft, and patrolling were stressed. A FARELF Training Center was created for individual and unit training. Advance echelons of newly arriving battalions flew out in advance to be trained as instructors for their units. Each battalion was given two months' initial training on the average before operational deployment.

The issue of *large- vs. small-unit operations* was a perennial one. In the early days, especially until new commanders learned the peculiar nature of Malayan jungle warfare, the army usually made the mistake of operating in too large formations. As Brigadier Clutterbuck himself attests, "the predilection of some army officers for major operations seems incurable."[10] Battalion- and even brigade-size task forces were often employed for jungle sweeps in 1948-1949, but seldom resulted in many kills or captures. Frequent changes of commanders and personnel slowed the learning process.[11] Also, the insurgents began operating in smaller groups, and in accord with Maoist doctrine usually withdrew rather than stand and fight for long. Systematic patrolling and small ambushes got better results. So, in October 1951, General Briggs laid down the principle that large-scale operations should be forsworn in favor of small ones acting on intelligence. His successors all shared this view. The most successful battalions almost invariably employed it.

By 1953, *food denial* — starving the guerrillas out — became the chief basis of military as well as other C-I operations (see Section VII). By stringently clamping down on the leakage of food to the guerrillas in a given area over perhaps many months, troops and police could drive them to risk coming out of hiding and thus exposing themselves to ambushes and patrols. Such techniques were gradually refined. Sunderland describes the unusually large and highly successful fifteen-month Operation GINGER in 1958-1959 in Perak State. It utilized an infantry brigade group of five battalions, a squadron (troop) of the Special Air Service, a troop of armored cars, two artillery batteries, and an engineer battalion, plus 1,899 police, Home Guard, etc. — a total of over 4,200 men. The ratio was about 20 to one. Little happened for about three months, but in the ensuing twelve months 222 guerrillas gradually were killed, captured, or surrendered.[12]

D. Artillery and Air Support

The military contribution in Malaya was predominantly from the army, and among army components it was chiefly an infantry war. Only two armored car units were used, mostly to patrol the roads. More surprising, only **six** two-gun troops of 25-pounder artillery were employed up to 1955, plus a few 5.5" guns. After 1955, nine two-gun troops were used. Instead of being sited in static positions, they were almost invariably attached to battalions on operations. Not until September 1957 was the millionth round fired off into the jungle. Compared to Vietnam, such small-scale artillery support is striking.

Air support was on but a modestly larger scale, except for air supply. Clutterbuck felt that "offensive air strikes . . . were the least important of all in Malaya" and "probably did more harm than good."[13] On the other hand, Colonel J. R. Shirley, who headed a British operations research team in Malaya during 1949-1951, recalled no evidence that air sorties had ever killed anyone but thought they had an undeniable psychological effect.[14] There simply weren't many good targets in the deep jungle where small guerrilla groups were widely dispersed. Inhabited villages were never bombed, strafed, or shelled. The combat aircraft available were mostly those assigned to Malaya and Singapore for more conventional contingencies. In 1957, for example, Malaya Air Command had one squadron of heavy prop-driven bombers and three squadrons of jet fighter bombers. Monthly ordinance expenditures peaked in 1951, averaging in January-September over 600 tons of bombs and over 1,700 rockets. A few successful bombing raids, one killing fourteen guerrillas and another ten, were made in 1956-1957.[15] But only 33,000 tons of bombs were dropped throughout the Emergency.[16]

Air supply, however, was indispensable. It gave the security forces an enormous advantage over the guerrillas in jungle operations. Only one squadron of eight transports was used for the purpose until December 1953, when a second was added. The monthly average of supplies delivered by air rose from around 13 short tons during the Emergency's first year to a peak of 324 short tons during 1955.

Casualty evacuation and air insertion, mostly by helicopter, were also important — not least to troop morale. Only between two and five small helicopters were available until 1954, when they were increased to two or three squadrons. Assault landings were not used, lest they prevent surprise. Other important uses of air were photo and visual reconnaissance, air observation of artillery fire, communications, and leaflet drops. Herbicides for spraying of guerrilla food plots in the jungle were first used in Malaya — though on a small scale. A comprehensive photo survey was completed early in 1953. Voice broadcasting to the guerrillas was also employed (see Section IX).

When SWECs and DWECs wanted air support for an operation, they could call on a mobile team of air planners. But Air Officer Commanding Malaya kept centralized control of air assets, and all bids for their use were channeled to a central Joint Operations Center set up next to HQ Malaya Command. The overall impression is one of imaginative use of a small but flexible air component.

VII. SEPARATING THE INSURGENTS FROM THEIR POPULAR BASE

In retrospect it is abundantly clear that one of the most effective U.K./GOM counterinsurgency techniques was the breaking of the links whereby the insurgents drew support from part of the Chinese community, especially the squatters.

Aside from security force operations aimed at enhancing local security in populated areas while driving the guerrillas back into the jungle, this was done through a series of carefully coordinated civil programs: (1) registration, travel control, curfews, ID card checks; (2) resettlement of the great bulk of the squatter population in protected new villages; (3) pervasive food and drug controls in "black" areas to deny the guerrillas access to food supplies; (4) accelerated social and economic development; (5) steady movement toward self-government and independence (see Section VII); and (6) public information and psywar programs designed to keep the population fully informed of what was under way (see Section IX). Each of these programs reinforced the others. Moreover, all were conducted within the framework of a rule of law which carefully spelled out what the government and security forces could and could not do.

This multifaceted civil/military effort is well illustrated by this account of Templer's first address to the Federal Legislative Council in March 1952:

> He began by saying that the Emergency could not be overcome by military measures alone, but must be fought on the social, economic, and political fronts as well. He spoke of the steps necessary to build up a united Malayan nation — such as an extension of citizenship rights to more non-Malays, the formation of a Federation Army, improvements in social services and education and the betterment of the economic position of the Malays. At the same time he outlined his plans for increasing the efficiency of the Police. Referring to political progress, he said that self-government must be built up from the bottom and local elections would have to be well established before elections to State and Federal Councils could be held.[1]

These programs reflected a dual strategy of control and accommodation — control of those people and resources which could fuel the insurgency and accommodation to those popular aspirations which were seen as helping rob the insurgency of its political appeals. This has been loosely called the carrot-and-stick approach. Great emphasis was placed on the former. Indeed, it was Templer who is believed to have first used the phrase about winning hearts and minds. He is cited as saying that "the answer [to the terrorists] lies not in pouring more soldiers into the jungle, but rests in the hearts and minds of the Malayan people."[2] But the enhancing of social, economic, and political opportunities was part of a carrot-and-stick approach designed at least partially to offset the adverse impact of a system of pervasive C-I controls. In this sense, the U.K./GOM approach fits as well into the Wolf-Leites model of how to cope with insurgency by organization and effective coercion as it does into the alternative model which they dub "hearts and minds."[3]

A. Resettlement of the Squatters

The crucial support being provided the insurgents by sympathizers or the coerced among the half-million Chinese squatters who lived largely unadministered along the jungle fringe quickly led the U.K./GOM to focus on how to break this link via regrouping or resettlement. But action was slow in coming, as land titles (a touchy issue under the jurisdiction of the various state governments) were involved. The Malay-dominated state governments were reluctant to appropriate funds or give up lands reserved for Malays to take care of Chinese squatters. A federal committee with state representation was formed, a report was made, proposals were approved, and the necessary Emergency Regulations were passed — but nothing very concrete had happened by the time Briggs arrived in April 1950.[4]

Briggs quickly agreed that the squatters and rubber tappers had to be relocated so that the guerrillas could not feed on them. He favored resettling the squatters in self-contained communities of about one thousand each, in which entry and exit could be strictly monitored and strict curfews enforced during night hours. Each settlement would be wired in, with entry only by special gates; if necessary, watchtowers, pillboxes, and floodlights would be provided. Each settler would get title to the land he tilled, and a sixth of an acre for his house and garden plot. But every effort would be made to see that the communities did not degenerate into mere detention camps. Schools, dispensaries, markets, electric light, and other facilities would be provided. Water would be piped in.

The success of the program was owing largely to careful planning and meshing of the efforts of many government agencies under strong central management.[5] Planning and execution was under the DWECs, but had to be approved at state level. Land was purchased in advance, and fortunately plenty of unused land was available. Actual resettlement was carried out as a military operation; surprise was essential so that the insurgents would not be forewarned. After an area was cordoned off by troops at first light, people were moved as short a distance as was consistent with security. Compensation was paid on the spot for anything (like growing crops) which could not be moved. If the squatters were moved more than two miles, a five-month subsistence allowance was paid while they raised new crops.

Resettlement's success was also owing to the fact that, in strong contrast to the later Strategic Hamlet program in Vietnam, it was carried out without undue haste. By the end of 1950 only 82 new villages with 117,000 people were complete or close to completion, and 58 more were in the pipeline. By end-1951 the number had risen to 429 villages with 395,000 people. By the end of 1952 there were 509 new villages with a population of 462,000.[6]

A select group of 430-odd resettlement officers, largely educated young Chinese, gradually were recruited to shepherd the new villages. Many were seconded from the Forestry, Game, Mines, and Survey departments, which were all but closed down anyway owing to insecurity in the countryside. An assistant resettlement officer, initially a European but later often a specially trained young Chinese, lived in the village as liaison with the government and to ensure adequate "aftercare" — the provision of improved services.[7] Local protection was initially provided from a police post established in each new village while a Home Guard was being trained. Then the Home Guard gradually took over. By 1955 about a quarter of the new villages had become responsible for their own defense. Still later, the Home Guard too was phased down to a largely standby basis as the area became secure. Equally important, the new villages were progressively accorded local self-government (see Section VIII).

In 1951 the GOM also developed a program to regroup the 650,000 rubber estate and mine workers. Locales that were capable of being protected were simply wired in and given additional protection, but in some cases workers had to be moved to resettlement areas like the squatters. Costs were shared between government and the employers according to an agreed formula. GOM costs for both programs over a three-year period are given officially as about $20 million.

Mistakes were made, especially in the early stages of the program, when some squatters were forcibly moved before adequate plans had been developed to settle them elsewhere. Many problems also arose over land tenure. Nor were the people happy about being uprooted. But they came to prefer the new villages, and almost none moved back to the old areas when these were later declared "white." Meanwhile, resettlement and regrouping greatly facilitated protection of the rural population, bringing it under effective GOM administration and separating it physically from the insurgents. Its success is suggested by the sharp drop in guerrilla-initiated incidents: As the program was completed, incidents fell from a 1951 average of over five hundred a month to around one hundred a month in 1953, though this drop is attributable to other factors as well.

By the end of the Emergency, around 530,000 people—over a tenth of the population—had been resettled in some 557 "new villages." Most were Chinese, but the Malays were not neglected; no fewer than 139 new villages were established for them (see table 3). Moreover, many of the new villages were in fact satellites of existing villages and towns (72 out of 139 Malay, and 198 out of 399 Chinese).[8] In sum, resettlement not only helped the C-I effort greatly but served as an instrument for local development and a means of integrating much of the rural population into Malayan society. Though sooner or later some form of resettlement probably would have had to be undertaken anyway to bring the squatters under normal administration, the effect of the Emergency was to force the government to carry out the bulk of the resettlement in a matter of months rather than years, and it has changed the face of Malaya.[9]

TABLE 3

Number of New Villages by Size of Population: 1959*

State	Population Under 1000	1000-1999	2000-4999	5000-9999	10,000+	Total
Malay						
Johore	5	1	1	-	-	27
Kedah	1	-	-	-	-	1
Kelantan	16	4	1	-	-	21
Negri Sembilan	6	1	-	-	-	7
Pahang	26	-	-	-	-	26
Perak	43	1	1	-	-	45
Selangor	7	2	2	-	-	11
Trengganu	1	-	-	-	-	1
Total	125	9	5	-	-	139
Chinese						
Johore	43	25	26	6	-	100
Kedah	11	11	7	-	-	29
Kelantan	-	-	1	-	-	1
Malacca	17	-	-	-	-	17
Negri Sembilan	20	8	5	-	-	33
Pahang	28	11	8	-	2	49
Penang**	3	3	3	-	-	9
Perak	29	27	33	12	3	104
Perlis	1	-	-	-	-	1
Selangor	15	16	14	6	2	53
Trengganu	2	1	-	-	-	3
Total	169	102	97	24	7	399
All Races*						
Johore	69	27	27	6	-	127
Kedah	14	12	7	-	-	33
Kelantan	16	4	2	-	-	22
Malacca	17	-	-	-	-	17
Negri Sembilan	26	9	5	-	-	40
Pahang	56	11	9	-	2	78
Penang**	3	3	3	-	-	9
Perak	80	29	34	12	3	158
Perlis	1	-	-	-	-	1
Selangor	23	18	17	6	2	66
Trengganu	3	1	-	-	-	4
Total	308	114	104	24	7	557

*Source: Data from the Malayan Christian Council, *A Survey of the New Villages in Malaya*, rev. Kuala Lumpur, 1959, pp. 21-46, as cited by Maynard Weston Dow, *Counterinsurgency and Nation-Building: A Comparative Study of Post-World War II Antiguerrilla Resettlement Programs in Malaya, The Philippines and South Vietnam*, University Microfilms, Inc., Ann Arbor, Michigan, 1965, p. 64ff.

**Including Wellesley Province.

***This table includes 7 Indian, 4 Thai, 2 Senoi, 2 Japanese, and 4 new villages of unknown racial composition. It excludes 28 new villages which had already been closed down.

B. FOOD CONTROL PROGRAMS

Close control of food and such other essentials as medicines was soon recognized as a valuable C-I measure, but as in the case of resettlement, some time elapsed before it was systematically applied. Not only was Malaya a rice deficit area, but the insurgents could not sustain themselves in any numbers in the jungle without external food supplies. Rice and food caches early became a major target of security force operations, and some controls were applied under the Emergency Regulations.

Yet not until June 1951, when squatter resettlement and growth of the police made it feasible, did General Briggs lay on a sweeping Federation-wide system of food and drug control, aimed at breaking the logistic links between the jungle guerrillas and their support in the populated areas. The system was administered by the SWECs and DWECs, which were allowed considerable local option. In "black" areas it involved strict rationing of certain foods at state discretion, village gate checks and curfew hours (also on roads), spot checks, careful inspection of road and rail traffic at checkpoints, mobile food-check teams, and strict accounting for all stocks and sales of specified foods and supplies. Food cans were even punctured when sold to prevent their being stored. Sales could be made only to people with ID cards, and records had to be kept for inspection in food-restricted areas.[10]

Curfews were an integral part of the system of control over movement of vehicles and people, the security forces assuming that anyone or anything moving after curfew was to be shot on sight — and to kill. The basic control document was the "food stuffs movement permit," which was used not only for food but for other materials and for hardware. At first such permits were issued only at district; as the system became more refined, food control offices were established at village level and the permits were issued there.

By 1953 Templer, refining the Briggs Plan, decided that the security forces should focus their efforts on the guerrilla supply parties operating near the jungle edge to force the insurgents to commit resources to defending their supply organization, thus making them vulnerable.[11] The guerrilla could not long exist — much less operate — on the natural food found in the deep jungle, which gave only an unbalanced diet. Nor could he live for long off the jungle aborigines — who were subsistence farmers with little or no surplus — except by confiscation and terrorist tactics which incited resentment and retaliation. Lastly, he could not cultivate any substantial area in the jungle without detection from the air.

In order to force the insurgents to make supply their major concern, the GOM turned to sizable food denial campaigns as the preferred form of security force operations. By July 1953 no less than 77 such operations had been mounted in the state of Negri Sembilan alone. "For the remaining years of the Emergency," says Sunderland, "patrol, ambush . . . inspections, cordon, and watch-and-ward activities associated with food denial became the major occupations of the Security Forces," replacing the earlier futile large-scale jungle sweeps.[12]

Sunderland gives a good account of some of the larger food control operations. He draws an analogy to a naval blockade. Briefly, each operation was preceded by weeks of secret planning and rehearsal. Choosing a proper target — one small enough for adequate deployment of the security forces available yet large enough to enforce denial of food to the guerrilla on a sufficiently punitive scale — was of primary importance.[13] Adkins states:

> Actually food denial was found to be too strong a word because it was almost physically impossible to deny food over large areas. This could be done only in small tightly controlled communities and even then seepage of small to even large amounts of food stuffs did occur.[14]

It did not take much "seepage" to feed a guerrilla who could subsist on a daily ration of a handful of rice. But he could store without detection only about six to eight weeks' supply, and the number of people, time, and effort involved in a "food lift" from village to jungle edge to deep jungle was such as to make the lift vulnerable to discovery.

Once the target was chosen (on the basis of careful intelligence), regulars moved out before dawn; by first light soldiers surrounded every village in their assigned areas. A heavy investment of police and soldiers was required to make the cordon effective. The system also demanded efficient and honest local administration. Food stocks over a certain specified amount were confiscated, and food rationing was instituted (sometimes at subsistence level), with strict accounting of all inventory, and sales limited to specified food and supplies. Sales could be made only to people with ID cards at shops where they were registered, and records had to be kept subject to inspection in food-restricted areas.

The police performed essentially police functions — maintaining checkpoints at village gates, inspecting road and rail traffic, and supervising and controlling the central cooking of rice in community kitchens (the rice was all stored by the government). This technique of community cooking as a control mechanism was based on the fact that cooked rice spoils in twenty-four hours in the tropical climate and thus could not be stored for any period of time. According to Adkins, however, central cooking was used in only a few, widely separated instances. It was apparently expensive in terms of manpower and required a high degree of control.

Meanwhile, the enlarged security forces would mount constant patrols and ambushes to keep pressure on the guerrillas, forcing them to keep on the move and making them vulnerable to ambush, destroying cultivated areas deep in the jungle, etc. The Home Guard protected and patrolled the perimeter of the "wired-in" villages.

All this took time. Seldom were there early results, as it was often months before the pressures told. Until the operation ended (some lasted for a year or more), every vehicle and every man, woman, and child in the village would be searched each time they left the village. (The authorities took great care not to offend local sensibilities; for example, only women searched the female villagers under the Emergency Regulations.)

Since food control was essentially unpopular (although in time it came to be appreciated as a blind behind which the people could refuse food to the guerrilla), an intense and continuing public relations program was conducted in each village. The people were told in advance what was expected of them, and the reasons for the imposition of the controls; the need to impose them was blamed on the guerrillas. Finally, they were promised that the controls would be lifted when the area was considered cleared of insurgents, there was little or no contact with the enemy, and the people had demonstrated a willingness to cooperate with the security forces by informing on the insurgents. The area would then be declared "white," under Templer's carrot-and-stick approach.

In 1956 an Emergency Food Denial Organization (EFDO) was created under the new Ministry of Defense and Internal Security to standardize and provide overall supervision of the food control effort.[15] It had food control officers on the SWECs and DWECs. But in 1958 the EFDO itself consisted of only 151 professionals and about 200 clerks; the actual conduct of food denial checks and operations was handled by the police and military under direction of the DWECs.

Over time, this complex of food and resource controls together with the food denial operations seem to have done a great deal to sap insurgent strength. It forced the guerrillas to expose themselves to patrols and ambushes, and eventually to surrender in increasing numbers under the pressure of hunger. The SEPs citing hunger as their reason for surrendering rose from none in 1949-1951 to 29 percent in January-February 1955. Those citing a corollary reason — hopelessness — increased from 21 to 36 percent over the same period.

C. Development and Assistance Programs

During the first few years the disruption caused by the insurgency probably had an adverse net effect on Malayan social and economic development. Various development projects had to be postponed because of diversion of resources to Emergency purposes and because of insecurity in rural areas.[16] Gradually, however, as it gained the upper hand, the GOM accompanied the controls imposed on the people with a series of programs designed to improve their lot. Of course, such programs were greatly facilitated by the availability of funds from the tin and rubber exports, which made Malaya unusually wealthy among South-east Asian nations. While the programs were intended primarily to help lead Malaya as a whole toward viability and stability, they also were designed with C-I benefits in mind. The "new villages" themselves were perhaps Malaya's greatest socioeconomic development project during 1948-1960.

Overall development was guided by a broad Federation Development Plan, which was drafted in 1950 and incorporated in the Colombo Plan for South and Southeast Asia. It was mostly locally financed, but received some help from the Colombo Plan donor nations, especially the United Kingdom. Included was a $200 million electric power program managed by an autonomous Central Electricity Board. [17]

One innovation was the Rural Industrial Development Authority (RIDA), begun on an experimental basis in 1950. It was designed mostly to help the Malay community; indeed a key aim was to meet the Malays' demand that they be helped to overcome their economic backwardness vis-á-vis the Chinese. From its inception it was based on the principles of self-help and response to local initiative. [18] It would assist local efforts, not dominate them. One of its major activities was the promotion of cooperatives, which the GOM encouraged. Some 2,123 had been formed by 1956. As early as 1953 RIDA was judged to have proved itself sufficiently to be converted from a government department to an autonomous corporation, backed by an annual subvention ($4.4 million through 1954) and a $3.3 million GOM loan but designed to be mostly self-financing. [19] RIDA established Development boards in every state and district, and in some places village boards, to which funds were allocated. Though a relatively small-scale activity in the early years, it probably had a positive psychological impact out of all proportion to its modest resources. After independence its activities were greatly expanded by the GOM, and the famous "Red Book" — a detailed rural development plan made up according to a standard format by each district's rural development committee — was one of the results.

Much attention was also paid to rejuvenation of the Malayan labor movement. When the Emergency was declared and the MCP banned, the MCP-dominated labor movement — which had used strikes so effectively in 1946-1948 — all but collapsed. The number of unions fell from 389 to 162, and membership declined by half. [20] There were many reservations about rebuilding incautiously what might again become a major threat. But with the advice of union officials brought over from England, a Malayan Trades Union Congress was formed in 1950. By 1956

union membership again exceeded that of 1947, though 62 percent of the members were Indian and only 16 percent Chinese. [21]

The full panoply of measures undertaken by the GOM with British advice and assistance is too much for discussion here; moreover, as already noted, many were aimed at general development, even though they also helped limit the insurgency's appeal. In this category fall the rapid postwar expansion of the educational system, greatly improved health services, social legislation limiting hours of work and regulating interest rates to prevent usury, public housing, and the like.[22] The essential point is that this wide range of improving services played a major role in creating a climate in which it was increasingly difficult for insurgency to gain popular appeal.

D. Dealing with the Aborigines

Until the Emergency little was known about most of the aborigines living in the deep jungle. Their numbers (which may be over 100,000) were grossly underestimated. But after 1951, as the insurgents retreated further into the deep jungle, they would persuade or force the aborigines to grow food for them, act as warning scouts, and serve in other ways. At one time, it was estimated that as many as 12-15,000 aborigines were under insurgent influence.[23]

The U.K./GOM response was quite different from that often taken by the GVN toward the much larger Montagnard population in South Vietnam. The small GOM welfare staff which worked with the aborigines was elevated to a government department in 1950 and was greatly increased. As Templer put it, "The control of aborigines in deep jungle will be achieved by taking protection and administration to them rather than resettling them in new areas."[24] Starting in 1952, police-manned deep-jungle forts (often air-supplied) were created to provide protection to the aborigines. Programs were developed to improve their living conditions and safeguard their rights. Over time these proved quite successful. Indeed, a small aborigine strike force of some three hundred was later established, which killed more guerrillas in the last two years of the Emergency than did all the rest of the security forces put together.[25]

VIII. STRATEGY OF POLITICAL ACCOMMODATION

At the same time that it helped Malaya deal with insurgency, Britain helped it move toward enfranchising its citizenry, self-government, and then independence — all in the brief space of ten years.[1] This would sooner or later have occurred in any case as part of the general postwar decolonization process which broke up the British Empire. But it is doubtful that Malaya would have moved as fast if there had been no insurgency. Sunderland cites John Morton, Director of Intelligence under Templer, as saying that the GOM could not have won without the positive political theme of a greater Malaya and that the U.K./GOM leadership saw its job as bringing the nationalist movement to the fore.[2] By deeds as well as words, the British managed to convince most of the people that Malaya was on the road to early independence. The visible progress in this direction — culminating in August 1957 — certainly helped limit the insurgency's appeal.

So too did simultaneous British efforts to settle the difficult communal problem created by the existence of large unfranchised Chinese and Indian minorities. Liberalizing the citizenship laws was seen by the British as essential to bringing these minorities into Malayan political life. Fortunately the felt need to counter the insurgency by stressing the benefits of responsive government also led the Malays to be more responsive to this endeavor and caused the Chinese community to be more interested than it would otherwise have been.

But it was the British rather than the Malays who initially forced the pace. Violent anticolonialism was notably absent among the Malays. The Malay aristocracy was in no hurry for independence. The rajahs of the various states held, in theory at least, all political power. No one had ever voted in an election. Moreover, it was Malayan resentment against the United Kingdom's pushing through enfranchisement of Chinese and Indians as well as Malays which caused the demise of the short-lived Malayan Union of 1946-1948.

It also led, in 1946, to formation of Malaya's first large political party, the United Malay National Organization (UMNO), a conservative grouping formed by wealthy Malays to oppose the Malayan Union. In turn a Malayan Chinese Association (MCA) was formed in 1949 both to agitate for improvement of Chinese status and to compete with the Communists for the allegiance of the Chinese community. Malcolm MacDonald encouraged its formation in order to help undermine the MCP's appeal. The MCA proved successful in this respect; it and UMNO came to form the political base of an emerging independent GOM.[3]

A. Broadening the Base of Government: 1951-1954

The 1948 *Federation of Malaya Agreements* between Britain and the eleven Malay states and settlements provided that "progress should be made towards eventual self-government" and that as soon as feasible legislative organs would become composed of elected members.[4] As the first step, a Federal Legislative Council was created with a majority of nominated "unofficial" members. The same was done with the eleven state/settlement councils. In contrast to the prewar councils (which had been advisory though influential), the new councils passed all laws and financial measures. In April 1951 six unofficial members of the Federal Legislative Council became in effect ministers responsible for various civil government departments, replacing the senior civil servants who had theretofore run them.

London's directive to General Templer in February 1952 stressed that Malaya should in due course become both "a fully self-governing nation" and a united one.[5] To this end Templer laid stress on developing the electoral process, and on enfranchising the Indians and Chinese. A compromise law in September 1952 extended federal citizenship to 50-60 percent of the Indians and Chinese.

In encouraging the parallel development of political responsibility through elected governments, of which Malaya had no experience, the British started at the local level. A federal ordinance of September 1950 provided for elections to municipal and town councils and later to rural boards. The first town elections were held in early 1952. The rural process began with appointment of village committees to handle local affairs. Then, in May 1952, legislation was passed for electing village councils in the Malay kampongs and in the "new villages" created by the resettlement policy. By 1955 more than 50 percent of the villages had elected local councils with an average 75 percent turnout at the polls. In the words of one student, this program "accelerated political change in Malaya and helped prepare it for self-government." [6]

Next came elections to state legislative councils, which were proposed by Templer in November 1952 and took place in 1954-1955, replacing the nominated unofficial members. The sultans became in effect constitutional rulers.

The electoral process also helped stimulate the development of political parties and coalitions. To contest the first municipal council election in January 1952 (in the capital of Kuala Lumpur), an alliance was formed between UMNO and the MCA. Later joined by the Malayan Indian Congress, this became Malaya's dominant political party — the Alliance Party. In 1953 it demanded an elected majority in the Federal Legislative Council and independence within three years. In 1954 it demanded a fully elected federal legislature.

B. Self-Government, Then Independence: 1955-1957

Templer was unwilling to go this far, but decided that the Federal Legislative Council would have an elected majority of 52, and 46 nominated members.[7] In the July 1955 federal election the Alliance Party swept into 51 of 52 elected seats. Though far more Malays than Chinese or Indians voted in proportion to their numbers, all the non-Malay Alliance candidates (15 Chinese, 1 Indian, and 1 Ceylonese) were elected. The Council's 98 members comprised 50 Malays, 26 Chinese, 12 Europeans, 7 Indians, 2 Ceylonese, and 1 Eurasian.

As majority party leader, the Tungku became Federation Chief Minister of an Executive Council (cabinet) composed of six Malayan and three Chinese ministers heading government departments, and five British officials. All were responsible to the legislature within its sphere. Though the High Commissioner retained his legal right of veto under the 1948 Federation Agreements, he never exercised it.

At a London conference in early 1956, the Tungku won further changes. Now all members of the Executive Council except the Attorney General and Chief Secretary became Malayan ministers (including Defense and Internal Security). This last raised an interesting problem of putting British troops under the authority of a Malayan minister. The solution was to leave the troops under the command of the British general serving as Director of Operations, but he would act (as before) under the general policy guidance of the top war council chaired by the Minister of Defense.

Many other thorny issues, especially communal ones, were resolved by a bargaining process before independence. A hard-fought compromise provided most Chinese and Indians with the franchise. The Chinese also won support for Chinese schools. On the other hand, numerous preferences were still allowed the dominant Malay community. The rajahs would become constitutional rulers and real power would reside in elected legislatures.

When independence was formally achieved on August 31, 1957, the administrative and legislative machinery was thus already in place and functioning. Hence little administrative change actually took place, except that remaining British officials became employees of an independent GOM. Though Malaya was the last country of South and Southeast Asia to become independent, it did so on a more stable and efficient administrative base — despite communal divisions — than most of the others.

C. Malayanization of the Administration

It proved a significant factor for stability that the basic political-administrative structure of the Federation was not radically altered by the sweep toward self-government and independence; it had been progressively Malayanized already. As early as 1948, most of the lower levels of the Federation administrative structure, and many of the higher, were occupied by local nationals. The highest level of the Malayan Civil Service numbered about 300, of whom 36 were Malays. The bulk of the larger Malayan Public Service (including the police) was local, though most of its higher positions were still held by Britons. In all there were about 2,500 British officials, mostly civil servants and police officers. A special problem was created by the limited number of Chinese.

Malayanization was accelerated during 1948-1957. Numerous students were sent to British higher schools. Entry into the Civil Service was liberalized in 1951. Over the period, the higher Civil Service ranks were progressively filled by local nationals as qualified men became available. The process was a gradual one. By June 1954 there were 107 Malayans to 161 British in the highest level of the Civil Service alone.[8] At the 1956 Malaya Constitutional Conference in London, a definite schedule was drawn up for the gradual withdrawal of remaining British personnel and their replacement by Malayans.[9] A Committee on the Malayanization of the Public Service was formed, with the Tungku as Chief Minister chairing it, to fill vacant posts and replace over time some 1,800 senior European personnel. In 1956 the entire Civil Service (all levels) numbered 106,600 of whom 61,000 were Malays, 29,000 Indians, 13,000 Chinese, and the rest largely Eurasians. 10

By the time independence arrived in 1957, most district police officers, infantry company commanders, and middle-level civil servants were already Malayans, largely owing to a crash training program concentrated on these levels in 1955-1957.[11]

IX. INFORMATION AND PSYCHOLOGICAL WARFARE

As part of their emphasis on multiple counterinsurgency techniques, the U.K./GOM gradually came to make extensive use of carefully designed information programs. These proved indispensable to explaining the "carrot-and-stick" approach. The purpose was to ensure that ample word on GOM activities reached all the people, on the principle that such knowledge could be a potent C-I weapon. Of course, for such information to be credible, it had to be accurate and reflect positive real-life acts. This was the case in Malaya, where progress toward damping down the insurgency, improving living conditions, and achieving self-government provided ample grist for the government propaganda mill.

Psychological warfare against the insurgents, aimed chiefly at weakening their morale and encouraging surrenders, was also extensively used. It became a major function of the information services. Leaflets dropped over jungle areas

were the means most frequently employed. Often quite sophisticated appeals were made, and a well-publicized reward system paid off handsomely. When Templer, in retrospect, "rated the information program as almost on a par with intelligence in combatting guerrillas. . . ,"[1] he doubtless also had these psywar aspects in mind.

Also interesting is how the U.K./GOM used their Emergency powers to keep a low profile on their protracted C-I effort both in Malaya and abroad. Strict censorship was enforced on the local media. The international press was provided with minimal access to news and services, and military communiqués were kept as uninformative and unexciting as circumstances allowed. As a result, not only was British domestic criticism of the war relatively low, but little international interest was aroused. Hence the MCP was unable to generate much significant leverage on London, a factor reinforced by its lack of any overt international sponsorship — a very different situation from that in Vietnam.

A. Information Programs

As in other aspects of the Emergency, it took some years for the information program to hit its stride. From the beginning the U.K./GOM saw the need to explain the rationale for the pervasive network of Emergency procedures to the affected population. In 1949 alone some 3.75 million copies of local newspapers and 50 million leaflets were distributed; public address trucks also reached 200,000 people a month by late 1949.[2] But for the first two years of the Emergency there was no information service and no coordinated antiguerrilla information campaign. In June 1950 a service was organized at the Federation level, with representatives in every state and increasingly in the districts.

Templer did much to strengthen information and psychological war. He brought in to head it in 1952 Mr. A. D. C. Peterson, who had psywar experience in Southeast Asia Command during World War II. All relevant activities were brought under his control. In 1953 Information became a full-fledged government department. Support of all media was provided by this one department. Information officers served on the SWECs and DWECs.[3] In 1955 Peterson was succeeded by the first Malayan to become head of a federal administrative department.[4]

Peterson regarded his aim as being "to detach the honest anti-colonialist from the Communists. . . . He believed that an information campaign had to have something to sell and that nationalism filled this need." This theme helped him to recruit young, progressive men who, after a six-week course, would go out into the villages and preach nationalism, using well-equipped mobile vans with a wide variety of equipment. By November 1958 there were ninety mobile vans and four boats, enough to permit field information officers to visit around a million people — one-sixth of the population — each month. These mobile field officers and their teams concentrated on the rural areas, especially the new villages, and mixed their information function with tailored psywar themes under the guidance of the local DWEC.[5]

Among other techniques a Malayan Film Unit produced topical movies; troops of SEPs would "satirize" guerrilla life; three radio stations produced programs in various languages and dialects; weekly and monthly newspapers were produced, besides booklets, pamphlets, and a multitude of press releases for the local vernacular press. Emergency expenditures of the Information Department from 1952 to 1960 were only $1.5 million, a comparatively modest sum compared to the impact achieved.[6] Perry Robinson notes this disproportion, commenting that the total annual cost of the Information Services was less than that of one jet fighter, and that allocating only a little more to psywar might have achieved even greater results.[7]

As part of the process of political education, the GOM also devised "civics courses." Selected local representatives were taken as GOM guests to visit government departments, hear lectures, and see demonstrations. Some 3,600 people attended civics courses in 1953 alone.[8]

B. Psychological Warfare

Although Peterson in retrospect saw the information program as more important to the C-I effort,[9] the government also put emphasis on psychological warfare aimed at the insurgents themselves. It not only made life as hard as it could for the insurgents but then proceeded to harry them in their loyalties, and (carrying this approach to its logical conclusion) made it as tempting as it could for them to surrender.

The primary objective of GOM psychological warfare was to increase the surrender rate.[10] But there were a number of obstacles to doing so. Insurgents feared the treatment they might be accorded after surrender. They also faced some danger in surrendering, for if they did not follow recognized procedures they might be shot by the security forces in the very act of giving themselves up. Psywar programs addressed themselves to both these problems, stressing the good treatment they would receive and giving specific instruction on how to surrender.

Secondary GOM psywar aims were to increase the tensions between the MRLA's leaders and its rank and file, and those between the MRLA and the Min Yuen, its covert supporters in the villages. Such efforts would no doubt have been far less effective if the British had not promised independence to the country, and begun as early as 1951 to make that promise into a commitment visible in the villages.

Psychological warfare functions were part of the work of the Information Services, which drew heavily on clues provided by Special Branch. The best psywar material was written by a Malayan Chinese team led by C. C. Too, which included several ex-insurgents.[11] The army was not allowed to establish its own information or psychological warfare service. However, a special Psychological Warfare Section was attached to the Director of Operations staff to plan operations against the insurgents in the jungle, while the Information Services remained responsible for carrying out the actual programs under the aegis of the DWECs and SWECs.

The size of these programs may be judged by the fact that in 1956 alone they included the recording of 639 separate voice messages, and more than 2,200 sorties by aircraft broadcasting these to insurgents in the jungle.[12] The main means of direct communication with the insurgents was the leaflet — thousands of which were dropped over suspect jungle base areas, promising amnesty to those who surrendered and telling about those who had already done so and others who had been killed. More general "strategic" themes were also used. Out of more than a hundred million leaflets dropped in 1956, one series of twenty million announced the outcome of the truce talks between Chin Peng and the Tungku, and the end of the GOM amnesty offer. Another series of ten million stressed the end of the amnesty and drew attention to the coming Chinese New Year and thoughts of family reunion. A third series of ten million warned that the coming of independence in the following year would in no way alter the determination of the government and people to destroy the MCP and to end terrorism.[13] The MPLA decreed the death penalty for anyone in its ranks found even picking such leaflets up.

C. The Rewards-for-Surrender Program

The heart of the government's psychological warfare was its rewards-for-surrender program. This addressed itself to the fact that killing an insurgent was — at least by any rational standards — exorbitantly expensive. Bribing insurgents to surrender, or others to provide information which would lead to their capture, was much cheaper. So bribes and rewards were set at levels which made them quite handsome by any standards. For bringing in an insurgent alive, they ranged from U.S. $28,000 for the Chairman of the Central Committee, down to $2,300 for a platoon leader and $875 for a soldier (see Table 4).

For information which led to the capture or killing of such officials by the authorities, the rewards averaged about 78 percent of these figures. When an agent brought about the capture or killing of two or more insurgents, these sums were cumulated. For one coup in which an agent's information concerning an insurgent camp led to an air strike that killed fourteen out of sixteen insurgents, the agent was awarded his bonus for all fourteen — a total of U.S. $20,000. According to an officer who knew of the incident, the agent became "no doubt a very prosperous man with his own business in Hong Kong or Singapore."[14]

The high scale of these rewards provoked some criticism that the entire approach was immoral. As one Australian soldier remarked, terrorists who were caught were treated like murderers, while those who surrendered were "treated like kings."[15] Even the smallest of the rewards — $875 — could have represented a lifetime of a worker's savings, but it would have been foolish to have made them any lower. For the dilemma which they were intended to resolve was that of money plus such safety as the gov-

	TABLE 4	

SCALE OF REWARDS FOR DEFECTION OR CAPTURE IN MALAYA*
(U. S. Dollars)

Group	Approximate Political or Military Rank	Malaya Bring in Alive, 100%
A	Chairman Central Committee	$28,000
B	Presidium Member	$22,700
C	Central Committee Member	$18,200
D	Province Secretary Regimental CO	$16,000
E	Province Current Affairs Member Front Chairman Battalion CO	$8,750
F	Province Committee Member District Secretary	$6,300
G	District Assistant Secretary Company CO	$4,550
H	District Committee Member Assistant Company CO	$2,800
I	Platoon Leader	$2,300
J	Cell, Squad Leader	$1,600
K	Ordinary Party Member Solider or Class A Laborer	$875

*Source: Stephen Enke, Vietnam's "Other" War, Tempo 66 TMP-112, General Electric Company, Santa Barbara, California, December 1966, p. 14.

ernment could provide versus no money and such safety as the insurgents could provide. Above a certain level the amount of money was often less important than the defector or informer's estimate of which side could protect him or hide him better from the other. Until the government could provide a defector or informer the protection he needed, the program got nowhere. But once it could do so — and make this clear to the insurgents — the program not only neutralized a large number of insurgents who might otherwise have continued fighting, but it also provided Special Branch with a large flow of intelligence (full cooperation with the police was the price of the reward).

The program thus began to pay dividends only slowly, and of course it was the totality of pressures exerted on the insurgents — not just psywar and rewards — which led to the growing toll. In the last half of 1948 only 56 insurgents surrendered. In 1949 the total increased to 251, but in 1950 it declined to 147. In the three following years it rose again to 201, then to 256, and in 1953 to its high of 372 (compared to 73 captured, 291 wounded, and 947 killed in that year).[16] During the twelve years of the Emergency, a total of 2,702 insurgents surrendered, compared to 6,710 killed and 1,287 captured. However, this total leaves out of account those who were captured, wounded, or killed on the basis of defector intelligence. It also ignores the profound effect which surrenders had on morale in the insurgents' camps, especially when SEPs were used for shrewd psywar appeals.

One observer calls the SEPs "the most potent propaganda weapon in the Emergency."[17] Statements by SEPs urging the insurgents to surrender were recorded and broadcast over the jungle treetops from planes; these "voice flights" were so effective that 70 percent of the SEPs said that they had some role in shaping their decision to surrender.[18]

To stop the rot the MRLA high command went to extraordinary lengths to maintain control of their followers. Checks, controls, and inquisitions multiplied; sentries watched sentries; watchers watched everyone. It will never be possible to calculate the loss of productivity which followed. But it seems safe to conclude that the program played a far larger role in the defeat of the insurgency than the total number of SEPs might indicate. It may not be quite true, as one writer has asserted, that "the war was won by bribing the rank-and-file Reds to give up."[19] But rewards undoubtedly advanced the cause of winning it.

X. MALAYA AND VIETNAM: A COMPARISON IN RETROSPECT

By now the key features of the Malayan counterinsurgency effort seem almost self-evident: (1) deliberate use of a long-haul, low-cost strategy employing a wide range of civil, police, and military programs; (2) their knitting together by an unusual civil/military and U.K./GOM management structure; (3) dominant emphasis on breaking the links between the guerrillas and their popular base, especially among the Chinese squatters; (4) great emphasis on the right kind of intelligence; (5) a carrot-and-stick approach com-

bining tough controls in black areas with a major campaign to win "hearts and minds"; and (6) extensive use of information and psywar programs. Though all this took considerable time to develop, it met the ultimate test.

No one element was decisive. Success was achieved by the meshing of many civil-military programs, each of which interacted with the others. If there was one element on which all others depended it was the increasingly effective Police Special Branch intelligence. But without improving local security and growing cooperation from the population such intelligence gathering would have been far more difficult. Improving local security, largely a police effort, freed the army to go after the insurgents in the jungle, which it did with growing success. Resettlement of the squatters, plus effective population and food controls, made it more and more difficult for the guerrillas to get support. Development programs, social services, and the move toward popular enfranchisement and political independence won increasing rural support. And all these programs were effectively integrated by a unified British-Malayan management system at all key levels — another essential ingredient of success.

All this did not spring full-blown from the head of Zeus, but resulted from a painful trial-and-error process over time. For the first few years the government effort was confused, inadequate, and lacking in direction, and it looked as though the U.K./GOM were losing. Yet the leadership showed flexibility and adaptability in learning from its mistakes and evolving a more successful C-I response.

Nonetheless, why did it take twelve years? The early mistakes took time to rectify. Many programs also needed years to achieve full impact. Moreover, the U.K./GOM opted deliberately for a long-haul, low-cost strategy largely dictated by financial constraints. In any event, would doubling the military effort in 1948-1950, for example, have produced much more than a doubling of the number of soldiers stumbling blindly about in the jungle? Better intelligence was the key, and this took time to develop. Clutterbuck avers that "if we had had in 1948 the Police Special Branch intelligence system that we had built up by 1954, the insurgency might never have gotten into its stride and would certainly have been ended more quickly."[1]

Combined U.K./GOM management during the Emergency was so successful that it was again promptly put into effect when Indonesian "confrontation" pressures developed on Borneo some six years after Malaya's independence. The threat from Indonesian cross-border operations looked ominous for a time. When the United Kingdom came to the aid of Malaya (now Malaysia), both parties were quite conscious of Malaysia's newfound political sensitivities as a sovereign nation.[2] By mutual agreement a British Director of Operations was again appointed, responsible to both Kuala Lumpur and London. Great stress was also laid on a multifaceted civil/military strategy. The first DO described his primary aim as being to prevent this small conflict "from escalating into open war"; to do this "it was vital to win not only the opening rounds of the jungle battle but at the same time the psychological battle in the kampongs of the up-country tribal people." His first principle was "to win the battle for hearts and minds. . . . It is because by winning over the people to your side you succeed in isolating your opponent from supplies, from shelter and from intelligence."[3] This strategy proved quite successful, though Indonesian guerrilla raids never reached critical proportions.

But the intriguing question with respect to drawing useful lessons for application elsewhere is how much the U.K./GOM's success can be attributed to the approaches they developed and how much to the special circumstances which limited the insurgency threat in Malaya, and later Borneo, and gave the U.K./GOM decisive advantages on which they capitalized. While both factors obviously are significant, do such special circumstances give the lessons of Malaya only limited transferability to quite different situations — such as Vietnam?

A. Underlying Dissimilarities between Malaya and Vietnam

Perhaps the best way to bring home this issue to an American audience is to compare the Malayan C-I effort briefly with the more ambiguous U.S. experience in Vietnam. The Vietnam conflict has been going on for some dozen years now, and the Malayan Emergency also lasted twelve years. Certain aspects of the two conflicts are sufficiently similar to permit comparison, and even the differences may prove instructive.*

It must be acknowledged that in many respects the United Kingdom confronted a quite different and more manageable situation in Malaya than did the French and then the Americans in Vietnam. Indeed, some observers argue that Malaya and Vietnam are so dissimilar as to make comparisons invalid. Bernard Fall has asserted that "any comparison between British victories in Malaya and the situation in Vietnam in the 1960s is nothing but a dangerous delusion, or worse, a deliberate over-simplification of the whole problem."[4] R. O. Tilman takes a similar view.[5] However, both critics focus more on the differences between the two countries and their insurgencies than on the different C-I approaches employed. In fact Fall's own critique of U.S. performance clearly suggests that what the British did in Malaya is far more in tune with his own thinking than what the United States did in Vietnam.

But there is little doubt that the Malayan insurgency was far more limited in nature, scale, and external support than was Vietnam after 1961 or 1962. First, its popular base was almost entirely limited to a portion of the ethnic Chinese minority; it never caught on among the dominant Malay element or even the Indians. The Viet Cong (VC) insurgency had far broader and deeper popular roots.

Second, the ethnic Chinese guerrillas in Malaya never received any significant outside aid. In contrast the VC insurgents had the inestimable advantage of nearby out-of-country sanctuaries, extensive outside logistic and personnel help (plus many thousands of South Vietnamese regroupees), and after 1964 increasing infiltration of North Vietnamese regular troops.

Third, the two insurgencies differed greatly in the degree of their legitimacy as seen through the eyes of the target population. With considerable success, the VC portrayed themselves as the heirs of the anticolonial revolution against the French, which had succeeded in liberating North Vietnam by 1954. The Malayan CP tried hard to do the same, but was never able to exert a comparable nationalist appeal — not even to most ethnic Chinese. Steady progress toward Malayan

---

* Since this study covers only Malaya, the points made on Vietnam are drawn from reports still in preparation.

independence robbed the MCP of credibility for its claim that violent revolution was the only way to achieve it.

Fourth, the VC benefited greatly from the feeble and often oppressive nature of GVN administration in the countryside. In neither popular appeal nor effectiveness could it compete effectively with the VC's own rural shadow administration. In Malaya, on the other hand, the U.K./GOM could rely on a viable and increasingly effective political/administrative structure, which had been largely rebuilt during 1946-1948. Rural administration never broke down in Malaya as it did in Vietnam. At the center, too, the government in Kuala Lumpur was at all times far more stable, effective, and responsive than that in Saigon. Thompson calls this political/administrative contrast "perhaps the greatest advantage which Malaya had over South Vietnam."[6]

Fifth, the United Kingdom had the inestimable advantage of being long and firmly entrenched in Malaya and enjoying a solid reciprocal relationship with its local rulers. This permitted Britain to provide effective leadership in the crucial stages under a Malay political umbrella. British troops participated from the outset too. While the GOM was being Malayanized, U.K. personnel operated from within the GOM structure, greatly simplifying the problems of joint administration and command. Thus there was no question of imperialist intervention. Indeed, one of the keys to Britain's success was the skillful manner in which it disengaged politically while fighting an insurgency. In contrast, the United States in Vietnam played a role till 1965 that was mostly advisory, and thereafter maintained an uneasy coalition relationship with a nation it treated as a sovereign ally.

Last but not least, largely because of these underlying differences, the VC insurgency grew to a scale far outstripping the Malayan — whereas the latter had begun declining in strength after the first few years. Of course, this must also in part be attributed to U.K./GOM success in containing the insurgency, as opposed to GVN/U.S. inability to do so. In any event, by 1962-1963, the VC insurgency had grown far larger and the GVN far weaker than had the insurgency in Malaya at its peak.

Thus the most valid comparison would be between Malaya 1948-1954 (when the insurgency peaked and was defeated) and Vietnam 1958-1962 (when it was still essentially a rural insurgency). Malaya is far less comparable to the later period in Vietnam, when a quasiconventional war was superimposed on the continuing rural insurgency and especially after North Vietnam and then the United States began intervening with regular forces. Almost inevitably, it now appears in retrospect, the focus on the "big-unit" war tended to crowd out focus on C-I programs. Not until mid-1967, after the United States had prevented a VC takeover and recaptured the initiative, was a counterinsurgency-oriented pacification program of any scale launched in Vietnam.

On the other hand, the differences between Malaya and Vietnam should not be allowed to obscure what U.S. Army Chief of Staff General H. K. Johnson called "the many similarities."[7] Especially if we compare the early periods in both cases, these similarities are striking. Both insurgencies pursued a Maoist strategy aimed essentially at the political objective of undermining the existing government. Both were organized on the Maoist pattern. Both were rural-oriented, and utilized remote and inaccessible jungle base areas.[8] Both stressed high ideological discipline and élan. Nor were the disparities in strength so great. Insurgent strength measured against total population in Malaya in 1948-1951 with its Min Yuen support organization was roughly comparable in size to that in Vietnam during 1958-1961 and maybe even including 1962. And the GOM was not very much stronger vis-á-vis the insurgents in the early phase than was the GVN. Diem's position looked pretty solid in 1958-1959.

Another often ignored similarity is that the insurgents had the early initiative in both cases. We have seen how the early U.K./GOM response was confused, unwieldy, and inadequate. Good intelligence was equally lacking. The large Malayan "squatter" areas were as virtually unadministered as remote areas in South Vietnam. For the first two or three years it looked as though the U.K./GOM were losing. But here we come again to a major difference. The U.K./GOM gradually contained the insurgency and then broke its back within four years, while in Vietnam the insurgency gradually grew to almost unmanageable proportions. Why was this?

B. Differing Approaches to the Problem

Granted that many of the reasons for these contrasting outcomes lie in the factors already mentioned, not least of them the internal weakness of the fledgling GVN and the mistakes of Ngo Dinh Diem. But to what extent can they also be attributed to the different approach taken by the GVN/U.S. as opposed to the U.K./GOM? Put another way, if the GVN/U.S. in Vietnam had followed an approach more like that followed successfully by the U.K./GOM in Malaya, might the outcome — at least during the pre-1965 period — have been significantly different?

For the two C-I approaches were of course quite different, particularly in the extent to which each relied on *military* means. In part this is owing to varying perceptions of the threat. The U.K./GOM, recognizing the limited scope of the insurgency (and its lack of outside support), opted to deal with it via a mixed strategy employing civil and police as much as military resources. The U.S. and GVN, influenced by the Korean War and Ho's victory over the French, worried far more during 1955-1960 over a conventional attack by North Vietnam. They devoted the bulk of their resources to military preparations against this external threat. Though insurgency developed instead, their efforts to meet it remained predominantly military, a tendency which grew further in the early sixties as rural insurgency developed into quasi-conventional war.

After 1964-1965, of course, any adequate U.S./GVN response had to be largely military, but this only reinforced the trend toward concentration on its more conventional military aspects to the neglect of other key aspects of the insurgency. The "big unit" war dominated the Vietnam stage.

This led to the second striking difference between the two C-I approaches — the notable disparity between the proportion of total effort which the U.K./GOM devoted to nonmilitary measures and that which the U.S./GVN allotted to similar measures, especially in the period before the Hanoi-backed VC military threat grew almost unmanageable. True, many small-scale efforts were undertaken in Vietnam, some of them directly inspired by Malaya. But not until 1967-1968 did the GVN/U.S. begin devoting major resources to what we termed a "pacification" program on a scale and with a priority more commensurate with the need. Only after our massive military effort had contained but failed to defeat the insurgency did we come to treat programs such as pacification as an indispensable corollary to our military response. And in terms of the proportion of total GVN/U.S. response allocated to it, it remained a poor second to the continuing investment in the big-unit war.

Granted that this weighting of the GVN/U.S. response was largely dictated by the exigencies of the situation. Nonetheless, in hindsight there seems to be much that was done in Malaya that might have been usefully stressed more heavily in Vietnam — with suitable adaptation to the local scene. It is painful to read British critiques of U.S. performance in Vietnam in the light of Britain's own experience in Malaya. One example is a seminar of friendly and experienced senior observers held by the Royal United Services Institution in February 1969. While conscious of the disparities between the two situations, its members, perhaps inevitably, tended to criticize the United States for neglecting such keys to earlier U.K./GOM success as: intelligence on the insurgent organization, the police in general and Special Branch in particular, effective and responsive local administration, the winning of rural support, and integrated civil/military conflict management at all levels.[9]

Only partly explicable by the more limited nature of the threat is the much greater reliance in Malaya than in Vietnam on police and paramilitary forces. Particularly in the 1955-1961 period, when the VC threat was mostly rural and guerrilla, strengthening the Civil Guard and the Self-Defense Corps in the GVN, plus a good police force, might have provided a more suitable response than building up ARVN. Proposals and even some modest efforts were made to this end. In 1961 the British Advisory Mission, for example, made establishment of a truly professional national police its first recommendation to Diem. Moreover, Civil Guard and Self-Defense Corps were increased from under 100,000 to some 180,000 by end-1963.[10] But both the ARVN generals and their MAAG advisers were far more attuned to meeting a threat of conventional North Vietnamese invasion across the DMZ, which never occurred in the way anticipated.

Lack of an effective C-I intelligence system in Vietnam, in such strong contrast to Malaya, is also attributable partly to the failure to build up police instead of military intelligence. Sir Robert Thompson argues that "no government can hope to defeat a communist insurgent movement unless it gives top priority to, and is successful in, building up such an organization."[11] U.K./GOM lack of one was a serious handicap in the early Emergency years, just as the growth of an outstanding Police Special Branch was crucial to later success. By the same token inadequate GVN/U.S. attention to the right kind of counterinsurgency intelligence has been a critical handicap even to the present day.[12] The British Mission recommended in 1962 that C-I intelligence be put under the police to replace the plethora of ineffective intelligence groups then existing, but again the military decided the issue. True, the problem in South Vietnam had proved far more difficult to remedy, but early adequate focus on it could not have helped but produce better results by now.

In Vietnam as well as in Malaya various efforts were made to break the links between the insurgents and the people through better local security for the villages, population and resource controls, resettlement, food denial, and the like. In fact, a conscious effort was made to apply Malayan experience in Vietnam. The attempt proved as unsuccessful in Vietnam, at least till very late in the day, as it had proved successful in Malaya. One example was the overambitious 1961-1963 "strategic hamlet" program, based largely on the Malayan experience but executed with striking differences. Thompson, who recommended the resettlement program, summarizes the reasons for its failure:

As we have seen, the major weakness in the Vietnamese implementation of the strategic hamlet programme was that it had no strategic direction, with the result that strategic hamlets were created haphazardly all over the country, and in no area was there a really solid block of them. This led to a situation where, instead of the hamlets on the perimeter of the advance forming the front line against the Viet Cong, almost every single hamlet was itself still in the front line and vulnerable to Viet Cong attack. The second weakness was that military operations, particularly in the Mekong Delta, were

not designed to support the advance of the strategic hamlet programme. The third weakness was that no real effort was made to separate the population in the strategic hamlets from the Viet Cong by eliminating their agents and supporters inside the hamlets, or by imposing controls on the movement of people and supplies. Even if some more overt Viet Cong agents and supporters moved out of a strategic hamlet at the time when it was established, they subsequently had no difficulty in re-penetrating the hamlet, continuing subversion and maintaining their organization and infrastructure.

Basically, the Vietnamese seemed unable to understand that the establishment of strategic hamlets would accomplish nothing unless the other necessary measures were taken to achieve their three objects: of protection, of uniting and involving the people, and of development, with the ultimate aim of isolating the guerrilla units from the population. Not only with regard to strategic hamlets but in other fields as well, the Vietnamese tended to confuse the means with the end. It took over three years to establish 500 defended Chinese villages in Malaya. In under two years in Vietnam over 8,000 strategic hamlets were created, the majority of them in the first nine months of 1963. No attention was paid to their purpose; their creation became the purpose in itself. A similar attitude prevailed with regard to defence posts. Hundreds of these had no function in the insurgency other than to defend themselves. This inability to think a thing through applied even to *coups d'etat*. Governments could be overthrown with increasing frequency without previous thought as to what should replace them or what policies should be adopted.[13]

As even British critics admit, such efforts were far more difficult in Vietnam, partly from sheer lack of adequate administration to carry out such programs under a firm rule of law.[14] It is hard to overestimate the importance of a viable administrative base to an effective C-I response. C. C. Too, the brilliant head of the Psywar Section of the Malayan Ministry of Internal Security, called good local administration "the first essential."[15] While the U.K./GOM started with the advantage of a more viable and effective local structure, they also paid far more attention to strengthening it continuously than did the U.S./GVN in Vietnam.

In gaining popular support through effective, equitable government and by satisfying popular aspirations, the Malayan experience was far more successful than the Vietnamese. In Malaya, of course, the dominant ethnic population was pro-British from the outset; moreover, the United Kingdom was in the driver's seat and could set the pace, whereas in Vietnam the United States was repeatedly frustrated in its efforts to move the GVN. Also, the recurrent U.S. attempts to encourage broadening the base and enhancing the appeal of the GVN were subordinated to the needs of a shooting war, which were often seen as requiring stability rather than risky change in Saigon.

The same held true in the field of information and psywar. Here too Britain did not have to deal with a separate government which it chose to treat as sovereign. The U.K./GOM psywar and rewards-for-surrender programs were notably successful, especially in luring high-level defectors who were put to good use. The Chieu Hoi program in Vietnam, again recommended by the British Mission, has had considerable success since its 1963 inception in garnering over 190,000 ralliers, but most of these have been quite low-level. Rewards for key enemy cadre were not used on any scale till 1971.

A last, striking difference between the two C-I approaches is that in Malaya all the many facets were pulled together by a unified U.K./GOM civil/military management on a scale which the United States never even sought in Vietnam. True, despite all the talk of its being a "U.S. puppet," the GVN regime was sovereign — and the U.S. role till 1965 was primarily one of advice and logistic support. Diem jealously guarded his independence, and our ability to sway him (or for that matter his successors) was limited — though we didn't try very hard. Moreover, at least till 1965 the United States felt that assumption of more than an advisory role might lead to overcommitment — an irony in the light of what happened later.

Even after massive U.S. intervention, however, little attempt was made to do more than coordinate the U.S. and GVN efforts. At times we almost seemed to be fighting two separate wars. As General Westmoreland has pointed out, there were many legitimate disadvantages to a single combined command, not least that it

would have been a step backward from the political aim of strengthening the independence of South Vietnam.[16] But from the standpoint of improving the C-I effort, is there much doubt in retrospect that some form of combined war direction would have done much to overcome one of the crucial flaws — the spotty nature of ARVN military leadership? The author, who served in the top U.S. management in Saigon, believes that some form of combined war direction could have helped greatly; in fact, he suggested it in 1966 and 1967. He also believes that, despite the great political sensitivities involved, the GVN would have accepted such proposals. Sir Robert Thompson had even earlier suggested a sort of Director of Operations on the Malayan model. Nor was civil/military management ever unified on either the U.S. or the GVN side, except late in the day and then only in the pacification field.

C. Summing Up

But whether a C-I approach more like that applied successfully in Malaya would have been as effective in Vietnam must remain an historical "if." Certainly, the enormous disparities between the two situations underline the dangers inherent in any comparison. Certainly, the threat in Vietnam also grew to proportions far transcending that in Malaya. Moreover, the underlying weaknesses of the GVN may have been so fundamental that no C-I effort, however well constructed and managed, could have overcome this handicap. Here lies another crucial variable on which opinions differ sharply. From a U.S. standpoint, would it ever have been possible during or even after the Diem period to get adequate performance out of the GVN?

But such a negative view may be overly influenced by American disillusionment with our tragic involvement in Vietnam. Even granting the disparities between Malaya and Vietnam, both the U.K./GOM and the U.S./ GVN confronted quite similar C-I needs — especially in the early phases. Both made similar initial mistakes. While the C-I approaches later evolved by the British to rectify these errors would have required modification for the Vietnamese environment, greater U.S./GVN emphasis on similar approaches would at the least have led to a less costly C-I effort. It is even conceivable that — if carried out consistently

—this could have made a decisive difference, *especially in the early years!* And the contention that the GVN was incapable of such an effort is partly contradicted by the GVN's ability to mount the belated pacification program of 1967-1971 — an essentially Vietnamese effort, though heavily supported by the United States.[17]

Indeed, the at least qualified success of the 1967-1971 pacification program is itself perhaps the most compelling evidence that our Vietnam response would have benefited from greater and earlier emphasis on certain features crucial to U.K./GOM success in Malaya: (1) a more balanced civil/police/military effort, rather than one so overwhelmingly military; (2) unified conflict management at all key levels; (3) far greater emphasis on the C-I type of intelligence and on efforts to root out the directing cadre of the insurgency; (4) more focus on breaking the links between the insurgents and the population, rather than so much on military operations against elusive enemy forces; and (5) far greater stress on outbidding the insurgents for popular support — not so much by massive economic development as by effective, equitable, and responsive government operating under a rule of law. Most of this was attempted in one way or another in Vietnam, but only as a secondary aspect of a primarily military C-I response.

In any case, by 1964-1965 Vietnam had become a different ball game, a quasi-conventional war superimposed upon insurgency which required far more than what had sufficed in Malaya. The United States felt compelled to intervene militarily to prevent a GVN collapse and restore the situation to a point where a major civil-military "pacification" effort could belatedly be set in train. But all things considered, it is hard to fault Clutterbuck's implicit judgment that, if the GVN with U.S. support had managed to do in 1958-1963 what the GOM backed by Great Britain did so well in 1948-1953, the Vietnam war might have taken on a quite different cast.[18] The British and Malayans learned from their early mistakes. Did we instead reinforce ours?

BIBLIOGRAPHY AND NOTES

The best source of data on the administrative and financial aspects of the Emergency is to be found in the official *Annual Reports* of the Federation Government to the Colonial Office for 1948 through 1956. Of course, these were discontinued after Malaya became independent in 1957. The *Annual Estimates* (budget) of the Government of Malaya (GOM), which fortunately were continued, are an exceptional source of cost data because the GOM carefully segregated Emergency expenditures (even of regular departments) from ordinary outlays.

Special mention should also be made of a series of classified Rand Reports prepared for DOD/ISA by Riley Sunderland: RM-4170-ISA, *Army Operations in Malaya, 1947–1960* (U); RM-4171-ISA, *Organizing Counterinsurgency in Malaya, 1947–1960* (U); RM-4172-ISA, *Antiguerrilla Intelligence in Malaya, 1948–1960* (U); RM-4173-ISA, *Resettlement and Food Control in Malaya* (U); and RM-4174-ISA, *Winning the Hearts and Minds of the People: Malaya, 1948–1960* (U), all classified Secret and dated September 1964. Their impressively comprehensive and detailed analysis of how the U.K./GOM coped with the Emergency has been used extensively for background purposes, but because they are classified, only unclassified references from them have been cited.

I. THE INSURGENT MOVEMENT

1. The most detailed account of these developments is the manuscript "Basic Paper on the Malayan Communist Party," Volume I, Part 2; cited in C. B. McLane, *Soviet Strategies in Southeast Asia: An Exploration of Eastern Policy Under Lenin and Stalin*, Princeton University Press, 1966, pp. 134-137. On Ho Chi Minh's role, see I. Milton Sacks, "Marxism in Vietnam," in *Marxism in Southeast Asia: A Study of Four Countries*, ed. by Frank N. Trager, Stanford University Press, California, 1960, pp. 118-124 and 318; and Jean Lacouture, *Ho Chi Minh: A Political Biography*, trans. by Peter Wiles, Random House, New York, 1968, pp. 52-61.

2. This was largely due to Rene Onraet, then Director of the Singapore Special Branch (police intelligence). His arrest and interrogation of Joseph Ducroux, a high Comintern official, on June 1, 1931, provided the British police with the names of the entire Comintern network in Southeast Asia and China, and led to the arrest of Ho Chi Minh in Hong Kong (where he was imprisoned until 1932), of a number of other Vietnamese Communist leaders by the French Surete; and of

most of the Central Committee of the Chinese Communist Party by the Kuomintang. It also led to the collapse of the Comintern's Far Eastern operations. Onraet tells a little of this story in Rene Onraet, *Singapore: A Police Background*, Dorothy Crisp and Company, London, 1947, pp. 113-114.

3. Onraet, *op. cit.*, p. 116.

4. Manuscript "Basic Paper," in McLane, *op. cit.*, p. 243.

5. See F. Spencer Chapman, *The Jungle Is Neutral*, Chatto and Windus, London, 1957. The official military history describes these talks only in the most general terms, without reference to the MCP, and suggests that they "produced very little," as the "Chinese representatives made demands for terms of service and amenities which . . . could not possibly be met." (Cf. Major General S. Woodburn Kirby, *The War Against Japan*, Volume 1: *The Loss of Singapore*, Her Majesty's Stationery Office, London, 1957, p. 155.) According to one source, the number of MCP members released from prison was "a hundred or so." (J. B. Perry Robinson, *Transformation in Malaya*, Secker and Warburg, London, 1956, p. 23.)

6. Chapman, *op. cit.*, pp. 214ff. and 365-372. The background is given in Major General S. Woodburn Kirby, *The War Against Japan*, Volume 4: *The Reconquest of Burma*, Her Majesty's Stationery Office, London, 1965, pp. 407-408.

7. McLane, *op. cit.*, p. 305 n. 136.

8. Vice-Admiral the Earl Mountbatten of Burma, *Report to the Combined Chiefs of Staff by the Supreme Allied Commander Southeast Asia, 1943-1945*, Philosophical Library, New York, 1951, pp. 142-145, 165-169, and 179-186; also Section E of the Report, "Post Surrender Tasks," 1969, pp. 300-302. (This section was considered so sensitive that it was not published until 1969.)

9. "The Chinese throughout Malaya," Chapman notes, "especially in the country districts, were filled with a most bitter hatred of the Japanese, and yet felt themselves completely impotent to do anything about it." *Op. cit.*, pp. 127-128.

10. Robinson, *op. cit.*, p. 14.

11. F.S.V. Donnison, *British Military Administration in the Far East, 1943-1946*, Her Majesty's Stationery Office, London, 1956, pp. 385-386. At the time, one Malayan dollar was worth approximately U.S. $0.30.

12. Cf. Mountbatten, "Post Surrender Tasks," *op. cit.*, p. 301; Donnison, *op. cit.*, pp. 385-386; A. H. Peterson *et al.*, eds., *Symposium on the Role of*

Airpower in Counterinsurgency and Unconventional Warfare, The Rand Corporation, RM-3651-PR, July 1963, pp. 4-5. Chin Peng's OBE was revoked soon afterwards.

13. Donnison, *op. cit.*, pp. 385-387. Approximately 6,800 MPAJA men were disarmed and paid their gratuities, and 5,497 weapons were surrendered (compared to 4,765 which had been issued), *ibid.*, p. 387.

14. *Annual Report on the Malayan Union 1947*, Government Printer, Kuala Lumpur, 1948, p. 12. This series of Colonial Office reports changed its title in the following year (when the Malayan Union was replaced by the Federation) to *Annual Report on the Federation of Malaya*, and continued through 1956, the year before Malaya received its independence. Volumes in this series are hereafter referred to as *Annual Reports*.

15. *Annual Report 1956*, p. 79.

16. *Annual Report 1948*, pp. 11 and 15.

17. Sir Robert Thompson, *Defeating Communist Insurgency*, Frederick A. Praeger, Inc., New York, 1966, pp. 26-27.

18. Brig. R. E. Clutterbuck, *The Long, Long War*, Frederick A. Praeger, Inc., New York, 1966, p. 35.

19. Cf. Ruth T. McVey, *The Calcutta Conference and the Southeast Asian Uprisings*, Cornell Modern Indonesia Project, Ithaca, New York, 1958.

20. *Annual Report 1948*, p. 13.

21. *Annual Report 1956*, p. 474.

22. *Annual Report 1947*.

23. Harry Miller in his *Menace in Malaya* (George G. Harrap, London, 1954, p. 104), gives a "conservative" estimate of 500,000 Min Yuen, including sympathizers. This seems far too high.

24. Clutterbuck, *op. cit., pp.* 90-92.

25. *Ibid.*, pp. 46-48.

26. Mills, *op. cit.*, p. 58.

II. MAIN LINES OF THE BRITISH/ MALAYAN RESPONSE

1. Sunderland, RM-4171, *op. cit.*, p. 11.

2. Lennox A. Mills, *Malaya*, University of Minnesota Press, Minneapolis, 1968, p. 40.

3. Robinson, *op. cit., p.* 150.

4. Mills, *op. cit.*, pp. 155-160.

5. Robinson, *op. cit.*, p. 103.

6. *Ibid., op. cit.*, p. 150.

7. Clutterbuck, *op. cit.*, p. 5.

8. Robinson, *op. cit.*, p. 126.

9. Cited in Miller, *op. cit.*, Preface.

10. *Ibid.*, p. 92.

11. Clutterbuck, *op. cit.,* pp. 55-56; also see Mills,*op. cit.,* pp. 58-61.
12. Miller, *op. cit.,* p. 196.
13. Colonial Office, *The Fight Against Communist Terrorism in Malaya.,* Colonial Office, London, November 1953 (hereafter called COI), p. 12.
14. Clutterbuck, *op. cit.,* p. 89.
15. *Ibid.,* p. 113.
16. *Ibid.,* p. 114.
17. *Ibid.,* p. 170.
18. Mills, *op. cit.,* pp. 208-210.
19. *Straits Times,* August 1, 1960 (Malayan $ converted at U.S.$0.33).
20. *Commonwealth Survey,* Vol. 6, No. 16, February 8, 1960 (£ converted at $2.80 rate).

III. MANAGING THE C-I EFFORT

1. Malcolm MacDonald, Commissioner General for Southeast Asia (resident in Singapore) representing the British Cabinet, did not play a direct leadership role in the Emergency, but commanded much influence behind the scenes. He had much to do with bringing the Chinese and Malayan communities together, and with the evolution of Malaya toward independence.
2. Robinson, *op. cit.,* p. 149.
3. *Ibid.,* p. 148.
4. G. N. Parkinson, *A Low Vote Themselves: Twelve Portraits,* Houghton Mifflin, Boston, 1966, p. 147.
5. Miller, *op. cit.,* pp. 138-139.
6. *Ibid.,* p. 140.
7. Robinson, *op. cit.,* pp. 116-117.
8. Mills, *op. cit.,* pp. 59-60, citing contemporary accounts.
9. Robinson, *op. cit.,* pp. 149-150.
10. Miller, *op. cit.,* p. 197.
11. *Straits Times,* January 17, 1952, cited in Mills, *op. cit.,* p. 61.
12. Major General S. Woodburn Kirby, *The War Against Japan,* Volume 2. *.India's Most Dangerous Hour,* Her Majesty's Stationery Office, London, 1958, p. 108.
13. Parkinson, *op. cit.,* p. 147.
14. Their meeting is described in Charles M. W. Moran, *Winston Churchill: The Struggle for Survival, 1940-1965,* Sphere Books, London, 1968, pp. 387-388.
15. Robinson, *op. cit.,* p. 204.
16. "Noll" (pseud.), "The Emergency in Malaya," *Army Quarterly,* Vol. 68, April 1954, pp. 44-63. Has good account of committee system in 1953.
17. Clutterbuck, *op. cit.,* p. 83.
18. *Ibid.,* pp. 83-84.
19. *Ibid.,* p. 146.
20. Commonwealth troops remained under separate command though operationally subordinate to the DO and the SWECs-DWECs. Their commanders had the right to appeal to their own higher echelons in the event of disagreement, but apparently it never had to be used *(ibid.,* pp. 146-147).

IV. ENFORCING THE RULE OF LAW

1. Clutterbuck, *op. cit.,* p. 36.
2. *Ibid.,* pp. 36-37.
3. E. H. Adkins, *The National ID Card Program: The Federation of Malaya,* Michigan State Advisory Group, Saigon, October 1961, Appendix VII.
4. *Annual Report 1948,* p. 187; *Annual Report 1950,* p. 160.
5. *Annual Report 1956,* pp. 30-31.
6. *Ibid.,* p. 31.
7. Clutterbuck, *op. cit.,* pp. 37-38.
8. Robinson, *op. cit.,* pp. 102-103; see also Miller, *op. cit.,* pp. 133-134.
9. Clutterbuck, *op. cit.,* pp. 38-41.
10. Miller, *op. cit.,* p. 196.
11. *Ibid.,* pp. 206-210.
12. K. E. Mackenzie, *Economic and Commercial Conditions in Malaya,* His Majesty's Stationery Office, London, 1952, pp. 21-22. Miller, *op. cit.,* p. 77.
13. *Annual Report 1950,* p. 16.
14. Robinson, *op. cit.,* p. 95; Miller, *op. cit.,* pp. 133-134 and 182-186.
15. Mills, *op. cit.,* p. 65.
16. *Annual Report 1950,* p. 16.

V. KEY ROLE OF THE POLICE IN SECURITY AND INTELLIGENCE

1. Clutterbuck, *op. cit.,* p. 178.
2. *Annual Report 1947.*
3. COI, *op. cit.,* p. 15; *Annual Report 1953,* p. 224.
4. COI, p. 15.
5. *Annual Estimates 1959.*
6. Clutterbuck, *op. cit.,* pp. 115-116.
7. *Annual Report 1949,* p. 203.
8. *Annual Report 1954,* p. 270.
9. *Annual Report 1951,* p. 211.
10. Robinson, *op. cit.,* pp. 95-98.
11. *Ibid.,* p. 164.
12. Onraet, *op. cit.,* pp. 74, 81-83.
13. *Annual Report 1948,* p. 124.
14. Robinson, *op. cit.,* p. 164.
15. *Ibid.,* pp. 162-163.
16. Clutterbuck, *op. cit.,* p. 131.

17. "Lessons from the Vietnam War," Report of a Seminar held at the Royal United Services Institution, London, February 12, 1970 (hereafter called the RUSI Seminar Report), p. 7.
18. Sunderland, RM-4170-ISA, *op. cit.*, D. 57.
19. Robinson, *op. cit.*, p. 159.

VI. THE ROLE OF THE MILITARY

1. For a brief overall account, see Clutterbuck, *op. cit.*, Chapter 6, "The Big Battalions," pp. 42-54. Sunderland, RM-4170-ISA, *op. cit.*, gives much more detail on matters covered in this chapter.
2. Sunderland, RM-4170-ISA, *op. cit.*, p. 31.
3. *Ibid.*, unclassified Figure 1 on p. 25.
4. Federation of Malaya, *Weekly News Letter*, April 3, 1953.
5. Thompson, *op. cit.*, p. 61.
6. Miller, *op. cit.*, p. 137.
7. M.C.A. Henniker, *Red Shadow over Malaya*, Wm Blackwood and Sons, Edinburgh and London, 1955, p. 33.
8. Sunderland, RM-4170-ISA, *op. cit.*, pp. 143-151.
9. See remarks of Col. J. R. Shirley on problems of adapting tactical radio to jungle warfare in Stephen T. Hosmer *et al.*, *Counterinsurgency: A Symposium*, The Rand Corporation, R-412-ARPA, January 1963.
10. Clutterbuck, *op. cit.*, pp. 51-52.
11. Robinson, *op. cit.*, pp. 129-131.
12. Sunderland, RM-4173-ISA, *op. cit.*, pp. 85-103.
13. Clutterbuck, *op. cit.*, pp. 157 and 160-161.
14. Hosmer, *op. cit.*, pp. 102-103.
15. Clutterbuck, *op. cit.*, pp. 162-164.
16. Air Commodore R. E. Warcup in Peterson, *op. cit.*, p. 49.

VII. SEPARATING THE INSURGENTS FROM THEIR POPULAR BASE

1. COI, p. 12.
2. Mills, *op. cit.*, p. 63.
3. Nathan Leites and Charles Wolf, Jr., *Rebellion and Authority: An Analytic Essay on Insurgent Conflicts*, Markham Publishing Company, Chicago, Illinois, 1970, pp. 149-152.
4. Robinson, *op. cit.*, pp. 80-81.
5. M. E. Osborne, *Strategic Hamlets in South Vietnam: A Survey and a Comparison*, Data Paper No. 55, Southeast Asia Program, Cornell University, Ithaca, New York, April 1965, compares the Malayan and SVN programs.
6. *Ibid.*, p. 34; *Annual Reports 1950, 1951, 1952.*
7. Miller, *op. cit.*, p. 148.
8. Maynard Weston Dow, *Counterinsurgency and Nation-Building: A Comparative Stud of Post World War II Anti-Guerrilla Resettlement Programs in Malaya, the Philippines and South Vietnam*, University Microfilms, Ann Arbor, Michigan, 1965, has a detailed discussion.
9. Robinson, *op. cit.*, p. 71; Miller, *op. cit.*, p. 145.
10. Miller, *op. cit.*, pp. 188-189.
11. Sunderland refers to these guerrilla supply parties as the "service elements" that were the link between the Min Yuen in the villages and the guerrillas in the deep jungle. Two of the four objectives of the Briggs Plan had been to deny the insurgents access to food and support, and to destroy the Communist forces by forcing him to fight.
12. Sunderland, RM-4173-ISA, *op. cit.*, p. 73.
13. *Ibid.*, *passim.*
14. E. H. Adkins, Jr., *The Police and Resources Control in Counterinsurgency*, USOM, Public Safety Division, Saigon, June 1964.
15. *Annual Report 1956*, pp. 475 and 479.
16. COI, pp. 28-31; MacKenzie, *op. cit.*, p. 4.
17. MacKenzie, *op. cit.*, pp. 118-121, and pp. 4-6.
18. Robinson, *op. cit.*, pp. 68-69.
19. Mills, *op. cit.*, pp. 77-78.
20. *Annual Report 1948*, pp. 13-15.
21. *Annual Report 1956.*
22. These are extensively discussed in MacKenzie, *op. cit.*, pp. 11-23, and COI, pp. 28-32.
23. Robinson, *op. cit.*, pp. 171-177.
24. *Ibid.*, p. 170; Miller, *op. cit.*, pp. 226-227.
25. Thompson, *op. cit.*, p. 153.

VIII. STRATEGY OF POLITICAL ACCOMMODATION

1. The underpinning in this Chapter is largely from Mills, *op. cit.*, Chapters IV and V.
2. Sunderland, RM-4174-ISA, *op. cit.*, p. 11.
3. Robinson, *op. cit.*, pp. 193-196.
4. *Annual Report 1950*, pp. 2 and 3-16.
5. Miller, *op. cit.*, pp. 203-204.
6. Dow, *op. cit.*, p. 80.
7. *Annual Report 1954*, pp. 6-7.
8. Robinson, *op. cit.*, p. 64.
9. Annual Report 1956, p. 483.
10. *Ibid.*, p. 34.
11. Clutterbuck, *op. cit.*, p. 148.

IX. INFORMATION AND PSYCHOLOGICAL WARFARE

1. Interview with Templer in Sunderland, RM-4174-ISA, *op. cit.*, p. 11.
2. *Annual Report 1949*, p. 208.
3. Sunderland, RM-4174-ISA, *op. cit.*, pp. 29-30; *Annual Report 1953*, p. 340; in 1956 the Infor-

mation Services were put under the Home Ministry (cf. *Annual Report 1956,* p. 477).

4. Robinson, *op. cit.,* pp. 64, 107-108, and 153-154.
5. Sunderland, RM-4174-ISA, *op. cit.,* pp. 30, and 50-51.
6. *Annual Estimates* for 1952 and thereafter. It is impossible to separate out psywar and information costs. Moreover, the cost of aircraft use and other services was budgeted elsewhere, while the cost of the psywar section of the DO staff (about $66,000 in 1958) was in the Ministry of Defence budget. But the overall costs are still surprisingly small.
7. Robinson, *op. cit.,* p. 154.
8. *Annual Report 1953,* pp. 317-318.
9. Sunderland, RM-4174-ISA, *op. cit.,* p. 31.
10. *Annual Report 1953,* p. 340.
11. Clutterbuck, *op. cit.,* p. 106.
12. Such aircraft were capable of delivering an audible message of approximately thirty seconds duration from a height of 2,500 feet *(Annual Report 1953,* p. 341).
13. *Annual Report 1956,* p. 440.
14. Peterson, *op. cit.,* p. 17.
15. Cf. Dan Kurzman, *Subversion of the Innocents: Patterns of Communist Penetration in Africa, the Middle East and Asia,* Random House, New York, 1963, p. 437.
16. Data from *Annual Report 1956,* p. 452.
17. Robinson, *op. cit.,* p. 47.
18. Edgar O'Ballance, *Malaya: The Communist Insurgent War: 1948-1960,* Faber and Faber, London, 1966, p. 151.
19. Kurzman, *op. cit.,* p. 437.

X. MALAYA AND VIETNAM: A COMPARISON IN RETROSPECT

1. R. E. Clutterbuck, "Communist Defeat in Malaya," in *Military Review,* Vol. 43, No. 9, September 1963.
2. Sir Claude Fenner, IG of Malayan Police, 1963-1965, in RUSI Seminar, pp. 5-6.
3. Lt. Gen. Sir Walter Walker, *ibid.,* p. 5.
4. Bernard Fall, *The Two Vietnams,* Frederick A. Praeger, Inc., New York, 1967 (2d rev. ed.), pp. 342 and *340ff.*
5. R. 0. Tilman, "The Non-Lessons of the Malayan Emergency," *Asian Survey,* Vol. 2, No. 8, August 1966, pp. 407-409.
6. Thompson, *op. cit.,* p. *80.*
7. Clutterbuck, *The Long, Long War, op. cit.,* p. ix.
8. *Ibid.,* pp. 5-9.
9. See RUSI Seminar.
10. Gen. W. C. Westmoreland, *Report on the War in Vietnam, 1964-1968,* Superintendent of Documents, Washington, D.C., 1970, p. 77.
11. Thompson, *op. cit.,* p. 84.
12. Clutterbuck, *op. cit.,* p. 100.
13. Thompson, *op. cit.,* pp. 141-142; see also Chapter 11 on "Strategic Hamlets."
14. Clutterbuck, *op. cit.,* p. 67.
15. Lecture of C. C. Too in *C-I Case History: Malaya, 1948-60,* U.S. Army Command and General Staff College, RB-2, November 1, 1965.
16. Westmoreland, *op. cit.,* p. 104.
17. A detailed treatment of this effort will be part of the author's forthcoming Rand report on "The Impact of Institutional Constraints on U.S./GVN Performance in the Vietnam War."
18. Clutterbuck, *op. cit.,* pp. 65-76.

The Hukbalahap Insurrection
A Case Study of a Successful Anti-Insurgency Operation in the Philippines, 1946–1955

Major Lawrence M. Greenberg
U.S. Army

INTRODUCTION

In 1950, the Philippine government was pushed to the verge of collapse by a well organized, popularly supported, communist insurgency known as the Hukbalahap. No stranger to internal rebellion, the nation again faced a direct challenge to democratic government. The United States, already at war in Korea, was threatened with the loss of a strategic stronghold in the Pacific, and the subversion of a longtime friend and ally.

This study analyzes the Hukbalahap (Huk) Insurrection to determine what conditions led to the near disaster of 1950 and to discover what steps were taken by the governments of the Philippines and the United States to bring the uprising to stop the revolt by 1955. It examines the insurgent movement; its origins, evolution, goals, tactics, and personality; in order to shed new light on a successful anti-insurgency operation. Philippine governments in power during this time are also examined to determine why their anti-Huk policies failed until the appointment of Ramon Magsaysay as Secretary of National Defense in September 1950. As this unique and extremely talented individual began to change the course of the rebellion, American military and economic assistance became vital to his success.

This study also includes an analysis of the functions and roles played by the Joint United States Military Assistance Group—Philippines (JUSMAG) and of a key U.S. advisor, Air Force Lieutenant Colonel Edward G. Lansdale. Without American aid and assistance, the Magsaysay government would not have been able to defeat the Huk—but aid alone did not stop the insurgency. It required a unique melding of personalities, a revitalization of the Armed Forces of the Philippines (AFP), dedicated efforts by the Philippine government to win back the people's allegiance, and the right combination of American military advice and economic aid. Lacking any of these essential ingredients, the anti-Huk campaign might well have failed.

This is the story of a once powerful indigenous communist insurgency, of American aid and advice, and of the Philippine government under Ramon Magsaysay. But most of all, it is a story about the Philippine people—a people frustrated by a string of uncaring and corrupt governments that showed little concern for the country's peasants. With hope and progress, the people would follow any authority regardless of political affiliation. Ramon Magsaysay understood the people he grew up with, and knew what their aspirations were. With American support and assistance he was able to provide what

Greenberg, Lawrence. (1986). *The Hukbalahap Insurrection: A Case Study of a Successful Anti-Insurgency Operation in the Philippines—1946-1955*. Washington, D.C.: United States Army Center of Military History, 1986. (Offered as a U.S. Army Publication, CMH Pub 93-8.)

his countrymen wanted and stop the Huk at the very peak of their influence and power.

To examine only military and political actions that occurred between 1946–1955, however, does not tell the entire story. To appreciate the insurrection fully, one must first consider the background and evolution of the Huk movement and of the people of central Luzon. With this preface, the story is placed in context, and one can understand the insurrection and the reasons for its rise and subsequent fall. Under Ramon Magsaysay's enlightened leadership and guidance, the guerrillas were beaten at their own game by Philippine armed forces reborn with pride, competence, professionalism, and a deep devotion to their fellow countrymen.

THE EVOLUTION OF THE HUKBALAHAP MOVEMENT

EARLY BACKGROUND

The Hukbalahap movement, known simply as the Huk (pronounced "hook"), was the culmination of events and internal Philippine conditions that predated World War II by centuries and was rooted in the country's pre-colonial period. Economic, social, and political inequities existed before the arrival of the Spanish, who further coopted it into their own variety of mercantilism, and were perpetuated into the twentieth century by American policy. This social and political history divided the Filipinos into classes where the "haves" reaped the nation's profits while the "have-nots" were left with little but their desperate desire for change.

In 1565, Spanish explorers landed in the Philippines (christening the islands for their monarch, King Philip II) and found a home-grown agricultural society that was easily adapted into their own *encomienda* system. The Spanish crown issued royal land-grants to colonists, who developed large plantations on the island of Luzon, the nation's agrarian heartland. Filipino landowners were disenfranchised and their tenant farmers were placed under the authority of the new landlords. Former native landlords were either retained by the Spanish to operate the *haciendas* for them, became sharecroppers themselves, or sought work elsewhere.

Filipinos were quick to react to their loss of land ownership, additional taxes placed upon them by the Spanish, and their worsening economic condition. The first of numerous revolts against the Spanish broke-out in 1583 and was dealt with in the manner of the times—bloody retaliation. A relatively small Spanish garrison, that did not exceed 600 troops during this period, employed the assistance of several native ethnic groups and ruthlessly crushed the revolt. Subsequent uprisings during the next three hundred years were handled by the Spanish colonial government in much the same manner.

Hints of social reform did not appear in the Philippines until the mid-19th century. A more liberal regime in Madrid allowed some wealthy Filipinos, who rose in social stature via employment as tax collectors and low level administrators for the colonial government, to seek education and operate small tracts of private farmland. The Spanish also started a few small development projects on some of the larger islands, such as Mindinao and Cebu. However, when the enlightened government in Madrid fell, attempts for even minimal reforms were forgotten and the near feudal, pre-reformed *status quo* returned.[1]

In 1870, Philippine opposition to Spanish rule erupted into a series of guerrilla wars. Despite harsh repression taken against peasant farmers, the fighting continued and by the outbreak of the Spanish-American War in 1898, the Katipunan Revolt (usually credited with beginning in 1896) spread from Luzon to the islands of Panay and Cebu as Spanish troops withdrew for the defense of Manila. In the same year, rebel leader Jose Rizal was captured and killed by the Spanish. During the Huk insurrection, his descendants again played a role.[2]

When the United States annexed the Philippines after the Spanish-American War, Filipinos were given greater responsibility for governing their own land. Local government was assisted by limited American efforts to improve both economic and social conditions. Philippine officials advanced in the civil service and many of these bureaucrats joined a growing number of prosperous businessmen to replace Spanish *haciendas* with their own large plantations. Collectively, they formed a new Philippine elite and sought to retain the *status quo* that had provided them the opportunity to succeed—whether through business, agriculture, or corruption in government.[3] There existed little indeed for honest government servants when the system rewarded corruption, nepotism, and favoritism so handsomely.

U.S. POLICY BEFORE WORLD WAR II

American policy toward the Philippines was first tested during the bloody 1899–1902 Philippine Insurrection. Although the nearly three year long war suppressed overt Philippine nationalism, at least for the time, the bitterness it produced among many Filipinos endured well into mid-century. As normalcy returned to the islands in 1903, the United States attempted to address one of the long-term problems faced by the islands—land-tenure. Many large parcels of Church-owned land that had been expropriated by the Spanish in the sixteenth century and given to the Church to administer were offered for public sale. However sincere the effort, few Filipinos were able to take advantage of this opportunity. Those who attempted to purchase land were often victims of usury and fraud at the hands of local officials more interested in graft than in helping the peasants acquire land.[4] The land sale program failed to transfer land ownership to the farmers but did allow those few Filipinos with resources to increase the size of their holdings. This had the effect of perpetuating the landlord-tenant relationship that had become synonymous with Philippine agriculture. Rampant corruption in government, coupled with an unchanging socio-economic climate, continued under the new American administration in Manila throughout the 1920s.

During the next few years, American concerns about the Philippines were limited almost entirely to economic matters and establishing a date for Philippine independence. In 1934, U.S. Congress passed Public Law 127, the Tydings-McDuffie Act. The act, ratified in May by the Philippine Congress, promised full Philippine independence on 4 July 1946 and established conditions under which the islands would be governed until that time—the Philippine Commonwealth. The United States retained control of Philippine foreign relations, defense, and major financial transactions but granted the

Philippine president and legislature power to administer internal affairs.[5] The Tydings-McDuffie Act created dissension within the Philippine government, for it promised independence at the price of formalizing economic ties with Washington for the next twelve years. Many critics in Manila, and in the growing communist and socialist parties as well, objected strongly to the near total disregard for Philippine nationalism that these strict controls mandated.

After the establishment of the Philippine Commonwealth in 1935, U.S. economic and political policy did little to alleviate the basic Philippine problems of poverty and land-tenure.

Although the Philippine economy showed marked improvements before World War II, internal distribution of wealth remained much as it always had been. Landlords grew rich at the expense of the peasant farmer who found it increasingly difficult to repay loans for seed or lease money made by the landlord. Confronted with these obstacles, individual initiative was stifled, productivity remained low, and whatever profits a farmer managed to scrape together went toward paying his landlord.

By 1941, 80 percent of Luzon's farmers were hopelessly indebted to their landlords with no

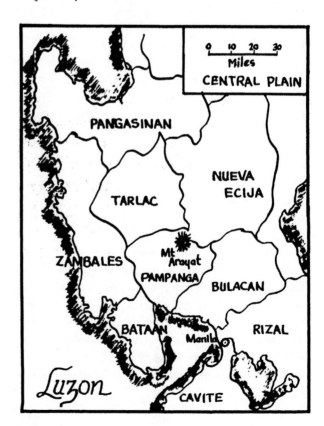

expectations of a brighter future at all. Although improvements had been made in education, transportation, health care and communications, the absence of social reforms served only to raise local frustrations with their central government. In Luzon's provinces of Balacan, Nueva Ecija, Cavite, Tarlac, Bataan, and Laguna, few farmers owned their land. The majority were either tenants or hired labor. In Pampanga Province, 70 percent of the farmers were tenants.[6] As a result, annual income during this period hovered at only 120 pesos, about $65. This agrarian region proved ripe for anti-government insurgencies as the local population continued to struggle against landlords and had little faith in the central government which the peasant saw as unconcerned with their plight.

PRE-WAR DEVELOPMENT OF THE HUK

Peasant farmers, many of whom were literate by this time thanks to American efforts to abolish mass illiteracy under Spanish rule, were demoralized by stagnant social conditions and the failure of the United States to grant Philippine independence after the war with Spain. They realized landlords were taking advantage of them and began to seek outlets for their frustrations. The farmer tilled land owned by an absentee landlord or by the Church, either of which demanded not less than half of his crop, sometimes 70 percent, as rent and payment for seed. Additionally, the landlord controlled almost every aspect of his life. A story recalled by the Huk supreme commander, Luis Taruc, shares the experiences of many Filipino farmers during the early 1920s. Taruc told of his family moving by carabao cart from their home in San Luis, Pampanga, to take over the farm worked by his uncle in Bataan. Although they moved with great expectations about the land's productivity, they realized that it was owned by the Pabalan family, landlords from San Miguel, Bulacan, who would exact their 50–70 percent of the crop as rent and interest payment. But because the land was more productive than that in Pampanga, they hoped to end up with a larger share than before.[7] Faced with a government content to maintain the *status quo,* it

was not surprising to find serious unrest on Luzon, Panay, Negros, and Mindanao by 1920.[8]

In 1920, the Third International, or Comintern, headquartered in Moscow, met in Canton, China. The worldwide growth of interest in communism coincided with the rising level of disaffection in the Philippines. Following the International, an American Comintern representative, Harrison George, joined with several Philippine socialists to form the base for the first Philippine communist party. Together with Isabelo de los Reyes, Dominador Gomez, Crisanto Evangelista, and Antonio Ora, he fought an influential Church and established a small foothold for the communist cause in Luzon. In May 1924 they founded the *Kapisanang Pambansa ng mga Magbudukid sa Filippinas* (KPMP), or National Peasant's Union in Nueva Ecija Province, a stronghold of peasant unrest and violence. Soon the National Peasant's Union spread across Luzon and into the Philippine capital of Manila.[9]

The Peasant's Union exploited social conditions, the continued colonial status of the islands, the land-tenure system, and the deteriorating climate between landlords and peasants, to become the leader of a confederation of labor unions, the Philippine Labor Congress. In 1927, the organization officially associated itself with the Comintern and organized the nation's first legal communist political party, the Worker's Party.[10] Within the year, Evangelista, as head of the Worker's Party, took advantage of his position and visited Chou En Lai and Stalin. Upon his return to Luzon, he organized four new socialist and communist organizations and began to plan the "class struggle" against the Manila government.[11]

On the 34th anniversary of the 1896 Katipunan Revolt, 26 August 1930, Evangelista announced the birth of the *Partido Komunista ng Filipinas,* the Communist Party of the Philippines (PKP). Less than three months later, on the 13th anniversary of the Russian Bolshevik Revolution, he formally established the PKP and proclaimed its objectives. In his address of 7 November, he set forth five guiding principles for the Philippine communist movement: to mobilize for complete national independence; to establish communism for the masses; to defend the masses against capitalist exploitation; to overthrow American imperialism in the Philippines; and to overthrow capitalism. With these guidelines and the PKP banner that displayed the communist hammer and sickle emblem on a red background, surrounded by the words "Communist Party of the Philippines," Evangelista set out on his mission.[12]

Exactly two years after the birth of the PKP, the Philippine Supreme Court declared it illegal and Evangelista and several of his chief lieutenants were imprisoned. They were charged with plotting the overthrow of the government and instigating large scale, bloody riots in Manila. Other PKP members went underground and began to fight against landlords on behalf of the peasants. Although not widespread, PKP attacks unsettled central Luzon. Landlords were murdered, farm animals slaughtered, and many fields were put to the torch. In reaction, President Quezon instituted several minor land reform measures, including putting a 30 percent limit on the amount of a tenant's crop that could be demanded by the landlord. Although highly lauded at its conception, this reform was all but ignored by landlords, courts, and the government.[13]

An unfortunate side-effect of the 1932 court decision was a dramatic rise in prestige and size of the heretofore weak Philippine Socialist Party (formed in April 1932 in Pampanga) and the militant Worker and Peasant's Union (WPU). With the PKP in an outlaw status, the socialists and WPU became the legal foci for many PKP supporters. Both organizations gained considerable influence during the next six years as poor socio-economic conditions remained unchanged for Luzon's tenant farmers and urban poor.[14]

Amidst increasing incidents of violent communist-sponsored demonstrations in Manila in 1938, Quezon released PKP leaders Evangelista, Taruc, and de los Reyes when they pledged their loyalty to the government and to American efforts to resist fascist and Japanese expansion.[15] This action soon proved less than desirable for Quezon. Almost immediately after his parole, Evangelista assumed leadership of a united socialist front when the PKP merged with the Socialist Party on 7 November. The new organization openly proclaimed the communist doctrine and spread from its traditional stronghold in central Luzon to Bataan, Zambales, and to the islands of Cebu, Panay, and Negros.

Communist Party Evolution Before 1941

* Canton Comintern

* KPMP founded

*Labor Congress founded

* KPMP joins Labor Congress and becomes the Worker's Party

* WP becomes PKP

Phil. Socialist Party founded *

PKP and PSP merge into CPP *

1910   1920   1930   1940

CHART 1

Evangelista's bitter opposition to Quezon and his administration continued until 1941 when the threat of Japanese invasion brought a temporary truce and offers from the PKP to support the Commonwealth. President Quezon, who trusted neither Evangelista nor the CPP coalition, refused the offer.[16] The stage had been set for the war with Japan that was sure to come. Evangelista was the leader of a small but growing socialist/communist organization that drew support from the large number of dissatisfied peasants in Luzon's heartland. The Philippine central government distrusted the CPP coalition and despite the growing clouds of war on the horizon, refused to negotiate any cooperative agreements with them. The peasant remained trapped by his poor social and economic status and perceived the Manila government as content to let this condition continue. Now, on top of all these concerns, the threat of Japanese invasion cast an even darker shadow over the Filipino peasant.

WORLD WAR II AND HUK EXPANSION

The Japanese invasion of the Philippines in December 1941 provided the impetus that enabled a small number of untrained, unorganized, communist rebels to become an effective guerrilla force. Although the CPP sought to expand its support base in Luzon before the war, the Japanese invasion provided the opportunity to do this. With an invader occupying Philippine soil, the CPP grasped the chance to continue their cause, but now as patriotic freedom fighters facing an evil and numerically superior foe.

Willing to fight the invaders but unable to secure agreement with the Quezon administration, Evangelista took to the mountains of Luzon with a small band of CPP activists. With few trained fighters and even fewer weapons, the communists established a base of operations in the vicinity of Mount Arayat and the neighboring Candaba Swamp. Protected by dense mountain jungles and vast swamps, Evangelista planned a campaign to harass the Japanese. Here he adopted the slogan, "Anti-Japanese Above All," and sought to form a united, nationalist organization that would integrate communist and non-communist groups alike. From his

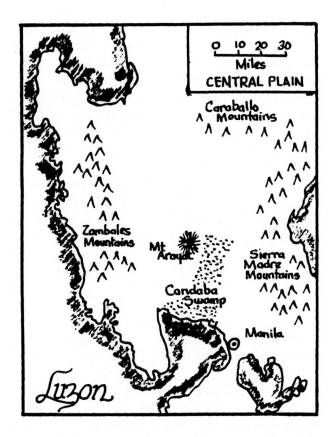

Mount Arayat stronghold, Evangelista and his forces launched small but annoying forays from this base against the Japanese as they advanced across Luzon toward Bataan and Corregidor. The KPMP and the socialist Peasant and Workers' Union, who merged into a united front in 1938, were consolidated totally and placed under the overall control of Evangelista and the CPP.[1]

Spurned by both the Quezon government and the retreating American forces, the communist guerrillas nevertheless fought the Japanese. On 10 December 1941, CPP leaders issued a manifesto in which they vowed to support the Commonwealth and U.S. efforts to resist the Japanese and urged the people to support their united anti-Japanese front.[2] Aware of his military weakness, Evangelista directed attacks against the Japanese-controlled Police Constabulary, whose mission was to suppress opposition in the countryside. His attacks, mainly raids and ambuscades, succeeded in a number of important areas. First, they allowed the accumulation of arms and ammunition, items that remained in constant shortage. Second, many individual members of the constabulary were convinced to join the guerrilla movement as an alternative to execution. Third, the raids showed the peasants that an organized resistance movement existed and kept many villages from accepting total Japanese domination. Finally, the raids intimidated the Police Constabulary. Taking casualties from an enemy who disappeared into the countryside, the constabulary developed a great deal of resistance to venturing far afield.[3]

By the end of 1941, Evangelista's raids gained his forces the respect of local peasants and, as often is the case with patriotic "Robin Hoods," their fame spread rapidly. The Japanese could do very little to suppress these popular feelings and often contributed to them through their harsh, often brutal, treatment of Luzon's peasantry. Time and time again, the *Kempei Tai* (Japanese secret police) committed atrocities against the populace in attempts to get information about Taruc's guerrillas. Often assisted by the *Makapili*, the Japanese secret police spread terror across Luzon and drove many Filipinos to the CPP guerrillas. Because the CPP were the best organized and most active resistance group on Luzon during the early years of the Japanese occupation, peasants often viewed them as the most effective and visible opposition to the Japanese.[4] In January 1942, Evangelista and his deputy, Abad Santos, were captured by a Japanese patrol and later put to death when they refused to call for the surrender of their guerrilla forces.[5]

On 29 March 1942, in a small forest clearing near the base of Mount Arayat where the provinces of Pampanga, Tarlac, and Nueva Ecija intersect, the CPP merged with Luzon's remaining socialist and peasant organizations to form the Hukbalahap, an acronym for the *Hukbo ng Bayan Laban sa Hapon* or the "Anti-Japanese Army." Following a week-long organizing conference, the newly formed Huk organization selected four of their leaders (three men and one woman) to become the Huk Military Committee. The Military Committee was at the apex of Huk structure and was charged to direct the guerrilla campaign and to lead the revolution that would seize power after the war. Luis Taruc; a CPP leader (although considered more socialist than pure communist) and peasant-organizer from a small barrio near San Luis in Pampanga; was elected to head the committee, and became the first Huk commander, "El Supremo."[6]

Organized into five 100-man squadrons, the Huks embarked on their anti-Japanese campaign. They obtained much needed arms and ammunition from Philippine army stragglers in exchange for civilian clothes, from battlefields on Bataan, from police deserters, and from ambushed enemy patrols. They began to recruit new followers and to seek popular support from the local population as patriots and freedom-fighters.[7] The Huk recruitment campaign progressed more slowly than Taruc expected, due in large measure to U.S. Army Forces Far East (USAFFE) guerrilla units. Most Filipinos who decided openly to oppose the Japanese recovered weapons carefully hidden in the jungles and joined the U.S. supported guerrillas in Luzon. The U.S. units already had recognition among the islands, had trained leaders and sergeants, and an organized command and logistic system. Although restrained by the American sponsored guerrilla units, the Huks nevertheless took to the field with only 500 men and even fewer weapons. Despite several setbacks at the hands of the Japanese and with less than enthusiastic support from USAFFE units, the Huk guerrillas grew in size and efficiency throughout the war, emerging at its conclusion as a well trained, highly organized force numbering some 15,000 armed fighters and capable of threatening the post-war Philippine government.[8]

As 1942 progressed, the Huks made concerted attempts to increase their number of personnel and armaments. Playing on what had become almost a Filipino past-time, "Jap sniping," the search for trained fighters soon went beyond simple recruitment on ideological grounds to include impressment and intimidation. Often, when an experienced Filipino fighter was located, he was given the choice of joining a Huk squadron or facing reprisals against himself or his family. Faced with these alternatives, many decided to join the guerrillas.[9] Others voluntarily joined as news of Japanese atrocities spread across the islands. After the fall of Bataan in April and Corregidor in May 1942, Taruc directed a major effort to collect weapons for his growing force. Battlefields were scoured, private weapons were confiscated, and on more than one occasion, USAFFE arms caches hidden in Luzon's central plain were looted. By the end of the year, the Huks managed to amass 2,000 assorted small arms and a few machine-guns. [10]

In an attempt to obtain American supplies and equipment in May 1942, Huk representatives contacted USAFFE guerrilla units, under the command of Lieutenant Colonel Charles A. Thorpe. General MacArthur instructed Thorpe, who before the war was in charge of U.S. Army investigations into communist labor unions near Ft. Stotsenburg, to organize a united guerrilla operation to harass the Japanese. Thorpe carried out this mandate from his base-camp west of Clark Field near Mount Pinatubo in Zambales Province.[11] This initial meeting—as recalled in later years by Colonel B. L. Anderson, an eyewitness to the event—was less than cordial and set the tone for subsequent Huk/USAFFE relations during the war.

Anderson and three other American officers met with a Huk delegation, led by Casto Alejandrino, for three weeks in the Candaba Swamp. The Huks requested arms and munitions from USAFFE units but refused to relinquish control of their own operations to Thorpe. They were willing, even anxious, to fight the Japanese with U.S. assistance but only in line with their own ultimate objective of seizing post-war control of the Philippines. After three weeks of negotiations a draft agreement was struck and delivered by two of the U.S. officers to Colonel Thorpe. In the proposed agreement Taruc's forces would follow U.S. military direction but would maintain independent control over their political program. Although a joint headquarters would be set-up to issue battle orders and regulations, the Huks would remain free to run their own organization and recruitment efforts.[12] The other two officers were to remain with the Huks as an example of American trust and goodwill until Thorpe's reply arrived. Knowing that Thorpe would not accept the proposed agreement and fearing for their lives, the two stay-behind officers escaped from the Huk camp and returned to the safety of a nearby USAFFE unit.[13]

Huk operations continued despite the lack of American support and, combined with USAFFE efforts, prevented the Japanese from establishing firm control over the important island of Luzon. In September 1942,. the Japanese launched a major anti-Huk offensive in the area of Mount Arayat. The results from this 1942 offensive were mixed. Although the operation yielded few dead or captured Huks, it totally disrupted their internal organization.[14] The September offensive taught Taruc a lesson he would long remember. If he was to maintain the guerrilla operation, he needed an effective and timely intelligence system. Following the return of the Japanese to Manila, Taruc reorganized his forces into Regional Commands (Recco) and took steps to improve his intelligence gathering ability.[15] What little cooperation existed between the two guerrilla organizations fell apart in late 1942 when Colonel Thorpe was captured by the Japanese. From that time on, the two groups coexisted in an atmosphere of mutual mistrust. Of the Huk units, only one, Recco 2, located in southern Luzon and less political than the others, managed any significant degree of cooperation with the USAFFE organization.[16]

Ironically for the Huks, the brightest point of the campaign came from several instances of Japanese atrocities that accompanied their search and destroy operations. Civilians were tortured, intimidated, and murdered by the Japanese as they sought information on guerrilla whereabouts and members. These terror tactics produced little information but drove many recruits to Taruc. In the two months that followed, Huk strength grew to approximately 5,000 active supporters, organized in thirty-five squadrons and support troops.[17]

The 100-man squadron remained the basis of Huk organization. The squadron was led by a commander, an executive officer, and an intelligence officer, and was organized into platoons and squads. Two squadrons formed a battalion and two battalions made a regiment. Regiments were organized into Military Districts based on geographic areas of responsibility. Five such districts were established: 1st District—southwest Pampanga; 2nd District—central Pampanga; 3rd District—northern Pampanga and part of Tarlac; 4th District—Nueva Ecija; and 5th District—northwest Pampanga and the rest of Tarlac. Atop this structure sat the Military Committee. Shortly after its conception in 1942, the Military Committee combined with CPP leadership to form the Huk General Headquarters (GHQ). Luis Taruc served as chairman of the GHQ, with Casto Alejandrino, a former middle-class landlord and mayor of Arayat, assisting him as vice-chairman. Political officers were placed at all levels of command to advise the commander on matters related to indoctrination and civil affairs.[18]

In January 1943, Huk attacks resumed against Police Constabulary garrisons and Japanese supply depots. As their tactical successes grew and the people saw them as more effective fighters, Huk strength grew again—doubling to 10,000 by March 1943. As their strength and popularity mounted, the Huks activated additional squadrons and helped form an all-Chinese force, the Overseas Chinese 48th Detachment of the People's Anti-Japanese Forces, or *Wachi*. This Chinese unit operated almost exclusively in the provinces of Bulacan and Laguna and, by war's end, included six 200-man squadrons.[19]

The Japanese mounted another major assault on Mount Arayat in March 1943. Five thousand Japanese regulars, police, and the *Makapali* (Japanese sponsored Filipino terrorists) surrounded northeast Pampanga, trapping an estimated fifteen Huk squadrons and most of the Huk GHQ. After ten days the Japanese withdrew with nearly one hundred guerrilla prisoners and several members of the GHQ staff. Despite these losses and the temporary disruption of at least fourteen squadrons, most Huks managed to slip between the Japanese lines to safety.[20] Turning a near rout into a moral victory, the Huks drew strength and confidence from the Japanese failure to destroy their stronghold. Following this episode, they intensified efforts to reestablish their military organization and to promote village defense forces throughout the region. These local forces provided the Huks with logistic and intelligence support and, proved invaluable to Huk operations for the duration of the war and well beyond.

Throughout 1943, Huk military organization matured and formalized in both function and structure. Reports generated at the Military Districts were systematized and increased the flow of information and supplies to Taruc's guerrilla army. Military training and education were emphasized throughout the organization. At "Stalin University" (a large, semi-permanent Huk camp in the Sierra Madres mountains) military training was accompanied by political

indoctrination under the watchful eyes of veterans from the Chinese Red Army. Just one year after the birth of the Huk movement, Taruc claimed 10,000 active supporters, approximately one-third of them armed.[21]

Huk military activity increased steadily through 1943 and into the following year until the organization faced a dilemma over strategy. Taruc desired to press the military attack while CPP leaders wanted to consolidate their control in central Luzon and expand the popular base. From that time until the U.S. invasion of Luzon in January 1945, anti-Japanese activity diminished although efforts to increase the area under Huk control continued. Huks continued to deny the Japanese unmolested access to the region but failed to expand their own areas to any great measure.[22]

Concurrent with guerrilla operations against the Japanese, Taruc and the Huk began to develop village defense forces throughout the region. These paramilitary units, called Barrio United Defense Corps (BUDC), were loose-knit local units composed of five to fifteen members. Formed ostensibly to protect the villagers, to provide law and order, to promote anti-Japanese sentiments, and to deny the enemy access to food and supplies, the corps provided bases for Huk recruitment, intelligence, and logistics support. Acting through the BUDC, Taruc established governments to run the daily activities of the villages.[23]

In larger villages, defense corps were organized into councils composed of "elected" officials. Besides a chairman, vice-chairman, secretary-treasurer, and chief of police, each BUDC had separate departments to administer recruitment, intelligence, transportation, communications, education, sanitation, and agriculture. Although instructed to avoid direct conflict with the Japanese, the councils organized public efforts to limit Japanese support, sought out local traitors, and administered the law as they saw it. Communication was maintained between the BUDC and Huk General Headquarters via a system of couriers who passed information and supplies to Huk squadrons in the vicinity. A major mission established for the councils was indoctrination of the local people. This mission was accomplished through a combination of education and coercion. That is, those peasants reluctant to embody the Huk cause out of devotion, were prevented from acting against it by the threat of force. Once the BUDC were established and running, Huk cadre left the village, but maintained contact through periodic visits.[24] BUDC leaders "elected" many local officials during this unsettled time, including provincial governors in Pampanga and Laguna. By establishing *de facto* governments, the Huks hoped to present advancing U.S. forces and the exiled Philippine government with a *fait accompli* by using this new power to influence subsequent national and regional elections.[25]

In 1944, Taruc refined Huk GHQ organization by adding subordinate departments responsible for specific functions and changed the Military Districts to Regional Commands. The new departments within the GHQ included: Training and Inspection; Maintenance and Supply; Information and Publicity; Communications; and Intelligence.[26] These departments dramatically improved the effectiveness of Huk operations. Having learned from the Japanese victories in 1942, the expanded GHQ moved frequently around Mount Arayat and in the Candaba Swamp.

Five Regional Commands (Recco) replaced the older Military Districts and assumed the following areas of responsibility: Recco 3—Tarlac: Recco 4—Nueva Ecija; Recco 7—Pampanga and Bulacan; Recco 8—central Pampanga and part of Nueva Ecija; and Recco 11—southern Luzon. Later, Recco 4 and 8 were combined into Recco 9, with control of all of Nueva Ecija, while Recco 11 expanded into Rizal and into the Manila barrios. At the height of Huk influence in the war, these Recco controlled the activities of thirty squadrons.[27]

Huk Organization
(ca. 1944)

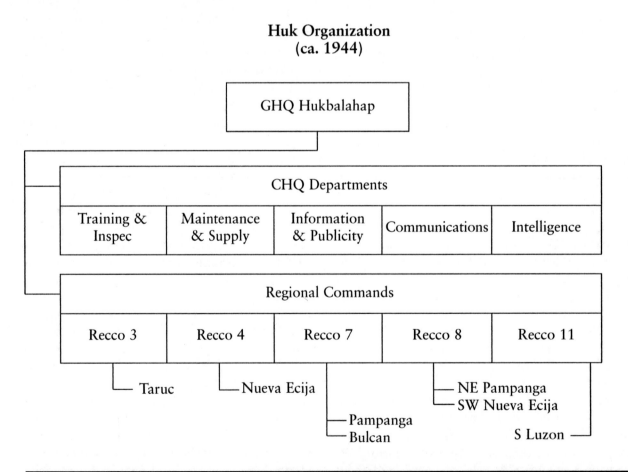

CHART 2

Following the reorganization, Huk activities slowed as internal differences between Taruc and CPP leaders reduced the organization's efficiency. Taruc wanted to continue military operations and, although hindered by the rift, he proceeded with a few attacks on Japanese and police garrisons. Most of his effort, however, was used to press on adjacent USAFFE areas. This developed into a low-level fight for control of central Luzon between the Huks and American sponsored units. Unlike the Huks who sought to intensify attacks during 1943–44, USAFFE units used this period to develop internal organization and to conduct training in preparation for the anticipated American invasion. As U.S. units were becoming active, they saw the decline in Huk activity as detrimental to the liberation effort and charged the Huks with passive collaboration. Although not supported by fact or events, these charges increased tension between the two groups.[28]

After the U.S. invasion in October 1944, Huk military and recruitment activity became more active. As the Japanese withdrew before American forces, Huk squadrons moved into villages and barrios declaring liberation. The fact that they engaged in very limited combat with the retreating forces or, that on the few occasions when Japanese troops reoccupied towns the Huks offered only token resistance, made little consequence to the people. That the Huks were there, establishing order amidst chaos, made the difference and gathered a great deal of local support for them.

An incident in the town of Tarlac illustrated how the Huks took advantage of the fluid situation in early 1945. On 21 January, forces from the U.S. 160th Infantry reached the almost deserted town. After clearing Tarlac of a few Japanese stragglers, the U.S. forces moved on toward Manila. Moving close on American footsteps, Huk forces occupied Tarlac and declared it liberated—but liberated as of 19 January, two days before the American arrival. The local inhabitants did not really care who took credit for their liberation, or for that matter on what date, they only cared that the Japanese were gone. In villages outside of Tarlac the Huks received credit for the liberation and the admiration of even more peasants.[29]

This is not to suggest, however, that every Huk guerrilla failed to support the liberation of the Philippines. In southern Luzon, two Huk squadrons cooperated closely with the U.S. 11th Airborne Division and helped rescue American and allied prisoners from Japanese prison-camps at Cabantuan and Los Banos. After these successful actions, members of these squadrons were detached to the U.S. 37th Infantry and served as guides and interpreters while the division drove toward Manila.

Feelings of mistrust and suspicion that developed during the war continued into liberation and laid the foundation for U.S. policy after 1945. Just six days after U.S. forces landed on Leyte in October 1944, MacArthur's headquarters, GHQ Southwest Pacific Area (SWPA), issued a report on the Huks and their political ambitions. In this report they were defined as aggressive, brutal communist bandits led by a large number of former *Sakdalistas* (pro-Japanese terrorists and thugs) whose objective was to establish a communist regime after the United States left the islands.[30]

The report continued to paint the Huks in an unflattering and biased manner. Besides being anti-American, Huks were described as indiscriminate robbers, plunderers, and killers "capable only of deceit, treachery, and arrogance in dealing with USAFFE guerrilla units." Although the report was correct in assessing them as the largest, most powerful, and best organized group in central Luzon (100,000 members and supporters), the report confused the issue by stating that the Huks were willing to accept arms and assistance from the Japanese in order to fight American units.[31] Greatly exaggerated and often misleading in regard to Japanese and *Sakdalista* connections, it was not surprising that by 9 January 1945 (the U.S. invasion of Luzon), Huk guerrillas were seen as little better than the Japanese by American military leaders. These feelings lasted well into the post-war era and they affected U.S. policy for years to come.

Two months before "V-J" Day, in June 1945, Taruc and his armed Huk forces joined CPP political leaders to form the Democratic Alliance. They founded this political organization to legitimate communist aspirations for the post-war era through a legal political party. Looking ahead to Philippine independence in 1946, as promised by the Tydings-McDuffie Act, Taruc realized that his organization could use the political system to gain a foothold in the government—a position from which he hoped later to seize total power.

BETWEEN LIBERATION AND INDEPENDENCE

CONDITIONS AT LIBERATION

When General MacArthur stepped ashore on Leyte on 22 October 1944, he was accompanied by Sergio Osmena, the former Philippine vice-president who succeeded President Manuel Quezon who died in August 1944 while in exile in the United States. With U.S. forces pushing the Japanese from the islands, Osmena was brought back to reestablish a legitimate civilian government, to oversee post-war recovery, and to prepare the Philippines for independence. Three days after his arrival in Leyte, MacArthur returned civil control of liberated areas to the commonwealth president and, on 27 February 1945, he granted Osmena civil control over the entire Philippines. Unfortunately, Osmena was considered by many to be a weak and ineffectual leader, lacking the skill and charisma of his predecessor.[1]

But what of the nation Osmena was given charge of? The islands were devastated. General Eisenhower remarked that, "Of all the wartime capitals, only Warsaw suffered more damage than Manila."[2] Essential services were in chaos. Transportation and communication systems were barely operational in most areas, food production was at a standstill, and the health system was horribly overtaxed. The economy was in shambles—unemployment was epidemic and the nation's export industry had collapsed during the war. In fact, only graft and corruption seem to have increased from pre-war days.[3] To accomplish anything, many hands in government had to be crossed with silver and assistance was provided to those with connections, not to those with the greatest need.

In January 1946, Paul V. McNutt, the U.S. High Commissioner to the Philippines, delivered a report to President Truman outlining conditions and their effects on the scheduled independence of the islands that July. "The situation is critical," McNutt reported, "it does not at this moment seem possible for the Filipino people, ravaged and demoralized by the cruelest and most destructive of wars, politically split between loyalists and enemy collaborators, with several well-armed dissident groups still at large, to cope with the coincidence of political independence and the tremendous economic demands of rehabilitation."[4]

During this trying period the United States Congress made sincere efforts to assist Philippine recovery through economic assistance programs. In October 1945, Senator Tydings (co-author of the 1934 Tydings-McDuffie Act) introduced legislation in the Senate for Philippine rehabilitation. Originally seeking $620 million in emergency economic aid, Tydings' bill was reduced in scope by $100 million.[5]

The act provided for several important actions to assist reconstruction. The first of these provisions established a Philippine War Damage Commission, chartered by Congress to investigate and pay claims for property lost as a result of military action. The commission owed its conception as much to an August 1943 promise by President Roosevelt to "assist in the full repair of ravages caused by war," as it did to concerns about conditions on the islands.[6] A second provision authorized the U.S. government to transfer surplus military equipment and property, at cost or as grants, to the Philippine government. Together, Congress hoped that the influx of economic aid and Philippine acquisition of cheap, reliable equipment would speed reconstruction and put the nation's economy back on track.[7]

This well intentioned program, as well as other smaller ones, however, did little to solve the problems faced by the Philippine people or promote an enlightened climate for political or social reforms. American money, supplies, and equipment were quickly absorbed by an economy starved for even the most basic commodities. Amidst a people hungry for all types of goods, black markets flourished, relief and rehabilitation materials disappeared, and the Osmena administration seemed unwilling to do anything about corruption. War damage claims, administered by a joint U.S.-Philippine War Damage Corporation, began business in June but, soon became hopelessly mired in bureaucratic red-tape. Although the U.S. Congress allocated $520 million for Philippine war claims, that figure fell far short of the $1.2 billion estimate made by President Osmena, or even the $800 million estimate submitted by the U.S. War Damage Commission that visited the islands shortly after liberation.[8]

During the corporation's four year life, more than one million private claims were processed. Each of some 685 daily claims had to be validated before payments were made. Although the first payment to the Philippine government was made in December 1946, payment of the first individual claim was not made until April 1947. When the commission finished its work in 1950, it had dispersed only $388 million against claims totaling $1.25 billion.[9] Slowness, inefficiency, and overt corruption within the Commission set public feelings against the central government and by extension against the United States. Needless to say, Huk propagandists combined these feelings of neglect and corruption with those about land-tenancy as they rebuilt their popular base. As the people's frustrations grew, so did their affinity for the communist cause—not so much from an ideological position, as from their desire for change and reform.

UNITED STATES POLICY TOWARD THE PHILIPPINES

The attitudes of U.S. policy-makers toward the islands in the period between liberation and independence was paternalistic, economically based, conservative, and anti-Huk. Post-war policy was aimed at returning the nation to normalcy through economic assistance that would, in essence, reestablish conditions as they existed before 1941. In short, American policy sought to return the *status quo* and cut the umbilical cord with Manila, by granting the nation independence, just as soon as it could. This policy resulted in the implementation of poorly administered assistance programs that often worked to the Huks' advantage.

Emergency assistance in the forms of food and aid were rushed to the islands on the heels of liberation. By mid-1945, 200 million pounds of food were shipped to Manila to relieve shortages caused by the near total breakdown of Philippine agriculture. However promising the effort, emergency programs suffered from a lack of American supervision once the aid reached the Philippines. Once unloaded, the distribution of aid was mismanaged by inept, usually corrupt, Filipino officials. These problems were aggravated by the release of several thousand Filipino collaborators by United States and Philippine

authorities when their skills were needed by the Osmena government.[10] However, as often is the case involving large sums of money and materiel flooding into an impoverished nation, many local officials took the opportunity to become wealthy through corruption and the black market at the expense of their countrymen.

Based on U.S. wartime experience with the Huk, intelligence reports produced in the closing days of the war by the Southwest Pacific Area staff, and in consultation with President Osmena (who had a narrow understanding of the Huks and their goals), MacArthur ordered the guerrillas disarmed and dispersed. Of all the Huk squadrons that participated in the war, only two from southern Luzon were offered official recognition and promised veteran benefits, back pay, and the opportunity to integrate into the Philippine armed forces. Conversely, most USAFFE veterans were integrated directly into the Philippine Military Police Command, and promised full benefits.[11] These seemingly arbitrary actions led to serious confrontations between Huk and U.S. forces and, when coupled with U.S. reluctance to even recognize them as *bona fide* anti-Japanese guerrillas, the stage was set for long-term disaffections.

It became official U.S. policy to ignore the Huks, considering them but bands of armed civilians. Several squadrons offered to join the AFP, but were refused and ordered instead to surrender their arms. In more than one instance, Huks were confronted by armed U.S. and Philippine forces sent to carry out U.S. policy regarding the disarmament of armed civilian groups. In Pampanga Province, American troops surrounded three squadrons who refused to lay down their arms. These Huks were finally disarmed at rifle-point. In mid-February, U.S. troops arrested members of the Huk GHQ and imprisoned them in San Fernando. When Taruc and Alejandrino were arrested, temporary control of the movement fell to Mariano Balges, Huk GHQ political commissar. Balges fled with many of his supporters to the jungles and swamps of central Luzon and began the process of rebuilding the Huk organization. Many local people, who just weeks before had applauded the arrival of U.S. forces, viewed the incarceration of the Huk leadership and other hard-handed American and Filipino actions with disdain and threw-in once again with the guerrillas.[12]

After twenty-two days of imprisonment, Taruc and Alejandrino were released when mass demonstrations threatened to undermine peace throughout central Luzon. United States and Philippine government authorities hoped that the two leaders would convince Huks to come-in and surrender their arms. Instead, Taruc reassumed his position as Hukbalahap "El Supremo," this time vowing to continue the fight against the government and the United States. Unfortunately for Taruc and Alejandrino, Huk intelligence suffered seriously during liberation and they were arrested once again by U.S. CIC agents in April. This time, they were sent to Iwahig Prison on the island of Palawan, far from their supporters. As harsh as American actions were toward the Huks, MacArthur had in fact resisted even stronger ones. He held sympathetic feelings for what the Huk were fighting for and told his biographer, William Manchester, that if he (MacArthur) were a Filipino, he would have been a Huk.[13]

Another problem faced by the government after liberation concerned local governments established by the Huks during the war. These Barrio United Defense Corps (BUDC) maintained a degree of order within the villages and were seen as legitimate by the local populace. In the provinces of Pampanga, Tarlac, Nueva Ecija, Bulacan, Rizal, and Laguna, entire government structures from provincial governor to local postal clerks were held by Huk/CPP officials or their supporters. President Osmena considered these local governments invalid and, with the consent of the U.S. High Commissioner, refused them recognition and ordered them replaced with his own appointees.[14]

At this critical point in Philippine reconstruction, U.S. policy makers failed to see the Huks and their popular, peasant-based movement for what it really was—a communist revolutionary struggle capable of mass support under current conditions. Instead, the Huks were treated as bandits, their mass support was seriously underestimated, and no real efforts were pursued to bring about socio-economic changes or reforms.[15] Few Americans understood the Huk movement or what was needed to defeat it. Those who did, men such as then Air Force Major Edward G. Lansdale, were few in number and not politically influential.[16]

American insensitivity to internal Philippine problems continued into 1946 when the U.S. Congress passed two measures that strained Philippine relations and fueled Huk propaganda fires. In February, the Congress addressed the issue of Filipino veteran rights. In a move that shocked people across the Philippines, Congress, initially at least, denied them GI Bill benefits, breaking a promise made to them by General MacArthur as he retreated from Bataan. The American decision also denied back-pay, hospitalization, mustering-out pay, and burial benefits. In the Philippines, this decision met widespread opposition. The U.S. Congress readdressed the veteran issue over the following five years, finally approving money for Philippine veteran hospitals in 1948, burial benefits in 1951, and later paid Filipino veterans $473 million in back-pay and allowances.[17]

A second action that inadvertently aided Huk calls for a Philippines free of U.S. domination was the Philippine Trade Act (or Bell Act) of 1946. Introduced by Missouri Representative C. Jasper Bell in September 1945, the highly controversial act underwent five revisions before being passed in April 1946. Designed to stabilize economic ties with the United States help Philippine recovery, the act formalized pre-war economic trading patterns and ensured U.S. economic hegemony over the country.[18] Provisions of the 1946 act fixed the Philippine peso to the dollar and prevented the Philippine government from changing the value of the peso without U.S. consent. As a final insult, the act legislated a twenty-eight year extension for duty-free trade between the nations and mandated equal and free access to Philippine markets by American businessmen and companies.[19] The Trade Act was the subject of hot debate in the Philippine legislature before being ratified on 18 September 1946, primarily due to the efforts of a coalition of local merchants, businessmen, and politicians (those most likely to benefit from a return to the old *status* quo).[20] Huks seized upon this legislation as just another example of the United States acting through the Philippine government to maintain a neo-colonial relationship for the benefit of Filipino landlords, rich businessmen, and corrupt government officials.

THE RESUMPTION OF HUK/CPP ACTIVITY

By summer of 1945, the people of central Luzon had serious doubts about the intentions of their newly reestablished central government. Local authorities were not recognized by President Osmena and Huk friends and relatives were being arrested—certainly unusual treatment for those regarded as brave, patriotic freedom-fighters. To make matters worse, peasants were now falling victim to government police and troops who often preyed upon the peasants for food and supplies much as the Japanese had done. As lawlessness increased, the peasants were forced to choose between supporting a central government that was legal but could not exert control, or to support the Huks, who although illegal, attempted to provide control and worked to enforce order.[21]

Sensing the growing climate of disaffection, the CPP moved its base of operations into the Manila barrios and began to organize new labor unions. In July 1945, the CPP formally joined with two of the more successful unions they helped establish before the war—the National Peasant's Union and the broad, socialist-based Congress of Labor Organizations. Together, the three groups formed the Democratic Alliance (DA). Under Lava's control, the Alliance set to plot a strategy for the upcoming November 1946 general elections as a major opposition party to the ruling *Partido Nacionalista*.[22] At the same time, Democratic Alliance leadership planned the timetable for the eventual overthrow of the Philippine government.

The Democratic Alliance timetable defined three periods in which an alliance of political and military activists would work toward specific goals. The first phase, from 1946–1949, would be devoted to organization. During this preparatory stage, the movement would attempt to win the support of the working and peasant classes. Once this support was well entrenched, they would set up a national revolutionary bloc of workers, peasants, and intellectuals to prevent the capitalist classes from extending their control over the nation.

The second stage of the strategy was to take place between 1949 and 1951, and would focus on the "political offensive." DA leaders planned to couple the mass political base, built during the first phase, with the military wing of the organization, the Hukbalahap. The planning document used for this strategy called for Huk strength to peak at 172,800 members by September 1951. Finally, in 1952, the communists planned to see their strategy through to fruition with the takeover of the government in the third and final stage. This takeover would be accomplished in a mass uprising—an uprising so grand in scale that the existing capitalist government could not stand in its path.[23]

Throughout the summer of 1946, the Democratic Alliance organized large demonstrations in Manila to demand the release of Taruc and Alejandrino. In September, following an especially violent and bloody riot, Osmena ordered the two Huk leaders released from Iwahig. They returned home and organized political campaigns for the November elections.

The communist political organization also took advantage of yet another sensitive issue that appeared after the war—collaboration. Questions over who collaborated with the Japanese and why, sparked violent debates and hatred in the post-war Philippines. For many Filipinos who suffered greatly at the hands of the enemy the slightest hint of collaboration by a public official was cause for deep resentment. This problem intensified in cases involving the Philippine Police Constabulary and members of the new government. The police had been used by the Japanese to control the countryside and, although they seldom cooperated fully with the enemy, they did operate under his control. Many members of the reconstruction government had also cooperated with the Japanese and were under similar suspicions.

Manuel Roxas, a politician and army brigadier general before the war, was a government administrator during the Japanese occupation. At liberation, Roxas, along with 5,000 others, was taken into custody by U.S. military authorities and imprisoned for collaboration. Due to his administrative skills, and evidence that he collaborated to minimize violence directed against Filipinos, he was among many former government officials released on the orders of President Osmena and General MacArthur in April 1945.[24] Roxas had strong support from MacArthur, and because of his administrative background was appointed to the Osmena administration and soon returned to a position of power in the Nationalist Party from which he challenged President Osema. During the first post-war election in 1945, Roxas was elected president and forty-five members of the occupation government were returned to the legislature.[25] The issue of collaboration played heavily on the minds of most Filipinos and quickly became a key element of the Huk propaganda campaign.

When the guerrillas returned to the jungles and swamps of central Luzon, they began to rebuild their wartime organization. Luis Taruc resumed his role as military commander while Jose Lava ran the movement's political campaign. Seeking shelter and protection in the same areas they used so effectively against the Japanese, Taruc's armed guerrillas ventured out to harass government forces, intimidate civilians who favored the Manila government, and raise supplies and money through taxes levied on villages, and an occasional robbery or kidnapping when voluntary contributions failed.[26] Concurrently, other armed units were formed that terrorized and murdered landlords returning to lay claim to the lands they abandoned during the war. The Huks received active support from the peasantry for these actions, since most of the peasants remained with the land and attempted to resist the Japanese when the landlords fled.[27]

Indoctrination and propaganda campaigns were conducted to support the armed struggle at every opportunity. Stalin University was reopened in the Sierra Madres mountains for promising recruits. Huk propagandists were quick to exploit even the most minor case of government abuse or corruption, and there was no difficulty in identifying these. Realizing that most of their support came from the peasant farming class, the movement adopted the slogans "Land for the Landless" and "Prosperity for the Masses".[28] This strategy proved most effective in the days prior to independence in 1946 as the people searched for socio-economic reforms that never came from Manila.

Thus, as the nation approached independence, little constructive change had taken place since 1941. If there was any dramatic change at all, it was a worsening condition for the peasant, brought about by the ravages of war. The Manila government was riddled with corruption and showed no visible concern for the peasant farmer. Landlords and wealthy Filipino businessmen continued to hold firm sway in government and, aided by post-war U.S. policy, had returned the Philippines to the *status quo* that most favored their own purposes. The peasant felt forgotten, abused, and saw no hope for substantive social or economic change coming from the current government once the islands achieved independence.

THE INSURRECTION—PHASE I (1946–1950)

CONDITIONS AT INDEPENDENCE

Amidst great fanfare, the Republic of the Philippines was born on 4 July 1946. After the celebrations ended however, the government had to face the realities of sovereignty, a faltering economy, and widespread poverty, especially in Luzon. In Manila, the city once called "the pearl of the Orient," a million people lived in shambles, little improved since the departure of the Japanese. The barrios were full of unemployed Filipinos who arrived during and after the war to seek shelter and jobs but, unfortunately, found neither. The youth grew restless and resented the government that expressed little concern for their plight.

The new Philippine government, that had run nearly all of the nation's internal affairs during the commonwealth period, now had sole responsibility for solving the people's problems. Established using the American model of government, an expected result of the country's association with the United States since the end of the nineteenth century, the Philippines had a bicameral legislature and an executive branch consisting of a president and vice-president elected for a four year term and limited to two consecutive terms of office. Beneath the office of the President were ten executive departments, much the same in form and function as U.S. cabinet departments. A singular departure from the American system was the right of the president to suspend, remove, or replace local mayors or governors at his discretion. The final government body, the judiciary, consisted of a supreme court and subordinate statutory courts scattered throughout the islands. All of the justices were appointed by the president and approved by the legislative Commission on Appointments.[1]

THE 1946 ELECTIONS

In preparation for the nation's first post-independence election, President Osmena released Taruc and Alejandrino from the Iwahig Prison in September. Both leaders had long anticipated the importance of the post-independence elections to establish a permanent position within the government for their movement. This had been the prime reason for the formation of the Democratic Alliance, the political alliance between the CPP and other socialist /communist groups during the liberation period. The two returned immediately to central Luzon and began to plan the Democratic Alliance's campaign for the November election but never fully regained absolute control of the political organization. However, the failure to recapture their political positions was made less dramatic because of a spilt within the ruling *Partido Nacionalista.*

President Osmena and Manuel Roxas, his chief opponent within the party, were divided on the issue of how to handle Huk resistance in Luzon. Osmena favored negotiation, while Roxas proposed elimination. After heated debate and intense internal maneuvering, Osmena retained control of the Nationalist Party and was nominated as its presidential candidate in 1946. Roxas, bitter after his failure to capture the party, left and formed the Liberal Party that, not surprisingly, nominated him as their candidate. Not yet strong enough to nominate a viable candidate for the presidency and afraid that a three way race would guarantee victory for Roxas, the Democratic Alliance threw its support behind Osmena, the more liberal of the two major candidates. For the time, the Alliance was content to run candidates for regional office throughout central Luzon.

Campaigning during the fall of 1946 was intense and often violent. Roxas promised that, if elected, he would eliminate Huk resistance within sixty days of his inauguration, and instituted a campaign of terror and intimidation to ensure victory. Huk members of the Democratic Alliance responded with their own counter-terror campaign directed against Roxas' supporters and increased their efforts on behalf of their own candidates in central Luzon. The peasant electorate was trapped between the two warring factions, becoming more and more alienated from the central government as the violence continued.[2]

In November, Roxas won the victory on the national level, but lost heavily in central Luzon. The Democratic Alliance elected six congressmen to the legislature in Manila from the provinces of Nueva Ecija, Tarlac, Pampanga, and Bulacan. Despite Roxas' victory, Huk supporters saw a glimmer of hope because of their regional success in the election. However, these hopes were dashed when Democratic Alliance congressmen-elect, including Luis Taruc, went to Manila to take their seats in Congress.[3]

Roxas intended to live up to his campaign promise of ridding the islands of the Huks after his inauguration in early 1947. His first step was to use his influence within Congress to deny the Alliance congressmen their seats, along with three *Nacionalista* senators whom he felt were allied with the DA. Refused his seat, Taruc returned to the mountains near Mount Arayat in May 1947 and reorganized the Huk General Headquarters. President Roxas then declared a virtual nationwide "open season" on the Huks. The Philippine Military Police Command, reorganized with the Police Constabulary after the war, joined Civil Guards (paramilitary units raised by provincial governors) on indiscriminate "Huk Hunts" wherever they thought Huks or their sympathizers were located. As these government-sanctioned groups scoured the countryside in search of Huks, they spread terror throughout local populations. Preying on the people for supplies, food, and information (often obtained through intimidation and torture) they provided opportune and popular targets for Taruc's forces. They proved the best recruiters for the Huks, who gained new members with each passing day.[7] This was the real start of the insurrection.

"HUKLANDIA" AND THE PEASANTS

When the Huk guerrillas again took to the mountains, they chose central Luzon for their base of operations—the traditional land from which they had fought against the Japanese and from which countless generations of guerrillas had sought sanctuary from oppressive regimes,

whether Spanish, American, Japanese, or Philippine. Just as the mountains near Mount Arayat and the Candaba Swamp protected them from the Japanese, so now the land protected them from President Roxas' forces. Surrounded by 6,000 square miles of the richest rice growing region in the Philippines, and supported by local villagers who felt the brunt of government frustrations and inequities, Taruc resumed his plans for the overthrow of the Philippine government.[8]

The key to Huk success and persistence stemmed almost entirely from the active support of the local people. Luis Taruc understood them, their desires, aspirations, and, at least during the first phase of the insurrection, used this intimacy to his advantage. When asked why people allied with the his movement, Taruc responded that "People in the barrios . . . joined because they had causes—like agrarian reform, government reform, anti-repression, recognition of the Hukbalahap— and, frequently, because they simply had to defend themselves, their very lives against repression."[9] Others joined him to revenge the death or abuse of friends and relatives. Still others were so poor and so deeply in debt that they had nothing to lose by backing the rebels. But the one overriding factor that seemed to be central for Huk supporters and converts was the issue of land-tenure. They wanted to own the land they had worked for generations. Luzon, with the country's highest rate of land-tenancy, provided an ideal recruiting ground for the movement.[10]

ORGANIZATION FOR THE INSURRECTION

At the onset of the insurrection, the Huk movement was made up of three general types of people—politicals (communists and socialists), former wartime guerrilla fighters, and a small criminal element of common thieves and bandits. Taruc would have preferred to avoid association with the latter group, but reality dictated that he accept help and recruits from whatever source. Several years later, after the government organized an effective anti-Huk campaign in late 1950, this diversity severely hurt the organization's cohesion and effectiveness.

The Huks were also divided along functional lines, that is, the organization was composed of fighters, supporters, and a mass civilian base. At the heart of the movement were the regulars— full-time fighters who conducted raids, ambuscades, kidnappings and extortion. The second group of Huks, the supporters, were divided between what may be called combat and service support activities. The combat support Huks were generally "die hard" followers who joined the regulars from time to time, but usually remained in their villages and carried on life as farmers. Those considered service supporters performed such non-combat duties as collecting taxes and acting as couriers—a most important function for the organization. Finally, there was the largest group of all, the mass support base. Although the people in this category rarely fought with the guerrillas, they provided them with food, information, and sanctuary. The number of supporters in the mass base was always a subject of either debate or boasting, but it was generally accepted to have peaked at the end of 1950 at some one million peasants and farmers. This was the foundation upon which Taruc built his movement and without which it could not have survived.[11]

To control far-flung Huk activities, Taruc developed an extensive and well organized structure. This structure drew heavily on wartime organization and fully integrated the militant Huk forces with the political CPP faction. The National Congress and the thirty-one member Central Committee, so common to communist movements, sat atop the organization. An eleven-member Politburo was subordinate to the Central Committee and provided day-to-day direction for the movement through its secretariat. Consisting of four major departments, the Secretariat was the level at which the movement's political and military branches met and may be considered the Huk operational level of command, with those levels above it working at the strategic level.

CPP/Huk Organization
(ca. 1950)

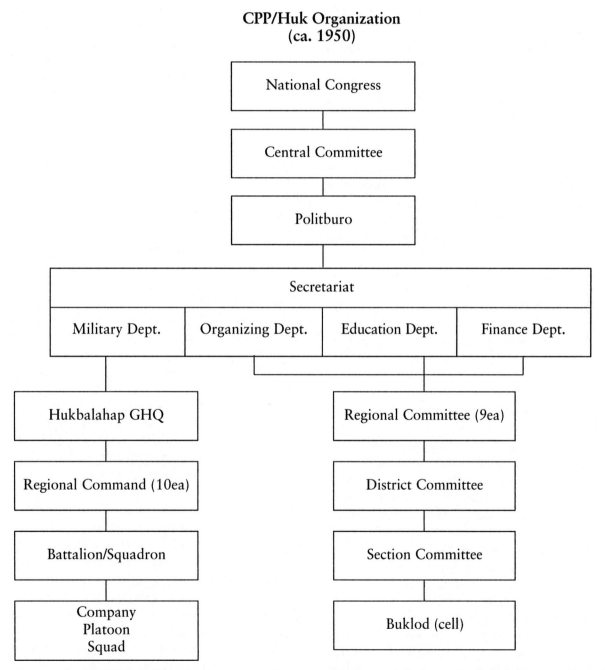

Source: Donald MacGrain, Anti-Dissident Operations in the Philippines, (Carlisle Barracks, PA: U.S. Army War College, [26 March 1956], p. 35.

CHART 3

The internal organization of the Huk Military Department was constructed similar to that of the overall body. Each Regional Command (Recco) was composed of a single regiment (almost totally concerned with administration and logistics) made up of two battalions of two squadrons each. The 100 man squadron (company) was nominally composed of two platoons, each platoon having four twelve-man squads.[12]

Despite this impressive organization, the movement suffered from two important deficiencies that worked to its detriment after 1951. These areas were armaments and communications, with armaments being the more pressing and constant problem. As during World War II, obtaining sufficient amounts of arms and ammunition remained a major obstacle. What weapons they had, they stole, found, or purchased in Manila's black market. To counter this shortcoming, Taruc relied heavily on obtaining weapons after battles, raiding government outposts, or simply picking up armed fighters on their way to a large engagement that occasionally saw Huk combat formations as large as 2,000 troops.[13] There exists little evidence to substantiate claims made by President Roxas that the guerrillas received external arms shipments from Chinese communists on the mainland. On the contrary, the matter of arming his available troops remained one of Taruc's chief concerns throughout the insurrection.

The other area in which Huk organization was deficient was communications. Although the insurgents acquired several radios during the course of the rebellion, including some purchased in Manila in 1948 but captured by government forces before they could be used, evidence showed that they were used primarily for intelligence gathering.[14] That is, Huks monitored government troops but did not use the radios for their own communications. They chose to do this for several reasons; they lacked trained radiomen, sufficient radios, or spare parts and batteries. Instead, Huks relied on the time-tested courier system to transfer information, orders, and supplies between their elements. This simple system worked well for several years, supplying squadrons with information about government movements and food but, lacked flexibility and responsiveness when later faced with new government tactics.

HUK INTELLIGENCE AND PSYOP

During the height of the insurgency, much of its success depended on good intelligence. Outnumbered, outgunned, and outsupplied, Taruc relied on information about government activities to plan his operations. Throughout Huklandia, his agents recruited local government officials and members of the Philippine Police Constabulary as informants. Not all of these officials offered their help voluntarily, but threats against them or their families often gained their cooperation.[15] Huks also attempted, sometimes successfully, to infiltrate government forces. Once in, agents sought weapons, information, and provoked ill feelings between officers and men by pointing out how differently were their respective life styles within the armed forces. Police and several Philippine Army officers and men collaborated by providing information, either to prevent trouble in their area of responsibility or for greed.[16]

During the early years of the insurgency, before 1951, Taruc found that good intelligence information was not hard to gather. Peasants were eager to help the Huks fight the government troops, who often treated the villagers worse than did common bandits. Information was transported up through the Huk or CPP organization via couriers. The couriers, either "illegals" (usually young, innocent looking men and women who traveled cross-country) or "legals" (couriers that used the highway and public transportation networks) passed their messages on at established relay points to the next courier. Knowing only two points of the entire system (their individual start and finish points), the couriers proved highly successful and remarkably secure until well after 1951.[17] The occasional government radio that fell into guerrilla hands also provided a wealth of information about AFP and police operations. In fact, it was one of these captured radios that led to the 1949 Huk ambush and killing of Senora Aurora Quezon, wife of the former president—an incident that proved a grave miscalculation.

The Huks were always quick to adapt local concerns into effective propaganda campaigns. The original slogan, "Land for the Landless," was catchy, to the point, and served the Huks well for many years. Following the violent and fraud-ridden 1949 election, Taruc adopted a new slogan for the movement—"Bullets, not Ballots." Again, Huk leaders identified a situation that the people felt strongly about and capitalized on it."[18] To supplement their propaganda campaign and to prove to the people that the Huk/CPP organization had authority, Huk headquarters published and widely distributed a series of newspapers and periodicals. These publications ran the gamut from the bi-weekly newspaper *Titus (Sparks)* to a monthly theoretical magazine for Huk cadre, *Ang Kommunista*. There was also *Mapagpalays (Liberation),* a monthly periodical that dealt with the Huk struggle and its goals, and a cultural magazine, *Kalayaan (Freedom),* that published short stories, poems, and essays. Huk propagandists also experimented with correspondence courses, producing two self-study pamphlets with monthly updates—one for Huk regulars, and one for CPP political workers.[19]

Taruc and the Huk leadership used poor social conditions and corruption within government to fuel their propaganda campaign. During 1948, and up until the general election of 1949, the Huks devoted great efforts to publicize examples of governmental excess and corruption. For example, in 1948 a full 75 percent of Luzon's population were peasants and, for these people, the post-war government had done little to mitigate their plight.[20] Tenancy had returned, landlords ignored laws that established debt ratios for the farmers, and the courts invariably decided in favor of influential landlords. The gap between the Philippine upper classes and the peasant majority had widened since the war and independence, not contracted as many had hoped.

Graft and corruption ran rampant in government. The Roxas administration seemed to condone it and did nothing to conceal its presence or depth. In a 1948 letter to General Omar Bradley, the Chief of Staff, Major General George F. Moore (Commander, U.S. Army Philippine-Ryukyus Command) reported that Philippine law enforcement and court systems were inadequate, applied arbitrarily, and did not protect the citizen. Rather, he reported they were being used as tools by government officials, wealthy landowners, and businessmen. General Moore cited an investigation into a criminal ring involved in stealing U.S. surplus jeeps and selling them on the black market. Sons of the mayor of Manila, the

Police Chief, and the Secretary of Labor were implicated as running the ring and of ordering the murder of an American investigator's infant daughter. Local police in San Luis confessed to taking part in the incident, and testified that the town mayor, Atilio Bondoc, fired the shot that killed the little girl. Local courts found the policemen guilty and gave them light sentences, but the mayor was released without action.[21]

General Moore also connected this criminal ring to the killing of a U.S. officer outside a supply depot in Manila and with discrepancies in the Philippine Foreign Liquidation Commission's books. The Commission, composed jointly of American and Filipino administrators, was established to oversee the disposal of surplus equipment in the country. At the time Moore wrote Bradley, there existed a shortage of some 6,000 jeeps that should have been accounted for in Commission records. When confronted with the evidence, the Commission failed to take any action. This corruption also extended into gasoline, hijackings of U.S. cargo trucks, spare parts, and incidents of U.S. equipment being thrown off moving trains to waiting thieves. Finally, when some culprits were brought to justice, the General found that they were either acquitted or given light fines and released.[22] These were examples of corruption and government sponsored crime that Huk propagandists ensured went before the "public's eye."

HUK FINANCING AND LOGISTICS

The widespread Huk structure required an extensive logistics system to support the guerrilla fighters as well as CPP political activities. Since Taruc received little if any outside aid or equipment, he relied on local support and the Manila based National Finance Committee. In and around Huklandia, the Huks levied quotas on villages for food and some money. Villagers unsympathetic to the cause were intimidated into making contributions by specially organized tax collectors—toughs and thugs. Collections were augmented by Huk agents who impersonated government tax collectors in areas not under their control and by occasional raids, holdups, or train robberies.[23]

In Manila, the National Finance Committee organized a series of Economic Struggle Units to gather funds and equipment. These units collected voluntary contributions, mainly from the 20,000 Chinese living in and around Manila, and conducted urban robberies, extortion rackets, and levied taxes in Manila's suburbs. Collected funds were divided equally between the Huk/CPP national headquarters and the local regional command (Recco).[24] To supplement food received by local sympathizers, Huks began to establish "production bases" in 1948. These "bases" were actually small farms run by Huks and protected from the government by their dispersed locations within Huklandia. The bases only became vital once the Philippine Army severed Huk logistic routes during and after 1951.

Weapons and ammunition posed a constant supply problem for the insurgents. There were never enough of either to go around and lacking outside assistance, Huks had to make do with weapons left over from the war, captured from the Army, or stolen from U.S. military depots intended for the invasion of Japan. However, showing the greatest of confidence in the solidarity of the international communist movement, Taruc established a secret base on Luzon's Pacific coast to receive clandestine arms shipments from submarines.[25] As best as can be determined, this base was never used and the Huks were forced to fight the battle with old Enfield and Springfield rifles, carbines (some of which were converted by Huk ordnance shops into fully automatic weapons), .45 caliber "tommy-guns," a few .30 caliber machine-guns, and small mortars, normally no larger than 60 mm.

HUK MILITARY OPERATIONS

Throughout the first phase of the insurrection, 1946–1950, Huk squadrons roamed freely across central Luzon harassing Philippine Army and Police Constabulary (PC) outposts at will and gaining support. The poorly led, underpaid government forces, with a combined total strength of only 37,000 in 1946, faced 10,000-15,000 Huk regulars and over 100,000 supporters in a region of two million inhabitants.[26] Following the first engagement between Huks and government forces (shortly after Manuel Roxas was inaugurated in May 1946), the tendency among government troops was to remain close to the campfires.[27] On those few occasions

when these forces ventured afield and encountered Huks, the outcome usually favored the insurgents. Having been ceded the initiative by the government, Huks seized town after town, establishing martial law and spreading their influence as they went.

In the first battle between government regulars and the guerrillas, a Huk squadron ambushed a 10th Military Police Company patrol in the town of Santa Monica in Nueva Ecija Province. Ten members of the patrol were killed and the patrol leader captured and beheaded. The Huks did not lose a single man in the engagement and the victory provided the fledgling Huks with a tremendous boost in morale. The Santa Monica ambush was followed quickly by other hit-and-run raids on Army patrols and outposts. Huk recruitment showed a dramatic increase because of these early military victories. Events that began in Santa Monica culminated when Huk Commander Viernes, alias "Stalin," captured the city of Nueva Ecija, the provincial capital, with 200 Huk regulars, and declared it Huk territory.[28] This overt challenge to the government went unanswered for years.

While coordinating activities with Taruc's fighters, the CPP began to expand rapidly in the fall of 1946. As political influence spread westward from the central plain into Bataan and Zambales provinces, propagandists were followed closely by organizers and Huk forces. This was the Huk pattern—to follow political agitators with Huk organizers and then establish the area as their own with HMB squadrons. Within a short time they exerted considerable political and military influence in Pangasinan Province to the north; in Nueva Vizcaya and Isebala; in Laguna, Batangas, and Tayabas provinces in southern Luzon; and on the island of Panay.[29]

Despite an occasional military setback during this phase of the insurrection, Huks worked constantly to build bonds with the people. Many times, squadrons would stay with villagers, working and playing with them, all the while developing stronger ties and indoctrinating them about the Huk/communist cause. Army forays against the insurgents usually caused few guerrilla casualties but often resulted in the frustrated soldiers taking vengeance on the local people. Military Police Command terrorism and constant demands from the soldiers for food and supplies, bolstered Huk claims that they, not the government, were trying to protect the people from abuse and lawlessness.[30]

Huk raids continued through the spring of 1947, steadily increasing in size and number. In April, the insurgents ambushed an Army patrol, killing six men. In May, a hundred-man squadron attacked the garrison at Laur, Nueva Ecija, looted the village bank and kidnapped the local police chief, who they held for ransom. At the same time, raids and ambushes took place in San Miguel, in Bulacan, and in other provinces across central Luzon.[31] President Roxas was outraged by the Huks' success and following the Laur raid, ordered the military to attack the guerrilla stronghold around Mount Arayat.

Two thousand Army and constabulary troops participated in OPERATION ARAYAT. The operation spanned two weeks but produced only meager results—twenty-one Huks were reported killed in action and small quantities of rice and weapons captured. Huk intelligence agents knew the government troops were coming, where they would be coming from, and about how long they would devote to the operation. As a result, almost all the Huks in the area slipped through government lines to safety. When contact was made, it usually happened by accident, thus the relatively low Huk losses considering the total number of insurgents in the affected area.[32]

In February 1947, Luis Taruc outlined his "five minimum terms for peace" to author and journalist Benedict Kerkvliet. Taruc demanded that the government: immediately restore individual rights; grant amnesty for all Huk members; replace police and government officials in central Luzon; restore the seats of the six Democratic Alliance congressmen elected in 1946; and institute land reforms that would abolish land-tenancy.[33] Taruc realized fully that Roxas would never concede to these demands, especially those concerning the DA congressmen and replacing officials but, the Huks were riding a swell of popular support and proclaiming the movement's demands gave it credibility outside central Luzon.

Huks felt so secure within Huklandia that, by 1948, training camps, command bases, schools, and production bases were reestablished across

"HUKLANDIA"
Expansion After 1946

central Luzon, much as was done during World War II.[34] With its center at the 3,400 foot tall Mount Arayat, the Huk stronghold spread south across the marshy and seasonally flooded Candaba Swamp, east to the Sierra Madre mountains, and west to the mountains of Zambales province.[35] As they solidified control over this broad area, the Huks increasingly integrated military and political/cultural activities to cultivate links with the towns and villages. If Taruc's movement was to succeed in the eventual overthrow of the government, he had to have a firm and resolute popular base from which to act.

President Roxas died unexpectedly of a heart-attack while visiting Clark Field in April 1948. Upon hearing the news, Taruc made clear his feelings about both Roxas and the United States when he eulogized the former president as "(dying) symbolically in the arms of his masters. . . . His faithful adherence to American imperialist interests and the excessive corruption in his government had exposed him to the people."[36] His successor, Elpido Quirino, was more moderate on the issue of the Huks, and after declaring a temporary truce, opened negotiations with

Taruc and Alejandrino for the surrender of Huk weapons. After four months of negotiations, during which time both sides violated the truce numerous times, the talks broke off. Taruc returned to the mountains on 29 August 1948 and rejoined his forces. Although Taruc blamed the failed talks on Quirino's bad faith, there was really no valid reason for the Huks to surrender—they were beating government troops in the field and expanding their support base almost at will. Taruc used the four months to reorganize and strengthen his position in Huklandia, establish new arms caches, and use public gatherings to spread propaganda and incite the crowds against the Quirino government.[37]

1948 proved a difficult year for Huk political/military cooperation. The Politburo, now under the leadership of Jose Lava, wished to pursue the Russian model of class struggle by concentrating on urban centers and disrupting government activities to bring about the communist overthrow. The Huks however, under Taruc, were more Maoist in outlook and, based on its peasant base, wanted to expand its rural base and continue the fight in the countryside. The argument over where to concentrate Huk efforts caused a rift within the organization. Although the rift did not prove fatal to either camp, it reduced the effectiveness of both the CPP Marxist-Leninists and the Huk Maoists. Furthermore, when the tide of battle turned to favor the government after 1950, old scars caused by this dissention opened once again and helped to bring about the end of the entire movement.

In November, the military wing of the movement changed its name to the *Hukbong Magapalaya ng Bayan*, the People's Liberation Army, commonly referred to as the HMB. Drawing on the support garnished during the summer truce, the HMB started a new series of raids on government troops and targets. Throughout the following year, 1949, HMB raids continued against government installations in and around central Luzon. Most of the raids were typical guerrilla operations, hit-and-run, and were usually conducted at night to avoid direct confrontation with AFP forces. Despite their numerous ambuscades and raids on banks and supply depots, the HMB did not participate in the old guerrilla favorite—sabotage. This was not only because they lacked trained demolition men or equipment, but also because the Huks relied heavily on government transportation and communication facilities for their own purposes.[38]

The Huk campaign that began in November 1948 reached its peak in April 1949, with the ambush of Señora Aurora Quezon, widow of the former Philippine president. Commander Alexander Viernes, alias Stalin, took two hundred men and laid an ambush along a small country road in the Sierra Madres mountains and waited for a motorcade carrying Sra. Quezon, her daughter, and several government officials. When the ambush ended, Señora Quezon, her daughter, the mayor of Quezon City, and numerous government troops lay dead alongside the road. Although Viernes claimed a great victory, people throughout the islands, including many in central Luzon, were outraged. Viernes misjudged his target's popularity. President Quezon left a strong nationalistic sentiment after his death in exile during the war, and his widow represented the spirit of Philippine nationalism and resistance. Feeling the swell of popular indignation about the death of a national hero's wife and family, Taruc denied responsibility and said that the ambush was conducted without HMB approval. Despite his attempts to disclaim the actions of an overzealous Commander Viernes, Taruc lost a great deal of popular support and confidence over the incident, confidence he never fully regained and support that he would need later, but would not find forthcoming.[39]

Huk political organizers took full advantage of conditions that accompanied the 1949 general election. In a race that pitted Jose Laurel, the Nacionalista Party candidate and former president under the Japanese occupation, against Quirino, the incumbent Liberal Party candidate, the Huks seemed to enjoy the violence and mudslinging that had become part of Philippine politics. Each new charge raised by one candidate against the other provided new ammunition for the Huk cause. The Politburo finally decided to support Quirino, the more liberal of the two candidates, and ordered the organization to work for his election. Huk goon-squads joined those from the Liberal Party and battled similar "political action groups" from the opposition for control of the election.[40]

On election day, thugs from both sides intimidated voters at the polls, ballot boxes were stuffed or disappeared mysteriously, and in more than one province the number of ballots cast far outnumbered the entire population.[41] Quirino won a slim victory, but at the cost of widespread popular despair about Philippine democracy. Many of the disillusioned turned to the communists as being the only hope for reducing corruption, violence, and the disregard for individual rights that had become ingrained in society.

Aided greatly by the horrible conditions that accompanied the 1949 election, Huk strength and influence grew by the end of the year, recovering somewhat from the Quezon ambush episode. HMB regular strength grew to between 12–14,000 and Taruc could rely on 100,000 active supporters in central Luzon. After the elections (fraught with fraud, terror, and rampant electioneering violations), Huk raids became more frequent and widespread. A Huk squadron occupied the town of San Pablo; Police Constabulary posts at San Mateo and San Rafael were attacked and the towns looted; and the mayor of Montablan was kidnapped and held for ransom.[42] After most of these attacks, Huks left propaganda pamphlets with the people seeking their aid and support, and playing on their growing sense of disaffection for the government that resulted from election fraud. As the guerrillas strengthened their control in Tarlac, Bulacaan, Nueva Ecija, and Pampanga provinces, most government officials left their offices every day before nightfall, returning to the relative safety of homes they maintained in Manila.[43]

Supporting communist claims, the election was a signal from the administration for corruption to run amuck. All forms of government permits and contracts were bought and sold openly, while favoritism and nepotism spread rapidly throughout the government.[44] Bolstered by new supporters that governmental policies provided, and against a backdrop of near governmental collapse into fraud and corruption, the Huk Politburo declared the existence of the "Revolutionary Situation" in January 1950, and called for the beginning of the armed overthrow of the government.[45] Jose Lava, the political leader of the CPP, advanced the communist timetable for the overthrow of the Philippine government by approximately two years and was met with immediate and harsh criticism from Taruc. Although Lava saw the situation favoring

increased communist initiatives for military actions, political expansion, and mobilization of the masses, Taruc did not. Rather, Taruc felt it premature to attempt the overthrow and desired to maintain the original agenda and limit activities to guerrilla operations and the expansion of their popular base.

The two leaders could not reconcile their differences and, in late January, Taruc broke ranks with the CPP dominated political wing of the movement. Undoubtedly, part of this rift was a result of long-standing political differences between the CPP from the HMB. As was the case surrounding an earlier rift between the two in 1948, the CPP tended to follow Marxist-Leninist strategy while Taruc and his HMB were more inclined to adhere to Maoist theory based on peasant revolt. Following the split, Taruc and the HMB continued to carry-on the guerrilla campaign against the Quirino government with almost daily raids across central Luzon. Attacks spread to both the north and south of the central plain and outlying districts of Manila were no longer spared from guerrilla intrusions. Even small Philippine Army outposts, usually avoided in the early years of the insurrection, now joined PC barracks on the Huk target list.

As the attacks increased to some ten times their pre-1950 frequency, President Quirino abandoned his conciliatory stance toward the rebels. In a last-ditch effort to stop the insurgency, he ordered the armed forces to assume the responsibility for combating the insurgents and to return to the terror tactics that the Roxas administration had once used so widely. Quirino's change of heart, taken out of pure frustration, did little to hinder Taruc's operations but did manage to remind the people why they had shifted their support to the Huks in 1946.[46] In response to renewed AFP/PC terror and intimidation tactics, the Huks also reverted to this most base form of warfare, leaving bodies in streets with tags on them that read: "He resisted the Huks." In one case they quartered a Catholic priest before a group of his parishioners who had assisted government forces.[47]

Attacks against three major cities by squadron sized or larger units took place in May, and were followed in August, by a series of large-scale attacks directed against Army barracks. On 26 August, two simultaneous attacks were launched against garrisons at Camp Macabulos (in Tarlac) and at Santa Cruz (in Laguna), involving no less than 500 Huk regulars. At Camp Macabulos, two squadrons killed twenty-three army officers and men and seventeen civilians before releasing seventeen Huk prisoners and burning and looting the camp's storehouse and hospital. Meanwhile at Santa Cruz, three hundred Huks sacked and looted the town, killed three policemen and fled to Pila in stolen vehicles before government reinforcements could be mustered.[48]

These attacks were examples of the first of three varieties of raids that Taruc planned to carry-out against the government— organized assaults. The second variety, terror raids, were conducted by smaller formations against undefended cities and barrios, with the intent of killing government officials and intimidating the populations. Finally, Taruc planned to conduct nuisance raids—small ambushes, roadblocks, or hijackings that would harass government forces and demonstrate Huk control over certain regions. These attacks were usually planned to coincide with national festivals or fiestas, when security would be lax or, during the rainy season when weather conditions would favor hit-and-run tactics by his HMB that now numbered 15,000 regulars (with 13,000 weapons), 100,000 active supporters, and a popular base estimated to number nearly a million peasants in central Luzon.[49]

While Taruc's HMB forces increased their military pressure on the government, Lava ordered party activists to increase the tempo of their activities to ease the path for the armed revolution—a revolution that the Politburo estimated would topple the Philippine government in 1951.[50] These grandiose plans; calling for a total Huk force of some thirty-six divisions that would have 56,000 cadre, 172,000 party members, and a mass base of 2.5 million supporters; fell apart quickly when the Politburo was unexpectedly captured by government troops in October 1950.[51]

ARMED FORCES OF THE PHILIPPINES OPERATIONS

In 1946, the Armed Forces of the Philippines consisted of only 25,000 poorly trained, armed, and led troops scattered throughout the islands.

The AFP was the remains of the war-time Philippine military and police forces, reduced rapidly after the war from their former strength of some 132,000.[52] The Philippine Military Police Corps was the result of General MacArthur's authorization to form thirteen military police companies, armed as police, to maintain internal peace and order.[53] In addition to the Army and MPC forces, the government had a small Navy (some 3,000 sailors), and an equally small and outdated Air Force (only 3,800 men). Other than participating in a few resupply missions, the Air Force did not play an important role during the initial phase of the insurrection. After 1950, the Air Force role increased in size and function as it assumed a larger part of the overall anti-Huk campaign.

In Manila, the government treated the Huk problem as simply a series of criminal acts, not an organized and well established insurrection. President Roxas vowed to attack the guerrillas with a "mailed fist" but, except for independent forays by ambitious local authorities and a few military police units, the mailed fist was stuffed with cotton. When the government mounted operations against the Huks, it seldom succeeded in anything but alienating the local villagers who felt the brunt of the troops' frustrations.[54] Roxas seemed more amenable to seeking the spoils of office for himself and his followers than to fighting Huks on their homeground.

In June 1946, Roxas admitted the futility of his plan to "exterminate" the guerrillas and attempted to negotiate an agreement with Taruc. Promises of agrarian reforms in exchange for the surrender of weapons were broken and negotiations ceased.

The government returned to its policy of haphazard operations in central Luzon, but with no better results than it had had before the truce. Government forces stayed close to their barracks and bands of "Civil Guards" (private armies hired by landlords), tried to protect plantations and went on occasional, and always unproductive, "Huk hunts."

After the November elections, both sides reduced military activities to consolidate and reorganize. The Army was exhausted from futile dashes into the swamps and mountains and needed the time to train with weapons they were receiving from U.S. stocks of surplus World War II arms. By January 1947, Roxas, always keen to improve his political standing, took advantage of the relative calm and declared the situation solved. His declaration was soon met by a resurgence of activity centered in Huklandia.[55]

Embarrassed over his premature declaration, Roxas ordered a major offensive in March, 1947. In the largest and most organized government effort since the end of the war, three battalions of regular forces and military police units advanced into the area around Mount Arayat. Accompanied on the expedition by numerous newspaper reporters, food vendors, and sightseers, the two thousand government troops waded ever so slowly into the Huk stronghold. Although they managed to capture about a hundred insurgents, the operation did not damage Taruc militarily—it merely made him more cautious and showed him that he needed a better intelligence organization.[56] Following this offensive, Roxas dismantled the Military Police Command and formed the Police Constabulary (PC) in its stead, with the mission to provide internal security for the country and to perform other police-style functions. The Constabulary was organized into ninety-eight man companies with from one to fifteen companies assigned to a Provincial Provost Marshall depending on the size and location of the province. In turn, the Provost Marshall worked directly for the Provincial Governor.[57]

In March 1948, after the collapse of another brief truce, Roxas declared the Hukbalahap illegal and announced that he was putting his "mailed fist" policy back into effect. Company after company of constabulary troops charged into Huklandia burning entire villages, slaughtering farm animals, and killing or imprisoning many innocent peasants in their search for the elusive insurgents.[58] They located few Huks, killed or captured even fewer, and alienated almost the entire population of the region from the central government.

Shortly after Roxas' death in April 1948, President Quirino offered the Huks another chance to negotiate a settlement. As was the established pattern for these truces, the negotiations proved fruitless but the Huks put the months of government inactivity to good use by increasing their internal training and organization. When this truce finally

broke-down, Quirino was forced to acknowledge that the insurgency was indeed a major problem, one too large for the constabulary to handle alone. To alleviate this shortcoming, he assigned one regular army battalion, the 5th Battalion Combat Team (BCT) to the PC.[59] Two years later, after the 5th BCT was badly beaten in an engagement with the guerrillas, Quirino reorganized the constabulary under the Secretary of National Defense, removing it from the jurisdiction of the Secretary of the Interior where it had languished since 1945.

"FORCE X"

Shortly after the Secretary of National Defense reorganized the constabulary, the government authorized the one truly successful anti-insurgent operation during the first phase of the insurrection—"Force X." This special force was envisaged to operate deep within enemy territory under the guise of being a Huk unit itself. As such, the force would be valuable in obtaining intelligence and carrying out small unit operations such as kidnappings of Huk leaders and ambuscades. "Force X" was created to take advantage of a period when Huks operated freely in central Luzon but when their command organization was loose and inexperienced.[60]

Philippine Army Colonel Napoleon Valeriano, commander of the Nenita Unit, a special constabulary force that operated in the area of Mount Arayat from 1946 until 1949, selected the 16th Police Constabulary company, under the command of Lieutenant Marana to become "Force X." Secretly screening his unit for the most devoted and aggressive men, Marana selected three officers and forty-four enlisted men who departed their barracks under the cover of darkness and moved to a secret training camp in the nearby jungle. The camp's location and purpose were known only to the president, the Army Chief of Staff, Col. Valeriano, and three of the president's closest staff officers. At the camp, the unit was stripped of issued clothing and equipment, and given captured weapons and old civilian clothes. Using three captured guerrillas as instructors, "Force X" received training in Huk customs, practices, and tactics to help them pass as the enemy. Each man assumed an alias as well as a nickname, a technique favored by the Huks, and began to live life as a guerrilla.[61]

After four weeks of intensive training and a careful reconnaissance into the area where "Force X" would initially venture, the unit was almost ready to go. To complete the scenario, Colonel Valeriano recruited two walking-wounded from an Army hospital in Manila and secretly transported them to the training camp. At 1700 hrs, 14 April 1948, "Force X" fought a sham battle with two police companies and withdrew with their "wounded" into Huk country. Four hours later they were met by Huk troops, interrogated as to who they were and where they had come from, and were taken into Candaba Swamp where they met Squadrons 5 and 17. Marana convinced the commander of his authenticity (a story based on the death of a genuine Huk leader) and was promised that he and his forces would be taken to Taruc. The cover was working better than expected.[62]

"Force X" spent two days at the base-camp learning a great deal about local officials, mayors, and police chiefs who were Huk sympathizers and about informants within the constabulary. As they awaited their appointment with Taruc, they were joined by two other squadrons, one of which was an "enforcement squadron" whose members specialized in assassination and kidnapping. On the sixth day in camp, Marana became suspicious of Huk attitudes and ordered his men to prepare to attack the assemblage. Quietly removing heavy weapons (including four 60mm mortars, two light machine-guns, 200 grenades, and a radio) from hidden compartments in their packs, "Force X" attacked the unsuspecting squadrons. In a thirty-minute firefight, "Force X" killed eighty-two Huks, one local mayor, and captured three squadron commanders.[63]

After radioing for reinforcements to secure the area, "Force X" took off on a two week long search and destroy mission, accompanied this time by two infantry companies. During seven engagements, government troops killed another twenty-one guerrillas, wounded and captured seven, and identified seventeen Huks in local villages. "Force X's" success did not stop when it withdrew at the end of the operation. Three weeks after the incident at the Huk base-camp, two squadrons stumbled onto each other and,

each assuming that the other unit was "Force X," opened fire. The panic and mistrust that "Force X" put into Huk ranks cost the insurgents eleven more dead from this chance encounter.[64]

AFP TACTICAL OPERATIONS

Unfortunately, "Force X" was practically the only bright spot for the government during 1946–1950 and it was fielded too infrequently. Most other operations remained bound to conventional tactics involving large units. Task forces continued to be ordered out only following some Huk victory or atrocity that made political waves in Manila. Even when an operation reached its announced objective, follow-up operations were rare and troops usually returned immediately to garrison. These conventional sweeps proved ineffective and left many other areas totally bare of government troops. As a final detriment, most of the large operations harmed civilians more than the guerrillas. This did very little to develop feelings of confidence or allegiance between the people and their central government.[65]

Poor tactical leadership, slow responsiveness, slipshod security, and inadequate logistic support characterized the majority of military operations during this period. Troops were forced to live off the land, or rather, to live off the villagers. Enlisted men lacked discipline while their officers, often engaged in large-scale corruption themselves, did little to correct the situation. Although these officers were often implicated in Manila-based scandals, Army leadership did nothing.[66]

Throughout 1948, the Philippine military remained ineffectual in Luzon's central plain. What little progress took place was instigated by President Quirino on a political level through negotiations with Taruc. For a brief time, Quirino returned Taruc's congressional seat and back-pay, but after months of debating and public denunciations from both sides, Taruc rejoined his guerrillas in the mountains in August to resume the fight.[67] His return to the countryside produced increased government actions that hurt relations between the people and the largely out-of-touch and uncaring central government.

Government forces changed little during 1949 with the exception that the Police Constabulary grew modestly in size. However, whatever increased effectiveness that could have been achieved from this expansion was lost when the police companies were broken into platoon sized units and scattered across the nation—in essence, losing their numerical and equipment advantage to the Huks, still concentrated in central Luzon. Too often, these new constabulary units were used solely to administer local law, serve warrants, and try to keep the peace in "their" village. This led to a tacit *modus vivendi* between the police and guerrillas in an area.[68] Dedicated anti-Huk operations by either the Philippine Army or the Police Constabulary remained few in number and insignificant in effect with the exception of the government operation mounted after Huks murdered Sra. Quezon on 28 April.

Ordered by President Quirino not to return to garrison until all the Huks who ambushed Señora Quezon were themselves either dead or captured, 4,000 troops (two constabulary battalions and one army battalion) went into the Sierra Madres mountains. Divided into three task forces, one to block and two to maneuver, the force scoured the mountain-sides. After two weeks of relentless patrolling, a Huk camp was discovered and while taking it, government troops captured a Huk liaison officer who told them the location of Commander Viernes' base-camp near Mount Guiniat.[69] Five companies converged on the mountain camp at dawn, 1 June 1949, but killed only eleven guerrillas before discovering the camp was only an outpost, not Viernes' base. The following day, government forces located the base-camp and attacked immediately. The troops captured the camp, that turned out to be "Stalin University," and in the ensuing week long search and destroy mission killed thirty-seven additional Huks. Commander Viernes, however, managed to elude the net once again. After two more months of searching the mountains, the Philippine Army cornered Viernes near Kangkong and killed him on 11 September. His death, along with the deaths of many of his captains and several other Huk commanders, ended the operation that had spanned nearly four months. All toll, 146 insurgents were killed, 40 captured, and an entire Huk regional command was destroyed during the operation.[70]

However, after the conclusion of the Sierra Madres offensive, conditions in the Philippine military returned to their old form of normalcy—ineffectiveness, corruption, and no efforts whatsoever to help the local villagers. Army checkpoints became "collection points" where troops extorted money from local citizens. The Philippine Chief of Staff discovered this situation when he (wearing civilian clothing) was stopped by a group of soldiers who demanded money from him. On Good Friday, 1950, army troops massacred 100 men, women, and children in Bacalor, Pampanga, and burned 130 homes in retaliation for the killing of one of their officers.[71] In Laguna, fifty farmers attending a community dance were placed before a wall and executed as "suspected Huk."[72] The Philippine Air Force also contributed to the government's loss of popular support. It acquired several P-51 Mustangs from the United States in 1947, and used them to strafe and bomb suspect locations. Unfortunately, these aerial raids caused more damage to civilians than to the Huks, and in mid-1950, the government placed tighter controls over the use of the fighter-bombers. In general then, government forces were treating the people worse than were the guerrillas, who while occasionally preying on a village, did try to maintain close ties with the majority of the population in central Luzon.[73]

By mid-1950 it was obvious that the Philippine armed forces simply were not holding their own against the Huks. They lacked both direction and an overall campaign strategy. Orders went directly from AFP GHQ in Manila to army units in the field. The intelligence effort was sadly lacking and no plans were in the offing to improve it. What plans were being made involved defensive operations around towns or the estates of large landowners or businessmen. The AFP was acting more as an army of occupation than as a combat force attempting to quell a rebellion. Patrols stayed close to base and invariably returned to garrison before dark. Local commanders were satisfied to continue this practice as long as their individual areas of responsibility remained out of the headlines in Manila.[74]

The Army suffered from neglected training in maneuver, communications, security, intelligence, and the use of available firepower.[75] Though they tended to remain in a single area for years, local forces never gained a working knowledge of the terrain, preferring instead to stick to known paths near the base. The soldiers were often antagonistic to the local population, whom they saw as Huk sympathizers and treated accordingly. And, compounding all of these deficiencies, the soldier was poorly educated as to the purpose of the campaign. He simply didn't understand his role and therefore lacked motivation. Those above him seemed as equally unconcerned, more interested in graft, corruption, and a comfortable life than with fighting.[76]

The Philippine armed forces, numbering a total of 30,952 men in July 1950, suffered from this variety of ailments to such a degree that it almost proved fatal. The appointment of Ramon Magsaysay as Secretary of National Defense in mid-1950 helped reverse this trend.[77] Faced with numerous, seemingly insurmountable problems within the armed forces, he had first to conquer these problems before he could begin his campaign against the insurgents in central Luzon.

RAMON MAGSAYSAY, EDWARD LANSDALE, AND THE JUSMAG

RAMON MAGSAYSAY

Born the son of a village school teacher in the small village of Iba, the capital of Zambales Province and in the very shadow of Mount Pinatubo, Ramon Magsaysay spent his formative years surrounded by the people of central Luzon. When Ramon was six years old, he learned about honesty and integrity from his father, who lost his teaching job in the public school when he refused to pass the school superintendent's son in his carpentry class. Outcast by the community, the Magsaysay family moved to Castillejas, where his father set up a small carpentry and blacksmith shop to support the family.[1] His father's example took root in Ramon and remained a cornerstone of his personality throughout his life.

Ramon entered Zambales Academy, an equivalent to high school, at the age of thirteen and graduated as salutatorian. In 1927, he enrolled in the Academy of Liberal Arts at the University of the Philippines but was forced to leave because of poor health. After recovering his health, Magsaysay transferred to Jose Rizal College, from which he was graduated in 1932 with a degree in commerce. The only job he could find was as a mechanic at the Try Transportation Bus Company in Manila. Within a few years, he rose to become the company's general manager.[2] At the outbreak of World War II, he quit his position in Manila and joined the Philippine 31st Infantry Division.

After the fall of Bataan, Magsaysay joined a USAFFE guerrilla unit. Commissioned at the grade of captain, he served as G-1, supply officer, was promoted to major, and eventually became the commander of the Zambales Military District, responsible for the actions of nearly 10,000 USAFFE fighters in the area near Mount Pinatubo. His prowess as a military commander became well known and resulted in the Japanese placing a 100,000 peso bounty on his life.[3] In February 1945, General MacArthur appointed Major Magsaysay the military governor of Zambales due to his honesty, integrity, and ability. During his tenure as military governor he became an outspoken champion for veteran rights and impressed the local population with his dedication to improving their life. A year later, President Roxas asked him to join the Liberal Party and run for a congressional seat in the November election. Magsaysay refused initially, stunning the president, but relented when he was presented a petition signed by 11,000 of his men asking him to run for Congress. Despite his personal differences with Roxas, whose policies Magsaysay saw as favoring only the rich, his men convinced him that he could best help the country by joining the government. He resigned his commission and won a seat in the Philippine House of Representatives with the largest popular margin in Zambales history.[4]

Once in Congress, he continued to fight for veteran rights and was soon appointed to the House Committee on National Defense, the committee with oversight responsibility for the armed forces. He became the committee's chairman after his re-election in 1949 and was instrumental in transferring the Police Constabulary from the Interior Department to the Department of National Defense. Magsaysay was also responsible for the reorganization of the Armed Forces of the Philippines into battalion combat teams, and its assumption of responsibility from the Police Constabulary for the anti-Huk campaign in Luzon.

While Chairman of the Armed Forces Committee, he traveled to Washington in April 1950 on a quest to obtain financial aid for the faltering government in Manila. The importance of this visit was twofold. First, after conferring with General George C. Marshall (who was still in retirement before becoming Secretary of Defense in the fall), and speaking with President Truman and the National Security Council, he received $10 million in emergency aid to pay the military and offer rewards for information about the insurgents and was promised additional assistance under the Military Assistance Agreement of March 1947. Second, and as important for the anti-Huk campaign, he met and befriended newly promoted Lieutenant Colonel Edward G. Lansdale, an Air Force intelligence officer familiar with the Philippines and her people, and who would very shortly become Magsaysay's personal JUSMAG advisor.[5]

On his return to Manila, Magsaysay told President Quirino that Philippine prestige in the United States was at a low ebb as a result of poor social conditions and Huk success in the Luzon countryside. He suggested that the president take immediate steps to purge the government of corrupt officials and institute needed agrarian reforms. The Philippine president suggested that Magsaysay confine his attentions to the military situation and promptly ignored Magsaysay's comments. After all, Magsaysay had succeeded in bringing home $10 million and the future seemed to promise even more American money and equipment.

Magsaysay and the Philippine Armed Forces

In September 1950, Magsaysay was approached by President Quirino and asked if he would become the Secretary of National Defense. Earlier that summer, the former secretary, Roberto Kangleon, resigned in a dispute with Quirino over reorganization. The President received pressure from many within his administration, as well as from Major General Leland Hobbs, Chief of the Joint U.S. Military Advisory Group to the Philippines (JUSMAG), to ask Magsaysay to take the position. Magsaysay

agreed to become the new secretary, but only if he was given a "free hand." Reluctantly, Quirino agreed to his terms.[6] Within a few days of his appointment, Magsaysay was approached by a group of officers who asked him if he would join them to overthrow President Quirino. Although he found it difficult to refuse them; not out of a desire for a military coup but, rather because he opposed so much the Quirino administration was doing, or failing to do; he made them a promise, "Give me ninety days. If I haven't done anything by then, go ahead. I promise you."[7]

There is no doubt that he accepted the office with clear-cut plans in mind. He wanted to shake the Philippine military from top to bottom, cleansing its ranks of corrupt, incompetent officers, and indeed, he wanted to change its very role.

Heretofore, the AFP conducted itself much like an army of occupation, seldom venturing afield in search of Huks, unless Manila headlines made it absolutely necessary, and most of the time preying heavily on the local populace. Magsaysay saw the military in a different light. He wanted it to become a major part of a large, coordinated development plan for the country, a plan that would incorporate the military as a participant in social reforms and public service.[8] Not only did he demand that his forces abandon corrupt practices, he set the example himself. He refused special treatment, lived from his government salary (about $500 per month) and a small stipend from being the Chairman of the Board of Philippine Airlines, and whenever possible presented a modest appearance in public.[9] Not surprisingly, many within the Philippine military felt nervous about his intentions but felt just as confident that one man could not bring about such dramatic changes. These doubters soon were not only proved incorrect, but became jobless as well.

On his first day as secretary, Magsaysay began to clean his new house. He relieved several high ranking officers, including the Chief of Staff and the Chief of the Constabulary, and ordered other "armchair strategists" to the field. Those reluctant to leave the safety of Manila, or implicated in graft and corruption, were likewise removed. He then began a personal routine that included extensive travelling, talking with troops and civilians alike, and taking quick and decisive actions when he found a situation that warranted it.[10] During these unannounced field trips Magsaysay became convinced that his plans for the AFP were correct. He found it suffering from low morale, ineffectiveness, poor leadership, and riddled with corruption. Under his enlightened leadership, these conditions changed rapidly.

The secretary personally selected many new, and younger, battalion commanders and ordered most of the units to new areas of operation. By doing this, Magsaysay hoped to destroy cliques within the service and reduce tensions that had built up between local people and Army units over a period of years when units remained assigned to a single area.[11] When Magsaysay discovered an officer under Huk influence, he got rid of him, along with those he considered reluctant to carry the fight to the guerrillas. Favoritism, long an established criteria for promotion, was halted and those who had advanced using it were advanced no further.[12]

On his almost daily excursions to the field, Magsaysay stopped at all AFP sites, regardless of size or location, and made thorough inspections of the men, their equipment, and their facilities. Officers derelict in their duties or involved in graft were relieved on the spot. During one such night visit he found a guard asleep at his post. The secretary took the man's rifle, replaced the soldier at his post, and ordered the soldier to fetch his commander. The soldier was disciplined and his commander was relieved that night.[13] These surprise inspections were so numerous and effective that leaders throughout the military began to improve the condition of their units. In the words of the commander of the 7th BCT, AFP Colonel Napoleon Valeriano, "No commander, even in the most isolated outpost could go to bed at night sure that he would not be awakened at dawn by an irate Secretary of National Defense."[14]

At the same time, Magsaysay was equally fast to reward as to punish. One captain was offered 150,000 pesos to "forget" about a Huk ammunition cache his men discovered. The officer accepted the money, but instead of keeping it, he went immediately to the secretary, who at that time was attending a state dinner to honor President Quirino. Between courses, Magsaysay awarded the captain a cash reward for his honesty and promoted him to major.[15]

In his first twenty days as secretary, he took two other steps that directly affected the soldier in the field. First, using money he acquired from U.S. military assistance funds, he increased pay from only 30 centavos to a full peso per day. Although the pay-scale seems meager, it allowed the soldier to purchase his daily ration from the local people rather than steal or demand it as had often been the case prior. Second, Magsaysay equipped each patrol leader with a camera to document enemy casualties. As has so often been the case in guerrilla wars, accurate numbers of enemy casualties (body counts) proved difficult to verify. Without photos, government claims were not verified unless, as was sometimes the case when the cameras broke, the patrol leader brought other positive proof back with him. This proof sometimes included Huk heads or ears strung on rattan cords.[16]

Magsaysay stopped and spoke to the local people during each of his inspection tours. He told the people that the police and military forces were there to protect them and, that if they had complaints about his forces, they could tell him and he would take appropriate action. To encourage this communication, Magsaysay authorized free telegrams from villagers and insured that each was answered quickly by himself or his key staff.[17] With programs such as these it did not take long for word to spread about the new secretary and what he expected from his armed forces. Within just a few months, the entire outlook of the AFP was changing for the better.

Soon after becoming Secretary of National Defense, Magsaysay decided that government tactics needed drastic adjustment. Although he had originally favored large-scale conventional sweep operations, he changed his mind as he examined the results from these operations on both the guerrillas and the local populace who seemed to suffer the brunt of such large actions. He was willing to try something new, something not in "the book." When he approached the president with his proposal to change their tactics, Quirino responded: "I have never heard of such tactics. General Castaneda (the Chief of Staff that Magsaysay fired) has never suggested anything like this to me." "Of course not," answered

Magsaysay, "Costanedo does not know anything about guerrilla warfare. He does not understand the kind of strategy that has to be practiced against the Huks if we are to defeat them."[18]

He decided to base government military tactics on small-unit operations, relying on large convention sweeps only when specific circumstances dictated its use. By doing this he hoped to maintain greater pressure on the Huks, reduce intelligence leaks associated with large operations, and remove the enemy's sense of security in Huklandia. In a speech delivered before the Philippine General Staff, Magsaysay summarized his new tactics: "Gentlemen, I know you all have graduated from military establishments here and in the United States. Now I am telling you to forget everything you were taught at Ft. Leavenworth, Ft. Benning, and the Academy. The Huks are fighting an unorthodox war. We are going to combat them in unorthodox ways. Whatever it was that hurt me most as a guerrilla is what we are going to do now to the Huk."[19]

To support his new strategy, Magsaysay began to increase the size of the Army to twenty-six battalions that would operate in four tactical

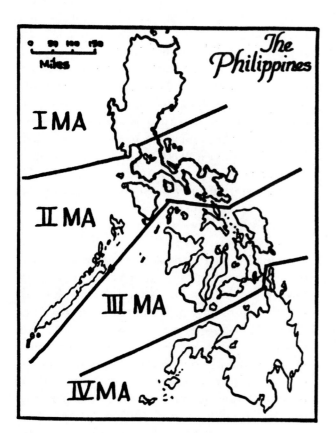

commands. With help from the JUSMAG, and monies from the Military Defense Assistance Program (MDAP), this ambitious plan was accomplished—28,000 troops were added to the AFP by 1955 and the number of constabulary companies increased to ninety-one. Of the twenty-six BCTs, twenty-three were concentrated on Luzon with only two deployed to the southern islands. The final battalion remained in Manila in a training/reserve status. Emphasis was placed on patrolling (especially at night), squad/platoon size operations, and hit-and-run tactics similar to those used by Luis Taruc.[20]

Above all other considerations, Magsaysay knew that government terror tactics had to be stopped. From his days as a guerrilla leader, he understood that the campaign depended on gaining the people's support and allegiance. In the past, government attempts to provide relief for the people were destroyed by just a few acts of barbarism against the villagers. He told the military that their function was to protect the people from the Huks and to assist them in whatever ways they could. Each soldier was given two duties: to act as an ambassador of good will toward the people and to kill Huks. Army legal officers were instructed to serve as civilian counsel, free of charge, in court cases involving peasants and landlords, while Magsaysay personally investigated cases of military crimes, harshly punishing those involved. Just three months into his term as secretary, children ran to greet Army trucks when they visited villages rather than running to hide in the jungle as they had done before.[21]

On 23 December 1950, Magsaysay ordered the Police Constabulary placed under Army control for the duration of the Huk campaign. Formed in 1901 as a national police force, the Constabulary was the oldest independent paramilitary organization in the country. By subordinating them to the military, a move police accepted only with great anxiety, Magsaysay demonstrated how far he was willing to go to improve the government's posture to fight the insurgency. In another attempt to improve the quality of the constabulary forces, regular army officers were placed in command of PC units and the PC was given additional training and newer weapons and equipment.[22]

The EDCOR Project

As part of his overall strategy to defeat the Huks, Magsaysay incorporated civil resettlement projects with his military campaign. His rural background told him that as long as the peasant felt no obligation to the central government, the guerrillas could continue to prosper in their midst. One of his first efforts to accomplish this began in December 1950 with the formation of the Economic Development Corps (EDCOR) that was implemented in conjunction with plans to provide captured or surrendered guerrillas better treatment. He envisioned the Corps operating under direct supervision of the Philippine Chief of Staff, who was strong enough to ensure military cooperation with this civil action. Magsaysay hoped that EDCOR would provide enough incentives for Huks to rejoin mainstream society. If successful, it might entice active Huks to give up their arms once they saw that the government was making progress toward land-reform and private land-ownership.

The program had four primary aims, all centered on resettling former insurgents on government land away from Luzon—government land to which settlers would be given title. Captured or surrendered Huks who were not wanted for criminal activities other than being a guerrilla, could participate in the program. Once screened by Army intelligence, they received a short re-education program and indoctrinated about the benefits of belonging to peaceful society. The Philippine Army transported those selected for the program, with their families, to one of the project sites and there gave them additional education on how to care for the land and advice on what to grow. To provide stability, and in some cases to keep control, the government allowed a small number of retired soldiers to participate in the EDCOR program as well.[23]

In February 1951, a reluctant President Quirino allowed army engineers to depart Luzon for the first EDCOR site on the southern island of Mindinao. Using equipment and supplies obtained through the JUSMAG, they cleared land, erected administration buildings, constructed roads, and prepared sites for settler's homes. Three months later, Magsaysay accompanied the first group of settlers to the project at Kapatangan. Using building materials supplied by the government and with the assistance of AFP troops, the new settlers began to raise their homes and clear their farmland. Each family was given 6-10 hectares (15–25 acres) of farmland, a home garden plot, free transportation, schools, medical care, electricity and clean water. Other basic necessities, such as farm animals, seed, and an initial supply of food, was sold to them on credit by the EDCOR administrators—always of course, under Magsaysay's watchful eyes. In exchange, the farmers promised, in writing, to farm the land, repay the government for start-up costs, and accept advice from the Philippine Department of Agriculture. Finally, the settlers had to guarantee that they would not sell or sub-divide his land—tenancy was strictly forbidden.[24]

This was truly a contractual agreement between the government and former Huks. Magsaysay hoped that since the program required all parties to work toward a common goal, the participants would develop pride in their accomplishments, unlike other give-away programs that did not require the recipient to devote his own time and labors. The Army helped clear the land, worked daily with the people, and provided the community with utilities. This became very important to the settlers, most of whom did not have the luxury of electricity before.[25] The farmers were given title to the land on condition they develop and live on it.

EDCOR's success came early and surpassed everyone's expectations. Applicants soon outnumbered available plots and many Luzon peasants paid their own way to Mindinao in attempts to get some land adjacent to EDCOR sites. By November 1951 it was obvious that the program needed to be expanded and a second EDCOR site was started on Mindinao. The second site proved as successful as the first and was itself followed by two more sites on Luzon, outside of contested areas, in 1954.[26]

EDCOR also provided Magsaysay with a great propaganda victory. It not only gave the farmer a chance to own land, it undercut the foundation upon which the Huk campaign was based. "Land for the Landless," once the Huk slogan, now belonged to the government. Although Huks tried several times to sabotage EDCOR projects and spread word that EDCOR projects were concentration camps, persistent rumors about the wonderful conditions at the projects made these Huk attempts counterproductive.[27] Glowing reports and stories about EDCOR spread beyond the Philippines to China and Malaya as well. British officials from Malaya came to see the "huge" generators they had heard were being used to power the settlements. What they found were small army generators providing electricity to the farmer's homes. The actual size of the generators was unimportant, that word of the good EDCOR conditions had spread throughout the Philippines and beyond was significant. Before the end of the insurrection, many guerrillas surrendered to government troops and the first thing that they asked was how they could get their own farm.[28]

By 1955, government officials estimated that 1,500 guerrillas had surrendered or simply quit the resistance to take advantage of EDCOR. Without this imaginative program, the Philippine government estimated it would have taken the efforts of 30,000 troops to eliminate that portion of the insurrection. Some five thousand-two hundred people (1,200 families) were resettled from central Luzon to EDCOR projects.[29] But the final results of EDCOR went beyond the number of people that were resettled. The program demonstrated the willingness and dedication of the Magsaysay administration to change the way government treated its peasant farmers. From the program's first success in Mindinao, the psychological effect on the people of Luzon was dramatic and served to undercut the support that Taruc and his guerrilla movement relied upon.

Magsaysay and the Filipino People

Few people have directly affected an entire population as Ramon Magsaysay. His honesty, unpretentious aire, and deep concern with the problems faced by his countrymen forged a bond with the common man that was unprecedented in Philippine history. He lived in an unprotected home (at least until he was convinced to move into Lansdale's guarded residence within the JUSMAG compound), wore simple clothes, frequently drove his own car, and spoke in a manner easily understood by all. To make sure that the people knew what he was striving for, he traveled daily across his nation, visiting military installations and civilian communities alike, asking questions and listening to what his people had to say. As one villager told a journalist about Magsaysay: "The government never comes here to see how we live. The only man who comes to these parts is Magsaysay," and adding a bit of prophecy, "Maybe he should be president. At least he knows how badly we need his help, and seems to be the only one interested in the welfare of the barrios."[30]

Magsaysay normally wore common civilian clothing on his travels—an "aloha" shirt and slacks. Unlike other government officials who traveled amidst great pomp, Magsaysay's ordinary appearance lent credence to his reform plans and helped him gain the people's trust. On one occasion, however, his appearance almost cost him a long and uncomfortable walk through the Philippine countryside. With his personal advisor, Lt. Col. Lansdale, he had flown by helicopter to what he thought was walking distance from a village. After walking for some time, the two realized that they had misjudged the distance and tried to catch a ride with passing motorists. Finally one driver stopped when he saw Lansdale, who was in uniform, but hesitated to give a ride to the other man, whom he did not recognize. Only after Lansdale convinced the Filipino that his companion was the secretary of national defense, did the wary driver permit Magsaysay to get into his car.[31]

Besides his concern for the people, Magsaysay's honesty became synonymous with his administration. When he found graft or corruption he was quick to act against those involved. "Everytime I sit here and look at my stamp drawer," recalled a local postmaster, "I start to think, well, I don't have much money and my family needs food, maybe I ought to swipe some. Then I start thinking that that damn Magsaysay might suddenly show up ... just as my hand is going into the petty cash drawer, and he'd throw me in jail."[32]

The new secretary of national defense's popularity and fame did not escape Taruc's notice. During his first year in office, Magsaysay was the target of several Huk assassination attempts. Fortunately, all of these attempts failed and in one case, the agent was "turned" after having a long discussion with Magsaysay.[33]

One of several young men sent to assassinate Magsaysay during his first year as secretary was Thomas Santiago, known as "Manila Boy." Santiago was one of Luis Taruc's personal bodyguards and totally dedicated to the Huk cause.

Leaving the mountains with grenades and pistols hidden in his clothing, he went to Manila where, while watching the secretary's office, he overheard a group of citizens talking about Magsaysay. To his great surprise, they were praising the secretary as a new national hero. When young Santiago challenged their contentions, he was taken aside by a former guerrilla leader and told that he should talk to Magsaysay to see if what he heard was indeed the truth. The following morning, Santiago did just that. After an hour of often heated debate, Santiago shook Magsaysay's hand, turned his weapons over to the secretary, and told him, "I came to kill you. Now please, let me work for you."[34] As was the case with several Huk personalities during Magsaysay's term, "Manila Boy" went to work for the secretary, touring the country and telling all who would listen to him of Magsaysay's dedication to the people and the nation.

This episode however, should not suggest that Magsaysay's personality and charisma overcame all adversity—it did not. Several other assassins arrived in Manila, but they too failed to kill Magsaysay. The secretary was by then living with Lansdale in a Manila residence quietly protected by a special team of Filipino bodyguards who specialized in stealth and night operations. Although never publicized, several "hit teams" were quietly dispatched by these extraordinary bodyguards. One might wonder why these attacks were kept secret—Lansdale recalls Magsaysay saying that it would be best to remain silent and let Taruc wonder what happened to his men, ie, were they killed or had they deserted.[35]

MAGSAYSAY'S RELATIONSHIP WITH EDWARD G. LANSDALE

A prominent factor in the successful anti-guerrilla campaign was the close, personal relationship that developed between Edward Lansdale and Ramon Magsaysay. This relationship provided an effective conduit through which American advice affected Philippine actions during this period. To overlook Lansdale's role would be to neglect a significant chapter of this story.

The relationship began in 1950 when they first met at a Washington reception for the visiting Secretary of National Defense. Magsaysay came to the United States to encourage U.S. support for his government's growing fight against the Huks. Lansdale, who served as an intelligence officer for the OSS and the Military Intelligence Service in the Philippines during the war and who had but recently been promoted to lieutenant colonel, was then teaching intelligence and counter-guerrilla operations at the Air Force Strategic Intelligence School at Lowry Air Force Base. Lansdale received a call from an old friend, Philippine Colonel Montemayor, telling him that he should meet the new Philippine secretary. "I'm with quite a man," Montemayor told Lansdale, "and you've got to get to know him."[36] At the Ft. Myer reception, Lansdale caught both Magsaysay's ear and imagination. Later that year, as the JUSMAG began to play a more prominent role in the anti-Huk effort, Magsaysay asked President Quirino to request Lansdale's assignment to the JUSMAG.

Shortly after his arrival in the Philippines with his assistant, U.S. Army Maj. Charles T.R. Bohannan, Lansdale was invited to dinner by Magsaysay at his home near Manila. Concerned with visible guerrilla activity in the neighborhood and the lack of security for the Secretary, Lansdale invited him to share his room in the house he lived in within the JUSMAG compound in Manila. Magsaysay accepted the offer, sent his wife and children back to his wife's family on Bataan, and moved in with the U.S. advisor. Thus began the intimate relationship that existed between the two military men until Magsaysay's untimely death in 1957.

Although assigned to the JUSMAG as a G-2 advisor, Lansdale was given exceptional freedom of action and quickly became Magsaysay's *de facto* personal advisor. Often the two talked long into the night about conditions that fostered the insurrection and about the real need for governmental and social reforms as a prelude to a permanent solution to the Huk problem. Early each morning the Secretary would rouse Lansdale from his bed and together they made daily inspection tours around the nation. To maintain this close personal contact, Lansdale obtained special permission from the Chief of JUSMAG, General Hobbs, to make these forays into contested areas to see firsthand the condition of the Philippine armed forces. Other than Lansdale and Bohannan, JUSMAG advisors were prohibited from taking the field with their counterparts. It was during these visits, and during frequent informal coffee-chats, that Lansdale was able to discuss the real causes for the insurrection with Magsaysay, his assistants, and other concerned government officials. Shortly thereafter, Magsaysay took steps to revitalize the military, improve pay and morale, eliminate corrupt officers, and foster his campaign to win the people back to the central government.

As part of the rejuvenation campaign, Lansdale, with Magsaysay's active support, helped establish intelligence schools and a Philippine Military Intelligence Corps. As graduates from these schools joined forces in the field, battalion combat team commanders became convinced of the importance of intelligence to their operations, the battle began to shift to the government. During the next few years, programs initiated by Magsaysay gradually took the revolution away from the Huks. The people saw clear evidence of military professionalism, competence, and honesty (quite a dramatic change) and through the military's behavior, began to realize that Magsaysay was working for their benefit. The soldiers became heroes to the people, "White Hats," and received more and more of their active support.

Late in 1953, Lansdale was ordered back to Washington to prepare for an assignment with the O'Daniel mission to Vietnam. After completing his first French lesson, Lansdale was called at home by President Magsaysay and asked to return to the Philippines. Lansdale told his old friend that he was unable to come back but, after the Philippine President made another call to President Eisenhower, Lansdale found himself in Manila early in 1954. This time, he was only able to remain until May, when he was ordered to continue on to Vietnam "to do there what you did in the Philippines."[37]

To what did Edward Lansdale credit his success? First and foremost, he dealt with Magsaysay and the Filipinos as friends and equals. Filipinos viewed friendship as a deeper and longer-lived relationship than Americans did. To them, friendship involved total acceptance into their most valued social institution— the family. Trusting the Filipinos, allowing them to form their own solutions to their problems with a minimum of interference, and always treating them as equals were Lansdale's keys to success. He advised them on counter-guerrilla tactics and helped them lessen their reliance on conventional operations, but he always made sure they were responsible for the decisions. He maintained a low-profile and allowed Filipinos to take credit for successful operations, concurrently building pride and confidence in the AFP and their fellow countrymen. As retired Maj. Gen. Lansdale so aptly put it, the Filipinos best knew the problems, best knew how to solve them, and did it—with U.S. aid and advice, but without U.S. domination of their effort.[38]

THE JOINT UNITED STATES MILITARY ASSISTANCE GROUP

The JUSMAG supported the Philippine governments during the first half of the 1950s through a multi-faceted approach that included advice to key military and government officials, both officially and otherwise, and through direct material and financial aid. Whether by purpose or default the combination of money, war surplus equipment, and good sound advice found fertile ground with Ramon Magsaysay. With the American assistance, he defeated the insurrection.

Evolution of the JUSMAG

JUSMAG-Philippines, originally called the Joint Advisory Group, was established by the JCS on 1 November 1947 to oversee a modest military assistance program under the Military Assistance Act of 1946.[39] Initially under the operational control of CINCFE, the JUSMAG worked in conjunction with U.S. economic programs and as a major participant in the total American effort that followed the war. Initially, the JUSMAG's small size, having less than twenty officers assigned until 1952, reflected American post-war philosophy of reducing U.S. military presence in the region to promote local development. The Huk insurrection prompted many changes in the JUSMAG and demonstrated shortcomings in post-war U.S.-Philippine policy. Of these failures, the greatest were misjudging the seriousness of the situation until 1950, and the importance of nationalism and land ownership to the average Filipino.[40]

The Department of Defense refined the JUSMAG's mission in late 1950 to reflect more closely U.S. support for the Philippine government in their growing battle against the Huk—a battle the Philippine government was losing. At the same time, Congress passed a special act permitting the sale at cost of surplus military equipment to the Philippines. In addition, Congress allocated an undetermined amount of grant aid for the government under the Military Defense Assistance Act. The JUSMAG, then under the command of General Hobbs, became the sole source of all military assistance to the Philippines.[41] Its responsibility grew rapidly as monies and materiel arrived to support the anti-Huk campaign. For example, the Army Materiel Program, the largest of the three service accounts, nearly doubled between fiscal years 1950 and 1951 from $12.6 million to $21.8 million. All of this was made easier after 25 June 1950 when North Korean troops crossed the international boundary into South Korea and the United States entered the Korean War.[42]

Shortly thereafter, the JUSMAG increased in size to seventeen officers and twenty-one enlisted men.[43] Its mission expanded to reflect a growing concern in Washington that the ineffectiveness of the Philippine armed forces was preventing victory over the Huks, who were growing in activity and popular support during 1949 and 1950. During the summer of 1950, while U.S. advisors helped Magsaysay reorganize the Army into battalion combat teams (BCT), officials of the Mutual Defense Assistance Program conducted a survey of conditions in the Philippines. They found the primary problem to be political-economic instability and concluded that progress would be impossible without broad-based American assistance.[44] They were proved correct. The Huks were suppressed only after

Luzon's peasant class was assisted by progressive social and economic changes that allowed them to shift their allegiance back to the central government and away from the guerrillas. Without this basic change, military operations alone could not have defeated the guerrillas, but it would require time to incorporate such a broad attack. Yet, the JUSMAG seemed to be ignoring non-military aspects of the insurrection before the MDAP report on the insurgency was published. Lansdale commented about the lack of attention even in the summer of 1950. Recalling his in-briefing at the JUSMAG, he mentioned that, ". . . curiously enough, Philippine and American officers barely mentioned the political and social factors in briefing me. They dwelt almost exclusively on the military situation. It was as though military affairs were the sole tangible factor they could grasp."[45]

In 1951, things began to change. Originally established by Public Law 454, the JUSMAG was reorganized when the Mutual Defense Assistance Act replaced PL 454 on 4 July 1951. The JUSMAG increased in size and became the executive agent for American military assistance to the Philippines under the general guidance of the ambassador, not the Commander-in-Chief Pacific as had previously been the case. The Chief of JUSMAG was designated by the Joint Chiefs of Staff and approved by the Secretary of Defense and the government of the Philippines.[46] Although removed from MacArthur's command, the JUSMAG continued to inform his headquarters of the situation by forwarding weekly and semi-annual reports through it on the way to the Director of the Office of Military Assistance and the JCS in Washington. In August 1951, Maj. Gen. Albert Pierson replaced General Hobbs as Chief Advisor/Chief of MAAG, but not before the JCS adopted Hobbs' proposed reorganization. His proposals to increase the size of the JUSMAG with officers to advise Philippine military service and branch chiefs were incorporated in 1952.

The JCS directed that the JUSMAG be composed of a chief, and three service related division appointed by the Services. Although

Organization of JUSMAG-Philippines

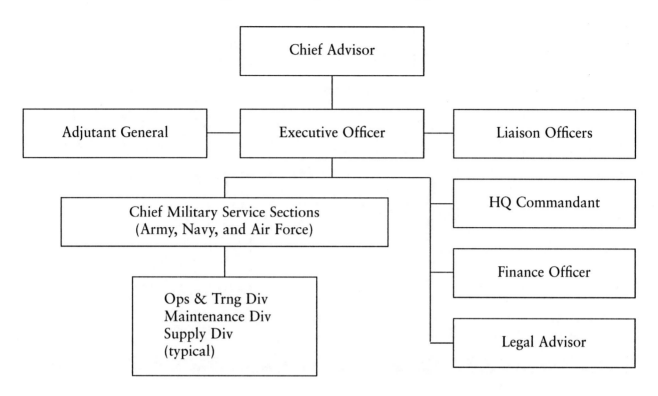

Source: JUSMAG. *Semi-Annual Report 1 Jun-30 Jul 52*, MMRD, RG 330, box 46, NARA, Washington, D.C.

CHART 4

documentation detailing the composition of the JUSMAG officially set its strength at "such numbers as required," an earlier draft showed the JUSMAG would consist of thirty-two officers and twenty-six enlisted men, nearly double the previous strength of seventeen and twenty-one.[47] During the remainder of the campaign, the JUSMAG retained this thirty-two officer/twenty-six enlisted structure, later adding nine civilian stenographers to assist in administrative duties. In May 1953, Maj. Gen. Robert M. Cannon succeeded General Pierson as Chief Advisor.

The reorganized JUSMAG was given four areas of major responsibility. Under the guidance of the American ambassador, it would provide advice and assistance to key members of the mil-

itary, administer the Mutual Defense Assistance Program that financed end items, help train the AFP, and promote standardization within it.

JUSMAG Support and Operations

JUSMAG requests for arms, ammunition, and vehicles rose in 1950 as Huk activity increased. Prior to this time, aid requested by JUSMAG was received, but the amounts were limited and consistently fell below the amount requested. For example, a fiscal year 1948 request for $9.4 million for food, fuel, and clothing for the Philippine military met the following response from Washington: ". . . it is felt very little justification exists at this time for favorable consideration. Also, it does not appear that denial of this request would

Organization of Army Section—JUSMAG

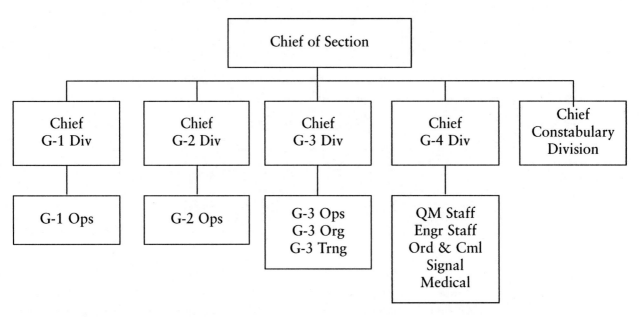

Source: JUSMAG. *Semi-Annual Report.*

CHART 5

seriously retard development of Philippine defense forces beyond the capability of the Philippine government to control."[48] Nearly a year later, in the fall of 1948 and despite a marked increase in Huk activity, U.S. policy remained largely unchanged. "Equipment in addition to that already furnished to the armed forces of the Philippines," wrote the War Department's Director of Plans and Operations to the Commander in Chief Far East, "can be provided only after more urgent requirements are met and after the necessary appropriations are obtained."[49] Finally, in 1950, requests for additional transfers of equipment and for AFP school quotas in the United States began to reap positive results.

With the exception of heavy engineer equipment that was diverted to Korea, the Department of Defense approved most of the new requests and shipped the equipment to Manila. For example, in the three months from April to July, the Philippine armed forces received fifteen million rounds of small arms and mortar ammunition, several armored cars, light trucks, and thirty-four F-51 aircraft from Pacific and CONUS war surplus

stocks.[50] At the same time, surplus cargo, training, and observation aircraft (C-47, T-6, and L-5) were delivered to the small Philippine Air Force. Other materials received by the JUSMAG and passed to the armed forces in 1950 included various types of small arms, machine guns, mortars, light artillery, wheeled cargo vehicles, and a few light and medium tanks.[51] Concurrently, JUSMAG advisors received permission from the JCS to participate in training the AFP in such vital functions as organization, tactics, logistics, and the use of the new weapons and equipment—a decision nearly as important as the arrival of the actual equipment.[52]

Beginning in 1950, the JUSMAG supported Philippine requests for additional monetary assistance. Magsaysay first sought these special funds in a letter to Secretary of Defense Johnson in April. These funds were not for the purchase of equipment, as might be expected, but rather, were earmarked to pay the existing government troops and to allow the government to increase the number of battalion combat teams in the Philippine Army from ten to twenty-six. Throughout 1950

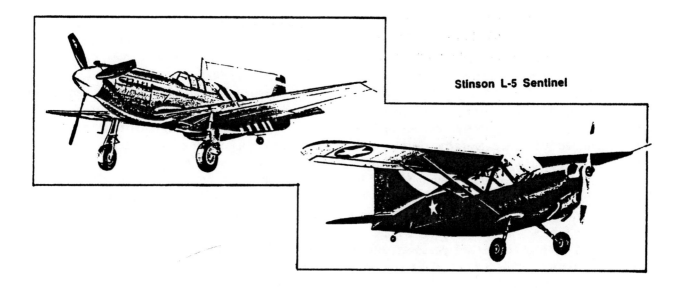

Stinson L-5 Sentinel

and well into the following year, MDAP money flowed into the Philippine Department of National Defense. These requests culminated in a special request for $10 million during the summer of 1951. Approved by President Truman, this special request seems to have put the Army over the top. Corruption began to decline, due to increased pay and the efforts of the new Secretary of National Defense; and the armed forces became more professional and effective. Soldiers, now able to purchase rations from the local villagers and provide for their families, began to feel better about their mission. This attitude change had far reaching effects for both the soldier and the peasant alike. The soldier gained prestige, a sense of nationalism, and felt that he was fighting Huks to protect his country and his fellow countrymen. The peasant was relieved as the police and military finally began to protect him, and no longer used him as a handy supply house.[53] As the trend continued, so did the erosion of Huk popular support.

In the fall of 1951 the JUSMAG began to train and equip a Philippine airborne infantry company. The unit, sparked by an idea passed to Secretary Magsaysay by Lt. Col. Lansdale, was intended to be emplaced behind enemy lines to act as a mobile blocking force during large operations. Although the necessary equipment and training was provided, the airborne company was never employed as planned.[54] Concurrently,

the JUSMAG funneled large amounts of equipment into the AFP, including nearly 200 wheeled and light tracked vehicles that greatly increased their mobility and helped alleviate two long-standing deficiencies—mobility and slow response time.

It was also during 1951 that the JUSMAG embarked upon an expanded program to provide the military with professional education and training. Quotas for officers and enlisted men from all three Philippine services were obtained for military and technical schools in the United States. In 1951 alone, 249 Philippine officers and men attended 85 courses in the United States at a cost of $930,300.[55] These courses ranged from the Command and General Staff College to branch advanced and basic courses, to NCO academies, and to courses on communications, maintenance, and supply. Encompassing schools from all three U.S. services, the education program paid high dividends as the AFP grew in capability and professionalism.

JUSMAG efforts to increase the amount of MDAP funds were successful, aided no doubt by growing government successes against the Huks. In 1952, the Department of Defense designated $48.9 million for the Philippines to raise sixteen additional battalion combat teams. This allowed Magsaysay to achieve the twenty-six BCTs that he desired. The appropriation included a supplemental request sent to President Truman by the

Secretary of Defense in February 1952, seeking an additional $5 million to be used to pay government forces and to finance a government program to purchase weapons from Huks and their supporters.[56]

By 1953, JUSMAG efforts could be judged through greater AFP effectiveness against the Huks and, to a larger extent, by overall conditions in the country. Luis Taruc saw the tide of battle changing and blamed the United States for the government's good fortunes. "He was given an American Military Advisory Group to train his armed forces," he said of Magsaysay, "to train them for war against the peasants, and he was backed up with the promise of greater aid if the people's movement got too strong for him."[57] American aid and advice were working—working too well for some.

At this junction, an important change took place in JCS philosophy. American military advisors were permitted, for the first time, to accompany government forces into the field, a suggestion first raised by the 1950 MDAP survey mission. Prior to this time, JCS policy prohibited advisors (with only two exceptions, Lt. Col. Lansdale and his assistant, Maj. Bohannan) from taking the field with their counterparts.[58] In February 1953, JUSMAG made the first official reference to granting a few advisors permission to accompany Philippine units afield. The *Country Statement FY 1954*, reported that "Periodically, JUSMAG officers accompany AFP tactical units as non-combatant observers during operations in the field against dissidents. At these times, they note and report on the tactics employed and utilization (made) of MDAP equipment. By accompanying AFP units in the field from time-to-time, ... (they) are thereby better able to advise Philippine Commanders."[59] The exact number of advisors or their specific actions while accompanying Philippine Army units were not detailed.

The situation in the Philippines had reversed by 1954 and was favoring the government, now under the leadership of President Magsaysay. Relying heavily on American aid and advice from the JUSMAG, Manila was winning the battle against the insurgents and improving the economy throughout the islands. The military had

been reorganized, increased in size and efficiency, and was now viewed by the peasants as a protector rather than as an oppressor. The AFP numbered some 51,000 troops, of which 37.000 were assigned to twenty-six BCTs. The remaining forces were divided between the Police Constabulary (7,300), general headquarters and special units (7,700), and combat support and service units and the small Air Force and Navy.[60] Due to American aid, Magsaysay was able not only to beat the Huks, but to devote thee majority of his country's finances to social programs and land reforms. Special community projects were funded that built schools, roads, and health clinics in areas long forgotten about by previous administrations. In yet another large development program, thousands of new wells were dug across Luzon and on the southern islands to provide the people with fresh, clean water. From 1951 until 1954, the Philippines received $94.9 million in non-military economic aid and assistance, assistance that enabled national spending on the military to remain below 50 percent of the total budget, even at the height of the insurrection.[61]

THE INSURRECTION—PHASE II (1950-1955)

Ramon Magsaysay 's appointment as Secretary of National Defense in 1950 marked the beginning of the second phase of the Huk insurrection. His appointment marked the beginning of the end of Huk supremacy and initiated the effective government offensive that crushed the rebellion during the following four years. The previous chapter discussed some of the changes Magsaysay dictated for the Philippine military and detailed new initiatives taken by the JUSMAG to support his effort. This chapter examines the military actions that took place between 1950, when President Quirino was a virtual prisoner in Malacanang, and the collapse of the insurgency in 1954/55.

AFP ORGANIZATION—PHASE II

Although the Philippine military began to reorganize before Magsaysay became the Secretary, it was during his tenure that the Philippine military matured and refined its role and function. Each of the 1,100-man battalion combat teams was organized to reflect the change in tactics from conventional, to a more unconventional mode that was based on small unit operations, mobility, and firepower at the unit level. Artillery and heavy mortar batteries were removed from the battalion and replaced with additional rifle and reconnaissance companies. When artillery was required for an operation, it was attached to the sector for use in that specific operation.[1] The following charts show the organization of the Armed Forces of the Philippines and of a typical Philippine Army battalion used as the basis for Magsaysay's anti-Huk campaign after 1950.

The Headquarters and Service Company provided the battalion various support detachments used to augment rifle companies, coordinate support for the battalion, and in the case of the intelligence detachment, to conduct independent operations for the battalion commander or the AFP general staff. Besides the intelligence detachment, the service company also included a medical detachment; a communications platoon, capable of establishing and repairing radio or wire communication and equipment; a transportation platoon with eighteen cargo vehicles; a heavy weapons platoon with automatic weapons, 81mm mortars, and two 75mm recoilless-rifles, used to augment the weapons company; a replace-

Armed Forces of the Philippines Organization
(ca. 1952)

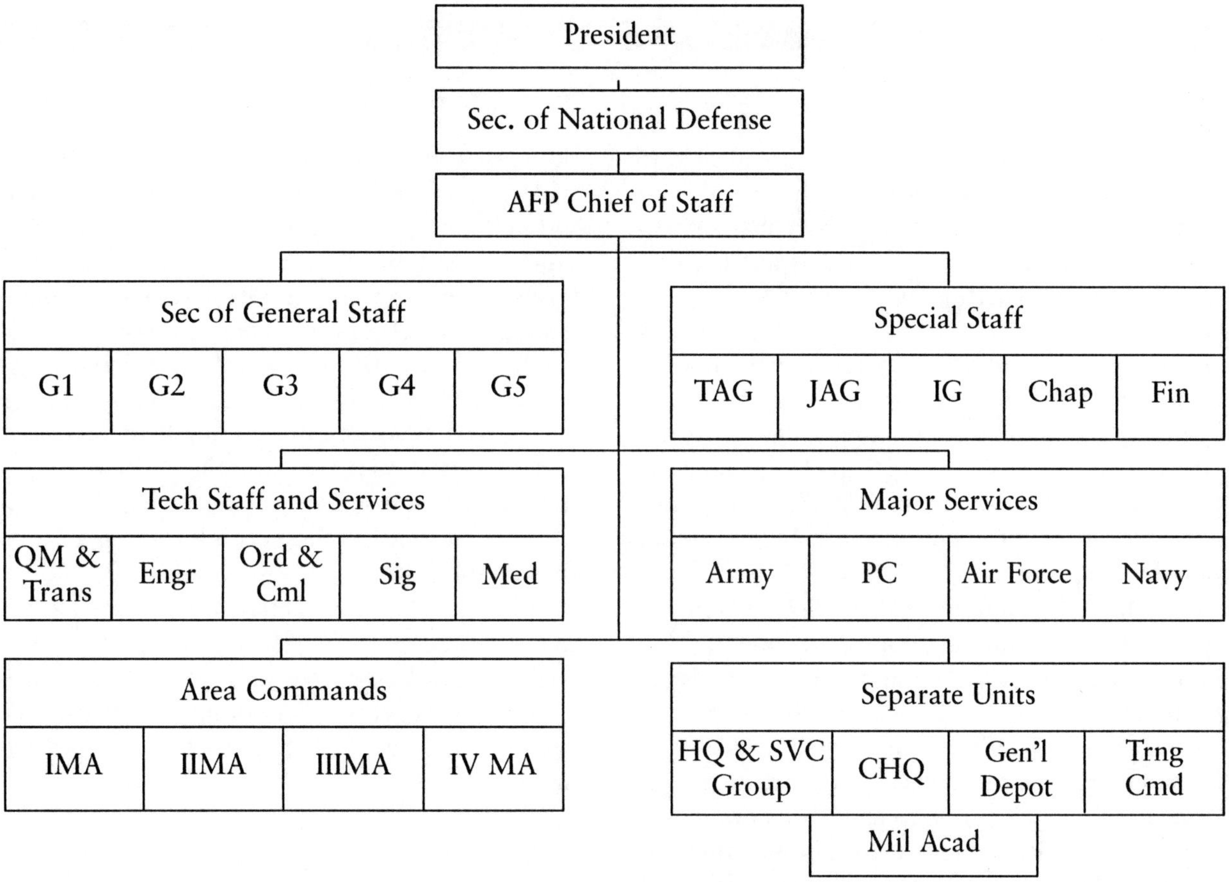

President

Sec. of National Defense

AFP Chief of Staff

Sec of General Staff						Special Staff				
G1	G2	G3	G4	G5		TAG	JAG	IG	Chap	Fin

Tech Staff and Services						Major Services			
QM & Trans	Engr	Ord & Cml	Sig	Med		Army	PC	Air Force	Navy

Area Commands					Separate Units			
IMA	IIMA	IIIMA	IV MA		HQ & SVC Group	CHQ	Gen'l Depot	Trng Cmd

Mil Acad

Source: JUSMAG, *Semi-Annual Report 1 Jan-30 Jun 1952*, 1 Aug 52.

CHART 6

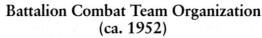

Battalion Combat Team Organization
(ca. 1952)

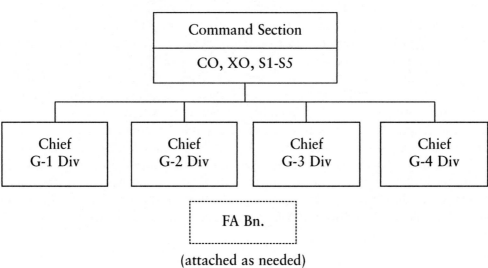

Source: Smith. *Philippine Operations*, p. 7.

CHART 7

ment pool; and an air support detachment with light observation helicopters and aircraft. The aircraft, usually WWII surplus L-5 artillery observation planes, provided aerial resupply and gathered intelligence information by observation or receiving "coded" messages from agents on the ground in guerrilla territory. Helicopters were used to evacuate wounded and proved a great morale builder for soldiers on long-range missions. Although the United States provided some heavy helicopters to the Philippine military, they were noisy, slow, and not employed in large numbers during the insurgency.[2]

With the exceptions of the S-2 section and pilots from the air support detachment, Magsaysay discontinued the old practice of leaving a battalion in one area for extended periods. Instead, he ordered them moved periodically, leaving only the Intelligence Service Team and the pilots in the old location to assist the new, incoming unit.[3] The Army found this allowed them the greatest flexibility to work closely with local police and constabulary units, while avoiding ill-feelings with the local populace. Within a BCT's defined area, companies or other smaller units were deployed to conduct independent operations, or the entire battalion could join quickly with others into larger formations when needed.

Each company consisted of approximately 200 men and was divided into four infantry platoons; a service platoon with intelligence, maintenance, civil affairs, and medical sections; and a small company headquarters. Additional transportation assets and heavier armaments were transferred from company and battalion level, and placed directly within the individual platoons. Each platoon was assigned four light utility vehicles, one 2 1/2 ton truck, radios, two .50 caliber machine guns, and one 60mm mortar. Combat platoons were made up of three squads, each squad capable of fielding two patrols. Typically, a combat patrol had an enlisted patrol leader, a radioman, a Browning Automatic Rifle man, a scout, a rifleman/grenadier, and an aidman/cook.[4]

AFP TACTICS

Beginning in 1950, AFP tactics underwent dramatic changes in both style and in combining purely military actions with psychological warfare activities. By combining the two, Magsaysay hoped to maintain pressure on the Huks, cause dissension within guerrilla ranks, and influence the people to favor the government. Patrols that once stayed close to home and usually near major roads became more effective as new, more aggressive leaders took command of BCTs. Patrolling was conducted on an irregular time-frame and a patrol often remained in the field for several days before returning to garrison. This in itself was a major change from the pre-Magsaysay days when patrols always returned home before nightfall. Instead of remaining road-bound, patrols ventured deep into the jungle in search of Huk camps and to gather information.[5]

BCT commanders relied on Scout-Rangers for long-range patrols that exceeded more than a few days in length. Five man teams were assigned to each battalion and often penetrated deep into guerrilla territory for several weeks at a time. One of their favorite methods of gaining information was to enlist the help of local minorities, who themselves were often victimized by Huk bands. Capitalizing on this ready-made animosity toward the Huks, the government often enlisted the assistance of Negritos, black pygmies who lived in Luzon's mountains, to gather intelligence or to act as guides for the Army.[6]

Magsaysay was also quick to implement novel methods of attacking Huk logistics and supply. About half of the money he received from the United States after his 1950 visit went toward the purchase of "loose" weapons. His "Cash for Guns" campaign was so successful during its five year lifetime that it is estimated to have reduced Huk weapon stores by up to 50 percent.[7] The remainder went to build the Philippine military. By the end of 1950, Philippine Army strength rose to almost 30,000 troops, nearly double its size of a year before. In addition to battalion combat teams, Army force structure contained a K-9 Corps (used occasionally to track Huks), a battalion of Scout-Rangers, and a horse cavalry squadron.[8]

PSYCHOLOGICAL WARFARE OPERATIONS

Long-range government patrols were also used to assist the government's psychological warfare program that was in full gear by 1951. The "Force X" idea was reborn by Col. Valeriano, now the commander of the 7th BCT, and psychological warfare officers, who reported directly to the Secretary of National Defense staff, were attached to each Army battalion. Scout-Ranger units within each battalion often adopted "Force X" tactics and ambushed enemy patrols and planted "dirty tricks" in Huk weapon caches. In addition, they were used covertly to distribute propaganda leaflets in areas thought secure by local guerrillas. The most successful of these leaflets was "The Eye." When a Huk found one of these simple leaflets, he was shaken at the thought of his secure territory being violated by some unseen enemy.[9] Another AFP favorite, originally used against the Moros, involved planting altered ammunition in enemy ammunition stockpiles. This modified ammunition contained dynamite in place of powder and exploded when it was fired. Besides destroying a weapon and injuring the man firing it, it sent chills of mistrust through the Huk ranks. Who could be sure that the cartridge he was about to fire had not been tampered with and, who was to blame? Was it planted into one of their secure depots or, was their supplier a government agent? They never could really be sure.[10]

The Philippine Army's research and development unit, known affectionately as "The Department of Dirty Tricks" developed several other

The "Eye" Leaflet

interesting items. Some of these involved exploding radios, flashlights, and doctored Huk weapons that were then secretly replaced into enemy stockpiles. Another of the inventions developed by the head of the R&D unit, whom Bohannan called ". . .the nicest man that I have ever known and with one of the nastiest minds," was a modified M1 carbine for use by Scout-Rangers. This weapon was equipped with dual barrels, made fully automatic, and was capable of firing 1,500 rounds per minute. They were greatly favored by the patrols who needed the firepower but not the weight of conventional weapons for their long excursions into Huklandia. Finally, the AFP produced a homemade napalm bomb that was dropped from L-5 light observation aircraft. These napalm bombs were made by filling coconut shells with gasoline and dropping them along with a couple of incendiary grenades on suspected Huk locations.[11]

Initial success with infiltration tactics prompted the government to experiment with expanding into large-scale infiltrations. Company C of the 7th BCT was selected for this project and moved to a secret training site in the Sierra Madre mountains. After eight weeks of intense training in all varieties of special operations and in impersonating the insurgents, four teams were dispatched on OPERATION COVER-UP. The teams moved into the area around the village of Pandi and settled into the local community as farmers and laborers. From their base in a house rented by the unit S-2, they reported on guerrilla activities, ambushed several Huk patrols, and carried out a number of "snatch" operations against local Huk officials. Before the operation ended, seventy Huk officials disappeared and almost all guerrilla activities in the area were documented. This one action literally took Pandi away from the Huks as an operational base.[12]

As the government realized benefits from promoting dissension and mistrust in the Huk organization, it increased its efforts in 1952. Rewards were paid for information leading to the capture of guerrilla leaders and were given wide publicity. Local officials known to sympathize with the Huk were often put into such compromising positions that they volunteered

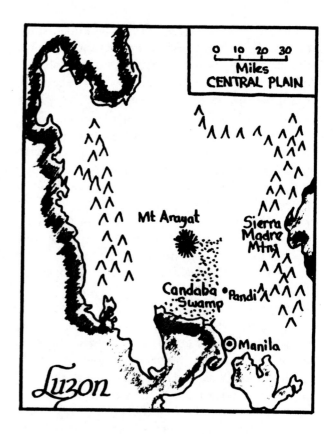

information in exchange for safe-conduct out of the area. In one instance, a local mayor was called into a village square and amidst great pomp and fanfare was thanked by Col. Valeriano for helping his troops kill a courier. Although totally unaware of the circumstances surrounding the courier's death, the mayor and his family appeared on the colonel's doorstep at 0300hrs the following morning. In exchange for information, the government resettled the mayor and his family to another island.[13]

In another example of psychological warfare, this time aimed at Huk cohesion, Magsaysay authorized a bounty of $50,000 for Luis Taruc. This was followed immediately by a more surprising move. He authorized even larger rewards for some Huk lieutenants and less important leaders. His plan worked. Jealousy sprang up between different groups whose members were upset that their leader's "price" was less than other leader's. However juvenile the effect, the reward program succeeded in disrupting guerrilla organization and did in fact lead to the capture of several Huk leaders.[14]

One enterprising BCT on Manila's outskirts managed to borrow several panel trucks from a local business and began making daily deliveries around the city. Early one morning, one of the trucks (with a fully armed squad concealed in its cargo compartment) was stopped by a Huk foraging party on a lonely country road and demanded the driver give them what he had in the back of his truck. This, he did graciously. The dead insurgents were left where they fell by the road and, after similar incidents happened around Manila's suburbs, hijackings of civilian vehicles almost came to a complete stop.[15]

In another episode, a plane flew over a small battle and called down to the surprised Huks below by name. As the pilot departed, he thanked several "informers" on the ground and wished them good luck in escaping injury as a result of helping the Army find their unit. The Huks stared at one another, especially those whose names were called out, and wondered how much of what they had just heard was true. Could their comrades be informers? They just couldn't be sure, and as the tide of battle turned against them, several mock trials were held and more than one innocent guerrilla was put before a convenient wall.[16] Those who watched the execution must surely have prayed that the next plane to fly over them didn't have a list with their names on it.

Late in the campaign, government L-5 aircraft dropped two series of leaflets on Huk forces trapped without food on Mount Arayat. The first set, addressed to the group's leaders, promised a choice of safe conduct if they surrendered, or death by starvation if they continued to resist. The second set of leaflets were addressed to the troops and promised them fair trials and just treatment, including food, if they surrendered. Magsaysay's object was to make the troops believe their leaders no longer cared about what happened to them and that they were willing to sacrifice them for a lost cause. In this case, the plan worked, at least partially. About half of the surrounded guerrillas surrendered, while others attempted to break-out of the government lines. Even though some escaped, their confidence in their leaders suffered.[17]

AFP INTELLIGENCE OPERATIONS

Secretary Magsaysay realized that intelligence was the key that could reverse the course of the insurrection. Without knowing where the Huks were, in what strength, and what their plans were, no amount of military reorganization or change in tactics would prove effective. Using Lansdale's practical advice, he made Huk order-of-battle the first concern of his intelligence officers. Commanders were told to study Huk organization in their areas and to compile complete information files on known or suspected members of the movement. Each battalion started a special intelligence file on 3x5 index cards on all of these people. The files contained information about specific people, about local Huk intelligence and logistic nets, and other information obtained by Scout-Ranger patrols. When the BCT was transferred to a new area, the card file, and the S-2 Intelligence Section, remained in the area to help the incoming BCT.[18] Periodically, these files were collected and their information consolidated at AFP GHQ.

Magsaysay presented his commanders with two sets of basic questions that were essential to the campaign. First, what can the enemy do to hurt me, what does he intend to do, and when will he do it? The second question was where is the enemy, what are his strengths that should be avoided, and what are his weaknesses that should be exploited?[19] As this information was compiled, other related data came to light—the Huk communication system and the location of local supply points and logistic drop-points were discovered. The information about order-of-battle became so complete by 1954 that Lansdale remarked that if the guerrillas wanted to know where any of their units were, all they needed do was ask AFP intelligence.[20]

"Force X's" rebirth was a direct result of this emphasis on intelligence. During this second phase of the insurrection, "Force X" operations supplied the government with both intelligence and erased Huk feelings of security even in their traditional strongholds around Mount Arayat, the Candaba Swamp, or in the Sierra Madre mountains. Realizing large-scale infiltration did not come easily for the military, Magsaysay required his commanders to devote more and more of their assets to its use. Much of the program's success can be credited to the work of the Philippine Intelligence Service and graduates from the intelligence school, both organizations revitalized through the efforts of Secretary Magsaysay and his personal advisor, Edward Lansdale. Intelligence school graduates were placed at all levels within the Army, the Constabulary, and the National Bureau of Investigation.[21] Soldiers were screened and trained, cover stories developed, and when conditions favored "Force X", they were employed. These conditions usually involved the temporary disruption of Huk communications in an area or a successful operation that destroyed a Huk unit and its leaders. But above all, "Force X" relied on secrecy in planning, training, and execution.[22]

On the island of Panay, the Philippine Army tried a variation of the "Force X" concept to break the local guerrilla structure. Accompanied by three military intelligence agents, a group of twenty former Huks were infiltrated into the island's interior. After three months of gathering information, establishing their cover as a *bona fide* Huk unit, and gaining the confidence of the island's Huk leadership, they hosted a "by invitation only" barbecue for the Panay High Command.[23] Between the ribs and potato salad, the covert government force sprang an ambush that killed or captured nearly all the Panay commanders and crippled the organization on the island for the duration of the campaign.

Magsaysay also resorted to planting spies within the Huk ranks to gain first-hand information. Employing the tightest of security, Magsaysay located a willing villager who was the cousin of a local Huk commander. The commander had joined the movement for personal rather than ideological reasons and was considered as the operation's target. After two months of training, Magsaysay's plan was put into action. Government troops burned the man's house, his brother was imprisoned, and his parents secretly moved to another island. With this as his cover, he sought refuge with his cousin, the guerrilla, and joined the movement. The local squadron made him a National Finance Committee collector and with money supplied to him by the government, he was soon promoted and

in a short time became one of Luis Taruc's personal bodyguards. Before this project was terminated and the informer ordered to escape to friendly lines, he supplied the government with the names of the 1,175 member Finance Committee, and information about the entire Huk operation in Candaba Swamp.[24]

The government also relied on information obtained from captured Huks and their friends and families. Direct intelligence came from the guerrilla or his immediate family. Although the amount of information received directly from these people was limited, when it was tendered, it was usually accurate and timely. The government tried to interrogate a captured Huk as soon after his capture as possible. By doing this, intelligence officers hoped to take full advantage of confusion and depression that normally accompanies capture. Once the man was convinced that he was going to be treated fairly and not tortured or summarily executed, he sometimes cooperated.

More information was gathered by using an indirect method that targeted friends, classmates, and more distant family members such as cousins, uncles, aunts, etc. While the guerrilla remained at large, these people were reluctant to divulge information but, once the guerrilla relative was captured, family members often volunteered information to help their friend or relative. To supplement this program, the government also planted agents in Manila prisons and questioned criminals about Huk activities. Since Huks sometimes employed common criminals to assist them with robberies and kidnappings, especially during the movement's decline, this tactic proved most helpful. Criminals frequently knew about Huk organization and were likely to exchange this information for reductions in sentences or improved living conditions.[25]

The Philippine Army was not beyond staging well planned production numbers to get information from hard-core Huk supporters. In San Luis, Luis Taruc's hometown, a local guerrilla unit killed four policemen and left the dismembered bodies scattered on a highway. In response, an AFP company surrounded the village, marshaled the villagers into the town square and proceeded to march them at gunpoint to a nearby riverbank. Across the river stood a squad of troops and twelve bound and hooded "Huks." One by one the soldiers bayoneted and shot the "Huk" prisoners while those awaiting execution shouted out names of local supporters amidst their cries for mercy. When the last "Huk" was killed, the people were marched back to the village and individually questioned by MIS officers. Out of fear, and probably more than a little shock, many of those named by the executed guerrillas began to spew forth information about local guerrilla activities, food and weapon caches, and anything else they could think of. The information broke the Huk hold over the village and hurt the movement throughout the region. Alas, what the villagers failed to see while they were being questioned was the scene at the execution site. As soon as the villagers left the riverbank, the executed "Huks" arose from the dead, went into the jungle, washed the animal blood from their clothing, and rejoined their units.[26] It had been a grand show, and it worked.

Together with other programs geared to gather information and influence the people, Magsaysay's intelligence campaign was a resounding success. By the end of the campaign in 1955, Luzon was flooded with informants, posters offering rewards for Huks still at large, and government troops carried out large covert operations throughout the region once known as Huklandia. The well organized and coordinated program gave the Army the information it needed to strike the Huks where they were most vulnerable and gradually severed the guerrillas from their food, arms, and most importantly, from the people.[27]

MILITARY OPERATIONS—PHASE II

On the day he was sworn into office as Secretary of National Defense, Magsaysay received an anonymous phone call from a man who wished to talk to him about the insurgent movement. An hour after the call, Magsaysay met Tarciano Rizal on a deserted back street in one of Manila's barrios. (Rizal was the grandson of Jose Rizal, a national folk hero and freedom fighter from the 1896 rebellion.) As proved the case with other would be assassins, Rizal came to Manila to kill Magsaysay but heard so many glowing reports about the Secretary that he decided to meet him

first. For several days the two men discussed the Huk movement, its roots, its goals, and what Magsaysay wanted to do for the Philippines. When their talks concluded, Rizal was convinced of Magsaysay's sincerity and offered to help him. He took the Secretary to his Manila apartment from which the two watched a local lady leave two baskets of food for CPP Politburo members.[28] When Magsaysay returned to his office and told the chief of Philippine intelligence what he had seen, he was informed of the ongoing government operation to try to keep track of this CPP group.

On 18 October 1950, using information compiled by Army Intelligence and from observations of the "basket lady," twenty-two simultaneous raids were launched on Politburo members and their meeting places. The raids totally disrupted the Politburo and prompted Magsaysay to get President Quirino to issue a presidential proclamation suspending the writ of *habeas corpus* for the duration of the anti-Huk campaign. This step allowed the government to hold captured guerrillas longer than twenty-four hours without *prima facie* evidence. Magsaysay could now hold Huks for extended periods while the government built judicial cases against them. Before the writ was suspended, it was not at all unusual for a captured Huk to be back with his unit within two days from the time he was taken into custody.[29]

The Manila raids spawned a rash of Huk retaliation. Having a strength of some 12,000 armed fighters and another 100,000 active supporters in Luzon, the Huks renewed their campaign of raids, holdups, kidnappings, and intimidation.[30] In Binan, Huks robbed the local bank of $76,000. Another Huk squadron attacked the village of San Marcelino and burned thirty-six homes, kidnapped ten people, and murdered seventy-two others before leaving. In Zambales, fifty guerrillas attacked the PC garrison at Palawig and killed two policemen and captured twenty-one rifles before being driven off.[31]

However, in its enthusiasm one squadron went too far. On 25 November, one hundred Huks attacked the small village of Aglao and massacred nearly the entire population. As word of this atrocity spread, people throughout central Luzon became outraged. There were no government troops in Aglao and the villagers had done nothing to anger the Huks. When Taruc heard of the massacre, he recalled the unit's commander, tried him by court martial, and sentenced him to confinement and hard labor. But Taruc's efforts to appease popular discontent came too late. The damage was done and the entire Huk organization suffered the consequences.[32]

The government responded to the new offensive and the Aglao massacre with an early 1951 offensive of its own. In January, Army units struck Huk locations near Mount Arayat and Mount Dorst that they had learned of from information gathered in the October Manila raid. OPERATION SABER, as this action was called, ended in February about the time the EDCOR program was formally launched. SABER demonstrated the military's new resolve to pursue the Huks into their strongholds, and showed that the government would no longer be satisfied with simply responding to guerrilla attacks but would initiate operations when and where it desired.[33]

At the same time, the AFP began to disrupt Huk supply lines between villages and their jungle hideouts. Using information collected through infiltration, informants, and from aerial reconnaissance, government troops tried to separate Huks from their food and popular base. Meanwhile, L-5 flights were used to locate "production bases" that Taruc started during the previous couple of years. When one of these farms was located, it was either attacked directly or was kept under aerial surveillance until just before harvest time. Then, when government agricultural consultants thought harvest was imminent, the farm would be raided and destroyed.[34] This procedure proved most effective. It kept guerrilla forces occupied guarding and working the "bases," only to have them destroyed just before they could harvest the crops. This not only cut deeply into Huk food supplies, but hurt morale as well.

Magsaysay continued to integrate the military into his civil affairs and psychological warfare campaigns throughout 1951. In the small hamlet of San Augustin, population fifty, the local Huk leader's wife was preparing to have her first child. Knowing that the hamlet lacked medical facilities, Magsaysay ordered the local battalion commander to send a five-man surveillance team to the village and to report when she delivered the baby. When the child was born, Magsaysay dispatched an Army ambulance, doctor, and nurse to help the woman. While the ambulance was en route, an AFP helicopter flew over the hamlet and told the surprised villagers that medical help was on the way for their newest citizen. When the ambulance arrived, siren blaring, it was met by cheering townspeople. Later, the new mother sent her thanks to the Secretary and apologized for her husband being a guerrilla. Shortly thereafter, the guerrilla peaceably surrendered with his entire unit to the area BCT commander.[35]

By the close of 1951, Army strength increased by nearly 60 percent over the preceding year to stand at twenty-six 1,047-man BCTs. In addition to the BCTs, one of which served in Korea, an airborne infantry battalion was activated in October, an engineer construction group with three construction companies was formed, and the Police Constabulary increased to ninety-one companies. The entire Department of National Defense had been successfully reorganized for internal defense. With a combined strength of over 53,700 men, the Philippine armed forces were beginning to make steady progress against the guerrillas. Professionalism and competence were improving in both officer and enlisted ranks and, during 1951, two hundred-sixty top graduates from Philippine military schools attended training courses in the United States. Another significant addition was made to the Philippine Air Force—they received fifty F-51 Mustang fighters to improve their ground support mission.[36]

The 1951 Elections

The 1951 off-year election played an important role in fighting the guerrillas and demonstrated increased public confidence in the Philippine military and the changing complexion of the insurgency. Magsaysay promised the nation an honest election and was determined to keep his word. Remembering the violent 1949 election that bolstered Huk propaganda, Magsaysay mobilized the military to guarantee the November election would take place in a more peaceful atmosphere.

Despite several Huk attempts to disrupt campaigning, and occasional political violence between the major parties in Manila, overwhelming military presence during the campaign and at the polls produced a surprisingly quiet election. Magsaysay activated the Philippine Army Reserve and mobilized ROTC cadets to secure the polls and ensure that ballot boxes arrived safely, and untampered with, at tally centers. In addition, Maj. Gen. Robert Cannon, then Chief of the JUSMAG, assigned twenty-five of his officers to poll-watching duties.[37]

Four million Filipinos cast ballots and only twenty-one people lost their lives during the election. This compared most favorably to the 1949 election during which several hundred Filipinos were killed. Aside from the lack of violence, the major surprise was that Quirino's Liberal Party lost considerable ground to the opposition *Nacionalistas* who carried every contested congressional seat and won control of the Philippine Senate.[38] The people distrusted Quirino and felt that the only reason he allowed some reforms was to stop the Huks, not to help them. Magsaysay on the other hand, who refused to campaign for Quirino's Liberals, was seen as acting to help the people by stopping the insurgents. His popularity grew from both his success against the Huks and from delivering the honest, peaceful election he promised the people.[39] Beginning that December, Huk surrenders increased, the number of active squadrons declined, and the combined government intelligence programs and PSYOP operations continued to erode guerrilla solidarity.

In 1952, AFP GHQ established a Public Affairs Office for Psychological Warfare and Public Relations. With considerable assistance from the U.S. Information Service, well equipped teams were assigned to areas where they conducted efficient public relations programs to gain the people's support for the government. Using pamphlets, posters, and public address systems, the teams held public rallies that were generally well received. Because the teams lived with the people and helped them construct schools and other public facilities, they became well liked and their influence grew accordingly. By the end of 1953, these public relations teams often found themselves in the middle of surrender negotiations, acting as go-betweens for the government and the guerrilla forces.[40]

A second program directly aimed at influencing the villagers also began in 1952. Army commanders were encouraged to set up Civilian Commando Units in friendly areas susceptible to Huk raids. Composed entirely of local volunteers, and led by Army NCOs, the volunteer units protected their barrios and thus relieved government forces from these stationary duties. By allowing the villagers to protect themselves, the program grew to include some 10,000 people by the end of the campaign in 1955.[41]

By the spring of 1952, the AFP was taking the initiative away from the Huks. Once again forced to fight as semi-autonomous bands, Huks no longer enjoyed the luxury of well-organized squadrons under Taruc's central control and guidance. Government intelligence continued to improve and provided GHQ with accurate and timely information about Huk strength and location. Huk casualties during the first few months of the year increased 12 percent, while AFP casualties declined by 23 percent. Training and education of officers and enlisted men began to pay benefits in professionalism and competence. As a result of the new professionalism and the success of village commando units in securing many local hamlets, fewer Army forces were required for static defense, thus allowing a larger proportion of government troops to undertake active pursuit operations. By year's end, the Army stood at 36,400 men and had a new M-4 medium tank platoon that was activated in May.[42]

On 11 April 1952, government forces raided Recco 1 headquarters in Nueva Ecija Province, capturing the Recco commander, William Pomeroy.[43] During the summer, the government conducted a two-day operation near Mount Arayat that demonstrated the increased effectiveness of the entire Philippine Armed Forces. Although the operation netted few guerrillas, it was the first major effort wherein the Philippine Air Force actively supported a ground operation with air cover. P-51 fighters flew air support for the BCT for the entire time the force was in the field. Response time was reduced to less than twenty minutes and the two forces cooperated to their fullest—due in no small measure to the fact that the Air Force commander was the son of the BCT commander on the ground. This cooperation, based as it was on familiarity and a singular goal, continued to grow throughout the remainder of the campaign.[44]

In August 1952, the 7th and 16th BCT mounted an offensive against guerrillas in Zambales Province. Supported on the west and south by other Army units, the 7th BCT moved into the mountains while the 16th BCT formed a blocking position around the perimeter. For seventy-two days the BCT searched the area for Huk camps and received daily resupply from L-5 aircraft whose pilots, lacking adequate parachutes, dropped supplies encased in woven rattan spheres. When the operation concluded in October, seventy-two of the estimated two hundred Huks in the area were captured or killed, and numerous enemy ordnance shops and caches were destroyed. As the battalion withdrew, it left behind platoon-sized units to continue the search. Although small, these stay-behind units were armed exceptionally well. Each unit had at least two automatic rifles, four sub-machine guns, a radio, and the ever present camera. This operation, along with other similar ones conducted throughout Huklandia, produced a Huk offer for a truce just before Christmas. Unfortunately, the government agreed to withdraw its forces during the negotiations and, when the talks broke down after New Year's, the Huks recovered somewhat from the government's fall offensive. Despite this reprieve, the Huk force had lost nearly 13,000 members to combat action or surrender since the day Magsaysay took office in 1950.[45]

Philippine military success continued throughout the following year. 1953 was marked by a major April offensive and the November elections. In early April, a captured guerrilla told 17th BCT officers where the main Huk headquarters was located near Mount Arayat. On 10 April, the battalion attacked the location while three companies of the 22d BCT held the north and east slopes of the mountain. Unfortunately, the camp was deserted, but rather than abandon the operation, the government force pressed its advance. Moving from area to area, discovering many smaller camps as they went, troops searched for the main enemy concentration. While they searched, two more battalions reinforced the perimeter around Mount Arayat.

On 24 April, the 17th BCT and two additional rifle companies attacked the barrio of Buena Vista on the mountain's western slope. Although they managed to engage a number of Huks, most of the leaders escaped through the perimeter five days later.[46] Again, the number of enemy casualties failed to tell the whole story of the offensive. The Army's real success came from doggedly pursuing the guerrillas through the very center of their former bastion. For even the most optimistic Huk, this meant the government now had relatively free access to any part of Luzon. The idea of an impenetrable Huk fortress was dashed and the remaining 2,300 guerrillas were forced to move constantly to avoid the persistent government troops.[47]

The 1953 General Election

1953 was the year the Philippines was scheduled to have its next presidential election and, other than the military situation with the insurgents, little had changed in Manila. The Quirino administration was still corrupt and made no attempts to clean its house or improve the people's plight in ways not directly connected to the insurrection. Early that year, Magsaysay was again approached by several Filipino statesmen who were planning a *coup d'etat* to avoid what they suspected would be a bloody election in November. True to his nature, Magsaysay responded to their advance as he had done in 1950.

> I know that it is true, as you say, that I can seize the government, should we try. There is no doubt about it in my mind. I should like to point out, however, that if we do this thing it will make us into a banana republic. It would be a precedent we would regret if we allow our young democracy to set out on such a dangerous undertaking . . . Let us work together to insure a clean election. If all else fails, and we have not tried all else yet, then, let us discuss the problem again.[48]

On the last day of February, Magsaysay resigned his position as Secretary of National Defense on the pretext of irreconcilable differences with President Quirino, but in reality, his resignation paved the way for his running for the presidency on the *Nacionalista* party ticket. In his letter of resignation, Magsaysay set the tone for the campaign: ". . . It would be futile to go on killing Huk while the administration continues to breed dissidence by neglecting the problems of our masses."[49] Thus, began his run for the presidency. During the next nine months, while his hand-picked senior Army officers continued to take the fight to the Huks, Magsaysay visited 1,100 barrios and spoke for more than 3,000 hours on issues close to the hearts of his countrymen—corruption, neglect, poverty, and land reform.[50]

On 10 November, more than four million voters cast ballots in another relatively quiet and clean election. As was the case in 1951, the military guarded the polls, ensured the integrity of ballot boxes, and prevented political thugs, or the remaining 2,000 Huks, from intimidating voters. When the ballots were counted, Magsaysay won the presidency by the largest popular margin in Philippine history—2.9 million to 1.3 million for Quirino. Six weeks later, on 30 December 1953, Ramon Magsaysay was inaugurated in a most unorthodox ceremony. Instead of the traditional tuxedo and tails, he wore an open shirt and slacks that were shortly thereafter torn from his body by an overly enthusiastic crowd of supporters. That night, five thousand people attended a state dinner to honor the new President and cleaned-out the kitchen completely, but Magsaysay loved every minute of it all.[51]

As president Magsaysay continued his practice of traveling and speaking with the people both while on the road and at his home in Manila. Each morning, people formed outside his home to discuss problems or suggestions they had with the president while he ate his breakfast. Magsaysay seemed everywhere at once—with troops on campaign, checking local officials, and talking with the people. It was on one of these trips aboard his C-47, *The Mount Pinatubo,* that he died at age forty-one in a crash on Cebu on 17 March 1957.[52]

Final Anti-Huk Military Operations

After assuming the presidency, Magsaysay was able to concentrate on civil relief operations and he devoted less of his time to purely military matters. During his first year in office, he dramatically reduced the amount of corruption in government and instituted many social and agrarian reforms. A quarter of a million hectares of public land were distributed to almost 3,000 farmers and two EDCOR projects on Mindinao flourished. EDCOR was by now so popular that several peasants admitted to joining the Huk movement simply as a means to participate in EDCOR when they turned around and surrendered to government forces. Outside of EDCOR project sites irrigation projects were started, 400 kilometers of new roads were constructed, and another 500 kilometers of existing roads were repaired and improved.

Late in 1953, the Philippine Congress passed the Elementary Education Act of 1953. This act, that received acclaim across the nation, called for free, compulsory elementary education, and provided seven years of intermediate and secondary education. During the following year, 1954, the government founded the Liberty Wells Association. Funded heavily by American aid, this organization supervised the digging of more than two thousand sanitary water wells in villages across Luzon and on larger islands to the south.[53] While his administration took action to improve the people's lives through these programs, Magsaysay continued to supervise the anti-Huk campaign by serving as his own Secretary of National Defense.

As 1954 began, Huks no longer presented a serious threat to the central government. They numbered less than 2,000 active guerrillas and their popular support base was all but dried up. Under these severe restrictions they were forced to limit operations to small raids aimed primarily at getting food and supplies, and they increasingly turned to simple banditry. In essence, the Huks were reduced in status to the level that the United States and the Philippine governments allotted to them before 1950.

In February, the Army began its largest anti-Huk operation to date in an area bounded by Mounts Dorst, Negron, and Caudrado, thirty miles west of Mount Arayat. OPERATION THUNDER-LIGHTNING lasted for 211 days and involved more than 5,000 troops. When it ended in mid-September, government forces had captured eighty-eight Huks, killed forty-three, accepted the surrender of fifty-four others, and destroyed ninety-nine production bases, burned

HMB/CPP Strength
1950–1955
(in thousands)

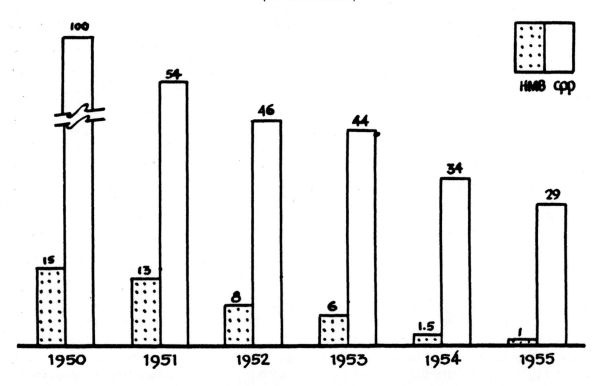

Source: Donald MacGrain, *Anti-Dissident Operations in the Philippines*, (Carlisle Barracks, PA: U.S. Army War college, [1967]), p.35.

CHART 8

more than five hundred enemy huts, and captured ninety-nine weapons. By comparison, government casualties were extremely light—five killed, four wounded, and one L-5 destroyed. But the high point of OPERATION THUNDERLIGHTNING came on 17 May when Luis Taruc surrendered to a young presidential assistant, Ninoy Aquino.[54] The following day, Taruc's Chief of Staff surrendered to government troops in Candaba Swamp and started a mass surrender of Huk leaders and guerrillas throughout central Luzon.

Concurrent with Taruc's surrender, Second Military Area forces conducted a six-week long operation centered on Mount Banahaw. There, two battalions pushed through the Sierra Madre mountains northeast toward the Pacific Ocean. By the time they reached the coast, they killed twenty-nine guerrillas, wounded eight, and captured another twenty-three. All toll, government

troops killed nearly 6,000 Huks, wounded an estimated 1,600, captured over 4,000, and accepted the surrender of yet another 16,000 as the campaign drew to a close in late 1954. During this same period, the AFP suffered 642 killed and another 710 wounded.[55]

Throughout 1955 the number of guerrillas remaining at large continued to diminish until by year's end less than 1,000 remained. Occasional sightings and some contact was made with these hold-outs, but they all but disappeared as a threat to either the region or the government. Their organization was destroyed and the former Huks were nothing more than roving bands of thieves and bandits trying to get enough food and support to simply survive. The number of Huk sympathizers in the region suffered a similar fate. Of the 250,000 Huk supporters in central Luzon in 1949, less than 30,000 could be found by December 1955.[56]

CONCLUSION

When one looks back on the insurrection, one sees that Ramon Magsaysay defeated the guerrillas through a campaign that combined American aid and assistance, domestic social reforms, and a revitalization of both the Philippine military and central government. Before mid-1950, Manila governments had neither the resources nor the inclination to attack the insurgents with such a broad socio-military program. Did the movement's rapid growth after World War II indicate that the people supported their form of change or does it indicate that Huk leaders merely took advantage of ineffectual governments in Manila? Perhaps a little of both was true. At various times the Huks were indeed effective and, at their peak of influence in 1950, kept the Philippine president in self-imposed seclusion within Malacanang. Finally, did Magsaysay's ultimate success indicate that American post-war policy was handled correctly? Indeed not, for although U.S. policy after mid-1950 allowed Magsaysay to win the battle, U.S. policy between 1945 and 1950 was certainly deficient. If instead, American policy had been less complacent and more sensitive to the needs and aspirations of the Filipino people, the Hukbalahap movement would simply have dried up and blown away after the war.

The entire insurgency suffered from a variety of ailments at different times during the course of the insurrection. Each of the key players in the rebellion; the Philippine government, the United States, and the guerrillas achieved victories between 1946 and 1955. It was this timing of neglect, reaction, victory, and defeat that eventually doomed the insurrection to failure. U.S. neglect of social problems on Luzon after the war combined with a series of uncaring governments in Manila to provide the Huks with fertile ground for their communist based insurgency. Only when the Philippine government was at the brink of collapse did U.S. policy makers tackle the real problems facing this allied nation and provide the necessary assistance that allowed Magsaysay to carry out his strategy to defeat the guerrillas.

THE HUK GUERRILLAS

By taking advantage of World War II to consolidate their organization, the Huks were able to adapt quickly to post-war conditions in the Philippines. The people of central Luzon were disillusioned with the post-war government and felt that no one but the Huks cared about their problems. That the guerrillas were communist inspired made little difference to a peasant farmer who lacked education, medical care, clean water, and was deeply in debt to uncaring landlords. The Huks understood this disaffection and made it the cornerstone for their movement.

At war's end, the Huks had a goal—the overthrow of the Philippine government and the establishment of a communist state—and they possessed the internal organization to mount an effective campaign to achieve it. Prior to 1951, they had sufficient logistic support to maintain their forces and to strike out against government police and military forces who at best, were reluctant to venture far afield to chase them. And, at least during the first stage of the insurrection, the Huks had the support of the local population—the key that made all of their actions possible. This was a population that had suffered at the hands of the Japanese and was then suffering at the hands of their own government and its poorly disciplined troops. In both instances, the Huks seemed the only force visibly fighting against those who were oppressing the peasants.

However, by mid-1950 the Hukbalahap movement began to suffer from symptoms that had afflicted it during World War II—over confidence and lapses of security. The October Manila raid hurt them seriously and disrupted their joint political-military strategy. Coupled with public outrage over the murder of Senora Quezon and other atrocities against civilians, the Huks' mass support base developed cracks. Later, when the government managed to mount a few successful operations, the cracks expanded and eventually led to the movement's collapse. Taruc knew that he depended on popular support to survive, but as government pressure built against him, he began demanding too much from the same peasants he had once vowed to protect from just that type of abuse. Once his mass support base began to crumble, the end was in sight. His chief opponent, Ramon Magsaysay, realized the importance of popular support from his own days as a guerrilla leader, and won it for the government.

RAMON MAGSAYSAY

It required two major changes to the post-war *status quo* for the Philippine government to defeat the Huks. First, the United States had to recognize the severity of the insurgency and provide appropriate amounts of advice and military and economic assistance to help counter it. Luckily, this American advice was sound and well received by an enlightened Filipino leader, Magsaysay. Second, a government victory required an administration in Manila that was more concerned with improving the quality of life for its citizens than with self-enrichment. Ramon Magsaysay provided the latter when he accepted the position of Secretary of National Defense and later won the office of President.

What attributes made this former Zambales resident and son of a village school teacher so successful in winning his fellow Filipinos' loyalty? Certainly his well-known honesty helped him achieve his position in the Congress. But it was his deep and sincere concern for his fellows that brought him to national attention and paved the way for his becoming the Secretary of National Defense. He was a man dedicated to duty and blessed with a personality that blended persistence and charisma with an ability to listen to those around him. Perhaps his greatest attribute, an attribute certainly reinforced by his own war-time experience as a guerrilla leader, was his ability to see the Huk guerrilla movement as symptomatic of greater diseases that were threatening his country—poverty, rising social expectations, and an uncaring and corrupt central government.

These were the targets that Magsaysay set his sights on. He combined military operations with civic-action projects to form his grand strategy, a strategy that, if successful, would improve Philippine living conditions and remove the base of guerrilla strength—popular support. He demanded that each soldier, regardless of rank, be dedicated first to the people, then, to killing the guerrillas. He changed the basic tactics used by the Philippine military and fostered unconventional operations, while concurrently developing a more professional and competent armed forces. The military and the government had first to win the respect of the people before their anti-Huk campaign could ever produce tangible

results. Military abuses ceased and soldiers or policemen implicated in abusing civilians were dealt with swiftly and harshly. Without the people's support, whatever gains the military made would vanish as soon as the last trooper returned to his garrison. Without the people's support, Huks would be unable to move freely or sustain themselves in the field.

With American assistance and the fortune of having Edward Lansdale's advice, counsel, and friendship, Magsaysay's strategy proved a resounding success. EDCOR provided land for reformed guerrillas. Other tracts of government land were sold to the people, schools were established, transportation and communication networks were repaired and improved and, for the first time, the armed forces worked side by side with the people to secure their mutual future.

As an epilogue to his remarkable life, Ramon Magsaysay was honored with a commemorative stamp issued by the United States shortly after his death in 1957. At the ceremony accompanying the stamp's issue, President Eisenhower eulogized this progressive leader and his contribution to Philippine democracy.

> If we are ready to do our full part in combating communism, we must as a unit stand not only ready, as Magsaysay did, to bare his chest to the bayonet, if it comes to that, but to work day by day for the betterment—the spiritual, moral, intellectual, and material betterment—of the people who live under freedom, so that not only may they venerate it but they can support it. This Magsaysay did, and in this I believe is his true greatness, the kind of greatness that will be remembered long after any words we can speak here will have been forgotten.[1]

UNITED STATES SUPPORT

Without American economic and military assistance to the Philippine governments after 1950, the Huks might well have succeeded in their rebellion. But, before we applaud the U.S. effort too quickly, perhaps we should consider that U.S. neglect and short sighted helped put the government in jeopardy. Before 1950, U.S. policy makers concentrated their attentions on Europe, were tired of war in the Pacific, and seemed blind to the many problems that tore at the islands. The land-tenure question had been present since the days the nation became an American protectorate and very little had been done to ease its burden on the Filipino farmer. Although land-tenure was a major factor in the years preceding WWII, after the war, U.S. policy ignored it and was intent on divestiture of responsibility for the islands.

Economic aid was made available to the government after the war but the programs were poorly managed and did little other than increase the size of many Filipino elite's bank balances. Other programs, such as the various economic trade acts and the issue of collaboration served only to widen the gap between the people and their government. American foreign policy makers simply did not understand Filipino concerns and aspirations and therefore chose to ignore them. Many incisive and worthwhile reports on conditions in the Philippines (such as that delivered by the Bell Mission) went unheeded until the government in Manila nearly fell in 1950.

Luckily, once the American government realized how close to collapse the Quirino administration was in 1950, Washington reacted. JUSMAG reports, long ignored or given only summary attention, suddenly gained new respect and concern. The JUSMAG was expanded, aid began to flow in, and opinions expressed by some of the JUSMAG's exceptional advisors began to receive attention. Thanks in great measure to the Korean War that was attracting the lion's share of attention in Washington, advisors found themselves with great latitude and were able to develop comprehensive assistance programs that worked hand-in-hand with Magsaysay's objectives for integrating the armed forces with social reforms.

Although the Philippines received large amounts of military aid and equipment from the United States during this period, most of it came from surplus WWII stocks. The equipment was simple to use and maintain, and allowed the AFP to adapt quickly to it and keep it operational. One should remember that the vast preponderance of newer equipment was committed elsewhere, Europe and Korea. Another result of the Korean War was that no U.S. troops were readily available for deployment to the Philippines and, with very few exceptions, American advisors were prohibited from taking the field with their Filipino counterparts until the latter stages of the insurgency. This was perhaps one of our greatest contributions to the Philippines during this period. Without foreign troops to assist them, the Philippine military was forced to develop on its own, under its own leaders, and fight to protect its own land and people. Once the Army became convinced that they were fighting to protect their countrymen, and not as an occupation force trying to subdue an unruly foreign population, they began to receive the people's support. As already described, the alliance of the military with the villagers, and in turn the villagers reliance on the government, spelled the end for the Huk movement.

JUSMAG advisors did all they could to foster a sense of Filipino self-reliance. Whenever possible, they assumed back-row seats for themselves so that government officials could look good and receive the credit for successful operations. Even when programs succeeded as direct results of American efforts, the advisors played down their own role and let a Filipino become the moment's hero. This built pride and self-esteem in both the officials involved and, more importantly, in the Filipino people. They saw themselves succeeding where others had failed and they tried to continue the pattern. When advice was given, it was given directly to the Filipino leader who needed it, as low in the organization as possible, and given by an advisor who the recipient knew and trusted. And how did they develop this trust? General Lansdale put it quite simply—treat them as equals, treat them fairly and honestly, never lie to them, and prove your intentions by displaying courage and willingly accepting the same hardships and inconveniences that they do. In essence then, you must demonstrate that you consider them as good as yourself and that you trust and respect them as much as you want them to trust and respect you.[2]

By following these guides the United States helped the Philippine government solve its internal insurgency. The American government provided most of the material with which the Philippine military fought, provided the money that paid them, and provided advice when it was needed. But, it was Filipinos who fought the battles and defeated the guerrillas under the leadership of an unusual man endowed with the insight to see the larger problem that fostered the resistance, and a leader who aggressively sought to remove the causes for internal unrest in the future.

NOTES

The Evolution of the Hukbalahap Movement

1. Robert R. Smith, *The Hukbalahap Insurgency: Economic, Political and Military Factors*, (Washington, D.C.: Office of the Chief of Military History, [1963]), pp. 3-9.
2. F. Landa Jocano, "Ideology and Radical Movements in the Philippines: An Anthropological Overview," *Solidarity* No. 102 (1985), p. 53.
3. Smith, *The Hukbalahap Insurgency*, pp. 7-8.
4. lbid., p. 13.
5. Clarence G. Barrens, *I Promise: Magsaysay's Unique PSYOP "Defeats" HUKS*, (Ft. Leavenworth, KS: U.S. Army Command and General Staff College, [1970]), p. 25.
6. Smith, *The Hukbalahap Insurgency*, p. 14.
7. Interview with Luis Taruc, 29 May 1974, by Bruce Nussbaum. Bentley Library, University of Michigan, Ann Arbor, Michigan.
8. Smith, *The Hukbalahap Insurgency*, p. 3.
9. Ismael Lapus (Colonel, AFP), "The Communist Huk Enemy," in *Counter-Guerrilla Operations in the Philippines 1946-53*, (Ft. Bragg, NC: U.S. Army Special Forces Center and School, [15 June 1961]). p. 11; and Smith, *The Hukbalahap Insurgency*, p. 17.
10. Smith, *The Hukbalahap Insurgency*, p. 18.
11. Lapus, "The Communist Huk Enemy," p. 12.
12. Rodney S. Azama, *The Huk and the New People's Army: Comparing Two Postwar Filipino Insurgencies*, (Quantico, VA: Marine Corps Command and Staff College, [26 April 1985]), p. 209; and Lapus, "The Communist Huk Enemy," p. 12.
13. Azama, *The Huk and the NPA*, p. 209; and Lapus, "The Communist Huk Enemy," p. 13.
14. Smith, *The Hukbalahap Insurgency*, p. 19.
15. Taruc, interview, p. 40.
16. Lapus, "The Communist Huk Enemy," p. 13; Eduardo Lachica, *The HUKS: Philippine Agrarian Society in Revolt*, (NY: Praeger Publishers, 1971), p. 103; and Smith, *The Hukbalahap Insurgency*, p. 19.

World War II and Huk Expansion

1. Luis Taruc, *Born of the People*, (Bombay: People's Publishing House, LTD, 1953), pp. 45-6; Rodney S. Azama, *The Huks and the New People's Army: Comparing Two Postwar Filipino Insurgencies*, (Quantico, VA: Marine Corps Command and Staff College, [26 April 1985]), p. 210; and Ismael Lapus (Colonel, AFP), "The Communist Huk Enemy," in *Counter-Guerrilla Operations in the Philippines 1946-53*, (Ft. Bragg, NC: U.S. Army Special Forces Center and School, [15 June 1961]), p. 13.
2. Robert R. Smith, *The Hukbalahap Insurgency: Economic, Political, and Military Factors*, (Washington, D.C.: Office of the Chief of Military History, [1963]), p. 22.
3. Ibid., p. 34.
4. Ibid., p. 22.
5. Lapus, "The Communist Huk Enemy," p. 13.
6. Interview with Luis Taruc by Bruce Nussbaum, 29 May 1974, (Ann Arbor, MI: Bentley Library, University of Michigan), p. 1; and Taruc, *Born of the People*, p. 51
7. Taruc interview, p. 41; and Taruc, *Born of the People*, p. 13.
8. Smith, *The Hukbalahap Insurgency*, p. 32; and Azama, *The Huk and the NPA*, p. 14.
9. Luis A. Villa-Real, "Huk Hunting," *Army Combat Forces Journal* V (November 1954), p. 32; Smith, *The Hukbalahap Insurgency*, p. 32; and Edward G. Lansdale, *In the Midst of Wars* (NY: Harper and Row, Publishers, 1972), pp. 6-7.
10. Smith, *The Hukbalahap Insurgency*, p. 32.
11. Taruc, *Born of the People*, p. 56; and Smith, The Hukbalahap Insurgency, p. 30.
12. Taruc, *Born of the People*, p. 56; and F. Sionil Jose, "The HUKS in Retrospect," *Solidarity* No. 102 (1985), p. 70.
13. A.H.Peterson, G.C. Reinhardt, and E.E. Conger, eds. *Symposium on the Role of Airpower in Counterinsurgency and Unconventional Warfare: The Philippine Huk Campaign*, (Santa Monica, CA: The Rand Corporation, [July 1963]), pp. 2-3.
14. Azama, *The Huk and the NPA*, p. 130.
15. Smith, *The Hukbalahap Insurgency*, p. 34.
16. Smith, *The Hukbalahap Insurgency*, p. 30.
17. Ibid.; and Taruc, *Born of the People*, p. 58.
18. Center for Research in Social Systems, *Internal Defense Against Insurgency: Six Cases*, (Washington, D.C.: The American University, [December 1966]).
19. Smith, *The Hukbalahap Insurgency*, p. 34; and Lapus, "The Communist Huk Enemy," p. 14.
20. Smith, *The Hukbalahap Insurgency*, p. 36.
21. Azama, *The Huk and the NPA*, p. 15; and Smith, *The Hukbalahap Insurgency*, p. 34.
22. Historical documentation. Maj. Gen. Edward G. Lansdale, 25 April 1971, by U.S. Air Force Oral History Program, Washington, D.C.
23. Smith, *The Hukbalahap Insurgency*, p. 24; and Lapus, "The Communist Huk Enemy," p. 15.

24. William J. Pomeroy, "Philippines: Hukbalahap and its Mass Base," in *Guerrilla Warfare and Marxism*, William J. Pomeroy, ed. (NY: International Publishers, 1969), p. 233; and Taruc, *Born of the People*, p. 101.

25. Smith, *The Hukbalahap Insurgency*, p. 53.

26. Ibid., p. 27.

27. Ibid., p. 30; and Reginald J. Swarbrick, *The Evolution of Communist Insurgency in the Philippines*, (Quantico, VA: Marine Corps Command and Staff College, [7 June 1983]), p. ii.

28. Smith, *The Hukbalahap Insurgency*, pp. 39 and 46.

29. Ibid., p. 51.

30. Ibid., p. 47.

31. Ibid., p. 48.

Between Liberation and Independence

1. Leo S. Comish, Jr., *The United States and the Philippine Hukbalahap Insurrection: 1946-54*, (Carlisle Barracks, PA: U.S. Army War College, [8 March 1971]), pp. 3-6.

2. Robert A. Smith, *Philippine Freedom 1946-1958*, (NY: Columbia University Press, 1958), p. 115.

3. William B. Steele, *Internal Defense in the Philippines: 1946-1954*, (Carlisle Barracks, PA: U.S. Army War College, [1967]), p. 2.

4. Comish, *The US and the Philippine Hukbalahap Insurrection*, p. 8.

5. Ibid., p. 26.

6. Milton W. Meyer, *A Diplomatic History of the Philippines*, (Honolulu: University of Hawaii Press, 1965), p. 5.

7. US Department of State, *The Philippine Rehabilitation Program: Report to the President by the Secretary of State*, Far Eastern Series, (Washington, D.C.: GPO, [31 August 1954]), p. 3.

8. Robert R. Smith, *The Hukbalahap Insurgency: Economic, Political, and Military Factors*, (Washington, D.C.: Office of the Chief of Military History, [1963]), p. 60.

9. Comish, *The US and the Hukbalahap Insurrection*, p. 27.

10. Ibid. p. 45.

11. Rodney S. Azama, *The Huks and the New People's Army: Comparing Two Postwar Filipino Insurgencies*, (Quantico, VA: Marine Corps Command and Staff College, [26 April 1985]), p. 42; and Smith, *The Hukbalahap Insurgency*, pp. 53-55.

12. Smith, *The Hukbalahap Insurgency*, pp. 53-58; and Luis Taruc, *Born of the People* (Bombay: People's Publishing House, LTD., 1953), p. 173.

13. Ibid., p. 55; and William Manchester, *American Caesar*, (Boston: Little, Brown and Company, 1978), p. 4.

14. Lapus, "The Communist Huk Enemy," p. 15; and Reginald J. Swarbrick, *The Evolution of Communist Insurgency in the Philippines*, (Quantico, VA: Marine Corps Command and Staff College, [7 June 1983]), p. 8.

15. Comish, *The US and the Hukbalahap Insurrection*, p. 17.

16. *Reference Book RB 31-3, Internal Defense Operations: A Case History, The Philippines 1946-1954*, (Ft. Leavenworth, KS: U.S. Army Command and General Staff College, [1967]), p. 37.

17. Smith, *The Hukbalahap Insurgency*, p. 62; and Comish, *The US and the Hukbalahap Insurrection*, p. 36.

18. Comish, *The US and the Hukbalahap Insurrection*, p. 31; and Smith, *The Hukbalahap Insurgency*, p. 62.

19. Azama, *The Huks and the N.P.A.*, p. 43; and Napoleon Valeriano (Colonel, AFP), "Military Operations," in *Counter-Guerrilla Operations in the Philippines 1946-53*, (Ft. Bragg, NC: U.S. Army Special Forces Center and School [15 June 1961]), p. 26.

20. Comish, *The US and the Hukbalahap Insurrection*, p. 34.

21. Center for Research in Social Systems, *Internal Defense Against Insurgency: Six Cases*, (Washington, D.C.: The American University, [December 1966]), p. 47.

22. Lapus, "The Communist Huk Enemy," p. 16; and Swarbrick, *Evolution of Communist Insurgency*, p. 10.

23. Donald MacGrain, *Anti-Dissident Operations in the Philippines*, (Carlisle Barracks, PA: U.S. Army War College, [26 March 1956]), p. 6.

24. Comish, *The US and the Hukbalahap Insurrection*, p. 10; and F. Sionil Jose, "The Huks in Retrospect," p. 67.

25. Smith, *The Hukbalahap Insurgency*, p. 59.

26. Medardo Justiniano (Major, AFP), "Combat Intelligence," in *Counter-Guerrilla Operations in the Philippines 1946-53*, (Ft. Bragg, NC: U.S. Army Special Forces Center and School, [15 June 1961]), p. 40.

27. Azama, The *Huk and the NPA*, p. 19.

28. Justiniano, "Combat Intelligence," p. 40.

The Insurrection—Phase I (1946-1950)

1. Military Assistance Institute, *Country Study and Station Report: Philippines*, (Washington, D.C.: American Institute for Research, [1964], p. 21.

2. Robert R. Smith, *The Hukbalahap Insurgency: Economic, Political, and Military Factors*, (Washington, D.C.: Office of the Chief of Military History, [1963]), p. 65

3. Reginald J. Swarbrick, *The Evolution of Communist Insurgency in the Philippines*, (Quantico, VA: Marine Corps Command and Staff College, [7 June 1983]), p. 10; and Smith, *The Hukbalahap Insurgency*, p. 65.

7. Smith, *The Hukbalahap Insurgency*, p. 67.

8. Swarbrick, *The Evolution of Communist Insurgency*, p. 19.

9. Benedict Kerkvliet, *The Huk Rebellion: A Study of Peasant Revolt in the Philippines*, (Berkeley, CA: University of California Press, 1977), p. 170.

10. A later study conducted among four hundred captured Huks (sixty percent of whom were under thirty years of age), found that a full ninety-five percent of the interviewees claimed to have joined the Huk as a means to pursue land reform. Rodney S. Azama, *The Huks and the New People's Army: Comparing Two Postwar Filipino Insurgencies*, (Quantico, VA: Marine Corps Command and Staff College, [26 April 1985]), p. 79; and John Jameson, *The Philippine Constabulary Force, 1948-1954*, (Carlisle Barracks, PA: U.S. Army War College, [1971]), p. 26.

11. Harvey Averch and John Koehler, *The Huk Rebellion in the Philippines: Qualitative Approaches*, (Santa Monica, CA: The Rand Corporation, [August 1970]), p. 2; and Azama, *The Huk and the NPA*, p. 84.

12. Donald MacGrain, *Anti-Dissident Operations in the Philippines*, (Carlisle Barracks, PA: U.S. Army War College, [26 March 1956]), p. 5.

13. Ismael Lapus (Colonel, AFP), "The Communist Huk Enemy," in *Counter-Guerrilla Operations in the Philippines 1946-53*, (Ft. Bragg, NC: U.S. Army Special Forces Center and School, [15 June 1961]), p. 23; and Clifford M. White, *Why Insurgency was Defeated in the Philippines*. (Carlisle Barracks, PA: U.S. Army War College, [1967]), p. 6.

14. Azama, *The Huk and the NPA*, p. 188.

15. Ibid., p. 139.

16. A.H. Peterson, G.C. Reinhardt, and E.E. Conger, eds. *Symposium on the Role of Airpower in Counterinsurgency and Unconventional Warfare: The Philippine HUK Campaign*, (Santa Monica, CA: The Rand Corporation, [July 1963]), p. 9.

17. Luis A. Villa-Real, "Huk Hunting," *Army Combat Forces Journal* V, (November 1954), p. 36; and Azama, *The Huk and the NPA*, p. 140.

18. Azama, *The Huk and the NPA*, p. 141.

19. Ibid., p. 143.

20. Leo S. Comish, *The United States and the Philippine Hukbalahap Insurrection: 1946-54*, (Carlisle Barracks, PA: U.S. Army War College, [8 March 1971]), p. 54.

21. Ltr, Maj. Gen. George F. Moore (Cdr. U.S.A. Philippine-Ryukyus Command) to CSA, 10 May 1948, sub: Review of Jurisdictional Problems in the Philippines. MMRD, RG 319, box 25, folder P&O P.I.TS. NARA, Washington, D.C.

22. Ibid.

23. Andrew Molinar, *et al.*, *Undergrounds in Insurgent, Revolutionary, and Resistance Warfare*, A special report prepared for the Army by the Special Operations Research Office, (Washington, D.C.: American University, [1963]), p. 321; and Villa-Real, "Huk Hunting," p. 36.

24. Azama, *The Huk and the NPA*, p. 184.

25. Peterson, *et al.*, *Symposium on the Role of Airpower*, p. 14.

26. Napoleon D. Valeriano and Charles T.R. Bohannan, *Counter-Guerrilla Operations: the Philippine Experience*, (NY: Frederick A. Praeger, Publisher, 1966), p. 23; and United States Army, *Reference Book RB 31-3, Internal Defense Operations: A Case History, The Philippines 1946-1954*, (Ft. Leavenworth, KS: U.S. Army Command and General Staff College, 1967), p. 46.

27. Lapus, "The Communist Huk Enemy," p. 10.

28. Ibid., p. 17.

29. Ibid., p. 71.

30. Valeriano, "Military Operations," p. 28.

31. Lapus, "The Communist Huk Enemy," p. 17.

32. Valeriano and Bohannan, *Counter-Guerrilla Operations*, p. 32.

33. Azama, *The Huk and the NPA*, p. 127.

34. MacGrain, *Anti-Dissident Operations*, p. 7.

35. Peterson, *et al.*, *Symposium on the Role of Airpower*, p. 7.

36. Luis Taruc, *Born of the People*, (Bombay: People's Publishing House, LTD., 1953), p. 258.

37. Smith, *The Hukbalahap Insurgency*, p. 69; White, *Why Insurgency Was Defeated*, p. 6; and Azama, *The Huk and the NPA*, p. 131.

38. Azama, *The Huk and the NPA*, p. 137.

39. Lapus, "The Communist Huk Enemy," p. 18.

40. MacGrain, *Anti-Dissident Operations*, p. 9.

41. Smith, *The Hukbalahap Insurgency*, p. 82.

42. Azama, *The Huk and the N.P.A.*, p. 84; and Lapus, "The Communist Huk Enemy," p. 18.

43. Peterson, *et al.*, *Symposium on the Role of Airpower*, p. 16.

44. Smith, *The Hukbalahap Insurgency*, p. 84.

45. Military Assistance Institute.

46. Smith, *The Hukbalahap Insurgency*, p. 84.

47. William O. Douglas, *North From Malaya: Adventure on Five Fronts*, (NY: Doubleday and Company, Inc., 1953), p. 107.

48. Lapus, "The Communist Huk Enemy," pp. 19-20.

49. Smith, *The Hukbalahap Insurgency*, p. 92; and Peterson, *et al, Symposium on the Role of Airpower*, p. 17.

50. From a captured document of the Communist Party of the Philippines, "Document on Strategy and Tactics of the Philippine Communist Party," 22 December 1950, in MacGrain, *Anti-Dissident Operations*, p. 10.

51. Lapus, "The Communist Huk Enemy," p. 19.

52. MacGrain, *Anti-Dissident Operations*, p. 1.

53. Valeriano, "Military Operations," p. 26.

54. Fred Poole and Max Vanzi, *Revolution in the Philippines: The United States in a Hall of Cracked Missors*, (NY: McGraw-Hill Book Company, 1984), p. 26.

55. Smith, *The Hukbalahap Insurgency*, p. 73.

56. Ibid.; and White, *Why Insurgency Was Defeated*, p. 5.

57. Valeriano and Bohannan, *Counter-Guerrilla Operations*, p. 114.

58. William Moore, *The Hukbalahap Insurgency, 1948-1954: An Analysis of the Roles, Missions, and Doctrine of the Philippine Military Forces*, Report of the Institute of Advances Studies (Carlisle Barracks, PA: U.S. **Army** War College, [1971]), p. 11.

59. Peterson, *et al., Symposium on the Role of Airpower*, p. 15.

60. Valeriano, "Military Operations," p. 27.

61. Ibid., p. 36.

62. Ibid.

63. Ibid., p. 36.

64. Ibid., p. 37.

65. Ibid., p. 27.

66. Ibid., p. 29.

67. Smith, *The Hukbalahap Insurgency*, p. 77.

68. Valeriano, "Military Operations," p. 26.

69. Valeriano and Bohannan, *Counter-Guerrilla Operations*, pp. 117-118.

70. Ibid., p. 121; and Swarbrick, *The Evolution of Communist Insurgency*, p. 17.

71. Douglas, *North From Malaya*, p. 118; and Valeriano and Bohannan, *Counter-Guerrilla Operations*, p. 97.

72. Edwin J. McCarren, *Personal Leadership: An Element of National Power*, (Carlisle Barracks, PA: U.S. Army War College, [8 April 1966]). p. 28.

73. Peterson, *et al, Symposium on the Role of Airpower*, p. 15.

74. MacGrain, *Anti-Dissident Operations*, p. 11.

75. As of July 1950, AFP weapons and equipment included: .30 carbines; .30 light machine-guns; .30 M1 rifles; .30 Springfield rifles; .45 pistols; .50 machine-guns; 20mm, 37mm, 40mm and 57mm guns; 60mm, 81mm, and 105mm mortars; 75mm and 105mm howitzers; scout and armored cars; half-tracks; light and medium M5 and M4 tanks; and a variety of utility and cargo vehicles. Report, US JUSMAG-PHIL, "Weekly Summary of Activities," 20 July 1950. MMRD, RG 334 (Interservice Agencies) JUSMAG-Phil, box 6, NARA, Washington, D.C.

76. MacGrain, *Anti-Dissident Operations*, pp. 12-13.

77. Report, US JUSMAG-Phil, "Weekly Summary of Activities," 8 June 1950. MMRD, RG 334 (Interservice Agencies) JUSMAG Phil, AG Section, box 6, NARA, Washington, D.C.

Ramon Magsaysay, Edward Lansdale, and the JUSMAG

1. Edwin J. McCarren, *Personal Leadership: An Element of National Power*, (Carlisle Barracks, PA: U.S. Army War College, [8 April 1966]), p. 20.

2. Clarence G. Barrens, *I Promise: Magsaysay's Unique PSYOP "Defeats" HUKS*, (Ft. Leavenworth, KS: U.S. Army Command and General Staff College, [1970]), p. 46.

3. Barrens, *I Promise*, p. 47; and McCarren, *Personal Leadership*, p. 21.

4. Carlos P. Romulo and Marvin M. Gran, *The Magsaysay Story*, (NY: Van Rees Press, 1956), p. 78.

5. Irwin D. Smith, *The Philippine Operation Against the Huks: Do Lessons Learned Have Application Today?*, (Carlisle Barracks, PA: U.S. Army War College, [24 January 1968]), p. 6; and McCarren, *Personal Leadership*, p. 29.

6. Robert R. Smith, *The Hukbalahap Insurgency: Economic, Political and Military Factors*, (Washington, D.C.: Office of the Chief of Military History, [1963]), p. 100; and Smith, *Philippine Operations*, p. 86.

7. William L. Wardon, "Robin Hood of the Islands," *Saturday Evening Post* CCXXIV (January 12, 1952), p. 76.

8. Ismael Lapus (Col., AFP), "The Communist Huk Enemy," in *Counter-Guerrilla Operations in the Philippines 1946-53*, (Ft. Bragg, NC: U.S. Army Special Forces Center and School, [15 June 1961]), p. 20.

9. Barrens, *I Promise*, p. 54.

10. McCarren, *Personal Leadership*, p. 26.

11. A.H. Peterson, G.C. Reinhardt, and E.E. Conger, eds. *Symposium of the Role of Airpower in Counterinsurgency and Unconventional Warfare: The Philippine Huk Campaign*, (Santa Monica, CA: The Rand Corporation, [July 1963]), p. 18.

12. Smith, *The Hukbalahap Insurgency*, p. 102.

13. Barrens, *I Promise*, p. 70.

14. William B. Steele, *Internal Defense in the Philippines: 1946-1954*, (Carlisle Barracks, PA: US Army War College, [1967]), p. 8.

15. Barrens, *I Promise*, p. 86.

16. Peterson, *et al.*, *Symposium on the Role of Airpower*, p. 25.

17. In the first year of the program, Magsaysay received 59,000 telegrams, each of which was answered in three days or less. Clifford M. White, *Why Insurgency Was Defeated un the Philippines*, (Carlisle Barracks, PA: U.S. Army War College, [1967], p. 10.

18. Romulo, *The Magsaysay Story*, p. 105.

19. Reginald J. Swarbrick, *The Evolution of Communist Insurgency in the Philippines* (Quantico, VA: Marine Corps Command and Staff College, [7 June 1983]), p. 30.

20. Donald MacGrain, *Anti-Dissident Operations in the Philippines*, (Carlisle Barracks, PA: U.S. Army War College, [26 March 1956]), p. 16; and White, *Why Insurgency Was Defeated*, p. 7.

21. Charles T.R. Bohannan, "Unconventional Warfare," in *Counter-Guerrilla Operations in the Philippines 1946-53*, p. 55; and Napoleon Valeriano and Charles T.R. Bohannan, *Counter-Guerrilla Operations: The Philippine Experience*, (NY, Frederick A. Praeger, 1966), p. 207.

22. Military Assistance Institute, *Country Study and Station Report: Philippines*, (Washington, D.C.: American Institute for Research, [1964]), p. 49.

23. Smith, *The Hukbalahap Insurgency*, p. 108.

24. Ibid., p. 109.

25. Peterson, *et al.*, *Symposium on the Role of Airpower*, p. 30.

26. Smith, *The Hukbalahap Insurrection*, p. 109.

27. Smith, *Philippine Operations*, p. 10.

28. Peterson, *et al.*, *Symposium on the Role of Airpower*, p. 30; and Lansdale interview, p. 17.

29. Fred Poole and Max Vanzi, *Revolution in the Philippines: The United States in a Hall of Cracked Mirrors*, (NY: McGraw-Hill Book Company, 1984), p. 32.

30. Richard M. Leighton, Ralph Sanders, and Jose N. Tinio, *The HUK Rebellion: A Case Study in the Social Dynamics of Insurrection*, (Washington, D.C.: Industrial College of the Armed Forces, [March 1964]), p. 23.

31. Lansdale interview.

32. Ibid.

33. Edward G. Lansdale, *In the Midst of Wars*, (NY: Harper and Row, 1972), p. 46.

34. William O. Douglas, *North From Malaya: Adventure on Five Fronts*, (NY: Doubleday & Company, Inc. 1953), pp. 103-105.

35. Lansdale interview.

36. Ibid.

37. Ibid.

38. Ibid.

39. Memo, Gen. Omar Bradley to Sec. Def., 2 Feb 51, sub: Semi-Annual Appraisal of the JUSMAG to the Republic of the Philippines, MMRD, RG 330, box 74, NARA, Washington, D.C.

40. Leo S. Comish, Jr., *The United States and the Philippine Hukbalahap Insurrection: 1946-54*, (Carlisle Barracks, PA: U.S. Army War College, [8 March 1971]), p. 74; and Memo, Col. F.T. Folk to P&A, 8 Oct 48, sub: Personnel for JUSMAG-Philippines, MMRD, RG 319, box 25, folder P&O P.I. TS, NARA, Washington, D.C.

41. Memo, Maj. Gen. S.L. Scott to Maj. Gen. Duff, 6 Dec 50, sub: Agency to Army Outstanding MDAA Fund, MMRD, RG 330, box 74, folder 091.3 Phil., NARA, Washington, D.C.

42. Memo, J.O. Bell to Maj. Gen. S.L. Scott, 30 Jun 51, MMRD, RG 330, box 74, folder 111 FY 50-52, NARA, Washington, D.C.

43. Memo, CSA for JCS, 24 Oct 50, sub: Proposed Installation of a Medium Wave Transmitter, JCS 1519/51, MMRD, RG 330, box 31, folder CCS 686.9 Phil Islands, NARA, Washington, D.C.

44. Memo, J.T. Forbes to Chairman of Mission and FMACC, 27 Sep 50, sub: MDAP Organization-Philippines, MMRD, RG 330, box 74, folder 0005-333 Phil, NARA, Washington, D.C.; and Valeriano and Bohannan, *Counter-Guerrilla Operations*, p. 123.

45. Lansdale, *Midst of War*, p. 19.

46. Memo, F.C. Nash to Sec Def, 16 Jun 52, sub: Modifications to JUSMAG to the Philippine Directive, MMRD, RG 330, box 74, NARA, Washington, D.C.

47. Memo, OSD to JCS, 14 Jan 52, sub: Modification to JUSMAG to the Philippines Directive, MMRD, RG 330, box 74, folder 121, NARA, Washington, D.C.; and Note, Sec of JCS to holders of JCS 1519/44 (The Philippines), 28 Jul 50, MMRD, RG 330, box 31, folder CCS 686.9, NARA, Washington, D.C.

48. Msg., War Department to CINCFE, 13 Aug 47, MMRD, RG 319, box 25, folder P&O P.I. TS, NARA, Washington, D.C.

49. Ltr., Lt. Gen. A.C. Wedemeyer to CINCFE, 11 Oct 48, sub: Defense Plans of the Philippines, MMRD, RG 319, box 25, folder P&O, NARA, Washington, D.C.

50. Memo, Maj. Gen. L.L. Lemnitzer to Sec Def, 25 Apr 50, sub: US Aid to the Philippines, MMRD, RG 330, box 74, NARA, Washington, D.C.

51. During 1950, the AFP received the following items from surplus US stocks: .30 M1 and M2 carbines; .30 M1 and 1903 rifles; .30 machine guns; .50 machine guns; 60mm, 81mm, and 105mm mortars; .45 pistols; 37mm, 57mm, 40mm, 75mm guns and recoilless rifles; and 75mm and 105mm howitzers; 1/4 ton, 3/4 ton, 2 1/2 ton utility and cargo trucks; scout and armored cars; half-tracks; and light and medium M4 and M5 tanks. Memo, Leffingwell to Gen. Lemnitzer, 17 Jul 50; and Memo, Col. M. W. Brewster to Director Military Assistance, OSD, 17 Jul 50, both in MMRD, RG 330, box 74, folder 0005-333 Phil., NARA Washington, D.C.

52. Ltr., Scott to Arthur Foye, Dec 50, MMRD, RG 330, box 74, folder 091.3, NARA, Washington, D.C.

53. Lansdale interview.

54. Ibid; and Memo, Col. Nyquist to Gen. Olmsted, undated, MMRD, RG 330, box 31, folder 091.3, NARA, Washington, D.C.

55. JUSMAG, *Proposed MDAP for the Republic of the Philippines FY 1951,* 25 Mar 50, MMRD, RG 330, box 74, NARA, Washington, D.C.

56. Memo, Col. K.R. Kreps to Sec. Army, 3 Mar 52, sub: Special Fund for the Armed Forces of the Philippines; and ltr., W.C. Foster to President Truman, 21 Feb 52, both in MMRD, RG 330, box 74, folder 091.3 and 121, NARA, Washington, D.C.

57. Luis Taruc, *Born of the People,* (NY: International Publishers, 1953), p. 251.

58. Ltr., Gen. Omar Bradley to Maj. Gen. Hobbs, 31 Aug 50; and Memo, J.T. Forbes to Chairman of Mission, both in MMRD, RG 330, box 31, folder CCS 686.9 Phil Islands, NARA, Washington, D.C.

59. American Embassy, Manila, *Country Statement,* 17 Feb 53, MMRD, RG 330, box 12, folder 111 FY 50 Phil, NARA, Washington, D.C.

60. JUSMAG, *Submission of the Director of Mutual Security - FY 1954 Program,* 6 Sep 54, MMRD, RG 330, box 74, folder 111 FY 53 Phil, NARA, Washington, D.C.

61. JUSMAG, *Country Statement.*

The Insurrection—Phase II (1950-1955)

1. Napoleon D. Valeriano and Charles T.R. Bohannan, *Counter-Guerrilla Operations: The Philippine Experience,* (NY: Frederick A. Praeger, Publisher, 1966), p. 133.

2. Ibid., pp. 132 and 257-266.

3. Reginald J. Swarbrick, *The Evolution of Communist Insurgency in the Philippines,* (Quantico, VA: Marine Corps Command and Staff College, [7 June 1983]), p. 33.

4. Valeriano and Bohannan, *Counter-Guerrilla Operations,* p. 68.

5. Irwin D. Smith, *The Philippine Operations Against the Huks: Do Lessons Learned Have Application Today?,* Carlisle Barracks, PA: U.S. Army War College, [24 January 1968]), pp. 1 and 8.

6. Charles T.R. Bohannan, "Unconventional Warfare," in *Counter-Guerrilla Operations in the Philippines 1946-53,* (Ft. Bragg, NC: U.S. Army Special Forces Center and School, [1961]), p. 61.

7. Donald MacGrain, *Anti-Dissident Operations in the Philippines,* (Carlisle Barracks, PA: U.S. Army War College, [26 March 1956]), p. 23.

8. Clarence G. Barrens, *I Promise: Magsaysay's Unique PSYOP "Defeats" HUKS,* (Ft. Leavenworth, KS: U.S. Army Command and General Staff College, [1970]), p. 41.

9. A.H. Peterson, G.C. Reinhardt, and E.E. Conger, eds. *Symposium on the Role of Airpower in Counterinsurgency and Unconventional Warfare: The Philippine HUK Campaign,* (Santa Monica, CA: The Rand Corporation, [July 1963]), p. 50.

10. Valeriano and Bohannan, *Counter-Guerrilla Operations,* p. 136.

11. The U.S. refused to sell napalm munitions to the Philippines. Bohannan, "Communist Insurgency in the Philippines," p. 50.

12. Ibid., pp. 67-69; and Napoleon D. Valeriano (Colonel, AFP), "Military Operations," in *Counter-Guerrilla Operations in the Philippines 1946-53,* (Ft. Bragg, NC: U.S. Army Special Forces Center and School, [15 June 1961]), p. 32.

13. Bohannan, "Communist Insurgency in the Philippines," p. 61.

14. William O. Douglas, *North from Malaya: Adventure on Five Fronts,* (NY: Doubleday & Company, Inc. 1953), p. 120.

15. Valeriano and Bohannan, *Counter-Guerrilla Operations,* p. 153.

16. Peterson, *et al., Symposium on the Role of Airpower,* p. 50.

17. Luis A. Villa-Real, "Huk Hunting," *Army Combat Forces Journal* V (November 1954), p. 35.

18. Peterson, *et al., Symposium on the Role of Airpower,* p. 29; and Valeriano, Military Operations," p. 32.

19. Valeriano and Bohannan, *Counter-Guerrilla Operations*, p. 45.
20. Valeriano, "Military Operations," p. 32; and Interview with Lansdale.
21. JUSMAG, *Semi-Annual Report, July - December 1951*, 15 Jan 52, MMRD, RG 334, box 6, NARA, Washington, D.C.; and Interview with Lansdale.
22. Valeriano, "Military Operations," p. 33.
23. Smith, *The Hukbalahap Insurgency*, p. 123.
24. Medardo Justiniano (Maj., AFP), "Combat Intelligence" in *Counter-Guerrilla Operations*, pp. 44-46.
25. Ibid., p. 42.
26. Ibid., p. 47.
27. MacGrain, *Anti-Dissident Operations*, p. 22; and Valeriano and Bohannan, *Counter-Guerrilla Operations*, p. 153.
28. Douglas, *North From Malaya*, p. 111.
29. Ismael Lapus (Col., AFP), "The Communist Huk Enemy," in *Counter-Guerrilla Operations*, p. 22; and Valeriano and Bohannan, *Counter-Guerrilla Operations*, p. 68.
30. Special Operations Research Office, *Peak Organized Strength of Guerrillas and Government Forces in Algeria, Nagaland, Ireland, Indonesia, South Vietnam, Malaya, Philippines, and Greece*, (Washington, D.C.: The American University, [1965]), p. 16.
31. Lapus, "The Communist Huk Enemy," p. 21.
32. Rodney S. Azama, *The Huks and the New People's Army: Comparing Two Postwar Filipino Insurgencies*, (Quantico, VA: Marine Corps Command and Staff College, [26 April 1985]), p. 148.
33. Ibid.
34. Valeriano and Bohannan, *Counter-Guerrilla Operations*, p. 134.
35. JUSMAG, *Semi-Annual Report, 1 July - 30 December 1951*, 11 Jan 52, MMRD, RG 334, box 6, NARA, Washington, D.C. ; and Valeriano and Bohannan, *Counter-Guerrilla Operations*, p. 155.
36. JUSMAG, *Semi-Annual Report Jul-Dec 51*.
37. Barrens, *I Promise*, p. 56.
38. Edwin J. McCarren, *Personal Leadership: An Element of National Power*, (Carlisle Barracks, PA: U.S. Army War College, [8 April 1966]), p. 30.
39. Smith, *The Hukbalahap Insurgency*, p. 111.
40. MacGrain, *Anti-Dissident Operations*, p. 25.
41. Ibid.
42. JUSMAG, *Semi-Annual Report, 1 January - 30 June 1952*, 1 Aug 52; and Smith, *The Hukbalahap Insurgency*, pp. 121-122.
43. Pomeroy later wrote of his Huk experience in *The Forest*. New York: International Publishers, 1963. This volume provides an interesting view of the insurrection and its causes from the guerrilla standpoint.
44. Peterson, *et al.*, *Symposium on the Role of Airpower*, p. 26.
45. Villa-Real, "Huk Hunting," p. 33 and Smith, *The Hukbalahap Insurgency*, p. 119.
46. Villa-Real, "Huk Hunting," pp. 34-35.
47. Report, JUSMAG to CINCPAC, "Monthly Summary of Activities for April," 9 May 53, MMRD, RG 334, box 8, NARA, Washington, D.C.
48. Carlos P. Romulo and Marvin M. Gran, *The Magsaysay Story* (NY: Van Rees Press, 1956), p. 192.
49. McCarren, *Personal Leadership*, p. 32.
50. Leonard S. Kenworth, *Leaders of New Nations*, (NY: Doubleday and Company, 1959), p. 210.
51. Smith, *The Hukbalahap Insurgency*, p. 113; and Barrens, *I Promise*, p. 60.
52. Barrens, *I Promise*, p. 63.
53. Report, JUSMAG to CINCPAC, "Monthly Report of Activities for January 1954," 10 Feb 54, MMRD, RG 330, box 46, NARA, Washington, D.C.; McCarren, *Personal Leadership*, p. 36; and Military Assistance Institute, *Country Study*, p. 5.
54. In August, Taruc was sentenced to twelve years imprisonment and given a 20,000 peso fine—considered a very light sentence. Reports, JUSMAG to CINCPAC, "Monthly Summary of Activities for August 1954," 10 Sep 54; and "Report for September 1954," 9 Oct 54, both in MMRD, RG 330, box 46, NARA, Washington, D.C.
55. Reports, JUSMAG to CINCPAC, "Monthly Summary for June 1954," 10 Jul 54; and "Monthly Report for February 1955."
56. Ibid.; and Swarbrick, *The Evolution of Communist Insurgency*, p. 38.

Conclusion

1. US Department of State Bulletin, *Remarks of President Eisenhower and Secretary of State Dulles on US Commemorative Stamp Honoring Magsaysay*, September 16, 1957, p. 472.
2. Interview with Edward G. Lansdale.

BIBLIOGRAPHY

BOOKS:

Blaufarb, Douglas S. *The Counter-Insurgency Era: U.S. Doctrine and Performance*. New York: The Free Press, 1977.

Douglas, William O. *North from Malaya: Adventure on Five Fronts*. New York: Doubleday, 1953.

Kerkvliet, Benedict J. *The HUK Rebellion: A Study of Peasant Revolt in the Philippines*. Berkeley: University of California Press, 1977.

Lachica, Eduardo. *The HUKS: Philippine Agrarian Society in Revolt*. New York: Praeger, 1971.

Lansdale, Edward G. *In the Midst of Wars: An American's Mission to Southeast Asia*. New York: Harper and Row, 1972.

Manchester, William. *American Caesar*, Boston: Little, Brown and Company, 1978.

Meyer, Milton W. *A Diplomatic History of the Philippines*. Honolulu: University of Hawaii Press, 1965.

Pomeroy, William J. ed. *Guerrilla Warfare and Marxism*. New York: International Publishers, 1969.

_____. *The Forest*. New York: International Publishers, 1963.

Poole, Fred and Vanzi, Max. *Revolution in the Philippines: The United States in a Hall of Cracked Mirrors*. New York: McGraw-Hill, 1984.

Romulo, Carlos P. and Gran, Marvin M., *The Magsaysay Story*. New York: Van Rees Press, 1956.

Smith, Robert A. *Philippine Freedom 1946-1958*. New York: Columbia University Press, 1958.

Taruc, Luis. *Born of the People*. Bombay: People's Publishing House, 1953.

Valeriano, Napoleon D. and Bohannan, Charles T.R. *Counter-Guerrilla Operations: The Philippines Experience*. New York: Frederick A. Praeger, 1966.

PERIODICALS:

Jocano, F. Landa. "Ideology and Radical Movements in the Philippines: An Anthropological Overview." *Solidarity* No.102 (1985), pp. 47-63.

Sionil, F. Jose. "The Huks in Retrospect." *Solidarity* No. 102 (1985), pp. 64-103.

Villa-Real, LTC Luis A. "Huk Hunting." *Army Combat Journal* V (November 1954), pp. 32-36.

REPORTS:

Averch, Harvey and Koehler, John. *The HUK Rebellion in the Philippines: Quantitative Approaches*. RM-6254-ARPA. Santa Monica, CA: The Rand Corporation, [August 1970].

Azama, Rodney S. *The Huks and the New People's Army: Comparing Two Postwar Filipino Insurgencies*. student thesis. Quantico, VA: Marine Corps Command and Staff College, [26 April 1985].

Barrens, Clarence G. *I Promise: Magsaysay's Unique PSYOP "Defeats" HUKS*. student thesis. Ft. Leavenworth, KS: U.S. Army Command and General Staff College, [1970].

Bohannan, Charles T.R. "The Communist Insurgency in the Philippines: The Hukbalahap, 1942-1955," in *Supporting Case Studies for Isolating the Guerrillas*. Washington, D.C.: Historical Evaluation and Research Organization, [1966].

Center for Research in Social Systems. *Internal Defense Against Insurgency: Six Cases*. Washington, D.C.: American University, Social Science Research Institute, [December 1966].

Comish, Leo S. Jr. *The United States and the Philippine Hukbalahap Insurrection: 1946-1954*. Carlisle Barracks, PA: U.S. Army War College, [8 March 1971].

Leighton, Richard M., Sanders, Ralph, and Tinio, Jose N. *The HUK Rebellion: A Case Study in the Social Dynamics of Insurrection*. Publication No. R-231. Washington, D.C.: Industrial College of the Armed Forces, [March 1964].

Lewis, Jesse W. Jr. *A Successful Approach Toward Countering Insurgency—Philippines, 1946-1955*. student research paper. Carlisle Barracks, PA: U.S. Army War College, [20 February 1973].

MacGrain, Donald. *Anti-Dissident operations in the Philippines*. student study. Carlisle Barracks, PA: U.S. Army War College, [26 March 1956].

McCarren, Edwin J. *Personal Leadership: An Element of National Power*. student thesis AWC Log. 66-4-48U. Carlisle Barracks, PA: U.S. Army War College, [8 April 1966].

Military Assistance Institute. *Country Study and Station Report: Philippines*. Washington, D.C.: American Institute for Research, [1964].

Peterson, A.H., Reinhardt, G.C., and Conger, E.E. eds. *Symposium on the Role of Airpower in Counterinsurgency and Unconventional Warfare: The Philippine HUK Campaign*. RM-3652-PR. Santa Monica, California: The Rand Corporation, [July 1963].

Sens, Andrew D. *A Summary of the U.S. Role in Insurgency Situations in the Philippine Islands 1899-1955*. Washington, D.C.: American University, [18 December 1964].

Smith, Irwin D. *The Philippine Operations Against the Huks: Do Lessons Learned Have Application Today?* student paper. Carlisle Barracks, PA: U.S. Army War College, [24 January 1968].

Smith, Robert R. *The Hukbalahap Insurgency: Economic, Political, and Military Factors.* Washington, D.C.: Office of the Chief of Military History, [1963].

Steele, William B. *Internal Defense in the Philippines: 1946-1954.* student paper. Carlisle Barracks, PA: U.S. Army War College, [1967].

Swarbrick, Reginald J. *The Evolution of Communist Insurgency in the Philippines.* student paper. Quantico, VA: Marine Corps Command and Staff College, [7 June 1983].

United States Army. *Reference Book RB-31-3, Internal Defense Operations: A Case History, The Philippines 1946-1954.* Ft. Leavenworth, KS: U.S. Army Command and General Staff College, [1967].

United States Department of State. *The Philippine Rehabilitation Program: Report to the President by the Secretary of State*, Far Eastern Series, Washington, D.C.: Government Printing Office, [31 August 1954].

White, Clifford M. *Why Insurgency Was Defeated in the Philippines.* student paper. Carlisle Barracks, PA: U.S. Army War College, [1967].

GOVERNMENT DOCUMENTS:

National Archives. Modern Military Records Division. Record Groups 218, 319, 330, and 334, Washington, D. C.

United States Army Special Warfare Center and School, *Counter-Guerrilla Operations in the Philippines, 1946-1953.* Ft. Bragg, NC: United States Army [15 June 1961].

UNPUBLISHED SOURCES:

Lansdale, Edward G., Maj. Gen. (Retired), United States Air Force. Historical Documentation. U.S. Air Force Oral History Program. 25 April 1971.

_____. McLean, Virginia. Interview. 3 March 1986.

Taruc, Luis. Interview by Bruce Nussbaum. 29 May 1974. Bentley Library, University of Michigan, Ann Arbor, Michigan.

CORDS in Charge
Vietnam, 1967–1972

Douglas S. Blaufarb

In the pages that follow, we will trace the course of the action program undertaken by the new CORDS organization with an inevitable emphasis upon American measures and policies, for this is the principal interest of our study, and, besides, the record is clear that pacification was, in the entire period from 1963 to the end, an American initiative. The Americans developed virtually all of the programs and concepts (sometimes, as in the case of Revolutionary Development, in collaboration with some exceptional Vietnamese), established priorities, and contributed most of the resources. On the other hand, it remained entirely an advisory program which would succeed or fail to the degree that the GVN willingly and energetically carried out its share which was, in number of people involved, overwhelmingly the larger part of the effort. The Americans could advise and prod and persuade but they could not do the job themselves. The story of the CORDS phase of pacification is thus the story of how the Americans organized, managed, and implemented an effort to induce the Vietnamese to do the right amounts of the right kinds of things so as to secure the countryside and gain the willing support of the rural population.

PROJECT TAKEOFF

Komer did not delay in putting to use the powers and resources of his new office. He moved rapidly to obtain certain policy decisions which were critical to his concept of the needs of pacification and to fill obvious gaps in the program array with new or revised programs. One such gap which had long concerned all participants was the absence of continuous security for the hamlets. In an attempt to provide the needed security capability he sought a major policy decision at the start, assigning to CORDS responsibility for support, advice, and training of ARVN's paramilitary auxiliaries, the Regional and Popular Forces. The decision was a critical addition to CORDS' ability to affect directly the security environment in the countryside and it led to a greatly enlarged program of support and development for these neglected rural units. Numbers were steadily increased, reaching a half million in 1970; weapons, which had consisted of World War II leftovers, were replaced by the M-16 and other modern light armament. The entire paramilitary force was re-trained by five-man mobile advisory teams, eventually number-

Blaufarb, Douglas. (1977). "CORDS in Charge: Vietnam, 1967-1972" *The Counter-insurgency Era: U.S. Doctrine and Performance, 1950 to Present* (pp. 243–312). London: The Free Press, 1977.

ing 355. They conducted the training in the field and often served in an advisory capacity to local commanders. ARVN was persuaded to upgrade its RF/PF staff and replace the colonel commanding with a lieutenant general.'

The decision was an early example of the value of the CORDS concept, for it is unlikely that MACV would have agreed otherwise to turn control of such a large military advisory program, intimately involved with ARVN, to a civilian pacification management. Even more remarkable was Westmoreland's agreement, early in the life of CORDS, to remove the MACV sector advisory teams from the chain of command which tied them to the division advisory teams and thus to the regular ARVN command channels. ARVN division commands, closely controlling the pacification activities in each province, had become enmeshed in province politics and power rivalries to the detriment of both their primary functions and of pacification. Although the Americans could not directly change ARVN's internal arrangements, the argument was made that ARVN would eventually follow any pattern established by MACV. Komer therefore made the recommendation and Westmoreland, previously opposed to the change, now accepted it.[2] Ultimately, ARVN did the same. Both chains of command were now in tandem and had eliminated a purely military link at a critical level.

These were significant improvements, although their impact should not be overstated. The RF and PF were substantially improved in the ensuing years and came to be a major factor in establishing better rural security; improved capability, however, by no means always guaranteed improved results. The better-trained and better-armed militia performed unevenly, depending on the quality of local leadership. Often they continued to button themselves up in their fortified outposts at night instead of patrolling and laying ambushes. They were sometimes slow to respond to calls for help from hamlets, especially at night, and they were frequently used for personal security and static duties at the pleasure of the province or district chiefs. Although division commands played a reduced role in local security arrangements, the local government was still in the hands of ARVN officers on active duty. CORDS could and did attempt to transfer individuals who had behaved corruptly or otherwise

demonstrated incapacity, but changing individuals did not change the system. In addition to being a national defense force, ARVN was also a political cabal whose first priorities were to perpetuate the system and to protect the safety, livelihood, and future prospects of those who con-trolled it. CORDS was thus able to bring about changes which were out of the reach of any previous American organization, but that very fact tended to highlight the outer limits of the technical, administrative approach to the fundamental problem of Vietnam which was, first and last, a political problem.

THE ORIGINS OF PHOENIX

Such considerations anticipate somewhat. Returning to our account, CORDS, while busying itself with the establishment of a headquarters staff, managed also to move systematically on substantive programs, committed to the principle that American resources, skills, and dedication, effectively focused, would eventually prevail upon the Vietnamese to alter their behavior patterns.

One of the early priorities was the attempt to improve the exploitation of the growing volume of intelligence on the Viet Cong and to focus that process on the most important target, namely, the enemy's directing organization, the government organs and structure of the Viet Cong. Earlier we noted that an elaborate and sophisticated network based on the People's Revolutionary Party organization managed all VC activity. Within the American bureaucracy it was dubbed "the VC infrastructure." In 1967 the CIA proposed that all U.S. intelligence agencies pool their information on the VC infrastructure at the district, province, and Saigon levels and agree on assigning responsibility for exploitation. Permanent centers were proposed at province and district levels staffed by the participating agencies. At Saigon, a permanent staff was to be established, headed by a CIA officer, to whom other agencies would also assign staff. Its function would be to support, monitor, and guide the local centers in the field. Exploitation—that is, the taking of action on the intelligence screened, collated, and put into usable form at the district centers—was the responsibility initially of the subsector adviser, who was to avail himself of the most suitable resources in the area. In a large number of cases the Provincial Reconnaissance Units were most readily available, for the Americans had a more direct role in their control, but police and military units could also be called on. It should be made clear at this point that this entire U.S. structure was intended to support and advise Vietnamese operating units. From the beginning of Phoenix, the Americans proposed but the Vietnamese disposed of the operating units and used or, as often happened, mis-used them in accordance with their own notions. At the outset no effort was made to persuade the Vietnamese to establish a counterpart staff structure.

This program in its origins was entirely American and largely the initiative of the CIA. It was first called the Intelligence Coordination and Exploitation Program (ICEX) and began to take shape in the regions during the last months of OCO. The Vietnamese were advised of the plan but were not pressed immediately to adopt it as their own. That, in brief, was the origin of the most controversial of the U.S. pacification efforts, the Phoenix program. To its originators it seemed the essence of straightforward common sense, a managerial device to pull together a scattered and diverse effort by often competing and duplicating units, to focus it, eliminate inefficiencies, and direct it precisely against what many believed to be the enemy jugular. In this spirit, Komer enthusiastically adopted it, obtained COMUSMACV's endorsement, and assigned it a high priority. For a new, more impressive name, he chose Phoenix, an approximate translation of Phung Hoang—"all-seeing bird"—already being used by the Vietnamese. He began discussions with the Vietnamese leading to their adoption in 1968 of a counterpart staff structure also bearing the name Phung Hoang. CORDS also proposed for it one of its preferred management techniques, that of assigning quotas of Viet Cong Infrastructure (VCI) members who were to be "neutralized," i.e., eliminated by whatever means (they were not specified), in each month.

This decision can stand as a symbol for the mismarriage of enthusiastic American managerial technique with Vietnamese indifference that produced the Phoenix failure. Phoenix made certain unexamined assumptions which proved to be damaging to its purposes and to pacification. These assumptions were shared by all of those who saw effective counterinsurgency as the heart of the matter in Vietnam, including the British experts led by Sir Robert Thompson.[3] The concept, in fact, owed much to British experience in Malaya and to the belief, frequently voiced by Thompson, that a program which ignored the enemy infrastructure was doomed to failure in the long term, if not the short. For, the theory held, the infrastructure of dedicated Communist cadres gave the enemy his staying power, his ability to adapt to new conditions, to regenerate his strength, and to stay the course of a "protracted war." The threat, therefore, could not finally be disposed of while the VCI survived intact.

Among the unexamined assumptions made by the program were several that related to operational matters. Thus, it was assumed that the various competing and jealous Vietnamese intelligence services could be forced to cooperate, share information, and contribute qualified personnel to a combined effort. In the event, lacking the power of command, the U.S. was unable to force cooperation. The sharing of information was meager and the Vietnamese police and military tended to assign their least valued personnel to the district and provincial centers. They had more urgent priorities, including the goal of advancing their own positions in competition with rival services. Pooling of effort in a center where service identity was merged in a larger whole did not serve that purpose. The Police Special Branch, which should have been the key to an improved effort, was a serious offender.

Again, it was assumed that the arrest of infrastructure members would remove them from the picture. The reality was quite different. The judicial and correctional systems were inadequate to cope with a large new influx of prisoners. Bribery and official indifference together with the shortage of facilities led to many prisoners being released soon after their apprehension. One estimate made by Phoenix advisers stated that in 1969 only 30 percent of the suspects brought in through the Phoenix mechanism were eventually sentenced and served jail terms.[4]

But the most serious misconception underlying Phoenix lay in the belief that the purpose of the Vietnamese police and intelligence services was the same as that of the Americans. With some honorable exceptions, it was the same as that of ARVN described above, to preserve the system and its benefits for the individuals and groups that controlled it, the benefits being understood to include in many cases the opportunity to squeeze the population and to appropriate the resources made available by the Americans. By establishing a nationwide organization and system and bringing pressure to bear through it upon the police everywhere, Phoenix was forcing the police and the local authorities to assume a task which those concerned apparently considered unrealistic and far too difficult. They believed, it would appear, that the Viet Cong infrastructure was so well dug in and so effective as to be beyond the reach of any tools available to them. To satisfy the demands of Phoenix, they merely had to fulfill a quota which they proceeded to do by a variety of techniques, the most common of which was to list as VCI individuals killed or captured in routine military sweeps. Although the purpose of the system was to generate *targeted* operations against specific high-level VCI members, a large number of each monthly "bag" was made up, in fact, of untargeted suspects labeled as VCI after the fact. Another technique that helped fill the quota was to arrest as VCI the low-level peasants who merely paid taxes or joined VC mass organizations because they had no choice. In fact, they were not VCI at all. Moreover, it later turned out that some of the VCI "eliminations" were completely faked.

Although, therefore, Phoenix was not a viable concept in the Vietnam of the 1960s, many misconceptions have seriously distorted its intent and structure. Thus, it was not a new organization or activity but a staff whose purpose was to rationalize and focus a confused tangle of ongoing police and intelligence operations against the Communist apparatus. It was not a large effort in terms of manpower and other resources: under five hundred advisers were assigned to it, most of them from the Army. Furthermore, while the concept was American, the execution was largely Vietnamese. The Americans had only the control they could generate through their corps of advisers at various levels. Often this amounted, in effect, to no control at all.

More remains to be said on the subject at a later point. In any event, the apparently reason-

able and straightforward case for a major effort against the VCI was embraced by the CORDS leadership, and the program became a priority in "Project Takeoff," the initial set of goals set for the new organization to be accomplished in 1967. In his account Komer summarizes these goals as "aimed principally at improving 1968 pacification planning, accelerating the Chieu Hoi program ... mounting the new attack on the VC infrastructure, expanding and improving RVNAF support of pacification—especially RF/PF—expanding the RD effort, stepping up aid to the mounting number of refugees, revamping and strengthening of the police and land reform."[5] The priorities comprised the most pressing immediate problems or represented essential foundations for future progress. "Project Takeoff" had the further purpose and effect of impressing upon both Americans and Vietnamese that a serious new effort was under way to realize the goals of pacification.

THE HES DILEMMA

Much prominence also came to be given at this time to a new addressing of the perennial problem of how to measure such progress—or lack of it—as the program may have achieved. The goal of pacification was to change attitudes and thus behavior. Good management practice requires that the managers of such a complex enterprise have readily available a measurement of how well their efforts are succeeding, if possible with sufficient accompanying detail to permit the pinpointing of problem areas. But attitudes, especially in so exotic a culture as Vietnam, are not easily pinned down and measured, much less as promptly, frequently, and comprehensively as the managers required. After unhappy experience with such devices as measuring incidents of violence, captured weapons, and the like, or of counting U.S. inputs (dollars, tin roofing, cement, and so on) a new approach was attempted. Down at district level, the U.S. staff (MACV advisers under CORDS) were given a list of factors, eighteen in all, which they were to rate on a six-point scale (A through F). The factors corresponded roughly to the criteria of the RD teams. Six concerned security, six social and economic factors, and six political factors. In effect, they evaluated some elements of village conditions relating to pacification, and they measured administrative success or failure in carrying out the requirements of the program or VC success in subversion and terrorism. The ratings were then averaged to produce a grade from A (secure) to F (VC-controlled) in some ten thousand hamlets throughout the country.

The effort was a bold and highly controversial attempt to become independent of the GVN. Its weakness lay in the fact that it depended on the inputs of hundreds of subsector advisers who were in effect judging their own work, whose tours were short, and who were often inexperienced. On the other hand, it strove, unlike earlier systems, to measure elements that were meaningful in relation to the goal. As a management tool it had its usefulness, especially over time, in indicating general trends; but as an absolute measurement of success, a way of determining how close or how far off lay final victory, it was inadequate. Unfortunately, this was the interpretation most often placed upon the figures in public discussion. Later, a more sophisticated version, called HES/70, developed over several years of experimentation, was put into operation. It was more reliable because it attempted to eliminate subjective judgment in assigning grades and simply posed questions of fact with the grading done in Saigon, using a "weighted formula not known to the field."[6]

HES attracted a great deal of attention and represented a considerable effort, but its main interest for us is as a symbol of the dilemma the U.S. found itself faced with in Vietnam, especially in regard to pacification, which was supported and advised but not managed or controlled by the Americans. Under such circumstances, a properly functioning allied government, reaching down to all levels of the rural community, should have routinely been able to provide the kind of rough-and-ready indicators that would adequately depict the trends in security and development and even in attitudes that CORDS needed to know. But the Vietnamese apparatus could not cope with the reality of its problems in the country-side, for the system, in effect, did not wish to know and confront the hard facts. Left to its own devices, it would simply produce the kind of information desired by the regime with little reference to actuality. The Americans were therefore obliged to institute a large new program which could only be a clumsy substitute for the natural feedback of functioning local government. The problem, in truth, traced to the rural/urban gap which split the governors from the governed and which underlay all the bitter dilemmas of Vietnam.

THE MILITARY SIDE OF THE COIN

The organization of CORDS in mid-1967 gave pacification activities a notable increase in relative importance, in visibility, and in vigor of address against the problems of the countryside. Although much of the activity was internal to the American mission, there was, in Saigon at least, a sense of progress which reflected organizational improvements as much as anything else. One indicator—the figure of persons rallying to the government side in 1967—showed a dramatic increase in the first half of the year and this contributed to the feeling of growing success, leading some to talk of "the smell of victory" in the air.

Pacification was only one element in the complex situation—although the critical one—and remained, despite its growing importance, a relatively minor facet of the war in terms of numbers of men, resources, and attention it absorbed. In 1967, U.S. armed strength in Vietnam increased by one hundred thousand reaching 486,000 by the end of the year.[7] Other Free World forces reached fifty-nine thousand.[8] The combat operations of these forces monopolized the attention of the press and the world in general. Several large operations in 1967, particularly those called "Cedar Falls" into the "Iron Triangle" and "Junction City" into "War Zone C," seemed to be major victories. They took the U.S. and accompanying ARVN units into zones which had long been enemy strongholds, caused heavy enemy casualties, and resulted in the capture of major supply caches, headquarters areas, tunnel complexes, and the like. Such operations contributed heavily to the feeling that success was near.

The strategy followed by the military was now firmly established. The bulk of the U.S. firepower and about half its combat force would be directed against Communist main force units to prevent them from concentrating for attack and to "drive . . . [them] away from the priority pacification area."[9] This "search and destroy" mission represented the offensive side of the military strategy and reflected the traditional U.S. Army concept of the proper use of its great superiority in technical capability, firepower, and mobility. It was used with the actual purpose of inflicting such heavy casualties on the enemy that he would be unable to sustain them and thus be forced to yield. In the absence of any other measure of how this phase of the war was succeeding (terrain, in this type of conflict, being irrelevant), the military focused on enemy casualties, or "body count." It was a notoriously inaccurate measurement, prone to exaggeration or even fabrication. In the pursuit of such goals, the troops were copiously supported by artillery and air power, including B-52 bombers which were used virtually as a tactical weapon in support of troops. These fearsome aircraft could each drop 100 five hundred-pound bombs. Released in carefully timed sequence, the bombs from one flight could churn up the earth for a square mile and do it with great precision. They flew at such great heights as to be inaudible and invisible from the ground and the sudden eruption of frightful destruction from a silent sky struck terror in the hearts of the victims. The use of chemical defoliants to strip the jungle of its cover, of Rome plows to clear large jungle areas which had been enemy sanctuaries, of helicopters to move troops into and out of quick-striking attacks, these were some of the technical triumphs deployed in the effort to punish the enemy so heavily that he would be unable to sustain his losses over any consider-able length of time. In order to employ such techniques effectively, the Army preferred to operate in remote, thinly populated areas. Said General Westmoreland, "This would enable the full U.S. fire-power potential to be employed without danger of civilian casualties."[10]

Some Vietnamese units, comprised largely of specialized elite units such as marines, airborne forces, and rangers also participated in the attempt to search out and destroy the enemy force. But in 1966, the Vietnamese command had, under American urging and with some reluctance, agreed to consecrate the bulk of its regular forces to the support of pacification, stationing them in populated areas where they would be available to protect the hamlets undergoing the process of reclamation from VC control. Other American and allied units, constituting more than half of

their combat strength, were supposed to be assigned to work with them in this task.

This division of labor seemed a reasonable one to the Americans. It used superior American firepower and mobility against the toughest element in the enemy array—the main forces—while it deployed the ARVN's divisions in intimate contact with their own people, whose language and customs they understood. At the same time these ARVN units benefited from considerable American support in their assignment although the numbers never actually came up to the half share promised.[11] Throughout 1967, therefore, while American and allied strength grew to over a half-million men and the ARVN was substantially upgraded along with its paramilitary auxiliaries, the new strategy and division of responsibility was put into effect. Firepower and its use in offensive operations was never greater; a great buildup of logistic capability was carried forward and pacification enjoyed more substantial and better-managed support than ever before. Yet shortly after the end of the year, at the beginning of Tet, the Vietnamese 1968 New Year holiday, the enemy unleashed a general offensive throughout the country which, while immensely costly for him, nevertheless showed the opposite of the declining power and capability one would have been led to expect from the massive effort carried on for more than a year against him. This surprise attack turned out to be a political and psychological blow from which the Americans never recovered. It changed the war, causing abandonment of the assumption that U.S. power could win in a time span and at a cost acceptable to the American public. After Tet, the Americans no longer talked of victory as the objective but of other, lesser goals.

Although many continue to maintain—and no doubt always will that this outcome resulted from the restrictions placed upon the military for political reasons, the analysis and description we have offered lead to another conclusion: U.S. military concepts and the style in which they were carried out were simply off the mark, played into the enemy's hands, and gave him the opportunity to bring Goliath down. Put differently, the course of the war would have at least been substantially altered—although one still hesitates to assert that it could have been won outright relying on purely military means—by a more sophisticated and flexible use of U.S. strength, avoiding the known pitfalls of counterguerrilla warfare. This would have required making the undoubtedly painful changes in the American approach which had long been formally and verbally accepted as the appropriate tactic but never carried out—fight the enemy with his own weapons, "set guerrillas to catch guerrillas."

What actually happened in the two phases of the war, the offensive "search and destroy" campaign in remote areas, and the dose-in phase of pacification? In the first phase, immense areas of jungle were pitted with bomb craters and swept with shrapnel, and substantial enemy casualties were inflicted, but they were spread out in time, never concentrated to the point that large units were overwhelmed and disappeared or a cost exacted that could not be sustained. The American style prevented such an outcome, in part, at least, because it required a softening-up process to precede each attack, thereby giving due warning, even if the enemy intelligence system had not already learned of an attack from its massive penetrations into the ARVN. By and large, then—and this is the essence of the VC/NVA's ability to survive in the teeth of American superiority—the enemy was able to control the pace and scope of combat and thus the level of combat losses by evading contact when it did not suit his purpose. By this means, he managed to keep losses within his capability to replace them, even despite the length of his supply and replacement lines and his lack of mobility and of heavy firepower. Generally alerted in advance to American intentions, he avoided battle until he was ready. To him, losses—at least up to a rather high level never actually reached—did not matter, terrain did not matter. What mattered was to keep the main force in being, its morale high, and its minimum supply requirements assured—and to exact a price from the Americans which in the long run would be felt painfully. To explain in detail how the VC/NVA was able to do this in 1967 and after would take us too far afield, but one thing is clear: during this phase of the war it could only assure the essential intelligence, supply, and manpower from the South Vietnamese population, and that required a substantial degree of local support secured by all the means described earlier.

The same factors were of importance in the close-in, pacification, phase of the war, but an equally critical element was the performance characteristics of the ARVN and the U.S. military. The regular ARVN units assigned to "support of pacification" maintained the predilection, derived from their training and doctrine, to operate in large units, to rely on air power and artillery to soften up the target prior to the attack, and to carry out set-piece attacks with concentrated force; and the Americans involved in the same mission for the most part did the same. Although nominally dedicated to pacification support—a type of duty that rarely called for as much as a battalion to fight in any action—the ARVN remained organized into divisions and the divisions into corps Commanders were free to interpret "pacification support" as might suit them. Frequently they diverted companies and battalions on pacification duties to such tasks as securing roads and canals or reinforcing large-scale attacks which had only a tenuous relationship to pacification. In fact, the pacification support mission was not popular with ARVN commanders who, naturally, derived their values from their American mentors. It seemed demeaning compared with the main-force war. It also called for tedious, very basic, small-unit operations with little opportunity for dramatic battles using the full panoply of weapons at their command. Success in pacification did not bring glory and promotions. It brought hard, tedious work, nighttime operations, and casualties. Division and regimental commanders generally contrived to slight it without directly opposing it. At the same time—and in spite of continuing U.S. training and support efforts—ARVN performance standards continued low. Reluctance of commanders to close with the enemy, corruption in handling pay and other requisites, poor combat leadership, poor troop behavior toward the population—all remained common characteristics of most units.

The Americans involved in close-in operations followed a similar pattern, although performance standards were, of course, higher and there was usually no reluctance among the Americans to close with the enemy. Nevertheless, the pattern remained one of keeping large units together to seek out and hopefully to destroy large enemy units, and of copious use of artillery and air power to soften up the target before the attack. The desire to use firepower freely led to the declaration of "free-fire zones," areas where no friendly population was believed to exist and where any human observed was subject to attack without warning. Populations were sometimes moved from their homes and resettled to permit the declaration of such a zone.

Another tactic frequently employed was "harassment and interdiction fire," the unobserved firing of artillery at night at targets believed to be in the vicinity of enemy concentrations, installations, or lines of communications. An enormous weight of shells was expended in this fashion. By the nature of the technique, results were unverifiable and the risk of hitting innocent civilians was great. Nevertheless the practice continued.

All regular forces—American, Korean, and ARVN—also conducted sweeps of areas where the enemy were suspected of hiding among the civilian population. These were usually called "cordon and search" operations and were often preparatory to the introduction of pacification teams into new areas. They called for the sealing off of an area with troops, searching all structures, and screening the entire population to comb out enemy weapons, supplies, soldiers, or infrastructure members. Surprise was sought though not often achieved. Again the fault probably lay with the penetration of ARVN staffs by Communist intelligence; usually the enemy's adherents were alerted and slipped away. Even if some of the enemy were caught, his organization was soon mended. The troops left, pacification units moved in, and the submerged and scattered VC waited—as the population was aware they did—for their opportunity to return. Often, before they left, they summoned the people and told them that they were going—but would be back. The purported goal of such operations, to "clear and hold" territory infested with VC, was thwarted by the failure of troops to stay and patiently and persistently patrol the area as long as necessary to establish true security. This was not seen as their proper mission and tended to be left to paramilitary forces, which in pre-Tet years were inadequately trained and led, together with the pacification teams, while the regulars moved on to additional "clear and hold" activity or to

larger, set-piece operations against VC/NVA main forces in their area of responsibility.

It was in this phase of the war, namely, pacification support, that the military demonstrated most clearly its inability to grasp the nature of the conflict it was attempting to fight. Studies of the Vietnamese war carried out long afterward and based on careful analysis of all statistics available in the Pentagon demonstrate conclusively that the military machine, in spite of all verbal assurances to the contrary, simply performed in Vietnam according to its normal and conventional combat repertoires. By far the largest part of the resources expended in South Vietnam were dedicated to the air war. The huge numerical superiority of the anti-VC/NVA forces was illusory because so many of the troops were involved in logistics, the air war, and other non-infantry combat activity. In 1971 the overall strength ratio of the two opposing forces was 6 to 1, but the "foxhole" strength ratio was a mere 1.6 to 1. Even more striking is the fact that combat results measured in terms of casualties improved *after* the U.S. had withdrawn the bulk of its combat forces because, at the same time, efforts to improve and enlarge Vietnamese territorial forces (the RF, PF, and People's Self-Defense Forces) reached their peak.[12] Pacification support was a bitter failure of both the U.S. Army and the ARVN. It never enjoyed the troop allocations claimed, and those troops which were employed in this duty, by the style in which they fought, made the pacification task more difficult rather than helping to advance it.

The futility of attempting to fight a guerrilla enemy with the wrong techniques, the poor psychological preparations of U.S. units, and the stark strangeness along with frequent hostility of the people whose rescue from Communist rule was supposed to be the purpose of all the sweaty, toilsome, and frequently bloody effort—these were the chief factors responsible for the poor morale, declining discipline, and grave operational lapses of U.S. forces, of which the My Lai episode is the best known. The troops—among the best-educated infantry ever put into the field—quickly learned that their dangerous work was not accomplishing its purpose, that the task was endless and the people unwilling, that, in fact, they were accomplices in a fraud being perpetrated upon the Vietnamese and American people by an army leadership which did not grasp the fundamentals of what it was supposed to be doing. Heroin addiction and a growing frequency of "fragging" episodes (a surreptitious attack upon an American officer by his own soldiers) against combat leaders were some of the eventual results.

THE IMPACT UPON THE PEOPLE

The tragic irony of the regular military effort, particularly in the close-in operations which were intended to support pacification, was that the manner in which it was carried out assured that the goals of pacification, instead of being brought closer, would be made vastly more difficult. That goal was to gain the willing support of the government's cause by the people brought into the pacification process. Instead, large numbers of them were bombed or shelled, forcibly resettled, or caught in the cross fire as contending forces clashed in or around their homes. Wherever American troops were stationed they had an inevitably powerful effect on the economy and social fabric of the surrounding communities. Inflation rates soared, "strips" featuring bars and bar girls sprang up, and a flow of ready cash overturned accustomed expectations and fostered a class of entrepreneurs battening on the Americans. For those shrewd enough to exploit the situation there was opportunity for fast profits, but for most it was simply a rather obscene assault on moral standards and an uprooting of normal life that brought few rewards.

The style of war of the regular forces thus, in a variety of ways and without anyone deliberately willing it, reinforced the sense of helplessness, of alienation from the authorities, of the Vietnamese caught in the powerful wake of the war machine. The tendency among military leaders was to dismiss the civilian toll as an unfortunate but inevitable cost of war, something that always accompanied battle, and to point to directives and practices MACV instituted to minimize it to the extent possible.

Their case was seriously weakened, however, by their inability bring about a decisive military result following the strategy and tactics they had adopted. It is impossible to measure the precise impact of the phenomenon we are discussing upon attitudes in the countryside and thus to

suggest the extent of the damage done to the effort by the way the military played its role. One must appeal finally to common sense: If the target was truly the people, was this the way to reach them?

COMBINED ACTION PLATOONS AND CID

Within the military itself there were many who questioned the conventional wisdom, and there were significant efforts to change the pattern. The one which came closest to answering the need involved the marines, who throughout their heavy combat commitment in the northern part of the country set aside a small group of men to work integrally with Vietnamese paramilitary units at hamlet level, performing the basic security tasks in communities undergoing pacification. These Combined Action Platoons came into existence in 1965, not long after marine combat units arrived in force. The marines operated in I Corps, the northernmost provinces of South Vietnam, in areas where the countryside had long been dominated by the enemy. They early discovered that the Viet Cong controlled villages on the margins of their bases and that local security forces were unable to dig them out. An experiment was launched to determine whether American soldiers assigned to selected hamlets to work with the local Popular Force militia could bring about a significant improvement. The results of the early experiments were encouraging, and a slow expansion of the program took place, reaching eventually a total of 114 Combined Action Platoons.[13] This small effort is nevertheless worth exploring in some detail for it represents the only sustained effort to fight guerrillas with guerrillas undertaken by any part of the United States armed forces in Vietnam. The experiment thus demonstrated the problems and the potential of such an attempt.

Each unit consisted of a squad of marines (fourteen men) under command of a sergeant, assigned to live and work with a Popular Force platoon of thirty-four Vietnamese. One navy corpsman was also included in the American component. The marines were volunteers and were required to have had previous combat experience in Vietnam. They were screened before acceptance with emphasis on eliminating those who disliked or were unable to work with Vietnamese. They received several weeks' training which tended to emphasize the basics of small-unit combat with a limited amount of attention to civic action. The trainees were then assigned to their locations which were usually selected because of proximity to an important military objective such as a base or a major road. The formal mission of the platoon was the same as that of the Popular Forces they worked with except that they had the additional task of improving the performance of the PF units themselves. That mission included—besides the obvious tasks of destroying the VC organization, protecting the government organization and installations, and enforcing law and order—the formation of "people's intelligence nets" and civic action and propaganda."

Regardless of the formal goals, the marines focused on patrolling the hamlets at night, on setting up ambushes, and, in whatever other way they could, preventing the enemy from moving in and out, collecting taxes, recruiting, or gathering information. They brought a higher degree of professionalism to the PFs as well as better weapons and support, particularly medical evacuation by helicopter. One of the superior combat narratives of the war, *The Village*, by F. J. West, Jr.,[15] gives a vivid account of the work of a single CAP assigned to the village of Binh Nghia in Quang Ngai province. It is very largely the story of a series of night patrols, many of them ending in no contact, during which marines and PF, in groups of six or eight, stalked an elusive enemy through the pathways and backyards of a handful of adjacent hamlets, finally forcing him to abandon the village which, thanks to persistent night patrolling by the CAP, had become exceedingly hazardous to him. This success took over a year to accomplish and was costly in American lives relative to the size of the unit. During the entire year, the village was not once bombed from the air, and only once did the CAP request artillery support. On that occasion, a single shell was fired, well off target, destroying a house and killing two villagers. Artillery was never again called in by the marines in Binh Nghia. Moreover, neighboring regular American units were instructed to leave Binh Nghia alone and only occasionally lapsed. On one occasion, an Army

battalion attempted a sweep, using tanks, one of which slipped off the dike road into a rice field, where it stuck. That ended the sweep.

After seventeen months, the marines at Binh Nghia reported that the local PF platoon, with which they had worked so closely, was fully capable of maintaining security without their help. The village officials were staying in the area at night, VC contacts occurred very seldom, and there was little left for the marines to do. They were transferred to a neighboring village and the militia was left to do the job on its own. The PF unit had difficulties at first which, its leaders claimed, were due to their inability to get quick reaction support from the Americans now that no American soldiers were stationed in the village. They dealt with that problem by organizing and arming a People's Self-Defense Force to supplement their own firepower. Under the leadership of the battle-tested PF, this solution worked and Binh Nghia remained secure.

The Village is a superb case history of the kind of tactics which, if used on a wider scale, could have made a vast difference in the war for the countryside. There were problems and weaknesses, of course, even in the small program that was actually carried out. The CAPs were not uniformly successful. Their lack of language capability was a serious handicap, training was inadequate, and confusion often existed about the purpose and mission of each unit—a matter the marines usually solved by focusing on combat as their *raison d'etre* and letting the rest go. More serious was the failure of the command to link the various CAPs together into an interlocking and mutually supporting network. They were too scattered and isolated to have maximum impact.[16]

Small as they were, the CAPs drew considerable command attention. Generals often dropped in by helicopter to be briefed by the units, for the experiment intrigued and puzzled the command levels. The combat record, the "kill ratios," and the fact that American soldiers were living and fighting in intimate contact with Vietnamese, all suggested an interesting phenomenon, but, despite this interest and its achievements, the program was kept small. The commanders were unable or unwilling to accept the conclusion implicit in the success of the CAPs, which was that their vast resources, equipment, and technology were essentially irrelevant to the kind of war they faced. Some months after the CAP program was launched, the marines noted a growing enemy buildup in the Demilitarized Zone, the northern frontier of South Vietnam. They shifted the axis of their effort to dealing with that threat and from then on the CAPs were considered a limited sideshow to the main-force war. What would have happened if the army had also adopted the experiment and if it were given a priority call on manpower up to, but not beyond, :he point where the combat divisions could no longer shield the CAP areas from heavy-unit attacks? All that remains a matter of speculation. It would certainly have been a different war.

THE CITIZENS IRREGULAR DEFENSE GROUPS

Throughout Vietnam, and indeed Southeast Asia, the majority of the people occupy lands suitable for the cultivation of "wet" rice. The vast mountainous areas are lightly populated by the more primitive tribal communities, and between the two lie age-old animosities encouraged by the colonial powers to ease their task of ruling huge territories with a handful of administrators. In South Vietnam this pattern prevailed throughout the mountainous provinces along the lone, remote frontier with Laos and Cambodia. Literally dozens of small tribes practiced shifting cultivation (slash-and-burn) remote from the densely populated Mekong Delta and coastal plains and were, until 1954, shielded by the French from penetration by the lowland Vietnamese. With independence these barriers were lifted, and Vietnamese began to filter into the upland valleys, a movement encouraged by the Diem government which sponsored resettlement projects in tribal lands. Inevitably, the tribal peoples felt victimized and exploited and became readily susceptible to Viet Cong appeals.

To the Communists the area was of critical military importance, controlling the entry points of their supply lines into the South and providing enormous-remote areas for bases, supply dumps, and concentration points. They quickly became active among the tribes, preaching a form of autonomy and employing cadres who spoke the tribal languages and were familiar with tribal ways. The VC did suffer from several disadvan-

tages: they spoke for a Vietnamese authority, and their intentions, which could not always be concealed, amounted to the establishment of a kind of control over the tribes which the latter had instinctively and traditionally sought to avoid. Into this rather explosive mix the CIA moved in the early sixties, establishing the first of the armed village programs which were described earlier.[17] In 1963 the CIA relinquished management of the tribal programs to the U.S. Special Forces which conducted them from then on in the role of advisers to the Vietnamese Special Forces. What had originally been a system of interlocked village defense groups supported by strike forces drawn from all the villages in the group became a rather different type of program. The CIDG volunteers became full-time soldiers numbering eventually some fifty thousand in all. They were stationed at special camps built in remote areas from which they patrolled, identifying targets for air strikes and conducting raids against VC installations. Their families usually lived in the camps with them, but in other respects the CIDG were full-time professionals fighting under the command of the Vietnamese. Fighting was an occupation to which the tribal populations took with more ease than the Vietnamese, especially in the mountains which were their homeland.

In the prevailing conditions of the highland areas, disrupted as they were by war and political turmoil, service in the CIDG became a means of livelihood for the troops. The commitment was by no means a political one, for the GVN was dilatory and inconsistent in evolving a program that went even part of the way to meet tribal demands for equality, representation, and some control of their own affairs. The CIDG soldiers were, in effect, mercenaries who performed useful service in the remote areas where otherwise the enemy would have had virtually a free hand. (In passing, we should note that in more stable and settled tribal communities closer to province towns and Vietnamese centers of population the Revolutionary Development program was active in a slightly modified form. Here the RD cadre were called *Truong Son*.) Similar forces had been used in insurgent and other types of war from time immemorial, and there was nothing particularly innovative about the device, although it was not one the U.S. had often employed in its previous martial experience. Nor did the CIDG in this latter form make any particular contribution to counterinsurgency as we have defined it.

The role of the Special Forces in this conventionalized war was therefore different in important ways from that envisioned in the early sixties, when they were seen as a key counterinsurgency force. Essentially, they trained and advised the Vietnamese Special Forces who, in turn, organized the CIDG. This, at least, was the formal relationship, although in the early days of USSF responsibility the Vietnamese role was often minimal. During this very confused period (1964 and 1965) the Special Forces, in fact, were caught in a major political confrontation between the Vietnamese government and CIDG units who were demanding autonomy or even independence. This tension was eventually resolved, but the episode had the effect of reducing the direct role of the USSF in the program.

Although the Vietnamese were thus mollified and accepted the program, it remained one conceived and planned largely by the U.S. The pattern it finally took thus inevitably became one that fit U.S. military criteria and met U.S. norms. The CIDG Strike Forces, as they were called, were simply light infantry companies constituting a military auxiliary organized to conduct scouting and raiding activity from fixed bases in difficult terrain. The Special Forces, in effect, devoted the larger part of their effort in Vietnam to a variant of standard military operations with a distinctly limited counterinsurgency function—a far cry from the role originally anticipated for them.

Some of the other missions they undertook were less conventional in nature. For example, they organized long-range patrols, small units operating for relatively long periods away from their bases. As the main component of the Special Operations Group (SOG) they were also deeply involved in the so-called 34A Operations, comprising secret raids and harassment into North Vietnam. None of this altered the fact that as a small specialized force the USSF in Vietnam had a restricted role compared to earlier expectations, the reason being the need to conform to prevailing military concepts in a command dominated by the regulars.

Indeed, something similar could be said of the entire U.S. military effort in Vietnam. Despite the public fanfare surrounding the "new form of warfare" with which the Vietnamese involvement began, the essence of the effort remained very much the old familiar form of warfare for which the military were long prepared. We can sum up by saying that counterinsurgency was not seriously attempted on a large scale by the U.S. combat forces in Vietnam. It was left to a few thousand civilian and military advisors with some military support, but they had only a limited influence on the way in which the military command, with its vast resources, conducted the phase of the war which it had defined as its responsibility. The war, in fact, was fought as two separate conflicts despite the fact that it was only one. What was done by the military in pursuit of victory over the main force impacted severely on the populace, so severely that we can conclude that the regular army's side of the war not only did not constitute counterinsurgency, it was a massive obstacle in the way of successful counterinsurgency. That is what the "new form of warfare" came to represent in the largest of U.S. involvements in people's war.

THE TET EARTHQUAKE

The massive nationwide Viet Cong offensive that began on January 30, 1968, ended the first phase of U.S. military involvement and began the long second phase of gradual withdrawal which finally played itself out in April and May 1975. The Tet offensive and its aftermath affected every phase of U.S. activity in Vietnam, pacification included. By the time the shock waves receded and the U.S. and GVN restored the losses of the attack, it was a much-changed war, most particularly in the countryside, where initially all the painfully won gains of the previous year seemed to vanish in a moment, until the reality of the changed situation dawned on all concerned: as a result of Tet, the government was stronger, not weaker, in the villages and hamlets. Many things which before had seemed impossible were now within reach and merely had to be energetically seized.

We need not rehearse in detail in this history the events of Tet 1968. Suffice it to say that, with a large degree of surprise, the VC/NVA forces unleashed coordinated attacks on thirty-four cities, Saigon very much included.[18] The focus of the "General Uprising and General Offensive," as the Communists called it, was the cities, hitherto largely exempt from the havoc of war. Most urban areas in the country and most towns were assaulted, as the major part of the armed strength of the enemy was moved up from remote bases and close-in hiding places and flung against the superior American and South Vietnamese firepower. Relying on surprise and on the massive nationwide fury of the assault, the Communists—for reasons still not well understood—took an incredible gamble. How one judges the results varies with the time scale and vantage point from which the judgment is made. No doubt, now that the war has ended victoriously for them, the Communists are entitled to view the gamble as a success. It was the turning point of U.S. involvement, and they had no chance of victory while the U.S. remained in strength. But there is also no doubt that as a result of the Tet gamble the relative strength of the two sides altered significantly in favor of the government and that by the end of 1968, psychologically as well as materially, the government side confronted new opportunities.

The initial impact of the Tet attacks in the countryside seemed to be a victory for the Viet Cong for the reason that the security forces were immediately preoccupied either with defending the embattled towns or preserving their own lives and left the villages with greatly reduced defenses. The relative vacuum that resulted partly reversed the gains of the reorganized pacification effort. But these initial results were, in a matter of months, rapidly overtaken by a new reality. With the reestablishment of security in the cities, units were released and returned to their original posts in the countryside. In the meantime, the recklessness of the offensive had taken an enormous toll of the enemy, a figure estimated at forty-five thousand men lost through the end of February 1968 out of a total deployment of eighty-four thousand.[19] This figure was put together from probably exaggerated body counts and needs to be discounted. Nevertheless, subsequent developments confirm that the losses were enormous. The larger part of the

Communist forces committed (though by no means all) comprised Viet Cong local and main force units whose losses were staggering and left them seriously depleted. A second wave of attacks occurred in May and increased the toll. A third wave, scheduled for August, was a hardly noticeable ripple. Hamlet Evaluation Survey statistics, which are useful to illustrate this kind of trend, tell the story concisely. At the end of 1967, HES reports showed over two-thirds of the hamlets (67.2 percent) in the secure or relatively secure category, the rest being contested or under VC control. At the end of February 1968, that figure had dropped by 7 percentage points to about 60 percent and was at the same level as the beginning of 1967. By the end of November, however, the total number of hamlets in the secure and relatively secure category was 73 percent, higher than it had ever been before.[20] The Tet losses had set back the Viet Cong in the countryside far below their strength at the time they had launched the offensive. Moreover, the enemy was not only physically but also morally depleted. The sacrifices called for at Tet had been justified in advance as a final, all-out surge which was to bring victory quickly.[21] But after the slaughter was over and victory still had not arrived, the VC faced the necessity of a period of retrenchment and rebuilding to restore enthusiasm and commitment.

Some students of the war point out that the Tet offensive was a strategic victory although a tactical defeat for the VC/NVA. They suggest that it is entirely plausible that Vo Nguyen Giap and his associates were not surprised by the heavy losses, having discounted them in their planning in order to achieve a result which would shock American opinion and greatly undermine support for the war.[22] This interpretation is plausible, although we will probably never be certain. In any event, the results were a major and significant blow to the VC organization in the South which, as we shall see, precipitated important changes in the course of pacification.

In the meantime, after some months of shock and confusion, the GVN side began to pull itself together. Encouraged by the fact that the government and the armed forces remained intact and had held on despite the ferocity of the attack, Saigon recovered its poise and gained increased confidence from the Tet ordeal. Although their performance was uneven, many ARVN units had fought well during the crisis with their backs to the wall. The government continued to function under adverse circumstances, and Communist propaganda calling for a nation-wide popular uprising to greet and support their general offensive proved unavailing. These among other factors encouraged the GVN to take measures long urged by the U.S. but put off because of political sensitivity. In effect, the enemy's loss of morale was paralleled by an eventual increase in morale on the GVN side and a turning point of sorts occurred which had major consequences for pacification.

NATIONAL MOBILIZATION

The drafting of men of military age was a perennial U.S. recommendation that no South Vietnamese government had felt strong enough to endorse. The effects of Tet and the popular reaction to it emboldened President Thieu to proceed where he had earlier hesitated. One feature of the reaction to Tet had been a sudden increase in volunteers for the army and, most noteworthy, demands from many areas for arms for the people. The National Mobilization Law of 1968 emerged from this experience, requiring all able-bodied men of military age to serve in the armed forces. This long-delayed mobilization resulted in the eventual increase of the armed forces to a million men and had the unintended beneficial effect for pacification of absorbing much of the manpower pool on which the VC as well as the government had depended.

Another important post-Tet decision, again at U.S. urging, was the creation of a nationwide program to arm villagers and city dwellers alike in units now called People's Self Defense Forces (PSDF). Although lip service had long been paid to the concept of arming the population, the national government now seemed to be serious about it. The new law required that all men of military age who were not in the armed forces participate in the defense of the country by joining the PSDF. Provision was also made to accept voluntary participation by women, old people, and children as young as twelve in noncombat support roles. By 1970 some three million persons were claimed to be enrolled in the PSDF.[23] The figure

was undoubtedly inflated, but some four hundred thousand arms were distributed, and this figure can be accepted with more certainty.

The PSDF was responsible to village chiefs and they in turn had the duty of assuring that the members received training and that their activities were effectively coordinated with the militia. American advisers, especially the Mobile Training Teams assigned to work with Popular and Regional Forces, were of assistance in many localities in putting the program on its feet. As did every other such activity in Vietnam, PSDF varied greatly in quality and performance but it had an undoubted impact. The spread of these rather informal and unmilitary village-based armed groups was one of the causes and, in turn, one of the most important indicators of improvement of the situation in the countryside. The act of issuing arms to the population was symbolic of a growing awareness of the importance of popular engagement in the government's cause and of the willingness of the government to take some chances to make progress along that road.

COUNTEROFFENSIVE IN THE COUNTRYSIDE

By the end of 1968 the government was sufficiently recovered to plan and launch a systematic pacification offensive to recover lost ground and exploit the Tet-generated enemy weakness in the countryside. The drive, called the Accelerated Pacification Campaign was Komer's final initiative. It was motivated in part by the realization that the opportunity to gain ground might be fleeting. It also stemmed in part from events in Paris, where peace talks appeared about to begin. The GVN wished, in the event of a cease-fire, to have established its presence in as many villages as possible. To release additional forces for this purpose, the RD team structure was altered and the teams reduced in size. In effect, a standard team no longer included a squad whose main duties were military. Instead, the reduced team— now consisting of thirty-five men and later reduced to thirty—was tied in more closely with the local militia platoon, which took over the defense functions. This step was made possible by the increase and improvement of the RF/PF militia. It permitted the rapid creation of additional teams needed to launch the Accelerated Pacification Campaign.

The campaign progressed rapidly, and soon the government, against little opposition, had moved back into all the communities it had abandoned at Tet and penetrated into areas over which its hold had never been reestablished. Originally scheduled to last only three months, the Accelerated Pacification Campaign became the basis for a far more vigorous and successful phase of pacification which had as its key a substantial upgrading of the process by President Thieu and his immediate advisers. For whatever reason—and some suggested that it was the galvanizing effect of the reality of gradual American withdrawal—President Thieu from 1968 to 1970 took decisive action on major issues which had caused pacification to lag in the past. As important was his personal involvement in the decision-making process, manifested by his presiding regularly over the Central Pacification and Development Council which coordinated the work of the various GVN agencies involved. He set the goals and helped to shape the details of the 1969 plan and those that followed. By personal appearances in the villages and at the training camps he sought to emphasize and reemphasize the priority he and the government attached to the program.

This commitment by the regime gave to the program a critical ingredient which had hitherto been absent—Vietnamese initiative and convinced leadership at the highest levels. In all of its many aspects, as we have noted, pacification was—and of necessity had to be—a Vietnamese program, with the Americans serving as advisers, expediters, and suppliers of material resources. Too often in the past, the ideas, initiatives, and sense of urgency had been contributed by the Americans, with much of the program considered by the Vietnamese to be an American hobbyhorse. Such a division of labor ill-suited an activity which sought to deal with the most intimate aspects of social life in thousands of Vietnamese communities. By making the program his own, President Thieu resolved some of the anomalies that had dampened the impact of the effort and gave it an injection of sorely needed elan. On the other hand, while his personal involvement had a noticeable impact, the resulting improvement—as always in Vietnam—remained relative to the earlier low levels of performance, efficiency, and honesty of administration.

Sweeping policy decisions continued into 1969 and 1970, focused on the village and aimed at the goal of giving the villagers greater control over their affairs and resources. First, the process of village elections to select a governing council, instituted in 1967, was pressed forward vigorously. By the end of 1969, 95 percent of the villages of Vietnam had elected their own councils which, in turn, elected the village chief.[24] By a decree of April 1, 1969, the elected village governments were given control of local armed forces which by now included the PF, PSDF, RD cadres, and police (where assigned to villages).[25] Village government was enlarged to handle the new responsibilities. A deputy chief for security managed the security forces, another deputy was created for administration, and a secretariat assisted village officials in processing their paperwork.[26]

The same decree delegated to the reorganized village governments control of a development fund which initially was set at one million piasters annually and later increased. This was to be spent at the discretion of the village council for local development with the proviso that the villagers themselves contribute their labor or other resources to each project. During the same period, reflecting the increased responsibilities of the village regimes, training of village officials became a large-scale program, mostly carried on at the RD Training Center at Vung Tau. In 1969 a total of seventeen thousand hamlet and village officials passed through the center, receiving instruction in the requirements of effective local government and indoctrination on nationalist themes and goals.[27] Persisting in his new pattern of personal involvement, President Thieu addressed each graduating class of village officials in succession.

Perhaps the most far-reaching policy initiative of this whole period of renovation of pacification, however, was Thieu's decision to throw his personal prestige and influence behind a new and sweeping land reform program. The passage of the new land reform law was delayed in the legislature and did not come until March 1970, but in its final form it was one of the most thoroughgoing undertaken anywhere. Its critical provision reduced landholdings to fifteen hectares per farmer and awarded title to that amount of property without cost to the new owner, the government assuming the burden of compensating the landlords.[28] Moreover, local land distribution under the reform became a responsibility of village government, which thus acquired a major new power over a critical aspect of village life. Long-delayed as it was, true land reform finally became a firm feature of GVN policy. Once passed, the law was implemented with a degree of vigor that surprised both Americans and Vietnamese. According to one authority "three years after the bill was signed, the GVN had redistributed nearly one million hectares of farmland. Well over two-thirds of the tenant farmer families in South Vietnam were to be significantly affected by the measures."[29]

Accompanying these basic structural changes in the government's rural policies was a steady improvement in levels of economic activity, reflecting better security as well as the payoff from many years of increasing development inputs and, not least important, the ingenuity and hard work of the peasant population. Among the most important material factors involved were the reopening of roads and canals, the spread of the so-called miracle rice of the IR5 and IR8 strains developed in the Philippines, and the spread of small tractors along with gas-powered irrigation pumps in the Delta. Official estimates placed the number of tractors in the Delta in mid-1970 at thirty-four hundred, representing a doubling of numbers in a little more than a year.[30] The decline of South Vietnamese agricultural production which had continued steadily since about 1960 was reversed, and signs of new prosperity and growth were visible almost everywhere. The prosperity was not evenly distributed, of course, and many, especially the refugees, continued to lead a life of hardship. Nevertheless, the trend was apparent and contributed significantly to the improved rural picture. These results were an outstanding success for CORDS which had invested a far larger proportion of its resources in such activities than in those such as Phoenix, which attracted more attention.

IMPACT ON THE VIET CONG

One significant political development that accompanied and underlay these changes was a sharp decline in the fortunes of and popular support for the Viet Cong. The Tet spasm backfired seriously in terms of popular faith and confidence in VC promises. The manpower losses resulting from Tet, together with the government's mobilization of the entire national manpower pool and the movement of population away from the scene of heavy fighting, had depleted VC ranks and made the recruitment of replacements exceedingly difficult. Loss of support meant loss of funds; consequently VC taxation in areas to which they still had access became so high that the peasants found the burden far greater than in government-controlled areas. Forcible recruitment into VC ranks be-came more common—in effect a form of a kidnapping which did not produce reliable adherents. In many provinces the VC concentrated merely on maintaining its organization, undertaking little aggressive activity. During 1970, for example, aggressive operations by the insurgents were concentrated in eleven provinces, while in the remaining thirty-three they were reduced to occasional harassment.[31] In 1969, forty-seven thousand VC personnel, mostly low level, voluntarily went over to the government side through the Chieu Hoi program. In 1970, the figure was thirty-two thousand.[32]

Nevertheless, despite the undoubted decline of the VC's hold, it would be an error to conclude that it had been defeated as an insurgency. As had happened more than once in their history, the Communists had sustained a serious setback but, as before, they adjusted rapidly to the new circumstances and developed a new set of tactics to deal with them. Their goal now appeared to be that of maintaining the existence of their organization at the least cost in manpower and to wait for the withdrawal of the Americans and the new situation that would then prevail. In the meantime, the burden of aggressive operations and of keeping up the pressure was assumed by the North Vietnamese, who also provided replacements for the depleted VC units.

In effect, the war entered a new phase of a markedly different character. Insurgency-style guerrilla warfare was no longer the prevailing mode of Communist operations, although it persisted in a few provinces where the capability still existed. In most areas, the VC conducted the minimum of operations necessary to maintain a reduced organization. Periodically, a regional or nationwide "highpoint," a flurry of mortarings and ambushes, would be carried out, often by North Vietnamese units. In effect, the war was conventionalized to a considerable degree in that the political link between the enemy and the population withered away, and forces which were largely foreign to the area conducted operations which more and more resembled incursions from outside. The North Vietnamese did not have the same capability as the VC to melt away when pursued and took greater risks in their operations for that reason. Believing it essential to keep up some pressure and to give evidence of continued strength and effectiveness, the Communists nevertheless took those risks.

CHANGE AND PERSISTENCE IN U.S. OPERATIONS

In the aftermath of Tet, U.S. forces also began to change their tactics, although there does not appear to have been a direct connection between one side's changes and the other's. The changes followed and reflected the rotation of commanders when General Creighton Abrams took over from General Westmoreland as COMUSMACV in June 1968. Under Abrams's leadership, U.S. forces modified their tactics to patterns more in keeping with the kind of war they faced. By mid-1969, most American units committed to locating and attacking large enemy units in remote areas were shifted from that duty. Instead, they were conducting saturation, small-unit operations in populated areas, working closely with ARVN and, particularly, with the regional and local paramilitary platoons and companies.[33] Constant patrolling by squads was ordained by the command and, according to one observer, many units were "entirely on night shift, as in one division where three battalions operate exclusively during the hours of darkness and schedule nothing but rest during daylight."[34] General Abrams also placed considerable command emphasis on military support for the Phoenix program although it remains unclear how army support of a police program was intended to function in practice. Certainly large numbers of troops were not an essential or even a useful ingredient for Phoenix purposes.

The implication of these changes is that General Abrams had formed certain convictions during his years as deputy to General Westmoreland relating to the appropriateness of U.S. military tactics in Vietnam. Some observers hold that the actual motivation was the instructions he received to hold down casualties during the U.S. withdrawal. In any event, the impact of the changes he made does not seem to have been great. The new emphasis on saturation patrolling and the accompanying deemphasis of "search and destroy" was in several respects ineffective. The commanders found that to change the tactics of an army already in the field was not merely a matter of issuing new orders. Frequently the new instructions, which violated ingrained habit, were given token compliance while the worst features of the old approach continued to be followed. "General Abrams," wrote one analyst of the problem, "has only partly succeeded in making his own ideas prevail over the traditional doctrine."[35] And again, "Our military institution seems to be prevented by its own doctrinal and organizational rigidity from understanding the nature of this war and from making the necessary modifications to apply its power more intelligently, more economically, and above all, more relevantly."[36] What this meant, among other things, was that the military forces often continued to operate against the enemy regulars as the primary target, concentrating firepower for this purpose and attempting to wear them down by exacting an intolerable rate of casualties. In the process, the population was victimized and the goals of pacification undermined. Within the military and CORDS many individuals, notably the veteran pacification expert John Vann, sought to alter this costly procedure, but the system, for many reasons, proved impossible to change fundamentally.

Within CORDS there were also changes in command personnel but no major alterations in the program or the organization. Robert Komer left Vietnam in late 1968 and was replaced by his deputy, William E. Colby, a senior CIA officer with many years of involvement in Vietnam affairs. Colby continued and refined the CORDS structure and program array that he had inherited. He sought to maintain a lower profile than his predecessor but doggedly pursued the main lines already established. Under his management, CORDS grew moderately in size, reaching an authorized personnel level of seventy-six hundred in 1970 with a budget of $891 million. This represented a near doubling of the U.S. contribution to pacification over the level of CORDS' first year. In the same period, the GVN total also doubled, from the piaster equivalent of $307 million to the equivalent of $628 million.[37] We have no information casting light on Colby's role in bringing about the GVN's policy departures of 1968–1970 other than that his public testimony suggests strong support for all of them. He also endorsed and strongly defended the Phoenix operation in congressional testimony and public statements during the years when it came under increasing public criticism.

ASSESSING THE ACHIEVEMENT

Pacification in Vietnam reached a plateau of achievement in 1970. The Hamlet Evaluation Survey for June of that year rated 91 percent of the hamlets in the country as "secure" or "relatively secure," 7.2 percent as "contested," and only 1.4 percent as "VC-controlled."[38] The evidence is impressive that a completely changed situation prevailed in the rural areas and that the insurgency in the countryside—the people's war—was effectively contained. This was certainly the impression of observers on the scene based on indicators evident to all. As early as October 1969, the *Washington Post* reporter in Saigon, like most American journalists a highly critical observer, prepared a series of three articles on pacification which he called "The New Optimists." It is largely a rehearsal of the facts summarized in the previous section—the new vigor of the government, the success of its changed policies, the improving prosperity of the population contrasting with the surprising weakness of the Viet Cong and its failure to respond vigorously to the spread of government presence and activity.[39] Quantitative measurements confirmed such impressions. In addition to the evidence of the HES, the number of internal refugees declined from the enormous total of 1.5 million in February 1969 to 217,000 in mid-1970, much of the improvement resulting from a movement of population back to homes in the country-side. Komer also notes the decline of the enemy-initiated incident rate and the localization of insurgency-type activity in some eleven provinces among other suggestive indicators of the reversal of the situation.[41]

Moreover, similar evidence confirms that these gains were firmly established and that the situation did not significantly change until shortly before the sudden collapse of 1975—underlining again the changed nature of the conflict in which conventionalized enemy tactics carried out by North Vietnamese replaced the techniques of people's war. From one viewpoint, by 1975 the situation in the countryside had become irrelevant to the outcome. This happened only after the enemy had lost the ability to prosecute a people's war and only after the departure of U.S. forces, which would have relished the challenge of meeting the NVA in conventional combat. The irony was no accident, of course. The enemy would not have risked meeting American forces "one on one," but felt no inhibitions about such a confrontation with ARVIN. Thus, although the war continued for over four more years, the story of U.S. counterinsurgency policy and practice in Vietnam can be concluded in 1970. In the years that followed, there were few innovations or departures from the pattern already described other than the orderly winding down of programs and the reversion of special organizations like the RD teams and the PRU to more normal formats.

To sum up, by 1970 a considerable measure of security had been restored and the ability of the insurgency to affect events, to mobilize the population, to fight, tax, and recruit had been eroded to the point where it was a manageable threat. On the other hand, neither in 1970 nor afterward was the VC apparatus—the infrastructure—dismantled or destroyed. It retained its structural integrity, albeit at far lower levels of strength and capability. And it still managed in a variety of ways to impress upon the population that it lurked in the wings, an alternative authority which could again become a threat. This residual presence *was* of importance to the enemy, for it maintained some credibility to the VC claim to represent the people and constituted a shadow government that, in the event of a sudden improvement of fortunes, could quickly provide a basis for a provisional Communist regime. Nevertheless, the population had substantially abandoned the VC cause which, it would appear, in the very same villages where once it had held on despite the overwhelming strength of its enemies, had now lost the "mandate of heaven."

At this point we face the question of the extent to which the pacification program could take credit for this outcome—and, in addition, whether the results represented a full achievement of the goals of the program. The first question has already been answered. VC errors and particularly the moral and material effects of the Tet gamble had a large but not precisely measurable share in the reversal of the situation. At the same time, however, the GVN moved effectively and broadly to exploit those errors and, in the process, jettisoned many of the political albatrosses that had hampered it in the past. It had also—urged on by the Americans—developed an organization and a series of programs which, under the improved circumstances of 1969 and 1970, realized broad gains. Not all of the programs were equally important or effective, as we will discuss at greater length below. But the combined impact of VC failures, an improved political approach, and improved programs vigorously prosecuted was responsible for the effects we have described.

A more difficult and complex matter is the extent to which the goals of the program were fully achieved. Specifically, the question is whether the GVN had succeeded in enlisting the voluntary support and commitment of a major part of the peasant population to its cause. This, of course, is a difficult question to answer convincingly, for it involves speculation about the attitudes and inner feelings of Vietnamese peasants. The conclusion of independent observers who studied the matter most thoroughly was that, while the VC lost much of its hold, the government was not able to replace it with a new loyalty to its cause. Thus, Samuel L. Popkin, a social scientist who conducted detailed interviews with some four hundred peasants in 1969, stated, "The increase in GVN control results in large measure from a drastic decline in the appeal to peasants of life in areas controlled by the Viet Cong, and from the grave danger of fighting for them."[42] In this writer's opinion, the effect of the programs and events described earlier was to develop a peasant opinion which was neutral with regard to national-level issues and thus considerably short of the goal of popular engagement on the government side. This view stems from the analysis given earlier and from the fact that the new autonomy of the villages had obvious limitations to go along with its advantages. In actual fact the village governments were forced into an overall structure which remained largely unchanged and which came into frequent conflict with the new aspirations of village self-government. At district level and in the province capital, the ARVN officers holding the key positions and responsible to an ARVN chain of command still dominated the power structure. The gap between peasant and urbanized army officer still existed. Favoritism, corruption, and manipulation of the laws for private purposes were the rule in this system. Despite persistent efforts by CORDS and by the Presidential Palace to remove the most notorious and ineffective of local and provincial officials, the system remained largely unchanged higher-caliber replacements still had to wink at corruption even if they did not participate, or risk earning the hostility of the command structure.

As a result, the villagers still saw themselves as being in the grasp of an alien power structure with little legal recourse. The ability of the peasants to influence the terms that shaped their lives was still severely circumscribed despite manifest improvements at the village level.

Some American observers thought that Vietnam's new constitution—despite the domination of the provincial structure by ARVN appointees—nevertheless offered a serious possibility of balancing the inequalities of rural power through the elected National Assembly. And indeed, a number of representatives systematically organized constituency services and began to act as a channel whereby villagers could obtain remedies for their grievances against the provincial government.[43] They remained a minority, however, and their efforts had limited effect. Thus, although the American view that a democratized government would eventually compete with the appeal of the VC system to the peasants began to demonstrate some validity, it was a long-term process requiring many years to bear fruit—too many, in fact.

The process, which was of vital importance to the goal of a committed peasantry, could have been greatly advanced if the central government had given positive encouragement to rural-based political organizations. Although President Thieu made several beginnings in that direction, he never followed through and eventually abandoned them all.[44] Without official encouragement no political group could survive the hostility of the provincial government. In the end, the peasant was left to his own resources, with no organization to speak for him above the village level. The government thus failed—despite the economic and development benefits of its programs, despite the increased security in the countryside—to create among the peasantry a strong, positive motivation to engage in the struggle on the official side. It was still, in peasant eyes, a government of "them," remote, arbitrary, and often abusive.

How could the same government which made such strenuous efforts to shore up its rural base have failed to get to the heart of the matter and left the peasant in a political limbo where he remained indifferent to national appeals and commitment? The answer seems to be the same as the one given earlier to the question of why President Diem, despite heavy pressure, had been unwilling to reform his overcentralized and increasingly isolated regime. Thieu could not change the system without putting his own position in serious jeopardy. His first political constituency was the military: if he attempted to strip it of power and privilege and access to wealth, he risked the development of a serious opposition to his leadership within the armed forces which could eventually bring him down. He seems to have considered more than once replacing his military base with a more open and broadly supported structure, but in the end he shrank from the risk. No doubt it was a real risk which would have required some daring and skill and perhaps some luck for him to succeed. The main justification for taking such risks in the mind of a practical politician would be the greater risk of not acting—but Thieu did not see matters in that light. The problem of self-reform in a situation of crisis, of fundamental change in a fragile political structure under great hostile pressure, remained as difficult as ever in the Vietnam of the 1970s.

REVOLUTIONARY DEVELOPMENT: AN UNREALIZED IDEA

The matter of political commitment concerned pacification in its broadest sense. Most of the American side of the effort had been invested in specific programs designed to accomplish specific goals in the area of performance which then, it was hoped, would change attitudes. Of these,

the two that attracted the most controversy, though they were not the most important, were Revolutionary Development and the Phoenix program. How had they fared?

At the heart of Revolutionary Development was a fundamental dilemma which was never resolved. The teams were trained, indoctrinated, and deployed in order to assist the villagers to take control of their own affairs, provide for their own defense, reorganize their government, cleanse the local power structure of corruption and abuse, and so on. But, according to the original concept, they were to do all this as an instrument of the province and district authorities who were themselves interested in retaining control of the village and, more often than not, in exploiting their power for personal advantage. Similarly, their role in local defense depended heavily on the support of the regular forces, which was often reluctant and delayed. These two factors, which we noted earlier as critical problems facing RD, were never satisfactorily resolved. After the revised strategies of 1968 and later, the RD teams were reduced in size, local defense was stiffened by the improvement and expansion of the militia, and control of the teams was assigned to the village chief. At this point the RD concept lost its central position in pacification, and the teams reverted to the role of an extra contribution of trained manpower at the disposition of the village government. As such they were helpful but not critical to pacification.

The RD program, in other words, had served as a device for mobilizing and organizing the pacification effort for a preliminary period, after which better means were found to do the job. The revised system developed in 1968 was better because it was simpler, more straightforward, and easier for all concerned to comprehend—and it conformed more closely to the realities of village life. The idea that an elite corps of some fifty thousand young men and women could be recruited, trained, and sent into the village to change the bases of life there in a period of six months to a year was attractive but quite unrealistic. Very soon the pool of suitable manpower was exhausted. The ranks of the RD teams were filled up with youth from the main towns of the province who lacked familiarity or even sympathy with village life. In many cases they obtained their assignments through favoritism; the position of RD cadre was, after all, a government job with steady pay and exemption from the draft. Once in place, the teams often lacked effective military support and, in many cases, were unable to do more than a token or cosmetic job in meeting their objectives. The system worked better after the teams were reduced in size and placed at the disposition of the village chiefs. With less responsibility they were still able to be useful, and although their contribution now became less critical it remained of substantial assistance.

PHOENIX: A CUCKOO IN THE NEST

The outcome of the Phoenix program was less constructive. There seems to be considerable agreement on one score, at least, and that is on the matter of Phoenix's lack of efficacy. Robert Komer, who had endorsed and successfully proposed it to the GVN, became an outspoken critic of it on grounds of ineffectiveness after he left the government. "To date," he said, writing in 1970, "*Phung Hoang* has been a small, poorly managed, and largely ineffective effort."[45] We have already discussed the reasons for this failure: they ranged from the inadequacy of the detention system to the lack of seriousness in the commitment of the Vietnamese services involved. The results were commensurate with the quality of the effort, namely, very poor.[46]

But there remains another and even more serious criticism of Phoenix to be dealt with. This is a charge maintained not by journalists, whose opportunity was slight for in-depth study of a specific subject, but by a number of social scientists who focused their researches on the rural areas. It is the allegation that Phoenix became a serious and additional obstacle in the pacification process. Here is the testimony of one such observer, based upon "several hundred discussions" with rural, political, and religious leaders with the object of identifying the principal problems of the peasant population:

> During 1969, the primary problem faced by the rural population involved the injustices suffered under the administration *of* the "Phoenix" program. . . . Often "Viet Cong" are arrested on the basis of anonymous denunciations received by the police from those who bear personal grudges against the "suspect." Of greater

concern, however, are the large numbers of persons arrested in connection with the efforts of each provincial security agency to fulfill the quota assigned to it, regardless of a suspect's political affiliation, and it has not been unknown for province or police chiefs to seek each month to exceed their quotas in order to demonstrate their competence. With large numbers of helpless persons detained in province or district jails, opportunities for corruption have proliferated. In some provinces the Phoenix program has been turned into a money-making scheme through which a villager's release can be obtained for the payment of a bribe, usually about $25 to $50.[47]

This is a very serious criticism indeed. It charges the pacifiers with controverting the purposes of their own program by mistaken zeal in pressing the attack against the infrastructure. Whether the actuality was fully as serious as charged remains questionable, for CORDS had its own means of checking public attitudes and problems and detected no such phenomenon.[48] We may with some plausibility conclude, however, that Phoenix did become a major problem to the peasantry in some areas where individual officials behaved abusively, but we question whether it was as general a matter as Goodman and others alleged.

As for the even more extreme charge that Phoenix was merely a machine for torture and murder, that it was responsible for the outright slaughter of some twenty thousand Vietnamese for political reasons, it should be clear from what has already been said that these charges were highly distorted and largely imaginary. The figures came from GVN claims which in turn were based largely on military actions, the labeling of the casualties as VC infrastructure being done after the fact in order to boost the quotas of the local authorities. This fact, of course, does not justify Phoenix, for it was a system seemingly made to order for manipulation and misinterpretation.

Clearly, then, Phoenix failed to eliminate the infrastructure that remained after the heavy losses of Tet and contributed to some degree to the difficulties confronting pacification. There is little evidence to suggest that it resulted in more eliminations of important infrastructure members than would have been achieved by conventional police operations. The advocates of

Phoenix at the time of its inception, and the author among them, were therefore mistaken in the belief that, in view of the critical role of the infrastructure in the enemy's system, the insurgency could not be brought under control without the elimination of the VC organization which directed it. From this belief, the concept of a hierarchy of local and regional centers where the work was to be done on a full-time and urgent basis emerged more or less naturally as simple administrative common sense. On the other hand, the author does not share the view that the members of an organization efficiently going about the destruction of an entire social system, and incidentally using terror and assassination routinely, are entitled to be dealt with gently, in accordance with the full protections of the Bill of Rights. The crime of Phoenix was not the use of harsh methods to apprehend or destroy the enemies of the GVN. Its crime was ineffectiveness, indiscriminateness, and, in some areas at least, the violation of local norms to the extent that it appeared to the villagers to be a threat to them in the peaceable performance of their daily business. The Americans involved erred in failing to appreciate the extent to which the pathology of Vietnamese society would distort an apparently sound concept. The GVN was guilty of both misfeasance and malfeasance in executing the program.

Believing what they did about the importance of the elimination of the infrastructure, those responsible thought they had no choice but to attack that objective with all the weapons they could devise. They did have an alternative, however, and that was to accept the unreality of the objective for the time being and concentrate on perfecting the tools before going at the target at full strength. This would have required a longer view and a more patient approach than prevailed at the time, delaying the final elimination of the infrastructure to a last "cleanup" phase after the main objectives of pacification had been completed.

Both Phoenix and Revolutionary Development suffered from a similar defect: a simplified view of the complexities of village life in Vietnam and of the ability of the central authority to intervene directly in the internal arrangements of thousands of villages simultaneously. Yet they were also overly complex programs for the American and Vietnamese personnel who were required to carry them out, demanding too much trained and dedicated manpower and a subtle approach which was only possible if attempted on a small scale. On the other hand, the programs which succeeded were more direct and straightforward in concept. Unfortunately, they evolved only after the Vietnamese leadership, particularly President Thieu, came to see pacification as an urgent and major priority, far too late for rapid achievement of the goals envisioned.

DID PACIFICATION SUCCEED OR FAIL?

A final judgment on the effort is not a simple matter, for it depends on how one sees the goals. The events of 1968 to 1970, of which pacification was a major element, broke the hold of the VC on the rural population. A striking contrast was established between the well-being enjoyed under government protection and the dangers and hardships of life with the Viet Cong, and certainly the pacification effort could take some if not all of the credit for that. According to a broader concept of pacification, however, the final goal of willing identification by the peasant of his interests with those of the government remained unachieved because of the regime's failure to devise a political framework that could express and bring the aspirations of the peasantry to bear on national decision-making. The government hold was extensive but thin, a little like Mark Twain's description of the Platte River: "an inch deep and a mile wide."

No doubt, on the other hand, the development of such a deep commitment was beyond the capability of a U.S. advisory and assistance program such as CORDS and depended upon the generation of indigenous, purely Vietnamese initiatives and leadership. These not only never emerged but were discouraged by the regime, which feared political movements it could not control and the threat they posed to its stability. The ultimate goals of pacification were thus beyond the reach of the program and depended on factors over which it had little influence.

It is problematical whether any foreign government could, under the circumstances of Vietnam, have brought into existence the indigenous policies and leadership required, but the American policymakers did not seriously try. They were convinced that stability was the first requirement for progress in any other field and therefore refrained from a persistent and determined attempt to force the Thieu regime in the desired direction, pinning their hopes on persuasion and on a gradual evolution toward democratic norms which never materialized. But as Thieu increased the repressiveness of his hold on political life, he fanned the flames of opposition in the United States to the Vietnam involvement. The upshot was the crisis of early 1975, which was precipitated by the refusal of the United States Congress to provide an assured supply of military aid in the amounts required. The tragic collapse of South Vietnam was ultimately a product of the crucial difficulty we have noted frequently on these pages, that of reforming and redistributing power in a political system under severe internal stress. If Thieu had gambled upon such a redistribution and won, his regime would both have answered the criticisms that undermined his support in the U.S. and deepened his hold upon the population in Vietnam. If he had gambled and lost, his honor would at least have shone a good deal brighter in exile, and he would have lost nothing he did not finally lose in any event.

The programmatic aspects of pacification in Vietnam were therefore a substantial success, but they were unable to come to grips with the most deep-seated problems of rural life in Vietnam. These could only have been solved by providing the villagers with political levers linked to the national political process, creating what one observer has called a "political community."[49] This failure lays bare in stark outline the basic dilemma implicit in counterinsurgency policy which was never seriously grappled with by U.S. policymakers, a matter which goes far beyond the programmatic and organizational questions that preoccupied the national security community during the "counterinsurgency era." Effective pro-grams require governmental stability, but successful counterinsurgency requires granting the rural population a strong voice in its own affairs. Steps toward the latter appear to threaten the former and are usually pushed aside with ultimately disastrous effects on counterinsurgency.

These considerations will be examined in more detail in what follows. As far as concerns the counterinsurgency in Vietnam, we may conclude that after unconscionable delays which granted the enemy an almost insurmountable head start, his own mistakes combined with—at long last—a revived and greatly strengthened "new model" U.S. pacification effort and a greatly improved GVN appreciation of the requirements, brought pacification a considerable degree of success. But pacification was only part of the story, and the total effort was still short of what was needed to sweep the enemy off the board or convince the American public of the value of its burdensome involvement. The limited nature of the success reflected, among other things, the inability of the U.S. to establish within its own apparatus a clear, consistent, and firm under-standing of the needs of the situation, most notably to knit together successfully the civilian and military efforts. In turn, that failure permitted the military to perform in a manner which aggravated the problem and brought public revulsion in the U.S. The mixed outcome also reflected the intractability of the political dilemma of Vietnam, the tension and opposition between political reform and stability. These failures brought the effort down in ruins and quite obscured the real accomplishments of the pacification effort, which were, in contrast to the rest, a notable achievement in a dark, confused, and tragic imbroglio from whose consequences it will take this country many years to recover.

Denouements

Douglas S. Blaufarb

LATIN AMERICA AND CIVIC ACTION

The involvement of the U.S. in pacification in Vietnam was the largest such involvement anywhere. It was not only costly but complex, a natural outcome of the attempt to spread its effects everywhere and to transform the daily lives of a large population through the intervention of the government. The involvements in Laos and Thailand were small relative to Vietnam, but both called for complex programs which posed considerable challenges to the U.S.'s ability to-coordinate and to respond flexibly in a wide range of activity, some of it (notably in Laos) entirely unprecedented in our history.

These episodes in Southeast Asia do not by any means exhaust the U.S. counterinsurgency experience, but they absorbed and deployed the greatest amounts of resources and attention. The threats that developed there were assessed to have a degree of seriousness not found elsewhere, and particularly not in Latin America, which is where almost all other such activity was concentrated.

It is true, however, that for a brief period in the early and mid-1960s insurgent activity in Latin America seemed to be a threat of major proportions. The urgings and appeals of Fidel Castro plus the indications that Cuba was providing training, weapons, and other assistance to insurgent groups were viewed in Washington as alarming. The countries where such signs were assessed as most threatening were Venezuela, Colombia, Peru, and Guatemala. Later, of course, Che Guevara's quixotic sally into Bolivia briefly revived concern. All these and other minor attempts to start Cuban-style insurgencies in Latin America quickly petered out in failure and disillusionment or else sputtered along uncertainly at a low level of activity, posing no credible threat. After a while the arguments for continued U.S. concern no longer seemed compelling. During the time of greatest concern, the U.S. involvements never advanced beyond the transfer of relatively small amounts of military aid, training by Mobile Training Teams, and by the assignment of Latin American officers to military schools in the Canal Zone and the continental United States, and police training and advice by both USAID and CIA. For this purpose AID made use of an international police school which it had established in Washington.

WHY CASTROISM FAILED

Various explanations have been advanced for the failure of Castro-style insurgency in Latin America. One study puts it simply in terms of the

Blaufarb, Douglas. (1977). "Denouements." *The Counter-insurgency Era: U.S. Doctrine and Performance, 1950 to Present* (pp. 243–312). London: The Free Press, 1977.

absence of a revolutionary situation in any of the countries of the area.[1] As we have seen in Chapter I, however, the theory developed by Castro, Guevara, et al. was designed to overcome that problem and to create a revolutionary situation by the activity of one or more guerrilla *focos* which would awaken the peasants to the possibility of achieving an overturn of existing authority by violent revolutionary action.

That theory failed entirely to prove itself for a number of reasons. One explanation, acknowledged by the Cuban leaders, was the absence of the element of novelty which, in Cuba itself, had seen the revolt against Batista develop rapidly and succeed before either Cubans or foreigners were aware of the seriousness of the threat or even that a Communist revolution was contemplated. To this day, in fact, many analysts believe that Communism was not Castro's conscious goal until some time after he came to power.[2] The effort to apply the tactics of the Cuban victory to other countries met with a far more alert and vigorous response by both the United States and the regimes concerned and shut off the possibility of a repetition of the Cuban surprise.

Equally important was the absence in these attempts of either a Castro on the side of the insurgents or a Batista in the seat of power. Castro's talents as a dramatic symbol of popular aspirations and as a figure around whom the opposition of all hues could rally was an essential ingredient of success in Cuba. It was lacking in all the other countries. Similarly, Batista's political and military ineptitude was a priceless asset to the Cuban revolutionaries. In contrast, we find in Venezuela, for example, the politically adept Romulo Betancourt, first freely elected president in his country's history, conducting a skillful campaign to isolate the revolutionaries and largely succeeding. Similar, if not so impressive, reactions resulted in the containment and isolation of revolutionaries in Colombia, Peru, and Bolivia. The Guatemalan situation has been more complex since the government at various times has tried different prescriptions ranging from the enlightened to the brutal. After much bloodshed a persistent guerrilla infection continues but makes little progress.

One of the shrewdest observers of these phenomena notes another major flaw in the revolutionary approach, namely, the origins of the revolutionists among the urban educated classes which made them, in the eyes of the peasantry, an alien force with little appeal.

> By and large they [the peasants] preferred to keep the little they had in life rather than to risk it in battle against the *patron* and his army. They believed it wiser to hope that those in power would grow more benign, rather than struggle to alter the hierarchy of things. Even where the peasants had already been politicized . . . they tended to look on the revolutionary insurgents as aliens. In most cases, the peasants would probably have preferred not to take sides; but when they did they usually favored the army with the information and co-operation needed to hunt down the guerrillas.[3]

A final point in explaining the failure of Castroism to catch on in Latin America is the large question which can be raised about the extent to which the revolutionary principles abstracted from their experience by the Castro group and broadcast far and wide as a surefire method of acquiring power in Latin America were actually responsible for the victory in Cuba. More important than the few *focos* fighting in the hills, according to some, was Castro's political skill which brought him the support of the anti-Batista forces throughout the island and resulted in the victory being handed to him after Batista fled, although at the time his guerrilla forces controlled only a small territory. The romantic predilection of the Castro brothers and Che Guevara for guerrilla heroics and—probably more important—their desire to take all the credit led them to attribute this success to the magic of guerrilla operations, but the story is far more complicated and probably not fully understood to this day.[4]

THE AMERICAN ROLE

The U.S.'s share in all of this was clearly secondary but nevertheless of some significance. The rash of Castro-style insurgencies coincided with the development, under President Kennedy's urgent insistence, of an interest and a capability on the part of the foreign affairs and national security agencies to guide and assist threatened governments in meeting the challenge. Missions were dispatched to survey the scene and to recommend U.S. assistance programs. In accordance with the procedure promulgated by the Special Group (C.I.),[5] the U.S. missions in designated countries developed Internal Defense Plans whose purpose was to design and put into effect an integrated program involving contributions from all concerned agencies. This then could provide a basis for monitoring and managing the ongoing American assistance effort.

Among the goals of the U.S. program was the education of the military leadership of the threatened countries in the concept of counterinsurgency as, among other things, a test of the army's ability to establish an improved relationship with the rural population. Civic action was one key concept of the prescription, along with rapid action to smother the insurgency at the earliest possible stage in its development and close pursuit to keep up the pressure. Of these, civic action received a large share of attention and resources—and also of the publicity. Presumably this was because it was considered an attractive concept with appeal to the public and thus a decorative embellishment of the armed forces' public image. It was, of course, also seriously intended as a counterinsurgency measure, and, in fact, as the decade progressed, the older justification of military aid to Latin American countries as a contribution to "hemispheric defense" was entirely superseded by the newer objective of improved internal defense against subversion of the Cuban type with emphasis on civic action. In a review of the military aid program, an assistant secretary of state for Latin American affairs said in 1969, "It is not . . . a program based on such an outdated rationale as 'hemispheric defense.' " And he added, somewhat more positively, "One primary purpose of our military aid program has been and is to help our Latin American neighbors to attain socioeconomic development by systematic evolution rather than in the volatile atmosphere of destructive revolution."[6] During much of the period roughly 15 percent of military aid was allocated to civic action. The total for all Latin America in 1964, a fairly representative year, was about $14 million.[7]

On the civilian side of the effort the most specifically counterinsurgency-oriented program was the police training activity of USAID. For this purpose, AID established an International Police Academy, first in the Canal Zone and later in Washington. The six-week basic course was given in Spanish. This was embraced within the larger Alliance for Progress programs which themselves were aimed at heading off insurgency by promoting development. In other words, one could look on the entire program of the U.S. in Latin America during these years as a broad counterinsurgency program at least in a preventive sense. We will not, however, include it as part of our story, for we are primarily concerned with actual insurgencies and the measures taken to deal with them.

As we have seen, all the Castro-inspired guerrilla insurgencies failed, and in most cases the U.S. contribution played a part, albeit a limited one. To review these episodes briefly, Venezuela was an early case and one in which the insurgents came closer to succeeding than anywhere else—although they did not actually come very close. It was not typical of this series of episodes in that, in the early phase, urban rebellion played a major role in the revolutionary scheme and rural guerrilla warfare was secondary. Clearly, Romulo Betancourt's contribution was essential, whereas that of the U.S. was merely useful. No civic action funds were committed in Venezuela during 1962 and 1963, although military aid was sizable. Probably the most important aspect of the American effort was the police program. The Venezuelan police were a principal target of the urban guerrilla operations. They were in woeful condition at the beginning of the insurgency for lack of training and because of the low quality of personnel, a condition due to the poor repute in which the police were held. Police programs were initiated by the U.S. (and also, curiously enough, by Chile) and carried out by both AID and CIA. Improvements, especially in equipment, were noticeable.[8]

All this was no doubt helpful to Betancourt, but not critical. The insurgency in Venezuela went through several phases, but an early turning point was the election of 1963 when a successor to Betancourt (Raul Leoni) was chosen in free national elections and then assumed the office as provided in the constitution—an unprecedented accomplishment in Venezuelan history. The Communists focused on the goal of preventing this election and failed. In the political and counterinsurgency campaign preceding the election, Betancourt mastered his enemies on all sides and did so without violating the constitution or democratic norms. On election day, 91 percent of the electorate turned out, dramatically demonstrating the failure of-the insurgent campaign. The Communists showed an appreciation for the reasons of their failure. They gave up urban insurgency and opted for "protracted war" in the countryside, which sputters on to this day. Meanwhile, democratic government has persisted in Venezuela, social and economic development have continued, and these have provided a political context in which the insurgency has been unable to flourish.

In neighboring Colombia the story is less dramatic and the role of the army more important. As recently as 1976 an American reporter in Colombia sought to develop an analysis to explain the failure of Castroite guerrilla warfare to progress in that country despite more than ten years of trying. She advanced such reasons as the traditional political loyalties of the population to either the Liberal or Conservative parties, the bloody years of civil war between 1948 and 1957 whose memory remains alive, and the shallowness of the commitment of the urban students to a cause which they quickly abandoned under pressure. Of considerable importance, she found, was the skill of the military handling of the peasantry.

> The initial government response to guerrilla action [she wrote] was careful, involving as much social and psychological action as military retaliation. The army . . . realized that "extremism feeds on broken promises," said one military source.
> The army brought roads, clinics and construction jobs along with the state of siege when it fought guerrillas in depressed areas. Soldiers were told to treat the population as allies against a few misguided but retrievable insurgents. Troops who manhandled villagers were court-martialled publicly in the towns where offenses occurred.[9]

This suggests that the training offered to Colombian officers at Fort Gulick, Panama, and Fort Bragg, North Carolina, was put into practice when they returned to their duty in Colombia. At the same time, another student of Colombia makes quite clear that the Colombian army had its own long and well-established tradition of civic action many years before it was exposed to North American concepts.[10] Colombia had been afflicted with bitter domestic violence and endemic banditry in the countryside for many years. Attempts to identify the underlying causes had led the military leadership to the concept that la Violencia reflected, among other things, social and economic disparities, and to the conclusion that the armed forces had a role to play in solving such problems. The theory was developed well before various leftist organizations moved in among the active guerrilla groups and became predominant in some of them. Nevertheless, there was close cooperation between U.S. counter-insurgency planners and the Colombian military in drawing up a comprehensive plan, called "Plan Lazo," which was adopted in 1962 and continued for three years. Although it succeeded in eliminating some of the bandit and guerrilla groups, it also appears to have had the effect of driving the remaining holdouts into the arms of the Castroites who, after 1965, became the dominant element in guerrilla activity.[11] The military continued, with some American help, the program of military pressure following a generally enlightened approach, and succeeded in reducing the threat to a lower but nevertheless persistent level which continues up to the present. As in Venezuela, the threat has been contained but not eliminated. American help, meanwhile, has been reduced to a trickle.

The experience in Peru was directly related to Communist exploitation of deep-seated peasant grievances in the department of Cuzco in the period 1963-1965. Spearheaded by the Trotskyist Hugo Blanco, there was an outbreak of strikes, demonstrations, and some violence against the authorities in the La Convencion valley which stimulated an army reaction characterized by both military repression and social action, including a local land reform, road-building, the opening of schools, and the like. Although the land reform was later criticized as being halfhearted and inadequate,[12] it succeeded for a while, along with the other measures taken, in dampening the revolt. Within a few years, however, another group of local Communists, this time modeling themselves on Cuba's fidelismo, launched an ill-timed and ill-led guerrilla-style revolt from the neighboring mountains. The leader was Luis de la Puente.

> The tactic failed [writes the same reporter]. Peru's army, one of the best-disciplined in Latin

America, had been getting ready for the guerrillas since 1963. Many Peruvian officers and noncoms were among the eighteen thousand Latin American soldiers trained at the U.S. Army Counterinsurgency School in Panama. Thousands more have undergone Special Forces training in the United States.... In addition, many agents of the Peruvian Investigative Police have attended a counterinsurgency school run by the Central Intelligence Agency.[13]

The military first attempted to bomb the guerrillas out of their fastness but succeeded in wrapping up the revolt only after sealing off the trails that led in and out. The victory in this one-sided affair stemmed from the overwhelming force brought to bear plus the failure of the guerrillas to attract support during a period when peasant hopes had been raised by partial land reform and promises of more.

This entire experience convinced the military that Peru was in a state of "latent insurgency" and played a role in establishing the viewpoints among some Peruvian officers which led them eventually to seize control of the government and to institute a socialist regime under military domination which remains in power to this day.[14] Although the training and indoctrination received by Peruvian officers at American schools can hardly be held responsible for this outcome, it was one element among several that led them in that direction.

Guatemala, too, conducted counterinsurgency operations during these years which were to some extent influenced by American concepts. Guatemala participated in the various training programs and experimented with civic action, offers of amnesty, and has even tried the unique tactic of ignoring the guerrillas entirely. The latter have been divided among themselves and have gone through various phases in which one or another of the existing varieties of Communism was adopted as the current ideology. Neither the government nor the guerrillas has been strong enough to prevail, however, no matter what approach was taken. The bloodshed has been heavy for a small country, with the urban supporters of the guerrillas resorting to assassinations (including several foreign ambassadors) and the regime retaliating by sponsoring vigilante-style terrorism. In the midst of this reign of terror and counter-terror the principles of enlightened counterinsurgency were overwhelmed and forgotten.[15]

A final case we must note is that of Bolivia and of Che Guevara's fatal intervention there. This famous episode has been repeatedly described and analyzed and does not require detailed review for our purposes. (The account we found most useful is that of Daniel James in his introduction to an edition of Guevara's captured diaries."[16]) In virtually every detail, Guevara's final adventure was based either on faulty concepts or mistaken estimates of the situation or poor technique. The fact is almost incidental that the U.S. contributed to his defeat by hastily training a ranger unit of the Bolivian army which was deployed in August 1967 (the *foco* was discovered by the authorities in March), and finally destroyed both of Guevara's armed groups in October. Similarly incidental is the reported involvement of the CIA in close monitoring and advice on the intelligence aspects of the operation. The attempt was foredoomed to failure and would certainly have collapsed of its own errors, particularly in the choice of a location and a situation in which no likelihood of peasant support existed.[17]

These five cases represent the most extensive of the various insurgencies attempted in Latin America following the Cuban model and the theories of Castro and Guevara. Several of them continue at a low and unpromising level to this day, kept alive by the desperate commitment of their leaders to a revolutionary concept of dubious origin and highly exaggerated potency. The Latin American peasantry, largely Indian in origin and culture and isolated from the Hispanic mainstream of the ruling cultures, has so far rejected this effort to overturn the immemorial patterns of society in the remote countryside. In the meantime, after Guevara's debacle, the interest of the urban and educated adherents of revolution turned from Castroism to urban terrorism, a variety of insurgency which is remote from people's war and has so far also failed in its goals. At the same time, attitudes toward the insurgent threat began to change in the United States. The programs launched by the Kennedy Administration, which had a distinct if secondary role in thwarting the insurgencies, have declined in importance and have largely been terminated. For most purposes the counterinsurgency era in Latin America is at an end.

THE WINDING DOWN
OF THE APPARATUS

If we confine ourselves to doctrine and theory, the interest in counterinsurgency of the U.S. military services, and most particularly of the army, remained high throughout the 1960s. A process of earnest study by military intellectuals of the available field experience, and reformulation of manuals and training courses in accordance with the lessons derived, went on throughout the decade and after. "Counterinsurgency" disappeared as a descriptive label to be replaced by "internal defense and development" as a general term for a whole range of activities related to assisting less-developed countries, and by "stability operations" to describe the specific operational activity of the armed forces. A field manual specifically called "Stability Operations—U.S. Army Doctrine" was prepared which gave liberal emphasis to noncombat roles for the military.[18] Among them were "civil affairs" activities which could encompass, among other things, the establishment of schools and public health systems, assistance to the police, or civic action by the army to improve the environment in a given locality.[19] All of this was to be fitted into an overall "internal defense and development plan" developed by the U.S. and the host government. In its elephantine way, the military system was attempting to adapt itself to the novel complexities of the new dispensation, but the adjustments quickly came up against unchangeable "laws" when the question of combat tactics arose. Unit integrity and the full use of available firepower, including armor, artillery, combat air support, and "aerial fire support" (armed helicopters) were all mandated.[20]

Even more novel notions began to emerge in some corners of the system. Serious staff attention was given to designing regional military organizations to be placed at the headquarters of some of the joint commands (e.g., CINCPAC in Pearl Harbor and CINCSOUTH in Panama) which would have a preplanned capability to intervene in insurgency situations. In association with these regional assistance commands, the planners talked of developing special combat units "as flexible and lightly equipped as possible. Light, fast, specially outfitted units are needed, rather than conventional fighting forces."[21] This concept, which has long been a secret dream of military men with an orientation toward counterinsurgency, never left the drawing boards. In fact, the notion of a regional assistance command, which was encouraged by General Howard K. Johnson when he was army chief of staff, died when General Westmoreland assumed that position in late 1968. The latter favored, instead, the development of a "nation-building" school.[22] There was, in fact, a brief period in the late 1960s when military intellectuals were advancing the notion that the U.S. Army was the arm of the government best equipped to carry out in the field the entire range of activities associated with "nation-building." According to two analysts who studied these trends:

> The new doctrine does, however, imply a greatly enlarged advisory role for the U.S. military, extending far beyond security and encompassing, in some variants, virtually every facet of life in the rebellion-beset country, even such purely civilian efforts as assistance in the conduct of the country's fiscal and economic affairs. By the beginning of the 1970's many thoughtful Army officers believed that, in view of the difficulty that U.S. non-military agencies had in deploying well-trained civilian advisers for these functions, the Army itself should be prepared to provide such assistance.[23]

In actual fact, Fort Bragg, the home of Special Forces and the Special Warfare School, absorbed the Civil Affairs School of Fort Gordon and became the Military Assistance School. The change had limited impact for, at the same time, public support for all such activities dwindled steadily in reaction to the growing frustration and sense of futility generated by the stalemate in Vietnam. In truth, the army had reacted far too slowly to the pressures that had been brought to bear upon it during the counterinsurgency era. It had taken three or four years of costly exposure to the reality of the battlefield in Vietnam for the import of "revolutionary war," i.e., people's war, to have an impact. By that time an impatient public and a disillusioned press were unwilling to hear of innovations to make future interventions more effective. They wanted no more such interventions. By the early 1970s, the army, after a brief, unconsummated flirtation with the notion of fighting in new or, perhaps more accurately, in more primitive ways, slipped back with some relief to a more familiar posture. Its principal concern again became the preparation for conventional, high-technology war against a conventional enemy on the familiar battlefields of Europe. Less and less was heard about giving the U.S. Army a predominant role in nation building. But even the novel departures of the late 1960s missed the main point. They accepted new roles for the army other than the application of force, but, at the same time, with the exception of a few voices which had begun to speak of a special light infantry, they clung to the assumption that the principal role of *military force* in a counterinsurgency situation is to find and destroy the armed enemy rather than accepting the prior importance of protecting the population in order to separate the insurgents from their base. The latter was viewed as a defensive strategy and anathema was pronounced upon it. Finally, even the achievement embodied in the new field manuals was illusory, for as Heymann and Whitson state:

> Even as late as 1966, most American unit commanders and division staff officers arriving in South Vietnam were not familiar with the standard doctrinal literature contained in Army field manuals. . . . In the view of these officers, the focal division staff problem was not that of understanding the nature of the conflict, but one of managing a division's resources according to prevailing practice.[24]

The genuine accomplishments of the military in Vietnam described in the last chapter were not the work of the line commanders and their staffs but of military men detached from their units and assigned to CORDS to work as advisers and members of Mobile Training Teams developing the capabilities of Regional and Popular Forces and assisting village chiefs with their security problems. The line units, despite adjustments made by General Abrams, remained fixated upon the large enemy divisions as their preeminent responsibility to be discharged in traditional fashion by the concentration of overwhelming force.

UNWINDING THE CIVILIAN AGENCIES

In those Civilian agencies which had participated heavily in the counterinsurgency effort, a similar process of deemphasis began in the late sixties, aided by the fact that they all had other major commitments and concerns which

reasserted their priority. For example, in AID, where the police training and advisory activity continued well into the mid-seventies, it nevertheless succeeded in gradually shifting emphasis away from counterinsurgency concerns—rural police, combat police, and the like—to more conventional goals summed up in the term "institution-building." These comprised training, administration, and the improvement of police support activities such as communications. Concurrently, the overall emphasis shifted from counterinsurgency to law and order. AID as a whole reverted to economic development as its primary task and gradually subordinated or dropped entirely its interest in the problems of rural environmental improvement for the sake of cementing popular loyalties.

This concept had always been a dubious proposition based on the unsupported belief that economic and social improvement, if seen as having been brought about by the government's efforts, would induce people to throw in their lot with the government rather than its enemies. But others were soon pointing out that development, or economic and social modernization, was a highly disruptive process usually accompanied by social upheaval.[25] Another view held that small-scale investment in local improvement, if properly institutionalized so as to become a permanent ongoing function of the threatened government, was a more appropriate response to a Communist rural insurgency. But many problems developed out of this concept as well, among them the undoubted fact that the insurgents were often able to exploit the aid, diverting some of it for their own use, terrorizing recipients to make increased contributions, and benefiting in many other ways.[26]

Still another point of view held, as does this writer, that the critical aspect of rural development aid for counterinsurgency purposes was the process by which decisions were made and the aid distributed, that an important part of the answer to Communist challenges in the countryside was to devise a means whereby the government side brought those affected into the decision-making process, thereby giving them some control over the terms of their existence. Land reform could be a major contributing factor in such an approach, depending on the degree to which tenancy and land ownership were a serious problem. A voice in the selection of the local officials who administered the program would be another, as would the availability of channels whereby a community could make its views known to a higher authority. Such an approach, however, is exceedingly difficult for a foreign power to launch within a host country. Inevitably it merges into issues of political reform, of changing the local power structure, and becomes anything but a neutral, administrative, and technical matter. In other words, it is a program beyond the capability of a foreign technical advisory and training agency such as AID to administer. AID had been called upon to accomplish a highly political task with a repertoire of techniques—the delivery of materials, advice, and technical training—which were not appropriate to the task, and the agency was not loath to see the emphasis on counterinsurgency gradually eased, permitting it to concentrate its efforts in areas in which it felt more competent.

A somewhat similar process occurred in CIA, where gradually the focus shifted in the late 1960s to the intelligence and counterintelligence aspects of counterinsurgency and away from efforts to support local popular paramilitary forces to fill the gaps caused by the central government's failure to provide local security. Symbolic evidence of this shift came to public light when a lengthy CIA analysis of the Vietnamese situation leaked out to the press in 1970.[27] The study made an extensively documented case for the view that Communist strategy in Vietnam had shifted from active military confrontation to the quiet penetration of government services by an estimated thirty thousand agents under Lao Dong control. The goal of the strategy was to establish a strong position from which the Communist organization could work to bring down the South Vietnamese regime after the American military withdrawal had been completed.

This study was the apparent fruit of a laborious and thorough intelligence collection and analysis effort made possible by a shift of CIA resources from training and advisory roles to *independent* intelligence collection, that is, collection carried on separate from and without the knowledge of the South Vietnamese. That type of effort, while it had always been part of the CIA program in Vietnam, acquired a high priority only in late 1968 when the CIA station informed

CORDS that it intended to withdraw the personnel who had been performing advisory and monitoring functions in the Phoenix program. CORDS replaced these officers with hastily trained army lieutenants and captains, and CIA put the personnel thus made available to work on the independent collection of information on the Viet Cong and Lao Dong. Similar transfers of effort took place as CIA and CORDS began the long process of withdrawal from the various cadre programs, particularly the Revolutionary Development teams. That shift represented the reassertion by elements within CIA of the preeminence of independent intelligence collection as the classic CIA function in any situation involving the U.S. national interest overseas. In effect, the lengthy report, completed in 1970, made the point by implication that the enemy had swept the boards in this subterranean contest of spying and counterspying and had thereby thwarted the immense and costly military and pacification efforts of the U.S. and South Vietnam. It stated that the enemy's penetration program had established Lao Dong–controlled agents at all key points in the South Vietnamese government structure, including the intelligence and counterintelligence services, and had done so in such strength that the very weapons by which they would ordinarily have been combated and neutralized were unable to achieve any lasting success against them. Whether or not that conclusion was true and fragmentary reports from Vietnam since the Lao Dong victory tend to confirm it—it implies a pointed criticism of CIA, and indeed of U.S. priorities in Vietnam up to 1968, and demonstrates both the trend away from counterinsurgency involvement by CIA as well as some of the arguments underlying that trend.

The evolution of national security and foreign policy concerns away from preoccupation with Communist insurgency was also evident in the Department of State. Indeed, although its public commitment had been as firm as that of the other agencies, foreign service officers as a body had included from the beginning a large number of skeptics, especially among the more experienced members of the career cadre. This attitude had been generated by the precise question which U. Alexis Johnson—the senior active foreign service officer at the time—had sought to combat as early as 1961.[28] This was the doubt, born of

Denouements **431**

experience, that ambassadors and their staffs could, with the means available to them, i.e., persuasion plus offers of aid, generate the enlightenment and breadth of view among host governments which were required to carry out a serious and effective counterinsurgency program. As Johnson himself had acknowledged in the early days of the policy, it was possible that foreign leaders might not be able or willing to take the risks of reforming their governments along the lines demanded by the urgencies of their situation.[29] Many foreign service professionals doubted that they would and remained quietly reserved toward the counterinsurgency enthusiasms of the moment, never taking their doubts to the public. An insight into this critical view was offered, somewhat after the fact, by Charles Maechling, Jr., who had served as "Director of Internal Defense" in the State Department during the Kennedy years, later left the government and in 1969 published "Our Internal Defense Policy—A Reappraisal," also in the *Foreign Service Journal*.[30]

Maechling's argument is a root-and-branch assault on the policy which he had played a senior role in implementing, and it strikes some shrewd blows. It suffers, however, from a failure to make adequate distinctions between differing situations and assumes an inability on the part of the U.S. to exercise choice between favorable and unfavorable circumstances. In fact, during the mid-sixties some advocates of the doctrine *did* more or less assume that counterinsurgency policies could be applied successfully anywhere, regardless of circumstances, but Maechling did not content himself with addressing the contradictions that resulted from this overly ambitious reach. He assumed that countries like Vietnam were the predominant type among nations endangered by insurgency and dwelled on the frustrations of intervention in a situation where the government services are corrupt, the army indifferent to the fate of the population, and "the ruling oligarchy is numerically so small that it has to keep the political opposition ... divided and neutralized in order to prevent being blown sky high." This is the government the United States has to rely on to achieve reforms that will make effective counterinsurgency operations possible. The result, in the author's view, "is the old horror of responsibility without authority,

elevated to the plane of high strategy." The final and tragic contradiction emerges when the situation deteriorates to the point that the U.S. believes itself obliged to intervene with troops, for that introduces all the horrors attendant on modern warfare, and visits them upon the hapless population.

In sum, Maechling sees counterinsurgency as envisaged by the then avowed policies of the U.S. as inevitably producing at best a prolonged and costly stalemate. He attributes this result to the reliance upon mere advice and persuasion to resolve the complex internal problems of sorebeset underdeveloped countries and to the destructive impact of foreign military intervention. Clearly, he had Vietnam in mind in making this indictment, and it had much validity as applied to that country. The view was representative of the opinion of many foreign service professionals who feelingly echoed the conclusion that an ambassador armed with nothing but his own eloquence and some economic and military aid could hardly rearrange the intimate internal power relationships of a foreign country at a time of crisis.

The Department of State did not resist the gradual drawing back from the open-ended and global commitments implied in the earlier formulations of counterinsurgency policy. On the contrary, many welcomed the trend as a delayed acknowledgment of reality. One of the clearer expositions of the new policy came from the under secretary of state in the early years of the Nixon Administration, Eliot Richardson. It was a version of the "Nixon Doctrine" first expounded by the president at Guam in 1969. Without disavowing anything that had been done in the past, Richardson said that while the U.S. would continue to aid its friends and allies threatened by internal subversion, such aid would

> hereafter depend on the realities of each separate situation. In some cases aid in economic and political development would be enough. In other cases aid in the form of training and equipment may be necessary. But the job of countering insurgency in the field is one which must be conducted by the government concerned, making use of its popular support, its resources and its men.[31]

The implications were further expounded in a later sentence: "We cannot, it seems clear, do the job of fighting insurgency for someone else." That, in fact, was the only new element of the policy. Despite the implications of Richardson's remarks, the character of American aid had usually depended upon the nature of the given situation.

The State Department continued for a while to offer the "counterinsurgency" course which had been launched by President Kennedy. Successive reorganizations brought about the establishment of the position of "Under Secretary for Security Assistance," whose function was to coordinate both military and economic assistance programs at a higher level than hitherto. Such bureaucratic rearrangements had little impact upon the reality of a steady decline in interest and concern which was reflected both in a reduction in appropriations and in high-level attention. An example of the latter is evidenced in President Nixon's report to Congress on U.S. foreign policy delivered on February 18, 1970. This document was unprecedented in the completeness of its survey of both foreign policy and defense policy. When published and distributed it comprised 160 pages. In the entire document a mere two paragraphs cover the matter which had stimulated such a copious flow of verbiage in the preceding years. They appear in the section devoted to defense policy and specifically concerned with "general purpose forces." Here they are *in toto*:

> We cannot expect U.S. military forces to cope with the entire spectrum of threats facing allies or potential allies throughout the world. This is particularly true of subversion and guerrilla warfare, or "wars of national liberation." Experience has shown that the best means of dealing with insurgencies is to preempt them through economic development and social reform and control them with police, paramilitary and military action by the threatened government.
>
> We may be able to supplement local efforts with economic and military assistance. However, a direct combat role for U.S. general purpose forces arises primarily when insurgency has shaded into external aggression or when there is an overt conventional attack. In such cases we shall weigh our interests and our commitments, and we shall consider the efforts of our allies, in determining our response.[32]

As we have already noted,[33] the reorganization of the National Security Council Staff by the Johnson administration had seen the dissolution of the Special Group (C.I.) set up by President Kennedy to oversee and energize the multiagency counterinsurgency effort. It had been replaced by a series of interdepartmental committees organized on a geographical basis, each one chaired by an assistant secretary of state. This structure ultimately disappointed its designer, General Maxwell Taylor, who had intended it as a means of concentrating effort and attention on the problems of Communist insurgency.[34] The result, he admitted, had been the opposite, not, one suspects, because of inherent defects, but because of the waning interest at the highest levels of the government after the departure from the scene of such true believers as John F. and Robert F. Kennedy. This trend was somewhat abetted, however, by the diffuseness of the new multicommittee structure.

In a desultory fashion an effort was made to bring up to date the policy document that governed U.S. activities formerly called counterinsurgency and now known as the Foreign Internal Defense Program. A formal paper was Brawn up, processed through all the agencies, approved by the NSC, and allowed to remain unimplemented.[35] It would appear that there was a reluctance at the higher levels of the system either to apply the global policies which remained formal commitments or to admit that they no longer carried the weight they once did. The rather indifferent and *pro forma* attitude of the policy levels is well illustrated by the language of the summation of counterinsurgency policy in the Nixon state paper cited above. The formula invokes the preemption of "wars of national liberation" through "economic development and social reform" and control "with police, paramilitary and military action by the threatened government." This approach was merely an iteration of conventional wisdom which ignored much of the hard-won experience of the preceding ten years, particularly the failure to establish any link between economic development and change in popular attitudes in favor of the government. It completely overlooks the political essence of the problem and once again implies that we are merely dealing with a technical and administrative matter rather than one that goes to the heart of the way power is distributed in the threatened country.

A final illustration of the eclipse of counterinsurgency as a foreign policy concern—without any public revision of the formal commitment—is an episode in which the author was personally involved. In May 1972, Henry Kissinger, then assistant to the president for national security affairs, signed an NSC Study Memorandum directing an interagency study of the insurgency situation in Thailand to include an array of U.S. government options for presidential decision. A study group was organized (the author was a member), traveled to Thailand, and began drafting its paper. By December 1972 a draft was circulating among the agencies concerned, but it did not complete the round of approvals. It simply disappeared into the bureaucratic maze and never emerged. For reasons still not clear, Dr. Kissinger lost interest and allowed it to expire for lack of high-level support. That experience convinced the author that no systematic program approach in this field could succeed without very high-level backing against the indifference of the bureaucracy to the subject as well as the resentment generated by the effort of the NSC staff to take the initiative in foreign policy formulation. Perhaps Dr. Kissinger concluded that any effort by him to bulldoze through the obstructions would probably not produce a worthwhile paper, or would take too much time and effort better spent on other matters, or, even if a workable policy emerged, it would be implemented half-heartedly—or perhaps his reasons partook of all three arguments. Not to be ignored is the possibility that concern over domestic political reaction was also involved, or even the impact on the new policy of rapprochement with China. At any rate, this abortive effort is the last initiative known to the author to generate new policy in the field of counterinsurgency. It represents the unmarked grave of a policy born amid much fanfare and high expectations twelve years earlier and now gone the way of "manifest destiny" and Theodore Roosevelt's Monroe Doctrine "corollary" and other forgotten policy urgencies in a changing world.

COULD COUNTERINSURGENCY BE REVIVED?

Behind the executive branch's retreat from counterinsurgency was the public identification of that policy with the involvement of the U.S. in the countries of former French Indochina and particularly Vietnam, an involvement which had generated such a powerful revulsion that any policy associated with it automatically shared the negative recoil. There were, however, less emotional reasons underlying the unavowed abandonment of the policy. Major changes had occurred in the world in the 1960s and in American perceptions of that world, changes which undermined most of the analysis by which the advocates had convinced two presidents of the seriousness of the threat and a third that enough of a residue remained to justify continued, if reduced, concern. No doubt the most momentous of these changes was the surfacing of the Sino-Soviet schism and the subsequent fragmentation of the international Communist movement. From a state in which the world was divided into two hostile camps and a third that strove to avoid commitment to either, one of the two major groupings, the Communist, split several ways and became polycentric. The hostility between the various centers made it appear certain that they could not combine their policies and resources against the United States and its allies, even though their verbiage continued to identify "imperialism" as a common enemy. Before this development, the power balance appeared to depend upon containing the threat of monolithic Communism and preventing it from spreading further. After the schism it no longer seemed momentous whether a given distant and obscure country became Communist unless some strategic or major economic factor also was apparent. The perception of the so-called domino theory—the belief that Communist victory in one country automatically placed its neighbors in immediate jeopardy—as an exaggerated extrapolation from questionable premises also played a part in allaying concern.

Sober second thought in the late sixties had also undermined the beliefs that the Communist world was unrelentingly expansive, that Maoist people's war was the preferred instrument of the Communists for the further expansion of their movement in the nuclear age which had rendered all-out war inconceivable, and finally that the less-developed world would be the scene of the critical struggle between Communist and non-Communist forces in which the side that mastered the secrets of people's war would win. Regarding Communist expansionism, the removal from the world scene of Khrushchev, together with his threatening bombast, made it easier to perceive and reflect on the fact that the Soviets were cautious rather than otherwise in taking risks for the sake of expansion, that they would become involved in extending their sway only if they could do so in a fashion so indirect that no provocation to justify war would be apparent. Nor were they at all wedded to people's war as a universal route to power. On the contrary, as we noted in the first chapter of this work, the Russians had never accepted the claims that Mao made for his formula for taking power in the less-developed world. Indeed, even China itself abandoned its immoderate pretensions to having devised an infallible method which all true Communists were obliged to put into prompt practice. Lin Piao, its great advocate, was disgraced and dead, and China had swung around almost 180 degrees in its approach to the United States. While guerrilla warfare and terrorism continued to be prominent features of the troubled world scene, more often than not they had become the instruments of extremist fanatics not only not under Communist discipline but looked upon by orthodox parties as both misguided and dangerous. Moreover, such failures of people's war as those of Castro in Latin America and the long-drawn-out but hardly significant efforts in Burma and Thailand, suggested that where the threat existed its success was far from guaranteed even without U.S. intervention, as was the case, for example, in Burma. A great deal depended on circumstances and on the capabilities of the two sides involved in the struggle. It began to be clear that the Communist movement, despite its sophisticated training and indoctrination methods and its tested organizational principles, performed unevenly throughout the world, and that in some countries its local representatives were downright incompetent.

Of these changes by far the most important was the split between the two major Communist countries. When the U.S. moved to take advantage of the schism by establishing contact with China and committing itself to "normalizing" relations, the fears of Chinese expansionism that had been a major justification for the Vietnam intervention were seen by all to have been more than somewhat exaggerated. As far as concerns his public commitment to the waging of unrelenting people's war until the West was surrounded and brought down, Mao Tse-tung himself, rather than the United States, was seen to have been the-paper tiger.

Thus, in the mid-1970s, very little if anything remained of the analytical structure which constituted the justification for the gravity with which, in the 1960s, the United States had viewed the threat of people's war and the urgency with which it sought to counter it. Rarely has there been so complete a reversal of strategic views and assumptions by a great power within so short a span of time. Many serious observers and analysts now look upon the brief preoccupation with counterinsurgency as an aberration stemming from cold-war fixations combined with the Kennedy style of policy development, a style emphasizing enthusiasm and faddishness at the expense of sober reflection.

Although perhaps containing some truth insofar as applies to the headlong attack and the breathless pursuit of the goal by hastily concocted techniques, the view nevertheless is an exaggeration based on the clarity of hindsight. In the early sixties the threat of a monolithic and expansionist Communism was not so easily dismissed. The expansionist thrust of Khrushchev's rhetoric, his pressure on Berlin, and his later effort to implant ballistic missiles in Cuba could not be waved aside. His verbal commitment to "wars of national liberation" was easily misread as a new global initiative in view of events in Vietnam, Laos, and Cuba—not to mention earlier Communist victories in China and Yugoslavia and the rash of insurgencies that had swept through Asia in Stalin's last years. In all these countries, attempts had been made—some successful, some still under way, and a few thwarted—to bring Communist parties to power by effective exploitation of the techniques of guerrilla warfare combined with skilled political organization and terrorism, all dominated by a shrewdly calculated political strategy. New episodes continued to manifest themselves throughout the 1960s, and even today we see the Soviets in particular providing encouragement and support to outbreaks of a similar type in Angola, Namibia, Mozambique, and Rhodesia, although actual Soviet control does not exist. It may have been largely coincidental that the combination of events on the eve and immediately following Kennedy's inauguration loomed so threateningly. No doubt the threat was partly in the eye of the beholder, the president, whose life had been lived in a time when World War II and its lessons were assumed to apply to all messianic totalitarians. Nevertheless, it cannot be dismissed as a mere figment in a later decade made wiser by further experience.

Although such movements, for the reasons just noted, no longer appear to pose a serious threat to the United States and its interests, there is no guarantee that this will always be so. The world continues to change, and the prominent and seemingly permanent features dominating one epoch can and do suddenly disappear, leaving a completely altered landscape. It is fruitless to speculate what such changes might be, but even in today's world, a Communist-sponsored and effective guerrilla insurgency, encouraged by the Russians in, for example, Panama or Mexico, could quickly reawaken U.S. concern. That being the case, it is not difficult to conceive of major changes in the world scene—a rapprochement between China and Russia leading to a close alliance between those two powers is one far-from-impossible development—under which a guerrilla insurgency even farther from our borders would have the effect of once again posing an apparent threat to vital interests.

In other words, it is imaginable, although far from likely in the near term, that some future White House may become interested in scrutinizing the counterinsurgency experience which we have been at some pains to recount and analyze in these pages, for lessons on both the pitfalls and the positive courses of action suggested by the successes and failures of the period. For several reasons it is much to be hoped that such does not turn out to be the case, and most especially for the reason that the lessons of our experience are clearly negative. Effective counterinsurgency, avoiding the brutalities of unadorned suppression, and seeking to deal with the genuine issues in a sophisticated manner which does no damage to our moral and democratic principles, is a complex and difficult maneuver for which the United States has shown no talent. Nevertheless, the world being the

unpredictable place that it is, let us review the terrain we have traversed to identify the lessons that seem common to most of the involvements discussed.

COPING WITH THE MILITARY AND THE BUREAUCRACY

To begin at home, involvement in counterinsurgency in any depth immediately confronts us with very difficult obstacles internal to our government and growing out of the nature of permanent bureaucracies. It cuts across the norms and hierarchies of the concerned agencies in several ways. First, it forces them to do things which are only indirectly related to their basic missions. Second, if organized in a properly integrated fashion it short-circuits normal command channels in favor of a new, temporary command structure that grievously flouts institutional loyalties and prerogatives. Unless dealt with early and firmly, these difficulties will quickly result in an apparatus that is merely going through certain motions without a considered strategy or appropriate priorities or operations effectively coordinated in the field. The foreign aid apparatus will focus on development for its own sake, placing emphasis on the transfer of things and of skills rather than on changing popular attitudes, for this latter is a goal which is extremely difficult to get hold of and to measure. The military will inevitably attempt to build the host government's armed forces in its own image, to shape a conventional army able quickly to concentrate its forces and spew forth heavy fire upon the terrain regardless of what is there. These agencies, together with the CIA and USIA, will be content to coordinate their operations at a regular committee meeting by a process of negotiation which leaves the internal and routine processes of their organizations undisturbed.

A central control point at a high level empowered to force new concepts through the system and monitor compliance is essential—even more so after the experiences of the counterinsurgency era than in 1962 when the Kennedy Administration innovated with the Special Group (C.I.). For the experience and lessons of the subsequent decade will largely be lost if no central authority exists to exhume them, reexamine them for lessons, and apply the lessons where appropriate.

Not only is institutional memory in our government of two-year or four-year stints in office extremely weak, but each agency will have its parochial view of the past as well as the present. Each will also have its own doctrine so designed as to disturb the institution the least. A common doctrine must be developed and enforced or the effort will be neutralized. Awareness of these problems must exist at the highest levels, that of the president himself, and he must be willing to take the heat that will result from imposing the necessary changes. If he shrinks from the political costs then he should not launch the effort at all, for he is courting failure, which will produce higher political costs in the long run.

APPLYING THE LESSONS TO THE MILITARY

The decision-makers' knottiest problem in the hypothetical situation we are discussing will be fitting the military into a revised organizational and doctrinal approach. At this writing, the U.S. military, in particular the army, has not acknowledged any degree of error in Vietnam or anywhere else and has dismantled the centers and training programs that might keep alive in some corners of the system a commitment to the notion that counterinsurgency calls for some modification the prevailing wisdom of "find 'em, fix 'em, and fight 'em," or "git thar fustest with the mostest."

Indeed, the way through this thicket is not easy to see. The military notoriously offer great resistance to change, especially if imposed from the outside. Moreover, as discussed in Chapter III, counterinsurgency war poses a conundrum for the higher commands with no solution that readily satisfies conflicting urgencies. The "solution" adopted in the 1960s was simply to deny the problem, to insist that standard military doctrines could readily be adapted to counterinsurgency warfare with only minor changes. Three and a half million tons of bombs dropped in South Vietnam alone were a monument to the belief voiced, for example, by General Wheeler when he was chairman of the Joint Chiefs, that "the essence of the problem is military."[36] Clearly, the solution chosen was no solution at all, and the problem will confront any future leadership attempting to avoid the mistakes of the past.

How can the U.S. Army best accommodate a mission which runs athwart its permanent and essential commitment to conventional war fought at the highest feasible technological level, and calls for it to strip down to a primitive and basic mode of combat, relying on small units, light weapons, and precise, measured fire? The matter is even further complicated over the uncertainty about whether any given situation will yield to a combination of material assistance and advice and training or whether it will escalate in seriousness until it becomes necessary once more—and in spite of repeated commitment to the contrary—to contemplate direct intervention with American forces.

Taking the second question first, it is impossible to be absolutely certain ahead of time that changed circumstances will not eventually force the U.S. to think again about the "unthinkable" alternative of deploying combat forces. Clearly, however, it is decidedly preferable for the United States to abstain from direct intervention if it is possible to do so without suffering a major setback. The best, if far from perfect, resolution of these conflicting requirements is to focus in the first instance upon developing suitable training and advisory capability, while at the same time perfecting a doctrine and a suitable plan for implementation in the event that intervention becomes inevitable. Both the advisory and training program and the plans for intervention must be consistent with each other and share a common doctrine and approach.

As for the nature of the approach, there is no single best solution. The principal alternatives all have drawbacks. One can create specialized units specifically pointed at this kind of warfare, a solution disfavored by the military hierarchy but one which was pressed upon it by President Kennedy. Such a solution tends to restrict the requisite skills and techniques to the specialized units which in the Kennedy years were the Special Forces. If such forces were given the full responsibility for dealing with U.S. commitments in counterinsurgency situations the approach might indeed meet the requirement. The record, however, shows a great unwillingness by the military hierarchy to permit the Special Forces a free hand in advising friendly governments on counterinsurgency. Its role has been limited to training and advising a counterpart organization, or simply to training any units that are assigned to receive such training. The broader task of helping an ally to develop a suitable armed forces structure pursuing a suitable strategy and encouraging systematic use of tactics appropriate to counterinsurgency operations has been preempted by the regular military. They, regrettably, conceive of the task as that of creating a mirror-image armed force functioning to the extent possible as the U.S. functioned in Vietnam.

Other alternatives have been discussed but never tried. Thus, it is imaginable but unlikely that the United States Army could fight or advise its clients to fight as the British fought in Malaya—breaking divisions up into smaller units, eschewing almost all artillery and combat air support, and totally merging the military side of the effort into a combined police and civilian organizational structure under civilian control. This alternative, which in theory is the one best fitted to the task, would involve the president in attempting to force down reluctant throats a drastic alteration in the military's procedures, their concept of their mission, and their traditional doctrine. The reaction of the officer corps to such an effort is suggested by the explosive comment of one general on the problem of adapting U.S. military operations to the task in Vietnam. "I'll be damned," he said, "if I permit the United States Army, its institutions, its doctrine, and its traditions, to be destroyed just to win this lousy war."[37]

Even if cooperation from the military institution were forthcoming, the policy would call for preparing the army, or parts of it, to fight at least two different kinds of war, which is obviously an extremely difficult if not an impossible burden. The mind shrinks from the complexities and the inevitable confusion and error that would result.

Another alternative would be to assign counterinsurgency functions neither to the army as a whole nor to any part of it but to another service entirely, which, in effect, means to the marines. Being a smaller force with a limited mission in contrast to the army's global security responsibility, the marines actually seem best suited to a limited and specialized task such as counterinsurgency. In their favor is their demonstrated flexibility, as shown in Vietnam, and their history of involvement in "nation building" in the Caribbean and Central America. The solution would face some practical difficulties but is

one that, we could hope, would be seriously studied should the government again be faced with the necessity of assisting a foreign government to deal with Communist rural insurgency.

WHO TO HELP

The American side of the coin thus still presents many dilemmas and difficulties, all of which would tend to reinforce our initial hope that the necessity to deal with them never does come up again. If we turn now to some of the lessons that should be absorbed and applied in approaching the foreign government and people to be helped, the situation is no better. Moreover, generalizations are far more uncertain because no two foreign countries will present identical sets of problems, and what may quickly prevail in one country may equally quickly fail in another.

No lesson is easier to state and harder to apply than that a decision to become involved once again in a counterinsurgency situation should be preceded by intense and prayerful study. Moreover, such a study should be in the form of an honest appraisal of whether or not U.S. assistance, knowing what we should have learned of its limitations in affecting the internal political arrangements of any foreign land, can truthfully be expected to perform what will be demanded of it if the intervention is to be successful. Merely suggesting such an approach immediately brings to the mind's eye the pitfalls it will be forced to confront. Call it "the arrogance of power" or the unwillingness to accept limitations in America's ability to deal with the backward and small and weak "as a great power should," it is simply impolitic to tell a president or a secretary of state of the "most powerful country in the world" that all our skill and wealth and know-how are to no avail, that country X is beyond saving because its own leadership is not up to the task, and no foreign government can substitute its own will for that of the native leadership. Nevertheless, unless the decision-makers are willing to ask such questions and probe beyond the easy responses to come to grips with the core problem, then we again invite failure.

Let us pursue the question further by asking what were the particular problems of Vietnam (as distinguished from the internal U.S. governmental problems just discussed) that made a mockery of our vast power, advanced technology, and willingness to spend resources lavishly. Some of them are obvious and are generally accepted. One is the advanced stage of the insurgency at the time we intervened militarily, with the South Vietnamese on the verge of defeat and the Lao Dong organization fully developed, experienced, and skillfully led, and operating from a firm base in North Vietnam. Another was the issue of nationalist feeling which, by the massiveness of our presence, as well as by our lack of familiarity with the people and the culture, we managed to exacerbate and reinforce so tragically. But by far the most critical problem, and one we never mastered, was the failure of the government we were bolstering and guiding at such great cost to rise to the opportunity, take hold, and move ahead with the task in vigorous and capable fashion. From beginning to end it remained unable to confront its problems effectively and to elicit an acceptable performance from its services, and was therefore hesitant, dependent on the U.S., and afraid, despite its great superiority in weaponry and the availability of massive technical and economic aid, to contemplate going it alone. Its services—military and civilian—were eaten out with corruption, favoritism, and petty politics. Its leadership also led in those categories, but not in the qualities necessary to grasp the opportunities offered and move forward confidently.

Why was this the case? Many reasons have been adduced—cultural or historical or keyed to the personalities involved. No doubt they all played some role. Without delving any more deeply into causes, however, we would point to the underlying political structure of the government and its paralyzing effect with regard to the compelling need for self-reform of its services and their relationship with the public.

The word reform is often employed by the school which sees successful revolution as preventable only by "social reform" or "thoroughgoing reform" or some such formula. We have something more specific in mind.. The problem stems from the precariousness of the regime's political base and the devices it employs to maintain itself in power. Three of the six governments in the case histories presented earlier were military dictatorships, and the fourth—the

Philippines—was a corrupt civilian regime ruling, behind a constitutional facade, by means of graft and cronyism. The Diem regime had similar structural weaknesses. The problem arises when a regime relies for its continued survival upon powerful subordinates whose support has to be purchased and who have to be carefully balanced in order to prevent combinations that might be tempted to reach for power themselves. The phenomenon is clearly a feature of political underdevelopment where sources of legitimacy via traditional means or constitutional processes are not available. Military dictatorships which have come to power by *coup d'etat* are particularly prone to this defect, for they have little moral claim to power and must devise a system to minimize the threat that others will attempt to duplicate their feat in seizing control by force and guile.

The effect upon the government's services of the system of purchased support is highly destructive of performance standards and of the relationship with the public; particularly in the armed forces and police, the two services which are closest to the leadership of a military regime and whose support is essential to any regime. At the top of any given service and filling the key posts are men who know that they enjoy their positions as a result of political loyalty and have been given within broad limits a free hand to make of it what they will. The quality of their performance has little to do with their continuance in office, and exploitation of their position for financial gain, if appearances are preserved, is expected rather than otherwise.

Once the top leadership of a service is of this character, it follows necessarily that the entire service will be permeated with the same attitudes. Subordinates down to the lower ranks are chosen to build a structure which will serve the private needs of their superiors. Their loyalties are purchased, too, thus permitting them to extract the most out of the bargain within the limits generally understood but never spelled out.

Even worse than corruption in its impact on the public is the effect of the system on performance. Part of the political bargain between superior and subordinate is the promise of prestige and ease of life, which reverses the normal order of the military in which the prestige is supposed to reward such qualities as courage, leadership, and competence in an arduous profession. When personal loyalty is offered in exchange for office, the martial qualities are the first to suffer. It is no part of the political bargain by which an officer obtains and keeps his job that he should take risks with his life, that he should work long and late, that he should put the comfort of his troops before his own, that the demands of duty, in other words, shall have first call on his time and energies. As a result, a political army—an army whose leaders play a critical role in keeping an existing regime afloat—is often a very poor army indeed. The low quality of its standards also impacts heavily upon the population it is supposed to be defending. Troops with poor leadership will normally not behave well in their contacts with the public, for their leaders are unconcerned and often take such poor care of the soldiers under them that the latter must steal in order to eat.

There are, of course, exceptions to this rule, most of which are found in countries with a proud military history and strong preexisting martial traditions. Pakistan is one such example, among several one could cite. Another exceptional case is Korea, whose present-day army is officered by men who survived and advanced during the testing time of the Korean War. Such countries as Laos, Thailand, and Vietnam, however, have no such proud past. Their armies had no traditions of valor and skill against which officers were judged and which they had to meet in order to be accepted into the charmed circle. Acceptability was determined by such criteria as class, family, relationships formed in military school, and the like.

In the case of Vietnam, these qualities persisted in the army and police throughout the long American involvement and proved impervious to the extraordinary efforts that were made to correct them. The ARVN combat patrols that were carefully signaled in advance to the enemy, the battalion and divisional commanders who were notorious incompetents but could not be removed, the frequent refusal to close with a trapped enemy, the great reluctance to risk casualties, and the apparent inability to raise the low standards of troop behavior toward the population, all were a result of the inherent flaws of a politicized army. They could not be eradicated

unless and until the army had been removed from politics and entirely reformed by a firm leadership in the style of Magsaysay. When the ARVN fought well—and it sometimes did—it was usually because it had no alternative, as at Tet or during the Easter offensive of 1972, when it had to fight to survive. There were also exceptions which resulted from intense American pressure favoring particular officers who performed above normal ARVN standards. But when the American soldiers were gone and the Congress sharply reduced its logistic support, panic quickly set in—panic caused, one can only surmise, by the realization of the Vietnamese officer corps that it was really not up to its job. In the final analysis, those who had played out the charade had never been fooled by it. Only the foreigners had been deceived, and deceived largely as a result of their own blindness to the political realities of a land where they had lived and worked for so many years without learning the most elementary truths of the scene about them.

Very similar problems—although for obvious reasons on a lesser scale also characterized the military and the police in Thailand. The Royal Thai Army was notoriously a garrison army and was not really intended by its superiors to fight in serious combat. The volunteer units sent to Vietnam, for instance, were quite inferior fighting forces. On the other hand, the volunteer units sent secretly to Laos were supposed to have given a good account of themselves. But these latter were not regular Thai units; the officers were RTA regulars assigned to the duty, while the men were volunteers. The accidental effect of this makeup was to produce a better-motivated and better-led force than the normal RTA regular battalions. The reason seems to have been that the officers were those with the least political influence in their original units. They could only hope that professional competence and a good combat record would help their careers in lieu of the political standing which they did not command.

Despite an enlightened doctrine relating to the role of the military in counterinsurgency, the Thai army has lapsed into firing into unarmed villages, and also into employing unobserved artillery fire and aerial bombardment against such targets. Such episodes violate Thai doctrine, but they nevertheless still happen on occasion. Notoriously, the RTA is reluctant to risk casualties. In one famous foray in 1971, the entire elite First Division sallied forth from its barracks outside Bangkok to eliminate an insurgent force in the northwest and returned months later without having accomplished its objective or having suffered a single casualty in direct combat; although losses were considerable, they all resulted from enemy booby" traps and the like. Casualties, particularly among the officer corps, cannot be distributed in accordance with political influence, and so are to be avoided even at the cost of failure of the mission.

Examples could be multiplied, but the point is clear enough. When the services of a regime have been politicized, a strong risk exists that they will be inadequate to the demands of dealing with a Communist insurgency—or any other serious military challenge. They must be reformed if the regime is to succeed against a well-established and well-led Communist insurgent movement. Such reforms are easy to prescribe but difficult to carry out. In effect, they require that the regime change the base of its power, a most problematical course to follow, especially at a time of internal crisis. This is the problem of "self-reform in crisis," to which we have frequently referred in the course of this history.

Reverting again to the example of Vietnam, it is well established that more than once between 1969 and 1975 General Nguyen Van Thieu launched apparently serious efforts to build a popular political base as an alternative to relying on the purchased loyalty of the armed forces. (See the preceding chapter.) Each time, however, he quailed before the risks and abandoned the effort. No doubt he saw that his chances for success were quite small, while the risks of provoking another military coup were very real. Thieu has more excuse for his failure than has the United States for its persistence in the hope that lavish weaponry and supply and massive training and retraining programs would transform the Vietnamese armed forces into a tough, well-ed, competent fighting machine and the police into an efficient, honest, and respected public service. Adding to the bitterness of the lesson is the fact that it is not understood or incorporated in any of the analyses of the Vietnam experience that have general acceptance.

The implications of this insight for any future involvement are not necessarily the imposition of a stark choice between intervention and abstention based on the political character of the armed forces of the threatened country. The matter is not that simple. What our findings mean is that an important additional consideration must be added to the preintervention analysis over and above such obvious considerations as the strength and quality of the Communist movement, the state of the threatened society, its cohesiveness, and its social and economic—as well as political—structure and state of health. For example, although it is quite clear that Thailand will never defeat its twelve-year-old insurgency unless it depoliticizes its armed forces and police, it is also clear that the insurgency is not quickly solving its problems and is making slow headway in a Thai society that retains its basic cohesiveness. Given the relatively weak condition of the insurgency, there may very well be a solution to the Thai problem which would quickly reduce the threat without the trauma involved in another major political upheaval—even in the unlikely event that the U.S. were able to induce the Thai leadership (since late 1976 once again a straight military dictatorship) to depoliticize the army. This would be to recruit a special paramilitary force under army sponsorship but—in the pattern of the units recruited especially for service in Laos—separate and apart from the internal political system of the armed forces.

This depoliticizing effect was accomplished inadvertently in the Laos intervention by assigning officers to what was understood to be a thoroughly dangerous and unpleasant duty rather than asking for *volunteers* as was done in forming the divisions sent to fight beside the U.S. Army in Vietnam. The Vietnam duty was not expected to be a particularly dangerous or arduous assignment, and there were known to be opportunities for profit from the easy access to PX goods. The complements were easily filled, and officers were accepted on the basis of political influence, which accounts for the inferior fighting quality of these units as compared with those formed for duty in Laos.

A unit recruited to fight against the insurgents inside Thailand on a basis similar to those sent earlier to Laos and totaling no more than a half dozen battalions would quickly reverse the slow growth of the insurgency and eventually reduce it to a hard-core remnant. Such a solution was opposed by the U.S. JUSMAAG in 1972[38] and probably would be opposed by the U.S. military today as being an unnecessary diversion from the priority task of building the Royal Thai Army into a proud and competent fighting force, at which point the insurgency would easily be mopped up. This view persisted despite the fact that some fifteen years of military aid had not had the desired effect.

The lesson suggested by these examples is the obvious one that the political structure of the country to be aided is of first importance in determining whether it can be successfully aided, and that the political role of the armed forces must be fully understood and taken into account in any aid decision. This view does not go so far as to insist that impeccable democratic credentials are essential for success in dealing with a people's war or that any degree of corruption will undermine the effort. If no political base exists other than the military, however, very grave questions are raised about the possibility of intervening successfully. At a minimum, the problem must be taken into account in reaching a decision and designing a program. A plausible solution must be proposed which goes to the central point and does not merely wish it aside by reference to training and advice to bring about better performance. Most discussions of counterinsurgency focus upon the programmatic details, and such matters do, indeed, have importance the same importance that good tactics have in military conflict. But good tactics cannot prevail when embedded in bad strategy. The strategic factors in counterinsurgency relate to politics and not to military concerns. In most cases it will be found that the basis of a successful strategy is the development of a political base that willingly supports the regime against its Communist enemies and that extends beyond the purchased loyalty of the senior military and police officers.

Nor is it satisfactory to decide to intervene hastily in order to rescue a seriously threatened regime in the expectation that the political problems can be straightened out later. Once assumed, the commitment, as we know, is not easily abandoned. American lives may be involved, not to mention pride and political stakes at home. We risk very quickly becoming the reluctant prisoners of an unsavory and incompetent regime which we continue to aid despite its obvious failures because it is too difficult to back out. At that point our ability to argue and persuade the regime into reforming itself and its military services becomes virtually nil. The client sees our advice as forcing him to face unacceptable risks of instability and loss of power, and so he evades and maneuvers to avoid our pressures, satisfying our demands with token adjustments which leave essentials unchanged.

Once these strategic political considerations have been dealt with in a fashion consistent with the lessons of our experience, the tactical matters can be addressed. We have seen that competent, professional police and military services are essential, and that they must proceed in accordance with the principle of "making the people the target." Conventional military operations are unsuited to this goal. Heavy weapons, tanks, artillery, and jet aircraft are worse than useless in most cases, for they impact at great cost upon the population while the enemy can usually evade their power. Small, lightly armed units, pinpointed operations assisted by "hunter-killer" squads, imaginative psychological warfare operations—and all of this based upon coordinated collection and exploitation of intelligence should be the main reliance of the military side of the effort. The police, if they have or can be brought to develop the capability, should play a major role in the intelligence effort and in other programs requiring frequent contact with the public. Both soldiers and police must be brought to recognize the overriding importance of good relations with the population and make consistent programmatic efforts in pursuit of that goal, which will probably include small-scale civic action. Part-time popular militia to maintain security in areas where the military have already done their job will also be essential. It is the best means of preventing the regular forces from being scattered about in static guard duties and it also serves to cement the population to the government's cause.

All of this still is not to suggest that counterinsurgency is, after all, essentially a military problem. As we have been at some pains to point out, competent and effective military operations are a product of a healthy political structure in which the army and police avoid behaving like an army of occupation and, instead, place themselves at the side of the people against a common enemy. Mere training and exhortation will not accomplish such a posture. It is a structural effect reflecting the fact that the power base of the regime is linked in some fashion to popular needs. Many brilliant students of counterinsurgency have somehow or other completely missed this point in their earnest and detailed advice to the U.S. and its clients on how to cope with insurgency. The last such effort was called *Rebellion and Authority: An Analytic* Essay *on Insurgent Conflicts* by Nathan Leites and Charles Wolf, Jr., of the Rand Corporation.[39] This erudite work dismisses the effort to gain public support for the purposes of defeating an insurgency—the so-called hearts and minds approach—as beside the point. It argues that stimulating certain kinds of popular behavior is the objective of the program and that such behavior can be brought about by various means, most effectively by making contrary behavior unprofitable to the individual. It argues for approaching the insurgency analytically as a system and focusing on four types of action to damage and bring it down without wasting effort and concern for whether or not the population supports the government's cause as a cause. The four actions are: reducing the supply of insurgent inputs, interfering with the conversion process whereby these inputs are turned into outputs, destroying the actual outputs (troops, but more importantly, leadership), and reducing the effectiveness of the insurgency's actions. The reader will see from this that the level of abstraction of the Leites and Wolf study is impressive. What they do not explain, however, is how all of these complex tasks can be accomplished by a regime with a level of competence that is extremely low and which is kept that way by the system's political dependence upon the purchased loyalty of military and police officers whose first priority is their private

well-being. That, of course, was the essence of the problem in Vietnam—a political problem from beginning to end which was never solved or even, in many cases, grasped by the most impressive official or academic minds.

This somewhat prolonged discussion of military aspects may give the impression that we see them as the major factor. In fact, they should be fully complemented by a program confronting the economic, social, and political problems of the affected regions, which, in the long run, is of equal importance. Military aspects have a priority in time, since other factors cannot progress far unless some measure of security exists. In the longer run, however, military and police operations, while they can greatly reduce and limit the insurgent movement, cannot be relied upon to eliminate it permanently. To do this, the regime must be shown to be deeply concerned about major popular needs and aspirations and also as able to do something effective to begin to meet them. Only in this way will the thrust of the Communist appeal be durably blunted and turned. For that reason, a successful counterinsurgency effort must combine the military and police actions already described with programs to tackle some of the serious problems pressing upon the rural population. In our opinion, major economic development programs are neither necessary nor, if they initially tend to disrupt the traditional patterns of rural life, desirable. The scale of rural assistance programs can be small if basic grievances are dealt with and if, in particular, the peasantry acquires, by means of the government's program, a role in determining its fate and its terms of living. How this is accomplished depends, of course, on the circumstances of particular cases. As we have already noted several times, land reform can be an important element, along with such reforms as rural self-government relating to local matters and an assured means of interaction between the local level and the higher levels of power and decision. Grievance procedures are also important, more so than the more common emphases on education, health services, roads, and the like, although these latter should not be ignored. In all the matters the process, to repeat what we have earlier stated more than once, is more important than the material details. It must be a process in which the beneficiaries are confirmed in their essential goal of achieving greater control over what is done for them and to them by the power structure.

Finally, all of this combined military, police, and civil effort must be managed and coordinated by a single civilian authority which has as its sole responsibility the task of assuring that the many parts of the complex effort mesh with each other, that a comprehensive plan is developed and faithfully followed. Simple efficiency requires such a management structure, but here, too, political obstacles exist. The authority which achieves control over such a major aspect of governmental activity automatically achieves great power within the system. Nevertheless, the highest levels of the threatened government must take the risk for the sake of an effective program which, after all, also has the objective of assuring its survival. Not to be overlooked is the fact that effectiveness also has political effect. A critical ingredient in gaining popular support—if you will, in winning hearts and minds—is competence on the part of the government and its services. The respect that is earned by a government which does the right amount of the right thing at the right time and place is more important to its cause than a vague liking or affection. Coercive measures such as forced population movements may also be necessary on occasion, and these need not harm the government's cause if they are seen to be controlled, fair and appropriate to the purposes sought. All of these factors go to underline the significance of a unified, well-managed effort, responsible to a single authority.

It should be starkly clear by now that counterinsurgency places unique demands upon a threatened regime, and that the governments which have most need of the courage, understanding, and cohesion required are the least likely to be able to muster these essential qualities. That, more likely than not, is why they have become targets of insurgency and why their defensive efforts will fail to the point where they require outside help. All the more reason why the United States, if it ever again sees its own vital interests intimately involved with the success of such a contest against a Communist people's war, should scrutinize the terrain with care, with an eye to the underlying fundamentals, and with a disabused realism in regard to its own abilities to provide suitable assistance.

THE AMBIGUOUS HERITAGE

The fundamental lesson to draw from our misadventures of the counterinsurgency era is the one already emphasized by many—the lesson of the limits of American power. It is also of importance that we should understand in what way our power, great as it is, can be challenged by a few thousand ragged jungle fighters armed with a dedicated leadership, a tested theory, and great patience. Too many have fallen back on the easy excuse that we failed in Indochina because our power was constrained and leashed, that more bombs, more destruction, more firepower was the answer. At the end of this account of what we tried to do, and how and why it fell short, it is to be hoped that some will be convinced that the failure was one of understanding: an inability to perceive the underlying realities of both our own system and that of the countries into which we thrust our raw strength. The scars of these failures will be a long time healing, but possibly, in time, understanding will take the place of revulsion in our thinking about the meaning of our unhappy experience. If, in addition, some turn of the wheel should once again bring us to the brink of such an involvement, the lessons which are our only return for all the blood and fortune that was spent will stand us in good stead, provided only that we finally have understood and digested them.